AN INTRODUCTION TO HIGH-FREQUENCY FINANCE

AN INTRODUCTION TO HIGH-FREQUENCY FINANCE

Michel M. Dacorogna
Zurich Re, Switzerland

Ramazan Gençay
University of Windsor, Canada
Olsen & Associates, Switzerland

Ulrich A. Müller
Olsen & Associates, Switzerland

Richard B. Olsen
Olsen & Associates, Switzerland

Olivier V. Pictet
Dynamic Asset Management, Switzerland

ACADEMIC PRESS
A Harcourt Science and Technology Company

San Diego   San Francisco   New York   Boston   London   Sydney   Tokyo

Academic Press
An imprint of Elsevier Science
525 B Street, Suite 1900, San Diego, California 92101-4495, USA
http://www.academicpress.com

Academic Press
84 Theobalds Road, London WC1X 8RR, UK
http://www.academicpress.com

Library of Congress Catalog Card Number: 2001088178

International Standard Book Number: 0-12-279671-3

PRINTED IN THE UNITED STATES OF AMERICA
02   03   04   05   06   EB   9   8   7   6   5   4   3

To our parents and families

CONTENTS

LIST OF FIGURES   xv

LIST OF TABLES   xix

PREFACE   xxi

ACKNOWLEDGMENTS   xxiii

I
INTRODUCTION

1.1	Markets: The Source of High-Frequency Data	1
1.2	Methodology of High-Frequency Research	2
1.3	Data Frequency and Market Information	3
1.4	New Levels of Significance	6
1.5	Interrelating Different Time Scales	8

2

MARKETS AND DATA

2.1	General Remarks on Markets and Data Types	10
	2.1.1 Spot Markets	11
	2.1.2 Futures Markets	12
	2.1.3 Option Markets	13
2.2	Foreign Exchange Markets	13
	2.2.1 Structure of the Foreign Exchange Spot Market	15
	2.2.2 Synthetic Cross Rates	19
	2.2.3 Multiple Contributor Effects	19
2.3	Over-the-Counter Interest Rate Markets	20
	2.3.1 Spot Interest Rates	21
	2.3.2 Foreign Exchange Forward Rates	22
2.4	Interest Rate Futures	23
	2.4.1 General Description of Interest Rate Futures	23
	2.4.2 Implied Forward Interest Rates and Yield Curves	25
2.5	Bond Futures Markets	28
	2.5.1 Bonds and Bond Futures	28
	2.5.2 Rollover Schemes	29
2.6	Commodity Futures	31
2.7	Equity Markets	32

3

TIME SERIES OF INTEREST

3.1	Time Series and Operators	34
3.2	Variables in Homogeneous Time Series	37
	3.2.1 Interpolation	37
	3.2.2 Price	38
	3.2.3 Return	40
	3.2.4 Realized Volatility	41
	3.2.5 Bid-Ask Spread	45
	3.2.6 Tick Frequency	46
	3.2.7 Other Variables	46
	3.2.8 Overlapping Returns	47
3.3	Convolution Operators	51
	3.3.1 Notation Used for Time Series Operators	53
	3.3.2 Linear Operator and Kernels	54
	3.3.3 Build-Up Time Interval	56
	3.3.4 Homogeneous Operators and Robustness	58
	3.3.5 Exponential Moving Average (EMA)	59
	3.3.6 The Iterated EMA Operator	59
	3.3.7 Moving Average (MA)	61

3.3.8	Moving Norm, Variance, and Standard Deviation	63
3.3.9	Differential	64
3.3.10	Derivative and γ-Derivative	66
3.3.11	Volatility	68
3.3.12	Standardized Time Series, Moving Skewness, and Kurtosis	71
3.3.13	Moving Correlation	71
3.3.14	Windowed Fourier Transform	74
3.4	Microscopic Operators	76
3.4.1	Backward Shift and Time Translation Operators	77
3.4.2	Regular Time Series Operator	77
3.4.3	Microscopic Return, Difference, and Derivative	78
3.4.4	Microscopic Volatility	79
3.4.5	Tick Frequency and Activity	79

4

ADAPTIVE DATA CLEANING

4.1	Introduction: Using a Filter to Clean the Data	82
4.2	Data and Data Errors	84
4.2.1	Time Series of Ticks	84
4.2.2	Data Error Types	85
4.3	General Overview of the Filter	86
4.3.1	The Functionality of the Filter	86
4.3.2	Overview of the Filtering Algorithm and Its Structure	88
4.4	Basic Filtering Elements and Operations	88
4.4.1	Credibility and Trust Capital	89
4.4.2	Filtering of Single Scalar Quotes: The Level Filter	91
4.4.3	Pair Filtering: The Credibility of Returns	93
4.4.4	Computing the Expected Volatility	96
4.4.5	Pair Filtering: Comparing Quote Origins	98
4.4.6	A Time Scale for Filtering	100
4.5	The Scalar Filtering Window	103
4.5.1	Entering a New Quote in the Scalar Filtering Window	104
4.5.2	The Trust Capital of a New Scalar Quote	104
4.5.3	Updating the Scalar Window	106
4.5.4	Dismissing Quotes from the Scalar Window	107
4.5.5	Updating the Statistics with Credible Scalar Quotes	108
4.5.6	A Second Scalar Window for Old Valid Quotes	108
4.6	The Full-Quote Filtering Window	109
4.6.1	Quote Splitting Depending on the Instrument Type	110
4.6.2	The Basic Validity Test	110
4.6.3	Transforming the Filtered Variable	112
4.7	Univariate Filtering	113

4.7.1 The Results of Univariate Filtering 114
4.7.2 Filtering in Historical and Real-Time Modes 115
4.7.3 Choosing the Filter Parameters 116
4.8 Special Filter Elements 116
4.8.1 Multivariate Filtering: Filtering Sparse Data 116
4.9 Behavior and Effects of the Data Filter 118

5

BASIC STYLIZED FACTS

5.1 Introduction 121
5.2 Price Formation Process 123
5.2.1 Negative First-Order Autocorrelation of Returns 123
5.2.2 Discreteness of Quoted Spreads 125
5.2.3 Short-Term Triangular Arbitrage 127
5.3 Institutional Structure and Exogeneous Impacts 127
5.3.1 Institutional Framework 127
5.3.2 Positive Impact of Official Interventions 129
5.3.3 Mixed Effect of News 129
5.4 Distributional Properties of Returns 132
5.4.1 Finite Variance, Symmetry and Decreasing Fat-Tailedness 132
5.4.2 The Tail Index of Return Distributions 135
5.4.3 Extreme Risks in Financial Markets 144
5.5 Scaling Laws 147
5.5.1 Empirical Evidence 147
5.5.2 Distributions and Scaling Laws 151
5.5.3 A Simple Model of the Market Maker Bias 154
5.5.4 Limitations of the Scaling Laws 158
5.6 Autocorrelation and Seasonality 160
5.6.1 Autocorrelations of Returns and Volatility 161
5.6.2 Seasonal Volatility: Across Markets for OTC Instruments 163
5.6.3 Seasonal Volatility: U-Shaped for Exchange Traded Instruments 167
5.6.4 Deterministic Volatility in Eurofutures Contracts 169
5.6.5 Bid-Ask Spreads 170

6

MODELING SEASONAL VOLATILITY

6.1 Introduction 174
6.2 A Model of Market Activity 175
6.2.1 Seasonal Patterns of the Volatility and Presence of Markets 175

6.2.2 Modeling the Volatility Patterns with an Alternative Time Scale and an Activity Variable   176
6.2.3 Market Activity and Scaling Law   177
6.2.4 Geographical Components of Market Activity   178
6.2.5 A Model of Intraweek Market Activity   179
6.2.6 Interpretation of the Activity Modeling Results   183
6.3 A New Business Time Scale (ϑ-Scale)   188
6.3.1 Definition of the ϑ-Scale   188
6.3.2 Adjustments of the ϑ-Scale Definition   189
6.3.3 A Ratio Test for the ϑ-Scale Quality   192
6.4 Filtering Intraday Seasonalities with Wavelets   193

7

REALIZED VOLATILITY DYNAMICS

7.1 Introduction   197
7.2 The Bias of Realized Volatility and Its Correction   198
7.3 Conditional Heteroskedasticity   204
7.3.1 Autocorrelation of Volatility in ϑ-Time   204
7.3.2 Short and Long Memory   207
7.4 The Heterogeneous Market Hypothesis   209
7.4.1 Volatilities of Different Time Resolutions   210
7.4.2 Asymmetric Lead-Lag Correlation of Volatilities   211
7.4.3 Conditional Predictability   215

8

VOLATILITY PROCESSES

8.1 Introduction   219
8.2 Intraday Volatility and GARCH Models   221
8.2.1 Parameter Estimation of GARCH Models   222
8.2.2 Temporal Aggregation of GARCH Models   224
8.2.3 Estimates of GARCH(1,1) for Various Frequencies   226
8.3 Modeling Heterogeneous Volatilities   231
8.3.1 The HARCH Model   231
8.3.2 HARCH and Market Components   234
8.3.3 Generalization of the Process Equation   237
8.3.4 EMA-HARCH Model   237
8.3.5 Estimating HARCH and EMA-HARCH Models   239
8.3.6 HARCH in Interest Rate Modeling   242
8.4 Forecasting Short-Term Volatility   243
8.4.1 A Framework to Measure the Forecasting Performance   243
8.4.2 Performance of ARCH-Type Models   246

9

FORECASTING RISK AND RETURN

9.1 Introduction to Forecasting 248
9.2 Forecasting Volatility for Value-at-Risk 250
    9.2.1 Three Simple Volatility Forecasting Models 250
    9.2.2 Choosing the Best Volatility Forecasting Model 254
9.3 Forecasting Returns over Multiple Time Horizons 255
    9.3.1 Intrinsic Time 255
    9.3.2 Model Structure 256
    9.3.3 A Linear Combination of Nonlinear Indicators 256
    9.3.4 Moving Averages, Momenta, and Indicators 257
    9.3.5 Continuous Coefficient Update 259
9.4 Measuring Forecast Quality 261
    9.4.1 Appropriate Measures of Forecast Accuracy 262
    9.4.2 Empirical Results for the Multi-Horizon Model 263
    9.4.3 Forecast Effectiveness in Intraday Horizons 264

10

CORRELATION AND MULTIVARIATE RISK

10.1 Introduction 268
10.2 Estimating the Dependence of Financial Time Series 269
10.3 Covolatility Weighting 270
    10.3.1 Formulation of an Adjusted Correlation Measure 272
    10.3.2 Monte Carlo and Empirical Tests 274
10.4 Stability of Return Correlations 277
    10.4.1 Correlation Variations over Time 278
    10.4.2 The Exponential Memory of Return Correlations 282
10.5 Correlation Behavior at High Data Frequencies 287
10.6 Conclusions 293

11

TRADING MODELS

11.1 Introduction 295
11.2 Real-Time Trading Strategies 297
    11.2.1 The Trading Model and Its Data-Processing Environment 299
    11.2.2 Simulated Trader 303
11.3 Risk Sensitive Performance Measures 304
    11.3.1 X_{eff}: A Symmetric Effective Returns Measure 305
    11.3.2 R_{eff}: An Asymmetric Effective Returns Measure 307
11.4 Trading Model Algorithms 309

11.4.1 An Example of a Trading Model 310
11.4.2 Model Design with Genetic Programming 311
11.5 Optimization and Testing Procedures 317
11.5.1 Robust Optimization with Genetic Algorithms 317
11.5.2 Testing Procedures 321
11.6 Statistical Study of a Trading Model 323
11.6.1 Heterogeneous Real-Time Trading Strategies 323
11.6.2 Price-Generation Processes and Trading Models 328
11.7 Trading Model Portfolios 338
11.8 Currency Risk Hedging 340
11.8.1 The Hedging Ratio and the "Neutral Point" 343
11.8.2 Risk/Return of an Overlay with Static and Dynamic Positions 344
11.8.3 Dynamic Hedging with Exposure Constraints 345
11.8.4 Concluding Remarks 346

12
TOWARD A THEORY
OF HETEROGENEOUS MARKETS

12.1 Definition of Efficient Markets 349
12.2 Dynamic Markets and Relativistic Effects 350
12.3 Impact of the New Technology 352
12.4 Zero-Sum Game or Perpetuum Mobile? 353
12.5 Discussion of the Conventional Definition 354
12.6 An Improved Definition of "Efficient Markets" 354

BIBLIOGRAPHY 356

INDEX 376

LIST OF FIGURES

1.1	Size and data frequency of different samples	4
1.2	Models versus time scale	5
1.3	Volatility with daily versus high-frequency data	7
3.1	Types of time series operators	36
3.2	Interpolation methods	38
3.3	Overlapping time intervals	48
3.4	One week of USD-CHF prices	53
3.5	Moving average (MA) kernel	61
3.6	MA kernel on a logarithmic scale	62
3.7	Schematic differential kernel	64
3.8	Kernel of a differential operator	65
3.9	Decay of a differential kernel	66
3.10	Differential and return	67
3.11	Distribution of derivative operator	68
3.12	Annualized volatility as a moving norm	71
3.13	Moving moments of returns	72
3.14	Kernel of a windowed Fourier operator	75
3.15	Normed windowed Fourier transform	77
3.16	Microscopic volatility	79
3.17	Tick activity	80
4.1	Flowchart of a data-cleaning filter	87

4.2	Schematic scalar filtering window	103
5.1	Short-term autocorrelation of returns	123
5.2	Comparison between quoted and transaction spreads	125
5.3	Scaling law exponent as a function of time	128
5.4	Seasonality in the interest rates	129
5.5	Intraday distribution of 15-min mean changes of absolute returns	130
5.6	Cumulative distributions of 10-min, 1-day, and 1-week USD-JPY returns	136
5.7	Order statistics for Student-t distribution	139
5.8	Scaling law for USD-JPY and GBP-USD	149
5.9	Wavelet variance at different scales	160
5.10	Autocorrelations of hourly returns, absolute returns, and squared returns	161
5.11	Autocorrelation as a function of the power of the absolute returns	162
5.12	Hourly intraday and intraweek distribution of absolute return, spread and the tick frequency	165
5.13	Intraday analysis of Eurofutures	168
5.14	Deterministic volatility of Eurofutures	169
5.15	Cumulative distributions of spreads	172
6.1	The USD-DEM intraweek activity pattern	178
6.2	Activity functions of geographical market components	182
6.3	Histograms of the average hourly activity for USD-JPY and USD-CHF	185
6.4	The activity model for USD-JPY and USD-CHF	186
6.5	Comparison of tick activity and volatility for different data sources	188
6.6	The ϑ-time versus physical time for USD-DEM	190
6.7	Hourly returns of USD-DEM in physical and ϑ-time	191
6.8	Seasonality and wavelet filtering	194
6.9	Autocorrelations of the 5-min absolute returns for USD-DEM and USD-JPY	195
6.10	Autocorrelations of the 5-min filtered absolute returns for USD-DEM and USD-JPY	195
7.1	Interaction of trader groups	199
7.2	The bias of realized volatility	201
7.3	The residual bias of bias-corrected realized volatility	203
7.4	Autocorrelation function of USD-DEM in physical-time	205
7.5	Autocorrelation function of USD-DEM in ϑ-time	206
7.6	USD-DEM autocorrelations from daily data	208
7.7	Coarse and fine volatilities	212
7.8	Asymmetric lagged correlation for USD-DEM	214

7.9 Asymmetric lagged correlation for Euromark IR futures   216
7.10 Asymmetry of lagged correlation   217
7.11 Conditional autocorrelation of returns   218
8.1 Estimated and theoretical GARCH coefficients in business time   226
8.2 Estimated and theoretical GARCH coefficients in ϑ-time   227
8.3 GARCH estimates on a moving sample   230
8.4 Moment conditions for a HARCH(2) process   234
8.5 Impacts of market components for HARCH processes   241
9.1 Standard RiskMetrics volatility at different daytimes   252
9.2 Momentum indicator for forecasting   258
10.1 Autocorrelation of absolute returns for USD-DEM   277
10.2 Linear correlation coefficients for USD/DEM/NLG   280
10.3 Linear correlation coefficients for USD/DEM/GBP   281
10.4 Linear correlation coefficients for USD/DEM/ITL   282
10.5 Linear correlation coefficients for DJIA/AMEX   283
10.6 Linear correlation coefficients for USD 3-6M/DEM 3-6M   284
10.7 Linear correlation coefficients for DEM 3-6M/DEM 9-12M   285
10.8 Autocorrelations of correlation coefficients   286
10.9 Exponential decay of the autocorrelation of correlation coefficients   287
10.10 Correlation coefficients as a function of return time interval   289
10.11 Correlation versus logarithmic return time interval   290
10.12 Correlation stabilization intervals versus data frequencies   292
11.1 Data flow within a real-time trading model   298
11.2 Crossover operator   313
11.3 Syntactic restrictions for basic arithmetic operators   314
11.4 Total return of a portfolio of 10 O&A trading models   341
11.5 Set of feasible portfolios with currency hedging   342

LIST OF TABLES

2.1 The traditional FXFX page of Reuters 16
2.2 FX data frequency 18
4.1 Data cleaning filter structure 89
4.2 Credibility addition 90
4.3 Trust capital as a function of price move size and time interval 96
4.4 Active periods of the three generic markets 101
4.5 Data cleaning filter parameters 117
4.6 Data cleaning rejection rates 119
5.1 Moments of return distributions for FX rates 133
5.2 Moments of return distributions for FX cross rates 134
5.3 Tail index of FX returns 140
5.4 Tail index of FX cross rates 141
5.5 Tail index of spot interest rates 143
5.6 Estimated tail index for different data frequencies and sample sizes 144
5.7 Extreme risks in the FX market 146
5.8 Drift exponents for FX rates 150
5.9 Drift exponents for Eurofutures 151
5.10 Timezone conversion table 163
5.11 Average number of ticks versus day of the week 164
5.12 Average volatility versus day of the week 166

5.13 Correlation coefficients between activity measures 167

5.14 Average spreads versus day of the week 171

6.1 Definition of the three generic markets 180

6.2 The ϑ-time parameter estimates for the three generic markets 184

6.3 The volatility ratio for the quality of the ϑ-scale 192

7.1 Difference between lagged correlations 213

8.1 Results of a GARCH(1,1) estimation in business time 228

8.2 Results of a GARCH(1,1) estimation in ϑ-time 229

8.3 Market components of a HARCH process 236

8.4 HARCH coefficients for USD-DEM 240

8.5 Results of the EMA-HARCH for the LIFFE Three-Month Euromark 242

8.6 Volatility forecasting performance for USD-DEM 246

9.1 The sampling periods of the forecast study 264

9.2 Forecast quality for 10 FX rates against the USD 265

9.3 Forecast quality for 10 FX cross rates 266

9.4 Significance of the forecast quality for 20 FX rates 267

10.1 Correlations from Monte Carlo simulations 275

10.2 Data sampling for correlation as function of time 278

10.3 Mean values, variances, maxima and minima of correlation 279

10.4 Estimation results of the autocorrelation of correlation 288

10.5 Correlation results characterizing the Epps effect 291

11.1 Market time constraints 299

11.2 Trading model results versus tree complexity 316

11.3 Performance comparison between models 324

11.4 Performance comparison between markets 325

11.5 The best X_{eff} as a function of opening hours 326

11.6 p-value Comparisons 331

11.7 Random walk Simulations for USD-DEM 332

11.8 GARCH(1,1) parameter estimates 334

11.9 GARCH(1,1) simulations for USD-DEM 335

11.10 AR(4)-GARCH(1,1) parameter estimates 337

11.11 AR(4)-GARCH(1,1) simulations for USD-DEM 338

11.12 Portfolio performance of O&A trading models 340

PREFACE

This book presents a unified view of high-frequency time series methods with a particular emphasis on foreign exchange markets as well as interest rate spot and futures markets. The scope of this book is also applicable to other markets, such as equity and commodity markets.

As the archetype of financial markets, the foreign exchange market is the largest financial market worldwide. It involves dealers in different geographic locations, time zones, and working hours who have different time horizons, home currencies, information access, transaction costs, and other institutional constraints. The time horizons vary from intraday dealers, who close their positions every evening, to long-term investors and central banks. In this highly complex and heterogeneous market structure, the market participants are faced with different constraints and use different strategies to reach their financial goals, such as by maximizing their profits or maximizing their utility function after adjusting for market risk.

This book provides a framework to the analysis, modeling, and inference of high-frequency financial time series. It begins with the elementary foundations and definitions needed for studying the fundamental properties of high-frequency financial time series. It extends into the adaptive data-cleaning issues, treatment of seasonal volatility, and modeling of intraday volatility. Fractal properties of the high-frequency financial time series are found and explored, and an intrinsic time is used to construct forecasting models. The book provides a detailed study of how the adopted framework can be effectively utilized to build econometric models of the price-formation process. Going beyond the price-formation process, the book presents the techniques to construct real-time trading models for financial assets.

It is designed for those who might be starting research in the area as well as for those who are interested in appreciating the statistical and econometric theory that underlies high-frequency financial time series modeling. The targeted audience includes finance professionals, including risk managers and research professionals in the public and private sectors; those taking graduate courses in finance, economics, econometrics, statistics, and time series analysis; and advanced MBA students. Because the high-frequency finance field is relatively new and the literature is scattered in a wide range of academic and nonacademic platforms, this book aims to provide a uniform treatment of the field and an easily accessible platform to high-frequency financial time series analysis — an exciting new field of research.

With the development of this field, a huge new area of research has been initiated, where work has hardly started. This work could not be more fascinating, and a number of discoveries are waiting to be made. We expect research to increase in this field, as people start to understand how these insights can dramatically improve risk-adjusted performances in asset management, market making, and treasury functions and be the foundation for other applications, such as an early warning system of financial markets.

Michel M. Dacorogna

Ramazan Gençay

Ulrich A. Müller

Richard B. Olsen

Olivier V. Pictet

ACKNOWLEDGMENTS

We should start by acknowledging that 15 years ago, when our research team at Olsen & Associates (O&A) first began using the amazing magnifying glass provided by high-frequency data to see if we could uncover possible patterns in the financial markets, none of us anticipated just how expansive the effort would become.

With the publication of this book originating from our work, sincere thanks are due to so many that we can only hope we have recognized most of the colleagues and friends who have advanced our work. Their help, their encouragement, their criticism, and their friendship have contributed to the style of teamwork we always favored.

We begin with Matthias Schwarz, a biology student who computed the first scaling law working with us in the autumn of 1986. Our first academic visitor was Claude Morgenegg, coming from the University of Geneva, who taught our group of physicists the right language to use to reach the economists. Thanks also to Casper de Vries, who opened up for us the world of extreme value theory; Cindy L. Gauveau, who prepared forecasting models for foreign exchange rates and also brought the economic touch to our work; Rakhal Davé, for his explorations of the LeBaron effect; Marco Tomassini and Bastien Chopard, who brought to our attention the genetic algorithms; Mark Lundin and his correlation studies; Gennady Samorodnitsky and Paul Embrechts, who were able to prove the sufficiency of the stationarity condition of HARCH processes; Giuseppe Ballocchi, who led us into the research on interest rate futures; and Wolfgang

Breymann, who has extended the ϑ-time concept and developed the idea of a heterogeneous market in his cascade model. A particular thanks goes to Gilles Zumbach, who has contributed many graphs to this book. He continues the work, bringing it to new levels and uncovering many more properties with the powerful operator framework and the software tools in C++ that he has developed over the years.

We also want to thank our colleagues who joined us at a later stage and have already reached out for other adventures: Lars Jaeger, Thomas Domenig, Peter Rice, and Hoss Hauksson. Our thanks extend also to Jørgen Olsen, whose wisdom and vast scientific culture has enlightened our seminars and whose road map for building a Richter scale for financial markets we implemented.

One very important and enriching experience has been the visits of many students who spent time with us and brought along their enthusiasm and eagerness to learn: Dominique Guillaume; Lukas Pulver; Petra Korndoerfer; Markus P. Herrchen; Jens Richelsen; Christian Jost; Jürg S. Füssler; Retus G. Sgier; Alexander Dimai; Jonathan Dawes; Jakob E. von Weizsäcker; Philipp Hartmann; Cătălin Stărică; Barbara Piccinato; Carl Hopman; Peter Rice, who later joined our research team; Simone Deparis; Fulvio Corsi; and Paul Lynch. Without them, we would never have been able to explore so many different time series and to accomplish so many studies.

Many of our academic friends around the world visited us and understood early on the interest in research on this type of data. They provided us with encouragement to continue and the sense that we were working in the right direction. Hermann Garbers was the first to invite us to give a seminar at the University of Zurich, where we presented the scaling law in December 1988. From Benoît Mandelbrot in 1989 to Gennady Samorodnitsky just prior to the publication of this book, we have been fortunate to share time and work at O&A with some fine scientists: Tim Bollerslev, William Brock, Hans Bühlmann, Peter Bühlmann, Frank K. Diebold, Christian Dunis, Rüdiger Frey, Hélyette Geman, Charles Goodhart, Rudolf Kalman, Hans Rudolf Lerche, Bruce Mizrach, John Moody, Salih Neftçi, Wolfgang Polasek, Remo Schnidrig, Albert N. Shiryaev, Gerhard Stahl, Massimo Tivegna, Murad Taqqu, Walter Wasserfallen, Andreas Weigend, and Diethelm Würtz. We would like to thank especially Charles Goodhart, whose support and insights led to the O&A "High-Frequency Data in Finance" conferences, but also Richard Baillie, Tim Bollerslev, Rob Engle, Joel Hasbrouck, Michael Melvin, and Maureen O'Hara. Gerhard Stahl has been a great partner in exploring new issues of risk management. His scientific rigor was always refreshing in this field where ad hoc arguments often dominate. Michel Dacorogna would like to thank particularly Blake LeBaron for the many e-mail exchanges we have had over the years on our research. They were always stimulating and encouraged us to think deeper into the problems and find the connections with the traditional economic approach. Manfred Härter and Mico Loretan have been always supportive of our work and have brought to us many ideas and opportunities for presenting it. Ramo Gençay would like to thank William Brock, Dee Dechert, Murray Frank,

Blake LeBaron, and Thanasis Stengos for many exciting research conversations, and Michael Charette, Ron Meng and Tibor Toronyi for research support. Ulrich Müller would like to thank Günter Schwarz for his contribution to our understanding of portfolio theory.

It is also clear that without the help and the dedication of our software team we would not have been able to access a database of such quantity and quality, covering more than 14 years of tick-by-tick prices. From Rob J. Nagler to Kris Meissner through J. Robert Ward, William H. Kelly, Daniel P. Smith, Martin Lichtin, Devon Bowen, and Michael Stumm, we learned the subtleties of object-oriented programming and have enjoyed their constant support in our efforts to make sense of all that we were seeing. Paul Breslaw has been so helpful with the data and improving our English. Our thanks go also to our friends from the operation group who kept alive our system, especially Jorge Mota, Jeff Courtade, and Gary Swofford. Whenever we had a problem with bulbs going out of function or air conditioning not working (especially when it was needed most), Filippo Guglielmo would always be here to solve it.

The trading model developments would not have been so interesting, nor so close to reality, without the contribution of our help desk: Pius Dall'Acqua, Stephan Schlatter, and last, but not least, Bernard Hechinger and his deep knowledge of the microstructure of financial markets. His interest in our models has brought us to rethink many aspects of their strategies and implement some of his ideas. In terms of market knowledge, we especially want to thank Dean LeBaron, whose vast experience and enthusiasm for new developments is a source of inspiration and encouragement. Our customers also brought many ideas to us, especially in the group who participated in the development of the interest rate project: Michael Brockmann, Dieter Heitkamp, Luciano Steve, and Giuseppe Ciliberto. We always enjoyed the exchanges with the practitioners who understood the need for a scientific approach to the markets. Another example of this fertile interaction was with Monique Donders, Tjark Tjin, and Marcel Vernooy during our project of building a currency overlay product based on trading models. Special thanks go also to Daniel Huber, who opened up so many doors for us.

There is no question that we benefited greatly from the structure and organization provided by our different administrative assistants over the years. Karin Jost, Rosemarie Arnold-Becker, and Melanie Käslin all brought a strong sense of service and dedication that made our teamwork possible.

The process of writing a book with many authors is complex and demanding but also very rewarding because it gave us the occasion to discuss, deepen our understanding of the matters and interact with interesting people. In this process, Scott Bentley's (the senior editor of Academic Press) help and feedback have been important for keeping the level of motivation high and for the success of this project. The care of Amy Hendrickson for many LaTeX formatting problems of a book of more than 400 pages and containing so many figures was essential for the resulting appearance of this book.

Before closing this page of gratitude, we do not want to forget Dina Weidmann and Elisa Guglielmo, who cooked so many fine dishes with the Italian touch and make O&A's famous "Friday family lunches" a genuine gourmet experience. Faced with mountains of data to unravel, this lovely tradition warmed the soul. Grazie.

Michel M. Dacorogna
Ramazan Gençay
Ulrich A. Müller
Richard B. Olsen
Olivier V. Pictet

1

INTRODUCTION

1.1 MARKETS: THE SOURCE OF HIGH-FREQUENCY DATA

A famous climber, when asked why he was willing to put his life in danger to climb dangerous summits, answered: "Because they are there." We would be tempted to give the same answer when people ask us why we take so much pain in dealing with high-frequency data. The reason is simple: financial markets are the source of high-frequency data. The original form of market prices is tick-by-tick data: each "tick" is one logical unit of information, like a quote or a transaction price (see Section 2.1). By nature these data are irregularly spaced in time. Liquid markets generate hundreds or thousands of ticks per business day. Data vendors like Reuters transmit more than 275,000 prices per day for foreign exchange spot rates alone.

Thus high-frequency data should be the primary object of research for those who are interested in understanding financial markets. Especially so, because practitioners determine their trading decisions by observing high-frequency or tick-by-tick data. Yet most of the studies published in the financial literature deal with low-frequency, regularly spaced data. There are two main reasons for this. First, it is still rather costly and time-consuming to collect, collate, store, retrieve, and manipulate high-frequency data. That is why most of the available financial data are at daily or lower frequency. The second reason is somehow more subtle but still quite important: most of the statistical apparatus has been developed and thought for homogeneous (i.e., equally spaced in time) time series. There is little work done to adapt the methods to data that arrive at random time intervals. Unfortunately in finance, regularly spaced data are not original data but artifacts derived from the original market prices. Nowadays with the development of computer technology, data availability is becoming less and less of a problem. For instance, most of the exchanges and especially those that trade electronically would gladly provide tick-by-tick data to interested parties. Data vendors have themselves improved their data structures and provide their users with tools to collect data for over-the-counter (OTC) markets. Slowly, high-frequency data are becoming a fantastic experimental bench for understanding market microstructure and more generally for analyzing financial markets.

That leaves the researcher with the problems of dealing with such vast amounts of data using the right mathematical tools and models. This is precisely the subject of this book.

1.2   METHODOLOGY OF HIGH-FREQUENCY RESEARCH

From the beginning, our approach has been to apply the experimental method which has been highly successful in "hard" sciences.[1] It consists of three steps, the first one being to explore the data in order to discover the fundamental statistical properties they exhibit with a minimum set of assumptions. This is often called finding the "stylized facts" in the econometric or finance literature. This first step was in fact not so important in the economic literature, because the sparseness of data made it either relatively simple or uninteresting due to the statistical uncertainty.

The second step is to use all of these empirical facts to formulate adequate models. By adequate models, we do not mean models that come from hand-waving arguments about the markets, but rather models that are directly inspired by the empirical regularities encountered in the data. It is the point where our understanding of market behavior and reality of the data properties should meet. There have been many debates between the time series approach and microstructure approach. The first one relying more on modeling the statistical properties of the data and the latter concentrating on modeling market behavior. Both approaches have their value and high-frequency data might be able to reconcile them by enabling us to actually test the microstructure models, Hasbrouck (1998); Rydberg and Shephard (1998).

The third step, of course, is to verify whether these models satisfactorily reproduce the stylized facts found in the data. The ultimate goal is not only a good descriptive model but the ability to produce reasonable *predictions* of future movements or risks and to integrate these tools into practical applications, such

---

[1] We refer here to experimental sciences such as physics, chemistry, or biology.

as risk management tools or option pricing algorithms. For decades, practitioners have been developing so-called technical analysis, which is a kind of empirical time series analysis based on rudimentary analytical tools. Although some new academic research has analyzed these trading rules,[2] they remain controversial and are looked down upon. We hope that this book will put on a new footing many ideas that have been developed in technical analysis.

We have organized this book along the same lines, we first present the empirical regularities, then we construct models, and lastly we test their power to predict market outcomes.

The novelty of high-frequency data demands to take such an approach. This was not usual in econometrics because so little data were available until the late 1980s. It was quite natural that the researcher's emphasis was to make sure that the methodology was correct in order to obtain the most information out of the sparse data that were available. Only recently the research community in this field has recognized the importance of the first step: finding empirical facts. This step can already be good research in its own right. A good example is the recent paper by Andersen *et al.* (2001), where the authors explore in detail the distributional properties of volatility computed from high-frequency data.

Thanks to the development of electronic trading and the existence of various data providers also on the Internet, it is now possible to follow the price formation in real-time. Ideally, the analysis and modeling of the price-generation process should, in real-time, produce results that add value to the raw data. There is strong demand from the market to have, next to the current price, a good assessment of the current risk of the financial asset as well as a reasonable prediction of its future movement. This means that the models should be made amenable to real-time computations and updates. Techniques for doing so will be presented in the remainder of the book. It is possible to develop methods that allow for the easy computation of models and can thus provide almost instantaneous reaction to market events. Although quite popular among practitioners who want to analyze the past developments of prices, those techniques have had little echo, until now, in the academic world. Very few research papers have studied the statistical foundations and properties of those "technical indicators." In this book (Chapter 3) we provide a unified platform for these methods.

1.3 DATA FREQUENCY AND MARKET INFORMATION

Relating the type of data available for researchers, the effects and the models that are discovered and developed with these different samples, provides insight into the development of research in finance. Figure 1.1 illustrates the sample size versus the measurement frequency of some well-known data sets used in finance. The

---

[2] Among others, here is a list of interesting papers on the issue of technical trading models: Neftci (1991), Brock *et al.* (1992), Taylor and Allen (1992), Levich and Thomas (1993b), Gençay and Stengos (1998), Gençay (1998a,b), Frances and van Griensven (1998), Allen and Karjalainen (1999), Gençay (1999), LeBaron (1999a), Sullivan *et al.* (1999), and Gençay *et al.* (2001c, 2002).

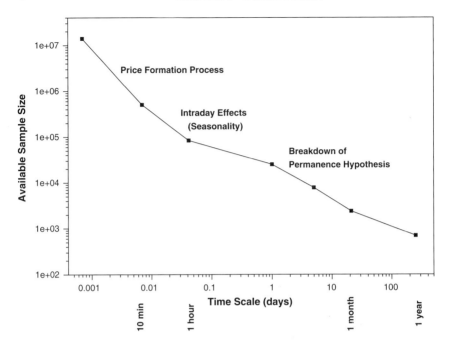

FIGURE 1.1   Available data samples with their typical sizes and frequency. The sample size and the frequency are plotted on a logarithmic scale. The first point corresponds to the O&A database, the last one to the 700 years of yearly data analyzed by Froot *et al.* (1995), the second to its left to the cotton price data of Mandelbrot (1963), and the daily data are computed from the sample used in Ding *et al.* (1993) to show long memory in the S&P 500. The text refers to the effects discovered and analyzed in the different segments of these samples.

double logarithmic scale makes the points lie almost on a straight line. The data sample with the lowest frequency is the one used by Froot *et al.* (1995) of 700 years of annual commodity price data from England and Holland. Beyond 700 years, one is unlikely to find reliable economic or financial data.[3] The data with the highest frequency is the Olsen & Associates (O&A) dataset of more than 14 years of high-frequency foreign exchange data. The tick-by-tick data are the highest frequency available. Between those two extremes, one finds the daily series of the Standard & Poors 500 from 1928 to 1991 used by Ding *et al.* (1993) or the monthly cotton prices used by Mandelbrot (1963) from 1880 to 1940. On this graph, we superimpose those effects that have been identified at these different time scales. One of the questions with data collected over very long periods is whether they really refer to the same phenomenon. Stock indices, for example, change their composition through time due to mergers or the demise of companies. When analyzing the price history of stock indices, the impact of these changes in

---

[3] Data can be found in natural sciences such as weather data up to a few hundred thousand years.

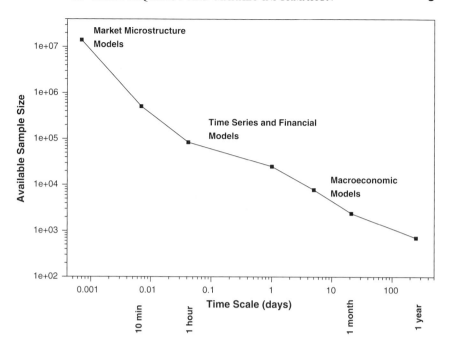

FIGURE 1.2   Available data samples with their typical sizes and frequency. The sample size and the frequency are plotted on a logarithmic scale. The text refers to the models developed and tested in the different segments of these samples.

composition is not obvious. We call this phenomenon the "breakdown of the permanence hypothesis." It is difficult to assess the quality of any inference as the underlying process is not stationary over decades or centuries. At the other end of the frequency spectrum (i.e. with high-frequency data), we are confronted with the details of the price generation process, where other effects, such as how the data are transmitted and recorded in the data-base (see Chapter 4) have an impact. With data at frequencies of the order of one hour, a new problem arises, due to the fact that the earth turns and the impact of time zones, where the seasonality of volatility becomes very important (as we shall see in Chapter 5) and overshadows all other effects.

Figure 1.2 relates the data to the models that are typically developed and tested with them. The high-frequency data have opened great possibilities to test market microstructure models, while traditionally low-frequency data are used for testing macroeconomic models.   In between lies the whole area of financial and time series modeling, which is typically studied with daily or monthly data as, for instance, option pricing or GARCH models. It is clear from this figure that we have a continuum of both samples and models. The antagonism that is sometimes encountered between time series and market microstructure approaches should slowly vanish with more and more studies combining both with high-frequency data. Yet the challenge is still open to build models that are simple to implement and describe to a reasonable degree the empirical behavior of the data at all time scales.

1.4   NEW LEVELS OF SIGNIFICANCE

High-frequency data means a very large amount of data. The number of observations in one single day of a liquid market is equivalent to the number of daily data within 30 years. Statistically, the higher the number of independently measured observations, the higher is the degrees of freedom, which implies more precise estimators. The large amount of data allows us to distinguish between different models (model validation) with a higher statistical precision. New statistical methods become possible, for example, tail statistics to examine the probability of extreme events. Almost by definition, extreme events are rare and doing statistics on such extreme events is a challenge. With high-frequency data one can have samples with as many as 400,000 independent observations[4] to study the 0.25% percentile and still have 1,000 observations with which to work. We shall see how important this is when we present the estimation of tail indices for return distributions. Similarly, when different models have to be ranked, the availability of a few hundred thousand observations allows us to find beyond a doubt which model provides the best description of the data-generating process (Müller *et al.*, 1997a).

Figure 1.3 demonstrates the importance of high-frequency data in model selection and inference within the context of Value-at-Risk (VaR) calculations. We report three different calculations all of which use the J. P. Morgan (1996) volatility model, which is in fact a 1-day volatility forecast as further discussed in Section 9.2. The three calculations differ in terms of the sampling and the data frequency. The Japanese volatility calculations are based on prices observed *daily* at 7 a.m. GMT, which corresponds to the afternoon Japanese time. The U.K. volatility calculations are based on prices measured *daily* at 5 p.m. GMT, which is the afternoon in the U. K. The high-frequency volatility calculations are based on the high-frequency tick-by-tick data recorded continuously on a 24-hour cycle. The top panel in Figure 1.3 reports the annualized volatility calculations and the bottom panel shows the underlying prices for January and February 1999. The top panel demonstrates that volatility can be extremely different depending on the time of the day at which it is measured with daily data. If observations are picked randomly once a day, the underlying volatility can be as small as 15% or as large as 22% for a given day and for the same currency. In mid-January 1999, the U.S. Dollar - Japanese Yen (USD-JPY) investors in the U.K. are assumed to be facing the risk of losing 56,676,400 USD in a portfolio of a hundred million USD with a 1% probability. In Japan, this risk would be reduced to 38,643,000 USD for the same day and for the same currency, a difference of approximately 18,000,000 USD between the two geographical locations! The utilization of high frequency leads to more robust

---

[4] This approximately corresponds to 10 years of returns measured over 10 minutes.

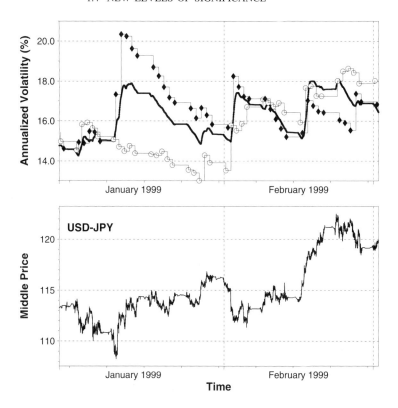

FIGURE 1.3 Top panel: Annualized USD-JPY volatility computed with daily prices observed at 7 a.m. GMT (afternoon Japan, circles), 5 p.m. GMT (afternoon U.K., diamonds) and with high-frequency data (solid line). The data period is from January 1999 to February 1999. Bottom panel: The USD-JPY high-frequency price series from January 1999 to February 1999.

annualized volatility estimations by minimizing the influence of the random noise in the market.

Another aspect of this is the choice of model. With few data, one tends to favor the simpler models because they contain few parameters and because tests like the likelihood ratio test would strongly penalize the increase of parameters. Of course, simplicity is a desirable feature of theoretical models, but one should not seek simplicity at the cost of missing important features of the data-generating process. Sometimes, it is useful to explore more complicated (nonlinear) models, which may contain more parameters. This increasing complexity is strongly penalized when explored with low-frequency data because of the loss of degrees of freedom. In the case of high-frequency data, however, the penalty is relatively small because the abundance of the independently measured observations approximates an asymptotic environment.

Researchers who want to use many observations with low-frequency data are using, for instance, daily observations of the Dow Jones Industrials from January 1897 like Ding *et al.* (1993) or LeBaron (1999a). In such a case, one is entitled to ask if the authors are actually analyzing the same market over the years. The huge technological changes that we experienced during this century have certainly affected the New York Stock Exchange and one is never sure, how this and any reconfiguration of the index has affected the results. To the contrary, high-frequency studies can be done for limited sampling periods with reasonably large samples. The market properties within such periods are nearly unchanged. The results are less affected by structural breaks or shifts in the overall economy than low-frequency studies with samples of many years. This is clearly an advantage when determining microstructure effects but also when examining the stability of some properties over time.

1.5   INTERRELATING DIFFERENT TIME SCALES

High-frequency data open the way for studying financial markets at very different time scales, from minutes to years. This represents an aggregation factor of four to five orders of magnitude.[5] Some empirical properties are similar at different scales, leading to fractal behaviors. Stylized facts observed for daily or weekly data gain additional weight when also observed with high significance for intraday data. An example of this is the long memory effect in 20-min absolute returns studied by Dacorogna *et al.* (1993). At the time, similar hyperbolic decay of the autocorrelation function was observed on daily returns in Ding *et al.* (1993). It is very difficult to distinguish rigorously in the data between long memory effects and regime shifts. Many mathematicians are working precisely on this problem such as Mansfield *et al.* (1999) and Mikosch and Starica (1999). Yet the fact that hyperbolic decay is empirically found at time scales that differ by two orders of magnitude in aggregation is definitely a sign that the process must include some long range dependence or that there are regime shifts at *all time scales*, which is equivalent.

Scaling properties and scaling laws have been new objects of study since the early work of Mandelbrot (1963) on cotton prices. In 1990, the research group of O&A published empirical studies of scaling properties extending from a few minutes to a few years (Müller *et al.*, 1990). These properties have shown remarkable stability over time (Guillaume *et al.*, 1997) and were found in other financial instruments like interest rates (Piccinato *et al.*, 1997). Mantegna and Stanley (1995) also found scaling behavior in the stock indices examined at high frequency. In a set of recent papers, Mandelbrot *et al.* (1997), Fisher *et al.* (1997) and Calvet *et al.* (1997) have derived a multifractal model based on the empirical scaling laws of different moments of the return distributions. Works on the scaling law of return

---

[5] By order of magnitude we mean the number of times the time horizon must be multiplied by 10 to achieve the lower frequency. For instance, a weekly frequency is aggregated three orders of magnitude from 10 minutes data (one week is 1008 times 10 minutes).

volatility have been flourishing in the past few years often coming from physicists who started venturing in the field of finance calling themselves "econophysicists." It is a sign that the field is moving toward a better understanding of aggregation properties. Unfortunately, the mathematical theory behind these empirical studies is not yet completely mature and there is still controversy regarding the significance of the scaling properties (LeBaron, 1999a; Bouchaud *et al.*, 2000). Thanks to high-frequency data, this kind of debate can now take place. The challenge is to develop models that simultaneously characterize the short-term *and* the long-term behaviors of a time series.

2

MARKETS AND DATA

2.1 GENERAL REMARKS ON MARKETS AND DATA TYPES

In the discussion of markets and data, we take the point of view of researchers studying high-frequency data rather than the view of traders or other practitioners. Instead of giving complete descriptions of markets (which are changing over time), we focus on those main markets that have produced consistent time series data over many years.

High-frequency data are direct information from markets. One logical unit of information is called a *tick*. This term originated from the language of practitioners and originally meant a number on a ticker tape, in a time before computers became an omnipresent tool. The term "tick" is more neutral and general than the particular terms "price," "interest rate," "quote," and so on. Whatever the quoted quantity, there is always a date and a time attached to every tick, a "time stamp." The sequence of time stamps is usually irregularly spaced. A large part of Chapter 3 deals with the consequences of this fact.

The quoted quantities are often prices, but other information such as transaction volume is also available from some markets. Detailed information on participants (e.g., the counterparty of transactions) is, however, rare because market participants often prefer anonymity.

Some markets are centralized in the form of exchanges or bourses. Other markets are decentralized interbank (over-the-counter) markets, where individual participants directly transact with no intermediary. Data from over-the-counter (OTC) markets are collected and provided in real time by data providers such as Reuters, Bloomberg, or Bridge. Data from centralized markets are available from the same sources and sometimes directly from the exchanges. The recent shift from floor trading to electronic trading helped to make this data more reliable and more easily available. Some data are released to a general audience only after a time delay when its direct value for traders has diminished. Exchanges such as London International Financial Futures Exchange (LIFFE) and the New York Stock Exchange (NYSE) also sell archived historical data, such as data from the TAQ database of the NYSE. There are also vendors of historical data such as O&A specializing in high-frequency data initially collected in real time from different sources.

The foreign exchange (FX) market has the highest market volume of all financial markets. A large part of this volume is traded over-the-counter between banks, but there is also electronic trading through centralized systems. The coexistence of interbank and centralized trading is found also in other markets. This implies that volume figures—if available—often refer to a market segment rather than all transactions of the whole market. Aside from FX, we discuss interest rate, bond, equity, and commodity markets; the latter two are scarcely treated in this book. All of these assets are directly traded in *spot* markets (see Section 2.1.1) and indirectly in *derivative markets*: *futures* and *option* markets as discussed in Sections 2.1.2 and 2.1.3.

In this book, there is no attempt to list all the changing types and trading mechanisms of markets and all the varying formats and availability conditions of data from different data suppliers.[1] Instead, we report stylized properties of time series data for markets with sampling periods of several years.

2.1.1 Spot Markets

Spot markets are direct markets for primary assets, such as foreign exchange or equity. The assets are traded immediately at the time of the transaction.[2] Spot trading is the most original form of trading, but it has some disadvantages. The timing is not flexible, traders have to deal with the physical delivery of the traded assets (such as commodities) and the interest rate spot market is affected by the counterparty default risk. For these reasons, derivative markets have become more important than spot markets in some cases. The FX market is a major example of a market where spot trading is still strong.

---

[1] A review is provided by Gwilym and Sutcliffe (1999).

[2] Transactions are actually booked at the *value date*, which is usually two days after the day of the spot transaction or, if that is a holiday, the first business day afterward. This fact hardly has an influence on prices, it just affects the timing of bookkeeping. Therefore, value dates can be ignored in most studies.

Some important spot markets are over-the-counter markets between individual institutions (banks), whereas many derivatives are traded at exchanges. However, this is not a general rule.

2.1.2 Futures Markets

In some cases such as most interest rates and commodities, futures markets have a higher liquidity and volume than the underlying spot markets and produce better high-frequency data. The following description of futures markets is quite general, and special features of particular futures markets are discussed in other sections.

Futures contracts are derivatives of an underlying asset, which can be defined as an agreement between two parties to buy or sell an asset at a certain time in the future for a certain price, Hull (1993). At this expiry time, the underlying asset has to be delivered according to settlement rules, after which the contract no longer exists. The expiry dates are regularly scheduled, often in a quarterly sequence. The contract with the nearest expiry is called the first position, the following contract the second position, and so on.

Most futures are traded at exchanges. Trading is typically geographically localized. There is no 24-hour trading, there are rigidly defined opening hours, although the trend is to effectively lengthen the active hours (e.g. with after-hours sessions). Given that futures contracts are exchange traded and each transaction is recorded centrally, futures markets offer a high price transparency. The historical data always include tick-by-tick transaction prices and, depending on the data source, bid and ask quotes and sometimes information on volumes and the flow of orders from the clients of the exchange.

The structure of many futures markets has changed due to the rapid growth of market volumes, some mergers of exchanges, and the shift from floor trading (open outcry) to electronic trading. For some researchers, this shift has been an object of study in itself.

All clients buying or selling futures contracts have to put some money in a collateral account. This account covers the counterparty default risk of the exchange. If the futures prices move to the disfavor of a client, the amount of money on the collateral account may no longer cover the risk, and the exchange will tell the client to increase it through a "call for margin." If the client fails to do this, the futures contract is terminated at its current market value. The flow of money to the collateral account (which earns some interest in its own right) makes the exact bookkeeping of returns (and risks) rather complicated, but this can be ignored in most studies.

The time series of prices coming from a single futures contract is not sufficiently long for certain statistical studies. Moreover, the behavior of a contract changes when approaching expiry and its price volatility systematically grows or shrinks according to the nature of the underlying asset. For these reasons, it is sometimes necessary to construct long samples joining several contracts together. Different empirical prescriptions are used by analysts and traders to join price histories of several futures contracts with successive expiries. Such prescriptions are typically based on rollover schemes – that is, they attempt to replicate the behavior of a trader holding a contract and switching ("rolling over") to the next contract before the expiry of the current contract. Section 2.5.2 gives such an example.

The opening hours of futures markets are sometimes modified, as those of other centralized markets. Long samples may extend over periods with different fixed opening hours. This fact leads to some difficulties in intraday studies, especially those related to daytime. Researchers should be aware of this and know the history of opening hours.

2.1.3 Option Markets

Option prices are very volatile and depend on parameters such as the strike price, the base spot price, and the expiry date. There are many types of options. The options markets are often too volatile for studying consistent time series over long samples and are not the subject of this book—except for the *implied volatility* aspect.

Unlike option prices, implied volatility figures are slowly changing over time. They are computed from option prices through the formulas introduced by Black and Scholes (1973) and some refined methods introduced later. The implied volatility figures provided by data vendors usually refer to at-the-money options (where the strike price is not far from the base spot price). For some markets, these data are available in high frequency with several quotes per day. Implied volatility can be interpreted as the market's forecast of the volatility of the underlying asset for the time period until expiry. Therefore, time series of implied volatility are interesting especially in comparison to historical or realized volatility computed from time series of underlying assets.

2.2 FOREIGN EXCHANGE MARKETS

The foreign exchange (FX) market is the largest financial market. Already in April 1992, its "traditional" part (FX spot and FX forward market, excluding the newer derivatives) had a daily net-net[3] turnover of 832 billion U.S. Dollar (USD) (Bank for International Settlements, 1993) which was more than the total non-gold reserves (USD 555.6 billion) of all industrial countries in 1992 (International Monetary Fund, 1993). Since that time, the FX net-net turnover had grown to USD 1190 billion in April 1995 and to USD 1500 billion in April 1998 (Bank for International Settlements, 1999).

The FX spot market produces high-frequency data that played and still play a central role in high-frequency finance. Unlike other data, these data are available over long sampling periods in high frequency, 24 hours per working day. The market is highly liquid and symmetric as both exchanged assets are currencies.

---

[3] This figure is adjusted for both local and cross-border double-counting.

Due to these favorable characteristics, new facts have often been found in FX spot data, and FX studies have served as a role model for the investigation of other high-frequency data with less favorable properties.

Since the beginning of the 1990s, academic researchers have been gaining new insights into the behavior of the FX markets through analyzing intraday data. Daily data, which were much used in the 1980s represent only a small subset of the information available at intraday frequencies, as they are only the average of a few intraday prices quoted by some large banks at a particular daytime. The number of data points available for intraday is larger by a factor of 1000.

On the basis of this information set, there is a rapidly growing body of literature in the study of the intraday FX markets, which opens new directions for understanding of financial markets and widening of concepts such as risk management or market efficiency. The analysis of intraday data also leads to insights into the market microstructure where it is possible to study the behavior of intraday traders, whose operations account for more than 90% of the FX market volume.

The stylized facts found for intraday FX rates shed some new light on different modeling approaches to the FX market.[4] Research studies have shown that known and well-accepted empirical regularities of daily or weekly data do not always hold up in intraday analysis. Looking at intraday data, the homogeneity of market agents (which is a working hypothesis for studying daily, weekly, or low-frequency data) disappears. A new wealth of structure is uncovered that demonstrates the complexity of the FX market at the intraday frequency. This complexity can be explained by the interaction of market agents with heterogeneous objectives resulting from different geographical locations, the various forms of institutional constraints, and risk profiles. This evidence will be presented in several chapters of this book. Indeed, the heterogeneous structure of intraday data may explain the fact that practitioners have effectively used methods of "technical analysis" over many years now. These intuitively designed methods try to take advantage of the interaction of different components of the markets, see Dunis and Feeny (1989); Neftci (1991); Surajaras and Sweeney (1992); Taylor and Allen (1992); Pictet *et al.* (1992); Levich and Thomas (1993b); Brock *et al.* (1992); Gençay and Stengos (1998) and Gençay (1998a,b, 1999); Gençay *et al.* (2001c, 2002).

The FX spot market is presented in Section 2.2.1. Aside from the spot market, there is also the over-the-counter FX forward market treated in Section 2.3.2 and the markets for FX futures and FX options. The contracts of these markets refer to a time period in the future, therefore they are affected by interest rate levels.

Exchange-traded FX futures follow the description of Section 2.1.2 and are not discussed here; their market volume is much lower than that of the FX spot market and the over-the-counter derivative markets, particularly the FX forward market.

As mentioned in Section 2.1.3, time series of implied volatility are available from the FX option markets. These are interesting objects of study, together with realized or historical volatility computed from FX spot rates.

---

[4] For surveys on the FX market at the daily or weekly frequencies, see, for example, the surveys of Mussa (1979); Hsieh (1988); Baillie and McMahon (1989), and de Vries (1992).

2.2.1 Structure of the Foreign Exchange Spot Market

The usual description of the FX markets made by international organizations such as the Bank for International Settlements (1999) or the International Monetary Fund (1993) emphasizes the presence of different geographical markets and different types of agents. However, these structural characteristics are not apparent from the inspection of daily or weekly data and their implications were seldom considered in theoretical modeling.

The FX market consists of two dominating parts, the FX spot and the FX forward market, and a smaller but growing market of FX derivatives. In 1992, both the FX spot and forward markets had a market share of roughly 50% each. In 1998, the FX forward market was moderately larger than the FX spot market, by a ratio 60:40% (Bank for International Settlements, 1999). However, the FX spot rates are used not only in the FX spot market but also for outright FX forward transactions, as explained in Section 2.3.2.

Nowadays, a growing segment of the FX spot transactions goes through automated, electronic order-matching systems,[5] such as the Electronic Broking Services (EBS) and Reuters Dealing 2000. These markets deliver good high-frequency data with transaction prices and volumes. These transaction data have become available to researchers to a limited amount.[6] Results based on these data are discussed in a few places in this book.

Aside from this electronic trading, the over-the-counter FX spot market is a direct market between banks (and brokers). The bid and ask offers of major financial institutions are conveyed to customers' screens by large data suppliers such as Reuters, Bloomberg, and Bridge (formerly Telerate and Knight Ridder) with as little time delay as possible and the deals are negotiated over the telephone. Many researchers have investigated data in various forms from this interbank market; there is no alternative way to obtain large FX samples, especially historical samples extending to the 1980s and early 1990s.

The bid-ask prices from the over-the-counter FX spot market are called *quoted* prices or quotes as opposed to transaction prices. One full tick contains the time stamp, a bid and an ask price and often some information on the origin of the tick (bank code, city, etc.). Transaction prices or volumes are not available, but some additional information such as financial news in text form is available from other pages of the data vendors.

The data suppliers offer a rather easy access to market data nowadays. The real-time data for a financial instrument can be obtained from Reuters, for instance, through the Reuters Instrument Code (RIC). The FX rate EUR-USD, for instance,[7] has the RIC "EUR=," the FX rate USD-JPY has the RIC "JPY=." Rates

---

[5] In April 1998, the share of deals going through such systems was "almost one quarter" in the United Kingdom, "almost one third" in the United States, and 36% in Japan, (Bank for International Settlements, 1999).

[6] Lyons (1995, 1996a,b); Goodhart *et al.* (1995), and Goodhart and Payne (1996) could obtain a few days of such data.

[7] For the currencies, we use the standard abbreviations of the International Organization for Standardization (ISO, code 4217).

TABLE 2.1   The traditional FXFX page of Reuters.

On this traditional page, the first column gives the time in GMT (for example, for the first line, "07:27"), the second column gives the name of a traded currency ("DEM" for USD-DEM), the third column the name of the bank subsidiary that publishes the quote as a mnemonic ("RABO"), the fourth column the name of the bank ("Rabobank"), the fifth column the location of the bank as a mnemonic ("UTR" for Utrecht), the sixth column gives the bid price with five digits ("1.6290") and the two last digits of the ask price ("00" which means 1.6300), the seventh column repeats the currency ("DEM"), and the last two columns give the highest ("1.6365") and the lowest ("1.6270") quoted prices of the day.

```
0727 CCY PAGE NAME   * REUTER SPOT RATES * CCY     HI*EURO*LO FXFX
0727 DEM RABO RABOBANK UTR    1.6290/00  * DEM    1.6365    1.6270
0727 GBP MNBX MOSCOW   LDN    1.5237/42  * GBP    1.5245    1.5207
0727 CHF UBZA U B S    ZUR    1.3655/65  * CHF    1.3730    1.3630
0727 JPY IBJX I.B.J    LDN    102.78/83  * JPY    103.02    102.70
0727 FRF BUEX UE CIC   PAR    5.5620/30  * FRF    5.5835    5.5582
0726 NLG RABO RABOBANK UTR    1.8233/38  * NLG    1.8309    1.8220
0727 ITL BCIX B.C.I.   MIL  1592.00/3.00 * ITL    1596.00   1591.25
0727 ECU NWNT NATWEST  LDN    1.1807/12  * ECU    1.1820    1.1774


XAU SBZG 387.10/387.60 * ED3  4.43/ 4.56 * FED    PREB  * GOVA 30Y
XAG SBCM     5.52/ 5.53 * US30Y YTM  7.39 * 4.31- 4.31 * 86.14-15
```

between two currencies other than the U.S. Dollar (USD) are called cross rates (see Section 2.2.2) and have both currencies in the RIC (e.g. "EURJPY=" for the rate EUR-JPY). There are also RICs serving as "tables of contents," called tiles. These contain information on other RICS. Once a real-time feed for a financial instrument is established, the data are transmitted in data records, each representing a tick. A data record contains several variables such as bid and ask prices and some side information. This data organization is used for all financial data, not just for FX.

Once the instrument codes and the variables of the data records are known, data collection is a straightforward operation. However, many results of this book are based on historical data collected at a time when data extraction was technically difficult. The traditional data feeds of the early 1990s and before were oriented to human users looking at full pages of information, such as the FXFX page of Reuters. Table 2.1 shows a snapshot of this traditional FXFX page. A quoted price of 1.6290/00 for the USD-DEM rate expresses the willingness of the market maker to buy USD at 1.6290 DEM and sell USD at 1.6300 DEM. Telerate also had a page-based feed at that time. Rather than using today's instrument codes, the data collector had to extract the desired information from full pages and from the many real-time updating messages associated to these pages. This implied a delicate text parsing task and also controlling for unexpected changes in the page layout. A large part of the data used in the studies of this book has been extracted and collected in this tedious way.

The FX market has no business-hour limitations. Any market maker can submit new bid-ask prices; many larger institutions have branches worldwide so that trading is continuous. Nevertheless, the bid-ask prices do emanate from particular banks in particular locations and the deals are entered into dealers' books in particular institutions. Although the FX market is virtually global through its electronic linkages, its activity pattern can be divided into three continental components, each with its typical group of time zones: East Asia, Europe, and America with Tokyo, London and New York as major trading centers[8] (Goodhart and Demos, 1990).

Except for some major currencies against the USD, currencies tend to be traded more specifically in their own geographical markets. Major currencies are USD, EUR (until 1998: DEM), JPY, GBP, and CHF. Both the global and local characteristics of the FX markets are reflected by the statistical properties of the data.

Actual trading prices and volumes are not known from the over-the-counter spot market. However, reputation considerations prevent market makers from quoting prices at which they would actually not be willing to trade. Therefore, real transaction prices tend to be contained within the quoted bid-ask spread (Petersen and Fialkowski, 1994). This is also shown by a comparison to simultaneous transaction prices of electronic dealing systems (where the bid-ask spread is narrower).

The growing volume of FX transactions has been increasingly made up of short-term, intraday transactions and results from the interaction of traders with different time-horizons, risk-profiles, or regulatory constraints. Nonfinancial corporations, institutional investors (mutual funds, pension funds, insurance companies), and hedge funds[9] have shifted their FX activities from long-term (buy and hold) investment to short-term (profit-making) transactions. This movement is both enabled and enhanced by the development of real-time information systems and the decrease of transaction costs following the liberalization of cross-border financial flows. This flow of short and long-term transactions initiated by nonfinancial institutions on the retail market is the origin of an even larger—by a factor of four to five times—flow of intradaily transactions between the dealers (the 50 largest banks and a few securities houses) on the wholesale market. These dealers, who are usually not allowed to take overnight positions, transact with each other to reduce the risk arising from their accumulated currency positions (Lyons, 1996a).

---

[8] In typical historical samples, the data contributors of "East Asia" are located in Australia, Hong Kong, India, Indonesia, Japan, South Korea, Malaysia, New Zealand, and Singapore. "Europe" covers Austria, Bahrain, Belgium, Germany, Denmark, Finland, France, Great Britain, Greece, Ireland, Italy, Israel, Jordan, Kuwait, Luxembourg, the Netherlands, Norway, Saudi Arabia, South Africa, Spain, Sweden, Switzerland, Turkey, and United Arab Emirates. "America" comprises Argentina, Canada, Mexico, and the United States.

[9] The high leverage and unregulated aspects of hedge funds distinguish their investors from other institutional investors.

TABLE 2.2 Numbers of archived ticks of main FX rates.

Tick frequencies of main FX rates: (1) main rates against the USD, (2) main cross rates, and (3) main rates against historical currencies now replaced by the Euro (EUR).

FX rate	Period	Number of ticks	Frequency per business day
EUR-USD	Jan 1999 – May 2000	4,794,958	13,300
USD-JPY	Jan 1987 – May 2000	9,585,136	2,800
GBP-USD	Jan 1987 – May 2000	7,892,919	2,310
USD-CHF	Jan 1987 – May 2000	8,310,226	2,430
EUR-JPY	Jan 1999 – May 2000	1,897,007	5,250
EUR-GBP	Jan 1999 – May 2000	1,740,209	4,820
USD-DEM	Jan 1987 – Dec 1998	18,416,814	6,020
USD-FRF	Jan 1987 – Dec 1998	3,655,638	1,190
DEM-JPY	Oct 1992 – Dec 1998	1,316,933	712

Still on the wholesale market, but in contrast to other players, central banks can afford relatively large open positions and can thereby have a significant impact on the market in the long run. The different types of traders can of course be found within similar types of institutions.[10]

To illustrate the enormous amounts of available FX spot ticks, Table 2.2 displays the size and frequencies of ticks in the Olsen & Associates (O&A) database. The FX rates of this table are between major currencies, the first one of a currency pair being the "exchanged" currency whose value is expressed in the second currency (which can be called the numeraire currency). The analyzed periods have been chosen with respect to the transition of some European currencies such as DEM and FRF to the Euro (EUR) at the beginning of 1999. On the largest market, EUR-USD, more than 10,000 ticks per business day are available; that is an average of almost 10 ticks per minute which can rise to 30 or more ticks per minute during the busiest periods. The daily tick frequencies of Table 2.2 are averages. The values of the 1980s and the early 1990s were distinctly smaller than the values nowadays. In today's data feeds, some of the ticks contain little information if they are copies of ticks from other contributors (as explained in Section 2.2.3) or repeatedly posted ticks (see Section 4.2.2). Minor FX rates have fewer ticks than the rates in Table 2.2, very few ticks if the liquidity is low.

In contrast to daily or weekly data, collecting tick-by-tick quotes presents a number of practical problems such as transmission delays and breakdowns or

---

[10] For example, Bank Negara of Malaysia was one of the most aggressive (short-term) speculators in the FX market for several years.

aberrant quotes due to human and technical errors. Therefore, it is important to implement a data cleaning filter to eliminate outliers. An extensive discussion of data cleaning is presented in Chapter 4.

2.2.2 Synthetic Cross Rates

FX rates between two currencies other than the U.S. Dollar (USD) are called *cross rates*. There are quotes for some important cross rates such as those in Table 2.2. For many other cross rates, there is little data or no data at all, either because the market for that cross rate is neglected by the data suppliers or because there is no direct market at all. In the second case, traders would go through a *vehicle currency* such as USD or EUR instead of making a direct transaction. A Canadian trader, for example, would obtain Japanese Yen (JPY) by buying USD from the USD-CAD market and selling USD on the USD-JPY market. The actual exchange rate in this case is

$$ p_{\text{JPY/CAD,bid}} = \frac{p_{\text{USD/CAD,bid}}}{p_{\text{USD/JPY,ask}}} , \quad p_{\text{JPY/CAD,ask}} = \frac{p_{\text{USD/CAD,ask}}}{p_{\text{USD/JPY,bid}}} \quad (2.1) $$

These formulas reflect the triangular relation between the three currencies USD, JPY, and CAD. If a direct market for JPY-CAD exists and its prices strongly deviate from this relation, the deviation can be profitably exploited through a set of riskless transactions. Such a strategy is called triangular arbitrage and leads to market adjustments that bring the prices back toward the relation of Equation 2.1. Traders are usally quick enough to make such arbitrage transactions before the prices strongly deviate from Equation 2.1. A trader calling market makers to execute an indirect transaction has to pay the bid-ask spreads of two markets, both USD-CAD and USD-JPY in our example. Both bid-ask spreads together may be higher than the bid-ask spread of a direct transaction.

In the case of cross rates with a direct market but bad data coverage, we are forced to compute synthetic cross rates through formulas such as Equation 2.1 which serve as proxies for the unknown direct rates. The two ticks used for the cross rate computation (a USD-CAD tick and a USD-JPY tick in the example of Equation 2.1) should be synchronous such that their time stamps deviate by no more than a few seconds or perhaps a minute. Otherwise, the synthetic cross rate is distorted by price moves in the time interval between the two ticks. The bid-ask spreads of the missing direct quotes can be expected to be lower than the synthetic bid-ask spreads. The data coverage for cross rates may only be bad during the active market hours of some time zones (e.g., due to the bad coverage of Asian markets by some data suppliers). In this case, we may have to mix quoted cross rate data with synthetic data (at certain daytimes).

2.2.3 Multiple Contributor Effects

The transactions of over-the-counter markets are between many individual institutions (banks and brokers). The market makers among these institutions publish their own price quotes. Data suppliers mix these data with the quotes of other contributors, thus creating a multicontributor data feed. Individual quotes are affected by the positions, views, and trading strategies of individual contributors, rather than behaving uniformly. Researchers using these data should be aware of this fact.

The FX spot market is the key example of a multicontributor market. The following multicontributor effects have been found in FX spot data:

- Depending on their inventory position, market makers have preferences for either selling or buying. They publish new quotes to attract traders to make a deal in the desired direction so that either the bid or the ask quote is competitive. The other price of the bid-ask pair is pushed away to a less attractive region by adding or subtracting a rather large, nominal spread. This leads to high unrealistic quoted bid-ask spreads and a negative autocorrelation of returns at lags of around one minute as discussed in Section 5.2.1.

- There are contributors of low reputation that abuse some quotes in attempts to manipulate the market into a desired direction.

- FX quotes lag behind the real market prices. This is confirmed by FX traders we have interviewed and from comparisons to transaction data from electronic trading systems. A closer look shows that some leading contributors do not have a considerable delay, whereas many other contributors lag behind by more than a minute. This can be shown through a *lead-lag* correlation analysis of returns of contributor-specific time series.

- Some contributors are laggards because they publish prices copied from the quotes of other contributors (e.g., moving averages of recent quotes with a tiny random modification). The motivation is to advertise the market presence of the contributor in the data feed (whereas true prices are negotiated over the telephone). These contributors often employ computers to publish fake quotes at high frequency. The described data-copying methods lead to lower data quality in general and lead to data-cleaning problems as discussed in Chapter 4.

Similar multicontributor effects are also found and expected in markets other than the FX spot market.

2.3 OVER-THE-COUNTER INTEREST RATE MARKETS

Two financial markets related to interest rates are over-the-counter (OTC) markets between individual banks.[11] These are the spot interest rate (IR) market and the FX forward market.

---

[11] This is similar to the interbank FX market.

2.3.1 Spot Interest Rates

Interest rate quotes have been directly available from the over-the-counter market for many years, for example, through the multicontributor "deposit" pages of Reuters. These interest rates are offered by banks to other banks who want to make either a deposit (at the bid interest rate) or take a credit (at the ask interest rate). The quotes come in bid-ask pairs and are called spot interest rates, cash interest rates, or interbank interest rates. Another traditional name, "Eurodeposits," suffers from possible confusion with the new currency named Euro. For quite some time, the spot interest rate (IR) market is no longer the most liquid IR market. This role is now taken by the IR futures market, see Section 2.4. The low liquidity of the spot IR market is reflected by the rather large spread between bid and ask quotes.

The actual rate at which a bank is ready to lend money to another one also depends on the credit rating of that bank. A bank with a low credit rating has to be ready to pay a higher IR in order to attract a lender; the IR level is increased by the *credit spread* . This fact makes the IR quotes less universally applicable than the FX quotes.

The credit spread can lead to serious data problems, which can lead to spurious statistical results. The story of the Japanese interest rates in the second half of the 1990s is the best illustration. There was a banking crisis in Japan that lowered the credit ratings of Japanese banks. In some data sources such as the Reuters deposit pages, these banks dominated some daytimes corresponding to the working hours of East Asian time zones. All of the IR quotes during these daytimes were systematically higher than the quotes at other daytimes. The market was split between low-rating banks and high-rating banks, causing two spurious statistical effects: (1) too high absolute values of returns (level changes) over time intervals of around 12 hr and (2) strong negative autocorrelation of returns at lags of around 12 hr. These spurious effects are solely due to periodically shifting credit ratings, which can be avoided by eliminating all the low-rating (or all high-rating) quotes from the sample. For a long time, Japanese Yen (JPY) interest rates were very low, below 1% for Japanese banks. The credit spread led to a strange effect around 1998 by pushing the IR levels for non-Japanese banks (dominating the European and American time zones) slightly *below zero*. Since then, this has been a classical example rejecting zero as an absolute minimum of IRs. Slightly negative interest rates can be possible and valid under special circumstances.

Spot interest rates always refer to a deposit of fixed duration, the maturity period. The following maturity periods are quoted in the market: overnight (O/N), "tomorrow next" (T/N, the next business day after tomorrow), 1 week (S/W), 1 month (1M), 2 months (2M), 3 months (3M), 6 months (6M), 9 months (9M), and 1 year (1Y). Among these maturity periods, the 3-month maturity often has the largest market and the best data followed by the 1-month, 2-month, 6-month, and 1-year maturities. Spot interest rates are the only IR instruments that always inform us on interest rate levels for time intervals starting now and extending over less than 3 months. Therefore, their use is inevitable when constructing yield curves; see Section 2.4.2.

Spot IRs are quoted in annualized form and in percentage terms. A 3-month IR of 6%, for example, means that the invested capital is multiplied by 1.015 after 3 months, because 3 months = 0.25 years and $0.25 \cdot 6\% = 1.5\% = 0.015$.

2.3.2 Foreign Exchange Forward Rates

Foreign exchange (FX) forward rates share some characteristics with the spot IRs. They also refer to the interbank market and are quoted for the same maturities as the spot IRs (see Section 2.3.1). They are quoted on the same traditional Reuters deposit pages.

FX forward transactions are similar to FX spot transactions, except that the actual transaction takes effect in the future, at maturity.[12] The timing of FX forward transactions leads to a difference in interest payments as compared to FX transactions. Due to the delayed transaction, the buyer of an FX forward contract earns some interest on the base currency of the FX rate (the currency in which the FX rate is expressed) instead of the exchanged currency. If the interest rates of the two currencies deviate, there is a net interest payment flow from or to the buyer during the maturity period. This fact determines the price of the FX forward contract, called the *outright* forward rate. In order to avoid riskfree arbitrage, the outright forward rate deviates from the simultaneously quoted FX spot price by an amount to offset the deviations in interest payments. The price deviation between FX spot prices and outright forward rates thus reflects the interest rate *differential* between the two exchanged currencies rather than the absolute level of those IRs.

The arbitrage relation between outright FX forward rates f, spot interest rates i and FX spot rates p can be formulated as follows:

$$
\begin{aligned}
f_{\text{bid}} &= p_{\text{bid}} \frac{1 + i_{\text{expr,bid}} \frac{m}{1\,\text{year}}}{1 + i_{\text{exch,ask}} \frac{m}{1\,\text{year}}} \\[2ex]
f_{\text{ask}} &= p_{\text{ask}} \frac{1 + i_{\text{expr,ask}} \frac{m}{1\,\text{year}}}{1 + i_{\text{exch,bid}} \frac{m}{1\,\text{year}}}
\end{aligned}
\tag{2.2}
$$

where m is the maturity period (e. g. 0.25 years for a 3-month period). This formula can be found in usual textbooks such as Walmsley (1992) but only for a middle price, not for bid and ask. It is valid for maturity periods up to one year. For longer periods, formulas based on compound interest are needed. The interest rates i should not be used in percentage (e.g., 0.05 should be used instead of 5%). The index "exch" denotes the exchanged currency of the FX rate; the index "expr" defines the (numeraire) currency in which one unit of the exchanged currency is expressed.

---

[12] The transaction is actually booked at the *value date*, which is usually two days after the maturity date or, if that is a holiday, the first business day afterward. This fact hardly has an influence on prices, it just affects the timing of bookkeeping. Therefore, value dates can be ignored in most studies.

Instead of outright FX forward prices f, the *difference* $f - p$ is usually quoted, which is the outright forward price minus the simultaneously valid FX spot price. This difference is less volatile than the outright forward price and can be positive or negative according to the sign of the interest rate differential. A positive difference is called *forward premium*, a negative difference is a *forward discount*. Both are also called "forward points." This formulation relates to the units of "basis points" in which they are usually quoted, which is the multiples of the last decimal digit of normal FX spot quotes. As an example, assume an FX spot rate of 1.5025/30 ($p_{\text{bid}} = 1.5025$, $p_{\text{ask}} = 1.5030$) and quoted forward points of -23/-20. The outright forward price is therefore $f_{\text{bid}} = 1.5002 (= 1.5025 - 0.0023)$ and $f_{\text{ask}} = 1.5010 (= 1.5030 - 0.0020)$.

FX forward premiums and discounts are also called FX swap rates , following another common view where an FX forward transaction is seen as a spot transaction plus a "swap" transaction (swapping two currencies during the maturity period). In fact, there is a large market for such FX swap transactions independent from spot or outright forward transactions.

Equation 2.2 can be used to compute synthetic forward rates from an FX spot rate and the spot IRs of both underlying currencies. Such synthetic FX forward rates are less reliable than direct quotes. They have a distinctly higher bid-ask spread. This implies that an FX forward transaction is more efficient than a substitute set of transactions, consisting of an FX spot transaction plus a deposit in one currency plus a loan in the other one. Direct forward quotes exist for most FX rates against the USD, but may not be available for some FX *cross* rates (see Section 2.2.2). For these currency pairs, synthetic forward rates are needed.

2.4 INTEREST RATE FUTURES

2.4.1 General Description of Interest Rate Futures

Short-term interest rate (IR) futures are the most liquid financial instrument for the interest rate markets. In particular, the IR futures markets with expiry periods of up to one year (or slightly longer) are more liquid than the over-the-counter spot IR market, as presented in Section 2.3.1. The transaction costs are lower; a typical bid-ask spread is about 10% (or less) of the quoted spread of cash interest rates.[13] The mechanism of price formation for futures is faster than for cash contracts (Fung and Leung, 1993; Garbade and Silber, 1985). As a consequence, IR futures markets yield high-quality intraday data.

IR futures markets are futures markets in the sense of Section 2.1.2. More specifically, an interest rate futures contract is a futures contract on an asset whose price is dependent solely on the level of interest rates, (Hull, 1993).

---

[13] The bid-ask spread on the Chicago Mercantile Exchange (CME) Eurodollar contract, for example, can be as small as half a basis point. A basis point corresponds to 1/100 of 1%, and its monetary value (in the case of three-month IR futures) is $25. The minimum price movement for the CME Eurodollar is half a basis point.

IR futures are traded at the Chicago Mercantile Exchange (CME),[14] the EU-REX (formerly the DTB, MATIF, etc.), the London International Financial Futures Exchange (LIFFE), the Singapore International Monetary Exchange (SIMEX), and other exchanges. In the first three quarters of 1997, the CME Eurodollar time deposit had a mean daily volume of 461,098 contracts,[15] with each contract corresponding to a notional 1 million dollar 3-month deposit. IR futures are exchange-traded contracts and this entails several differences with respect to over-the-counter (OTC) instruments, as already explained in Section 2.1.2. IR futures are linked to a specific exchange, except when a fungibility agreement is in effect.[16] Trading is typically limited to opening hours. Most IR futures exchanges have replaced or are replacing floor trading (open outcry) with electronic trading. In studies of long data samples, we may be forced to use a first half of data originating from floor trading and a second half from electronic trading.

IR futures are traditionally known under the name *Eurofutures*; the contracts were called "Eurolira," "Euroyen," and similar after the underlying currency. In statistical studies based on historical samples, these names may still be used, but nowadays, they lead to confusion with the new currency named the Euro.

Information on IR futures is particularly valuable for financial institutions and above all for banks. A quick analysis of a typical balance sheet would often reveal a higher exposure to IR risk than, for example, to foreign exchange risk. IR futures can also be used as hedging instruments. From a practical point of view, there is widespread need for a better understanding of the empirical behavior of IR futures on an intraday basis; nevertheless, in the literature there is little material on intraday IR futures markets. The studies by Ballocchi *et al.* (1999a,b), and Ballocchi *et al.* (2001) offer deep insights. The impact of scheduled news releases has been investigated by Ederington and Lee (1993, 1995).

IR futures refer to an underlying deposit (usually a 3-month deposit). An IR future price f (bid, ask, or transaction price) is quoted as a number slightly below 100 according to the following formulas

$$f = 100 \left(1 - \frac{r}{100\%}\right), \quad r = \left(1 - \frac{f}{100}\right) 100\% \qquad (2.3)$$

where r is the annualized forward interest rate[17] with a forward period of usually 3 months. There are four main settlement months in a year (March, June, September, and December), known as *quarterly expiries*. Serial expiry contracts (i.e., contracts expiring in months that do not correspond to the quarterly sequence) have been introduced more recently and typically have lower liquidity.

Unlike the spot IRs, the futures prices are not affected by the individual credit ratings of clients, because the collateral account required by the exchange already

---

[14] They are traded at the International Monetary Market (IMM) Division of the CME.

[15] All expiries combined, as reported in the January 1, 1998, issue of *Futures* magazine.

[16] One example of a fungibility agreement is the mutual offset system between CME and SIMEX, through which contracts opened in one exchange can be liquidated on the other one.

[17] For instance, a value $r = 3\%$ implies a futures price of 97.00.

covers the credit risk. The existence of the collateral account can usually be ignored in studies of IR futures data.

Unlike other futures markets contracts, IR futures contracts are settled in cash. The notional deliverable asset is a (3-month) deposit starting at expiry, but the exchange or the party with the short position does not deliver such a contract at expiry. Instead, a cash payment corresponding to the value of the notional deposit is made. This value is determined by the short-term offered rate (e.g., EURIBOR or LIBOR) at expiry.

As for futures in general, single contracts have a nonstationary time series of limited lifetime (e.g., Fung and Leung, 1993). A typical nonstationary effect of IR future contracts is the systematic decrease of mean volatility when moving closer to the expiry (which is fixed in calendar time). In order to study long time series, we have to connect the data from several contracts. Rollover schemes as suggested in Section 2.1.2 are not the most suitable method in the case of IR futures, because several contracts with different expiries trade at the same time with comparable liquidity, unlike what happens in bond futures and other futures markets, where basically only one contract (or at most two) are actively traded at any given time.

In the case of IR futures, the problem is inherently multivariate such that the interplay of several contracts with different expiries but simultaneous high open interest levels cannot be neglected. The method followed here is to infer *implied interest rates* from the prices of futures as discussed in the next section.

2.4.2 Implied Forward Interest Rates and Yield Curves

Implied interest rates have some advantages over IR futures prices. They can be studied in long time series. The behavior of their returns is closer to stationary, although more subtle effects such as local volatility peaks before expiry dates may still remain in time series of implied rates. Implied interest rates can be studied in two different forms:

- Forward interest rates: The interest rate for a period of usually 3 months, with a starting point always shifted to the future by a fixed time interval;
- Yield curve: Spot interest rates for periods starting now. The yield curve is the full term structure of interest rates of different maturities.

Both forms need to be computed as discussed next. Futures prices alone are not sufficient to construct implied spot rates (points on the yield curve), because the IR futures market does not convey any information about the applicable spot rate for the period from the current time to the next futures expiry. The necessity to use data from other instruments (spot IRs) can be avoided by studying forward IRs, with a minimum starting point of 3 months in the future.

There are many methods to construct forward interest rates or full yield curves from IR futures. Instead of presenting the wide field of methods in the literature, we explain the method that was actually used to obtain the results presented in this book, the *polynomial* method. To use the information from IR futures to construct a yield curve of forward (or spot) rates, a timing problem needs to be dealt with.

Futures are defined in terms of the contract expiry date (a fixed quarterly date, every 3 months for the major contracts) and the maturity period of the underlying reference rate (a fixed time interval, usually 3 months), whereas the implied forward rates are defined in terms of fixed time intervals, not in terms of fixed calendar dates. Those time intervals (forward periods) can be written as $[t_{exp}, t_{exp} + \Delta T_m]$. They start at time $t_{exp} = t + T_{exp}$ (t is the current time) where T_{exp} is called the time-to-start for the implied forward rate and ΔT_m is the maturity[18] period of the notional deposit.

The polynomial method presented here is based on the interpolation of rates between points on the expiry time axis. Polynomials of degree 2 are used for the interpolation. The choice of polynomial rather than linear interpolation is motivated by the seasonal behavior of returns. Forward IR series generated by linear interpolation exhibit some 3-month seasonalities, which are weak but distinctly stronger than those of forward IR series generated by polynomial interpolation. The seasonality of linearly interpolated data turns out to be an artifact due to insufficient modeling within the 3-month interpolation intervals.

A continuously compounded forward interest rate ϱ is assumed and modeled as a function of the time T where T is the size of the time *interval* from the time when the quote was issued to the time point of interest. The annualized implied forward rate r, whose relation to futures prices f is given by Equation 2.3, can be expressed by

$$r = \frac{1 \text{ year}}{T_{end} - T_{start}} \left\{ \exp\left[\int_{T_{start}}^{T_{end}} \varrho(T)\, dT \right] - 1 \right\} 100\% \qquad (2.4)$$

where the forward period is from T_{start} to T_{end}. For a futures contract, $T_{start} = T_{exp}$ is the expiry time and $T_{end} = T_{mat}$ is the maturity time, which terminates at the maturity period, $T_{mat} = T_{exp} + \Delta T_m$, with the forward period ΔT_m (often 3 months). The inverse formula is

$$\bar{\varrho} = \frac{\ln(1 + \frac{T_{mat} - T_{exp}}{1 \text{ year}} \frac{r}{100\%})}{T_{mat} - T_{exp}} \qquad (2.5)$$

which gives the mean value $\bar{\varrho}$ of $\varrho(T)$ within the forward period. The function $\varrho(T)$ consists of piecewise, continuously connected, quadratic polynomials

$$\varrho(T) = a\, t^2 + b\, t + c, \quad \text{with } t = \frac{2\, T - T_{exp} - T_{mat}}{T_{mat} - T_{exp}} \qquad (2.6)$$

for $T_{exp} \leq T \leq T_{mat}$ (i.e., $-1 \leq t \leq 1$). The polynomial coefficients should obey the requirements of Equation 2.4 and all quoted forward rates are reproduced by integration of Equation 2.6. The other requirement is the continuity of $\varrho(T)$ at the

---

[18] We do not use the term "maturity" as a synonym of "expiry," but we reserve it to denote the duration of deposits, including the underlying deposits of futures contracts. The maturity period of a futures contract thus starts at expiry.

edge points T_{exp} and T_{mat}, where the forward period meets the forward periods of the neighbor contracts. The value of ϱ at the meeting point T_{exp} is determined from the four implied forward rates nearest to T_{exp} (in a regular sequence of 3-month futures contracts) by polynomial interpolation

$$\varrho(T_{exp}) = \frac{9\,(\bar{\varrho}_2 + \bar{\varrho}_3) - \bar{\varrho}_1 - \bar{\varrho}_4}{16} \tag{2.7}$$

where $\bar{\varrho}$ is computed by Equation 2.5 and its index $(1, 2, 3, 4)$ indicates the position in the series of the four nearest forwards. For instance, $\bar{\varrho}_3$ refers to the forward from T_{exp} to T_{mat}. Equation 2.7 can be interpreted as the interpolation of a cubic polynomial going through the values $\bar{\varrho}_1 \ldots \bar{\varrho}_4$, located at the midpoints of the corresponding forward periods. The same equation if shifted by one forward period leads to $\varrho(T_{mat})$. If a contract at the edge ($\bar{\varrho}_1$ or $\bar{\varrho}_4$ in Equation 2.7) is not available from the data source, we extrapolate

$$\bar{\varrho}_1 = \frac{3\,\bar{\varrho}_2 - \bar{\varrho}_3}{2} \tag{2.8}$$

and analogously for $\bar{\varrho}_4$. The numerical impact of an extrapolation error is small, as $\bar{\varrho}_1$ and $\bar{\varrho}_4$ have little impact in Equation 2.7. By fulfilling all the mentioned requirements, the coefficients of the polynomial $\varrho(T)$ of Equation 2.6 can be formulated as

$$a = \frac{3}{4}\,[\varrho(T_{exp}) + \varrho(T_{mat}) - 2\,\bar{\varrho}] \tag{2.9}$$

$$b = \frac{1}{2}\,[\varrho(T_{mat}) - \varrho(T_{exp})]$$

$$c = \frac{1}{4}\,[6\,\bar{\varrho} - \varrho(T_{exp}) - \varrho(T_{mat})]$$

where $\bar{\varrho}$ follows from Equation 2.5 ($\bar{\varrho} = \bar{\varrho}_3$, using the indexing of Equation 2.7).

Now we can compute the annualized forward rate r for a given forward period by substituting Equations 2.5 through 2.9 into Equation 2.4. The integration is simple because the integrand, Equation 2.6, is a simple polynomial. The forward period to be considered (from T_{start} to T_{end}) may typically extend over many original forward periods of the futures contracts. In this case, we need to integrate over several piecewise polynomials.

A consequence of the polynomial interpolation is the potential overshooting of the yield curve. If the forward rates implied by a series of IR futures have a maximum somewhere around medium-term expiries, an interpolated forward rate (for a period close to that maximum) may exceed all the implied forward rates corresponding to original futures quotes. The modest overshooting of polynomial interpolation is not undesirable as it leads to a strong reduction of the 3-month seasonalities obtained for a forward IR series generated by linear interpolation (which has no overshooting). We conclude that polynomials with their smooth but sometimes overshooting behavior represent true yield curves better than piecewise linear interpolation with hard corners at the nodes. In our method, overshooting is a local effect—distant contracts cannot affect the behavior of $\varrho(T)$. This is better than some methods based on spline interpolation, where even very distant contracts have an influence on the local behavior.

A special case of overshooting might be "undershooting" of (forward) interest rates. Some parts of $\varrho(T)$ might have values below zero. The method should include an element to avoid strongly negative $\varrho(T)$, although interest rates can move *slightly* below zero under extreme circumstances.

The polynomial method relies on a regular quarterly sequence of expiries. It can be adapted to include also irregular contracts such as contracts based on serial months. The period from the current time to the first expiry cannot be covered by IR futures. We need spot IRs to fill that gap, which is a method described by Müller (1996). After filling the gap, the described methods to compute implied forward interest rates can also be used to compute implied spot rates, simply by choosing $T_{\text{start}} = 0$, which implies the current time. The yield curve consists of a set of implied spot rates with different T_{end}.

There is an interesting application for the yield curve of implied interest rates by comparing the curve derived from IR futures at any point in time with the curve derived from other instruments (such as deposits or over-the-counter forward rate agreements), which allows an investigation of arbitrage opportunities.

Convexity corrections of the yield curve, which represent the difference between futures and forward contracts due to the presence of margining arrangements for futures (collateral accounts, see Burghardt and Hoskins, 1995), are negligibly small in our case, because the futures contracts under consideration are never more than 18 months from expiry.

Time series of forward rates share many properties of FX time series, as studied in later chapters of this book.

2.5 BOND FUTURES MARKETS

2.5.1 Bonds and Bond Futures

Bonds are the dominating financial instrument related to long-term interest rates.[19] There is a wealth of *bonds* issued by governments or individual companies with different credit ratings. Bonds are interest-paying contracts. After a lifetime of several *years*, the capital is paid back to the holder of the contract. Some bonds are complicated financial constructions including special option contracts. The world of bonds is not simple enough to be studied in the form of few, long, consistent time series.

The bond *futures* market, on the other hand, is more standardized. Similar to the short-term interest rate futures discussed in Section 2.4, bond futures are a

---

[19] There is also a market for interest rate swap transactions with maturities of few years (with a focus on shorter maturities than those of bonds). The IR swap rates of this market constitute yet another source of high-frequency IR data.

liquid financial instrument in the area of interest rate markets, traded at the same exchanges. High-frequency, high-quality intraday data are available in the form of transaction prices, sometimes bid and ask prices, and volume figures. Bond futures markets supply more accurate and more frequent information on bonds than the cash market for bonds. In spite of this, there is little published research on the intraday behavior of bond futures, Ballocchi and Hopman (1997).

Bond futures are futures contracts as discussed in Section 2.1.2. As for most short-term IR futures, there are four settlement months in a year (March, June, September, and December) known as quarterly expiries. The exact settlement and delivery rules can be obtained from the exchanges (or their web sites). A practical introduction to the bond futures markets can be found in LIFFE (1995a,b). Active trading of bond futures is focused on the first two positions which are the contracts with the nearest expiries.

The underlying instruments of bond futures are often government bonds with maturity periods of years, for example the 30-year U.S. Treasury bond futures traded at Chicago Board of Trade (CBOT). This long duration is the main difference from short-term IR futures where the underlying instruments are notional 3-month deposits. Three-month interest rates are strongly influenced by monopolistic players such as the central banks with powers to set short-term rates. In this respect, the bond market and thus the bond futures market is "freer" than the short-term IR futures market. The underlying instrument of some typical bond futures is the cheapest bond(s) available to the exchange under certain conditions, the "cheapest-to-deliver." Unfortunately, the choice of the cheapest-to-deliver can change sometimes, leading to a disruptive behavior of bond futures prices.

For studying long samples, we need to create continuous time series.[20] A theoretically appealing method to construct such a series is to use arbitrage formulas such as in Hull (1993), with input from both short-term and long-term interest rates, as well as from the underlying deliverable instrument, to find a relationship between two successive bond futures contracts. Such an approach, which could be seen as an extended variation of the approach of Section 2.4.2 based on forward IRs, would require data input from several sources and imply considerable methodological efforts. Instead of this, we suggest using rollover schemes, which allow for an analysis based on bond futures data only.

2.5.2 Rollover Schemes

As mentioned in Section 2.1.2, a rollover scheme is a general way to create a continuous time series from the time series of futures contracts with different expiries. The proposed schemes have been mainly applied to bond futures in Ballocchi and Hopman (1997). The schemes are recommended to researchers but not necessarily to traders or investors who pay transaction costs. Investment strategies may also include rollovers, but the different optimization goal leads to different schemes.

---

[20] As before, the word "continuous" means a consistent behavior as close to stationary as possible. The series should not suffer shocks unrelated to market movements when crossing the contract expiries.

The rollover algorithm must follow an essential economic constraint imposing that the value of the portfolio changes only when the market prices of the individual bond futures move, with no change arising solely from the rollover procedure. When a rollover occurs, the number of new contracts to be bought is calculated so that the total amount of capital invested is constant, that is, the number of new contracts is given by the number of old contracts being sold multiplied by their middle price, divided by the middle price of the new contracts being bought. For bid-ask data, middle prices are defined as means of bid and ask prices.[21] Middle price are used because traders can go long or short; the continuous series should not only reflect one of the two directions.

Two different schemes are presented:

- A simple scheme involving a conversion factor to render continuous the transition from one contract to the next one, at a fixed date before the first contract's expiry.

- The construction of bond futures portfolios with "constant mean time-to-expiry," through a daily partial rollover, whereas the constituent bond futures have a fixed calendar date expiry.

The timing of the rollover determines the character of the obtained continuous time series. It is possible to make a "first position series" or a "second position series" or something in between. Typically there is not sufficient data in the third position to allow for a serious study.

The proposed simple rollover scheme has just one contract in the reference portfolio at once. At a fixed delay D_1 before the expiry of the contract in the portfolio, we roll over the entire holdings to the next expiry. If we start with one contract and the price at the rollover time is F_{1,T_1-D_1}, we can afford to buy a number α_{12} of new contracts at a price F_{2,T_1-D1},[22] where

$$\alpha_{12} = \frac{F_{1,T_1-D_1}}{F_{2,T_1-D1}} \tag{2.10}$$

Clearly the number of contracts we hold at any time can be calculated as the product of the α factors of all past rollovers.

The execution of rollover procedures (even if it happens only in theory, not in real transactions) requires the approximate simultaneous availability of reliable market prices for the two involved contracts. This is not always guaranteed, but it is likely if the rollover time is chosen when both contracts are liquid. The α factors computed by Equation 2.10 are slowly varying over time, often slower than the prices themselves. This fact can be used to take a mean α from those daytimes where simultaneous quotes of both contracts are found, rather than an α determined at only one fixed daytime.

---

[21] In the case of transaction data, the transaction prices take the role of middle prices.

[22] In reality, we can only buy an integer number of contracts. This does not matter for our theoretical rollover formula: α may be a fraction.

In empirical studies, however, few discontinuities of α factors over time are detected. Ballocchi and Hopman (1997) explain these discontinuities by asynchronicities in the underlying bonds, the "cheapest-to-deliver." If the underlying bonds of two successive contracts do not change exactly at the same time, the α factor is affected by the difference. When analyzing a continuous series, the exact knowledge of the underlying bonds (cheapest-to-deliver, or benchmark bonds) is helpful.

The second scheme based on a "constant time-to-expiry" is to have a portfolio that does not expire at a fixed calendar date, but keeps a constant mean time-to-expiry as time moves on, by means of an appropriate daily rollover procedure.[23] The time-to-expiry (or horizon) h for a portfolio is defined as a weighted average of the time-to-expiry of the constituents. We consider a constant time-to-expiry portfolio consisting at time t of two contract expiries, with a number $\beta_{i,t}$ of contracts in the first expiry, corresponding to time T_i and a number $\gamma_{i+1,t}$ of contracts in the second expiry, corresponding to time T_{i+1}. The time-to-expiry of this reference portfolio is then

$$h \; = \; \frac{\beta_{i,t}}{\beta_{i,t} + \gamma_{i+1,t}}(T_i - t) + \frac{\gamma_{i+1,t}}{\beta_{i,t} + \gamma_{i+1,t}}(T_{i+1} - t) \qquad (2.11)$$

Each day we arrange a partial rollover procedure, selling a proportion of the holdings in the first expiry and buying the second one, in order to keep h constant.

Some tools for generating long samples from several contracts through rollover schemes are commercially available, such as the Liffestyle program from LIFFE, see Gwilym and Sutcliffe (1999). This software also offers volume-dependent timing of the rollover (e.g., rolling over when the volume of a new contract overtakes that of an old contract).

2.6 COMMODITY FUTURES

Commodity futures are similar to the futures contracts presented in Section 2.1.2. The settlement at expiry means physical delivery of the underlying commodity. Commodities such as raw materials or agricultural products often exist in different variations and quality levels. Therefore a typical holder of a long position in commodity futures does not want to receive the commodity exactly in the form delivered at expiry. Most commodity futures traders offset their contracts (or roll them over) before expiry, in some markets so early that the second position (the contract with the second next expiry) has a higher liquidity than the first position.

A purpose of commodity futures trading is hedging. A manufacturer confronted with rapidly rising raw material prices is protected by holding some corresponding futures of simultaneously increasing value. Some investors use commodity futures as a vehicle for portfolio diversification.

---

[23] The related high transaction costs are irrelevant, since this rollover procedure does not need to be executed in practice.

Futures of agricultural commodities may have an irregular schedule of expiry dates due to the seasonality of agricultural production. The cocoa futures market of New York, for example, has five irregularly spaced expiry dates per year, in March, May, July, September, and December.

As in other futures markets, contracts with different expiry dates are not independent. A contract with distant expiry, for instance, cannot be *much* more expensive than a near contract; otherwise traders would buy the near contract and profitably store the commodity afterward in a warehouse. This condition is similar to the condition that forward interest rates cannot be far below zero.

Commodity futures markets are often much smaller than FX or money markets. They are not liquid enough for huge transactions. Large orders often cause considerable *slippage* with immediate price movements to the unfavorable direction.

High-frequency commodity futures data are available from the exchanges and from data vendors. Rollover schemes similar to those of Section 2.5.2 are needed to build long time series from different contracts.

2.7 EQUITY MARKETS

Equity markets are a major source of high-frequency data. The authors of this book have only casually investigated time series from equity markets. Therefore, only a brief description is given.

Equities are traded at stock exchanges of different kinds. Also the instruments derived from equities are exchange-traded. High-frequency data are mainly produced during the opening hours of the exchanges. In some main markets, there is also some electronic trading outside the normal opening hours, which yields some sparse additional data.

High-frequency data are available from the following markets:

- Equity of *individual companies* as traded by stock exchanges. This data type is strongly determined by the specific behavior of an individual firm and some general trends of the market and the economy. Stock splits (e.g. five new equity units replacing one old unit) and dividend payments affect the equity prices, and price series can only be understood with a full account of all these events. Only the most traded individual equities have a data frequency high enough to be called high-frequency.

- Equity *indices*, also called stock indices. These are weighted sums of individual equity prices according to a formula. The basket of equities includes important equities of specific countries or industry sectors. The basket and the weights are adapted from time to time, according to the changing size of the companies. A *performance index* reflects the value of a realistic portfolio of investments according to the basket, including all dividend payments and reinvested profits. It is thus possible to replicate the behavior of an equity index by a real portfolio (it is a better approximation if the index is a performance index). Equity indices represent large segments of an economy rather than individual companies and their behavior is less erratic than that of individual equities. High-frequency data for the main indices are available and are interesting objects of research. Due to their mathematical definition, they often show a positive autocorrelation of returns at a lag of up to 15 minutes. This may be a consequence of a lag structure between leading main equities and the less liquid equities of the basket.

- Individual equity *futures* or equity index futures are liquid instruments with high-quality, high-frequency data that have been studied by many researchers.

- *Options* also exist for individual equities as well as equity indices. Their implied volatility figures can be investigated by time series methods.

3

TIME SERIES OF INTEREST

An adequate analysis of high-frequency data relies on explicit definitions of the variables under study. In this chapter, we study the common mathematical framework used to analyze these variables.

Some aspects of preparing and preprocessing a time series are rather technical. Readers interested in economic results may prefer to skip the technical Chapters 3 and 4 and continue their reading in Chapter 5.

Researchers conducting their own high-frequency studies may profit from Chapters 3 and 4. If they have no access to preprocessed time series (i.e., cleaned time series with regular spacing in time), they will need the techniques described in these chapters. The literature often ignores technicalities of dealing with irregularly spaced high-frequency data, so we have a good reason to discuss them in two chapters of this book.

3.1 TIME SERIES AND OPERATORS

Many types of time series data can be obtained at high frequency, often intraday, at market tick-by-tick frequency. For most methods, these raw time series are not suitable to work with, because market ticks arrive at random times.[1] The

---

[1] There are models for the stochastic nature of these times, such as Engle and Russell (1997, 1998).

time series operator formalism developed by Zumbach (1996) and Zumbach and Müller (2001) offers a powerful way to deal with irregularly spaced data. Section 3.3 is based on this formalism and the notations of Zumbach and Müller (2001).

In time series analysis, a first important classification is done according to the spacing of data points in time. Regularly spaced time series are called *homogeneous*, whereas irregularly spaced series are called *inhomogeneous*. The concept of inhomogeneous time series also has to be distinguished from two other concepts, which are the concept of missing observations (where a series is essentially homogeneous with few gaps) and the concept of continuous-time finance (which belongs to theory rather than data sampling). When considering the spacing of data in time, a discussion of the time scale is necessary. Many time series of daily data in finance, for example, have only five observations per week; there are no observations on Saturdays and Sundays. Such a time series is homogeneous only if using a special "business time" scale, which omits weekends (and holidays). Even more sophisticated business time scales can be introduced in order to cope with some characteristics of intraday data such as the seasonality of volatility, (see Chapter 6 and Dacorogna *et al.*, 1993), the heteroskedasticity (Zhou, 1993), or both seasonality and heteroskedasticity (Guillaume *et al.*, 1997; Müller *et al.*, 1993a). Time is denoted by t in Chapter 3, but t may stand for any choice of time scale, not only physical time or clock time. The terms "homogeneous" and "inhomogeneous" have to be understood in the context of the chosen time scale. Inhomogeneous time series by themselves are conceptually simple. The difficulty lies in efficiently extracting and computing information from them. *Time series operators* are a major tool used to transform a raw, inhomogeneous time series to the (homogeneous *or* inhomogeneous) time series of the variable to be analyzed.

In most books on time series analysis, the field of time series is restricted to homogeneous time series.[2] In Section 3.2, we follow this restriction, which induces numerous simplifications, both conceptually and computationally. There, we need only one time series operator type: an operator to transform an inhomogeneous time series to a homogeneous one, type (a) of Figure 3.1.

In Sections 3.3 and 3.4, we follow Zumbach and Müller (2001) and build a computational toolbox for directly and efficiently treating inhomogeneous time series. In practice, this toolbox is attractive enough to be applied to any time series, including homogeneous ones. Given a time series z, such as an asset price, the general point of view is to compute another time series, such as the volatility of the asset, by the application of an operator $\Omega[z]$ where the resulting series stays inhomogeneous with the same time points as the original series. This operator type is called type (b) in Figure 3.1.

---

[2] Classical textbooks on homogeneous time series are Granger and Newbold (1977); Priestley (1989); Hamilton (1994).

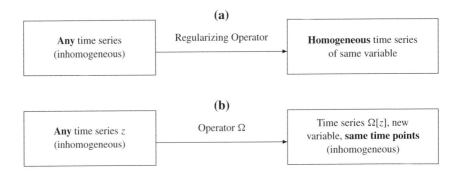

FIGURE 3.1 Different operator types to study time series:

(a) Sampling an inhomogeneous time series at regular time intervals. The resulting homogeneous time series can be treated by standard methods of time series analysis.

(b) Computing a new variable from the initial variable while keeping the initial (inhomogeneous) time points. Example: computing a series of local volatility values from the initial price series.

An important distinction between operators has to be made. We introduce two operator types:

- Microscopic operators depend on the actual sampling of the inhomogeneous time series. Eliminating some random ticks leads to very different results.
- Macroscopic operators extract *average* behaviors of their time series argument. They are essentially immune to small variations of the individual ticks, including adding or eliminating few ticks.

A possible technical definition of macroscopic operators is that they have a well-defined limit when the price quotes become infinitely dense. Practically, if the price quotes are sufficiently dense inside the range of the operator, we are close enough to this limit. For inhomogeneous time series, macroscopic operators are better behaved and more robust than microscopic operators. For homogeneous time series, this distinction is unnecessary because the sampling frequency is fixed and there is no reason to take a continuous-time limit or to formally add or remove ticks. Moreover, because homogeneous time series analysis is based on the backward shift operator $\mathcal{B}$ (which is microscopic), most of the conventional time series analysis becomes unusable for inhomogeneous time series. The classification between operators is further explored by Zumbach and Müller (2001).

Macroscopic operators can be represented by convolutions and are discussed in Section 3.3. The archetype of a macroscopic operator is the exponential moving average (EMA) that computes a moving average with an exponentially decaying weight of the past.

Microscopic operators are presented in Section 3.4. Examples are the time difference δt between ticks (e.g., in $\delta t_j = t_j - t_{j-1}$) and the backward shift operator $\mathcal{B}$ defined in Section 3.4.1.

3.2 VARIABLES IN HOMOGENEOUS TIME SERIES

Basic variables such as the price, the return, the realized volatility, and the spread are defined in Section 3.2. In order to capture the dynamics of the intraday market, some more variables such as the tick frequency are of interest.

3.2.1 Interpolation

Before defining different variables, the generation of homogeneous time series has to be explained. A homogeneous time series, although taken for granted in time series analysis, is an artifact that has to be constructed from the raw data, which is an inhomogeneous series with times t_j and values $z_j = z(t_j)$. The index j refers to the irregularly spaced sequence of the raw series. By utilizing an *interpolation* method, we construct a homogeneous time series with values at times $t_0 + i\,\Delta t$, regularly spaced by Δt, rooted at a time t_0. The index i refers to the homogeneous series.

The time $t_0 + i\,\Delta t$ is bracketed by two times t_j of the raw series

$$j' = \max(j \mid t_j \le t_0 + i\,\Delta t) \quad , \quad t_{j'} \le t_0 + i\,\Delta t < t_{j'+1} \tag{3.1}$$

We interpolate between $t_{j'}$ and $t_{j'+1}$. The two most important interpolation methods are *linear interpolation*

$$z(t_0 + i\,\Delta t) = z_{j'} + \frac{t_0 + i\,\Delta t - t_{j'}}{t_{j'+1} - t_{j'}} (z_{j'+1} - z_{j'}) \tag{3.2}$$

and *previous-tick interpolation* (taking the most recent value),

$$z(t_0 + i\,\Delta t) = z_{j'} \tag{3.3}$$

which was already proposed by Wasserfallen and Zimmermann (1985).

Both methods which are illustrated by Figure 3.2 have their merits. Previous-tick interpolation respects causality as it exclusively uses information already known at time $t_0 + i\,\Delta t$, whereas linear interpolation uses information from time $t_{j'+1}$, which lies in the *future* of time $t_0 + i\,\Delta t$. When using previous-tick interpolation over a gap (a long period of missing data) in the raw data, a spurious jump of z may be observed at the end of the gap, which may spoil a statistical analysis of extreme returns of z. In this example, linear interpolation would be the appropriate choice. As advocated in Müller *et al.* (1990), linear interpolation is the appropriate method for a random process with identically and independently distributed (i.i.d.) increments. Many statistical studies and model estimations can be alternatively done with both interpolation methods, in practice. The difference between the results indicates the sensitivity to the choice of the interpolation method. The difference is often small, even negligible thanks to high-frequency data. In the empirical studies of the book, the choice of the interpolation method is discussed whenever it matters.

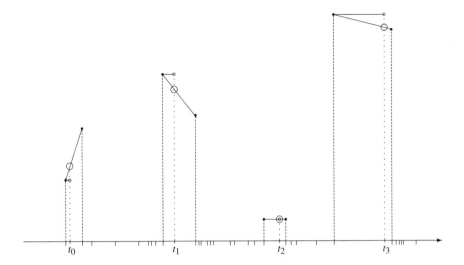

FIGURE 3.2 Interpolation methods to obtain a homogeneous time series: selecting values at equally spaced time points t_i, indicated by dotted vertical lines. The inhomogeneous time sequence of raw observations is indicated by ticks below the horizontal time axis and by dashed vertical lines (only for the observations bracketing the time points t_i). Two important interpolation methods are illustrated by empty circles: linear interpolation (big circles) and previous-tick interpolation (small circles).

The transformation of an inhomogeneous time series to a homogeneous one can also be understood as the result of a special microscopic time series operator which is discussed in Sections 3.3.1 and 3.4.2.

3.2.2 Price

Prices of assets are the most important variables explored in finance. Depending on the market structure and the data supplier, prices are available as quotes in different forms:

- Bid-ask price pairs: p_{bid} and p_{ask}
- Transaction prices (which may or may not be former bid or ask quotes)
- Bid, ask, transaction prices in irregular sequence (not in pairs, not synchronous)
- Middle prices

One individual observation at a time t_j, also in the case of bid-ask pairs, is called a *tick*.

Bid-ask price pairs are discussed first. FX prices and other asset prices, as well as nonprice variables such as spot interest rates and implied volatility figures from option markets, are quoted as bid-ask pairs. The most important variable under study is the logarithmic middle price x. At time t_j, it is defined as

$$x(t_j) \;=\; \frac{\log p_{\text{bid}}(t_j) + \log p_{\text{ask}}(t_j)}{2} \;=\; \log \sqrt{p_{\text{bid}}(t_j)\, p_{\text{ask}}(t_j)} \qquad (3.4)$$

where t_j is the inhomogeneous sequence of the tick recording times. The variable x may simply be called the *price* in a context where its logarithmic nature is obvious and not explicitly relevant. It is based on the (geometric) average of the bid and ask price rather than either the bid or the ask price alone; this is a better approximation of the true price. The best choice, even better than Equation 3.4, might be a so-called effective price as discussed at the end of this Section 3.2.2.

In the foreign exchange (FX) market, a further advantage of Equation 3.4 is obvious. FX prices can be seen from two sides, the value of the U.S. Dollar (USD) in Japanese Yen (JPY) and the value of the JPY in USD. Equation 3.4 is perfectly antisymmetric: if x is the USD-JPY price, the JPY-USD price is simply $-x$. Statistical results based on absolute differences of x (or volatility) are identical for USD-JPY and JPY-USD. This is a desired property because USD-JPY and JPY-USD are the same market. If the logarithmic transformation was avoided or the logarithm of the arithmetic average of bid and ask was taken instead of Equation 3.4, the antisymmetry would be violated and the statistical results of USD-JPY and JPY-USD would differ. The logarithmic transformation has the additional advantage of making returns (differences of x) dimensionless—that is, independent of the original units in which the price is measured.

In the case of transaction or middle prices, Equation 3.4 is obviously replaced by $x(t_j) = \log p_{\text{transact}}(t_j)$ or $\log p_{\text{middle}}(t_j)$. For certain data types, the logarithmic transformation is less suitable; it is avoided or made in a mathematically different form. For spot interest rates as discussed in Section 2.3.1, the logarithm of the capital increase factor can be taken:

$$x_{\text{bid}}(t_j) \;=\; \log[1 + i_{\text{bid}}(t_j)] \qquad (3.5)$$

and analogous for the ask quote, where the interest rate i is inserted as a plain value, not in percent (e.g., 0.05 instead of 5%). Alternative definitions of x are explained whenever they are applied in this book.

The inhomogeneous series $x(t_j)$ can be transformed to a homogeneous time series by using an interpolation method as explained in Section 3.2.1, using Equation 3.2 or 3.3. For the homogeneous series of prices, we use the index i:

$$x(t_i) \;=\; x(\Delta t, t_i) \;=\; \frac{\log p_{\text{bid}}(t_i) + \log p_{\text{ask}}(t_i)}{2} \qquad (3.6)$$

where t_i is the homogeneous sequence of times regularly spaced by time intervals of size Δt. As already mentioned, t and Δt may refer to any definition of the time scale, not only physical time.

In some markets such as the FX spot market, bid and ask prices are just indicative quotes produced by market makers who are often interested primarily in either the bid or the ask price; the other price acts as a noncompetitive dummy value. This leads to a small error that affects Equation 3.4. Moreover, the quoted spread (ask minus bid price) does not exactly reflect the real spread, which is usually smaller as reported in Goodhart *et al.* (1995).[3] Furthermore, because of transmission delays, it may be, for example, that market maker B enters a quote after market maker A, but that the quote of market maker B is the first to appear on a multi-contributor data feed. Data gaps due to transmission breakdowns become more significant at high frequencies.

All these effects can be modeled in the form of an *effective price* which is closer to the transaction price than the price x of Equation 3.4. In the absence of real transaction prices, we may define an effective price algorithm by looking at the properties of the prices and the market organization. All quotes have a finite lifetime, which is roughly around two minutes during periods of average FX market activity and can strongly vary depending on the market and its state. We can define the effective price as consisting of the best bid and ask quotes available (or the averages of bid and ask) in a time window of the size of a quote lifetime. Another idea for such an algorithm would be to eliminate the negative first-order autocorrelation of the returns present at very high frequencies (see Section 5.2.1). An example of an algorithm for the computation of effective price is given in Bollerslev and Domowitz (1993) where the trade-matching algorithm of the interbank market system "Reuters Dealing 2000" is used. Interestingly, the prices generated by this algorithm exhibit a positive rather than negative first-order autocorrelation. In contrast, Goodhart *et al.* (1995) still obtain a negative first-order autocorrelation, though less pronounced, in their analysis of the Dealing 2000-2 system. In this book, no definition of an effective price is given, but the behavior of prices in the very short term (seconds to minutes) is discussed in several aspects at several places.

3.2.3   Return

The *return* at time t_i, $r(t_i)$, is defined as

$$r(t_i) \;=\; r(\Delta t; t_i) \;=\; x(t_i) - x(t_i - \Delta t) \tag{3.7}$$

where $x(t_i)$ is a homogeneous sequence of logarithmic prices as defined by Equation 3.6, and Δt is a time interval of fixed size. In the normal case, Δt is the interval of the homogeneous series, and $r(t_i)$ is the series of the first differences of $x(t_i)$. If the return interval is chosen to be a multiple of the series interval, we obtain overlapping intervals as discussed in Section 3.2.8. Returns are sometimes also called price changes.

The return is usually a more suitable variable of analysis than the price, for several reasons. It is the variable of interest for traders who use it as a direct measure of the success of an investment. Furthermore, the distribution of returns

---

[3] In their one-day study of real transaction prices, Goodhart *et al.* (1995) found that although the actual spread is usually within the quoted spread, it could be larger in highly volatile periods.

is more symmetric and stable over time than the distribution of prices. The return process is close to stationary whereas the price process is not.

3.2.4 Realized Volatility

The *realized volatility* $v(t_i)$ at time t_i is computed from historical data and it is also called *historical volatility* . It is defined as

$$v(t_i) \;=\; v(\Delta t, n, p; t_i) \;=\; \left[\frac{1}{n} \sum_{j=1}^{n} |r(\Delta t; t_{i-n+j})|^p \right]^{1/p} \tag{3.8}$$

where the regularly spaced returns r are defined by Equation 3.7, and n is the number of return observations. There are two time intervals, which are the return interval Δt, and the size of the total sample, $n\Delta t$. The exponent p is often set to 2 so that v^2 is the variance of the returns about zero. In many cases, a value of $p = 1$ is preferred, although p may also be a fraction, $p > 0$. The choice of p is further discussed below.

In order to compute realized volatility, the return interval, Δt and a sample of length $n\Delta t$ need to be chosen. By inserting $\Delta t = 10$ min in Equation 3.8, one can compute the volatility of regularly spaced 10-min returns. One important issue is that many users want their realized volatility in *scaled* form. Although the volatility may be computed from 10-min returns, the expected volatility over another time interval (e.g., 1 hr or 1 year) may also be calculated. Through a Gaussian scaling law, $v^2 \propto \Delta t$, the following definition of scaled volatility is obtained:

$$v_{\text{scaled}} \;=\; \sqrt{\frac{\Delta t_{\text{scale}}}{\Delta t}} \, v \tag{3.9}$$

The most popular choice of the scaling reference interval Δt_{scale} is $\Delta t_{\text{scale}} = 1$ year. If this is chosen, v_{scaled} is called an *annualized* volatility, v_{ann}:

$$v_{\text{ann}} \;=\; \sqrt{\frac{1 \text{ year}}{\Delta t}} \, v \tag{3.10}$$

Practitioners often use annualized volatility in percent (multiplying v_{ann} by 100%). Typical annualized volatility values for some FX rates are around 10%.

In practice, various volatility definitions may lead to confusion. Terms such as "one-day historical volatility" should be avoided because they do not express whether "one day" refers to the return measurement interval Δt, the sample size $n\Delta t$ or the scaling reference interval Δt_{scale}. In order to clarify this, we give a detailed recipe to compute realized volatility in practice:

- Consider and choose *three* time intervals:
    - The time interval of return observations, Δt

- The sample size $n \Delta t$ (the number n of return observations)
- The scaling interval Δt_{scale}, e.g., 1 year if annualized volatility is desired

- Choose the exponent p of Equation 3.8 (often 2 or 1 as discussed below) and the basic time scale of the computation. Instead of physical time, a business time omitting the weekends may be used.
- Compute realized volatility according to Equation 3.8.
- Scale the result by applying Equation 3.9. If $\Delta t_{\text{scale}} = 1$ year, this means annualization.
- If the volatility has to be expressed in percentage, multiply the result by 100%.

A traditionally popular choice of realized volatility is the annualized volatility of daily returns on a yearly sample (using $p = 2$): $\Delta t = 1$ working day, $n \approx 250$, sample size $n \Delta t = 250$ working days ≈ 1 year, $\Delta t_{\text{scale}} = 1$ year. It should be noted that a business time scale with approximately 250 working days per year is used in this example instead of physical time.

The following examples illustrate the computation of realized volatility. Suppose we have regularly spaced 10-min returns from January 1, 1998 to December 31, 1999. This two-year sample has a total of $n = 105120$ return observations. From this data, we want to compute realized volatility in three forms:

1. Volatility of 10-min returns on May 12, 1999, scaled to one day. The return interval is $\Delta t = 10$ min, $n = 144$, and therefore, the sample size is $n \Delta t = 1440$ min $= 1$ day. v is computed from 144 returns according to Equation 3.8. To obtain the desired scaling, Equation 3.9 is used to compute $v_{\text{scaled}} = \sqrt{1 \, \text{day}/10 \, \text{min}} \, v = \sqrt{144} \, v = 12 \, v$.

2. Annualized volatility of 10-min returns over the whole sample where $\Delta t = 10$ min. All return observations, i.e., $n = 105120$ are used to calculate v according to Equation 3.8. The sample size is $n \Delta t = 1051200$ min $= 2$ years. To obtain annualization according to Equation 3.10, $v_{\text{ann}} = \sqrt{1 \, \text{year}/10 \, \text{min}} \, v = \sqrt{52596} \, v \approx 229.3 \, v$ is computed. This reflects the fact that an average year contains about 365.25 days and thus 52596 10-min intervals. Note that physical time is used in this particular example and weekends are not omitted.

3. Annualized volatility of 20-min returns over the whole sample. This is analogous to the example above, except for the different time interval $\Delta t = 20$ min. The 20-min returns R_j can be obtained by taking the sum of two 10-min returns: $R_1 = r_1 + r_2$, $R_2 = r_3 + r_4$, and so on.[4] The number of R_j observations is half that of the 10-min returns: $n = 52560$. The sample size is $n \Delta t = 52560 \times 20$ min $= 2$ years, as above. v is computed

---

[4] An alternative scheme to obtain 20-min returns from 10-min returns would be as follows: $R_1 = r_1 + r_2$, $R_2 = r_2 + r_3$, $R_3 = r_3 + r_4$ and so on. This scheme leads to overlapping 20-min returns and will be treated in Section 3.2.8.

from Equation 3.8 from the 20-min returns R_j instead of r_j. To obtain annualization according to Equation 3.10, $v_{ann} = \sqrt{1 \text{ year}/20 \text{ min}}\, v = \sqrt{26298}\, v \approx 162.2\, v$ is computed. One average year contains 26298 20-min intervals, hence the annualization factor.

All of these examples are static and based on calculating realized volatility values at a fixed time t_i. Of course, we can treat realized volatility as a time series and compute it for a sequence of time points: $t_i, t_{i+1}, t_{i+2}, \ldots$. For each of these realized volatility computations, the sample is shifted by one interval Δt.

The concept of historical or realized volatility is rather old. We find it already in Taylor (1986)[5] and in early high-frequency studies such as Müller *et al.* (1990). We distinguish three main types of volatility:

- Realized volatility, also called historical volatility: determined by past observations by a formula such as Equation 3.8.

- Model volatility: a virtual variable in a theoretical model such as GARCH or stochastic volatility (but there may be means to estimate this variable from the data).

- Implied volatility: a volatility forecast computed from market prices of derivatives such as options (see e.g., Cox and Rubinstein, 1985), based on a model of the underlying process such as the log-normal random walk assumed by Black and Scholes (1973).

The *term* "realized volatility" has recently been popularized by Andersen *et al.* (2000) and others. By exploring realized volatility, Andersen *et al.* (2000) show that this is more than a conveniently measured quantity; it can also be used for process modeling.

An alternative definition of realized volatility is

$$
v'(t_i) = \left\{ \frac{1}{n-1} \sum_{j=1}^{n} \left| r(\Delta t; t_{i-n+j}) - \frac{1}{n} \left[\sum_{k=1}^{n} r(\Delta t; t_{i-n+k}) \right] \right|^p \right\}^{1/p}
$$

(3.11)

For $p = 2$, this is the standard deviation of the returns about the sample mean. This definition is popular in portfolio analysis where the risk is measured in terms of deviations of the return from the average. In most other applications such as risk management and in the examples of this book, Equation 3.8 is preferred to Equation 3.11. The two definitions essentially differ only in the presence of a strong linear drift (i.e., if the returns have an expectation far from zero).

---

[5] There, absolute values of returns and squared returns were explicitly introduced as proxies of volatility in autocorrelation studies. Note that these quantities are special cases of Equation 3.8 with $n = 1$ and $p = 1$ (absolute return) or $p = 2$ (squared return).

Realized volatility $v(t_i)$ is based on a homogeneous series of returns as defined by Equation 3.7 and is a homogeneous time series in its own right. As an alternative, we can also compute a homogeneous series of realized volatility based on overlapping returns (see Section 3.2.8) or directly compute volatility from an inhomogeneous series with the help of convolution operators (see Section 3.3.11). The parameters of Equation 3.8 have to be carefully chosen. A large exponent p gives more weight to the tails of the distribution. If p is too large, the realized volatility may have an asymptotically infinite expectation if returns have a heavy-tailed density function. In practice, p should stay below the tail index of the distribution, which is empirically estimated to be around 3.5 for typical high-frequency FX data (as explained in Section 5.4). The fourth moment of the return distribution often diverges. Moreover, there are studies where realized volatility appears in the squared form (as in autocorrelation studies of volatility). There, p should be limited to the *half* of the tail index. The empirical autocorrelation of squared returns is of little relevance. Instead, autocorrelation studies can be made with absolute values of returns ($p = 1$), as already done by Taylor (1986), Müller *et al.* (1990) and, Granger and Ding (1995).

The choice of Δt and n is also important. Given a constant total sample size $T = n\Delta t$, Andersen *et al.* (2001) recommend choosing Δt as small as possible. This means a large number n of return observations and thus high precision and significance. However, realized volatility results become *biased* if Δt is chosen to be too small, as found by Andersen *et al.* (2000). Therefore, the best choice of Δt is somewhere between 15 min and 2 hr, depending on the market and the data type. The bias has several implications, among them the negative short-term autocorrelation found for some financial data (see Section 5.2.1). Corsi *et al.* (2001) propose a bias-corrected realized volatility with Δt around 5 min, in order to maintain the high precision gained due to a large n. Interval overlapping is a further method to make realized volatility more precise by a limited amount (see Section 3.2.8).

A more fundamental question has to be discussed. Does a realized volatility with a constant $T = n\Delta t$ essentially stay the same if the time resolution, Δt, is varied? "Coarse" realized volatility (with large Δt) predicts the value of "fine" volatility (with small Δt) better than the other way around, as discussed in Section 7.4.1. This lead-lag effect indicates that the dynamics of volatility are complex, and realized volatility with one choice of Δt is not a perfect substitute for realized volatility with another value of Δt.

The relative merits of realized, modeled, and implied volatility are discussed at several places in this book. For low-frequency (including daily) data, models such as GARCH (Bollerslev, 1986) and option markets may yield volatility estimates that are as good or better than realized volatility. For high-frequency, intraday data, realized volatility is superior. Intraday data cannot be described by one homogeneous GARCH model because of the seasonality and heterogeneity of the markets, as shown by Guillaume *et al.* (1994) and Gençay *et al.* (2001c, 2002).

3.2.5 Bid-Ask Spread

In bid-ask price pairs, the ask price is higher than the bid price.[6] The bid-ask spread is their difference. A suitable variable for research studies is the *relative spread* $s(t_j)$:

$$s(t_j) = \log p_{ask}(t_j) - \log p_{bid}(t_j) \tag{3.12}$$

where j is still the index of the original inhomogeneous time series. This definition has similar advantages as the definition of the logarithmic price x, Equation 3.4. The nominal spread ($p_{ask} - p_{bid}$) is in units of the underlying price, whereas the relative spread is dimensionless; relative spreads from different markets can directly be compared to each other. In the FX market, another advantage is obvious. If the relative spread of USD-JPY, for example, is s, the relative spread of JPY-USD is also s, because the roles of bid and ask are interchanged. Results of spread studies are invariant under inversion of the rate. Other spread definitions do not have this perfect symmetry. The relative spread is sometimes just called the "spread" if its relative nature is obvious from the context.

For spot interest rates, we can adapt the relative spread definition in the same sense as Equation 3.5:

$$s(t_j) = \log[1 + i_{ask}(t_j)] - \log[1 + i_{bid}(t_j)] \tag{3.13}$$

The relative spread is a positive bounded quantity that has a strongly skewed distribution. This can be a problem for certain types of analysis. A further transformation leads to the "log spread," $\log s(t_j)$. For bid-ask prices, the log spread is

$$\log s(t_j) = \log[\log p_{ask}(t_j) - \log p_{bid}(t_j)] \tag{3.14}$$

Müller and Sgier (1992) have shown that its distribution is much less skewed and closer to symmetric than the distribution of s.

The bid-ask spread reflects the transaction and inventory costs and the risk of the institution that quotes the price. On the side of the traders who buy or sell at a quoted price, the spread is the only source of costs as intraday credit lines on the foreign exchange markets are free of interest.[7] The spread can therefore be considered as a good measure of the amount of friction between different market participants, and thereby as a measure of market efficiency. The relatively high efficiency of the major FX spot markets is reflected by the small average size of s.

---

[6] Some data sources have prices of minor markets in the spurious technical form of bid-ask pairs with bid = ask, presumably because only one of the two prices is available at a time. These quotes are not true bid-ask pairs.

[7] A trader taking a forward position will, of course, have to pay the interest on his or her position between the trade and the settlement as well as the additional spread on the forward rate.

In markets with indicative quotes from different market makers, individual spreads $s(t_j)$ are often affected by individual preferences of market makers and by habits of the market (see Section 5.6.5). Therefore, a homogeneous time series of spreads $s(t_i)$ generated by interpolation contains a rather high level of noise. A more suitable alternative is to compute *average* spreads within time windows and to build a homogeneous time series of these average spreads.

3.2.6   Tick Frequency

The *tick frequency* at time t_i, $f(t_i)$, is defined as

$$ f(t_i) \;=\; f(\Delta t; t_i) \;=\; \frac{1}{\Delta t}\, N\{x(t_j) \mid t_i - \Delta t < t_j \le t_i\} \tag{3.15} $$

where $N\{x(t_j)\}$ is the counting function and Δt is the size of the time interval in which ticks are counted.

The "log tick frequency," $\log f(t_i)$, has been found to be more relevant in Demos and Goodhart (1992). We can also define the average time interval between ticks, which is simply the inverse tick frequency, $f^{-1}(t_i)$. Tick frequency can also be computed by a time series operator as explained in Section 3.4.5.

The tick frequency is sometimes taken as a proxy for the transaction volume on the markets. As the name and location of the quoting banks are also available, the tick frequency is also sometimes disaggregated by banks or countries. However, equating tick frequency to transaction volume or using it as a proxy for both volume and strength of bank presence suffers from the following problems. First, although it takes only a few seconds to enter a price quotation in the terminal, if two market makers happen to simultaneously enter quotes, only one quote may appear on the data collector's screen; second, during periods of high activity, some operators may be too busy to enter the quote into the system; third, a bank may use an automatic system to publish prices to advertise itself on the market; fourth, the representation of the banks depends on the coverage of the market by data vendors such as Reuters or Bridge.   This coverage is changing and does not entirely represent the whole market. For example, Asian market makers are not as well covered by Reuters as their European counterparts; they are more inclined to contribute to the local financial news agencies such as Minex. Big banks have many subsidiaries; they may use one subsidiary to quote prices made by a market maker in another subsidiary on another continent. Quotes from differently reliable and renowned sources have very different impacts on the market. For all these reasons, we should be cautious when drawing conclusions on volume or market share from tick frequency.

3.2.7   Other Variables

A set of other variables of interest are as follows:

- The "realized skewness" of the return distribution. Roy (1952) evaluates the extreme downside risk in portfolio optimization in terms of the cubic root of the third moment of returns. The skewness of returns can also be measured by a time series operator (see Section 3.3.12).

- The volatility ratio, the ratio of two volatilities of different time resolutions: $v_{ann}(m\,\Delta t, n, p)/v_{ann}(\Delta t, mn, p)$, based on Equations 3.8 and 3.10, with an integer factor $m > 1$. This is a generalization of the variance ratio studied in Lo and MacKinlay (1988), Poterba and Summers (1988) and Campbell *et al.* (1997). The volatility ratio is around 1 for a Brownian motion of x, higher if x follows a trend, lower if x has mean-reverting noise. The volatility ratio (or an analogous volatility difference) is thus a tool to detect trending behavior.

- The direction change indicator, counting the number of essential trend reversals within a time interval as defined by Guillaume *et al.* (1997).

3.2.8 Overlapping Returns

Some variables, notably returns, are related to time intervals, not only single time points. When statistically investigating these variables, we need many observations. The number of observations can be increased by choosing overlapping intervals. For returns, a modified version of Equation 3.7 is used:

$$r_i \;=\; r(t_i) \;=\; x(t_i) - x(t_i - m\,\Delta t) \;=\; x_i - x_{i-m} \qquad (3.16)$$

where t_i is again a regular sequence of time points (for any choice of the time scale), separated by intervals of size Δt. The interval of the return, however, is $m\,\Delta t$, an integer multiple of the basic interval Δt. If r_i is considered for every i, we obtain a homogeneous series of overlapping returns with the overlap factor m. The corresponding series of nonoverlapping returns would be $r_m, r_{2m}, r_{3m}, \ldots$.

Figure 3.3 illustrates the concept of overlapping intervals. Does a statistical study gain anything from using overlapping as opposed to non-overlapping returns? The number of observations can be increased by using overlapping intervals with a growing overlap factor m, thereby keeping the return interval $m\,\Delta t$ constant. At the same time, neighboring return observations become increasingly dependent. Thus a gain in statistical significance is not obvious. The problem was discussed in Hansen and Hodrick (1980), where a method of estimating parameters and their significance limits from overlapping observations has been developed and applied. In Dunis and Keller (1993), a "panel regression" technique is presented and applied where the overlapping observations are grouped in several nonoverlapping series with phase-shifted starting points.

Müller (1993) has investigated this question under the simplifying assumption that x is drawn from an identical and independent distribution

$$r_i' \;=\; x(t_i) - x(t_{i-1}) \;\in\; \mathcal{N}(0, \sigma^2) \qquad (3.17)$$

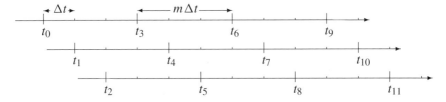

FIGURE 3.3 An overlapping scheme of time intervals to compute a homogeneous time series of overlapping returns. All returns are measured over a time interval of size $m\,\Delta t$. The intervals on the top time axis alone are not overlapping; an overlapping scheme arises when the phase-shifted intervals on the two lower time axes are added. In this example, the overlap factor is $m = 3$.

where the r'_i are independent. The investigated returns are sums of small-interval returns:

$$r_i = \sum_{i'=1}^{m} r'_{i-m+i'} \tag{3.18}$$

The conclusion of Müller (1993) is that the method of overlapping leads to a distinct but not overwhelming increase of precision and significance in most applications. Some main derivations and results of that study are presented here. There is one special case where overlapping does not help, which is the empirical *mean* of returns. Assume a large sample with n nonoverlapping intervals, covering the mn small intervals of size Δt with returns from r'_1 to r'_{mn}. The same information can be used to compute the $m(n-1)+1$ overlapping returns from r_m to r_{mn}. The mean of these overlapping returns is

$$\frac{1}{m(n-1)+1} \sum_{i=m}^{mn} r_i = \frac{1}{m(n-1)+1} \sum_{i=m}^{mn} \sum_{i'=1}^{m} r'_{i-m+i'} = \tag{3.19}$$

$$\frac{1}{m(n-1)+1} \sum_{i=1}^{m-1} [i\,(r'_i + r'_{mn+1-i})] + \frac{m}{m(n-1)+1} \sum_{i=m}^{m(n-1)+1} r'_i$$

The corresponding nonoverlapping mean is

$$\frac{1}{n} \sum_{i=1}^{n} r_{mi} = \frac{1}{n} \sum_{i=1}^{mn} r'_i \tag{3.20}$$

by using Equation 3.18. A comparison to the last term of Equation 3.19 shows that both means are essentially equal for $n \gg 1$; they are based on the sum of the small-interval returns r'. The remaining difference vanishes with n^{-1} in the large-sample limit, whereas the error of both means is proportional to $n^{-0.5}$ in the same limit.[8] Overlapping remains a valid method, but it is unable to reduce the error of the empirical mean.

---

[8] Müller (1993) has more details of this analysis.

Applications other than the computation of mean returns are more interesting. The most important example is realized volatility. A special version of Equation 3.8 is used:

$$v_i^p \;=\; v^p(t_i) \;=\; \frac{1}{N} \sum_{j=1}^{N} |r_{i-N+j}|^p \tag{3.21}$$

where the returns r_i are defined by Equation 3.16 and the returns are overlapping if $m > 1$. An analytical exploration of this realized volatility is possible under the assumption of Equation 3.17 and the special choice $p = 2$. By substituting Equation 3.18, we obtain

$$v_i^2 \;=\; \frac{1}{N} \sum_{j=1}^{N} \left(\sum_{j'=1}^{m} r'_{i-N-m+j+j'} \right)^2 \tag{3.22}$$

The expectation value of v_i^2 can be computed by expanding this expression where the cross products of r' vanish due to the iid assumption. The result is

$$\mathrm{E}[v_i^2] \;=\; m\,\sigma^2 \tag{3.23}$$

This is the theoretical expectation of the squared return of the Brownian motion over an interval of size $m\,\Delta t$. Equation 3.21 is thus an unbiased estimator, at least for $p = 2$.

The realized volatility v_i^2 of Equation 3.21 has an error whose variance is

$$\mathrm{E}\{[v_i^2 - m\,\sigma^2]^2\} \;=\; \mathrm{E}[v_i^4] - m^2\,\sigma^4 \;=\; \tag{3.24}$$

$$\frac{1}{N^2}\,\mathrm{E}\left\{ \left[\sum_{j=1}^{N} \left(\sum_{j'=1}^{m} r'_{i-N-m+j+j'} \right)^2 \right]^2 \right\} - m^2\,\sigma^4$$

where Equations 3.22 and 3.23 have been used. The further computation of this expression is somewhat tedious because of the two squares. A long sum is obtained where each term is a constant times four factors of the type r'_i. The expectation values of these terms follow from the Gaussian i.i.d. assumption: (1) r'^4_i has an expectation of $3\sigma^4$ (the fourth moment of the Gaussian random variable), (2) $r'^2_i r'^2_j$ has an expectation of σ^4 (if $i \neq j$), and (3) each term with a factor x_i to an odd power has the expectation zero. The resulting variance of the error is

$$\mathrm{E}\{[v_i^2 - m\,\sigma^2]^2\} \;=\; \frac{2\,m\,(2\,m^2+1)\,\sigma^4}{3\,N} \left[1 - \frac{m\,(m^2-1)}{2\,(2\,m^2+1)\,N} \right] \tag{3.25}$$

for $N \geq m$.

This has to be compared to the corresponding error of an overlap-free computation from the same sample. There are only n nonoverlapping return observations (with $N = mn$). The variance of the error is

$$
E\left\{\left[\frac{1}{n}\sum_{j=1}^{n}r_{mj}^2 - m\,\sigma^2\right]^2\right\} = \frac{2\,m^2\,\sigma^4}{n} = \frac{2\,m^3\,\sigma^4}{N} \tag{3.26}
$$

This has been computed as a special case of Equation 3.25 (case $m = 1$ with only n observations, but with a variance $m\sigma^2$ where m is the original overlap factor).

Equations 3.25 and 3.26 are now compared. The ratio of the two error variances is

$$
\frac{E\{[v_i^2 - m\,\sigma^2]^2\}}{E\{[\frac{1}{n}\sum_{j=1}^{n}r_{mj}^2 - m\,\sigma^2]^2\}} \approx \frac{2}{3} + \frac{1}{3\,m^2}, \quad \text{for } N \gg m \tag{3.27}
$$

This ratio is ≤ 1, so overlapping is indeed a means to reduce the stochastic error of realized volatility to a certain extent. In the limit of a very high overlapping factor m, the error variance is reduced to a minimum of two-thirds of the value without overlapping. An overlap factor of only $m = 2$ already reduces the error variance to 75%.

This finding can also be formulated by defining the *effective number of observations*, n_{eff}. This is the number of nonoverlapping observations that would be needed to reach the same error variance as that based on overlapping observations. From Equations 3.25 and 3.26, we obtain

$$
n_{\text{eff}} = \frac{3\,m\,N}{2\,m^2 + 1} = \frac{3\,m^2}{2\,m^2 + 1}\,n, \quad \text{for } n \gg 1 \tag{3.28}
$$

This can be expressed as a rule of thumb. Using the method of overlapping enhances the significance of realized volatility like adding up to 50% of independent observations to a nonoverlapping sample.

In Müller (1993), an analogous study was made for "realized covariance," the empirically measured covariance between two time series, based on simultaneous overlapping returns of both series. The result is similar. The estimator based on overlapping returns is unbiased and has a reduced error variance. The effective number of observations is again given by Equation 3.28.

In two cases, we have found an error reduction due to overlapping intervals. This provides a motivation for a general use of overlapping returns, also in other cases such as realized volatility with another exponent p (see Equation 3.8) and in other studies such as the analysis of the distribution of returns. The user has to be aware of and to account for the serial dependence due to overlapping and its possible effects on the results, as we have done in the derivations presented earlier. The increase in significance can roughly be expected to be as given by Equation 3.28, with some deviations due to the non-Brownian nature of the raw data. Heavy-tailed distributions, serial dependence, and heteroskedasticity as well as the choice of p may affect the behavior of the stochastic error. The statistical significance can alternatively be increased by choosing return intervals shorter than $m \Delta t$. However, these short-term returns would be a different object of study. The technique of overlapping has the advantage of leaving the object of study unchanged while increasing the precision.

3.3 CONVOLUTION OPERATORS

The original inhomogeneous data can be processed by convolution operators to build new inhomogeneous time series. This approach, developed by Zumbach and Müller (2001), is fundamentally different from the construction of homogeneous time series as discussed in Section 3.2. A set of basic convolution operators is defined that can be combined to compute more sophisticated quantities, for example, different kinds of volatility or correlation. A few stylized properties of these operators are explored, but the main emphasis is to build a sufficient vocabulary of operators well suited to high-frequency data analysis.

In this process, we should keep in mind a few important considerations:

- The computations must be efficient. Even if powerful computers are becoming cheaper, typical tick-by-tick data in finance are 100 or even 10,000 times more dense than daily data. Clearly, we cannot afford to compute a full convolution for every tick. For this reason, our basic workhorse is the exponential moving average (EMA) operator, which can be computed very efficiently through an iteration formula. A wealth of complex but still efficient operators can be constructed by combining and iterating the basic operators.

- A stochastic behavior is the dominant characteristic of financial processes. For tick-by-tick data, it is not only the values but also the time points of the series which are stochastic. In this random world, pointwise values are of little significance and we are more interested in average values inside intervals. Thus the usual notion of return also has to be changed. With daily data, a daily return is computed by Equation 3.7, as a pointwise difference between the price today and the price yesterday. With high-frequency data, a better definition of the daily return may be the difference between the average price of the last few hours and an average price from one day ago. In this way, it is possible to build smooth variables well suited to random processes. The calculus has to be revisited in order to replace pointwise values by averages over some time intervals.

- Analyzing data typically involves a characteristic time range; a return $r[\tau]$, for example, is computed on a given time interval τ. With high-frequency data, this characteristic time interval can vary from a few minutes to several weeks. This is taken care of by making explicit all of these time range dependencies in the formulation of operators.

- We usually want smooth operators with smooth kernels (weighting functions of moving averages). A simple example of a discontinuous operator is an average with a rectangular weighting function, say of range τ. The second discontinuity at "now $-\tau$," corresponding to forgetting events, creates unnecessary noise. Instead, we prefer kernels with a smooth decay to zero. Only at $t = $ now, we often prefer a jump in the kernel form. This jump gives a positive weight to the last piece of information and thus a rapid response in real time. For a discontinuous kernel, the weight at $t = $ now is inversely proportional to the range of the operator. Therefore, there is a trade-off between a fast reaction, which has more noise, and a smooth average behavior with a slow reaction time. Besides this fundamental noise created by the advance of events, it is better to have continuous and smooth operators.

The generalization to inhomogeneous time series introduces a number of technical peculiarities. In this Section 3.3, only macroscopic operators are treated, which, because of their time-translation invariance, can be represented by convolutions. A convolution is defined as an integral, therefore the series should have representation in continuous time. Actual data is known only at discrete sampling times, so some interpolation needs to be used in order to properly define the convolution integral. The same problem is present when constructing an artificial homogeneous time series from inhomogeneous data as in Section 3.2.1. Another technical peculiarity originates from the fact that our macroscopic operators are ultimately composed of iterated moving averages. All such EMA operators have noncompact kernels where the kernels decay exponentially, but strictly speaking they are positive. This implies an infinite memory; a build-up must be done over an initialization period before the error of an operator value becomes negligible.

The examples of Sections 3.3 and 3.4 are from the foreign exchange market. The data set is USD-CHF for the week of Sunday, October 26, to Sunday, November 2, 1997. This week has been selected because on Tuesday, October 28, some Asian stock markets crashed, causing turbulences in many markets around the world, including the FX market. Yet the relation between a stock market crash originating in Asia and the USD-CHF foreign exchange rate is quite indirect, making this example interesting. The prices of USD-CHF for the example week are plotted in Figure 3.4. When not specified otherwise, all figures from Figure 3.4 to 3.17 display quantities for the same example week. All of these figures have been computed using high-frequency data. The results have been sampled each hour using linear interpolation. The computations have been done in physical time, therefore exhibiting the full daily and weekly seasonalities contained in the data.

Finally, we want to emphasize that the techniques presented in this section are suitable for application to a wide range of statistical computations in finance such as in risk management. An early application can be found in Pictet *et al.* (1992) and a recent application is in Zumbach *et al.* (2000).

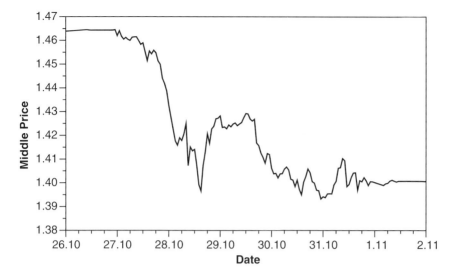

FIGURE 3.4 The FX rate USD-CHF for the week of Sunday, October 26, to Sunday, November 2, 1997. The high-frequency data are sampled hourly, using linear interpolation with geometric middle price $\sqrt{\text{bid} \cdot \text{ask}}$.

3.3.1 Notation Used for Time Series Operators

For time series operators in Sections 3.3 and 3.4, we use a suitable notation that sometimes differs from the conventions used for homogeneous time series. The letter z is used to represent a generic time series. The elements or ticks, (t_j, z_j), of a time series z consist of a time t_j and a scalar value z_j. As everywhere in Chapter 3, t may stand for any (business) time scale, not only physical time. The generalization to multivariate inhomogeneous time series is fairly straightforward (except for the business time scale aspect) and will not be discussed. The value $z_j = z(t_j)$ and the time point t_j constitute the j-th element of the time series z. The sequence of sampling (or arrival) times is required to be growing, $t_j > t_{j-1}$. The strict inequality is required in a true univariate time series and is theoretically always true if the information arrives through one channel. In practice, the arrival time is known with finite precision, say of a second, and two ticks may well have the same arrival time. Yet for most of the formulae that follow, the strict monotonicity of the time process is not required. In the special case where the time series is homogeneous, the sampling times are regularly spaced, $t_i - t_{i-1} = \delta t$. If a time series depends on some parameters θ, these are made explicit between square brackets, $z[\theta]$.

An operator Ω, from the space of time series into itself, is denoted by $\Omega[z]$, as already illustrated by Figure 3.1(b). The operator may depend on some parameters $\Omega[\theta; z]$. The value of $\Omega[z]$ at time t is $\Omega[z](t)$. For linear operators, a product notation Ωz is also used. The average over a whole time series of length T is denoted by $E[z] := 1/T \int dt\, z(t)$. For the probability density function (pdf) of z, we use $p(z)$. A synthetic regular (or homogeneous) time series (RTS), spaced by δt, derived from the irregular time series z, is denoted by $RTS[\delta t; z]$. For a standardized time series for z, we use the notation $\hat{z} = (z - E[z])/\sigma[z]$ and $\sigma[z]^2 = E[(z - E[z])^2]$. The letter x is used to represent the logarithmic middle price as defined by Equation 3.4.

3.3.2 Linear Operator and Kernels

We focus on operators with the following useful properties:

- Linear operators, where $\Omega[z_1 + c\, z_2] = \Omega[z_1] + c\, \Omega[z_2]$
- Time-translation invariant operators, where $\Omega[z(t - \Delta t)](t) = \Omega[z(t)](t - \Delta t)$
- Causal operators, where $\Omega[z](t)$ exclusively depends on information already know at time t. If $\Omega[z](t)$ depends on future events after t, it does not respect causality at time t and is noncausal.

An operator with all these three properties can be represented by a convolution with a kernel $\omega(t)$:

$$
\begin{aligned}
\Omega[z](t) &= \int_{-\infty}^{t} dt'\, \omega(t - t')\, z(t') \qquad (3.29) \\
&= \int_{0}^{\infty} dt'\, \omega(t')\, z(t - t')
\end{aligned}
$$

The causal kernel $\omega(t)$ is defined only on the positive semiaxis $t \geq 0$ and should decay for t large enough. With this convention for the convolution, the weight given to past events corresponds to the value of the kernel for positive argument. The value of the kernel $\omega(t - t')$ is the weight of events in the past, at a time interval $t - t'$ from t. In this convolution, $z(t')$ is a continuous function of time. Actual time series z are known only at the sampling time t_i and should be interpolated between sampling points. As in Section 3.2.1, we can define different interpolation procedures for the value of z(t) between t_{j-1} and t_j. Three are used in practice:

- Previous value, $z(t) = z_{j-1}$
- Next value, $z(t) = z_j$
- Linear interpolation, $z(t) = z_{j-1} + (z_j - z_{j-1})(t - t_{j-1})/(t_j - t_{j-1})$

The linear interpolation seems preferable as it leads to a continuous interpolated function. Moreover, linear interpolation defines the mean path of a random walk, given the start and end values. Unfortunately, it is non-causal, because in the interval between t_{i-1} and t_i, the value at the end of the interval z_i is used. Only the previous-value interpolation is causal, as only the information known at t_{i-1} is used in the interval between t_{i-1} and t_i. Any interpolation can be used for historical computations, but for the real-time situation, only the causal previous-value interpolation is defined. In practice, the interpolation scheme is almost irrelevant for good macroscopic operators, (i.e., if the kernel has a range longer than the typical sampling rate).

The kernel $\omega(t)$ can be extended to $t \in \mathbb{R}$, with $\omega(t) = 0$ for $t < 0$. This is useful for analytical computation, particularly when the order of integral evaluations has to be changed. If the operator Ω is linear and time-translation invariant but noncausal, the same representation can be used except that the kernel may be nonzero on the whole time axis.

We often use two broad families of operators that share general shapes and properties:

- An average operator has a kernel which is nonnegative, $\omega(t) \geq 0$, and normalized to unity, $\int dt\, \omega(t) = 1$. This implies that Ω[Parameters; Const] =Const.

- Derivative and difference operators have kernels that measure the difference between a value now and a value in the past (with a typical lag of τ). Their kernels have a zero average, $\int dt\, \omega(t) = 0$, such that Ω[Parameters; Const] $= 0$.

The integral in Equation 3.29 can also be evaluated in scaled time. In this case, the kernel is no more invariant with respect to physical time translation (i.e., it depends on t and t'), but it is invariant with respect to translation in business time. If the operator is an average or a derivative, the normalization property is preserved in scaled time.

The n-th moment of a causal kernel ω is defined as

$$\langle t^n \rangle_\omega := \int_0^\infty dt\, \omega(t)\, t^n \tag{3.30}$$

The range R and the width w of an operator Ω are defined, respectively, by the following relations:

$$R[\Omega] = \langle t \rangle_\omega = \int_0^\infty dt\, \omega(t)\, t \tag{3.31}$$

$$w^2[\Omega] = \langle (t - R)^2 \rangle_\omega = \int_0^\infty dt\, \omega(t)\, (t - R)^2$$

For most operators $\Omega[\tau]$ depending on a time range τ, the formula is set up so that $|R[\Omega[\tau]]| = \tau$.

Linear operators can be applied *successively*:

$$\Omega_C[z] = \Omega_2 \circ \Omega_1[z] = \Omega_2\, \Omega_1\, z := \Omega_2[\Omega_1[z]]$$

It is easy to show that the kernel of Ω_C is given by the *convolution* of the kernels of Ω_1 and Ω_2.

$$\omega_C = \omega_1 \star \omega_2 \qquad \text{or} \tag{3.32}$$

$$\omega_C(t - t') = \int_{-\infty}^{\infty} dt'' \, \omega_1(t - t'') \, \omega_2(t'' - t') \tag{3.33}$$

For causal operators,

$$\omega_C(t) = \int_{-t/2}^{t/2} dt' \, \omega_1(\frac{t}{2} - t') \, \omega_2(t' + \frac{t}{2}) \qquad \text{for } t \geq 0 \tag{3.34}$$

and $\omega_C(t) = 0$ for $t < 0$. Under convolution, range and width obey the following simple laws:

$$
\begin{array}{rcl}
R_C & = & R_1 + R_2 \\
w_C^2 & = & w_1^2 + w_2^2 \\
\langle t^2 \rangle_C & = & \langle t^2 \rangle_1 + \langle t^2 \rangle_2 + 2r_1 r_2
\end{array}
\tag{3.35}
$$

3.3.3 Build-Up Time Interval

As our basic building blocks are EMA operators, most kernels have an exponential tail for large t. This implies that, when starting the evaluation of an operator at time T, a build-up time interval must be elapsed before the result of the evaluation is accurate enough (i.e., the influence of the initial error at T has sufficiently faded). This heuristic statement can be expressed by quantitative definitions. We assume that the process $z(t)$ is known since time $-T$ and is modeled before as an unknown random walk with no drift. Equation 3.29 for an operator Ω needs to be modified in the following way:

$$\Omega[-T; z](t) = \int_{-T}^{t} dt' \, \omega(t - t') \, z(t') \, . \tag{3.36}$$

The "infinite" build-up corresponds to $\Omega[-\infty; z](t)$. For $-T < 0$, the average build-up error ϵ at $t = 0$ is given by

$$\epsilon^2 = E[(\Omega[-T; z](0) - \Omega[-\infty; z](0))^2] = E\left[\left(\int_{-\infty}^{-T} dt' \, \omega(-t') \, z(t')\right)^2\right] \tag{3.37}$$

where E is the expectation operator. For a given build-up error ϵ, this equation is the implicit definition of the build-up time interval T. In order to compute the expectation, we need to specify the considered space of random processes. We assume simple random walks with constant volatility σ, namely

$$E[(z(t) - z(t + \delta t))^2] = \sigma \frac{\delta t}{1y} \tag{3.38}$$

The symbol $1y$ denotes one year, so $\delta t / 1y$ is the length of δt expressed in years. With this choice of units, σ is an annualized volatility, with values roughly from 1% (for bonds) to 50% (for stocks), and a typical value of 10% for foreign exchange. For $t < -T$, $t' < -T$, we have the expectation

$$E[z(t)z(t')] = z(-T)^2 + \sigma \min(\frac{-t - T}{1y}, \frac{-t' - T}{1y}) \qquad (3.39)$$

Having defined the space of processes, a short computation gives

$$\epsilon^2 = z(-T)^2 \left(\int_T^\infty dt\, \Omega(t) \right)^2 + 2\sigma \int_T^\infty dt\, \omega(t) \int_T^t dt'\, \omega(t') \frac{t' - T}{1y} \qquad (3.40)$$

The first term is the "error at initialization" corresponding to the decay of the initial value $\Omega[-T](-T) = 0$ in Equation 3.36. A better initialization is $\Omega[-T](-T) = z(-T) \int_0^\infty \omega(t)$, corresponding to a modified definition for $\Omega[T](t)$:

$$\Omega[T; z](t) = z(-T) \int_{-\infty}^T dt'\, \omega(t - t') + \int_T^t dt'\, \omega(t - t')\, z(t') \qquad (3.41)$$

Another interpretation for the above formula is that z is approximated by its most probable value $z(-T)$ for $t < T$. With this better definition for Ω, the error reduces to

$$\epsilon^2 = 2\sigma \int_T^\infty dt\, \omega(t) \int_T^t dt'\, \omega(t') \frac{t' - T}{1y} \qquad (3.42)$$

For a given kernel ω, volatility σ and error ϵ, Equation 3.42 is an equation for T. Most of the kernels introduced in the next section have the scaling form $\omega(\tau, t) = \tilde{\omega}(t/\tau)/\tau$. In this case, the equation for $\tilde{T} = T/\tau$ reduces to

$$\epsilon^2 = 2\sigma \frac{\tau}{1y} \int_{\tilde{T}}^\infty dt\, \tilde{\omega}(t) \int_{\tilde{T}}^t dt'\, \tilde{\omega}(t')\, (t' - \tilde{T}) \qquad (3.43)$$

Because this equation cannot be solved for general operators, the build-up interval should be computed numerically. This equation can be solved analytically for the simple EMA kernel, and it gives the solution for the build-up time

$$\frac{T}{\tau} = -\ln \epsilon + \frac{1}{2} \ln \left(\frac{\sigma}{2} \frac{\tau}{1y} \right) \qquad (3.44)$$

As expected, the build-up time interval is large for a small error tolerance and for processes with high volatility. For operators more complicated than the simple EMA, Equation 3.43 is in general not solvable analytically. A simple rule of thumb can be given such that the heavier the tail of the kernel, the longer the required build-up. A simple measure for the tail can be constructed from the first two moments of the kernel as defined by Equation 3.30. The aspect ratio $AR[\Omega]$ is defined as

$$AR[\Omega] = \langle t^2 \rangle_\omega^{1/2} / \langle t \rangle_\omega$$

Both $\langle t \rangle$ and $\sqrt{\langle t^2 \rangle}$ measure the extension of the kernel and are usually proportional to τ; thus the aspect ratio is independent of τ and dependent only on the shape of the kernel, in particular its tail property. Typical values of this aspect ratio are $2/\sqrt{3}$ for a rectangular kernel and $\sqrt{2}$ for a simple EMA. A low aspect ratio means that the kernel of the operator has a short tail and therefore a short build-up time interval in terms of τ. This is a good rule for nonnegative causal kernels; the aspect ratio is less useful for choosing the build-up interval of causal kernels with more complicated, partially negative shapes.

3.3.4   Homogeneous Operators and Robustness

There are many ways to build nonlinear operators; an example is given in Section 3.3.13 for the (moving) correlation. In practice, most nonlinear operators are homogeneous of degree p, namely $\Omega[ax] = |a|^p \Omega[x]$ (here the word "homogeneous" is used in a sense different from that in the term "homogeneous time series"). Translation-invariant homogeneous operators of degree pq take the simple form of a convolution

$$\Omega[z](t) = \left[\int_{-\infty}^{t} dt' \, \omega(t - t') \, |z(t')|^p \right]^q \tag{3.45}$$

for some exponents p and q. An example is the moving norm (see Section 3.3.8) with ω corresponding to an average and $q = 1/p$.

Nonlinear operators can also be used to build robust estimators. Data errors (outliers) should be eliminated by a data filter prior to any computation, as discussed in Chapter 4. As an alternative or in addition to prior data cleaning, robust estimators can reduce the dependency of results on outliers or the choice of the data cleaning algorithm. This problem is acute mainly when working with returns, because the difference operator needed to compute returns (r) from prices (x) is sensitive to outliers. The following modified operator achieves robustness by giving a higher weight to the center of the distribution of returns r than to the tails:

$$\Omega[f; r] = f^{-1} \{ \Omega[f(r)] \} \tag{3.46}$$

where f is an odd, monotonic function over $\mathbb{R}$. Possible mapping functions $f(x)$ are

$$\text{sign}(x)|x|^\gamma = x \, |x|^{\gamma - 1} \tag{3.47}$$

$$\text{sign}(x) \quad \text{when} \quad \gamma \to 0 \tag{3.48}$$

$$\tanh(x/x_0) \tag{3.49}$$

Robust operator mapping functions defined by Equation 3.47 have an exponent $0 \leq \gamma < 1$. In some special applications, operators with $\gamma > 1$, emphasizing the tail of the distribution, may also be used. In the context of volatility estimates, the usual L^2 volatility operator based on squared returns can be made more robust by using the mapping function $f = \text{sign}(x)\sqrt{|x|}$ (the signed square root); the resulting volatility is then based on absolute returns as in Equation 3.67. More generally, the signed power $f(x) = \text{sign}(x)|x|^p$ transforms an L^2 volatility into an L^{2p} volatility. This simple power law transformation is often used and therefore included in the definition of the moving norm, moving variance or volatility operators, Equation 3.60. Yet some more general transformations can also be used.

3.3.5 Exponential Moving Average (EMA)

The basic exponential moving average (EMA) is the simplest linear operator, the first one in a series of linear operators to be presented. It is an averaging operator with an exponentially decaying kernel:

$$\text{ema}(t) = \frac{e^{-t/\tau}}{\tau} \tag{3.50}$$

This EMA operator is our foundation stone, because its computation is very efficient and other more complex operators can be built with it, such as moving averages (MAs), differentials, derivatives, and volatilities. The numerical evaluation is efficient because of the exponential form of the kernel, which leads to a simple iterative formula first proposed by Müller (1991):

$$\text{EMA}[\tau; z](t_n) = \tag{3.51}$$
$$\mu \, \text{EMA}[\tau; z](t_{n-1}) + (\nu - \mu) \, z_{n-1} + (1 - \nu) \, z_n$$

with

$$\alpha = \frac{t_n - t_{n-1}}{\tau}$$

$$\mu = e^{-\alpha}$$

where ν depends on the chosen interpolation scheme,

$$\nu = \begin{cases} 1 & \text{previous point} \\ (1 - \mu)/\alpha & \text{linear interpolation} \\ \mu & \text{next point} \end{cases} \tag{3.52}$$

Due to this iterative formula, the convolution is never computed in practice; only few multiplications and additions have to be done for each tick. In Section 3.3.14, the EMA operator is extended to the case of complex kernels.

3.3.6 The Iterated EMA Operator

The basic EMA operator can be iterated to provide a family of iterated exponential moving average operators $\text{EMA}[\tau, n]$. Practitioners of technical analysis have applied simple and (occasionally) iterated EMA operators to homogeneous time series for a long time. Iterated EMA operators for inhomogeneous time series were first explored by Müller (1991) and systematically developed and discussed by Zumbach and Müller (2001). A simple recursive definition is

$$\text{EMA}[\tau, n; z] = \text{EMA}[\tau; \text{EMA}[\tau, n-1; z]] \tag{3.53}$$

with $\text{EMA}[\tau, 1; z] = \text{EMA}[\tau; z]$. This definition can be efficiently evaluated by using the iterative formula in Equation 3.51 for all its basic EMAs. There is one subtle point related to the choice of the interpolation scheme in Equation 3.52. The EMA of z necessarily has an interpolation scheme different from that used for z. The correct form of $\text{EMA}[\tau; z]$ between two points is no longer a straight line but a nonlinear (exponential) curve. (Theoretically, it is straightforward to derive the corresponding exact interpolation formula.) When using one of the interpolation schemes of Equation 3.52 after the first iteration, we are making a small error. Yet if the kernel is wide as compared to $t_n - t_{n-1}$, this error is indeed very small. As a suitable *approximation*, we recommend using linear interpolation in the second and all further EMA iterations, even if the first iteration was based on the next-point interpolation. The only exception occurs if z_n is not yet known; then we need a causal operator based on the previous-point interpolation.

The kernel of $\text{EMA}[\tau, n]$ is

$$\text{ema}[\tau, n](t) = \frac{1}{(n-1)!} \left(\frac{t}{\tau} \right)^{n-1} \frac{e^{-t/\tau}}{\tau} \tag{3.54}$$

This family of functions is related to Laguerre polynomials, which are orthogonal with respect to the measure e^{-t} (for $\tau = 1$). Through an expansion in Laguerre polynomials, any kernel can be expressed as a sum of iterated EMA kernels. Therefore, the convolution with an arbitrary kernel can be evaluated by iterated exponential moving averages. Yet the convergence of this expansion may be slow, namely high-order iterated EMAs may be necessary, possibly with very large coefficients. This typically happens if one tries to construct operators that have a decay other (faster) than exponential. Therefore, in practice, we construct operators empirically from a few low-order EMAs, in a way to minimize the build-up time. The set of operators provided by Section 3.3 covers a wide range of computations needed in finance. The range, width, and aspect ratio of the iterated EMA are

$$
\begin{aligned}
R &= n\tau \\
\langle t^2 \rangle &= n(n+1)\tau^2 \\
w^2 &= n\tau^2 \\
AR &= \sqrt{(n+1)/n}
\end{aligned}
\tag{3.55}
$$

The iterated $\text{EMA}[\tau, n]$ operators with large n have a shorter, more compact kernel and require a shorter build-up time interval than a simple EMA of the same range

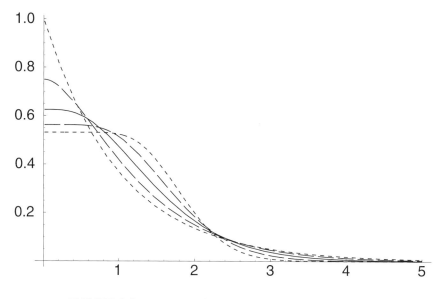

FIGURE 3.5 ma[τ, n](t) for $n = 1, 2, 4, 8$, and 16, for $\tau = 1$

$n\tau$. This is indicated by the aspect ratio AR, which decreases toward 1 for large n. Each basic EMA operator that is part of the iterated EMA has a range τ, which is much shorter than the range $n\tau$ of the full kernel. Even if the tail of the kernel is still exponential, it decays more quickly due to the small basic EMA range τ.

To further extend our computational toolbox, we build another type of compact kernel by combining iterated EMAs, as shown in the next section. As the iterated EMAs, these combined iterated EMAs have a shorter build-up time interval than a simple EMA of the same range.

3.3.7 Moving Average (MA)

A very convenient moving average is provided by

$$\text{MA}[\tau, n] = \frac{1}{n} \sum_{k=1}^{n} \text{EMA}[\tau', k] \qquad \text{with } \tau' = \frac{2\tau}{n+1} \qquad (3.56)$$

The parameter τ' is chosen so that the range of MA[τ, n] is $R = \tau$, independently of n. This provides a family of more rectangular-shaped kernels, with the relative weight of the distant past controlled by n. Kernels for different values of n and $\tau = 1$ are shown in Figure 3.5. Their analytical form is given by

$$\text{ma}[\tau, n](t) \quad = \quad \frac{n+1}{n} \frac{e^{-t/\tau'}}{2\tau} \sum_{k=0}^{n-1} \frac{1}{k!} \left(\frac{t}{\tau'} \right)^k \qquad (3.57)$$

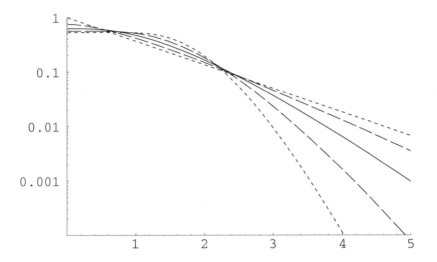

FIGURE 3.6   ma[τ, n](t) for $n = 1, 2, 4, 8$, and 16, for $\tau = 1$, on a logarithmic scale.

For $n = \infty$, the sum corresponds to the Taylor expansion of $\exp(t/\tau')$, which cancels the term $\exp(-t/\tau')$, making the kernel constant. For finite n, when t/τ' is small enough, the finite sum will be a good approximation of $\exp(t/\tau')$. Small enough means that the largest term in the sum is of order one: $(t/\tau')^n/n! \sim 1$. For large n, the condition $(t/\tau')^n/n! \sim 1$ corresponds to $t \sim 2\tau$ (using Stirling's approximation $n! \sim n^n$). Therefore, for $t \ll 2\tau$, the series approximates well the Taylor expansion of an exponential

$$\sum_{k=0}^{n-1} \frac{1}{k!} \left(\frac{t}{\tau'} \right)^k \rightarrow e^{t/\tau'}$$

$$\text{ma} \rightarrow \frac{n+1}{n} \frac{1}{2\tau}$$

This explains the constant behavior of the kernel for $t < 2\tau$. For $t > 2\tau$ large, the exponential always dominates and the kernel decays to zero. Therefore, for large n, this operator tends to a rectangular moving average for which $AR = 2/\sqrt{3}$. For n values of $n \sim 5$ and higher, the kernel is rectangular-like more than EMA-like; this can be seen in Figure 3.5. These rectangular-like kernels are preferred to the rectangular kernel itself because they fade smoothly rather than abruptly. Abrupt "forgetting" of past events leads to superfluous noise in the operator results.

The decay of MA kernels is also shown in Figure 3.6. The aspect ratio of the MA operator is

$$AR = \sqrt{\frac{4(n+2)}{3(n+1)}} \tag{3.58}$$

Clearly, the larger n, the shorter the build-up.

This family of operators can be extended by "peeling off" some EMAs with small k:

$$\mathrm{MA}[\tau, n_{\mathrm{inf}}, n_{\mathrm{sup}}] = \frac{1}{n_{\mathrm{sup}} - n_{\mathrm{inf}} + 1} \sum_{k=n_{\mathrm{inf}}}^{n_{\mathrm{sup}}} \mathrm{EMA}[\tau', k]$$

with

$$\tau' = \frac{2\tau}{n_{\mathrm{sup}} + n_{\mathrm{inf}}}$$

and with $1 \leq n_{\mathrm{inf}} \leq n_{\mathrm{sup}}$. By choosing such a modified MA with $n_{\mathrm{inf}} > 1$, we can generate a lagged operator with a kernel whose rectangular-like form starts after a lag rather than immediately. At the same time, the kernel loses its abrupt behavior at $t = 0$ and becomes fully continuous, thus reducing noise in the results even further. However, the time delay implied by the lag makes such kernels less attractive for real-time applications.

Almost everywhere, a moving average operator can be used instead of a sample average. The sample average of $z(t)$ is defined by

$$\mathrm{E}[z] = \frac{1}{t_e - t_s} \int_{t_s}^{t_e} dt' \, z(t') \tag{3.59}$$

where the dependency on start-time t_s and end-time t_e is implicit on the left-hand side. This dependency can be made explicit, for example with the notation $\mathrm{E}[t_e - t_s; z](t_e)$, thus demonstrating the parallelism between the sample average and a moving average $\mathrm{MA}[2\tau; z](t)$. The conceptual difference is that when using a sample average, t_s and t_e are fixed, and the sample average is a number (the sample average is a functional from the space of time series to $\mathbb{R}$), whereas the MA operator produces another time series. Keeping this difference in mind, we can replace the sample average $\mathrm{E}[\cdot]$ by a moving average $\mathrm{MA}[\cdot]$. For example, we can construct a standardized time series $\hat{z}$ (as defined in Section 3.3.1), a moving skewness, or a moving correlation (see the various definitions below). Yet be aware that sample averages and MAs can behave differently, for example $\mathrm{E}\left[(z - \mathrm{E}[z])^2\right] = \mathrm{E}[z^2] - \mathrm{E}[z]^2$, whereas $\mathrm{MA}[(z - \mathrm{MA}[z])^2] \neq \mathrm{MA}[z^2] - \mathrm{MA}[z]^2$.

3.3.8 Moving Norm, Variance, and Standard Deviation

With the efficient moving average operator, we can define the moving norm, moving variance, and moving standard deviation operators:

$$\begin{aligned}
\mathrm{MNorm}[\tau, p; z] &= \mathrm{MA}[\tau; |z|^p]^{1/p} \\
\mathrm{MVar}[\tau, p; z] &= \mathrm{MA}[\tau; |z - \mathrm{MA}[\tau; z]|^p] \\
\mathrm{MSD}[\tau, p; z] &= \mathrm{MA}[\tau; |z - \mathrm{MA}[\tau; z]|^p]^{1/p}
\end{aligned} \tag{3.60}$$

The norm and standard deviation are homogeneous of degree 1 with respect to z. The p-moment is related to the norm by $\mu_p = \mathrm{MA}[|z|^p] = \mathrm{MNorm}[z]^p$. Usually, $p = 2$ is taken. Lower values for p provide a more robust estimate (see

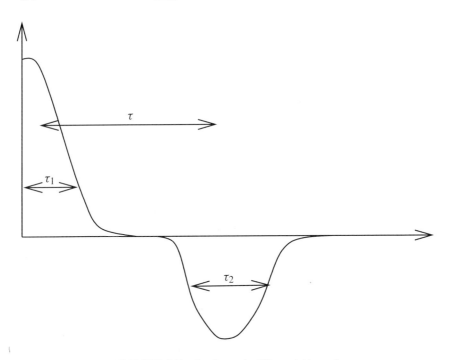

FIGURE 3.7   A schematic differential kernel.

Section 3.3.4), and $p = 1$ is another common choice. Yet even lower values can be used, for example, $p = 1/2$. In the formulae for MVar and MSD, there are two MA operators with the same range τ and the same kernel. This choice is in line with common practice for the calculation of empirical means and variances in the same sample. Yet other choices can be interesting, for example the sample mean can be estimated with a longer time range.

3.3.9   Differential

As argued in the introduction, a low-noise differential operator suitable to stochastic processes should compute an "average differential", namely the difference between an average around time "now" over a time interval τ_1 and an average around time "now $- \tau$" on a time interval τ_2. The kernel may look like that in Figure 3.7. Kernels of a similar kind are used for wavelet transforms. This analogy also applies to other kernel forms and is further discussed in Section 3.3.14.

Usually, τ, τ_1 and τ_2 are related and only the τ parameter appears, with $\tau_1 \sim \tau_2 \sim \tau/2$. The normalization of the differential Δ is chosen so that $\Delta[\tau; c] = 0$ for a constant function $c = c(t) = $ constant, and $\Delta[\tau; t] = \tau$. Note that our point of view is different from that used in continuous-time stochastic analysis. In continuous time, the limit $\tau \to 0$ is taken, leading to the Ito derivative with its subtleties. In our case, we keep the range τ finite in order to be able to analyze

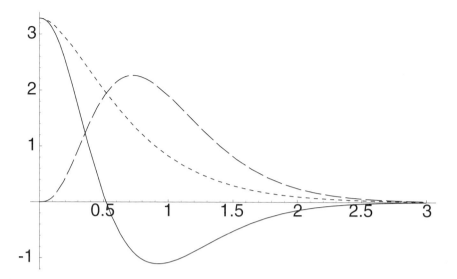

FIGURE 3.8 An example of a differential operator kernel (full line) for $\tau = 1$. The dotted curve corresponds to the first two terms of the operator $\gamma(\text{EMA}[\alpha\tau, 1] + \text{EMA}[\alpha\tau, 2])$, the dashed curve to the last term $2\gamma\ \text{EMA}[\alpha\beta\tau, 4]$.

a process at different time scales (i.e., for different orders of magnitudes of τ). Moreover, for financial data, the limit $\tau \to 0$ cannot be taken because a process is known only on a discrete set of time points (and probably does not exist in continuous time).

The following operator can be selected as a suitable differential operator:

$$\Delta[\tau] = \gamma\ (\text{EMA}[\alpha\tau, 1] + \text{EMA}[\alpha\tau, 2] - 2\ \text{EMA}[\alpha\beta\tau, 4]) \qquad (3.61)$$

with $\gamma = 1.22208$, $\beta = 0.65$ and $\alpha^{-1} = \gamma(8\beta - 3)$. This operator has a well-behaving kernel that is plotted in Figure 3.8.

The value of γ is fixed so that the integral of the kernel from the origin to the first zero is one. The value of α is fixed by the normalization condition and the value of β is chosen in order to get a short tail. The tail can be seen in Figure 3.9. This shows that after $t = 3.25\tau$, the kernel is smaller than 10^{-3}, which translates into a small required build-up time of about 4τ.

In finance, the main purpose of a Δ operator is computing returns of a time series of (logarithmic) prices x with a given time interval τ. Returns are normally defined as changes of x over τ; we prefer the alternative return definition $r[\tau] = \Delta[\tau; x]$. This computation requires the evaluation of six EMAs and is therefore efficient, time-wise and memory-wise. An example using our standard week is plotted in Figure 3.10, demonstrating the low noise level of the differential. The conventionally computed return $r[\tau](t) = x(t) - x(t - \tau)$ is very inefficient to evaluate for inhomogeneous time series. The computation of $x(t - \tau)$ requires a high, unbounded number of old t_i, x_i values to be kept in memory, and the t_i

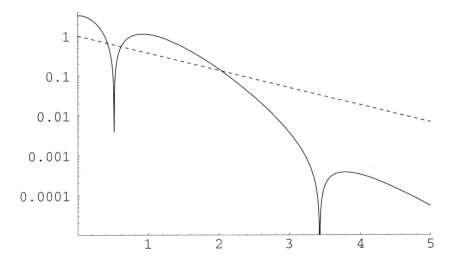

FIGURE 3.9   The absolute value of the kernel of the differential operator (full line), in a logarithmic scale. The dotted line shows a simple EMA with range τ, demonstrating the much faster decay of the differential kernel.

interval bracketing the time $t - \tau$ has to be searched for. This return definition corresponds to a differential operator kernel made of two δ functions (or to the limit $\tau_1, \tau_2 \to 0$ of the kernel in Figure 3.7). The quantity $x(t) - x(t - \tau)$ can be quite noisy, so a further EMA might be taken to smooth it. In this case, the resulting effective differential operator kernel has two discontinuities, at 0 and at τ, and decays exponentially—that is, much slower than the kernel of $\Delta[\tau; x]$. Thus it is cleaner and more efficient to compute returns with the Δ operator of Equation 3.61. Another quantity commonly used in finance is $x - \text{EMA}[\tau; x]$, often called a momentum or an oscillator. This is also a differential with the kernel $\delta(t) - \exp(-t/\tau)/\tau$, with a δ function at $t = 0$. A simple drawing shows that the kernel of Equation 3.61 produces a much less noisy differential. Other appropriate kernels can be designed, depending on the application. In general, there is a trade-off between the averaging property of the kernel and a short response to shocks of the original time series.

3.3.10   Derivative and γ-Derivative

The derivative operator

$$D[\tau] = \frac{\Delta[\tau]}{\tau} \tag{3.62}$$

behaves exactly as the differential operator, except for the normalization $D[\tau; t]$ = 1. This derivative can be iterated in order to construct higher order derivatives:

$$D^2[\tau] = D[\tau; D[\tau]] \tag{3.63}$$

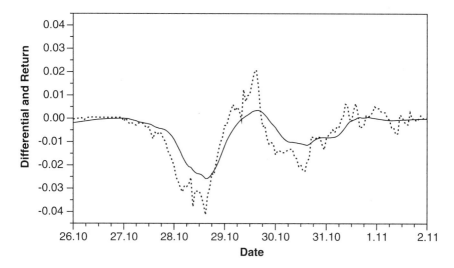

FIGURE 3.10 A comparison between the differential computed using the formula in Equation 3.61 with τ = 24hr (full line) and the pointwise return $x(t) - x(t - 24\text{h})$ (dotted line). The time lag of approximately 4hr between the curves is essentially due to the extent of both the positive part of the kernel ($0 < t < 0.5$) and the tail of the negative part ($t > 1.5$).

The range of the second-order derivative operator is $2\,\tau$. More generally, the n-th order derivative operator D^n, constructed by iterating the derivative operator n times, has a range $n\tau$. As defined, the derivative operator has the dimension of an inverse time. It is easier to work with dimensionless operators and this is done by measuring τ in some units. One year provides a convenient unit, corresponding to an annualized return when $D[\tau]x$ is computed. The choice of unit is denoted by $\tau/1y$, meaning that τ is measured in years, yet other units may also be used. For a random diffusion process, a more meaningful normalization for the derivative is to take $D[\tau] = \Delta[\tau]/\sqrt{\tau/1y}$. For a space of processes as in Section 3.3.3, such that Equation 3.38 holds, the basic scaling behavior with τ is eliminated, namely $E\left[(D[\tau]z)^2\right] = \sigma^2$. More generally, we can define a γ-derivative as

$$D[\tau, \gamma] = \frac{\Delta[\tau]}{(\tau/1y)^\gamma} \tag{3.64}$$

In particular

$$
\begin{array}{lll}
\gamma = 0 & \quad \text{differential} & \\
\gamma = 0.5 & \quad \text{stochastic diffusion process} & \tag{3.65} \\
\gamma = 1 & \quad \text{the usual derivative} &
\end{array}
$$

An empirical probability density function for the derivative is displayed in Figure 3.11. We clearly see that the main part of the scaling with τ is removed when using the γ-derivative with $\gamma = 0.5$.

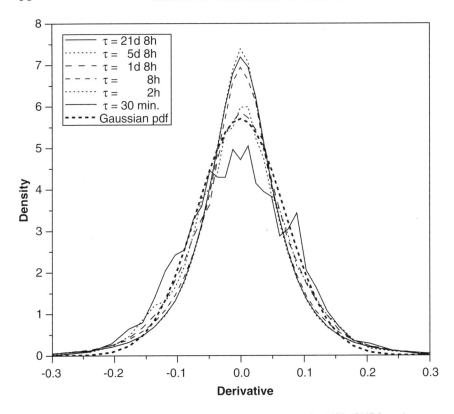

FIGURE 3.11   The annualized derivative $D[\tau, \gamma = 0.5; x]$ for USD-CHF from January 1, 1988 to November 1, 1998. The shortest time intervals τ correspond to the most leptokurtic curves. In order to discard the daily and weekly seasonality, the time scale used is the business time ϑ as explained in Chapter 6 and in Dacorogna *et al.* (1993). The data were sampled every 2 hr (in ϑ-time) to construct the curves. The Gaussian probability density function added for comparison has a standard deviation of $\sigma = 0.07$, similar to that of the other curves.

3.3.11   Volatility

The most common computation of realized or historical volatility is given by Equation 3.8 in Section 3.2.4, based on regularly spaced (e.g., daily) observations. Realized volatility can also be defined and measured with the help of convolution operators.

Volatility is a measure widely used for random processes, quantifying the size and intensity of movements, namely the current "width" of the probability distribution $P(\Delta z)$ of the process increment Δz, where Δ is a difference operator yet to be chosen. Often the volatility of market prices is computed, but volatility is a general operator that can be applied to any time series. There are many ways to turn this idea into a definition, and there is no unique, universally accepted definition of volatility in finance. In our new context, we can reformulate the realized volatility of Equation 3.8 as an L^2 norm,

$$\text{Volatility}[\tau, \tau'; z] = \left(\frac{1}{n} \sum_{i=0}^{n-1} \left(\delta \ \text{RTS}[\tau'; z] \right)_i^2 \right)^{1/2} \quad \text{with} \quad \tau = n \, \tau' \quad (3.66)$$

where the operator δ computes the difference between successive values (see Section 3.4.3), τ' is the return interval, and τ is the length of the moving sample. $\text{RTS}[\tau'; z]$ is an artificial regular time series, spaced by τ', constructed from the irregular time series z. The construction of homogeneous time series was discussed in Sections 3.2.1 and 3.2.2; it is reformulated in Section 3.4.2 in terms of the RTS operator. Realized volatility based on artificially regularized data suffers from several drawbacks:

- For inhomogeneous time series, a synthetic regular time series must be created, which involves an interpolation scheme.
- The difference is computed with a pointwise difference. This implies some noise in the case of stochastic data.
- Only some values at regular time points are used. Information from other points of the series, between the regular sampling points, is thrown away. Resulting from this information loss, the estimator is less accurate than it could be.
- It is based on a rectangular weighting kernel—that is, all points have constant weights of either $1/n$ or 0 as soon as they are excluded from the sample. A continuous kernel with declining weights leads to a better, less disruptive, and less noisy behavior.
- By squaring the returns, this definition puts a large weight on large changes of z and therefore increases the impact of outliers and the tails of $P(z)$. Also, as the fourth moment of the probability distribution of the returns might not be finite (Müller *et al.*, 1998), the volatility of the volatility might not be finite either. In other words, this estimator is not very robust. These are reasons to prefer a realized volatility defined as an L^1 norm:

$$\text{Volatility}[\tau, \tau'; z] = \frac{1}{N} \sum_{i=0}^{N-1} |\Delta[\text{RTS}[\tau'; z]]_i| \quad \text{with} \quad \tau = N \, \tau'$$

$$(3.67)$$

There are various ways to introduce better definitions for inhomogeneous time series. These definitions are variations of the following one:

$$\text{Volatility}[\tau, \tau', p; z] = \text{MNorm}[\tau/2, p; \Delta[\tau'; z]] \quad (3.68)$$

where the moving norm MNorm is defined by Equation 3.60. For Δ, we can take the differential operator of Equation 3.61 or a similar operator. Let us emphasize that no homogeneous time series is needed, and that this definition can be computed simply and efficiently for high-frequency data because it ultimately involves only EMAs. Note the division by 2 in the MNorm of range $\tau/2$. This is to attain an equivalent of Equation 3.66, which is parametrized by the total sample size rather than the range of the (rectangular) kernel.

The volatility defined by Equation 3.68 is still a *realized* volatility although it is now based on inhomogeneous data and operators. The kernel form of the differential operator Δ has a certain influence on the size of the resulting volatility. A "soft" kernel will lead to a lower mean value of volatility than a "hard" kernel whose positive and negative parts are close to delta functions. This has to be accounted for when applying operator-based volatility.

The variations of Equation 3.68 mainly include the following:

- Replacing the norm MNorm by a moving standard deviation MSD as defined by Equation 3.60. By this modification, the empirical sample mean is subtracted from all observations of $\Delta[\tau'; z]$. This leads to a formula analogous to Equation 3.11, whereas Equation 3.68 is analogous to Equation 3.8. Empirically, for most data in finance such as FX, the numerical difference between taking MNorm and MSD is very small.

- Replacing the differential Δ by a γ-derivative $D[\tau, \gamma]$. The advantage of using the gamma derivative is to remove the leading τ dependence, for example by directly computing the annualized volatility, independent of τ. An example is given by Figure 3.12.

Let us emphasize that the realized volatility in Equations 3.66 through 3.68 depends on the two time ranges τ and τ' and, to be unambiguous, both time intervals must be given. Yet, for example, when talking about a daily volatility, the common language is rather ambiguous because only one time interval is specified. Usually, the emphasis is put on τ'. A daily volatility, for example, measures the average size of daily price changes (i.e., $\tau' = 1$ day). The averaging time range τ is chosen as a multiple of τ', of the order $\tau \geq \tau'$ up to $\tau = 1000\tau'$ or more. Larger multiples lead to lower stochastic errors as they average over larger samples, but they are less local and dampen the time variations in the frequent case of nonconstant volatility. In empirical studies, we find that good compromises are in the range from $\tau = 16\tau'$ to $\tau = 32\tau'$.

On other occasions, for example in risk management, one is interested in the conditional daily volatility. Given the prices up to today, we want to produce an estimate or forecast for the size of the price move from today to tomorrow (i.e., the volatility within a small sample of only one day). The actual value of this volatility can be measured one day later; it has $\tau = 1$ day by definition. To measure this value with acceptable precision, we may choose a distinctly smaller τ', perhaps $\tau' = 1$ hr. Clearly, when only one time parameter is given, there is no simple convention to remove the ambiguity.

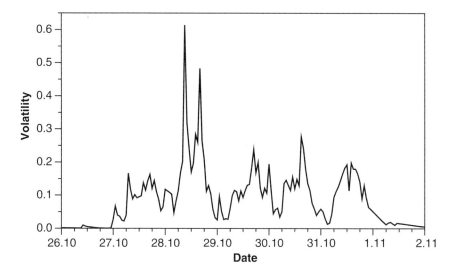

FIGURE 3.12 The annualized volatility computed as $MNorm[\tau/2; D[\tau/32, \gamma = 0.5; x]]$ with $\tau = 1hr$. The norm is computed with $p = 2$ and $n = 8$. The plotted volatility has five main maxima corresponding to the five working days of the example week. The Tuesday maximum is higher than the others, due to the stock market crash mentioned in the introductory part of Section 3.3.

3.3.12 Standardized Time Series, Moving Skewness, and Kurtosis

From a time series z, we can derive a moving standardized time series:

$$\hat{z}[\tau] = \frac{z - MA[\tau; z]}{MSD[\tau; z]} \tag{3.69}$$

In finance, z stands for the price or alternatively for another variable such as the return. Having defined a standardized time series $\hat{z}[\tau]$, the definitions for the moving skewness, and moving kurtosis are straightforward:

$$\begin{aligned} MSkewness[\tau_1, \tau_2; z] &= MA[\tau_1; \hat{z}[\tau_2]^3] \\ MKurtosis[\tau_1, \tau_2; z] &= MA[\tau_1; \hat{z}[\tau_2]^4] \end{aligned} \tag{3.70}$$

Instead of this kurtosis, the excess kurtosis is often used, whose value for a normal distribution is 0. We obtain the excess kurtosis by subtracting 3 from the MKurtosis value. The three quantities for our sample week are displayed in Figure 3.13.

3.3.13 Moving Correlation

Several definitions of a moving correlation can be constructed for inhomogeneous time series. Generalizing from the statistics textbook definition, we can write two simple definitions:

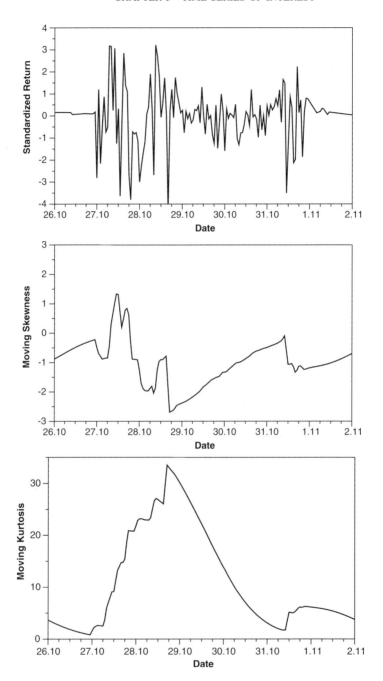

FIGURE 3.13 The standardized return, moving skewness, and moving kurtosis. The returns are computed as $r = D[\tau = 15\ \text{min};\ x]$ and standardized with $\tau_1 = \tau_2 = 24\text{hr}$.

$$\text{MCorrelation}_1[\tau; y, z] = \frac{\text{MA}[\ (y - \text{MA}[y])(z - \text{MA}[z])\ ]}{\text{MSD}[y]\ \text{MSD}[z]} \qquad (3.71)$$

$$\text{MCorrelation}_2[\tau; y, z] = \text{MA}\left[\frac{(y - \text{MA}[y])\ (z - \text{MA}[z])}{\text{MSD}[y]\ \text{MSD}[z]}\right]$$

$$= \text{MA}[\ \hat{y}\ \hat{z}\ ] \qquad (3.72)$$

where all of the MA and MSD[9] operators on the right-hand sides are taken with the same decay constant τ. These definitions are not equivalent because the MSD operators in the denominator are time series that do not commute with the MA operators. Yet both definitions have their respective advantages. The first definition obeys the inequality $-1 \leq \text{MCorrelation}_1 \leq 1$. This can be proven by noting that $MA[z^2](t)$ for a given t provides a norm on the space of (finite) time series up to t. It happens because the MA operator has a strictly positive kernel that acts as a metric on the space of time series. In this space, the triangle inequality holds $\sqrt{MA[(y+z)^2]} \leq \sqrt{MA[y^2]} + \sqrt{MA[z^2]}$, and, by a standard argument, the inequality on the correlation follows. With the second definition (Equation 3.72), the correlation matrix is bilinear for the standardized time series. Therefore, the rotation that diagonalizes the correlation matrix acts linearly in the space of standardized time series. This property is necessary for multivariate analysis, when a principal component decomposition is used. In risk management, the correlation of two time series of returns, x and y, is usually computed without subtracting the sample means of x and y. This implies a variation of Equations 3.71 and 3.72

$$\text{MCorrelation}_1'[\tau; y, z] = \frac{\text{MA}[\ y\ z\ ]}{\text{MNorm}[y]\ \text{MNorm}[z]} \qquad (3.73)$$

$$\text{MCorrelation}_2'[\tau; y, z] = \text{MA}\left[\frac{y\ z}{\text{MNorm}[y]\ \text{MNorm}[z]}\right] \qquad (3.74)$$

where again the same τ is chosen for all MA operators. In general, any reasonable definition of a moving correlation must obey

$$\lim_{\tau \to \infty} \text{MCorrelation}[\tau; y, z] \to \rho[y, z] \qquad (3.75)$$

where $\rho[y, z]$ is the theoretical correlation of the two stationary processes x and y. Generalizing the definition (Equation 3.72), the requirements for the correlation kernel are to construct a causal, time translation invariant, and a linear operator for $\hat{y}$ and $\hat{z}$. This leads to the most general representation

$$\text{MCorrelation}[\hat{y}, \hat{z}](t) = \int_0^\infty \int_0^\infty dt'\, dt''\, c(t', t'')\, \hat{y}(t - t')\, \hat{z}(t - t'') \qquad (3.76)$$

[9] See Equation 3.60.

We also require symmetry between the arguments where $\text{MCorrelation}[\hat{z}, \hat{y}] = \text{MCorrelation}[\hat{y}, \hat{z}]$. Moreover, the correlation must be a generalized average, namely $\text{MCorrelation}[\text{Const}, \text{Const}'] = \text{Const}\,\text{Const}'$, or, formulated for the kernel, $\int \int_0^\infty dt'\, dt''\, c(t', t'') = 1$. There is a large choice of possible kernels that obey these requirements. For example, Equation 3.72 is equivalent to the kernel $c(t', t'') = \delta(t' - t'')\, \text{ma}(\frac{t'+t''}{2})$.

3.3.14   Windowed Fourier Transform

In order to study a time series and its volatility at different time scales, we want to have a tool similar to a wavelet transform,[10] which adapts to causal signals. The motivation is to reveal structures of price movements related to certain frequencies. Similar to wavelet transforms, we want a double representation in time and frequency, but we do not require an invertible transformation because our aim is to analyze rather than further process the signal. This gives us more flexibility in the choice of the transformations. A simple causal kernel with such properties is like $\text{ma}[\tau](t)\,\sin(kt/\tau)$, where $\text{ma}[\tau](t)$ is still the MA kernel of Equation 3.57. Essentially, the sine part is (locally) analyzing the signal at a frequency k/τ and the MA part is taking a causal window of range τ. As we want a couple of oscillations in the window 2τ, we choose k between $k \sim \pi$ and $k \sim 5\pi$. Larger k values increase the frequency resolution at the cost of the time resolution. The basic idea is to compute an EMA with a complex τ; this is equivalent to including a sine and cosine part in the kernel. The nice computational iterative property of the moving average is preserved. The first step is to study complex iterated EMAs. The kernel of the complex ema is defined as

$$\text{ema}[\zeta](t) = \frac{e^{-\zeta t}}{\tau} \qquad \text{where} \quad \zeta = \frac{1}{\tau}(1 + ik) \qquad (3.77)$$

where ζ is complex but τ is again a real number. The choice of the normalization factor $1/\tau$ is somewhat arbitrary (a factor $|\zeta|$ will produce the same normalization for the real case $k = 0$) but leads to a convenient definition of the windowed Fourier kernel that follows. By using the convolution formula, one can prove iteratively that the kernel of the complex $\text{EMA}[\zeta, n]$ is given by

$$\text{ema}[\zeta, n](t) = \frac{1}{(n-1)!} \left(\frac{t}{\tau}\right)^{n-1} \frac{e^{-\zeta t}}{\tau} \qquad (3.78)$$

which is analogous to Equation 3.54. The normalization is such that, for a constant function $c(t) = c$,

$$\text{EMA}[\zeta, n; c] = \frac{c}{(1 + ik)^n} \qquad (3.79)$$

---

[10] An introduction to wavelet methods is studied extensively in Gençay *et al.* (2001b).

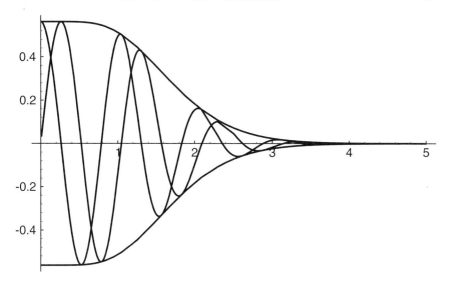

FIGURE 3.14 The kernel wf(t) for the windowed Fourier operator, for $n = 8$ and $k = 6$. Three aspects of the complex kernel are shown: (1) the envelope (= absolute value), (2) the real part (starting on top), and (3) the imaginary part (starting at zero).

Similar to Equation 3.51, we obtain an iterative computational formula for the complex EMA:

$$EMA[\zeta; z](t_n) = \tag{3.80}$$
$$\mu \, EMA[\zeta; z](t_{n-1}) + \frac{\nu - \mu}{1 + ik} z_{n-1} + \frac{1 - \nu}{1 + ik} z_n$$

with

$$\alpha = \zeta \, (t_n - t_{n-1})$$
$$\mu = e^{-\alpha}$$

where ν depends on the chosen interpolation scheme as given by Equation 3.52. We define the (complex) kernel wf(t) of the windowed Fourier transform WF as

$$wf[\tau, k, n](t) = ma[\tau, n](t) \, e^{-ikt/\tau} \tag{3.81}$$
$$= \frac{1}{n} \sum_{j=1}^{n} \frac{1}{(j-1)!} \left(\frac{t}{\tau}\right)^{j-1} \frac{e^{-\zeta t}}{\tau}$$
$$= \frac{1}{n} \sum_{j=1}^{n} ema[\zeta, j](t)$$

The kernel is shown in Figure 3.14. Another appropriate name for this operator might be CMA for "complex moving average." The normalization is such that, for a constant function $c(t) = c$,

$$N_{WF} = WF[\zeta, n; c] = \frac{c}{n} \sum_{j=1}^{n} \frac{1}{(1 + ik)^j}$$

To provide a more convenient real quantity, with the mean of the signal subtracted, we can define a (nonlinear) normed windowed Fourier transform as

$$NormedWF[\zeta, n; z] = |WF[\zeta, n; z] - N_{WF} \, MA[\tau, n; z]| \qquad (3.82)$$

The normalization is chosen so that

$$NormedWF[\zeta, n; c] = 0$$

In Equation 3.82, we are only interested in the amplitude of the measured frequency; by taking the absolute value we have lost information on the phase of the oscillations.

Windowed Fourier transforms can be computed for a set of different τ values to obtain a full spectrum. However, there is an upper limit in the range of computable frequencies. Results are reliable if τ clearly exceeds the average time interval between ticks. For τ values smaller than the average tick interval, results become biased and noisy; this sentence applies not only to windowed Fourier transforms but also to most other time series operators.

Figure 3.15 shows an example of the normed windowed Fourier transform for the example week. The stock market crash is again nicely spotted as the peak on Tuesday, October 28.

Using our computational toolbox of operators, other quantities of interest can be easily derived. For example, we can compute the relative share of a certain frequency in the total volatility. This would mean a volatility correction of the normed windowed Fourier transform. A way to achieve this is to divide NormedWF by a suitable volatility, or to replace z by the standardized time series $\hat{z}$ in Equation 3.82.

3.4 MICROSCOPIC OPERATORS

As discussed in Section 3.1, it is in general better to use macroscopic operators because they are well behaved with respect to the sampling frequency. Some microscopic operators allow the extraction of tick-related information at the highest possible frequency. An example of such an operator is the microscopic volatility defined later. The computation of the tick frequency requires (by definition) microscopic operators. We also want to extend to inhomogeneous time series the usual operators applied to homogeneous time series, such as the shift operator.

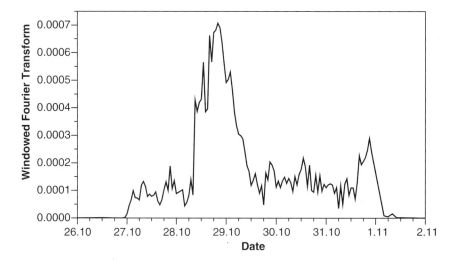

FIGURE 3.15 The normed windowed Fourier transform, with $\tau = 1$ hr, $k = 6$ and $n = 8$.

3.4.1 Backward Shift and Time Translation Operators

The backward shift operator $\mathcal{B}$ shifts the value of the time series by one event backward $\mathcal{B}[z]_i = (t_i, z_{i-1})$, but the time associated to each event is not changed. Some authors use the equivalent *lag* operator L instead. It shifts the time series values but leaves the time part untouched. The inverse operator $\mathcal{B}^{-1}$ will shift the series forward. It is well defined for regular and irregular time series. Only for a homogeneous time series spaced by δt, this operator is equivalent to a time translation by $-\delta t$ (followed by a shift of the time *and* value series by one event with respect to the irrelevant index i).

The operator $\mathcal{T}$ translates the time series by δt forward $\mathcal{T}[\delta t; z]_i = (t_i + \delta t, z_i)$; namely it shifts the time part but leaves the time series values untouched. Note that for an inhomogeneous time series, this operator defines a series with another set of time points.

3.4.2 Regular Time Series Operator

From the time series z, irregularly spaced in time, the operator $RTS[t_0, \delta t]$ constructs an artificial homogeneous time series at times $t_0 + k\delta t$, regularly spaced by δt, rooted at t_0. This involves an interpolation scheme as discussed in Section 3.2.1. Depending on this scheme, the RTS operator can be causal or not. The regular time series can also be constructed as being regular on a given business time scale rather than in physical time.

The RTS operator allows us to move from inhomogeneous to the homogeneous time series as presented in Section 3.2.2. For many computations, it is mandatory to have homogeneous data, for example when modeling financial data with ARMA or GARCH processes. Another example is the computation of empirical probability distributions. Such computations are done with a smooth version of the formula

$$p(z) = \frac{1}{T} \int_0^T dt \, \delta(z - z'(t)) \tag{3.83}$$

with $z'(t)$ the (continuously interpolated) empirical data. In the time integral, a measure can be added, or the integral can be evaluated in business time to account for the seasonalities. The evaluation of the time integral is computationally heavy, and it is much simpler to generate a regular time series and to use the familiar binning procedure to obtain a histogram of z. Note also that a moving probability distribution can be defined by replacing the time integral by an MA operator (see the remark at the end of Section 3.3.7).

3.4.3   Microscopic Return, Difference, and Derivative

From the tick-by-tick price time series, the microscopic return for a quote is defined as $r_j = x_j - x_{j-1}$. This return can be attributed to one quote, even if, strictly speaking, it is related to two subsequent quotes. Note that this is a "microscopic" definition that involves neither a time scale nor an interpolation scheme. Using the backward shift operator $\mathcal{B}$, the return time series can be defined as

$$r = x - \mathcal{B}[x] = (1 - \mathcal{B}) \, x = \delta x \tag{3.84}$$

where the microscopic difference operator[11] is $\delta = (1 - \mathcal{B})$. The lag n difference operator is defined by $\delta[n] = (1 - \mathcal{B}^n)$.

The microscopic derivative operator ∂ is defined as

$$\partial[\delta t_0] x_j = \frac{x_j - x_{j-1}}{\delta t_0 + t_j - t_{j-1}} = \frac{\delta x}{\delta t_0 + \delta t} \bigg|_j \tag{3.85}$$

The constant δt_0 regularizes the expression when $t_i = t_{i-1}$. A reasonable value of δt_0 must be small; the actual choice depends on the application. Similar to the macroscopic γ-derivative, a microscopic γ-derivative can be defined as

$$\partial[\delta t_0, \gamma] x = \frac{\delta x}{(\delta t_0 + \delta t)^\gamma} \tag{3.86}$$

The best parameters should follow a study yet to be done for the random process of x. The constant δt_0 regularizes the expression when $t_j = t_{j-1}$.

These derivatives are potentially very noisy and can be averaged. In general, the macroscopic derivative D (Equation 3.64) seems more relevant for applications to random processes.

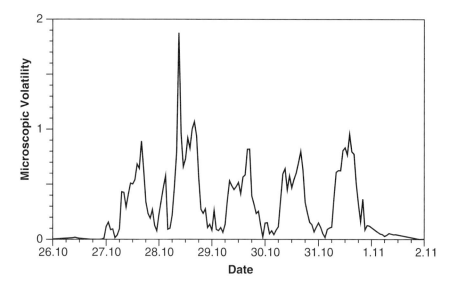

FIGURE 3.16 Microscopic volatility, computed with $\gamma = 0.5$, $\delta t_0 = 0.001$ seconds, the time interval expressed in years (annualized), and $\tau = 1$ hr.

3.4.4 Microscopic Volatility

The microscopic volatility is defined as the norm of the microscopic derivative,

$$\text{Microscopic volatility}[\tau; z] = \text{MNorm}[\tau/2; \partial z] \qquad (3.87)$$

which also depends on the implicit parameters δt_0 and γ of ∂z. Let us emphasize that this definition does not require a regular time series (and that it is not an MA of the macroscopic definition of volatility). In a way, this definition uses all of the information available on the process z. The constant τ controls the range on which the volatility is computed. The microscopic volatility for our standard example week is displayed in Figure 3.16.

3.4.5 Tick Frequency and Activity

The tick frequency $f(t_j)$ counts the number of ticks per time unit. One definition based on regular time intervals is already given by Equation 3.15 (see also Guillaume *et al.* (1997), for example). In general, the tick frequency at time t_j is defined as

$$f[T](t) = \frac{1}{T} N\{t_j \mid t_j \in [t - T, t]\} \qquad (3.88)$$

where $N\{t_j\}$ counts the number of elements in a set and where T is the sample time interval during which the counting is computed. The tick frequency has

---

[11] The operator δ should not be confused with the δ function used in Chapter 3.

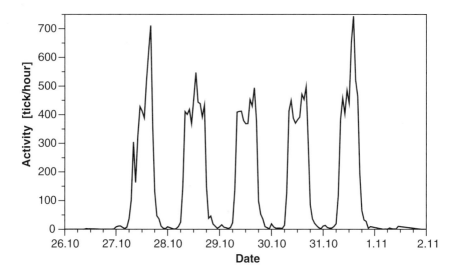

FIGURE 3.17 Tick activity A as defined by Equation 3.90, ticks per hour, computed with $\tau = 1\,\text{hr}$. The five working days of the example week can be clearly seen.

the dimension of an inverse time and is expressed in units such as ticks/minute or ticks/day. This simple definition has some properties that may not always be desired:

- The formula is computationally cumbersome when computed on a moving sample, especially for large T.
- It is an average over a rectangular window. We often prefer moving averages whose kernel (= weighting function) fades more smoothly in the distant past.
- If no quotes are in the interval spanned by T, this definition will give $f = 0$. A related problem is the unusable limit $T \to 0$ if one wants to measure an instantaneous quote rate.

For these reasons, we prefer the definition in Equation 3.90. The tick rate is defined as

$$a[\delta t_0]_j = \frac{1}{\delta t_0 + t_j - t_{j-1}} \tag{3.89}$$

The tick rate has the same dimension as the tick frequency. This definition has the advantage of being related only to the time interval between two subsequent ticks. Following Equation 3.89, an activity can be attributed to one tick, analogous to a return that is attributed to the jth tick by $r_j = x_j - x_{j-1} = (\delta x)_j$. The activity A is the average tick rate during a time interval τ:

$$A[\tau; z] = \text{MA}[\tau/2; a[z]] \tag{3.90}$$

To avoid the spurious singularity when $t_{j-1} = t_j$, the MA operator has to be evaluated with the next-point interpolation (see Equation 3.52). This makes the computation numerically stable even when an extremely small value of δt_0 in Equation 3.89 is chosen.

Figure 3.17 shows the behavior of A in our example week. At first glance, the activity A looks rather different from the tick frequency f. Yet an interesting feature of this definition is to be equivalent to the tick frequency f when the MA operator is a rectangular moving average with $\tau = T/2$ (this is easy to prove by computing the integral of the piecewise constant function a). However, the activity A has some advantages such that it is much simpler to compute on a moving window, and the weighting function of the past can be controlled through the choice of the MA kernel.

4

ADAPTIVE DATA CLEANING

4.1 INTRODUCTION: USING A FILTER TO CLEAN THE DATA

High-frequency data are commercially transmitted as a piece of real-time information to human users, usually traders. These data users are professionals who know the context (e.g., the market state and the likely level of a quoted price). If bad data is transmitted, professional users immediately understand, and implicitly clean the data by using information they have in their personal information set. They do not need additional human or computerized input to check the correctness of the data.

The situation changes if the data users are different, such as researchers investigating historical high-frequency data or computer algorithms that extract real-time information for a given purpose (e.g., a trading algorithm, risk assessment). If bad quotes are used, the results are inevitably bad and totally unusable in the case of aberrant outliers. In the experience of the authors and many other researchers, almost every high-frequency data source contains some bad quotes. Data cleaning is a necessity; it has nothing to do with manipulation or cosmetics.

Data cleaning is a very technical topic. Readers interested in economic results rather than methods and researchers enjoying the privilege of possessing cleaned high-frequency data may skip the remainder of Chapter 4.

A data cleaning methodology requires some criteria to decide on the correctness and possible elimination of quotes. As long as the data set is not too large, human judgment may be a sufficient criterion. In this book, however, we focus on high-frequency data with thousands and millions of observations. Therefore, the criteria have to be formalized through a statistical model that can be implemented as a computer algorithm. Such an algorithm is called a data *filter*. In this chapter, the term "filter" is exclusively used within the context of data cleaning and the term "filtering" is a synonym of "cleaning." Data cleaning is done as a first, independent step of analysis, before applying any time series operator as studied in Chapter 3 and before statistically analyzing the resulting time series. We choose this approach because it is universally applicable, regardless of the type of further analysis. There is a less favorable alternative to prior data filtering: *robust statistics*, where all the data (also outliers) are included in the main statistical analysis. The methods of robust statistics depend on the nature of the analysis and are not universally applicable.

Cleaning a high-frequency time series is a demanding, often underestimated task. It is complicated for several reasons:

- The variety of possible errors and their causes

- The variety of statistical properties of the filtered variables (distribution functions, conditional behavior, structural breaks)

- The variety of data sources and contributors of different reliability

- The irregularity of time intervals (sparse/dense data, sometimes data gaps of long duration)

- The complexity and variety of the quoted data as discussed in Chapter 2: transaction prices, indicative prices, FX forward points (where negative values are allowed), interest rates, figures from derivative markets, transaction volumes, bid-ask quotes versus single-valued quotes

- The necessity of real-time filtering (some applications need instant information before seeing successor quotes)

The data cleaning algorithm presented here is *adaptive* and also presented in Müller (1999). The algorithm learns from the data while sequentially cleaning a time series. It continuously updates its information base in real time.

Further guidelines are needed in a filtering methodology:

- The cause of data errors is rarely known. Therefore the validity of a quote is judged according to its *plausibility* given the *statistical properties* of the series.[1]

---

[1] We have to distinguish true, plausible movements from spurious movements due to erroneous quotes. Brock and Kleidon (1992) suggest decomposing observed movements in the data according to three causes: (1) erroneous quotes, (2) bid-ask spread dynamics due to the pressure on trading factors, and (3) other economic forces.

- A neighborhood of quotes, called the *filtering window*, is needed to judge the credibility of a quote. Such a data window can grow and shrink according to data quality.

- Quotes with a complex structure (i.e., bid-ask) are split into scalar variables to be filtered separately. The filtered variables are derived from the raw variables (e.g., the logarithm of a bid price or the bid-ask spread). Some special error types may also be analyzed for full quotes before data splitting.

- Numerical methods with convergence problems (such as model estimation and nonlinear minimization) are avoided. The chosen algorithm produces well-defined results in all situations.

- The filter needs to be computationally fast. This requirement excludes algorithms starting from scratch for each new incoming tick. The chosen algorithm is *sequential* and *iterative*. It uses the existing filter information base when a new tick arrives, with a minimum amount of updating.

- The filter has two modes, which are the *real-time* and the *historical* modes. Due to the windowing technique, both modes are supported by the same filter. In historical filtering, the final validation of a quote is delayed until successor quotes have been seen.

4.2 DATA AND DATA ERRORS

4.2.1 Time Series of Ticks

The object of data cleaning is a time series of *ticks*. The term "tick" stands for "quote" in a very general sense: any variable that is quoted, from any origin and for any financial instrument. The time-ordered sequence of ticks is inhomogeneous in the general case where the time intervals between ticks vary in size. Normally, one time series is filtered independently from other series. The multivariate cleaning of several time series together is discussed in Section 4.8.1.

The ticks of the series must be of the same type. They may differ in the origins of the contributors, but should not differ in important parameters such as the maturity (of interest rates, etc.) or the moneyness (of options or implied volatilities). If a data-feed provides bid or ask quotes (or transaction quotes) alternatively in random sequence, we advise splitting the data stream into independent bid and ask streams. Normal bid-ask *pairs*, however, are appropriately handled inside the filter.

The following data structure of ticks is assumed:

1. A time stamp.

2. The tick level(s) of which the data cleaning algorithm supports two kinds:

    (a) Data with one level (a price or transaction volume, etc.), such as a stock index.

(b) Data with two levels: bid-ask pairs, such as foreign exchange (FX) spot rates.

3. Information on the origin of the tick, e.g. an identification code of the contributor (a bank or broker). For some financial instruments, notably those traded at an exchange, this is trivial or not available.

A data feed may provide some other information which is not utilized by the filter.

4.2.2 Data Error Types

A *data error* is a piece of quoted data that does not conform to the real situation of the market. A price quote has to be identified as a data error if it is neither a correctly reported transaction price nor a possible transaction price at the reported time. We have to tolerate some transmission time delays and small deviations especially in the case of indicative prices.

There are many causes for data errors. The errors can be separated into two classes:

1. Human errors: Errors directly caused by human data contributors, for different reasons:

   - Unintentional errors, such as typing errors

   - Intentional errors, such as dummy ticks produced just for technical testing

2. System errors: Errors caused by computer systems, their interactions and failures

Human operators have the ultimate responsibility for system errors. However, the distance between the data error and the responsible person is much larger for system errors than for "human" errors. In many cases, it is impossible to find the exact reason for the data error even if a tick is very aberrant. The task of the filter is to identify such outliers whatever the reason. Sometimes the cause of the error can be guessed from the particular behavior of the bad ticks. This knowledge of the error mechanism can help to improve filtering and, in few cases, allow the correction of bad ticks.

The following error types are so particular that they need special treatment.

1. Decimal errors: Failure to change a "big" decimal digit of the quote. For instance, a bid price of 1.3498 is followed by a true quote 1.3505, but the published, bad quote is 1.3405. This error is most damaging if the quoting software is using a *cache* memory somewhere. The wrong decimal digit may stay in the cache and cause a long series of bad quotes. Around 1988, this was a dominant error type.

2. "Test": Some data contributors sometimes send test ticks to the system, usually at times when the market is not liquid. These test ticks can cause a lot of damage because they may look plausible to the filter, at least initially. Two important examples follow:

- "Early morning test": A contributor sends a bad tick very early in the morning to test whether the connection to the data distributor is operational. If the market is inactive overnight, no trader would take this test tick seriously. For the filter, such a tick may be a major challenge. The filter has to be very critical to first ticks after a data gap.

- Monotonic series: Some contributors test the performance and the time delay of their data connection by sending a long series of linearly increasing ticks at inactive times such as overnight or during a weekend. This is hard for the filter to detect because tick-by-tick returns look plausible. Only the monotonic behavior in the long run can be used to identify the fake nature of this type of data.

3. Repeated ticks: Some contributors let their computers repeat the last tick in more or less regular time intervals. This is harmless if it happens in a moderate way. In some markets with coarse granularity of tick values (such as short-term interest rate futures), repeated tick values are quite natural. However, some contributors repeat old ticks thousands of times with high frequency, thereby obstructing the validation of the few good ticks produced by other, more reasonable contributors.

4. Tick copying: Some contributors employ computers to copy and re-send the ticks of other contributors, as explained in Section 2.2.3. If these ticks are on a correct level, a filter has no reason to care—with one exception. Some contributors run computer programs to produce slightly modified ticks by adding small random corrections. Such slightly varying copy ticks are damaging because they obstruct the clear identification of fake monotonic or repeated series made by other contributors.

5. Scaling problem: Quoting conventions may differ or be officially redefined in some markets. Some contributors may quote the value of 100 units, others the value of 1 unit. Scaling factors are often integer powers of 10, but other values may occur (for stock splits in equity markets). The filter will run into this problem "by surprise" unless a human filter user anticipates all scale changes and preprocesses the data accordingly.

A complete data cleaning tool has to include algorithmic elements to deal with each of these special error types.

4.3 GENERAL OVERVIEW OF THE FILTER

4.3.1 The Functionality of the Filter

The flowcharts in Figure 4.1 illustrate some typical applications of a data cleaning filter in a larger context. Normal users simply want to eliminate "invalid" data from the stream, but the chart on the right-hand side shows that the filter can also deliver more information on the ticks and their quality.

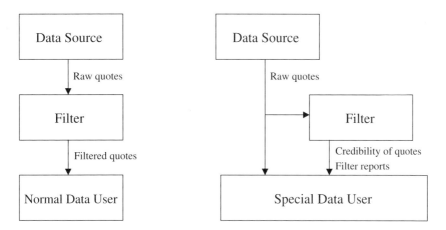

FIGURE 4.1 Data cleaning (filtering): Normal users want to eliminate bad ticks from the application (left chart). In special cases, users want to know filtering results such as the credibility or the reason for rejecting a tick (right chart).

A filter has some configuration parameters depending on the type of instrument, as to be shown later. Once it is created, it performs the following operations:

1. It receives financial ticks in the ordered sequence of their time stamps.
2. It delivers the same ticks in the same ordered sequence, plus the filter results. For each tick, the following results are delivered:

   - Credibility values of the tick and of its individual elements (such as bid, ask, bid-ask spread); the credibility is defined between 0 (totally invalid) and 1 (totally valid)

   - The value(s) of the tick, whose errors can possibly be *corrected* in some cases where the error mechanism is well known

   - The "filtering reason," which is a formalized piece of text explaining why the filter has rejected (or corrected) the tick

Normal users use only those (possibly corrected) ticks with a credibility exceeding a threshold value (which is often chosen to be 0.5). They ignore all invalid ticks and all side results of the filter such as the filter report. The timing of the filter operations is nontrivial. In *real-time* operation, the result of a filter is used right after the tick has entered the filter. In *historical* operation, the user takes the corrected result after the filter has seen a few newer ticks and adapted the credibility of older ticks.

The filter needs a *build-up period* to learn from the data. This is natural for an adaptive filter. If the data cleaning operation starts at the first available tick (beginning of data series), the build-up means to run the filter for a few weeks from this point, storing a set of statistical variables in preparation for restarting the filter from the first available tick. The filter will then be well adapted because it can use the previously stored statistical variables. If the data cleaning operation starts at some later point in time, the natural build-up period is a period immediately preceding the first tick needed.

The filtering algorithm can be seen as one whole block that can be used several times in a data flow such as the following:

- Mixing already filtered data streams from several sources where the mixing result is again filtered. The danger is that the combined filters reject too many quotes, especially in the real-time filtering of fast moves (or price jumps).

- Filtering combined with computational blocks: raw data → filter → computational block → filter → application. Some computational blocks such as cross rate or yield curve computations require filtered input and produce an output that the user may again want to filter.

Repeated filtering of the same time series is rather dangerous because it may lead to too many rejections of quotes. If it cannot be avoided, only one of the filters in the chain should be of the standard type. The other filter(s) should be configured to be weak (i.e., they should eliminate not more than the obviously aberrant outliers).

4.3.2 Overview of the Filtering Algorithm and Its Structure

The filtering algorithm is structured in a hierarchical scheme of subalgorithms. Table 4.1 gives an overview of this structure for a univariate filter for one financial instrument. A higher hierarchy level at the top of Table 4.1 can be added for multivariate filtering, as discussed in Section 4.8.1.

Details of the different algorithmic levels are explained in the next sections. The sequence of these sections follows Table 4.1, *from bottom to top*. Some special filter elements are not treated there, but are briefly described in Section 4.8.

4.4 BASIC FILTERING ELEMENTS AND OPERATIONS

The first element to be discussed in a bottom-to-top specification is the scalar filtering window. Its position in the algorithm is shown in Table 4.1.

The basic filtering operations utilize the quotes in the simplified form of *scalar quotes* consisting of the following:

1. The time stamp
2. One scalar variable value to be filtered (e.g., the logarithm of a bid price), here denoted by x
3. The origin of the quote (as in the full quote of Section 4.2.1)

The basic operations can be divided into two types:

1. Filtering of single scalar quotes: considering the credibility of one scalar quote alone. An important part is the *level filter* where the level of the filtered variable is the criterion.
2. Pair filtering: comparing two scalar quotes. The most important part is the *change filter* that considers the change of the filtered variable from one

TABLE 4.1 Basic structure of the filtering algorithm used for data cleaning. The data cleaning algorithm has three main hierarchy levels, each with its specific functionalities.

Hierarchy level	Level name	Purpose, description
1	Univariate filter	The complete filtering of one time series: Passing incoming ticks to the lower hierarchy levels Collecting the filter results of the lower hierarchy levels and packaging them into the right output format Supporting real-time and historical filtering Supporting one or more filtering hypotheses, each with its own full-tick filtering window
2	Full-tick filtering window	A sequence of recent full ticks (bid-ask), some of them possibly corrected according to a general filtering hypothesis. The tasks are as follows: Tick splitting: splitting a full tick into scalar quotes to be filtered in their own scalar filtering windows Basic validity test (e.g., whether prices are positive) A possible mathematical transformation (e.g., logarithm) All those filtering steps that require full ticks (not just bid or ask ticks alone)
3	Scalar filtering window	A sequence of recent scalar quotes whose credibilities are still being modified. The tasks are as follows: Testing new, incoming scalar quotes Comparing a new scalar quote to all older quotes of the window (using a business time scale and a dependence analysis of quote origins) Computing a first credibility of the new scalar quote; modifying the credibilities of older quotes based on new information Dismissing the oldest scalar quotes when their credibility is finally settled Updating the statistics with good scalar quotes when they are dismissed from the window

quote to another one. Filtering depends on the time interval between the two quotes and the time scale on which this is measured. Pair filtering also includes a comparison of quote origins.

The basic filtering operations and another basic concept of filtering, credibility are presented in the following sections. Their actual application in the larger algorithm is explained later, starting from Section 4.5.

4.4.1 Credibility and Trust Capital

Credibility is a central concept of the filtering algorithm. It is expressed by a variable C taking values between 0 and 1, where 1 indicates validity and 0 invalidity. This number can be interpreted as the probability of a quote being valid according to a given criterion. For two reasons, we avoid the formal introduction of the term "probability." First, the validity of a quote is a fuzzy concept (e.g., slightly deviating quotes of an over-the-counter spot market can perhaps be termed valid even if they are very unlikely to lead to a real transaction). Second, we have no model of

TABLE 4.2   Adding independent credibility values.

The total credibility C_{total} resulting from two independent credibility values C_1 and C_2. The function $C_{total} = C[T(C_1) + T(C_2)]$ defines an addition operator for credibilities, based on Equations 4.1 and 4.2. The values in brackets, (0.5), are in fact indefinite limit values where C_{total} may converge to any value between 0 and 1.

C_{total}	$C_1 =$				
	0	0.25	0.5	0.75	1
$C_2 =$					
1	(0.5)	1	1	1	1
0.75	0	0.5	0.75	0.878	1
0.5	0	0.25	0.5	0.75	1
0.25	0	0.122	0.25	0.5	1
0	0	0	0	0	(0.5)

probability even if validity could be exactly defined. Credibility can be understood as a "possibility" in the sense of fuzzy logic as proposed by Zimmermann (1985), for example.

Credibility is not additive; the credibility of a scalar quote gained from two tests is not the sum of the credibilities gained from the individual tests. This follows from the definition of credibility between 0 and 1. The sum of two credibilities of, say, 0.75 would be outside the allowed domain.

For internal credibility computations based on different tests, an additive variable is needed to obtain the joint view of all tests. We define the additive *trust capital* T, which is unlimited in value. There is no theoretical limit for gathering evidence in favor of accepting or rejecting the validity hypothesis. Full validity corresponds to a trust capital of $T = \infty$, full invalidity to $T = -\infty$. We impose a fixed, monotonic relation between the credibility C and the trust capital T of a certain object

$$C(T) = \frac{1}{2} + \frac{T}{2\sqrt{1 + T^2}} \tag{4.1}$$

and the inverse relation

$$T(C) = \frac{C - \frac{1}{2}}{\sqrt{C(1 - C)}} \tag{4.2}$$

There are possible alternatives to this functional relationship. The chosen solution has some advantages in the formulation of the algorithm that will be shown later.

The additivity of trust capitals and Equations 4.1 and 4.2 imply the definition of an addition operator for credibilities. Table 4.2 shows the total credibility resulting from two independent credibility values.

4.4.2 Filtering of Single Scalar Quotes: The Level Filter

There is only one analysis of a single quote called the level filter. Comparisons between quotes (done for a pair of quotes, treated in Section 4.4.3) are often more important in filtering than the analysis of a single quote.

The level filter computes a first credibility of the value of the filtered variable. This only applies to those volatile but mean-reverting time series where the levels as such have a certain credibility in the absolute sense—not only the level changes. Moreover, the timing of the mean reversion should be relatively fast. Interest rates or interest rates futures prices, for example, are mean-reverting only after time intervals of years; they appear to be freely floating within smaller intervals (see Ballocchi, 1996). For those rates and for other prices, level filtering is not suitable.

The obvious example for fast mean reversion and thus for using a level filter is the bid-ask spread, which can be rather volatile from quote to quote but tends to stay within a fixed range of values that varies only very slowly over time. For spreads, an adaptive level filter is at least as important as a pair filter that considers the spread change between two quotes.

The level filter first puts the filtered variable value x into the perspective of its own statistical mean and standard deviation. Following the notation of Section 3.3.8, the standardized variable $\hat{x}$ is defined by

$$\hat{x} \; = \; \frac{x - \bar{x}}{\text{MSD}[\,\Delta\vartheta_r, 2;\, x\,]} \; = \; \frac{x - \bar{x}}{\sqrt{\text{EMA}[\,\Delta\vartheta_r;\, (x - \bar{x})^2\,]}} \tag{4.3}$$

where the mean value of x is also a moving average:

$$\bar{x} \; = \; \text{EMA}[\,\Delta\vartheta_r;\, x\,] \tag{4.4}$$

The time scale used for this computation is called ϑ. Taking a business time scale ϑ as introduced in Section 4.4.6 leads to better data cleaning than taking physical time. The variable $\Delta\vartheta_r$ denotes the configurable range of the kernel of the moving averages and should cover the time frame of the mean reversion of the filtered variable; a reasonable value for bid-ask spreads has to be chosen. The iterative computation of moving averages is explained in Section 3.3.5. Here and for all the moving averages of the filtering algorithm, a simple exponentially weighted moving average (EMA) is used for efficiency reasons.

A small $|\hat{x}|$ value deserves high trust; an extreme $|\hat{x}|$ value indicates an outlier with low credibility and negative trust capital. Before arriving at a formula for the trust capital as a function of $\hat{x}$, the *distribution* of $\hat{x}$ has to be discussed. A symmetric form of the distribution is assumed at least in coarse approximation. This is ensured by the definition of the filtered variable x, which is a mathematically transformed variable. The exact definition of x is deferred to Section 4.6.3 in the chosen structure of this chapter.

The amount of negative trust capital for outliers depends on the tails of the distribution at extreme (positive and negative) $\hat{x}$ values. A reasonable assumption is that the credibility of outliers is approximately the probability of exceeding the outlier value, given the distribution function. This probability is proportional to $\hat{x}^{-\alpha}$ where α is called the tail index. We know that density functions of level-filtered variables such as bid-ask spreads are fat-tailed (see Müller and Sgier, 1992). Determining the distribution and α in a moving sample would be a considerable task, certainly too heavy for filtering software. Therefore, we choose an approximate assumption on α that was found acceptable across many rates, filtered variable types and financial instruments: $\alpha = 4$. This value is also used in the analogous pair filtering tool (e.g., for price changes, and discussed in Section 4.4.3).

For extreme events, the relation between credibility and trust capital, Equation 4.1, can be asymptotically expanded as follows

$$ C \; = \; \frac{1}{4 \, T^2} \quad \text{for} \; T \ll -1 \tag{4.5} $$

Terms of order higher than $(1/T)^2$ are neglected here. Defining a credibility proportional to $\hat{x}^{-\alpha}$ is thus identical to defining a trust capital proportional to $\hat{x}^{\alpha/2}$. Assuming $\alpha = 4$, we obtain a trust capital proportional to $\hat{x}^2$. For outliers, this trust capital is negative, but for small $\hat{x}$, the trust capital is positive up to a maximum value we define to be 1.

Now, we have the ingredients to come up with a formulation that gives the resulting trust capital of the ith quote according to the level filter:

$$ T_{i0} \; = \; 1 - \xi_i^2 \tag{4.6} $$

where the index 0 of T_{i0} indicates that this is a result of the level filter only. The variable ξ_i is $\hat{x}$ in a scaled and standardized form:

$$ \xi_i \; = \; \frac{\hat{x}_i}{\xi_0} \tag{4.7} $$

with a constant ξ_0. Equation 4.6 together with Equation 4.7 is the simplest possible way to obtain the desired maximum and asymptotic behavior. For certain rapidly mean-reverting variables such as hourly or daily trading volumes, this may be enough.

However, the actual implementation for bid-ask spreads has some special properties. Filter tests have shown that these properties have to be taken into account in order to attain satisfactory spread filter results:

- Quoted bid-ask spreads tend to cluster at "even" values (e.g., 10 basis points,) whereas the real spread may be an odd value oscillating in a range below the quoted value. A series of formal, constant spreads can therefore hide some substantial volatility that is not covered by the statistically determined denominator of Equation 4.3. We need an offset Δx_{min}^2 to account for the typical hidden volatility in that denominator. A suitable choice is $\Delta x_{min}^2 = [\text{constant}_1 (\bar{x} + \text{constant}_2)]^2$.

- High values of bid-ask spreads are worse in usability than low spreads, by nature. Thus the quote deviations from the mean as defined by Equation 4.3 are judged with bias. Deviations to the high side ($\hat{x}_i > 0$) are penalized by a factor p_{high}, whereas no such penalty is applied against low spreads.

- For some (minor) financial instruments, many quotes are posted with zero spreads (i.e., bid quote = ask quote). This is discussed in Section 4.6.1. In some cases, zero spreads have to be accepted, but we set a penalty against them as in the case of positive $\hat{x}_i$.

We obtain the following refined definition of ξ_i

$$
\xi_i = \begin{cases} \dfrac{\hat{x}_i}{\xi_0} & \text{if } \hat{x}_i \leq 0 \text{ and no zero-spread case} \\[2ex] p_{high}\dfrac{\hat{x}_i}{\xi_0} & \text{if } \hat{x}_i > 0 \text{ or in a zero-spread case} \end{cases} \tag{4.8}
$$

where $\hat{x}_i$ comes from a modified version of Equation 4.3,

$$
\hat{x} = \frac{x - \bar{x}}{\sqrt{\text{EMA}[\,\Delta\vartheta_r;\ (x - \bar{x})^2\,] + \Delta x_{\min}^2}} \tag{4.9}
$$

The constant ξ_0 determines the size of an $\hat{x}$ that is just large enough to neither increase nor decrease the credibility.

Equation 4.8 is general enough for all mean-reverting filterable variables. If we introduced mean-reverting variables other than the bid-ask spread, a good value for $\Delta x_{\min}^2$ would probably be much smaller or even 0, p_{high} around one and ξ_0 larger (to tolerate volatility increases in absence of a basic volatility level $\Delta x_{\min}^2$).

4.4.3 Pair Filtering: The Credibility of Returns

The pairwise comparison of scalar quotes is a central basic filtering operation. The algorithm makes pairwise comparisons also for quotes that are not neighbors in the series, as explained in Section 4.5.

Pair filtering contains several ingredients, the most important one being the change filter. Its task is to judge the credibility of a variable change (= return if the variable is a price). The time difference between the two quotes plays a role, so the time scale on which it is measured has to be specified. The criterion is *adaptive* to the statistically expected volatility estimate and therefore uses some results from a moving statistical analysis.

The change of the filtered variable x from the jth to the ith quote is

$$
\Delta x_{ij} = x_i - x_j \tag{4.10}
$$

The variable x may be the result of a transformation in the sense of Section 4.6.3. The time difference of the quotes is $\Delta\vartheta_{ij}$, measured on a time scale to be discussed in Section 4.4.6.

The expected variance $V(\Delta\vartheta)$ of x around zero is determined by the on-line statistics as described in Section 4.4.4. The relative change is defined by

$$\xi_{ij} = \frac{\Delta x_{ij}}{\xi_0 \sqrt{V(\Delta\vartheta_{ij})}} \tag{4.11}$$

with a positive constant ξ_0, which has a value of around 5.5 and is further discussed later. Low $|\xi|$ values deserve high trust, extreme $|\xi|$ values indicate low credibility and negative trust capital; at least one of the two compared quotes must be an outlier.

The remainder of the algorithm is similar to that of the level filter as described in Section 4.4.2, using the relative change ξ_{ij} instead of the scaled standardized variable ξ_i.

The amount of negative trust capital for outliers depends on the density function of changes Δx, especially the tail of the distribution at extreme Δx or ξ values. A reasonable assumption is that the credibility of outliers is approximately the probability of exceeding the outlier value, given the distribution function. This probability is proportional to $\xi^{-\alpha}$, where α is the tail index of a fat-tailed distribution. We know that distributions of high-frequency price changes are indeed fat-tailed (see Dacorogna *et al.*, 2001a). Determining the distribution and α in a moving sample would be a considerable task beyond the scope of filtering software. Therefore, we make a rough assumption on α that is good enough across many rates, filtered variable types and financial instruments. For many price changes, a good value is around $\alpha \approx 3.5$, according to Dacorogna *et al.* (2001a) and Müller *et al.* (1998). As in Section 4.4.2, we generally use $\alpha = 4$ as a realistic, general approximation.

As in Section 4.4.2 and together with Equation 4.5, we argue that the trust capital should asymptotically be proportional to ξ^2 and arrive at a formula that gives the trust capital as a function of ξ:

$$U_{ij} = U(\xi_{ij}^2) = 1 - \xi_{ij}^2 \tag{4.12}$$

which is analogous to Equation 4.6. This trust capital, depending only on ξ, is called U to distinguish it from the final trust capital T that is based on more criteria. At $\xi = 1$, Equation 4.12 yields a zero trust capital, neither increasing nor decreasing the credibility. Intuitively, a variable change of a few standard deviations might correspond to this undecided situation; smaller variable changes lead to positive trust capital, larger ones to negative trust capital. In fact, the parameter ξ_0 of Equation 4.11 should be configured to a high value, leading to a rather tolerant behavior even if the volatility V is slightly underestimated.

The trust capital U_{ij} from Equation 4.12 is a sufficient concept under the best circumstances, independent quotes separated by a small time interval. In the general case, a modified formula is needed to solve the following three special pair filtering problems.

1. Filtering should stay a local concept on the time axis. However, a quote has few close neighbors and many more distant neighbors. When the additive

trust capital of a quote is determined by pairwise comparisons to other quotes as explained in Section 4.5.2, the results from distant quotes must not dominate those from the close neighbors; the interaction range should be limited. This is achieved by defining the trust capital proportional to $(\Delta \vartheta)^{-3}$ (assuming a constant ξ) for asymptotically large quote intervals $\Delta \vartheta$.

2. For large $\Delta \vartheta$, even moderately aberrant quotes would be too easily accepted by Equation 4.12. Therefore, the aforementioned decline of trust capital with growing $\Delta \vartheta$ is particularly important in the case of positive trust capital. Negative trust capital, on the other hand, should stay strongly negative even if $\Delta \vartheta$ is rather large. The new filter needs a selective decline of trust capital with increasing $\Delta \vartheta$: fast for small ξ (positive trust capital), slow for large ξ (negative trust capital). This treatment is essential for data holes or gaps, where there are no (or few) close neighbor quotes.

3. Dependent quotes: if two quotes originate from the same source, their comparison can hardly increase the credibility (but it can reinforce negative trust in the case of a large ξ). In Section 4.4.5, we introduce an independence variable I_{ij} between 0 (totally dependent) and 1 (totally independent).

The two last points imply a certain asymmetry in the trust capital; gathering evidence in favor of accepting a quote is more delicate than evidence in favor of rejecting it.

All of these concerns can be taken into account in an extended version of Equation 4.12. This is the final formula for the trust capital from a change filter:

$$T_{ij} \;=\; T(\xi_{ij}^2, \Delta \vartheta_{ij}, I_{ij}) \;=\; I_{ij}^{\star} \, \frac{1 - \xi_{ij}^4}{1 + \xi_{ij}^2 + \left(\frac{d \, \Delta \vartheta_{ij}}{v}\right)^3} \tag{4.13}$$

where

$$I_{ij}^{\star} \;=\; \begin{cases} I_{ij} & \text{if } \xi_{ij}^2 < 1 \\ 1 & \text{if } \xi_{ij}^2 \geq 1 \end{cases} \tag{4.14}$$

The independence I_{ij} is always between 0 and 1 and is computed by Equation 4.23. The variable d is a quote density explained in Section 4.4.4. The configurable constant v determines a sort of filtering interaction range in units of the typical quote interval ($\approx 1/d$).

Table 4.3 shows the behavior of the trust capital according to Equation 4.13. The trust capital converges to zero with an increasing quote interval $\Delta \vartheta$ much more rapidly for small variable changes $|\xi|$ than for large ones. For small $\Delta \vartheta_{ij}$ and $I_{ij} = 1$, Equation 4.13 converges to Equation 4.12.

The approach of Equation 4.13 has been tested for almost all available types of financial data, not only FX. We find that it works for all data types with the same values of the parameters.

TABLE 4.3   Trust capital as a function of two variables.

The trust capital T resulting from a comparison of two independent ($I^\star = 1$) scalar quotes, depending on two variables: the relative variable change ξ and the time interval $\Delta\vartheta$ between the quotes. ξ is defined by Equation 4.11, and d and v are explained in the text.

T	$d\,\Delta\vartheta\,/\,v\,=$				
	0	0.5	1	2	4
$\|\xi\| =$					
4	-15.0	-14.9	-14.2	-10.2	-3.2
2	-3.0	-2.9	-2.5	-1.2	-0.22
1	0	0	0	0	0
0.5	0.75	0.68	0.42	0.10	0.014
0	1	0.89	0.50	0.11	0.015

4.4.4   Computing the Expected Volatility

The expected volatility is a function of the size of the time interval between the quotes and thus requires a larger computational effort than other statistical variables. Only credible scalar quotes should be used in the computation. The updates of all statistics are therefore managed by another part of the algorithm that knows about final credibilities as explained in Section 4.5.5.

Choosing an appropriate business time scale ϑ is important for measuring the time intervals between quotes and for all other computations of this section. This is explained in Section 4.4.6.

Although the expected volatility computation can be implemented with various methods of different degrees of sophistication, we adopt a simple method. The first variable needed is the quote density

$$d = \mathrm{EMA}\left[\,\Delta\vartheta_r;\,\frac{c_d}{\delta\vartheta}\,\right] \qquad (4.15)$$

This is a moving average in the notation of Section 3.3.5; $\delta\vartheta$ is the time interval between two "valid" (as defined on a higher level) neighbor quotes on the chosen time scale. $\Delta\vartheta_r$ is the configurable range of the kernel of the moving average. The variable c_d is the weight of the quote, which normally has a value of $c_d = 1$ and is lower only in the case of repeated quote values. The iterative computation of moving averages is explained in Section 3.3.5. The value $1/\delta\vartheta$ has to be assumed for the whole quote interval, which implies using the "next point" interpolation. It can be shown that a zero value of $\delta\vartheta$ does not lead to a singularity of the EMA.

An annualized squared "micro"-volatility is defined as a variance in the form of a moving average

$$v = \text{EMA}\left[\Delta\vartheta_r; \frac{(\delta x)^2}{\delta\vartheta + \delta\vartheta_0} \right] \tag{4.16}$$

where the notation follows Sections 3.3.5 and 3.4.3 and the range $\Delta\vartheta_r$ is the same as in Equation 4.15. δx is the change of the filtered variable between (sufficiently credible) neighbor quotes. There is a small time interval offset

$$\delta\vartheta_0 = \max\left(\frac{d_0}{d}, \delta\vartheta_{\min} \right) \tag{4.17}$$

The small positive term $\delta\vartheta_0$ accounts for some known short-term behaviors of markets: (1) certain asynchronicities in the quote transmissions, (2) some temporary market level inconsistencies that need time to be arbitraged out, (3) a negative autocorrelation of many market prices over short time lags (see Section 5.2.1). However, $\delta\vartheta_0$ is not needed to avoid singularities of v; even a zero value of both $\delta\vartheta$ and $\delta\vartheta_0$ would not lead to a singularity of the EMA. The "next point" interpolation is again appropriate in the EMA computation.

Strictly speaking, v can be called annualized only if ϑ is measured in years, but the choice of this unit does not matter in our algorithm. The exponent of the annualization is not too important because the different values of $\delta\vartheta$ share the same order of magnitude.

Experience shows that the volatility measure of the filter should not rely only on one variance v as defined here. It is more stable to use three such volatilities: v_{fast}, v and v_{slow}. All of them are computed by Equation 4.16, but they differ in their ranges, $\Delta\vartheta_r$, where v_{fast} has a short range, v a medium-sized range, and v_{slow} a long range. Our expected volatility is defined to be the maximum of the three:

$$v_{\text{exp}} = \max(v_{\text{fast}}, v, v_{\text{slow}}) \tag{4.18}$$

This is superior to taking only v. In case of a market shock, the rapid growth of v_{fast} allows for a quick adaptation of the filter, whereas the inertia of v_{slow} prevents the filter from forgetting volatile events too rapidly in a quiet market phase.

From the annualized v_{exp}, we obtain the expected squared change as a function of the time interval $\Delta\vartheta$ between two quotes. At this point, the filter needs a special element to prevent the filter from easily accepting price changes over large data gaps, time periods with no quotes. Data gaps are characterized by a large value of $\Delta\vartheta$ and very few quotes within this interval. In case of data gaps, an upper limit of $\Delta\vartheta$ is enforced:

$$\Delta\vartheta_{\text{corr}} = \min\left[\frac{2.5\, Q}{d}, \max\left(\frac{0.1\, Q}{d}, \Delta\vartheta \right) \right] \tag{4.19}$$

where d is taken from Equation 4.15 and Q is the number of valid quotes in the interval between the two quotes; this is explained in Section 4.5.2. Equation 4.19

also sets a lower limit of $\Delta\vartheta_{corr}$ in case of a very high frequency of valid quotes. It is important to validate fast trends with many quotes.

The corrected quote interval $\Delta\vartheta_{corr}$ is now used to compute the expected squared change V

$$V = V(\Delta\vartheta_{corr}) = (\Delta\vartheta_{corr} + \delta\vartheta_0) \, v_{exp} + V_0 \qquad (4.20)$$

This function $V(\Delta\vartheta_{corr})$ is needed in the trust capital calculation of Section 4.4.3 and inserted in Equation 4.11. The positive offset V_0 is small and could be omitted in many cases with no loss of filter quality. However, a small $V_0 > 0$ is desirable. Some quotes are quoted in coarse granularity (i.e., the minimum step between two possible quote values is rather large as compared to the volatility). This is the case in some interest rate futures and also for bid-ask spreads (in FX markets), which often have a rounded size of 5, 10, or 20 basis points with rarely a value in between. Quotes with coarse granularity have a *hidden* volatility such that a series of identical quotes may hide a movement of a size smaller than the typical granule. The term V_0 thus represents the hidden volatility:

$$V_0 = 0.25 \, g^2 + \varepsilon_0^2 \qquad (4.21)$$

where the granule size g is also determined by adaptive methods. (The granularity analysis is also needed in the analysis of repeated ticks, which is not explained here.) The extremely small term ε_0^2 just has the numerical task to keep $V_0 > 0$.

The term ε_0^2, however, plays a special role if the scalar variable to be filtered is a bid-ask spread. The spread filter is the least important filter, but leads to the highest number of rejections of FX quotes if it is configured similar to the filter of other scalars. This fact is not accepted by typical filter users who want a more tolerant spread filter. A closer inspection shows that different contributors of bid-ask quotes often have different spread quoting policies. They are often interested only in the bid or ask side of the quote and tend to push the other side off the real market by choosing a spread too large. Thus the spreads of neighbor quotes may have different sizes even in quiet markets. In some minor FX markets, some contributors even mix retail quotes with very large spreads into the stream of interbank quotes. In order not to reject too many quotes for spread reasons, we have to raise the tolerance for fast spread changes and reject only extreme jumps in spreads. This means raising ε_0^2: $\varepsilon_0 = \text{constant}_1 (\bar{x} + \text{constant}_2)$, where $\bar{x}$ is defined by Equation 4.4. This choice of ε_0 can be inferred from the mapping of the bid-ask spread in Equation 4.45. When a filter is initialized, we set $V_0 = \varepsilon_0^2$ and replace this by Equation 4.21 as soon as the granule size estimate g is available, based on statistics from valid quotes.

4.4.5 Pair Filtering: Comparing Quote Origins

Pair filtering results can add some credibility to the two quotes only if these are independent. Two identical quotes from the same contributor do not add substantial confidence to the quoted level—the fact that an automated quoting system sends the same quote twice does not make this quote more reliable. Two nonidentical quotes from the same contributor may imply that the second quote has been produced to correct a bad first one. Another interpretation might be that an automated quoting system has a random generator to send a sequence of slightly varying quotes to mark presence on the information system. Different quotes from entirely different contributors are the most reliable case for pair filtering.

The basic tool is a function to compare the origins of the two quotes, considering the main source (the information provider), the contributor ID (bank name), and the location information. This implies that available information on contributors has a value in data cleaning and should be collected rather than ignored. An "unknown" origin is treated just like another origin name. The resulting independence measure I'_{ij} is confined between 0 for identical origins and 1 for clearly different origins. In some cases (e.g., same bank but different subsidiary), a value between 0 and 1 can be chosen.

I'_{ij} is not yet the final formulation but has to be put in relation with the general origin *diversity* of the time series. An analysis of data from only one or very few origins must be different from that of data with a rich variety of origins. The general diversity D can be defined as a moving average of the $I'_{i\ i-1}$ of valid neighbor quotes,

$$D = \text{EMA}[\text{tick-time}, R; I'_{i\ i-1}] \tag{4.22}$$

where R is the range (center of gravity) of the kernel. The "tick-time" is a time scale that is incremented by one at each new quote. The "next point" interpolation is again appropriate in the EMA computation. Only "valid" quotes are used; this is possible on a higher level of the algorithm (see Section 4.5.5). By doing so, we prevent D from being lowered by bad mass quotes from a single computerized source. Thus we are protected against a difficult filtering problem. The high number of bad mass quotes from a single contributor will not force the filter to accept the bad level.

The use of D makes the independence variable I_{ij} adaptive through the following formula:

$$I_{ij} = I'_{ij} + f(D)(1 - I'_{ij}) \tag{4.23}$$

with

$$f(D) = \frac{0.0005 + (1 - D)^8}{2.001} \tag{4.24}$$

If the diversity is very low (e.g., in a single-contributor source), this formula (reluctantly) raises the independence estimate I_{ij} to allow for some positive trust capital to build up. For a strictly uniform source ($I' = D = 0$), I_{ij} will reach 0.5, which is one half of the I_{ij} value of truly independent quotes in a multicontributor series.

The output variable I_{ij} resulting from Equation 4.14 is always confined between 0 and 1 and is generally used in Equation 4.14. Some special cases need a special discussion:

- Repeated quotes. Rarely, the raw data contains long series of repeated quotes from the same contributor, and the obtained value of I_{ij} may still be too high. A solution would be a special filtering element focused on repeated ticks.

- High-quality data. The collected data may be mixed with old, historical, commercially available daily data that were of distinctly higher quality than the data from a single, average-quality contributor. When comparing two quotes from this historical daily data, we may force $I'_{ij} = 1$ although these quotes come from the same "contributor." This special filtering element is necessary only if there are huge, proven quality differences between contributors.

- In multivariate filtering (see Section 4.8.1), artificial quotes that might be injected by a multivariate covariance analysis should have $I'_{ij} = 1$ when compared to each other or to any other quote.

4.4.6   A Time Scale for Filtering

Time plays a role in the adaptive elements of the level filter as well as in almost all parts of the change filter. Value changes are tolerated more easily when separated by a large time interval between the time stamps. When using the term "time interval," we need to specify the time scale to be used.

The algorithm works with any time scale, but some are more suitable than others. If our tolerance for quote level changes is as large over weekends as over working hours, we have to accept almost any bad quote from the few weekend contributors. These weekend quotes are sometimes test quotes or other outliers in the absence of a liquid market. Our solution is a time scale that compresses the weekends and other inactive periods and thus leads to a lower tolerance.

Accounting for the low weekend activity is vital, but the exact treatment of typical volatility patterns during working days is less important. Therefore, we cannot accept using only physical time (= calendar/clock time), but the following solutions are possible:

1. A very simple business time with two states: active (working days) and inactive (weekend from Friday 21:00:00 GMT to Sunday 21:00:00 GMT, plus the most important and general holidays). The speed of this business time as compared to physical time would be either 1.4 (in active state) or 0.01 (in inactive state).

2. An adaptively weighted mean of three simple, generic business time scales ϑ with smoothly varying weights according to built-in statistics. This solution suits those filter developers that prefer to avoid the complex ϑ technology of Chapter 6.

TABLE 4.4 Active periods of the three generic markets.

Daytimes limiting the active periods of three generic, continent-wide markets; in Greenwich Mean Time (GMT). The scheme is coarse, modeling just the main structure of worldwide financial markets. The active periods differ according to local time zones and business hours. The Asian market starts on the day before from the viewpoint of the GMT time zone.

Market	k	$t_{\text{start},k}$	$t_{\text{end},k}$
East Asia	1	21:00	7:00
Europe	2	6:00	16:00
America	3	11:00	21:00

3. An adaptively weighted mean of three generic business time scales ϑ as defined by Chapter 6 or Dacorogna *et al.* (1993).

The second solution differs from the third one only in the definition of the basic ϑ-time scales. The adaptivity mechanism is the same for both solutions.

Three generic ϑ-times are used, based on typical volatility patterns of three main markets: Asia, Europe, and America. In the second solution, these ϑ times are defined as follows:

$$
\frac{d\vartheta_k}{dt} = \begin{cases} 3.4 & \text{if } t_{\text{start},k} \leq t_d < t_{\text{end},k} \text{ on a working day} \\ 0.01 & \text{otherwise (inactive times, weekends, holidays)} \end{cases} \tag{4.25}
$$

where t_d is the daytime in Greenwich Mean Time (GMT) and the generic start and end times of the working-daily activity periods are given by Table 4.4. They correspond to typical observations in several markets. The active periods of exchange-traded instruments are subsets of the active periods of Table 4.4. The time scales ϑ_k are time integrals of $d\vartheta_k/dt$ from Equation 4.25. Thus the time ϑ_k flows either rapidly in active market periods or very slowly in inactive periods. Its long-term average speed is similar to physical time. The implementation of Equation 4.25 requires some knowledge about holidays. The database of holidays to be applied may be rudimentary (e.g., Christmas holidays) or more elaborate to cover all main holidays of the financial centers on the three continents. The effect of daylight saving time is neglected here as the market activity model is coarse.

If the three ϑ_k-times are chosen as defined by Chapter 6 (the third solution of the list), effects like daylight saving time and local holidays (i.e., characteristic for one continent) are also covered. The activity in the morning of the geographical markets is higher than in the afternoon—a typical behavior of FX rates and, even more so, interest rates, interest rate futures, and other exchange-traded markets.

Once the three scales ϑ_k are defined (by the integrals of Equation 4.25 in our suggestion), their adaptively weighted mean is constructed and used as the time scale ϑ for filtering. This ϑ-time is able to approximately capture the daily and weekly seasonality and the low volatility of holidays. High precision is not required as ϑ is only one among many ingredients of the data cleaning algorithm, many of which are based on rather coarse approximations. This is the definition of ϑ-time:

$$\vartheta = \sum_{\text{all } k} w_k \, \vartheta_k \qquad (4.26)$$

with

$$\sum_{\text{all } k} w_k = 1 \qquad (4.27)$$

where "all k" means "all markets." This is three in our case, but the algorithm also works for any other number of generic markets. The weights w_k are adaptive to the actual behavior of the volatility. A high w_k reflects a high fitness of ϑ_k, which implies that the volatility measured in ϑ_k has low seasonal variations.

The determination of the w_k might be done with methods such as the maximum likelihood estimation of a volatility model. However, this would be unreliable given the local convergence issues and the existing modeling limitations of Equation 4.26. The proposed heuristic method always returns an unambiguous solution. The volatility of changes of the filtered variable is measured on all ϑ_k-scales in terms of a variance similar to Equation 4.16:

$$\sigma_k = \sqrt{\text{EMA}\left[\Delta\vartheta_{\text{smooth}}; \; \frac{(\delta x)^2}{\delta\vartheta_k + \delta\vartheta_0} \right]} \qquad (4.28)$$

where $\delta\vartheta_k$ is the interval between validated neighbor quotes in ϑ_k-time, δx is the corresponding change of the filtered variable, $\delta\vartheta_0$ is defined by Equation 4.17 and the time scale of the EMA is ϑ_k-time. The notation is as in Sections 3.3.5 and 3.4.3. Smoothing with a short range $\Delta\vartheta_{\text{smooth}}$ is necessary to diminish the influence of quote-to-quote noise. The EMA computation assumes a constant value of $(\delta x)^2/(\delta\vartheta_k + \delta\vartheta_0)$ for the whole quote interval. This means the "next point" interpolation of Equation 3.52.

The fluctuations of the variable σ_k indicate the badness of the ϑ_k model. In the case of a bad fit, σ_k is often very low (when the ϑ_k-scale expands time) and sometimes very high (when the ϑ_k-scale compresses time). The fluctuations are quantified in terms of the variance F_k,

$$\begin{aligned} F_k &= \text{EMA}[\, \Delta\vartheta_r; \; (\, \sigma_k - \text{EMA}[\, \Delta\vartheta_r; \; \sigma_k \,] \,)^2 \,] \qquad (4.29) \\ &= \text{MVar}[\, \Delta\vartheta_r, \; 2; \; \sigma_k \,] \end{aligned}$$

where the time scale is ϑ_k-time; the MVar operator is explained in Section 3.3.8.

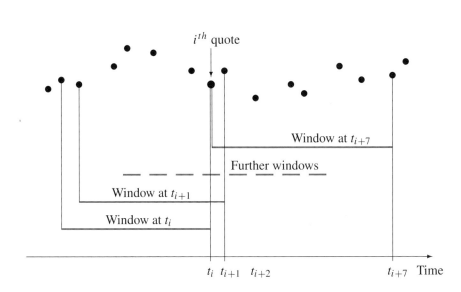

FIGURE 4.2   The scalar filtering window moves forward in time by including new scalar quotes and dismissing old ones.

The range $\Delta\vartheta_r$ has to be suitably chosen. In our approximation, the fluctuations directly define the weight of the kth market:

$$w_k = \frac{1}{F_k \sum_{\text{all } k'} \frac{1}{F_{k'}}} \tag{4.30}$$

which satisfies Equation 4.27 and can be inserted into Equation 4.26.

4.5   THE SCALAR FILTERING WINDOW

The scalar filtering window is located at the bottom of the hierarchical structure of the algorithm as shown in Table 4.1. It covers the set of all recent scalar quotes contained in a time interval. This neighborhood of quotes is used to judge the credibility of new incoming scalar quotes. In the course of the analysis, these new quotes are included and old quotes are dismissed at the back end of the window following a certain rule. Thus the window is moving forward in time. This mechanism is illustrated by Figure 4.2.

All the scalar quotes within the window have a provisional credibility value, which is modified with new incoming quotes. When the quotes leave the window, their credibilities are regarded as finally determined. Sufficiently credible quotes are then used to update the statistics needed for adaptivity.

At the initialization of a filter from scratch, the window is empty. When the first scalar quote enters, it cannot be filtered by pair filtering yet, only the level filter applies.

4.5.1 Entering a New Quote in the Scalar Filtering Window

Whenever a new scalar quote enters the window, an analysis is made based on earlier results and the new quote.

There are two possible ways in which a new quote enters the scalar filtering window:

1. The normal update. A new scalar quote from the data source enters, is analyzed, and finally becomes the newest member of the scalar filtering window. The window variables are updated accordingly. These operations are described by Sections 4.5.2 through 4.5.6.

2. A filter test. A new scalar quote from any source is merely tested. It is analyzed as in a normal update, but it does not become a member of the window. No window variable is changed by this test. Thus we execute the steps of Section 4.5.2 and avoid those of Sections 4.5.3 through 4.5.6. The resulting trust capital of the new scalar quote is returned.

4.5.2 The Trust Capital of a New Scalar Quote

The algorithm of the filtering window is organized in an iterative way. Whenever a new quote enters the window, an update is made based on earlier results and an analysis of the new quote.

When the new, i^{th} scalar quote arrives, it already satisfies certain basic validity criteria (e.g., a price is not negative) and has possibly been transformed to a logarithmic value. This is ensured by the higher-level quote splitting algorithm explained in Section 4.6. The following filtering operations are done with the incoming i^{th} scalar quote:

1. The base trust capital T_{i0} is computed as the result of the level filter, Equation 4.6, if the scalar quote is a bid-ask spread. Otherwise, $T_{i0} = 0$. The resulting T_{i0} of Equation 4.6 is multiplied by a configured constant c_{level} that determines the importance of level filtering.

2. The new quote is compared to all old quotes of the window through pair filtering steps as described in Section 4.4.3. The trust capitals T_{ij} resulting from Equation 4.13 determine the trust capital T_i of the new quote and also affect the trust capitals T_j of the old quotes.

For computing T_{ij}, we need the expected squared value change V from Equation 4.20 and $\Delta\vartheta_{corr}$ from Equation 4.19 and therefore the number Q of valid quotes in the time interval from quote j to quote i. For this, we use the valid-quote age Q_j of the old quotes

$$Q = Q_j + 1 \tag{4.31}$$

The increment by 1 stands for the new quote, which is not yet included in the window. The computation of Q_j is explained at the end of Section 4.5.3. The resulting value of Q is inserted in Equation 4.19.

The trust capital of the new, i^{th} quote is computed additively as follows

$$T_i' = c_{\text{level}} T_{i0} + \sum_{j=i-n}^{i-1} C_j T_{ij} \qquad (4.32)$$

T_i' is not termed T_i because it is not yet the final trust capital in some cases. Equation 4.32 is a weighted sum with weights $C_j = C(T_j)$ from Equation 4.1, which are the current credibilities of the n other quotes of the window.

The number n of quotes used for comparison to the ith quote has an influence on the trust capital and thus the credibility. The higher the value of n, the higher the trust capital according to Equation 4.32 (provided that we are in a series of good data). This effect reflects the fact that the more comparisons to other quotes, the more certain our judgment on credibility. However, the effect of increasing n by adding more and more remote quotes is marginal. The remoteness of quotes implies a high term proportional to $(\Delta \vartheta_{ij})^3$ in the denominator of Equation 4.13, so the resulting T_{ij} values are close to zero. The choice of n is further discussed in Section 4.5.4.

Equation 4.32 is a conservative concept insofar as it judges the credibility of a new quote in the light of the previously obtained credibilities C_j of the earlier quotes. In the case of an unusually large real move or price jump, new quotes on a new level might be rejected for a prolonged time. To prevent this, there is special treatment of "after-jump" situations, which may lead to a correction of the resulting trust capital T_i and a quicker acceptance of a new level after a jump.

The first step of the after-jump algorithm is to identify the location of a possible real jump within the scalar filtering window. This is done during the computation of Equation 4.32. At every j, we test whether the incomplete sum of that equation

$$T_{i,\text{at }j}' = T_{i0} + \sum_{j'=i-n}^{j-1} C_{j'} T_{ij'} \qquad (4.33)$$

is less than the critical value T_{crit}

$$T_{\text{crit}} = \mu \, c_{\text{level}} T_{i0} - 1 \qquad (4.34)$$

(where μ is defined below). At the same time, we test $T_{ij} > 0$ (this indicates having reached a new, stable level after the jump rather than an outlier). At the first j where *both* conditions are satisfied, we conclude that a value jump must have taken place somewhere before quote $j - 1$. Although this jump certainly happened before quote j, we define $j_{\text{jump}} = j$ because this is the index of the first quote where we have a reason to believe that the jump was real. In order to validate this possible real value jump, we initialize an *alternative* trust capital T_i''

$$T_{i,\text{at } j_{\text{jump}}}'' = T_{\text{crit}} - 0.5 + \mu \, (T_{i,\text{at } j}' - T_{\text{crit}}) \tag{4.35}$$

We *dilute* the normal trust capital $T_{i,\text{at } j}'$ by a small dilution factor μ. When the filter is initialized (before seeing some 10 acceptable quotes), we choose a slightly larger μ value in order to prevent the filter from being trapped by an initial outlier. The offset term -0.5 in Equation 4.35 prevents the alternative hypothesis from being too easily accepted. For all values of $j \geq j_{\text{jump}}$, we set

$$T_j'' = \mu \, T_j \tag{4.36}$$

and insert these diluted trust capitals T_j'' of old quotes in Equation 4.1. The resulting credibilities C_j'' are used to complete the computation of the alternative trust capital T_i'':

$$T_i'' = T_{i,\text{at } j_{\text{jump}}}'' + \sum_{j=j_{\text{jump}}}^{i-1} C_j'' \, T_{ij} \tag{4.37}$$

analogous to Equation 4.32.

Now, we decide whether to take the normal, conservative trust capital T_i' or the alternative T_i''. The resulting, final trust capital is

$$T_i = \begin{cases} T_i'' & \text{if } T_i'' > T_i' \text{ and } T_i'' > 0 \\ T_i' & \text{otherwise} \end{cases} \tag{4.38}$$

The alternative solution prevails if its trust capital exceeds 0 and the trust capital of the conservative solution. The trust capital T_i of the new quote is the end result of a pure filter test. In the case of a normal update, the window has to be updated.

4.5.3   Updating the Scalar Window

A new quote affects the trust capitals of the old quotes of the window. The most dramatic change happens in the case of accepting the alternative hypothesis according to Equation 4.38. In this case, a real value jump is acknowledged, which leads to a major reassessment of the old quotes. First, the pairwise trust capital of quote comparisons across the jump is diluted

$$T_{\text{corr},ij} = \begin{cases} \mu \, T_{ij} & \text{for } j < j_{\text{jump}} \\ T_{ij} & \text{otherwise} \end{cases} \tag{4.39}$$

In the normal case with no jump, $T_{\text{corr},ij} = T_{ij}$. Afterward, the quotes after the newly detected jump get a new opportunity

$$T_{j,\text{new}} = \begin{cases} \mu \, T_j & \text{if } j \geq j_{\text{jump}} \text{ and } T_j < 0 \\ T_j & \text{otherwise} \end{cases} \tag{4.40}$$

In the case of a jump, this new value $T_{j,\text{new}}$ replaces T_j.

In every case, whether there is a jump or not, the trust capitals of all quotes are finally updated additively following Equation 4.32

$$T_{j,\text{new}} = T_j + C_i \, T_{\text{corr},ij} \, , \quad \text{for } j = i - n \ldots i - 1 \qquad (4.41)$$

where $C_i = C(T_i)$ follows from Equation 4.1 by substituting T_i from Equation 4.38. The result $T_{j,\text{new}}$ of Equation 4.41 is replacing the old value T_j. It should also be clarified that the diluted values T_j'' from Equation 4.36 are never directly used to modify the trust capitals T_j.

In historical filtering, Equations 4.39 through 4.41 may lead to the rehabilitation of an initially rejected old quote. Even in real-time filtering, the corrected trust capital of an old quote indirectly contributes to the filtering of new quotes through Equation 4.32 and through the use of only sufficiently credible old quotes in the statistics of adaptive filtering.

The valid-quote age Q_j of all the old quotes is also updated

$$Q_{j,\text{new}} = Q_j + C_i \, , \quad \text{for } j = i - n \ldots i - 1 \qquad (4.42)$$

where $C_i = C(T_i)$. The more credible the new quote, the higher the increment of the valid-quote age Q_j.

After all these updates, the new quote with index i and with its newly computed trust capital T_i is inserted in the window as its newest member, with the valid-quote age Q_i initialized to zero.

4.5.4 Dismissing Quotes from the Scalar Window

The window does not grow infinitely. At the end of a normal update as described in Section 4.5.3, a rule for dismissing scalar quotes is applied. There are three criteria for obtaining a properly sized window: (1) a sufficient time interval, (2) a sufficient number of quotes, and (3) a sufficient *overall* credibility of all scalar quotes. These criteria are listed here in the sequence of increasing importance.

In our general quote dismissal rule, we use the product of the criteria. At the end of an update with a new quote, the following condition for dismissing the oldest quote (with index $i - n$) is evaluated:

$$(\vartheta_i - \vartheta_{i-n+1}) \, n^2 \left(\sum_{j=0}^{n-1} C_{i-j} \right)^6 \geq W \qquad (4.43)$$

The sum of credibilities, the overall credibility, is the most important criterion and is therefore raised to the sixth power. This exponent is a parameter as many others; the value 6 has been found optimal in tests of samples of different data frequencies and qualities. The configuration parameter W defines the sufficient size of the window and has the dimension of a time. The parameter W is somehow related to the parameter v of Equation 4.13, which determines a filtering range. Choosing a very large W when v is limited does not add value because the distant quotes have a negligible weight in this case.

A few considerations may illustrate the behavior of Equation 4.43. If the data in the window are of good quality, the window is of small size. As soon as a cluster of low-quality or doubtful data enters the window, it will grow (sometimes to a very large size) until the situation becomes clearer and most old quotes can be dismissed again. In the case of a sparse time series, the window may contain few quotes but these quotes will extend further in time than for a dense time series. After dismissing the oldest quote when Equation 4.43 is fulfilled, the whole quote dismissal procedure is repeated as long as the remaining window still satisfies Equation 4.43.

In very rare cases, the window grows to a very large size and the filtering algorithm becomes slow. This problem and its solution are discussed in Section 4.5.6. Aside from this, another safety measure is taken where a quote older than 300 days is dismissed from the window even if Equation 4.43 is not fulfilled, as long as the remaining window still has at least two quotes.

Dismissed scalar quotes are also reported to the higher level of the filtering algorithm. This is necessary in the case of historical filtering for producing the final filtering results.

4.5.5 Updating the Statistics with Credible Scalar Quotes

When a scalar quote is dismissed from the window, its credibility C_i has reached a final value that will no longer be changed where $C_i = C(T_i)$ results from Equation 4.1. This is the right moment to update all the statistics needed for the adaptivity of the filter.

Invalid quotes are excluded from these statistics and they are simply ignored when updating the statistical variables. We set a critical credibility level C_{crit} where only quotes with credibility values above C_{crit} are used for updating the statistics. However, we should not be too rigid when excluding quotes. The filter has to adapt to unexpected events such as sudden volatility increases, but this requires including also some mildly rejected quotes. In fact, tests have shown that only the totally invalid quotes should be excluded here. We choose a low critical credibility level. In the initial phase, right after a filter starts from initialization (before having seen 10 acceptable quotes), we take a larger, more cautious value.

If a dismissed quote has a credibility $C_i > C_{crit}$, we update all the statistics. These updates typically imply the computation of moving average iteration formulas, and the statistics are explained in Sections 4.4.2 through 4.4.6.

4.5.6 A Second Scalar Window for Old Valid Quotes

The quote dismissal rule of Equation 4.43 makes sure that the scalar window stays reasonably small—except in the case of a very long series of bad quotes. Such long, rarely occurring series usually consist of computerized quotes (e.g., repeated or monotonic quotes). The filtering window technology as described so far is well able to handle this case, but the computation time of the filter grows very much in the case of a very large window. In real time, this does not really matter, but historical filtering becomes slow.

For efficiency reasons, the filter therefore supports a second queue of old valid quotes. The normal scalar window size is strictly limited to a maximum number of quotes, but an old quote dismissed from the normal window is stored in a second scalar window if its credibility exceeds a low threshold value. Otherwise, the dismissed quote is treated as any dismissed quote, as explained before, including the updating of statistics and the final reporting of its credibility.

This second scalar window of old valid quotes is normally empty. As soon as one or more dismissed quotes are in this window, it is treated as a part of the normal scalar window in all computations. The trust capital computation of Equation 4.32, for example, has a sum over both scalar windows, starting at the window of old valid quotes. The window of old valid quotes stays and possibly grows as long as the quote dismissal condition (applied to the two joined scalar windows) is not fulfilled. When the condition is fulfilled, the oldest quote of the scalar window of old valid quotes is deleted. After deleting all of its quotes, the second window is again empty and filtering is back to the normal mode.

The concept of a second scalar filtering window for old valid quotes adds quite some complexity to the filter and is motivated only by computational efficiency.

4.6 THE FULL-QUOTE FILTERING WINDOW

The full-quote filtering window is managed on hierarchy level 2 of Table 4.1. It is basically a sequence of recent full quotes plus a set of algorithmic methods of managing and processing this sequence. The full-quote filtering window has the following tasks:

- Splitting the quotes into scalar quotes that can be used in the filtering operations of Section 4.4.

- A first basic validity test for the filtered variables. This is usually a domain test (e.g., rejecting negative prices). Rejected scalar quotes are marked as invalid ($C_i = 0$) and eliminated from all further tests. They do not enter a scalar filtering window.

- In many cases, a transformation of the quoted level such as taking logarithms of prices instead of raw price values.

- Creating independent filtering environments for all types of scalar quotes, each with its own scalar filtering window.

- Storing the credibility of dismissed scalar quotes until all the other scalar quotes belonging to the same full quote have also been dismissed. (The spread filter may dismiss quotes before the bid price filter, for example.)

- Storing the full quotes as long as two or more filtering hypotheses coexist, until one of them wins. This is decided by the next higher hierarchy level (see Section 4.7). The decision between filtering hypotheses can also be made fast enough to make this point superfluous.

- When a full quote is finally dismissed, reporting it, together with its filtering results, to the higher level (needed only in historical filtering).

In principle, the full-quote filtering window also offers the opportunity of analyzing those data errors that affect full quotes in a way that cannot be analyzed when just looking at scalar quotes after splitting. In our experience, we have never found a good reason to implement this (aside from the filtering hypotheses discussed in Section 4.7).

The full quotes may enter a full-quote filtering window in a form already corrected by a filtering hypothesis. This fact plays no role here since the algorithm of the full-quote window does not care about quote corrections. This is managed on a higher level. The most important task of the full-quote filtering window is *quote splitting*.

4.6.1 Quote Splitting Depending on the Instrument Type

Quotes can have complex structures as explained in Section 4.2.1. The filter follows the guideline of quote splitting, which is motivated by the goals of modularity and transparency. Instead of trying to formulate complex algorithms for complex data structures, we split the quotes into scalar quotes that are individually filtered, wherever possible. Some filtering operations are done on a higher level before splitting as explained in Section 4.7.

The quote splitting unit has the task of splitting the stream of full quotes into streams of different filtered variables, each with its scalar quotes that are used in the filtering operations of Section 4.4.

Some quotes, such as bid-ask or open/high/low/close quotes, are splittable by nature. Only the bid-ask case is discussed here as many instruments come in the form of bid-ask quotes. Other instruments have single-valued quotes. Bid-ask quotes are split into three scalar quotes:

- Bid quote
- Ask quote
- Bid-ask spread

Other instruments have single-valued quotes, which are "split" into one scalar quote:

- The "level" quote

This is not as trivial as it looks because quote splitting is coupled with two other operations: basic validity testing and mathematical transformations, as will be explained. The user of the filter has to know whether an instrument has single-valued or bid-ask quotes and has to select or configure the filter accordingly.

4.6.2 The Basic Validity Test

Many quotes have a natural lower limit in a predetermined *domain*. This instrument-dependent information has an impact on quote splitting and needs to be configured by the user. The lower limit of the allowed domain is called p_{min}. For some instruments, there is no limit (or $p_{min} = -\infty$). The choice of the lower limit is rather obvious for most instruments. A list of important examples is presented here:

Prices. Genuine asset prices of whatever kind, including FX and equity prices, are never negative. This means: $p_{min} = 0$.

FX forward premiums/discounts. As explained in Section 2.3.2, the "forward points" can be positive or negative. There is no lower limit ($p_{min} = -\infty$).

Interest rates. These can be *slightly* negative in extreme cases such as the JPY case discussed in Section 2.3.1 (but these negative interest rates were above -1%). Some theories rely on interest rates staying always positive, but a filter is not allowed to reject slightly negative interest rates if these are posted by reasonable contributors. The filter should use a moderately negative value of p_{min} here, e.g. -5%.

Short-term interest-rate futures. These can normally be handled as ordinary prices (where $p_{min} = 0$), but are in fact defined by Equation 2.3 to have no lower limit (but an upper one). In practice, futures prices are quite far from 0, so it does not matter whether we assume a lower limit of 0 or none.

The choice of the lower limit is important for the further treatment. The following errors lead to complete invalidity:

- Quotes that violate the monotonic sequence of time stamps (i.e., quotes with a time stamp before the previously treated quote). In some software environments, this is an impossible error.

- A domain error. An illegal level p of the filtered variable (i.e., $p < p_{min}$) as opposed to a merely implausible level.

Invalid scalar quotes with an error of this kind do not enter a scalar filtering window and are completely ignored in all further filtering steps. We mark them by setting $C_i = 0$. This is a fundamentally stronger statement than merely giving a very low credibility as a result of the scalar filtering window.

In the case of bid-ask quotes, the three resulting scalar quotes are tested individually:

- Bid quote. Domain error if bid quote $p_{bid} < p_{min}$.
- Ask quote. Domain error if ask quote $p_{ask} < p_{min}$.
- Bid-ask spread. Domain error if $p_{ask} < p_{bid}$.

Thus it is possible that the same quote leads to a valid bid quote passed to the scalar filtering window of bid prices and an invalid ask quote that is rejected.

The domain test of bid-ask spreads needs to be further discussed. First, we might interpret bad values ($p_{ask} < p_{bid}$) as the result of a sequence error. In other words, if the contributor typed ask-bid instead of bid-ask, this would be an error that could be corrected by the filter. This interpretation, although being true in many cases, is dangerous as a general rule. We prefer to reject all ask quotes that are less than the bid quote.

On the other hand, a more rigid test might also reject *zero* spreads. However, there are some quote contributors to minor markets interested only in either bid or ask or middle quotes. These contributors often produce formal quotes with $p_{bid} = p_{ask}$. In some markets, such quotes are the rule rather than the exception. A filter that rejects all of those quotes is throwing away some valuable and irreplaceable information.

The solution looks as follows. First, there is a filtering option of generally rejecting zero spreads (i.e., the case $p_{bid} = p_{ask}$). If the user chooses this option, the quote splitting algorithm will act accordingly. Otherwise, zero spreads can be accepted, but they have low credibilities in a market dominated by positive spreads. This is further explained in the next section.

4.6.3 Transforming the Filtered Variable

The filtered variable is mathematically transformed in order to reach two goals:

1. A simpler (e.g., more symmetric) density function. The basic filtering operations (e.g., Equation 4.6), assume a roughly symmetric distribution of the scalar quote values (and their changes). Some variables, mainly the bid-ask spread, have a skewed distribution. The filtering method contains no full-fledged analysis to determine the exact nature of the distribution. This would be too much for an efficient filter algorithm. The idea of the transformation is that the mathematically transformed variable has a more symmetric distribution than the raw form. For the logarithm of bid-ask spreads, this has been demonstrated in Müller and Sgier (1992).

2. The transformed variable should not depend on units such as Japanese Yens per U.S. Dollar. *Relative* changes have the advantage of being comparable between different financial instruments and different time periods of the same instrument. They do not depend on the units in which the different rates are expressed. A usual way to work with relative, unit-free variables is to take the logarithm of the raw variables such as prices.

The rules of the mathematical transformation are closely related to the validity tests of Section 4.6.2. The transformation never fails because all illegal quotes have already been removed by the domain tests. The transformed quote value is denoted by x and used in many formulas of Section 4.4.

For single-valued quotes, bid quotes, and ask quotes, the following transformation is made:

$$x = \begin{cases} \log(p - p_{min}) & \text{if } p_{min} > -\infty \text{ exists} \\ p & \text{otherwise} \end{cases} \qquad (4.44)$$

For bid-ask spreads, the transformation is

$$x = x_{spread} = 45.564\sqrt{x_{ask} - x_{bid}} \qquad (4.45)$$

where x_{bid} and x_{ask} are results from Equation 4.44. Equation 4.45 has been chosen to return a value similar to $\log(x_{\text{ask}} - x_{\text{bid}}) + \text{constant}$ for a wide range of arguments $x_{\text{ask}} - x_{\text{bid}}$ of typically occurring sizes. Indeed, a logarithmic transformation of spread values would be a natural choice. The reason to use Equation 4.45 rather than a logarithmic transformation is related to zero spreads.[2] A logarithmic transformation would make zero spreads impossible (as $\log(0) = -\infty$). When inserting a zero spread in Equation 4.45, we obtain the legal result $x = 0$. This value is far away from typical ranges of values obtained for positive spreads, so its credibility is likely to be low in normal situations. When zero spreads become a usual event, the filter will start to accept them.

4.7 UNIVARIATE FILTERING

Univariate filtering is the top level of the filter. All the main filtering functions are managed here. The full-quote filtering window with its quote splitting algorithm of Section 4.6.1 is on a lower hierarchy level (see Table 4.1). Thus the univariate filter sees full quotes before they are split; it has access to all components of a full quote in their raw form (with no transformation).

The tasks of univariate filtering are as follows:

- Serving as the main configuration of a filter.
- Analyzing those data errors that affect not only individual quotes but a whole continuous sequence of quotes. The presence (or absence) of such a general error defines the *filtering hypothesis*. Two such cases were found in financial data and are therefore covered by the filter:

  1. Decimal errors. A wrong decimal digit of the quote, corresponding to a constant offset from the true quote.

  2. Scaling factor. The quote deviates from the true level by a constant factor, often a power of 10.

  Both cases are further discussed here.

- Creating a new full-quote filtering window for a newly detected filtering hypothesis.
- Managing filtering hypotheses and their full-quote filtering windows during their lifetimes, selecting the winning hypothesis.
- In the case of an error hypothesis, correcting the error of new incoming quotes according to the hypothesis and passing the corrected quotes to the full-quote filtering window.
- Packaging the filtering results to be accessed by the user.
- Recommending a suitable build-up period of the filter prior to the desired start date of the filtering result production, based on the filter configuration. Typical sizes are from weeks to months.

---

[2] The treatment of zero spreads is discussed at the end of Section 4.6.2.

The errors affecting a continuous sequence of quotes cannot be sufficiently filtered by the means described in the previous sections; they pose a special challenge to filtering. The danger is that the continuous stream of false quotes is accepted to be valid after a while because this false series appears *internally* consistent.

A filtering hypothesis is characterized by one general assumption on an error affecting all its quotes. This can lead to another unusual property. Sometimes the cause of the error is so clear and the size of the error so obvious that quotes can be *corrected*. In these cases, the filter produces not only credibilities and filtering reasons but also corrected quotes that can be used in further applications. This will discussed further.

The errors leading to a filter hypothesis are rare. Before discussing the details, we should evaluate the relevance of this filtering element in general. Such an evaluation may lead to the conclusion that the filtering hypothesis algorithm is not necessary in a new implementation of the filter.

Decimal errors have been the dominant error type in the page-based data feed from Reuters in 1987–1989. In later years, they have become rare; they hardly exist in modern data feeds. The few remaining decimal errors in the 1990s often were of short duration so they could successfully be filtered also through the standard data filter. Thus there is no convincing case for adding a decimal error filter algorithm to a filter of modern data. A decimal error filter is needed if old, historical data have to be cleaned.

The scaling filter is also superfluous if the user of the filter has a good organization of raw data. If a currency is rescaled (e.g., 1000 old units = 1 new unit as in the case of the Russian Ruble), a company with good data handling rules will not need the data cleaning filter to detect this; this rescaling will be appropriately handled before the data is passed to the filter. Rescaled currencies (or equity quotes after a stock split) can be treated as a *new* time series. However, the transition between the two definitions may not be abrupt, and there may be a mixture of quotes of both scaling types for a while. A scaling analysis within the filter can serve as an additional element of safety to treat this case and detect unexpected scale changes.

There is the possibility of having coexisting hypotheses, for example, the hypothesis of having a decimal error and the hypothesis of having none. If an immediate decision in favor of one hypothesis is always made, there is no need to store two coexisting hypotheses. Note that the filtering hypothesis algorithms are executed for each new quote before quote splitting.

4.7.1　The Results of Univariate Filtering

The output of the univariate filter consists of several parts. For every quote entered, the following filtering results are available:

1. The credibility of the quote

2. The value(s) of the quote, possibly corrected according to a filtering hypothesis such as a scaling factor or a decimal error as explained in 4.2.2

3. The filtering reason, explaining why the filter has rejected a quote
4. Individual credibilities of scalar quotes (bid, ask, spread)

Users may only want a minimum of results, perhaps just a yes/no decision on using or not using the quote. This can be obtained by simply checking whether the credibility of the quote is above or below a threshold value, which is usually chosen to be 0.5.

In the case of bid-ask data, the credibility C of the full quote has to be determined from the credibilities of the scalar quotes, usually applying the following formula:

$$C = \min(C_{\text{bid}}, C_{\text{ask}}, C_{\text{spread}}) \qquad (4.46)$$

This formula is conservative and safe; valid quotes are meant to be valid in every respect. The timing of the univariate filtering output depends on whether it is in a historical or real-time mode.

4.7.2 Filtering in Historical and Real-Time Modes

The terms "historical" and "real-time" are defined from the perspective of filtering here. A filter in real-time mode may be applied in a historical test. The two modes differ in their timing:

- In the real-time mode, the credibilities of a newly included quote resulting from Equations 4.38 and 4.1 are immediately passed to the univariate filtering unit. If there is only one filtering hypothesis, these credibilities are directly accessible to the user. If there are several hypotheses, the hypothesis with the highest overall credibility will be chosen.
- In the case of historical filtering, the initially produced credibilities are modified by the advent of new quotes. Only those quotes are output whose credibilities are finally determined. At that time, the quotes leave the full-quote filtering window and this implies that their components have also left the corresponding scalar filtering windows. If several filtering hypotheses coexist, their full-quote windows do not dismiss any quotes and so we get filtering results only when conflicts between filtering hypotheses are finally resolved in favor of one winning hypothesis.

Although these modes are different, their implementation and selection is easy. In the historical mode, we retrieve the oldest member of the full-quote window only after a test on whether this oldest quote and its results are ready. In the real-time mode, we pick the newest member of the same full-quote window. Thus it is possible to get both modes from the same filter run.

A special option of historical filtering should be available by obtaining the last quotes and their results when the analysis reaches the most recent available quote. It should be possible to output the full-quote window (of the dominant filtering hypothesis) for that purpose, even if the credibilities of its newest quotes are not finally corrected.

This leads to another timing mode that might frequently occur in practice. A real-time filter might be started from historical data. In this case, we start the filter in historical mode, flush the full-quote window as soon as the filter time reaches real time, and then continue in real-time mode. This can be implemented as a special mode if such applications are likely.

4.7.3　Choosing the Filter Parameters

The filter algorithm as a whole depends on many configuration parameters. Table 4.5 summarizes the definitions and explanations. The parameters are listed in the sequence of their appearance in Chapter 4. Some less important parameters have no symbol and appear directly as numbers in the text; nevertheless they have been included in Table 4.5. The same parameter values can be chosen for the different financial markets. Tests have shown that we need no parameter adjustments because the adaptive algorithm successfully adjusts to different financial instruments.

Filter users may choose the parameter values in order to obtain a filter with properties suited to their needs. A higher value of ξ_0 in Equation 4.11, for instance, will lead to a more tolerant filter. For a sensitivity test, we define different filters, for example, a weak (tolerant) filter and a strong (fussy) filter. This is explained in Section 4.9.

4.8　SPECIAL FILTER ELEMENTS

The filter described so far is flexible enough for most cases, but not for some of the special error types presented at the end of Section 4.2.2. These errors can be identified by additional algorithmic elements, which are discussed by Müller (1999). Moreover, there can be disruptive events such as the redefinition of financial instruments that pose some additional problems. For these rare cases, the data cleaning environment should provide the possibility of human intervention.

4.8.1　Multivariate Filtering: Filtering Sparse Data

Multivariate filtering is a concept that has not been used in the empirical results of this book, and univariate filtering as described in Section 4.7 remains the highest algorithmic level. Multivariate filtering requires a more complex and less modular software than univariate filtering—but it seems the only way to filter very sparse time series with unreliable quotes. Some concepts of a possible implementation are presented here.

In the financial markets, there is a quite stable structure of only slowly varying correlations between financial instruments. In risk management software packages, a large, regularly updated covariance matrix is used to keep track of these correlations. Covariance matrices between financial instruments can also be applied in the data cleaning of sparse quotes. Although univariate filtering methods work well for dense quotes, they lose a large part of their power when the density

TABLE 4.5   List of filter parameters.

Description of parameter	Symbol	Equation number
Range of mean x	$\Delta \vartheta_r$	4.3, 4.4
Parameters of Δx^2_{min} used in the level filter		(after Equation 4.7)
Critical deviation from mean x	ξ_0	4.8
Critical size of value change	ξ_0	4.11
Interaction range in change filter (normal value, special value for bid-ask spread)	ν	4.13
Range of quote density	$\Delta \vartheta_r$	4.15
Weight of new quote in quote density (normal value, special value for repeated quotes)	c_d	4.15
Range of short-term, standard and long-term volatility (v_{fast}, v, v_{slow})	$\Delta \vartheta_r$	4.16
Relative time interval offset for volatility	d_0	4.17
Absolute time interval offset for volatility	$\delta \vartheta_{min}$	4.17
Relative limits of quote interval $\Delta \vartheta$ (upper, lower)		4.19
Weight of squared granule in volatility offset		4.21
Parameters used for volatility offset ε_0 for bid-ask spreads		(after Equation 4.21)
Range (memory) of the quote diversity analysis	R	4.22
All parameters of the impact of quote diversity		4.24
Activity of active periods, for ϑ_k		4.25
Activity of inactive periods, for ϑ_k		4.25
Range of short-term volatility used for ϑ	$\Delta \vartheta_{smooth}$	4.28
Range of the variance of volatility fluctuations used for ϑ	$\Delta \vartheta_r$	4.29
Weight of the level filter	c_{level}	4.32
Trust capital dilution factor (normal value, special value at initialization from scratch)	μ	4.34 – 4.36
Window size parameter	W	4.43
Critical credibility for statistics update (normal value, special value at initialization from scratch)	C_{crit}	(Section 4.5.5)
Lower limit of allowed domain (prices, FX forwards, interest rates)	p_{min}	4.44 (and Section 4.6.2)
Factor in transformation of bid-ask spreads		4.45
Standard credibility threshold for accepting a quote		(Section 4.7.1)

of quotes is low. When a new quote of a sparse series comes in, there are only few quotes to compare and these quotes can be quite old and thus not ideal for filtering. This is the place where some additional information from the covariance matrix becomes useful. This can technically be done in several ways.

The only method outlined here is the *artificial quote* method. If the sparse rate (e.g., in form of a middle price) is included in a covariance matrix that also covers some denser rates, we can generate some artificial quotes of the sparse series by exploiting the most recent quotes of the denser series and the covariance matrix. The expectation maximization (EM) algorithm of Morgan Guaranty (1996) is a method to produce such artificial quotes; there are also some alternative methods. Results are good if all the series included in the generation of artificial quotes are highly correlated or anticorrelated to the sparse series.

Artificial quotes may suffer from three uncertainties: (1) they have a stochastic error in the value because they are estimated, (2) there is an uncertainty in time due to asynchronicities in the quotes of the different financial instruments (Low *et al.*, 1996), and (3) only a part of the full quote is estimated from the covariance matrix (e.g., the middle price, whereas the bid-ask spread has to be coarsely estimated as an average of past values). Therefore, an additional rule may be helpful by using artificial quotes only if they are not too close to good quotes of the sparse series.

In some cases, we can simply use arbitrage conditions to construct an artificial quote, such as the triangular arbitrage of FX cross rates explained in Section 2.2.2. The following algorithmic steps are done in the artificial quote method:

- Define a basket of high-frequency time series which are fairly well correlated or anticorrelated to the sparse series.

- Generate artificial quotes from the correlation matrix and mix them with the normal quotes of the sparse series, thus reinforcing the power of the univariate filtering algorithm.

- Eliminate the artificial quotes from the *final* output of the filter (because a filter is not a gap-filler).

This algorithm has the advantage of leaving the univariate filtering algorithm almost unchanged. The multivariate element only enters in the technical form of additional quotes. Quotes are the usual input of univariate filtering.

4.9   BEHAVIOR AND EFFECTS OF THE DATA FILTER

Data cleaning is a necessity because unfiltered outliers would spoil almost any data application. However, there is a legitimate concern about unwanted side effects caused by data cleaning. Are too many ticks rejected? Does filtering open a door to arbitrary data manipulation?

The rejection rates are low as shown by the typical examples presented in Table 4.6. The investigated data filter is a standard filter developed and used by Olsen & Associates (O&A), following the guidelines of Chapter 4. A proper build-up time is essential for such an adaptive filter as explained in Section 4.3.1. In all

TABLE 4.6   Data cleaning: Rejection rates.

Percentage of ticks rejected by a standard data cleaning filter of Olsen & Associates, for different financial markets. The analyzed test samples always consist of irregularly spaced high-frequency data over a period of one year. The reported rejection rates originate from the filter working in real-time mode.

Market	Financial instrument	Analyzed time period	Number of all ticks in period	Rejected outlier ticks	All rejected ticks
Major FX rates	EUR-USD	Mar 99 – Feb 00	3,457,116	0.07%	0.30%
	USD-JPY	Jan 89 – Dec 89	683,555	0.24%	0.49%
	USD-JPY	Jan 99 – Dec 99	1,324,421	0.06%	0.48%
Minor FX rates	USD-MYR	Jan 99 – Dec 99	1,950	7.59%	8.41%
	USD-MXP	Jan 99 – Dec 99	55,227	1.14%	1.66%
Spot interest rates	GBP (3 months)	Jan 99 – Dec 99	10,471	0.08%	50.27%
Short-term interest rate futures	CHF (Mar 00, LIFFE)	Jan 99 – Dec 99	34,561	8.54%	8.54%

examples, the build-up period was the 3 months preceding the analyzed period. All the examined raw data have been collected from the Reuters real-time data feed. Two rejection rates are indicated: (1) the rejection rate of "classical" outliers only, and (2) the rate of all rejected ticks, including those monotonically drifting or excessively repeated ticks identified by special parts of the cleaning algorithm. These "nonclassical" data errors are explained in Section 4.2.2 and can directly or indirectly lead to bad data quality, as the normal outliers. Therefore, they are eliminated by a good data filter.

For frequently quoted, major financial instruments, less than 0.5% of the ticks are rejected, as indicated by examples of major FX rates (EUR-USD and USD-JPY) in Table 4.6. The two analyzed USD-JPY samples are separated in time by 10 years. The percentage of outliers has clearly decreased over these 10 years. Data quality seems to have improved. However, the percentage of *all* rejected ticks has remained almost stable, due to an increase of monotonically drifting and excessively repeated ticks. These bad ticks are generated by improper computerized quoting, which has obviously become more widespread over the years. Minor FX rates such as USD-MYR and USD-MXP in Table 4.6 typically have higher rejection rates, which may exceed 5%. In less liquid markets, the competitive pressure to publish high-quality data seems to be lower. The spot interest rate of GBP with a maturity of 3 months in Table 4.6 has the high rejection rate of 50%, but there are just 0.1% true outliers. The high number of 50% is solely due to the quoting habit of one single bank that excessively repeated few quotes at high frequency over long periods. This behavior is also found for other, similar financial instruments. Market data from exchanges are often more reliable because of the centralized data generation. The percentage of outliers is smaller, and there are no monotonically drifting or excessively repeated quotes. This latter observation can be made for the Swiss Franc (CHF) interest rate futures of Table 4.6, where all the rejected ticks are true outliers. However, the outlier rate is rather high, about 8.5%. A closer look shows that most of these rejected ticks are empty ticks with formally quoted values of zero. Whatever the reason of the data supplier to post these empty ticks, the filter rightly rejects them as outliers. The rejection rates of Table 4.6 have been computed for the filter running in real-time mode. The corresponding rejection rates of historical filtering (see Section 4.7.2) are similar—usually slightly lower. A data filter needs a testing environment to analyze its statistical behavior. Table 4.6 presents a simple example of results produced by such a testing environment.

A good general method to test the effects of filtering in practice is a *sensitivity* analysis of the following kind. The data application, whatever it is, is implemented twice, using two *different* filters. Both filters may follow the same algorithm, but one of them is weak with more tolerant parameters, leading to a lower rejection rate, perhaps only half the rejection rate of the other filter. Then the results of both applications are compared to each other. The deviations between analogous results directly reflect the sensitivity or robustness of the analysis against changes in the data cleaning algorithm, and indirectly the possible degree of distortion by the filter.

This has been done, for example, in the case of an extreme value study of FX returns—a type of analysis very sensitive to outliers (which naturally lead to extreme return observations). Fortunately, the results for both filters are very similar, which means that both filters successfully eliminate the true outliers. The doubtful ticks that are accepted by one filter and rejected by the other one have little influence on the final results.

5

BASIC STYLIZED FACTS

5.1 INTRODUCTION

Gathering basic stylized facts on the behavior of financial assets and their returns is an important research activity. Without such facts it is not possible to design models that can explain the data. High-frequency data opened up a whole new field of exploration and brought to light some behaviors that could not be observed at lower frequencies. In this chapter we review the main stylized facts for foreign exchange (FX) rates, interbank money market rates, and Eurofutures contracts.

These stylized facts can be grouped under four main headings: autocorrelation of return, distributional issues, scaling properties, and seasonality. We find a remarkable similarity between the different asset types. Hence, we shall examine each of the properties first for FX rates and then show how they are present or modified for the others. FX rates have been the subject of many studies. However, these studies do not present a unified framework of the return distributions of the data-generating process. Most of the earlier literature analyzed daily time series, but, more and more, recent publications deal with intraday prices. They essentially confirm the findings of this chapter. Here, we use a set of intraday time series covering a worldwide 24 hr market,[1] and we present a study of fundamental statistical

---

[1] For a full description of the data, we refer the reader to Chapter 2.

properties of the intraday data. More specifically, this chapter demonstrates the following:

- At the highest frequency, the middle price is subject to microstructure effects (e.g., the bouncing of prices between the bid and ask levels). The price formation process plays an important role and overshadows some of the properties encountered at lower frequencies.

- The distributions of returns are increasingly fat-tailed as data frequency increases (smaller interval sizes) and are hence distinctly unstable. The second moments of the distributions most probably exist while the fourth moments tend to diverge.

- Scaling laws describe mean absolute returns and mean squared returns as functions of their time intervals (varying from a few minutes to one or more years). We find that these quantities are proportional to a power of the interval size.

- There is evidence of seasonal heteroskedasticity in the form of distinct daily and weekly clusters of volatility. This effect may partly explain the fat-tailedness of the returns and should be taken into account in the study of the return distributions. Daily and weekly patterns also exist in quote frequency.

- Daily and weekly patterns are also found for the average bid-ask spread, which is negatively correlated to the volatility. The trading activity in terms of price quoting frequency has a positive correlation to the volatility and a negative one to the spread. These findings imply that the trading volume is also positively correlated to the volatility. The daily patterns of all these variables may be explained by the behavior of three main markets— America, Europe, and East Asia—whose active periods partially overlap. Our intraday and intraweek analysis shows that there are systematic variations of volatility, even within what are generally considered business hours.

The literature presents a number of views regarding the distributions of FX returns and the corresponding data-generating process. Some papers claim FX returns to be close to Paretian stable ones, for instance, (McFarland *et al.*, 1982; Westerfield, 1997); some to Student distributions that are not stable (Rogalski and Vinso, 1978; Boothe and Glassman, 1987); some reject any single distribution (Calderon-Rossel and Ben-Horim, 1982). Most researchers now agree that a better description of the data generating process is in the form of a conditional heteroskedastic model rather than being from an unconditional distribution. Among the earliest to propose this for the FX rates were Friedmann and Vandersteel (1982); Wasserfallen and Zimmermann (1985); Tucker and Scott (1987) and Diebold (1988). On distributional issues, the only agreement seems to be that daily returns are fat-tailed and that there are substantial deviations from a Gaussian random walk model. Moreover, all of the literature on GARCH agrees that the distribution is not stable. Many of the studies of the late 1980s have been limited to daily or even weekly data except for

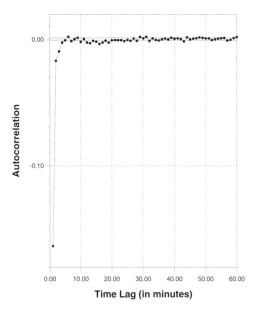

FIGURE 5.1 The autocorrelation function for the USD-DEM returns is plotted for different time lags in minutes up to 60 min. The returns are computed with prices interpolated using the previous tick interpolation method (see Chapter 3). The two horizontal lines represent the 95% confidence interval of an i.i.d. Gaussian process. The sampling period runs from January 5, 1987, to January 5, 1993. The autocorrelation is significantly negative up to a time lag of 4 min.

Wasserfallen and Zimmermann (1985); Feinstone (1987); Ito and Roley (1987), and Wasserfallen (1989). These papers analyze intradaily samples restricted to particular local markets and their local business hours. Recently the group of Barndorff-Nielsen has come up with the normal inverse Gaussian distribution that seems to capture some of the features we describe here, as observed in Eberlein *et al.* (1998); Barndorff-Nielsen (1998), and Barndorff-Nielsen and Prause (1999).

5.2 PRICE FORMATION PROCESS

The following three facts pertain to the short-term (less than 10 min) behavior of the foreign exchange intradaily returns. They highlight the difficulties inherent in tick-by-tick analysis.

5.2.1 Negative First-Order Autocorrelation of Returns

Goodhart (1989) and Goodhart and Figliuoli (1991) first reported the existence of negative first-order autocorrelation of returns at the highest frequencies, which disappears once the price formation process is over. In Figure 5.1, the autocorrelation function of returns measured at a 1 min interval is plotted against its lags. The returns are computed using the previous tick interpolation. There is significant autocorrelation up to a lag of 4 min. For longer lags, the autocorrelations mainly lie within the 95% confidence interval of an identical and independent (i.i.d.) Gaussian distribution. Goodhart (1989) also demonstrated that this negative autocorrelation is not affected by the presence (or absence) of major news announcements. Finally, Goodhart and Figliuoli (1992) showed that the resulting oscillations of the prices are not caused by bouncing prices between different geographical areas with different information sets. In Figure 5.1, negative autocorrelation is observed not only at the first lag (1 min) but also at further lags up to about 3 or 4 min. This is due to irregular spacing of ticks. If *tick time* is taken (i.e., an artificial time scale that moves by one unit with every tick), the negative autocorrelation is observed only at the first lag and rarely at larger lags, thus justifying the term "first-order." This behavior is characteristic if individual ticks randomly deviate from the market average while return clusters of longer duration are absent.

A first explanation of this fact is that traders have *diverging opinions* about the impact of news on the direction of prices—contrary to the conventional assumption that the FX market is composed of homogeneous traders who would share the same views about the effect of news so that no negative correlation of the returns would be observed. A second—and complementary—explanation for this negative autocorrelation is the tendency of market makers to skew the spread in a particular direction when they have order imbalances (Bollerslev and Domowitz, 1993; Flood, 1994). A third explanation is that even without order imbalances or diverging opinions on the price, certain banks systematically publish higher bid-ask spreads. This could also cause the prices to bounce back and forth between banks (Bollerslev and Domowitz, 1993). An early model for this bid/ask bounce was proposed by Roll (1984) in modeling transaction data in the stock market. The idea is that the two prices, bid and ask, can be hit randomly according to the number of buyers and sellers in the market. If the number of buyers is equal the number of sellers, which is the case most of the time in the market without exogeneous news, this model will produce a negative autocorrelation of transaction returns at high-frequency.

This negative autocorrelation is also seen in FX-rate transaction prices (Goodhart *et al.*, 1995) and in Eurofutures contracts (Ballocchi *et al.*, 1999b). For some stock indices such as the S&P 500, Bouchaud and Potters (2000) finds the autocorrelation of returns to be positive while it is not found in stock returns themselves or in futures contracts on indices (Ahn *et al.*, 2000). The explanation for the positive autocorrelation of stock indices is that some of them are constructed from equities that have very different liquidity. The model is called the *lagged adjustment model* (Ahn *et al.*, 2000). In this model one group of stocks reacts more slowly to aggregate information than another group of stocks. Because the autocovariance of a well-diversified portfolio is just the average cross-covariance of the stocks that make up the portfolio, this results in positive autocorrelations. In any case, the autocorrelation of returns is directly related to microstructure effects

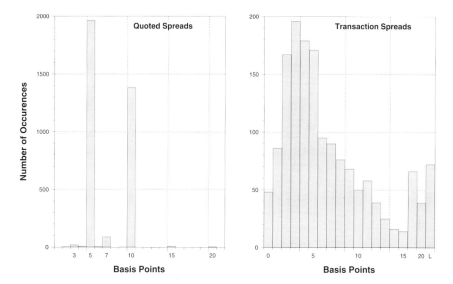

FIGURE 5.2   The figure on the left presents the spread size frequencies for USD-DEM *quotes* during June 16, 1993, collected from Reuters FXFX page. The figure on the right presents the spread size frequencies for USD-DEM *transactions* during June 16, 1993, from an analysis of Reuters Dealing 2000-2 by Goodhart *et al.* (1995).

in the market and should be carefully considered before using data at very high frequency.

The negative first-order autocorrelation can be seen as unwanted noise to be removed in a further study. An *effective price* can be defined in a way to eliminate the negative autocorrelation, as already discussed at the end of Section 3.2.2.

5.2.2   Discreteness of Quoted Spreads

Bid-ask spreads have discrete values. For studying this, we use the spread in its raw form, defined as ask price minus bid price, rather than the relative spread defined by Equation 3.12. In the example of Figure 5.2, bid-ask spreads of FX quotes are discretely distributed with the major peak at 5 basis points, followed by peaks at 10 and 7 basis points. A basis point is the smallest quoted decimal digit, which is 0.0001 German Marks per U.S. Dollar in the case of USD-DEM. In other, longer sampling periods and for other FX rates, we additionally observe spreads of 3, 8, 15, and 20 basis points with noticeable frequency. In a sample investigated by Bollerslev and Melvin (1994), the peaks at 5, 7, 10, and 15 basis points account for more than 97% of the distribution. These conventional spread values have evolved over the years, depending on the markets. For USD-DEM and some other major FX rates, the highest spread frequency peak shifted from 10 to 5 basis points during the 1990s, partly because the price levels became lower (Müller and Sgier, 1992). As explained in Section 3.2.5, spreads mainly depend on the cost structure of the market making banks and the habits of the market. Goodhart and Curcio (1991) have shown that individual banks usually quote two or three different spreads. Market makers who want to attract buyers more than sellers, or the other way around, tend to publish a skewed quote where only either the bid or the ask price is competitive and the other price is pushed away by a spread of conventional size, often 5 or 7 basis points. When they are uncertain about the direction the price should take, they may quote larger spreads with conventional values such as 10 or 15 (Lyons, 1998). Because different banks have different conventions and market situations change over time, the distribution of spreads has 4 or 5 peaks instead of 2 or 3.

A possible way to approximately *model* the *real* spreads, that is the difference between *traded* bid and ask prices, could be an analysis of the market *microstructure* which is discussed in detail by Flood (1991). Such a real spread model would analyze the microoscillations of (almost) simultaneous prices from different market makers. The *effective spread* would be something like the difference between the lowest ask and the highest bid prices currently quoted by any market maker—a model that would complement the effective price model proposed in Section 5.2.1. We did not try to set up such a subtle model, although we think that this would be the only way to overcome the limitations of quoted spreads. In a recent paper, Hasbrouck (1998) precisely proposes a market microstructure model for the clustering of the spreads based on a similar idea of a latent continuous efficient price.

Although the distribution of the spreads is discrete and consistent with theory (Admati and Pfleiderer, 1988; Subrahmanyam, 1991) market makers will cover themselves by conventional larger spreads in periods of higher risk such as in the release of important news (Goodhart, 1989), the closing or opening of markets (Bollerslev and Domowitz, 1993) and lunch breaks, (Müller *et al.*, 1990). More generally, the size of the spread is inversely related to market activity as measured by the tick frequency or the mean hourly volatility (Müller *et al.*, 1990). The size of the spread is directly related to the (instantaneous) volatility, which also measures the risk (Bollerslev and Domowitz, 1993).

In Figure 5.2, very different pictures emerge from the quoted spreads, which are only *indicative*, and the spreads as obtained from the electronic dealing system Reuters Dealing 2000-2. The different behaviors of the spread constitute the most pronounced difference between quoted prices and transaction prices. In Figure 5.2, the spread of actual transaction prices is uniformly distributed as one would expect. In their paper, Goodhart *et al.* (1995) note that, contrary to spreads, the volatility of middle prices does not exhibit substantial differences when transaction prices are used instead of quotes.

In the case of exchange-traded instruments such as Eurofutures (IR futures), there is no well-defined spread because the bid and the ask quotes are not synchronized and, depending on the market state, there may be only bid quotes or only ask quotes for a while. Nevertheless, a spread can be computed from bid and ask quotes that are few seconds apart. This effective spread is usually very small, typically less than one basis point on the Eurofutures market (Ballocchi *et al.*, 1999b), which represents relative spreads of the order of 10^{-4} according to the definition in Equation 3.12. Similar values are found for bond futures traded on the Deutsche Termin-Börse (DTB) (Franke and Hess, 1997).

5.2.3 Short-Term Triangular Arbitrage

The extremely short-term dynamics of price processes is also reflected in the significant predictive power of the USD-DEM in contrast to the other currencies (Goodhart and Figliuoli, 1991). A short delay is needed before traders in smaller currencies adjust themselves to the patterns of the two leading currencies. It is an effect comparable to the one we described in Section 5.2.1 for the positive autocorrelation of high-frequency returns of stock indices. Eben (1994) also finds evidence of triangular arbitrage opportunities at very high frequencies arising from very short-term trend reversals between two USD-rates, which are not yet reflected in the quoted cross rates. Although the detection of triangular arbitrage opportunities is rather easy and quick with a unique vehicle currency, it takes more time when the rates between two vehicles (e.g., USD and DEM) change (Suvanto, 1993; Hartmann, 1998).

Triangular arbitrage opportunities detected in quoted data do not necessarily reflect riskless profit-taking opportunities in real markets. The transaction costs may exceed the profits and the transaction prices may adjust more quickly than the quotes.

5.3 INSTITUTIONAL STRUCTURE AND EXOGENEOUS IMPACTS

5.3.1 Institutional Framework

An example of an institutional framework is the European Monetary System (EMS) introduced in the 1990s to keep some intra-European FX rates within certain bands. An intradaily analysis of FX rates within the EMS gives some insights into the distinct characteristics of this monetary system at a time when the bands were still quite narrow. As illustrated in Figure 5.3 (b), the EMS achieved a smaller *drift exponent* of the scaling law.

The scaling law relates the mean absolute return $E[|r|]$ observed over time intervals of a certain size to the size Δt of these intervals: $E[|r|] = \text{const} (\Delta t)^D$. The exponent D is called the drift exponent and empirically estimated using data samples. Low drift exponents indicate that the EMS successfully reduced the size of returns over large time intervals as compared to the volatility of short-term returns. A further, detailed discussion of drift exponents and their empirical estimation can be found in Section 5.5.

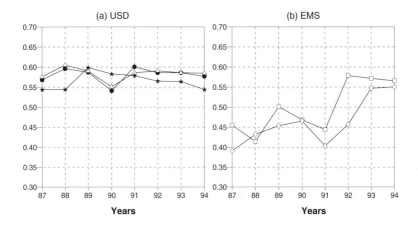

FIGURE 5.3 Drift exponents of the scaling law as a function of time, empirically estimated for yearly samples. (a): Drift exponents of freely floating rates against the USD,
DEM (•), FRF (△), JPY (⋆). (b): Drift exponents of EMS rates against the DEM, ITL (□)
and FRF (◇).

When the Italian Lira (ITL) left the EMS in 1992 and the EMS bands of the
French Franc (FRF) were broadened in 1993, the values of the drift exponents
went up and approached those of freely floating rates, as can be seen in Figure 5.3.

The drift exponent and the long-term volatility under the EMS were reduced,
however, at the cost of a larger probability of extreme events. This is further
explained in Section 5.4.2. The statistical analysis of EMS rates shows that institutional setups such as the EMS can be distinguished from freely floating markets
by purely statistical criteria in a robust way, independent of assumptions on the
generating-process.[2]

Another effect of the market framework can be seen in other financial high-
frequency data such as interbank spot interest rates. In this market, money market
quotes coming from East Asia are systematically higher than those from Europe or
America. Figure 5.4 clearly indicates that for USD 3-month money market rates
(spot interest rates collected from Telerate) the last bid quote before 2 a.m. GMT
(Greenwich Mean Time) almost always exceeds the last bid quote before 8 p.m.
GMT. On average, the early quote is larger by one-eight of a percent. The interest
rate intraday seasonality is caused by a geographical market segmentation between
East Asia on one side and Europe and America on the other side. This segmentation
is justified by market practitioners as being due to institutional constraints and
credit risks, making it less appealing on average for a European bank to place a
deposit with an East Asian counterparty than with a European counterparty. The
temporary difficulties in the Japanese banking sector were a likely cause of the
segmentation. The segmentation became very pronounced in the last half of 1995
and again during the "Asian crisis" in 1998 (with interest rate deviations of about

---

[2] See Svensson (1992) for a review of the literature on the modeling of target zones, and in particular,
of the European Monetary System.

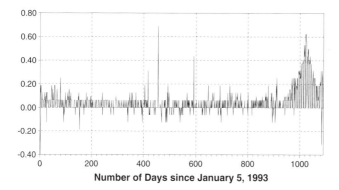

FIGURE 5.4 Daily difference between the last bid quote before 2 a.m. GMT and the last bid quote before 8 p.m. GMT. The early quote is systematically higher than the later one. Data sample: Quotes of the USD 3-month interbank money market rates published by Telerate. The analysis runs from January 5, 1993, to January 31, 1995.

0.5%). As explained in Section 2.3.1, the segmentation even caused negative JPY interest rates in the European and American markets.

5.3.2 Positive Impact of Official Interventions

One special type of trader is the central banks, as the time and the size of their interventions can be measured on an intradaily basis. Central banks may operate either directly through officially announced interventions or indirectly through unannounced interventions. Official interventions operate essentially as signals given to the markets and are therefore difficult to measure, see Edison (1993) for a review of the literature on central bank interventions. Some evidence is given in Goodhart and Hesse (1993) of the positive effects in the long run of official interventions, although they may result in short-term losses for the central bankers. One could, however, easily extend the analysis to any other long-term trader. A trader who can afford to keep a large open position for a long time will have some impact on the market through his reputation, even if he doesn't have a large share of the market. This is the case of some hedging funds, for example. Peiers (1997) shows the positive impact of unannounced interventions and interventions of a central bank, the Bundesbank, through the biggest player on the market, namely the Deutsche Bank.

5.3.3 Mixed Effect of News

News is a very broad concept covering a phone call of a customer who wants to make a large FX transaction (due to inventory imbalances, for instance), a conversation with a colleague, price forecasts and histories when used in technical analysis programs or the economic forecasts of the research department of a bank, general economic and political news, and major economic news announcements.

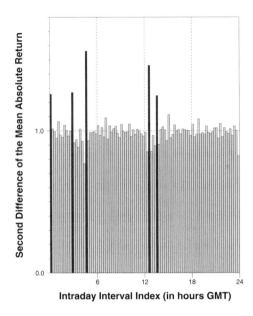

FIGURE 5.5 Intraday distribution of 15-min mean *changes* for the absolute returns (Equation 5.1 for the USD-DEM). Sudden peaks are darkened. The values are averages over all weeks of a sampling period of many years.

News is therefore difficult to quantify. Goodhart (1989) first tried to quantify news by looking at the "news" pages of Reuters. General economic and political news was displayed on the AAMM page (until February 1997). Goodhart (1989) found that "small" news does not have a significant effect on the behavior of the foreign exchange rates. Distinct and relatively large price movements unrelated to any news are indeed apparent. The price formation process seems to prevail, notwithstanding the presence or absence of news. In contrast, major economic news announcements such as trade, unemployment, budget deficit, or gross domestic product growth have significant impact (Goodhart, 1989). Economic news announcements along with the market expectations and the effect of the previous announcement were displayed in Reuters' FXNB page. Effective news—that is, the difference between the market expectation and the actual figure that is released—increases the volatility as the dispersion of traders' views on the impact of the effective news widens.

In Figure 5.5 we study the systematic effect of news release over a full day. We plot as a function of daytime (in GMT) a quantity that reflects the *change* of volatility by examining its relation to the neighboring values. This quantity is defined as

$$h_i = \exp\left[\ln |r_i| - \frac{1}{2}\ln |r_{i-1}r_{i+1}|\right] \tag{5.1}$$

where the index i represents the time of day (in steps of 15-min), and the h_i are averaged over all working days of a long sampling period. The three right peaks in Figure 5.5 show the clear-cut effect of news release in New York and Japan. News is not released every working day, but when it is, this happens at the typical daytimes indicated by peaks. The two peaks for the United States are separated by 1 hr and reflect the change of daylight saving time, which does not exist in Japan. The first two peaks on the left correspond to the beginning of the Japanese trading session and to the time just after the Japanese lunch. Goodhart *et al.* (1993) further show that major economic news announcements, such as release of the U.S. trade figures or changes in the U.K. base interest rate, have a significant impact on the return process. This effect however extends over 3 or 4 days as markets eventually incorporate the effects of the news. Moreover, the direction of the effect on the level of the price is difficult to predict. This can be explained by the highly nonlinear dynamics of the FX rates (Guillaume, 1994).

An alternative way to quantify the impact of news is with the mixture of distribution hypothesis (Clark, 1973; Tauchen and Pitts, 1983; Andersen, 1996). In this framework, the clustering of the volatility results from the clustering of the news arrival process. Because the news arrival process is an unobserved variable, proxies for the market activity such as the volume of trade are used (volume is not available in the FX markets). Moreover, as shown in Jones *et al.* (1994), volume can be rather noisy. Therefore, empirical studies in the FX intradaily markets use the tick frequency or the spread as proxies for the level of activity. Although a certain correlation between these variables and the volatility is obvious from the simple inspection of Figure 5.12, severe limitations harm the use of these variable as noted earlier. Moreover, Davé (1993) shows that tick frequency can only be a good approximation of the volume when markets are analyzed as separate geographical entities. Thus, there is no overlap between markets and the data are not disaggregated by individual bank subsidiary. Goodhart (1989) also shows that tick frequency does not specifically rise when news is released. Therefore, empirical evidence in favor of this mixture of distribution hypothesis is only partial, (Demos and Goodhart, 1992; Bollerslev and Domowitz, 1993). A more recent paper by Melvin and Yin (2000) provides new support for the link between news arrival frequency and quote frequency.

In another study, Almeida *et al.* (1998) are able to quantify the effect of news to a short-lived response of 15 min on average, confirming the results of Figure 5.5. The peaks of that figure disappear if longer time intervals are examined. This is also confirmed in a study by Franke and Hess (1998) on other very liquid markets such as the U.S. treasury bond market and the German Bund futures market. By studying the effect of scheduled U.S. macroeconomic news releases, these authors were able to detect an increase of volatility of the U.S. Treasury bond futures contracts. This anomalous volatility would last from few minutes to a maximum of an hour. Moreover, they show that the futures Bund price reacts significantly to an American news announcements. They attribute this reaction to the increasing integration of the German bond market. It is only with the use of more sophisticated indicators, rather than purely examining the returns, that it is possible to detect a significant impact of the news. Recently, Zumbach *et al.* (2000) have developed a scale of market shocks by integrating different volatility measures and relating a shock to its probability of occurrence. This measure is able to clearly identify turbulences on the market as well as to quantify the effect of news (Zumbach *et al.*, 2000).

5.4 DISTRIBUTIONAL PROPERTIES OF RETURNS

We mentioned in the introduction to this chapter the variety of opinions about the distributions of FX returns and the corresponding data-generating process. In this section, we do not want to propose a new model for the probability distribution function, but rather examine empirically what type of behavior is observed when returns are measured at different frequencies. We shall first present general results on the entire distribution and note that they are fat-tailed. Then, instead of looking at the center of the distribution, we shall present an alternative way to characterize the distribution by looking at the behavior of the tails.

There are many possible models of distribution functions, but this variety is greatly reduced when considering the tails of the distributions. The tail of a distribution can be described by using only one parameter, the tail index α. The empirical estimation of the tail index is difficult and requires large numbers of observations. The availability of high-frequency data makes this possible in practice. The methods, the empirical results, and their interpretation are presented in Section 5.4.2.

5.4.1 Finite Variance, Symmetry and Decreasing Fat-Tailedness

In this subsection, we analyze the probability distribution of returns of financial assets. The probability distribution associates each movement size with a certain probability of occurrence. In the case of empirical data, the domain of possible return values is divided into boxes, and one counts the frequency of occurrence in each box. One important issue in the case of tick-by-tick data is that this data are irregularly spaced in time, t_j. We have already discussed in Chapters 2 and 3 the different ways of constructing a homogeneous time series. Here we chose to take linearly interpolated prices. This is the appropriate method for interpolating in a series with independent random increments for most types of analyses. An alternative method discussed earlier, taking the last valid price before the gap as representative for the gap interval, must be avoided in a study of distributions as it would lead to a spurious large return from the last valid price within the gap to the first real price after the gap.

In Tables 5.1 and 5.2, we present the empirically computed moments of the distributions for the major FX rates against the USD and the major FX rates against the DEM.[3] The means are close to zero, as compared to the standard deviations,

---

[3] At least three of these cross rates have disappeared with the introduction of the Euro. Nevertheless, we think it is still interesting to report the results for them because they show the convergence of those

TABLE 5.1 Moments of return distributions for USD FX rates

This table gives an empirical estimation of the first 4 moments of the unconditional return distribution at different time intervals for the major currencies against the USD for the period from January 1, 1987, to December 31, 1993. The term kurtosis refers to the excess kurtosis, so a normal distribution has a kurtosis value of zero.

Rate	Time interval	Mean	Variance	Skewness	Kurtosis
USD-DEM	10 min	$-2.73 \cdot 10^{-7}$	$2.62 \cdot 10^{-7}$	0.17	35.10
	1 hr	$-1.63 \cdot 10^{-6}$	$1.45 \cdot 10^{-6}$	0.26	23.55
	6 hr	$-9.84 \cdot 10^{-6}$	$9.20 \cdot 10^{-6}$	0.24	9.44
	24 hr	$-4.00 \cdot 10^{-5}$	$3.81 \cdot 10^{-5}$	0.08	3.33
	1 week	$-2.97 \cdot 10^{-4}$	$2.64 \cdot 10^{-4}$	0.18	0.71
USD-JPY	10 min	$-9.42 \cdot 10^{-7}$	$2.27 \cdot 10^{-7}$	-0.18	26.40
	1 hr	$-5.67 \cdot 10^{-6}$	$1.27 \cdot 10^{-6}$	-0.09	25.16
	6 hr	$-3.40 \cdot 10^{-5}$	$7.63 \cdot 10^{-6}$	-0.05	11.65
	24 hr	$-1.37 \cdot 10^{-4}$	$3.07 \cdot 10^{-5}$	-0.15	4.81
	1 week	$-9.61 \cdot 10^{-4}$	$2.27 \cdot 10^{-4}$	-0.27	1.30
GBP-USD	10 min	$-6.91 \cdot 10^{-9}$	$2.38 \cdot 10^{-7}$	0.02	27.46
	1 hr	$7.61 \cdot 10^{-7}$	$1.40 \cdot 10^{-6}$	-0.23	21.53
	6 hr	$4.63 \cdot 10^{-6}$	$8.85 \cdot 10^{-6}$	-0.34	10.09
	24 hr	$1.72 \cdot 10^{-5}$	$3.60 \cdot 10^{-5}$	-0.26	4.41
	1 week	$6.99 \cdot 10^{-5}$	$2.72 \cdot 10^{-4}$	-0.66	2.77
USD-CHF	10 min	$-2.28 \cdot 10^{-7}$	$3.07 \cdot 10^{-7}$	-0.04	23.85
	1 hr	$-1.37 \cdot 10^{-6}$	$1.75 \cdot 10^{-6}$	0.05	18.28
	6 hr	$-8.23 \cdot 10^{-6}$	$1.11 \cdot 10^{-5}$	0.05	7.73
	24 hr	$-3.38 \cdot 10^{-5}$	$4.51 \cdot 10^{-5}$	-0.04	2.81
	1 week	$-2.58 \cdot 10^{-4}$	$3.16 \cdot 10^{-4}$	0.09	0.34
USD-FRF	10 min	$-1.98 \cdot 10^{-7}$	$2.08 \cdot 10^{-7}$	0.35	43.31
	1 hr	$-1.18 \cdot 10^{-6}$	$1.28 \cdot 10^{-6}$	0.47	28.35
	6 hr	$-7.13 \cdot 10^{-6}$	$8.29 \cdot 10^{-6}$	0.23	9.69
	24 hr	$-2.91 \cdot 10^{-5}$	$3.40 \cdot 10^{-5}$	0.06	3.22
	1 week	$-2.32 \cdot 10^{-4}$	$2.44 \cdot 10^{-4}$	0.16	0.88

and the absolute values of the skewness are, except in very few cases, significantly smaller than 1. We can conclude from these facts that the empirical distribution is almost symmetric. The mean values are slightly negative (except for GBP-USD where the currencies are inverted) because during this period (from January 1, 1987, to December 31, 1993) we have experienced an overall decline of the USD. For all time horizons, the empirically determined (excess) kurtosis exceeds the value 0, which is the theoretical value for a Gaussian distribution. For the shortest

currencies to the Euro by exhibiting lower variances than the others. They present a good example of the influence of external factors on the statistical behavior of financial asset prices.

CHAPTER 5 BASIC STYLIZED FACTS

TABLE 5.2 Moments of return distributions for DEM FX rates

This table gives an empirical estimation of the first 4 moments of the unconditional return distribution at different time intervals for the major currencies against the DEM for the period from January 1, 1987, to December 31, 1993. The term kurtosis refers to the excess kurtosis, so a normal distribution has a kurtosis value of zero.

Rate	Time interval	Mean	Variance	Skewness	Kurtosis
DEM-FRF	10 min	$9.84 \cdot 10^{-8}$	$1.91 \cdot 10^{-8}$	0.54	86.29
	1 hr	$5.89 \cdot 10^{-7}$	$1.14 \cdot 10^{-7}$	0.79	69.70
	6 hr	$3.53 \cdot 10^{-6}$	$6.53 \cdot 10^{-7}$	1.41	36.87
	24 hr	$1.07 \cdot 10^{-5}$	$2.84 \cdot 10^{-6}$	1.15	24.26
	1 week	$8.94 \cdot 10^{-5}$	$1.93 \cdot 10^{-6}$	1.92	3.95
DEM-NLG	10 min	$-5.19 \cdot 10^{-8}$	$1.42 \cdot 10^{-9}$	-5.68	9640.85
	1 hr	$-3.11 \cdot 10^{-7}$	$7.54 \cdot 10^{-9}$	2.76	4248.12
	6 hr	$-1.86 \cdot 10^{-6}$	$2.48 \cdot 10^{-8}$	0.74	124.35
	24 hr	$-7.80 \cdot 10^{-6}$	$9.66 \cdot 10^{-8}$	-0.30	30.02
	1 week	$-4.57 \cdot 10^{-5}$	$6.63 \cdot 10^{-7}$	0.03	0.06
DEM-ITL	10 min	$1.07 \cdot 10^{-6}$	$1.75 \cdot 10^{-7}$	0.86	64.03
	1 hr	$6.46 \cdot 10^{-6}$	$1.24 \cdot 10^{-6}$	1.83	89.92
	6 hr	$3.88 \cdot 10^{-5}$	$7.16 \cdot 10^{-6}$	1.03	37.26
	24 hr	$1.18 \cdot 10^{-4}$	$2.53 \cdot 10^{-5}$	-0.51	13.08
	1 week	$9.42 \cdot 10^{-4}$	$1.37 \cdot 10^{-4}$	-0.25	0.17
GBP-DEM	10 min	$4.53 \cdot 10^{-7}$	$9.86 \cdot 10^{-8}$	-0.32	25.97
	1 hr	$2.69 \cdot 10^{-6}$	$7.12 \cdot 10^{-7}$	-0.34	16.90
	6 hr	$1.56 \cdot 10^{-5}$	$4.62 \cdot 10^{-6}$	-0.02	7.48
	24 hr	$7.04 \cdot 10^{-5}$	$1.79 \cdot 10^{-5}$	0.27	3.15
	1 week	$1.17 \cdot 10^{-4}$	$1.29 \cdot 10^{-4}$	0.07	0.59
DEM-JPY	10 min	$-3.39 \cdot 10^{-6}$	$2.21 \cdot 10^{-7}$	-0.09	12.35
	1 hr	$-2.03 \cdot 10^{-5}$	$1.46 \cdot 10^{-6}$	-0.03	88.58
	6 hr	$-1.21 \cdot 10^{-4}$	$9.12 \cdot 10^{-6}$	-0.04	6.57
	24 hr	$-4.85 \cdot 10^{-4}$	$3.56 \cdot 10^{-5}$	0.12	2.52
	1 week	$-3.15 \cdot 10^{-3}$	$2.67 \cdot 10^{-4}$	-0.07	0.03

time intervals, the kurtosis values are extremely high. Another interesting feature is that all of the rates show the same general behavior, a decreasing kurtosis with increasing time intervals. At intervals of around 1 week, the kurtosis is rather close to the Gaussian value.

Tables 5.1 and 5.2 suggest that the variance and the third moment are finite in the large-sample limit and that the fourth moment may not be finite. Some solid evidence in favor of these hypotheses is added by the tail index studies that follow, mainly the results of Table 5.3. Indeed, the larger the number of observations, the larger the empirically computed kurtosis. At frequencies higher than 10 min, there seems to be some contradiction between the work of Goodhart and Figliuoli (1991), which claims that the fat tails start to decrease at these frequencies, and the paper of Bollerslev and Domowitz (1993), which gives some evidence of a still increasing fat-tailedness. One can show, however, that both results hold depending on whether one uses the linear interpolation method or the previous tick to obtain price values at fixed time intervals at such frequencies. This is an example of the difficulty of making reliable analyses of quoted prices at frequencies higher than 10 min. The divergence of the fourth moment explains why absolute values of the returns are often found to be the best choice of a definition of the volatility (i.e., the one that exhibits the strongest structures).[4] Indeed, because the fourth moment of the distribution enters the computation of the autocorrelation function of the variance, the autocorrelation values will systematically decrease with a growing number of observations.

To complement Tables 5.1 and 5.2, we plot on Figure 5.6 the cumulative frequency of USD-JPY for returns measured at 10 min, 1 day, and 1 week on the scale of the cumulative Gaussian probability distribution. Normal distributions have the form of a straight line, which is approximately the case for the weekly returns with a moderate (excess) kurtosis of approximately 1.3. The distribution of 10-min returns, however, has a distinctly fat-tailed form and its kurtosis in Table 5.1 is very high. If the data-generating process was a random walk with increments from a stable distribution, which is defined by the law that *scaled* returns $r/(\Delta t)^{\gamma}$ for a certain γ have the same distribution irrespective of the measurement interval Δt, we would obtain a uniform distribution with identical moments within the significance limits.[5] Considering all the presented results, this is clearly not the case. This instability of distributions was also found by other authors. McFarland *et al.* (1982) and Boothe and Glassman (1987) suggest that distributions are composed of reactions to different flows of information. Calderon-Rossel and Ben-Horim (1982) are in agreement with our findings and claim that the returns cannot be accurately described by a unique type of stable distribution.

5.4.2 The Tail Index of Return Distributions

The tails of all possible distributions can be classified into three categories:[6]

i. Thin-tailed distributions for which all moments are finite and whose cumulative distribution function declines exponentially in the tails

ii. Fat-tailed distributions whose cumulative distribution function declines with a power in the tails

iii. Bounded distributions which have no tails

---

[4] We shall see some evidence of this in Section 5.6.1 and in Chapter 7.

[5] Here there is no need to further characterize stable distributions in addition to the described scaling behavior. Section 5.5.2 has a definition and discussion of stable distributions.

[6] The interested reader will find the full development of the theory in Leadbetter *et al.* (1983), and de Haan (1990).

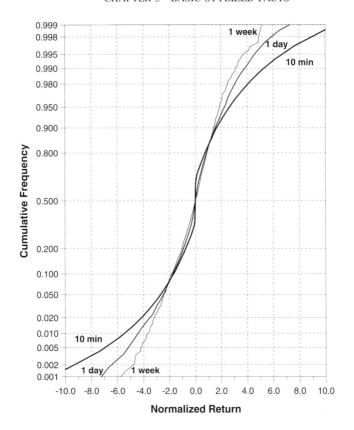

FIGURE 5.6 The cumulative distributions for 10-min, 1-day, and 1-week USD-JPY returns shown against the Gaussian probability on the y-axis. On the x-axis the returns normalized to their mean absolute value are shown. The mean absolute return for 10 min is 2.62×10^{-4}, for 1 day 3.76×10^{-3}, and for 1 week 1.14×10^{-2}. The three curves are S-shaped as typical of fat-tailed distributions. The S-shapes of the three curves are very differently pronounced.

A nice result is that these categories can be distinguished by the use of only one parameter, the tail index α with $\alpha = \infty$ for distributions of category (i), $\alpha > 0$ for category (ii), and $\alpha < 0$ for category (iii). The empirical estimation of the tail index and its variance crucially depends on the size of the sample (Pictet *et al.*, 1998). Only a well chosen set of the most extreme observations should be used. The very large sample size available for intradaily data ensures that enough "tail observations" are present in the sample. An important result is that the tails of a fat-tailed distribution are invariant under addition although the distribution as a whole may vary according to temporal aggregation (Feller, 1971). That is, if weekly returns are Student-t identically and independently distributed, then monthly returns are not Student-t distributed.[7] Yet the tails of the monthly return

---

[7] This is an implication of the central limit theorem.

distribution are like the tails of the weekly returns, with the same exponent α, but the *real tail* might be very far out and not even seen in data samples of limited size.[8] Another important result in the case of fat-tailed distributions concerns the finiteness of the moments of the distribution. From

$$
\mathrm{E}\left[X^k \right] \;=\; M_0 + c \int_s^\infty x^{k-\alpha-1} dx + o\left(x^{k-\alpha} \right) \tag{5.2}
$$

where X is the observed variable, M_0 is the part of the moment due to the center of the distribution (up to s), c is a scale variable and α is the tail index. It is easily seen that only the first k-moments, $k < \alpha$, are bounded.

How heavy are the tails of financial asset returns? The answer to this question is not only the key to evaluating risk in financial markets but also to accurately modeling the process of price formation. Evidence of heavy tails presence in financial asset return distributions is plentiful (Koedijk *et al.*, 1990; Hols and De Vries, 1991; Loretan and Phillips, 1994; Ghose and Kroner, 1995; Müller *et al.*, 1998) ever since the seminal work of Mandelbrot on cotton prices (Mandelbrot, 1963). He advanced the hypothesis of a stable distribution on the basis of an observed invariance of the return distribution across different frequencies and the apparent heavy tails of the distribution. A controversy has long been going on in the financial research community as to whether the second moment of the distribution of returns converges. This question is central to many models in finance, which heavily rely on the finiteness of the variance of returns. The risk in financial markets has often been associated with the variance of returns since portfolio theory was developed. From option pricing models (Black and Scholes, 1973) to the Sharpe ratio (Sharpe, 1994) used for measuring portfolio performance, the volatility variable is always present.

Another important motivation of this study is the need to evaluate extreme risks in financial markets. Recently, the problem of risk in these markets has become topical following few unexpected big losses like in the case of Barings or Daiwa. The Bank for International Settlements has set rules to be followed by banks to control their risks, but most of the current models for assessing risks are based on the assumption that financial assets are distributed according to a normal distribution. In the Gaussian model the evaluation of extreme risks is directly related to the variance, but in the case of fat-tailed distributions this is no longer the case.

Computing the tail index is a demanding task but with the help of high frequency data it is possible to achieve reasonable accuracy (see Pictet *et al.*, 1998; Dacorogna *et al.*, 2001a), where a theorem is proved which explicitly shows that more data improve the estimation of the tail index. Here, we present the main framework[9].

---

[8] See, for instance, the simulations done in Pictet *et al.* (1998) where for a high enough aggregation level, it is not possible to recover the theoretical tail index for Student-*t* distributions even if one can use 128 years of 10-min data.

[9] The interested reader can find the details in two recent papers by Pictet *et al.* (1998) and Dacorogna *et al.* (2001a).

Let $X_1, X_2, \ldots, X_n$ be a sequence of n observations drawn from a stationary i.i.d. process whose probability distribution function F is unknown. We assume that the distribution is fat-tailed—that is, the tail index α is finite.[10] Let us define $X_{(1)} \geq X_{(2)} \geq \ldots \geq X_{(n)}$ as the descending order statistics from $X_1, X_2, \ldots, X_n$.

Extreme value theory states that the extreme value distribution of the ordered data must belong to one of just three possible general families, regardless of the original distribution function F (Leadbetter *et al.*, 1983). Besides, if the original distribution is fat-tailed, there is only one general family it can belong to

$$G(x) = \begin{cases} 0 & x \leq 0 \\ \exp(-x^{-\alpha}) & x > 0, \quad \alpha > 0 \end{cases} \tag{5.3}$$

where $G(x)$ is the probability that $X_{(1)}$ exceeds x. There is only one parameter to estimate, α, which is called the tail index. The stable distributions (excluding the Gaussian distribution), the Student-t model, and the unconditional distribution of the ARCH-process all fall in the domain of attraction of this type of distribution.

To give more intuition to these statements, we plot the logarithm of the order statistics m as a function of the difference between the logarithms of the most extreme observation, $\ln X_{(1)}$, and the mth observation in the ordered sequence, $\ln X_{(m)}$. Such a plot is shown on Figure 5.7 for the case of a Student-t distribution with 4 degrees of freedom. Because we are in the domain of attraction of $\exp(-x^{-\alpha})$, it is trivial to see that the problem of estimating α becomes the problem of estimating the slope of the tangent at $m \rightarrow 0$ of the curve shown in Figure 5.7. We see that a straight line with a slope equal to 4 is indeed a good tangent to the curve, as it should be because the theoretical tail index of the Student-t distribution is equal to the number of degrees of freedom. Although the behavior of $\ln X_{(m)}$ is quite regular on Figure 5.7 because we took the average values over 10 Monte Carlo simulations, it is not always so and the problem of how to choose the number of points that are far in the tail is not trivial. One needs a more formal way to estimate the tail index. The estimator we present here is a way of estimating the slope of the tangent shown in Figure 5.7. There are other ways of studying the tail index by directly fitting the distribution of ordered data to some known distribution.[11]

We concentrate our efforts on the estimator first proposed by Hill (1975)

$$\hat{\gamma}_{n,m}^H = \frac{1}{m-1} \sum_{i=1}^{m-1} \ln X_{(i)} - \ln X_{(m)} \quad \text{where } m > 1 \tag{5.4}$$

This estimator was proven to be a consistent estimator of $\gamma = 1/\alpha$ for fat-tailed distributions in Mason (1982). From Hall (1982) and Goldie and Smith (1987), it follows that $(\gamma_{n,m} - \gamma)m^{1/2}$ is asymptotically normally distributed with mean zero

---

[10] A good review of the definitions used in this chapter can be found in Leadbetter *et al.* (1983).

[11] A good reference to learn about these methods is the book by Embrechts *et al.* (1997).

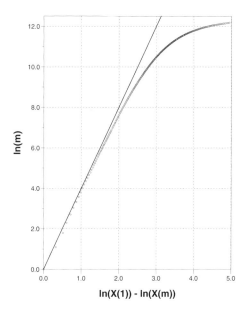

FIGURE 5.7 The logarithm of the order statistics m is plotted as a function of the difference between the logarithm of the most extreme observation and the logarithm of the ordered random observations. The data are drawn from a Student-t distribution with 4 degrees of freedom averaged over 10 replications of a Monte-Carlo simulation. The straight line represents the theoretical tangent to this curve.

and variance γ^2. In fact the Hill estimator is the maximum likelihood estimator of γ and $\alpha = 1/\gamma$ holds for the tail index. For finite samples, however, the expected value of the Hill estimator is biased. As long as this bias is unknown, the practical application of the Hill estimator to empirical samples is difficult. A related problem is that $\hat{\gamma}_{n,m}$ depends on m, the number of order statistics, and there is no easy way to determine which is the best value of m. Extending a bootstrap estimation method proposed by Hall (1990), Danielsson *et al.* (1997) solved the problem by means of a subsample bootstrap procedure, which is described and discussed by Pictet *et al.* (1998). Many independent subsamples (or resamples) are drawn from the full sample and their tail behaviors are statistically analyzed, which leads to the best choice of m. For such a statistical analysis, the subsamples have to be distinctly smaller than the full sample. On the other hand, the subsamples should still be large enough to contain some representative tail observations, so the method greatly benefits from a large sample size to begin with.

Tail index values of some FX rates have been estimated by a subsample bootstrap method and are presented in Table 5.3. The confidence ranges indicated for all values are standard errors times 1.96. Assuming a normally distributed error, this corresponds to 95% confidence. The standard errors have been obtained through the jackknife method, which can be characterized as follows. The data

TABLE 5.3   Estimated tail indices of FX rates

Estimated tail index values α and their 95% confidence ranges, for main FX rates against the USD, gold (XAU), and silver (XAG) and some of the main (computed) cross rates against the DEM, Müller *et al.* (1998). The tail index values are based on the subsample bootstrap method using the Hill estimator, the confidence ranges result from the jackknife method. Computed cross rates are obtained via the two bilateral rates against the USD, see Equation 2.1. The estimations are performed on samples from January 1, 1987, to June 30, 1996. The time intervals are measured in ϑ-time (see Chapter 6).

Rate	30 min	1 hr	2 hr	6 hr	1 day
USD-DEM	3.18 ±0.42	3.24 ±0.57	3.57 ±0.90	4.19 ±1.82	5.70 ±4.39
USD-JPY	3.19 ±0.48	3.65 ±0.79	3.80 ±1.08	4.40 ±2.13	4.42 ±2.98
GBP-USD	3.58 ±0.53	3.55 ±0.65	3.72 ±1.00	4.58 ±2.34	5.23 ±3.77
USD-CHF	3.46 ±0.49	3.67 ±0.77	3.70 ±1.09	4.13 ±1.77	5.65 ±4.21
USD-FRF	3.43 ±0.52	3.67 ±0.84	3.54 ±0.97	4.27 ±1.94	5.60 ±4.25
USD-ITL	3.36 ±0.45	3.08 ±0.49	3.27 ±0.79	3.57 ±1.35	4.18 ±2.44
USD-NLG	3.55 ±0.57	3.43 ±0.62	3.36 ±0.92	4.34 ±1.95	6.29 ±4.96
DEM-JPY	3.84 ±0.59	3.69 ±0.87	4.28 ±1.49	4.15 ±2.20	5.33 ±3.74
GBP-DEM	3.33 ±0.46	3.67 ±0.70	3.76 ±1.17	3.73 ±1.59	3.66 ±1.70
GBP-JPY	3.59 ±0.63	3.44 ±0.70	4.15 ±1.32	4.35 ±2.27	5.44 ±4.12
DEM-CHF	3.54 ±0.54	3.28 ±0.54	3.44 ±0.82	4.29 ±1.84	4.21 ±2.43
GBP-FRF	3.19 ±0.46	3.33 ±0.62	3.37 ±0.90	3.41 ±1.27	3.34 ±1.65
XAU-USD	4.47 ±1.15	3.96 ±1.13	4.36 ±1.82	4.13 ±2.22	4.40 ±2.98
XAG-USD	5.37 ±1.55	4.73 ±1.93	3.70 ±1.52	3.45 ±1.35	3.46 ±1.97

sample is modified in 10 different ways, each time removing one-tenth of the total sample. The tail index is separately computed for each of the 10 modified samples. An analysis of the deviations between the 10 results yields an estimate of the standard error, which is realistic because it is based on the data rather than restrictive theoretical assumptions. The methodology is explained by Pictet *et al.* (1998).

All the FX rates against the USD as well as the presented cross rates have a tail index between 3.1 and 3.9 (roughly around 3.5). These values are found in the 30-min column of Table 5.3. The other columns are affected by lower numbers of observations and thus wider confidence ranges. The chosen cross rates are computed from USD rates according to Equation 2.1. None of them was part of the European Monetary System (EMS), except GBP-DEM for a period much shorter than the analyzed sample. Gold (XAU-USD) and silver (XAG-USD) have higher tail index values above 4. These markets differ from FX. Their volatilities were very high in the 1980s, followed by a much calmer behavior in the 1990s, a structural change that may have affected the tail statistics.

TABLE 5.4   Estimated tail indices of cross rates.

Estimated tail index values and their 95% confidence ranges, for cross FX rates. The tail index values are based on the subsample bootstrap method using the Hill estimator, and the confidence ranges result from the jackknife method. All the cross rates of the lower part were subject to the regulations of the European Monetary System (EMS). The computed cross rates are obtained via the two bilateral rates against the USD (see Equation 2.1). The estimations are performed on samples from January 1988 to June 1994 ($6\frac{1}{2}$ years). The time intervals are measured in ϑ-time (see Chapter 6).

Rate	30 min	1 hr	2 hr	6 hr
DEM-JPY	4.17 ±1.13	4.22 ±1.48	5.06 ±1.40	4.73 ±2.19
GBP-DEM	3.63 ±0.46	4.09 ±1.98	4.78 ±1.60	3.22 ±0.72
GBP-JPY	3.93 ±1.16	4.48 ±1.20	4.67 ±1.94	5.60 ±2.56
DEM-CHF	3.76 ±0.79	3.64 ±0.71	4.02 ±1.52	6.02 ±2.91
GBP-FRF	3.30 ±0.41	3.42 ±0.97	3.80 ±1.34	3.48 ±1.75
FRF-DEM	2.56 ±0.34	2.41 ±0.14	2.36 ±0.27	3.66 ±1.17
DEM-ITL	2.93 ±1.01	2.60 ±0.66	3.17 ±1.28	2.76 ±1.49
DEM-NLG	2.45 ±0.20	2.19 ±0.13	3.14 ±0.95	3.24 ±0.87
FRF-ITL	2.89 ±0.34	2.73 ±0.49	2.56 ±0.41	2.34 ±0.66

In Section 5.3.1, we have seen that cross rates behaved differently when both exchanged currencies were members of the EMS in the 1990s. A difference is also found when considering the tail behavior, as shown in Table 5.4. The sample was chosen accordingly, during the lifetime of the EMS. The upper block of Table 5.4 has non-EMS cross rates for comparison, the lower block has EMS cross rates. The 1-day column is missing in Table 5.4 as the sample size is smaller than that of Table 5.3. The tail index values of EMS cross rates are around 2.7, distinctly lower than the typical value of 3.5 found for other cross rates in the upper part of Table 5.4 and other FX rates in Table 5.3. The 30-min columns of both tables should mainly be considered, but the values of the other columns confirm the same fact that EMS cross rates have fatter tails.

The cross rates are computed from USD rates according to Equation 2.1. As compared to direct quotes, these computed cross rates have larger spreads and an artificially generated volatility (i.e., noise due to the price uncertainty within the spread and asynchronous fluctuations of the used USD rates). Therefore we have also analyzed direct cross rate quotes in the limited sample (since October 1992) where they are available. These direct quotes have less short-term noise and lead to slightly but systematically lower tail index values than those of computed cross rates. The small tail index of EMS cross rates indicates that the reduced volatility induced by the EMS setup is at the cost of a larger probability of extreme events, which may lead to realignments of the system. This is an argument against the credibility of institutional setups such as the EMS.

Like the drift exponent as a function of time, the tail index reflects the institutional setup and, in a further interpretation, the way different agents on the markets interact. The tail index can therefore be considered as another empirical measure of market regulation and market efficiency. A large tail index indicates free interactions between agents with different time horizons, with a low degree of regulation and thus a smooth adjustment to external shocks. A small tail index indicates the opposite.

With very few exceptions, the estimated tail indices are between 2 and 4. A few confidence ranges extend to values outside this range, but this is due to the limited number of observations mainly for the longer return measurement intervals. Using Equation 5.2, we conclude that the second moment of the return distribution is finite and the fourth moment usually diverges. In Section 5.6.1, this fact leads us to preferring the autocorrelation of absolute returns to that of squared returns, which relies on the finiteness of the fourth moment.

Tables 5.3 and 5.4 indicate that the distribution of FX returns belongs to the class of fat-tailed nonstable distributions that have a finite tail index larger than 2. Furthermore, the very high values of the kurtosis in Tables 5.1 and 5.2 and the growth of these values with increasing sample size provide additional evidence in favor of this hypothesis.[12] From Tables 5.3 and 5.4, one can also verify the invariance of the tail index under aggregation, except for the longest intervals, where the small number of observations becomes a problem in getting significant estimates of α. The smaller number of data for large intervals forces the estimation algorithm to use a larger fraction of this data, closer to the center of the distribution. Thus the empirically measured tail properties become distorted by properties of the center of the distribution, which, for $\alpha > 2$ and under aggregation, approaches the normal distribution (with $\alpha = \infty$) as a consequence of the central limit theorem.

In Table 5.5, we present the results of α estimations of interbank money market cash interest rates for five different currencies and two maturities. Although generally exhibiting lower α's, the results are close to those of the FX rates. The message seems to be the same: fat tails, finite second moment,[13] and nonconverging fourth moment. . We also find a relative stability of the tail index with time aggregation. The estimations for daily returns give more consistent values than in the case of the FX rates. Yet the estimations are more noisy as one would expect from data of lower frequency, and this is reflected in the high errors displayed in Table 5.5. The tail index estimation is quite consistent but can significantly jump from one time interval to the next as is the case for GBP and CHF 6 months. This market is much less liquid than the FX market. Interest rate markets with higher liquidity can be studied in terms of interest rate derivatives, which are traded in

---

[12] Simulations in Gielens *et al.* (1996) and McCulloch (1997) show that one cannot univocally distinguish between a fat-tailed nonstable and a thin-tailed distribution only on the basis of low estimated values of the tail index. However, the confidence intervals around the estimated tail index values and the diverging behavior of the kurtosis are strong evidence in favor of the fat-tail hypothesis.

[13] In most of the cases, except perhaps the 6-month interest rate for JPY, α is significantly larger than 2. In the JPY case, if the first 2 years are removed, we get back to values for α around 3.

TABLE 5.5   Estimated tail index for cash interest rates.
Estimated tail index values of cash interest rates and their 95% confidence ranges, for five different currencies and two maturities. The tail index values are based on the subsample bootstrap method using the Hill estimator, and the confidence ranges result from the jackknife method. The time intervals are measured in ϑ-time (see Chapter 6). The estimations are performed on samples going from January 2, 1979, to June 30, 1996; "m" refers to a month.

Currency	Maturity	1 day	1 week	Maturity	1 day	1 week
USD	3m	4.03 ±2.99	3.53 ±3.46	6m	4.10 ±2.84	3.50 ±3.07
DEM	3m	2.54 ±0.73	2.88 ±1.63	6m	2.39 ±0.76	2.62 ±1.82
JPY	3m	3.16 ±2.07	3.43 ±3.01	6m	2.03 ±0.85	3.60 ±3.53
GBP	3m	2.61 ±0.84	3.86 ±3.78	6m	4.04 ±2.64	6.65 ±7.53
CHF	3m	3.69 ±2.41	5.24 ±5.13	6m	3.02 ±1.26	7.46 ±7.31

futures markets such as London International Financial Futures Exchange (LIFFE) in London or Singapore International Monetary Exchange (SIMEX) in Singapore.

To study the stability of the tail index under aggregation, we observe how the estimates change with varying sample size. We do not know any theoretical tail index for empirical data, but we compare the estimates with the estimation done on the "best" sample we have, 30-min returns from January 1987 to June 1996. To study the tail index of daily returns, we use an extended sample of daily data from July 1, 1978, to June 30, 1996. The small-sample bias can be studied by comparing the results to the averages of the results from two smaller samples: one from June 1, 1978, to June 30, 1987, and another one from July 1, 1987, to June 30, 1996. These two short samples together cover the same period as the large sample. The results are given in Table 5.6.[14] When going from the short samples to the long 18-year sample, we see a general decrease of the estimated α toward the values reached for 30-min returns. The small-sample bias is thus reduced, but probably not completely eliminated. We conclude that, at least for the FX rates against the USD, the α estimates from daily data are not accurate enough even if the sample covers up to 18 years. The case of gold and silver is different because the huge fluctuations of the early 1980s have disappeared since then. The picture in this case is blurred by the changing market conditions.

A similar analysis of 30-min returns reinforces the obtained conclusions. In this case, the two shorter samples are from July 1, 1988, to June 30, 1992, and from July 1, 1992, to June 30, 1996. The large sample is again the union of the two shorter samples. A certain small-sample bias is found also for the 30-min returns of most rates comparing the two last columns of Table 5.3, but this bias is rather small. This is an expected result because the number of 30-min observations is much larger than that of the daily observations.

---

[14] For the short samples we do not give the errors because we present only the average of both samples. The errors are larger for the short samples than for the long sample.

TABLE 5.6   Estimated tail index for different samples sizes.

Estimated tail index for the main FX rates, gold (XAU) and silver (XAG) on different samples for both daily and 30-min returns. The time intervals are measured in ϑ-time (see Chapter 6).

| FX rates | Daily returns | | 30-min returns | |
	Short samples	7/1978–6/1996	7/1988–6/1996	Short samples
USD-DEM	4.84	4.34 ±2.46	3.27 ±0.50	3.29
USD-JPY	7.81	5.69 ±3.94	3.86 ±0.71	3.94
GBP-USD	4.79	4.35 ±3.02	3.37 ±0.53	3.57
USD-CHF	5.24	4.15 ±2.71	3.63 ±0.55	3.61
USD-FRF	4.48	4.37 ±2.85	3.52 ±0.54	3.59
USD-ITL	3.82	3.97 ±1.94	3.38 ±0.44	3.56
USD-NLG	4.17	4.05 ±1.98	3.56 ±0.66	3.57
XAU-USD	3.65	3.88 ±2.53	4.24 ±0.99	4.00
XAG-USD	3.94	3.40 ±1.92	4.12 ±0.75	3.54

5.4.3   Extreme Risks in Financial Markets

From the practitioners' point of view, one of the most interesting questions that tail studies can answer is what are the extreme movements that can be expected in financial markets? Have we already seen the largest ones or are we going to experience even larger movements? Are there theoretical processes that can model the type of fat tails that come out of our empirical analysis? The answers to such questions are essential for good risk management of financial exposures. It turns out that we can partially answer them here. Once we know the tail index, we can apply extreme value theory *outside* our sample to consider possible extreme movements *that have not yet been observed historically.* This can be achieved by a computation of the quantiles with exceedance probabilities.[15]   Although this chapter focuses on stylized facts, it is interesting to show an example of the application of some of these empirical studies, which is very topical to risk management. There is a debate going on to design the best hedging strategy against extreme risks. Some researchers suggest using a dynamic method by utilizing conditional distributions (McNeil and Frey, 2000). We think that for practical purposes the hedge against extreme risk must be decided on the basis of the *unconditional* distribution. For a large portfolio, it would be impossible to find counterparties to hedge in very turbulent states of the market. Like in the case of earthquakes, hedging this type of risk needs to be planned far in advance.

Let us consider the expansion of the asymptotic cumulative distribution function from which the X_i observations are drawn as

$$F(x) = 1 - a x^{-\alpha} \left[1 + b x^{-\beta} \right] \qquad (5.5)$$

---

[15] We follow here the approach developed in Dacorogna *et al.* (2001a).

We denote by x_p and x_t quantiles with respective exceedance probabilities p and t. Let n be the sample size and choose $p < 1/n < t$; that is, x_t is inside the sample, while x_p is not observed. By definition (we concentrate on the positive tail),

$$p = ax_p^{-\alpha}\left[1 + bx_p^{-\beta}\right], \quad t = ax_t^{-\alpha}\left[1 + bx_t^{-\beta}\right] \qquad (5.6)$$

Division of the two exceedance probabilities and rearrangement yields

$$x_p = x_t\left(\frac{t}{p}\right)^{1/\alpha} \left(\frac{1 + bx_p^{-\beta}}{1 + bx_t^{-\beta}}\right)^{1/\alpha} \qquad (5.7)$$

Given that t is inside the sample, we can replace t by its empirical counterpart m/n, say; that is, m equals the number of order statistics X_i, which are greater than X_t. An estimator for x_p is then as follows

$$\hat{x}_p = X_m\left(\frac{m}{np}\right)^{\hat{\gamma}} \qquad (5.8)$$

where m equals the $\hat{m}$ obtained from the tail estimation corresponding to $\hat{\gamma}$. To write this estimator we ignore the last factor on the right-hand side of Equation 5.7. This would be entirely justified in the case of the Pareto law when $b = 0$. Thus $\hat{x}_p$ is based on the same philosophy as the Hill estimator. For an m sufficiently small relative to n, the tails of Equation 5.5 are well approximated by those of the Pareto law, and hence Equation 5.8 is expected to do well. In fact, it is possible to prove (de Haan *et al.*, 1994) that, for the law in Equation 5.5

$$\frac{\sqrt{m}}{\ln\frac{m/n}{p}}\left(\frac{\hat{x}_p}{x_p} - 1\right) \qquad (5.9)$$

has the same limiting normal distribution as the Hill estimator. Equation 5.9 gives us a way to estimate the error of our quantile computation.

Table 5.7 shows the result of a study of extreme risk using Equation 5.8 to estimate the quantiles for returns over 6 hr. This time interval is somewhat shorter than an overnight position (in ϑ-time) but is a compromise between the accuracy of the tail estimation and the length of the interval needed by risk managers. The first part of the table is produced by Monte Carlo simulations of synthetic data where the process was first fitted to the 30-min returns of the USD-DEM time series. The second part is the quantile estimation of the FX rates as a function of the probability of the event happening once every year, once every 5 years, and so on. Because we use here a sample of 9 years, the first two columns represent values that have been actually seen in the data set, whereas the other columns are extrapolations based on the empirically estimated tail behavior. Although the probabilities we use here seem very small, some of the extreme risks shown in Table 5.7 may be experienced by traders during their active life.

TABLE 5.7 Extreme risks in the FX market.

Extreme risks over 6 hr for model distributions produced by Monte-Carlo simulations of *synthetic* time series fitted to USD-DEM, compared to empirical FX data studied through a tail estimation.

| | Probabilities (p) | | | | | |
	1/1 year	1/5 year	1/10 year	1/15 year	1/20 year	1/25 year
Models:						
Normal	0.4%	0.5%	0.6%	0.6%	0.7%	0.7%
Student 3	0.5%	0.8%	1.0%	1.1%	1.2%	1.2%
GARCH(1,1)	1.5%	2.1%	2.4%	2.6%	2.7%	2.9%
HARCH	1.8%	2.9%	3.5%	4.0%	4.3%	4.6%
USD rates:						
USD-DEM	1.7%	2.5%	3.0%	3.3%	3.5%	3.7%
USD-JPY	1.7%	2.4%	2.9%	3.2%	3.4%	3.6%
GBP-USD	1.6%	2.3%	2.6%	2.9%	3.1%	3.2%
USD-CHF	1.8%	2.7%	3.1%	3.5%	3.7%	4.0%
USD-FRF	1.6%	2.3%	2.8%	3.0%	3.3%	3.4%
USD-ITL	1.8%	2.8%	3.4%	3.8%	4.1%	4.4%
USD-NLG	1.7%	2.5%	2.9%	3.2%	3.4%	3.6%
Cross rates:						
DEM-JPY	1.3%	1.9%	2.2%	2.5%	2.6%	2.8%
GBP-DEM	1.1%	1.7%	2.1%	2.3%	2.5%	2.6%
GBP-JPY	1.6%	2.3%	2.7%	3.0%	3.2%	3.4%
DEM-CHF	0.7%	1.0%	1.2%	1.3%	1.4%	1.5%
GBP-FRF	1.1%	1.8%	2.2%	2.5%	2.7%	2.9%

An interesting piece of information displayed in Table 5.7 is the comparison of empirical results and results obtained from theoretical models.[16] The model's parameters, including the variance of the normal and Student-t distributions, result from fitting USD-DEM 30-min returns. For the GARCH (1,1) model (Bollerslev, 1986), the standard maximum likelihood fitting procedure is used (Guillaume *et al.*, 1994) and the GARCH equation is used to generate synthetic time series. The same procedure is used for the HARCH model (Müller *et al.*, 1997a). The model's results are computed using the average $\hat{m}$ and $\hat{\gamma}$ obtained by estimating the tail index of 10 sets of synthetic data for each of the models for the aggregated time series over 6 hr. As expected, the normal distribution model fares poorly as far as the extreme risks are concerned. Surprisingly, this is also the case for

---

[16] The theoretical processes such as GARCH and HARCH are discussed in detail in Chapter 8. Here they simply serve as examples for extreme risk estimation.

the Student-t distribution with 3 degrees of freedom. The GARCH (1,1) model gives results closer to those of USD-DEM but still underestimates the risks by a significant amount. The HARCH model slightly overestimates the extreme risk. This is probably due to its long memory, which does not allow the process to modify sufficiently its tail behavior under aggregation. Obviously, further studies need to be pursued to assess how well models such as HARCH can predict extreme risks. In general, ARCH-type processes seem to capture the tail behavior of FX rates better than the simple unconditional distribution models. The advantage of having a model for the process equation is that it allows the use of a dynamic definition of the movements and it can hopefully provide an early warning in case of turbulent situations.

Paradoxically, in situations represented by the center of the distribution (nonextreme quantiles), the usual Gaussian-based models would overestimate the risk. Our study is valid for the tails of the distribution, but it is known that far from the tails the normal distribution produces higher quantiles than actually seen in the data.

5.5 SCALING LAWS

In this section, we examine the behavior of the absolute size of returns as a function of the frequency at which they are measured. As already mentioned, there is no privileged time interval at which the data and the generating process should be investigated. Thus it is important to study how the different measures relate to each other. One way of doing this is to analyze the dependence of mean volatility on the time interval on which the returns are measured. For usual stochastic processes such as the random walk, this dependence gives rise to very simple scaling laws (Section 5.5.2). Since Müller et al. (1990) have empirically documented the existence of scaling laws in FX rates, there has been a large volume of work confirming these empirical findings, including Schnidrig and Würtz (1995); Fisher et al. (1997); Andersen et al. (2000) and Mantegna and Stanley (2000). This evidence is confirmed for other financial instruments,[17] as reported by Mantegna and Stanley (1995) and Ballocchi et al. (1999b). The examination of the theoretical foundations of scaling laws are studied in Groenendijk et al. (1996); LeBaron (1999b), and Barndorff-Nielsen and Prause (1999).

Before discussing the literature, we present the empirical findings.

5.5.1 Empirical Evidence

The scaling law is empirically found for a wide range of financial data and time intervals in good approximation. It gives a direct relation between time intervals

---

[17] Brock (1999) has extensive discussions of scaling in economics and finance. He points out that most of these regularities are unconditional objects and may have little power to discriminate between a broad class of stochastic processes. Brock (1999) points out that the main object of interest in economics and finance is the conditional predictive distribution as in Gallant et al. (1993). Scaling laws may help in restricting the acceptable classes of conditional predictive distributions.

Δt and the average volatility measured as a certain power p of the absolute returns observed over these intervals,

$$\left\{E[|r|^{p}]\right\}^{1/p} \;=\; c(p)\,\Delta t^{D(p)} \tag{5.10}$$

where E is the expectation operator, and $c(p)$ and $D(p)$ are deterministic functions of p. We call D the drift exponent, which is similar to the characterization of Mandelbrot (1983, 1997). We choose this form for the left part of the equation in order to obtain, for a Gaussian random walk, a constant drift exponent of 0.5 whatever the choice of p. A typical choice is $p = 1$, which corresponds to absolute returns.

Taking the logarithm of Equation 5.10, the estimation of c and D can be carried out by an ordinary least squares regression. Linear regression is, in this case, an approximation. Strictly speaking, it should not be used because the $E[|r|]$ values for *different* intervals Δt are not totally independent. The longer intervals are aggregates of shorter intervals. Consequently, the regression is applied here to slightly dependent observations. This approximation is acceptable because the factor between two neighboring Δt is at least 2 (sometimes more to get even values in minutes, hours, days, weeks, and mean months), and the total span of analyzed intervals is large: from 10 min to 2 months. In addition, we shall see in Chapters 7 and 8 that volatility measured at different frequencies carries asymmetric information. Thus we choose the standard regression technique,[18] as Friedmann and Vandersteel (1982) and others do. The error terms used for $E[|r|]$ take into account the approximate basic errors of our prices[19] and the number of independent observations for each Δt.

The results presented here are computed for the cases $p = 1$ and $p = 2$. It is also interesting to compute instead of $\{E[|r|^{p}]\}^{1/p}$ the interquartile range as a function of Δt. Such a measure does not include the tails of the distribution. Recently, the development of the multifractal model (Fisher *et al.*, 1997) has brought researchers to study a whole spectrum of (also noninteger) values for the exponent p. In the same line of thought, multicascade models (Frisch, 1995) are also multifractals and involve different drift exponents for different measures of volatility. This feature is a typical signature of multifractality.

In Figure 5.8, we present empirical scaling laws for USD-JPY and GBP-USD for $p = 1$. Both the intervals Δt and the volatilities $E[|r|]$ are plotted on a logarithmic scale. The sample includes 9 years of tick-by-tick data from January 1, 1987, to December 31, 1995. The empirical scaling law is indeed a power law as indicated by the straight line. It is well respected in a very wide range of time intervals from 10 min to 2 months. The standard errors of the exponents D are less then 1%. The 1-day point in Figure 5.8 can be identified only by the corresponding label, not by any change or break between the intraday and interday behaviors.

---

[18] See Mosteller and Tukey (1977, Chapter 14).

[19] In Section 5.5.3, we give a full treatment of this problem.

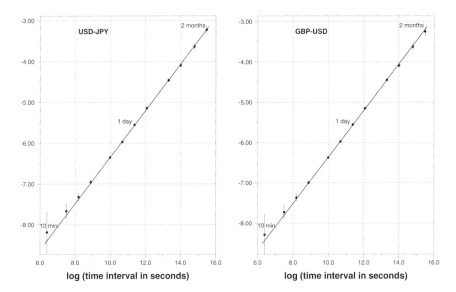

FIGURE 5.8 Scaling law for USD-JPY (right) and GBP-USD (left). On the y-axis, the natural logarithm of the mean absolute return ($p = 1$ in Equation 5.10) is reported. The error bars correspond to the mode described in Section 5.5.3. The sample period is January 1, 1987, to December 31, 1995.

Small deviations for the extreme interval sizes can be explained. The data errors grow on both sides, as discussed in Section 5.5.3. For long intervals, the number of observations in the sample becomes smaller and smaller, leading to a growing stochastic error. For very short intervals, the price uncertainty within the bid-ask spread becomes important. In fact, researchers such as Moody and Wu (1995) studied the scaling law at very high frequencies and obtained different exponents because they did not take into account the problem of price uncertainty. Recently, Fisher *et al.* (1997) also found a break of the scaling law around 2 hr. It is clear on both plots of Figure 5.8 that for time intervals shorter than 1 hour the points start to depart from a straight line. This deviation can be treated in two ways. In a first approach, we treat the price uncertainty as a part of the measurement error, leading to error bars that are as wide as to easily include the observed deviation at short time intervals. In a second approach, the deviation is identified as a bias that can be explained, modeled, and even eliminated by a correction. Both approaches are presented in Section 5.5.3.

In Table 5.8, we report the values of the drift exponent for four of the major FX rates against the USD and for gold for three different measures of volatility. Each of these measures treats extreme events differently. The interquartile range completely ignores them. The measure with $p = 2$ gives more emphasis to the tails than $p = 1$. The scaling law exponents D are around 0.57 for all rates and for $p = 1$, very close to 0.5 for $p = 2$, and around 0.73 for the interquartile range.

TABLE 5.8   Drift exponents for FX rates.

Drift exponents with standard errors found for the USD against DEM, JPY, CHF, and GBP and XAU against USD for two different powers and for the interquartile range. The sampling period extends from January 1, 1987, to December 31, 1995.

Currency	$E[|r|]$	$\left\{E[|r|^2]\right\}^{1/2}$	Interquartile
DEM	0.575 ± 0.006	0.501 ± 0.003	0.725 ± 0.017
JPY	0.570 ± 0.005	0.480 ± 0.035	0.691 ± 0.012
GBP	0.578 ± 0.004	0.514 ± 0.003	0.718 ± 0.011
CHF	0.574 ± 0.005	0.500 ± 0.002	0.737 ± 0.015
XAU	0.576 ± 0.005	0.491 ± 0.002	0.754 ± 0.012

These numbers are somewhat lower than those published by Müller *et al.* (1990), but this earlier study only covered 3 years of data. It seems that over the years the drift exponent for $p = 1$ has slightly decreased from typically 0.59 to 0.57.

The lower the weight of tails in the statistics, the more the empirically determined drift exponent deviates from the Gaussian random walk value of 0.5. This behavior is a consequence of the changing form of the distribution under aggregation and can also be seen as a sign of multifractality, as mentioned earlier. We repeated our analysis with only studying either negative returns or positive ones. The results show no significant asymmetry of positive and negative changes in accordance to the studies of Section 5.4.1. All results indicate a very general scaling law that applies to different currencies as well as to commodities such as gold and silver (which was additionally tested with a smaller sample). This *phenomenological* law becomes more important as the return distributions are unstable and the scaling law cannot be explained as a trivial consequence of a stable random process. This point will be discussed further in Section 5.5.2. Besides the evidence presented in Section 5.4, we find further evidence here for an unstable distribution because the drift exponent changes for the different measures of volatility. We find lower exponents $D \approx 0.5$ for $\left\{E[|r|^2]\right\}^{1/2}$ and higher exponents $D \approx 0.7$ for the interquartile ranges, and these can only be explained by varying distribution forms for different time intervals.

Similar scaling laws have been found by Ballocchi *et al.* (1999b) in a study of Eurofutures contracts[20] on the London International Financial Futures Exchange (LIFFE) and the Chicago Mercantile Exchane (CME) and in stock indices by Mantegna and Stanley (2000). We report here the results for the drift exponent for $p = 1$ for various contracts in Table 5.9. Here again the scaling law displays a drift exponent significantly larger than that expected for a Gaussian random walk and very close to the values obtained for foreign exchange rates. The table

---

[20] For a full description of these data and how they are treated for such a study, see Section 2.4.

TABLE 5.9   Drift exponents for Eurofutures.

Drift exponents with standard errors found for Eurofutures contracts. The drift exponent is for $E[|r|]$ ($p = 1$). All values are significantly larger than 0.5.

Expiry	Eurodollar	Euromark	Sterling
March 1995	0.60 ± 0.02	0.60 ± 0.01	0.61 ± 0.02
June 1995	0.66 ± 0.02	0.65 ± 0.01	0.62 ± 0.02
September 1995	0.68 ± 0.02	0.66 ± 0.01	0.62 ± 0.02
December 1995	0.64 ± 0.02	0.66 ± 0.01	0.64 ± 0.02
March 1996	0.57 ± 0.03	0.66 ± 0.01	0.63 ± 0.02
June 1996	0.70 ± 0.01	0.62 ± 0.01	0.62 ± 0.02
September 1996	0.70 ± 0.01	0.65 ± 0.01	0.62 ± 0.01
December 1996	0.69 ± 0.01	0.63 ± 0.02	0.60 ± 0.02
March 1997	0.66 ± 0.02	0.62 ± 0.02	0.63 ± 0.02

presents quite a dispersion of the exponents because the sample for each contract is relatively short. As a second step, we have repeated the scaling law analysis on an average of contracts. We averaged the mean absolute values of the returns (associated with each time interval) on the number of contracts. When the analysis referred to single Eurofutures, the average was computed on 9 contracts; when it referred to all Eurofutures and all contracts together, the average was computed on 36 contracts. Then we performed a linear regression for the logarithm of the computed averages against the corresponding logarithm of time intervals, taking the following time intervals: 1 day, 2 days, 1 week, 2 weeks, 4 weeks, 8 weeks, and half a year. The resulting drift exponent is 0.599 ± 0.007, remarkably close to the FX results. Ballocchi (1996) performed such studies for interbank short-term cash rates and computed the drift exponent of the mean absolute return averaged over 72 rates (12 currencies and 6 maturities from 1 month to 1 year), and the result is again 0.569 ± 0.007, close to the numbers listed in Table 5.8. To summarize, we find drift exponents of the mean absolute return of around 0.57 for FX rates and for cash interest rates, and 0.6 for Eurofutures.

5.5.2   Distributions and Scaling Laws

In this section we discuss how the distributions relate to the scaling law. There are remarkably few theoretical results on the relation between the drift exponents and the distribution aside from the trivial result for Gaussian distributions where all the exponents are 0.5. We only know of two recent papers that deal with this problem, Groenendijk *et al.* (1996) and Barndorff-Nielsen and Prause (1999). The latter gives $E[|r|]$ as a function of the aggregation and the parameters of the Normal Inverse Gaussian (NIG) Lévy process. The data generated from this process do not exhibit a scaling behavior, but the relationship is very close to a straight line when expressed in a double-logarithmic scale. The authors show that, with a particular choice of parameters, they can reproduce what they call the "apparent scaling" behavior of the USD-DEM data. There are other processes that present "apparent scaling" behavior. An example of such a process is given by LeBaron (1999a). In the literature, most scaling law results are of an empirical nature and are stylized facts directly obtained from the actual data. These results do not assume any particular data-generating process. Therefore, formal statistical tests are needed to test whether the empirically observed scaling laws are consistent with a particular type of null distribution. Although the findings of these statistical tests would not change the presence of empirical scaling laws, they would provide guidance for modeling return and volatility dynamics with those distributions consistent with the observed data dynamics.

We shall use here the approach of Groenendijk *et al.* (1996) to present a theorem they prove, which gives a good understanding of the relation between the drift exponent and other distributional properties for i.i.d. distributions. If we assume a simple random walk model

$$x(t) = x(t - \Delta t) + \varepsilon(t) \tag{5.11}$$

where x is the usual logarithmic price and the innovations $\varepsilon(t)$ are i.i.d., then the n-period return $r[n\Delta t](t)$ has the form

$$r[n\Delta t](t) = x(t) - x(t - n\Delta t) = \sum_{i=0}^{n-1} \varepsilon(t - i\Delta t) \tag{5.12}$$

where we have used Equation 5.11. In particular, if the ε_i's follow a normal distribution with mean zero and variance σ^2, the variance of $r[n\Delta t](t)$ is equal to $n\sigma^2$.

Groenendijk *et al.* (1996) consider the following quantity:

$$\ln\left(E\left[|r(n\Delta t)|^p\right]\right) - \ln\left(E\left[|r(\Delta t)|^p\right]\right) \tag{5.13}$$

where Δt is the smallest time interval and $\{r(n\Delta t)\}$ is the sequence of returns aggregated n-times. This quantity is directly related to the left-hand term of the scaling law shown in Equation 5.10.

The theorem they prove is related to the notion of stable distributions. Let us briefly state what this notion means. This class of distributions has the following attractive property. Let $\{a_n\}_{n=1}^{\infty}$ denote a sequence of increasing numbers such that $a_n^{-1} \sum_{i=1}^{n} \varepsilon_i$ has a nondegenerate limiting distribution, then this limiting distribution must belong to the class of stable distributions (Ibragimov and Linnik, 1971, p. 37). Ibragimov and Linnik (1971) show that the numbers a_n, which satisfy this requirement, are of the form $a_n = n^{1/\alpha} s(n)$, where $s(n)$ is a slowly varying function, that is,

$$\lim_{n \to \infty} \frac{s(tn)}{s(n)} = 1$$

with $t > 0$. Therefore, as $r(n \Delta t)$ is of the form $\sum_{i=1}^{n} \varepsilon_i$, we can expect $r_t(n \Delta t)$ to be of the order a_n (i.e., of the order $n^{1/\alpha}$), for large values of n. As a result, the dominating term in Equation 5.13 will be $p \ln(n)/\alpha$, such that the relationship between Equation 5.13 and $\ln(n)$ will be linear with slope p/α for all distributions that satisfy a generalized central limit law.

Theorem: *Let $\{\varepsilon_t\}_{t=1}^{\infty}$ denote a sequence of i.i.d. random variables with common distribution $F(.)$. Let $F(.)$ belong to the domain of attraction of a stable law with index α. Let p be such that $0 \le p < \alpha$ for $\alpha < 2$ and $0 \le p \le 2$ for $\alpha = 2$. Then*

$$\lim_{n \to \infty} \frac{\ln(E[|r(n \Delta t)|^p]) - \ln(E[|r(\Delta t)|^p])}{\ln(n)} = \frac{p}{\alpha} \tag{5.14}$$

Let us now consider the case $p = 2$. Following the theorem, the class of distributions of $\varepsilon(t)$ must now be restricted to the distribution with finite variance. Using the independence assumption, we can easily obtain the following result:

$$E[|r(n \Delta t)|^2] = E\left[\left|\sum_{i=0}^{n-1} \varepsilon(t - i \Delta t)\right|^2\right] = \sum_{i=0}^{n-1} E[\varepsilon^2(t - i \Delta t)] = n\sigma^2 \tag{5.15}$$

Consequently, the numerator in Equation 5.14 reduces to $\ln(n)$ and the fraction to 1. This is in accordance with the theorem, as it follows from the standard limit theory that distributions with finite variance lie in the domain of attraction of the normal distribution, which has an $\alpha = 2$, which, in this particular case, should not be confused with the tail index α of Section 5.4.2. In our study of tail indices, the conclusion was that the second moment of the distribution was finite (our tail indices were all largely above 2). Also, the results lead to a value of 0.5 (Table 5.8), which is the value one should theoretically obtain for $p = 2$ (as we were studying the square root of the second moment). There is, though, a difference between our empirical results and this theoretical result for $p = 1$ and for the interquartile range. There are at least three explanations for this. The first is that the distribution $F(.)$ of the random variable is not really common, which can be caused by heteroskedasticity. The second explanation is that the theorem is an asymptotic result and we might not have converged with our data to the limit. The third explanation is related to the i.i.d. assumption for the innovations under which the theoretical result is obtained. A drift exponent for $E[|r|]$, which is different from 0.5, could be an indication that there is a certain dependence between consecutive prices. We have already seen some of these dependencies for the very short-term (negative autocorrelation of returns) and we shall see some more in this and in the next chapter.

5.5.3 A Simple Model of the Market Maker Bias

In Section 5.5.1, we reported the findings published in Müller *et al.* (1990) about the scaling law of volatility measures. The parameters of this law seem very stable (see Guillaume *et al.*, 1997) but depend on the way the statistical quantities are computed and on the errors that enter the evaluation through the least square fit of the scaling law parameters. In Müller *et al.* (1990), we briefly mention the problem but in order to help people reproduce our results, we give here the full derivation of the error, which consists of a stochastic component and a market maker bias.

When making statistical studies of returns, researchers only consider the usual statistical error due to the limited number of observations. This error is clearly dominant when the return is measured over time intervals of a day or more. When the time interval is reduced to a few minutes, however, the *uncertainty* of the price definition due to the spread must be also considered. The market makers are biased toward one of the two prices, either the bid or the ask, thus introducing a bouncing effect that reflects in a negative autocorrelation of the returns in the very short-term (see Section 5.2.1, Goodhart and Figliuoli, 1991; Guillaume *et al.*, 1997). The true market price is between the bid and the ask quotes but not necessarily in their exact midpoint.[21] This uncertainty can be assessed to a considerable fraction of the nominal bid-ask spread. For short horizons, the amplitudes of price movements become comparable to the size of the spread. If spreads are large (especially minor FX rates), the uncertainty implies an important measurement error. For bid-ask data from electronic exchanges and transaction price data, the measurement error due to uncertainty is smaller or even negligible.

The purpose of this section is to derive the error on the statistical quantity entering the scaling law computation when the measurement error is also taken into account. We derived this model independently (Müller *et al.*, 1995) but it turns out that it is very similar to the model developed by Roll (1984) for equity prices.

We rely here on the definitions provided in Chapter 3 for the quantities we are going to use. The scaling law (see Equation 5.10) is empirically computed by fitting its logarithmic form,

$$\log(\overline{|\Delta x|}) \;=\; D \log \Delta t \;+\; \log c \tag{5.16}$$

The law becomes linear in this form. For the linear regression, we need to know the errors of $\log \overline{|\Delta x|}$. We saw that there is a similar scaling law for $(\langle |r|^2 \rangle)^{1/2}$:

$$\frac{1}{2} \log \left(\langle |r|^2 \rangle \right) \;=\; D' \log \Delta t \;+\; \log c' \tag{5.17}$$

The problem is to find the error on $\overline{|\Delta x|}$ knowing that we have an uncertainty related to the price definition and to the spread. Expressions with absolute values

---

[21] For a discussion of this point, see Müller *et al.* (1990); Bollerslev and Domowitz (1993); Goodhart and Payne (1996).

such as $\overline{|\Delta x|}$ are known for their poor analytical tractability. Therefore, the whole error computation is done for the analogous case of $(\langle |r|^2 \rangle)^{1/2}$. Following the arguments given in the introduction, let us assume that x_i^* is the series of true logarithmic market prices whereas the observed middle values x_i as defined by Equation 3.6 are subject to an additional market maker bias ε_i:

$$x_i = x_i^* + \varepsilon_i \tag{5.18}$$

The true return is defined analogous to Equation 3.7:

$$r_i^* \equiv r^*(t_i) \equiv x_i^* - x_{i-1}^* \tag{5.19}$$

Its relation to the observed return follows from Equations 3.7 and 5.18,

$$r_i = r_i^* + \varepsilon_i - \varepsilon_{i-1} \tag{5.20}$$

To compute the error, a minimum knowledge on the distribution of the stochastic quantities is required. We know that the returns r_i and r_i^* follow a Gaussian distribution only as a crude approximation (see Section 5.4), and the market maker bias ε_i might also be nonnormally distributed. Nevertheless, we shall assume Gaussian distributions (the same assumption is used in Roll, 1984) as approximations to make the problem analytically tractable:

$$r_i^* \in \mathcal{N}\left(0, \varrho^{*2}\right) \tag{5.21}$$

and

$$\varepsilon_i \in \mathcal{N}\left(0, \frac{\eta^2}{2}\right) \tag{5.22}$$

where $\mathcal{N}(\mu, \sigma^2)$ is the Gaussian probability distribution with mean μ and variance σ^2. The maximum deviation of the market maker bias is the distance between the middle price and the bid price (or ask price), that is half the spread. As a coarse approximation, we assume that the standard deviation is half that value, that is one-fourth of the typical value of the relative spread (Equation 3.12). This means that η^2 is assumed to be one-eighth of the squared relative spread.[22] Studies with transaction prices have shown that the "true" spread is very different from the quoted spread (see Section 5.2.2). This quantity is a kind of convention; the market maker is really interested in one of the bid or ask prices and adds or subtracts a canonical value to the price she or he wants to use. In normal market conditions, the price is settled with an equal distribution of buyers and sellers (same assumption as in Roll, 1984). Thus, in a first approximation, the two random variables, the true returns and the market maker bias as it appears in quoted prices can well be assumed to be independent. The choice of the market maker bias is somewhat

---

[22] We neglect spread changes.

arbitrary and depends on the model used. In the context of an efficient market with no arrival of information, Roll (1984) has assumed a similar bias.

Now, we are ready to compute the expectation of r_i^2 from Equation 5.20, using Equations 5.21 and 5.22 and the independence of r_i^* and ε_i,

$$\varrho^2 \equiv \mathrm{E}\left(r_i^2\right) = \mathrm{E}\left(\langle r^2 \rangle\right) = \varrho^{*2} + \eta^2 \tag{5.23}$$

The squared observed returns are thus biased by the positive amount of η^2.

Empirical measures of $\langle r^2 \rangle$ are not only biased but also contain a stochastic error, which is defined as the deviation of $\langle r^2 \rangle$ from its expectation ϱ^2. The variance of this stochastic error can be formulated

$$\sigma^2 \equiv \mathrm{E}\left[\left(\langle r^2 \rangle - \varrho^2\right)^2\right] = \mathrm{E}\left(\langle r^2 \rangle^2 - 2 \langle r^2 \rangle \varrho^2 + \varrho^4\right) \tag{5.24}$$

The last form of this equation has the expanded terms of the square. The first term, $\langle r^2 \rangle^2$, can be explicitly written by inserting Equations 5.12 and 5.20; the other two terms can be simplified by inserting Equation 5.23. We obtain

$$\sigma^2 = \mathrm{E}\left\{\left[\frac{1}{n} \sum_{i=1}^{n}\left(r_i^* + \varepsilon_i - \varepsilon_{i-1}\right)^2\right]^2\right\} - \varrho^4 \tag{5.25}$$

The first term is somewhat tedious to compute because of the two squares and the sum. We expand the squares to get many terms for which we have to compute the expectation values. All of those terms that contain r^* or ε to an odd power have a zero expectation due to the symmetry of the normal distribution and the independence of r^* and ε. The expectations of r^{*2} and ε^2 can be taken from Equations 5.21 and 5.22. The expectations of the fourth moments of normal distribution are

$$\mathrm{E}\left(r_i^{*4}\right) = 3 \left[\mathrm{E}\left(r_i^{*2}\right)\right]^2 = 3 \varrho^{*4} \tag{5.26}$$

$$\mathrm{E}\left(\varepsilon_i^4\right) = \mathrm{E}\left(\varepsilon_{i-1}^4\right) = 3 \left[\mathrm{E}\left(\varepsilon_i^2\right)\right]^2 = \frac{3}{4} \eta^4 \tag{5.27}$$

as found in (Kendall et al., 1987, pp. 321 and 338), for example. By inserting this and carefully evaluating all the terms, we obtain

$$\sigma^2 = \frac{n+2}{n} \varrho^{*4} + \frac{2(n+2)}{n} \varrho^{*2} \eta^2 + \frac{n^2 + 3n + 1}{n^2} \eta^4 - \varrho^4 \tag{5.28}$$

By inserting Equation 5.23, we can express the resulting stochastic error variance either in terms of ϱ^*,

$$\sigma^2 = \frac{2}{n} \varrho^{*4} + \frac{4}{n} \varrho^{*2} \eta^2 + \left(\frac{3}{n} - \frac{1}{n^2}\right) \eta^4 \tag{5.29}$$

or in terms of ϱ,

$$\sigma^2 = \frac{2}{n} \varrho^4 + \left(\frac{1}{n} - \frac{1}{n^2}\right) \eta^4 \tag{5.30}$$

Now, we know both the bias η^2 of an empirically measured $\langle r^2 \rangle$ and the variance of its stochastic error. For reporting the results and using them in the scaling law computation, two alternative approaches are possible:

1. We can *subtract* the bias η^2 from the observed $\langle r^2 \rangle$ and take the result with a stochastic error of a variance following Equation 5.30, approximating ϱ^2 by $\langle r^2 \rangle$. We do not recommend this here because η^2 is only approximately known and thus contains an unknown error. However, the idea of bias modeling and bias elimination is further developed in Chapter 7.

2. We can take the originally obtained value of $\langle r^2 \rangle$ and regard the bias η^2 as a *separate error component* in addition to the stochastic error. This is an appropriate way to go, given the uncertainty of η^2.

Following the second approach, we formulate a total error with variance σ^2_{total}, containing the bias and the stochastic error. The stochastic error is independent of the bias by definition, so the total error variance is the sum of the stochastic variance and the squared bias

$$\sigma^2_{\text{total}} = \sigma^2 + \eta^4 = \frac{2}{n} \varrho^4 + \left(1 + \frac{1}{n} - \frac{1}{n^2}\right) \eta^4 \tag{5.31}$$

This is the final, resulting variance of the total error of $\langle r^2 \rangle$.

For the application in the scaling law, we can use a good approximation for large values of $n \gg 1$, which is reasonable even for small values of n. By dropping higher order terms from Equation 5.31, we obtain

$$\sigma^2_{\text{total}} \approx \frac{2}{n} \varrho^4 + \eta^4 \approx \frac{2}{n} \langle r^2 \rangle^2 + \eta^4 \tag{5.32}$$

In the last form, the theoretical constant ϱ^2 has been replaced by its estimator $\langle r^2 \rangle$, see Equation 5.23.

The mean squared return with error can be formulated as follows:

$$\langle r^2 \rangle_{\text{with error}} = \langle r^2 \rangle \pm \sqrt{\eta^4 + \frac{2}{n} \langle r^2 \rangle^2} \tag{5.33}$$

where the second term is the standard deviation of the error according to Equation 5.32.

The scaling law is usually formulated for $(\langle r^2 \rangle)^{1/2}$ rather than $\langle r^2 \rangle$, as in Equation 5.10. Applying the law of error propagation, we obtain

$$\langle r^2 \rangle^{1/2}_{\text{with error}} = \langle r^2 \rangle^{1/2} \pm \frac{d\langle r^2 \rangle^{1/2}}{d\langle r^2 \rangle} \sqrt{\eta^4 + \frac{2}{n} \langle r^2 \rangle^2}$$

$$= \langle r^2 \rangle^{1/2} \pm \sqrt{\frac{\eta^4}{4 \langle r^2 \rangle} + \frac{\langle r^2 \rangle}{2 n}} \tag{5.34}$$

The scaling law fitting is done in the linear form obtained for $\log(\langle r^2 \rangle)^{1/2}$ (see Equation 5.17). Again applying the law of error propagation, we obtain

$$
\begin{aligned}
\log\langle r^2 \rangle_{\text{with error}}^{1/2} &= \log\langle r^2 \rangle^{1/2} \pm \frac{d\log\langle r^2 \rangle^{1/2}}{d\langle r^2 \rangle^{1/2}} \sqrt{\frac{\eta^4}{4\,\langle r^2 \rangle} + \frac{\langle r^2 \rangle}{2\,n}} \\
&= \log\langle r^2 \rangle^{1/2} \pm \sqrt{\frac{\eta^4}{4\,\langle r^2 \rangle^2} + \frac{1}{2\,n}}
\end{aligned}
\tag{5.35}
$$

which gives rise to the following expression for the error variance of this quantity:

$$
\text{Var}\left(\log\langle r^2 \rangle^{1/2}\right) = \frac{\eta^4}{4\,\langle r^2 \rangle^2} + \frac{1}{2\,n}
\tag{5.36}
$$

The assumption is now that the variance of the error for $\log \overline{|\Delta x|}$ is approximately the same as that of $\log(\langle r^2 \rangle)^{1/2}$ in Equation 5.36 and that we only need to replace there the empirically obtained $(\langle r^2 \rangle)^{1/2}$ by the empirically obtained $\overline{|\Delta x|}$. This approximation is justified by the similar sizes and behaviors of both quantities. We obtain

$$
\text{Var}\left(\log \overline{|\Delta x|}\right) \approx \frac{\eta^4}{4\,\overline{|\Delta x|}^4} + \frac{1}{2\,n}
\tag{5.37}
$$

This expression has interesting properties. In the case of long time intervals, $\overline{|\Delta x|} \gg \eta$, and the term $1/(2n)$ becomes the essential cause for errors. In the case of short time intervals, n is very big but $\overline{|\Delta x|}$ is of the same order as η, and the first term of the right-hand side of the equation plays the central role. This explains the peculiar form of the errors in Figure 5.8, very large for high-frequency points, then diminishing (almost undistinguishable because of the high number of observations) and eventually increasing again when the number of observations becomes small.

5.5.4   Limitations of the Scaling Laws

We have already mentioned that the empirical results indicate a scaling behavior from time intervals of a few hours to a few months. Outside this range, the behavior departs from Equation 5.10 on both sides of the spectrum. Many authors noticed this effect, in particular, Moody and Wu (1995) and Fisher *et al.* (1997) for the short time intervals. It is important to understand the limitations of the scaling laws because realized volatility is playing more of an essential role in measuring volatility and thus market risk. It also serves as the quantity to be predicted in volatility forecasting and quality measurements of such forecasts, as we shall see in Chapter 8.

In the previous section, we saw that the bid and ask bounce generates an uncertainty on the middle price, and we have estimated its contribution to the error of the volatility estimation. For most risk assessment of portfolios, a good estimation of the *daily volatility* is required. Unfortunately, in practice, departures from the i.i.d. diffusion process make the realized volatility computed with returns measured at very short intervals no longer an unbiased and consistent estimator of the daily volatility. It is thus interesting to go one step further than in the previous section and to model the bias in order to obtain an easy correspondence between volatilities estimated at different frequencies. Recently, Corsi *et al.* (2001) have investigated and modeled the bias and its effect on measurements of realized volatility.

There are two limitations to the precision of the estimation of realized volatility. The number of return observations in the measurement period is limited and leads to a stochastic error (noise). One can easily see that for long time intervals (a year and more) it becomes difficult to assess the statistical significance of the volatility estimation because there are not more than a handful of independent observations. This number grows and the noise shrinks when the return measurement intervals shrink, but then the bias starts to grow. Until now, the only choice was a clever trade-off between the noise and the bias, which led to typical return intervals of about an hour. Tick frequency and data gaps play a major role. The goal is to define a superior realized volatility, which combines the low noise of short return interval sizes with the low bias of large return intervals. We shall not enter in the details here since it is still a research in progress. It suffices to mention that this is a crucial issue for a widespread use of high-frequency data in volatility estimation.

Gençay *et al.* (2001d) also provide evidence that the scaling behavior breaks for returns measured at higher intervals than 1 day. Figure 5.9 reports their decomposition of the variance on a scale-by-scale basis through the application of a nondecimated discrete wavelet transform.[23] This methodology does not assume any distributional form to the returns. The wavelet variance for each absolute return series is plotted on a log-log scale in Figure 5.9. For example the first scale is associated with 20-min changes, the second scale is associated with 2*20=40-min changes, and so on. Each increasing scale represents lower frequencies. The first six scales capture the frequencies $1/128 \le f \le 1/2$; that is, oscillations with a period length of 2 (40 min) to 128 (2560 min). Because there are 72*20 = 1440 min in a day, we conclude that the first six scales are related with intraday dynamics of the sample.

In the seventh scale, an apparent break is observed in the variance for both series which is associated with 64*20 = 1280-min changes. Because there are 1440 min in a day, the seventh scale corresponds to 0.89 day. Therefore, the seventh and higher scales are taken to be related with 1 day and higher dynamics.

For a power law process, $\nu^2(\tau_j) \propto \tau_j^{-\alpha-1}$ so that an estimate of α is obtained by regressing $\log \nu^2(\tau_j)$ on $\log \tau_j^{-\alpha-1}$. Figure 5.9 plots the ordinary least squares (OLS) fits of the sample points for two different regions. Estimated slopes for the smallest six scales are -0.48 and -0.59 for USD-DEM and USD-JPY series,

---

[23] A extensive study of wavelet methods within the context of time series analysis and filtering is presented in Gençay *et al.* (2001b).

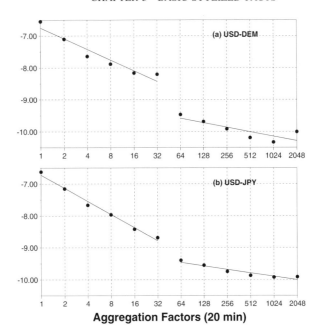

Aggregation Factors (20 min)

FIGURE 5.9   Wavelet variance for 20-min absolute returns of (a) USD-DEM and (b) USD-JPY from December 1, 1986, through December 1, 1996, on a log-log scale. The circles are the estimated variances for each scale. The straight lines are ordinary least squares (OLS) fits. Each scale is associated with a particular time period. For example the first scale reflects 20-min changes, the second scale reflects $2 * 20 = 40$-min changes, the third scale reflects $4 * 20 = 160$-min changes, and so on. The seventh scale is $64 * 20 = 1280$-min changes. Because there are 1440-min per day, the seventh scale corresponds to approximately one day. The last scale shows approximately 28 days.

respectively. This result implies that $\alpha = -0.52$ for the USD-DEM series and $\alpha = -0.40$ for the USD-JPY absolute return series for the first six scales (intraday).

5.6 AUTOCORRELATION AND SEASONALITY

Before closing this chapter, we investigate the autocorrelation and the seasonality of high-frequency data. Are returns and the volatility serially correlated, beyond the negative short-term autocorrelation in Section 5.2.1? Are there periodic patterns, seasonality, in the data? Clearly, we expect to find very little data during weekends and holidays, but what else can be said about different weekdays and daytimes? We answer these questions by using two types of statistical analysis. The autocorrelation function of a stochastic quantity reveals at the same time serially dependence and periodicity. The autocorrelation function signals a periodic pattern by peaking at lags that are integer multiples of the particular period. We call the other type of analysis an intraday-intraweek analysis. It relates quantities to the time of the day (or the week) when they are observed. We thus obtain average quantities evaluated for every hour of a day or of a week.

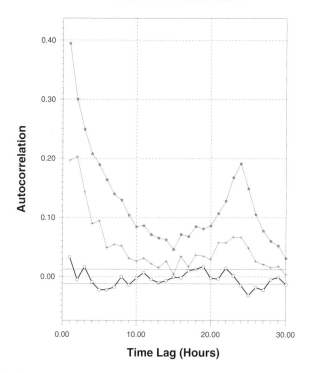

FIGURE 5.10 Autocorrelations of hourly returns (○), their absolute values (⋆), and their squares (+) as functions of the time lag, for XAU (gold) against USD. The band about the zero autocorrelation line represents 95% significance of the hypothesis of independent Gaussian observations.

5.6.1 Autocorrelations of Returns and Volatility

A convenient way to discover stylized properties of returns is to conduct an autocorrelation study. The autocorrelation function examines whether there is a linear dependency between the current and past values of a variable:

$$\rho_x(\tau) = \frac{\sum [x(t-\tau) - \langle x \rangle][x(t) - \langle x \rangle]}{\sqrt{\sum [x(t-\tau) - \langle x \rangle]^2 \sum [x(t) - \langle x \rangle]^2}} \qquad (5.38)$$

where $x(t)$ can be any time series of a stochastic variable and τ is the time lag. The autocorrelation function peaks at lags corresponding to the periods of seasonal patterns.

Here we present an analysis of the autocorrelation function ρ of hourly returns, their absolute values, and their squares over a sample of 3 years from March 1, 1986, to March 1, 1989. We see in Figure 5.10 that the last two variables have a significant, strong autocorrelation for small time lags (few hours), which indicates the existence of volatility clusters or patterns. More interesting is the significant peak for time lags of and around 24 hr. This is a strong indication of *seasonality* with a period of 1 day. The autocorrelation of the returns

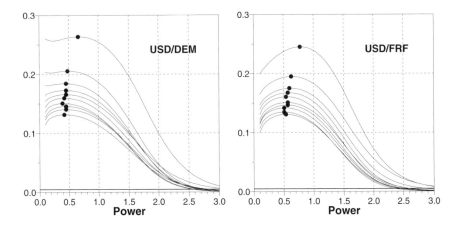

FIGURE 5.11 The first 10 lags of the autocorrelation function of $|r|^p$ as a function of the power p for USD-DEM and USD-FRF (first lag on top, 10th at the bottom). The maxima are shown by bullet signs (•). The returns are measured over 30 min (in ϑ-time, see Chapter 6). Right above the bottom, at a very low autocorrelation value, there is a horizontal line in both graphs. This is the upper limit of the 95% confidence band of the hypothesis of independent Gaussian observations.

themselves is insignificant as it stays mostly inside the confidence band of Figure 5.10.

Because the autocorrelation function varies when the absolute returns are raised to a different power, as can be seen in Figure 5.10, we systematically studied the influence of the power p on the autocorrelation function. Some studies on the influence of the power of absolute returns on the autocorrelation have been published (Granger and Ding, 1995; Müller et al., 1998; Bouchaud and Potters, 2000). Granger and Ding (1995) conclude that the exponent $p = 1$ leads to the highest autocorrelation. Here, as in Müller et al. (1998), we report a full analysis of the autocorrelation coefficients as a function of the power p of absolute returns. Figure 5.11 shows how the tails of the distribution influence autocorrelation. Increasing the power of the absolute returns boils down to increasing the relative importance of extreme events in the statistics. In Figure 5.11, we see that the autocorrelation, for the 10 lags considered, decreases when the influence of extreme returns is increased. In other words, extreme events are less correlated with each other than average or small absolute returns. From this study, it seems that the heteroskedasticity is mainly due to the average behavior, not the extreme events. This is represented by a low exponent p smaller than 1; the maximum autocorrelation is for values of p close to one-half.

The results presented in Table 5.3 can well explain a feature shown in Figures 5.10 and 5.11 where the positive autocorrelation of absolute returns is stronger than that of squared returns. The tail index α being almost always below 4, the

TABLE 5.10 Time conversion table.

Time conversion table between Greenwich Mean Time (GMT), Europe (MET), USA (EST), and Japan (JPT). The letter D indicates a particular day. Note that GMT and JPT are not subject to daylight saving changes whereas the regions under MET and EST are.

GMT		MET		EST		JPT	
D	0:00	D	1:00	D-1	19:00	D	9:00
D	3:00	D	4:00	D-1	22:00	D	12:00
D	6:00	D	7:00	D	1:00	D	15:00
D	9:00	D	10:00	D	4:00	D	18:00
D	12:00	D	13:00	D	7:00	D	21:00
D	15:00	D	16:00	D	10:00	D+1	0:00
D	18:00	D	19:00	D	13:00	D+1	3:00
D	21:00	D	22:00	D	16:00	D+1	6:00

fourth moment of the distribution is unlikely to converge.[24] The denominator of the autocorrelation coefficient of squared returns is only finite if the fourth moment converges, whereas the convergence of the second moment[25] suffices to make the denominator of the autocorrelation of absolute returns finite. The second moment is finite if α is larger than 2. Indeed, besides the empirical evidence shown in Figure 5.11, we find that the difference between the autocorrelations of absolute returns and squared returns grows with increasing sample size. This difference computed on 20 years of daily data is much larger than that computed on only 8 years. For a lag of 9 days, we obtain autocorrelations of 0.11 and 0.125 for the absolute returns over 8 and 20 years, respectively, while we obtain 0.072 and 0.038 for the squared returns, showing a strong decrease when going to a larger sample. The same effect as for the daily returns is found for the autocorrelation of 20-min returns, where we compared a 9-year sample to half-yearly samples.

5.6.2 Seasonal Volatility: Across Markets for OTC Instruments

The most direct way to analyze *seasonal heteroskedasticity* in the form of daily volatility patterns is through our *intraday statistics*. We construct a uniform time grid with 24 hourly intervals for the statistical analysis of the volatility, the number of ticks, and the bid-ask spreads.

The low trading activity on weekends implies a weekly periodicity of trading activity and is a reason for adding *intraweek* statistics to the intraday statistics. Both statistics are technically the same, but the intraweek analysis uses a grid of

---

[24] Loretan and Phillips (1994) come to a similar conclusion when examining the tail behavior of daily closing prices for FX rates.

[25] For a more formal proof of the existence of the autocorrelation function of stochastic variables obeying fat-tailed probability distribution, see Davis *et al.* (1999).

TABLE 5.11   Average number of ticks.

Average number of ticks for each day of the week (including weekends) for the USD against DEM, JPY, CHF, and GBP and XAU (gold) against USD. The sampling period is from January 1, 1987, to December 31, 1993. The tick activity has increased over the years except for XAU (gold).

	DEM	JPY	GBP	CHF	XAU
Monday	4888	2111	1773	1764	607
Tuesday	5344	2438	2043	2031	698
Wednesday	5328	2460	2033	2022	717
Thursday	5115	2387	1948	1914	702
Friday	4495	1955	1633	1670	675
Saturday	17	16	15	14	27
Sunday	168	181	46	34	6

seven intervals from Monday 0:00-24:00 to Sunday 0:00-24:00 (GMT). With this choice, most of the active periods of the main markets (America, Europe, East Asia) on the same day are included in the same interval. The correspondence of the hours between main markets is shown in Table 5.10. The analysis grids have the advantage of a very simple and clear definition, but they treat *business holidays* outside the weekends (about 3% of all days) as working days and thus bias the results. The only remedy against that would be a worldwide analysis of holidays, with the open question of how to treat holidays observed in only one part of the world. Another problem comes from the fact that daylight saving time is not observed in Japan while it is in Europe and in the United States. This changes the significance of certain hours of the day in winter and in summer when they are expressed in GMT. An alternative here would be to separate the analysis according to the winter and the summer seasons.

An analysis of trading volumes in the daily and weekly grids is impossible as there is no raw data available. The average numbers of ticks, however, give an idea about the worldwide market activity as a function of daytime and weekdays. They are counts of original quotes by representative market makers, though biased by our data supplier. The two bottom graphs of Figure 5.12 improve our knowledge of the intraday and intraweek studies. They show, for example, that even the least active hour, 3:00 to 4:00 GMT (noon break in East Asia), contains about 20 ticks for DEM, a sufficient quantity for a meaningful analysis. The intraweekly results are shown in Table 5.11. The ranking of the FX rates according to the amount of published quotes corresponds fairly well to the ranking obtained by the Bank of International Settlements (BIS) with its survey of the volume of transactions on the FX market (Bank for International Settlements, 1995, 1999).

Intraday volatility in terms of mean absolute returns is plotted in the two top histograms of Figure 5.12 for USD-DEM. Both histograms indicate distinctly uneven intraday-intraweek volatility patterns. The daily maximum of average

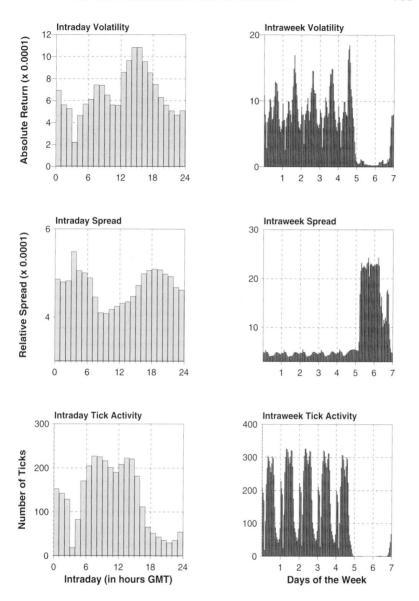

FIGURE 5.12 Hourly intraday and intraweek distribution of the absolute return, the spread and the tick frequency: a sampling interval of $\Delta t = 1$ hour is chosen. The day is subdivided into 24 hours from 0:00 − 1:00 to 23:00 − 24:00 (GMT) and the week is subdivided into 168 hours from Monday 0:00 − 1:00 to Sunday 23:00 − 24:00 (GMT) with index i. Each observation of the analyzed variable is made in one of these hourly intervals and is assigned to the corresponding subsample with the correct index i. The sample pattern does not account for bank holidays and daylight saving time. The FX rate is USD-DEM and the sampling period covers the 6 years from 1987 to 1992.

TABLE 5.12   Average volatility.

Average volatility for each day of the week (including weekends) for the USD against DEM, JPY, CHF, and GBP and XAU (gold) against USD; for the period from January 1, 1987, to December 31, 1993. The volatility figures have to be multiplied by 10^{-3}. They refer to one day. Corresponding *annualized* volatility figures are obtained through another multiplication by the factor $\sqrt{365.25} \approx 19.11$.

	DEM	JPY	GBP	CHF	XAU
Monday	6.12	4.66	5.44	6.04	5.75
Tuesday	5.28	5.17	5.49	5.88	5.48
Wednesday	4.93	5.02	5.04	5.52	5.47
Thursday	5.83	5.15	5.04	5.91	5.39
Friday	6.62	5.00	5.86	6.53	5.87
Saturday	0.58	0.74	0.76	0.88	1.19
Sunday	2.25	2.04	1.77	1.70	1.25

volatility is roughly four times higher than the minimum. The patterns can be explained by considering the structure of the world market, which consists of three main parts with different time zones: America, Europe, and East Asia. Even the lunch-break familiar to the European and East Asian markets, but not to the American one, can be detected in the form of the two minima of the histogram for USD-DEM. The main daily maximum occurs when both the American and the European markets are active. Other markets have similar patterns with characteristic differences in the weights of the markets, such as a higher volatility for the USD-JPY when the East Asian markets are active (as to be shown in Chapter 6). The patterns for USD-CHF and USD-DEM are similar, as expected. The pattern for XAU-USD reflects the well-known fact that the East Asian gold market is less active than the European and American ones. Different volatilities across the American, European, and Japanese markets were also detected by Ito and Roley (1987),[26] in their intraday study of the Japanese Yen.

Table 5.12 shows quite similar volatilities for the working days of the week. It does not confirm the weekend effect found by McFarland *et al.* (1982) with systematically lower volatilities on Fridays.[27] Their analysis was however different by taking daily changes at 18:00 GMT and putting together Saturdays, Sundays, and Mondays. The volatility is low on weekends, but, for FX rates, higher on Sundays than on Saturdays. This is due to the early Monday mornings in East Asia and in Australia, which coincide with Sunday nights in GMT.

The intraweek volatilities of Table 5.12 are correlated with the activities measured in terms of the number of ticks (Table 5.11). The analogous correlation

---

[26] For these authors volatility is measured by both the standard deviation and the mean absolute returns.

[27] The effect seems to be the reverse on the stock market (high returns on Fridays).

TABLE 5.13   Correlation coefficients for activity measures.

Correlation coefficients computed for the different intraday analyses for the USD against DEM, JPY, CHF, and GBP and XAU (gold) against USD. Sampling period: from January 1, 1987, to December 31, 1993.

	DEM	JPY	GBP	CHF	XAU
$E(|r|)$-ticks	+0.540	+0.421	+0.779	+0.755	+0.885
$E(|r|)$-spread	−0.220	−0.485	−0.570	−0.704	−0.287
Ticks-spread	−0.693	−0.018	−0.881	−0.707	−0.450

coefficients between the intradaily histograms of Figure 5.12 are also positive, as explicitly shown in the first line of Table 5.13. We conjecture that both variables are positively correlated to a third one, the worldwide intraday transaction volume, which is not known for the FX market. Transaction volume figures are, however, available for the stock market; their positive correlation to squared returns (and hence the volatility) has been found by Harris (1987) and other authors. Recently, Hasbrouck (1999) examined the data of the New York Stock Exchange and found similar correlations as in Table 5.13 for his transaction data, but the correlations did not uniformly increase when the data were aggregated.

The statistics show that an analysis of return distributions that neglects the large differences between the hours of a day and the days of the week is inappropriate. In Chapter 6, we will introduce a new time scale to solve this problem.

5.6.3   Seasonal Volatility: U-Shaped for Exchange Traded Instruments

Intradaily seasonalities were also found in the stock markets by Ghysels and Jasiak (1995), Andersen and Bollerslev (1997b) and Hasbrouck (1999). Unlike the FX market, stock exchanges and money market exchanges are active less than 24 hr a day. Thus the shape of the seasonality is different. It is called the U-shape because the high volatility of the opening is followed by a decrease, which is in turn followed by an increase of volatility just before closing. Ballocchi *et al.* (1999b) study the Eurofutures markets and find the expected intraday seasonality. For all contracts traded on LIFFE the hourly tick activity displays the U-shape with its minimum around 11 a.m. to 1 p.m. (GMT) and a clustering of activity around the beginning and the end of the trading day. There are differences among Eurofutures between the levels and widths of the peaks and the level of the minimum. The Eurodollar (a contract type traded on CME, see section 2.4.1) displays similar behavior but the activity in the first half of the working day, which takes place when the European markets are still open, is higher than during the second half of the day, when European markets have already closed and Asian markets are not yet open.

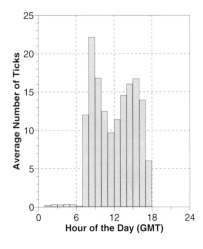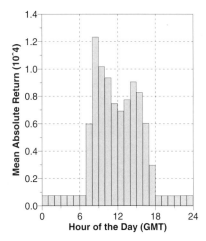

FIGURE 5.13 Intraday analysis of Short Sterling in position two. The intraday tick activity (left histogram) displays the average number of ticks occurring in each hour of the day whereas the intraday volatility (right histogram) shows the mean absolute return. Both plots display similar U-shapes, the only difference being that the minimum appears one hour later for intraday returns. The time scale is GMT (not UKT, the local time used by LIFFE in London). The sampling period starts on January 1, 1994, and ends on April 15, 1997. The total number of ticks is 184,360.

Intraday returns follow a pattern similar to that presented by intraday tick activity. In general, opening hours show the highest price variation (the difference with respect to the average of the other hours is around one basis point); only in some cases does the largest return occur toward closing time (usually in the last positions). Differences occur in some positions[28] for Short Sterling, Eurolira, and Three-Month Ecu,[29] which display the minimum of the U-curve 1 hour later than in the tick-activity case. This can be seen in Figure 5.13, which displays intraday tick activity and intraday returns for Short Sterling in position two. Note that the U-shapes in this figure are blurred by the fact that Greenwich Mean Time (GMT) is used. The observations do not only cover winter months but also summers where the time scale used by LIFFE in London is shifted by 1 hour (daylight saving time). If the time scale was local time (UKT) instead of GMT, the U-shapes would be more pronounced with clearer peaks at opening and closing.

The first two positions of the Euromark display less regularity in the intraday return behavior. This behavior is confirmed also by correlation results: on the whole, the correlation between hourly tick activity and hourly returns is above 0.96; only Euromark for the first two positions and Three Month-Ecu for the fourth position show a lower correlation around 0.90. In general, for Eurodollar, Euromark and Short Sterling, hourly returns tend to increase from position 1

---

[28] For an explanation of the word "position," see Section 2.1.2.

[29] Short Sterling, Eurolira, Three Month-Ecu, and Euromark are names of LIFFE contracts, all with an underlying 3-month deposit. Ecu is the European Currency Unit that preceded the Euro.

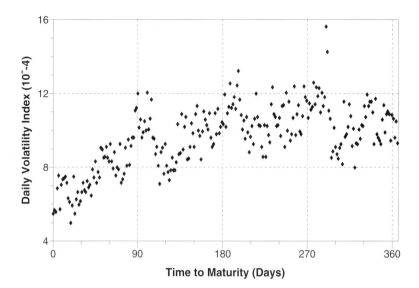

FIGURE 5.14 Volatility as a function of time to expiry. The volatility values are daily averages over 36 contracts (9 for Eurodollar, 9 for Euromark, 9 for Short Sterling, and 9 for Eurolira). The abscissa corresponds to the time to expiry: the farther on the right-hand side, the farther away from expiry.

to position 4; Eurodollar and Short Sterling display a decrease for some hours in position 4.

Looking at intraweek tick activity, there is evidence of a day-of-the-week effect. In general, the level of activity displays a minimum on Monday and a maximum on the last two working days of the week, usually on Thursday for LIFFE contracts and on Friday for CME contracts. The difference is definitely significant for the Eurodollar; in fact, for positions 1 and 2 the tick activity on Friday is almost double that on Monday and it becomes more than double for positions 3 and 4. In general, there is a gradual increase from Monday to Friday.

5.6.4 Deterministic Volatility in Eurofutures Contracts

Ballocchi *et al.* (2001) provide evidence that the volatility of futures prices systematically depends on the time interval left until contract expiry. We call these systematic volatility patterns *deterministic*, as opposed to the also existing stochastic fluctuations of volatility. In order to probe the existence of a seasonality related to contract expiry, a sample consisting of many futures contracts is needed. For several Eurofutures contact type (Eurodollar, Euromark, Short Sterling, and Eurolira) and for each contract expiry, we build a series of hourly returns using linear interpolation. Then we compute daily volatilities taking the mean absolute value of hourly returns from 00:00 to 24:00 (GMT) of each working day (weekends and holidays are excluded). These daily volatilities are plotted against time to expiry. The result is shown in Figure 5.14. The vertical axis represents the mean volatility computed from all Eurofutures and all contracts together. The horizontal axis represents the time left to expiry, as we move towards the left the number of days to expiry decreases.

Figure 5.14 spans a period of about 360 days because only within that period we are able to compute our mean volatility based on a full set of contracts. Some contracts have bad data coverage for times to expiry exceeding 360 days. The results obtained are quite interesting. There is a downward trend in volatility as the time to expiry decreases (moving from right to left in Figure 5.14). This downward trend is weak between about 300 and 180 days before expiry but becomes strong as we move toward the expiry date. There is also an unexpected behavior consisting of oscillatory movements with peaks every 90 days corresponding to rollover activities near the ending of contracts. These results are confirmed also by a deterministic volatility study on each single Eurofutures type—except Eurolira, which displays an increment in volatility as we move toward expiry. Eurodollar, Euromark, and Short Sterling show a decreasing volatility at least for the last 300 days before expiry. All Eurofutures display oscillatory movements with peaks around expiry dates (this appears particularly evident for Short Sterling).

A possible explanation for this effect is that these markets are all "cash settled" and therefore have no "delivery risk"; this means there is no risk of holding these futures on expiry day. Due to transaction costs, it is cheaper to take the cash at expiry than to close the position and realize the cash the day before. In other future markets such as the Deutsche Termin-Börse or the commodity markets, people who hold long positions to expiry actually take physical delivery of the underlying commodity or bond. There is a risk as expiry approaches as to which bond or type of commodity will be delivered. This may cause an increase in volatility as expiry approaches—a behavior opposite to that of Figure 5.14.

5.6.5   Bid-Ask Spreads

The bid-ask spread reflects many factors such as transaction costs, the market maker's profit, and the compensation against risk for the market maker, see (Glassman, 1987; Glosten, 1987). The subject of the intraday and intraweek analysis is the relative spread s_j (Equation 3.12). It is usually below or around 0.1%, and its distribution is not symmetric. Negative changes are bounded as spreads are always positive, but the spread can exceed 0.5% in times of low market activity. The arithmetic mean of s_j weights these low-activity spreads too strongly and therefore we choose the *geometric* mean as a more appropriate measure:

$$\overline{s_i} = \left(\prod_{j=1}^{n_i} s_{i,j} \right)^{\frac{1}{n_i}} \tag{5.39}$$

The index i indicates the hour of a day (or a week) or the day of the week, depending on the analysis. The total number of ticks that belong to the ith interval is n_i. j is the index and $s_{i,j}$ the spread of these ticks.

TABLE 5.14 Average spreads.

Geometric average of the relative spread for each day of the week (including weekends) for the USD against DEM, JPY, CHF, and GBP and XAU (gold) against USD; for the period from January 1, 1987, to December 31, 1993. The relative spread figures have to be multiplied by 10^{-4}.

	DEM	JPY	GBP	CHF	XAU
Monday	4.57	5.72	4.82	6.32	12.58
Tuesday	4.52	5.64	4.77	6.28	12.51
Wednesday	4.57	5.71	4.81	6.32	12.49
Thursday	4.64	5.77	4.84	6.38	12.62
Friday	4.79	6.00	4.99	6.49	12.59
Saturday	7.69	17.91	17.32	18.02	13.26
Sunday	5.28	6.78	9.60	10.99	14.04

Müller and Sgier (1992) analyze in detail the statistical behavior of the quoted spread. Here we shall present their main conclusions. First, it is important to remember that all the statistical analyses are dominated by one property of quoted FX spreads, which is the discontinuity of quoted values (see Section 5.2.2). This data set contains price quotes rather than traded prices. The banks that issue these price quotes are facing the following constraints:

- Granularity: FX prices are usually quoted with five digits—that is, 1.6755 (USD-DEM) or 105.21 (USD-JPY). The lowest digit sets the granularity and thus the unit *basis points*.

- Quoted spreads are wider than traded spreads as they include "safety margins" on both sides of the real spread negotiated in simultaneous real transactions. These margins allow the FX dealers, when called by a customer during the lifetime of the quote, to make a fine adjustment of the bid and ask prices within the range given by the wide quoted spread. They can thus react to the most recent market developments.

- FX dealers often have biased intentions: while one of the prices, bid or ask, is carefully chosen to attract a deal in the desired direction, the other price is made unattractive by increasing the spread.

- Because quoted spreads are wider than traded spreads, they do not need the high precision required in the direct negotiation with the customer on the phone. Hence, there is a tendency to publish formal, "even" values of quoted spreads as discussed in Section 5.2.2.

The strong preference for a few formal spread values, mainly 5 and 10 basis points, clearly affects every statistical analysis.

The results are shown in the middle histograms of Figure 5.12 and in Table 5.14. The general behavior of spreads is opposite to those of volatility and tick frequency. Spreads are high when activity is low, as already noticed by

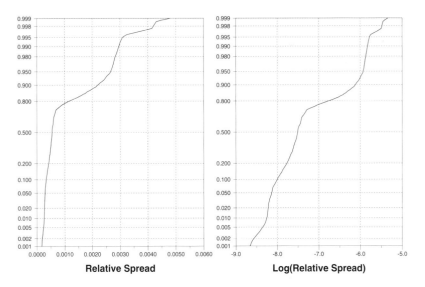

Relative Spread **Log(Relative Spread)**

FIGURE 5.15 Cumulative distributions of relative spreads (left) and logarithm of the relative spread (right) shown against the Gaussian probability on the y-axis. The distribution is computed from a time series of linearly interpolated spread sampled every 10 min for USD-DEM. The sample runs from March 1, 1986, to March 1, 1991.

Glassman (1987). FX spreads on Saturdays and Sundays can have double and more the size of those on weekdays and, as in Table 5.12, Sundays differ slightly less from working days than Saturdays. Sunday in GMT also covers the early morning of Monday in East Asian time zones. Unlike the volatilities, the average FX spreads exhibit a clear weekend effect in the sense that the Friday figures are higher, though still much lower than those of Saturday and Sunday. The spreads of gold vary less strongly, but they have double the size of the FX spreads on working days. The FX rate with the smallest spreads, USD-DEM, was the most traded one according to all the BIS studies (until it was replaced by EUR-USD in 1999). The histograms in Figure 5.12 have intraday patterns that are less distinct than those of volatility, but still characteristic. We analyze their correlations with both the volatilities and the numbers of quoted ticks. All the correlation coefficients on the second line of Table 5.13 and most of them on the third line are negative, as one would expect. The FX rates have different spread patterns. For USD-CHF, for instance, there is a general spread increase during the European afternoon when the center of market activity shifts from Europe to America, while the USD-JPY spreads decrease on average at the same daytime. This indicates that American traders are less interested in Swiss Francs and more in Japanese Yens than other traders. Hartmann (1998) uses the spreads to study the role of the German Mark and the Japanese Yen as "vehicle currencies," as compared to the USD.

An analysis of the empirical cumulative distribution function of the relative spread s is shown in the left graph of Figure 5.15 for USD-DEM and for ln s in the right graph of Figure 5.15. The resulting cumulative distribution functions have the following properties:

1. They are not Gaussian, but convex (s strongly, $\ln s$ slightly), indicating a positive skewness and leptokurticity (of the tail on the positive side).

2. They look like a staircase with smooth corners. For the nominal spread in basis point, s_{nom}, we would expect a staircase with sharp corners, the vertical parts of the staircase function indicating the preferred "even" values such as 10 basis points. Although s is a relative spread ($\approx s_{nom}/p_{bid}$), where the bid price p_{bid} fluctuates over the 5-year sample, and although we use linear interpolation in the time series construction (see Section 3.2.1), the preferred "even" s_{nom} values are still visible.

6

MODELING SEASONAL VOLATILITY

6.1 INTRODUCTION

The intradaily and intraweekly seasonality of volatility is a dominant effect that overshadows many further stylized facts of high-frequency data. In order to continue the research for stylized facts, we need a powerful treatment of this seasonality.

Many researchers who study daily time series implicitly use, as a solution, a business time scale that differs from the physical scale in its omission of Saturdays, Sundays, and holidays. With the ϑ-scale we extend this concept to the intraday domain, thereby allowing us to tackle a fundamental source of seasonality originating from the cyclical nature of the 24-hr hour trading around the globe in different geographical locations.

There are, therefore, three main motivations for our model:

- To provide a tool for the analysis of market prices by extending the concept of business time scale to intraday prices

- To make a first step toward formulating a model of market prices that also covers the intraday movements

- To gain insight into the interactions of the main market centers around the world and their relevance to each particular foreign exchange (FX) rate

A number of papers such as Andersen and Bollerslev (1997b, 1998b), Taylor and Xu (1997), and Beltratti and Morana (1999) propose alternative approaches for dealing with volatility seasonalities. They are based on a factorization of the volatility into an essentially deterministic seasonal part and a stochastic part, which is (more or less) free of seasonalities. The former is then modeled by a set of smooth functions. Cutting out the inactive periods of the time series and gluing together the active parts, Andersen and Bollerslev (1997b) succeeded in applying their method also to the S&P 500 index. This procedure is not fully satisfactory for a number of reasons: time series have to be preprocessed, there is no treatment of public holidays and other special days, the model fails when the opening or closing time of the market changes, and it is not adequate for instruments with a complex, hybrid volatility pattern. Gençay et al. (2001a) use the wavelet multiresolution methods for dealing with volatility seasonalities which is studied in Section 6.4.

6.2 A MODEL OF MARKET ACTIVITY

6.2.1 Seasonal Patterns of the Volatility and Presence of Markets

The behavior of a time series is called seasonal if it exhibits a periodic pattern in addition to less regular movements. In Chapter 5 we demonstrated daily and weekly seasonal heteroskedasticity of FX prices. This seasonality of volatility has been found in intradaily and intraweekly frequencies. In the presence of seasonal heteroskedasticity, autocorrelation coefficients are significantly higher for time lags that are integer multiples of the seasonal period than for other lags. An extended autocorrelation analysis is studied in Chapter 7.

As studied in Chapter 5, the intraweek analysis indicates that the mean absolute returns are much higher over working days than over Saturdays and Sundays, when the market agents are hardly present. The intraday analysis also demonstrates that the mean absolute hourly returns have distinct seasonal patterns. These patterns are clearly correlated to the changing presence of main market places of the worldwide FX market. The lowest market presence outside the weekend happens during the lunch hour in Japan (noon break in Japan, night in America and Europe). It is at this time when the minimum of mean absolute hourly returns is found.

Chapter 5 also presents evidence of a strong correlation between market presence and volatility such that the intraday price quotes are positively correlated to volatility when measured with mean absolute hourly returns. Market presence is related to worldwide transaction volume which cannot be observed directly. In the literature, a number of papers present substantial evidence in favor of a positive correlation between returns and volume in financial markets, see the survey of (Karpoff, 1987).

The correlation of market presence and volatility requires us to model and explain the empirically found seasonal volatility patterns with the help of fundamental information on the presence of the main markets around the world. We know the main market centers (e.g., New York, London, Tokyo), their time zones, and their usual business hours. When business hours of these market centers *overlap*, market activity must be attributed to their cumulative presence; it is impossible to assign the market activity to only one financial center at these times. The typical opening and closing times of different markets can be determined from a high-frequency database (such as the O&A database), which also contains the originating locations of the quoted prices.

In many of the approaches cited in the introduction, in particular in Baillie and Bollerslev (1990) where the seasonality of volatility is modeled by dummy variables, no further explanation of this seasonal pattern is given. We consider it advantageous to try to identify at every moment of the day *which* markets are responsible for the current volatility.

6.2.2 Modeling the Volatility Patterns with an Alternative Time Scale and an Activity Variable

Before relating the empirically observed volatility to the market presence, we introduce a model of the price process, which will be used for describing and analyzing the seasonal volatility patterns. A return process with strong intraday and intraweek volatility patterns may not be stationary. Our model for the seasonal volatility fluctuations introduces a new *time scale* such that the transformed data in this new time scale do not possess intraday seasonalities.

The construction of this time scale utilizes two components: the *directing process*, $\vartheta(t)$, and a *subordinated* price process generated from the directing process. Let $x(t)$ be the tick-by-tick financial time series that inherits intraday seasonalities. The directing process, $\vartheta(t) : \mathbb{R} \to \mathbb{R}$, is a mapping from physical time to another predetermined time scale. Here, it is defined such that it contains the intraday seasonal variations.[1] $\vartheta(t)$, when used with the subordinated price generating process $x(t) = x^*[\vartheta(t)]$, leads to the x^* process, which has no intraday seasonalities. Although this is not the only possible model to treat the observed seasonality, other traditional deseasonalization techniques are not applicable as the *volatility* is seasonal, not the raw time series.

In the literature, a variety of alternative time scales have been proposed, in different contexts. In the early 1960s, Allais (see, for instance, Allais, 1974) had proposed the concept of *psychological time* to formulate the quantity theory of money. Mandelbrot and Taylor (1967) suggested to cumulate the *transaction volume* to obtain a new time scale which they call the *transaction clock*. Clark (1973) suggested a similar approach. Stock (1988) studied the postwar U.S. GNP and interest rates and proposed a new time scale to model the conditional heteroskedasticity exhibited by these time series. Here we propose to use a new time scale to account for the seasonality.

---

[1] The $\vartheta(t)$ process can assume different roles in different filtering environments. If, for instance, the interest is to simply filter out certain holiday effects from the data, then $\vartheta(t)$ can be defined accordingly. Under such a definition, the transformation will only eliminate the specified holiday effects from the underlying $x(t)$ process. The ϑ type time transformations are not limited to seasonality filtering. They can also be used within other contexts such as the modeling of intrinsic time or transaction clock.

Because the ϑ-scale fully accounts for the seasonality of x, x^* has no seasonal volatility patterns. The process x^* may however have *nonseasonal* volatility patterns; it may be conditionally heteroskedastic. No attempt is made in this chapter to determine its exact nature. The time scale $\vartheta(t)$ is a strictly monotonic function of physical time t. Any time interval from t_1 to $t_2(> t_1)$ corresponds to a ϑ-time interval of the positive size $\vartheta_2 - \vartheta_1$. The new *activity* variable a is defined as the ratio of the interval sizes on the different scales,

$$a_{1,2} \equiv \frac{\vartheta_2 - \vartheta_1}{t_2 - t_1} \tag{6.1}$$

This activity reflects the seasonal volatility patterns. Its relation to other "activity" variables such as market presence or transaction volume was mentioned in Section 6.2.1 and is discussed below.[2]

6.2.3 Market Activity and Scaling Law

The volatility-based activity defined by Equation 6.1 can be computed with the empirical *scaling law* (see Chapter 5) for returns, which relates (for $p = 1$) $\langle |\Delta x| \rangle$, the mean absolute returns over a time interval to the size of this interval, Δt,

$$E[|r|] = c \, \Delta t^D \tag{6.2}$$

where E is the expectation operator, c is a constant depending of the specific time series. D is the drift exponent, which determines the scaling properties of the underlying process across different data frequencies. The drift exponent D is about 0.6 for major FX rates, whereas the pure Gaussian random walk model would imply $D = 0.5$. The scaling law expressed in Equation 6.2 holds for all time series studied and for a wide variety of time intervals ranging from 10 min to more than a year.

The scaling law is applied to subsamples in a so-called *intraweek* analysis that allows us to study the *daily* seasonality (open periods of the main markets around the world) as well as the *weekly* seasonality (working days – weekend). Here, we choose a sampling granularity of $\Delta t = 1$ hr. The week is subdivided into 168 hr from Monday 0:00 – 1:00 to Sunday 23:00 - 24:00 (Greenwich Mean Time, GMT) with index i. Each observation of the analyzed variable is made in one of these hourly intervals and is assigned to the corresponding *subsample* with index i. The 168 subsamples together constitute the full 4-year sample. The sample pattern is independent of bank holidays and daylight saving time. A typical intraday and intraweek pattern across the 168 hr of a typical week is shown in Figure 6.1.

---

[2] In skipping Saturdays and Sundays, other researchers use an implicit activity model with zero activity on the weekends.

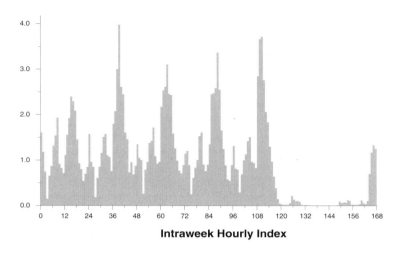

Intraweek Hourly Index

FIGURE 6.1   Histogram of the average hourly activity (as defined in Equation 6.4 for a statistical week (over 4 years) for the USD-DEM rate.

The scaling law, Equation 6.2, is applied to the ith hourly subsample instead of the full sample and mathematically transformed to

$$\Delta\vartheta_i = \left(\frac{E[|r_i|]}{c^*}\right)^{1/D} \tag{6.3}$$

From Chapter 5, we know that r_i can strongly vary for the different hours of a week. The time interval $\Delta t = 1$ hr (for the hourly sampling) is nevertheless constant. Therefore, it is replaced by the interval $\Delta\vartheta_i$ on the new time scale ϑ. The size of $\Delta\vartheta_i$ is no longer constant, but reflects the typical volatility of the ith hour. The constant c^* is essentially the c of Equation 6.2, but can differ slightly as it is calibrated by a normalization condition presented later.

The *activity* of the ith hourly subsample directly follows from Equation 6.1,

$$a_{\text{stat},i} \equiv \frac{1}{\Delta t}\left(\frac{E[|r_i|]}{c^*}\right)^{1/D} \quad , \quad \Delta t = 1 \text{ hr} \tag{6.4}$$

This is the volatility-based activity definition used in the following analysis. The constant c^* is calibrated to satisfy the following, straightforward normalization condition:

$$\frac{1}{168}\sum_{i=1}^{168} a_{\text{stat},i} = 1 \tag{6.5}$$

6.2.4   Geographical Components of Market Activity

In Figure 6.1, the histogram of the average hourly activity defined by Equation 6.4 is plotted for the USD-DEM rate. Although the activity definition is based only on return statistics, the histogram exhibits clear structures where there is very low activity over the weekends and strongly oscillating activity patterns on normal business days. The most active period is the afternoon (GMT) when the European and American markets are open simultaneously. We have varied the Δt granularity of this analysis from 15 min to 4 hr and found no systematic deviations of the resulting activity patterns from the hourly ones. Furthermore, the activity patterns are remarkably stable for each of the 4 years of the total sample. The strong relation between return activity and market presence leads to the explanation of activity as the *sum* of *geographical components*. Although the FX market is worldwide, the actual transactions are executed and entered in the bookkeeping of particular market centers, the main ones being London, New York, and Tokyo. These centers contribute to the total activity of the market during different market hours that sometimes overlap.

Goodhart and Figliuoli (1992) have explored the geographical nature of the FX market to look for what they call the *island hypothesis*. They studied the possibility that the price bounces back and forth from different centers when special news occurs before finally adjusting to it. Along the same idea, Engle *et al.* (1990), in a study with daily opening and closing USD-JPY prices in the New York and Tokyo markets and a market-specific GARCH model, investigate the interaction between markets. They use the terms *heat wave hypothesis* for a purely market-dependent interaction and *meteor shower hypothesis* for a market-independent autocorrelation. They find empirical evidence in favor of the latter hypothesis. Both studies have not found peculiar behavior for different markets. This encourages us to model the activity with geographical components exhibiting *similar* behavior.

The activity patterns shown in Figure 6.1 and the results reported in Chapter 5 suggest that the worldwide market can be divided into *three* continental components: East Asia, Europe, and America. The grouping of the countries appearing on the Reuters pages in our three components can be found in Table 6.1. This division into three components is quite natural and some empirical evidence supporting it will be presented in Chapter 7.

The model activity of a particular geographical component k is called $a_k(t)$; the *sum* of the three *additive* component activities is $a(t)$:

$$a(t) \equiv \sum_{k=1}^{3} a_k(t) \tag{6.6}$$

This total activity should model the intraweekly pattern of the *statistical* activity $a_{\text{stat},i}$ as closely as possible. Unlike a_{stat}, which has relatively complex behavior (see Figure 6.1), the components $a_k(t)$ should have a simple form, in line with known opening and closing hours and activity peaks of the market centers.

6.2.5 A Model of Intraweek Market Activity

Each of the three markets has its activity function $a_k(t)$. For modeling this, we use quantitative information on market presence. A statistical analysis of the number

TABLE 6.1 Definition of the three generic markets.

Grouping of the different countries appearing in the multicontributor pages or record from Reuters according to the three components of the worldwide market.

Index k	Component	Countries
1	East Asia	Australia, Hong Kong, India, Indonesia, Japan, South Korea, Malaysia, New Zealand, Singapore
2	Europe	Austria, Bahrain, Belgium, Germany, Denmark, Finland, France, Great Britain, Greece, Ireland, Italy, Israel, Jordan, Kuwait, Luxembourg, Netherlands, Norway, Saudi Arabia, South Africa, Spain, Sweden, Switzerland, Turkey, United Arab Emirates
3	America	Argentina, Brazil, Canada, Mexico, United States

of price quotes originating from each of the three markets defined by Table 6.1 reveals two aspects on market presence:

- A market has opening times that are *longer* than those of a particular submarket (e.g., an individual bank in one financial center such as Tokyo, Paris, or Chicago). The market opening time is the *union* of the opening times of all relevant institutions of the market.

- Two markets (East Asia and Europe) have a local price quote frequency minimum in the middle of their working day, corresponding to a *noon break*. This local minimum is very pronounced in East Asia and moderate in Europe. In America, there is no minimum around noon. These differences reflect the well-known, different business habits concerning lunch breaks.

Each of the three markets is modeled to have two basic states, either open or closed. The activity does not completely go to zero when the market is closed because it is defined in terms of returns. The activity during the closing hours is modeled to stay on a *small* constant base level $a_{0,k}$. During the opening hours, a much stronger, varying, positive activity $a_{1,k}$ adds to the base level,

$$a(t) \equiv \sum_{k=1}^{3} [a_{0,k} + a_{1,k}(t)] \equiv a_0 + \sum_{k=1}^{3} a_{1,k}(t) > 0 \qquad (6.7)$$

The joint base level a_0 is regarded as one model parameter. There is no need to analyze components $a_{0,k}$.

The activity during opening hours, $a_{1,k}$, is modeled with a polynomial with smooth transition to the constant behavior of the closing hours. This choice is mathematically convenient because such functions are easily differentiable and analytically integrable. For parsimony, the number of parameters of this polynomial is kept at a minimum to model the smooth transitions, the lunch break, and the skewness to account for the relative weights of morning and afternoon hours.

In the subsequent analysis, the statistical week is considered from $t = 0$ on Monday 00:00 to $t = 168$ hr on Sunday 24:00 (GMT), as shown in Figure 6.1. In order to define the opening and closing conditions of the markets in a convenient form, an *auxiliary* time scale T_k is introduced. Essentially, it is GMT time; the following market-dependent transformations are only done for technical convenience:

$$T_k \equiv [(t + \Delta t_k) \text{ modulo } (24 \text{ hr})] - \Delta t_k \qquad (6.8)$$

where Δt_k has the value of 9 hr for East Asia, 0 for Europe, and -5 hr for America. (The result of the modulo operator is the left-hand side argument *minus* the nearest lower integer multiple of the right-hand side argument.) The *weekend* condition (WEC) also depends on the market:[3]

$$(t + \Delta t_k) \text{ modulo } (168 \text{ hr}) \geq 120 \text{ hr} \qquad (6.9)$$

Now the model for an individual market component can be formulated by

$$a_{1,k}(t) \equiv \begin{cases} 0 & \text{if } T_k < o_k \text{ or } T_k > c_k \text{ or (WEC)} \\ a_{\text{open},k}(t) & \text{if } o_k < T_k < c_k \text{ and not (WEC)} \end{cases} \qquad (6.10)$$

where o_k and c_k are the parameters for the opening and closing hours, respectively. The polynomial function is

$$a_{\text{open},k}(t) \equiv \frac{\omega_k}{\frac{o_k+c_k}{2} - s_k} (T_k - o_k)^2 (T_k - c_k)^2 (T_k - s_k) [(T_k - m_k)^2 + d_k^2] \qquad (6.11)$$

where ω_k represents the scale factor of the kth market, s_k the skewness of the activity curve, m_k fixes the place of the relative minimum around the noon break, and d_k determines the depth of this minimum. The special form of the first factor is chosen to avoid too strong a dependence of the scale factor on s_k.

In Figure 6.2, the panel on the left illustrates the shape of the geographical seasonality in the European market. The opening and closing times are where the activity level is zero. These parameters are illustrated with "*o*" and "*c*" signs. The seasonality has two peaks with the second peak higher than the former. The relative minimum between the two peaks is the lunch break effect. The location and depth of this relative minimum are controlled by the parameters "*m*" and "*d*" of the last term of Equation 6.11. The activity starts to peak with the opening

---

[3] The Japanese markets were open on some Saturday mornings according to certain rules in earlier years. These Saturdays, which are noticeable in Figure 6.1, are neglected here, but discussed in Section 6.3.2.

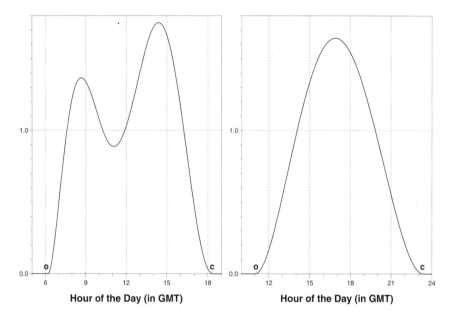

FIGURE 6.2 The geographical seasonality patterns. The panel on the left illustrates the shape of the geographical seasonality in the European market. The seasonality has two peaks with the second peak higher than the former. The relative minimum between the two peaks is the lunch break effect. In the right panel, the North American geographical seasonality is plotted. It has no lunch break effect.

of the market in the morning, slows down during the lunch break and it peaks in the afternoon again. As the market closing time approaches, the level of activity gradually goes down and reaches zero. In the right panel of Figure 6.2, the North American geographical seasonality is plotted, which has no lunch break effect. The parameter s controls the asymmetry of the peaks for the European market, whereas in the case of the North American market, it controls the skewness of the overall pattern.

This polynomial model applies to all markets. The European and Asian markets ($k = 1, 2$) have finite d_k values in the fitting process, but for the American one, the parameter d_3 always diverges to very high values. This reflects the missing noon break in this market, which has already been found in the tick frequency statistics.

The Equation 6.11 for America thus degenerates to a simpler form with no local activity minimum

$$a_{open,3}(t) \equiv \frac{\omega_3}{\frac{o_3 + c_3}{2} - s_3} (T_3 - o_3)^2 (T_3 - c_3)^2 (T_3 - s_3) \qquad (6.12)$$

Some of the model parameters, the opening and closing times, are already known from the quote frequency statistics. For the other parameters, there are constraints.

To ensure positive activities, a_0 and ω_k must be positive and s_k outside the opening hours,

$$a_0 > 0 , \quad \omega_k > 0 , \quad s_k \leq o_k \text{ or } s_k \geq c_k \qquad (6.13)$$

The parameter m_k in Equation 6.11 should be within the opening hours as it models the noon break:

$$o_k < m_k < c_k \qquad (6.14)$$

The functions $a_{1,k}(t)$ must be fitted to the results of the statistics, $a_{\text{stat}}(t)$, by minimizing the integral of the weighted square deviation of $a(t)$ from $a_{\text{stat}}(t)$. A continuous function $a_{\text{stat}}(t)$ is not available but rather the hourly series $a_{\text{stat},i}$ from Equation 6.4. Therefore, the sum over the intraweekly sample is used instead of the integral:

$$\sum_{i=1}^{168} \frac{\left[a_{\text{stat},i} - a_0 - \sum_{k=1}^{3} a_{1,k}(t_i) \right]^2}{\sigma_{\text{error},i}^2} = \min , \quad t_i = (i - \frac{1}{2}) \, \text{hr} \qquad (6.15)$$

The hourly intervals are represented by their middle points in this approximation. The least square model has 11 parameters, three ω_k's, three s_k's, two m_k's, two d_k's, and the base activity a_0. The values of opening, o_k, and closing, c_k, are subject to random measurement error originating from the price quote frequency statistics. Therefore, these values are allowed to vary *slightly* for adjusting the fit. The minimization problem of Equation 6.15 is nonlinear in some of the parameters. It can be solved by the Levenberg-Marquardt method (see Press *et al.*, 1986, Section 14.4), but in complex cases a simple genetic search algorithm provides the optimum parameters much more efficiently.

The main American and European markets observe daylight saving time during summer, whereas the main East Asian markets do not. This fact is ignored for the fitting. Only the GMT scale is used. A posterior daylight saving time correction is proposed in Section 6.3.2.

The resulting parameter estimates for four major FX rates and gold (XAU-USD) are presented in Table 6.2 together with the relative weights of the different markets (to be defined in Section 6.3.1). In the top panel of Figure 6.3, the resulting activity model together with the statistical activity for the USD-JPY is shown, and the bottom panel of Figure 6.3 shows the same quantity for the USD-CHF. Figure 6.4 displays the activity model over 48 hr (outside the weekend) with its different components for the same rates.

6.2.6 Interpretation of the Activity Modeling Results

The resulting parameters of the activity model and Figures 6.3 and 6.4 confirm the close relation between market presence and intraweekly volatility patterns. The market-specific tick frequency analysis and the activity fitting results compare favorably taking into account the Reuters coverage and the limitations of our model.

TABLE 6.2   The parameter estimates for the three generic markets.

The parameter estimates for the major FX rates and gold (XAU-USD) with the corresponding market weights. The sum of the market weights is less than 100 percent. The rest is accounted for by the basic activity a_0. The residual activity a_0, the scale factor ω, and the parameter d, which determines the depth of the minimum at lunch time, are dimensionless numbers. The ω values are a factor of 10^{-4}.

Rate	a_0	k	Market	Weight	ω	o	c	m	d	s
USD-DEM	0.03	1	East Asian	24.1%	1.69	-3:32	8:24	3:33	0.97	-3:33
		2	European	38.5%	1.07	5:54	18:39	11:07	2.06	20:21
		3	American	34.1%	12.46	11:24	23:25	—	—	40:44
USD-JPY	0.03	1	East Asian	35.4%	1.40	-4:14	8:43	3:35	1.01	-4:17
		2	European	27.6%	5.37	6:55	16:40	11:02	1.51	17:23
		3	American	33.4%	18.73	11:48	22:50	—	—	34:55
GBP-USD	0.02	1	East Asian	24.3%	1.05	-3:48	8:59	3:40	1.08	-4:02
		2	European	39.1%	0.98	6:00	18:19	11:13	2.85	20:05
		3	American	34.0%	13.88	11:24	23:11	—	—	31:43
USD-CHF	0.01	1	East Asian	22.0%	1.12	-4:00	9:00	3:40	1.06	-4:00
		2	European	45.1%	1.04	5:00	18:00	11:23	2.45	-4:45
		3	American	31.6%	13.71	12:00	24:00	—	—	24:00
XAU-USD	0.02	1	East Asian	9.7%	0.14	-3:43	9:36	4:05	3.17	-4:15
		2	European	54.8%	2.98	5:36	17:19	11:10	1.54	2:42
		3	American	33.8%	354.9	15:21	21:30	—	—	21:32

In both cases and for all FX rates, the local minima around noon have the following properties: they are pronounced in East Asia, moderate in Europe, and do not exist in America.

The USD-DEM and the USD-CHF have close parameter values as would be expected with a larger weight for Europe in the case of the USD-CHF, whereas the USD-DEM shows a higher weight for the American market. Gold (XAU-USD) has a very small East Asian market, which extends late because it is mainly traded with Europe. In general, its active trading periods in the individual markets seem to be less extended than for the FX rates. A similar effect is detected with silver. The USD-JPY has a strong East Asian component with a strong overlap with the American market. It is for this rate that the earliest opening of the East Asian market is found. The first example in Figure 6.4 (USD-JPY) has its main market in East Asia. The second example in Figure 6.4 (USD-CHF) has it in Europe, in line with the common sense expectation.

An alternative measure of market activity could also be based on the frequency of price quotes. According to the study in Chapter 5 (Table 5.13), this variable is highly correlated to the volatility. Yet we do not recommend it as an activity measure for two reasons.

1. This number depends on the coverage of the FX market by Reuters and its policy to publish prices on its FXFX page. For instance, a new price was

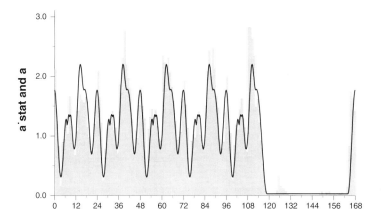

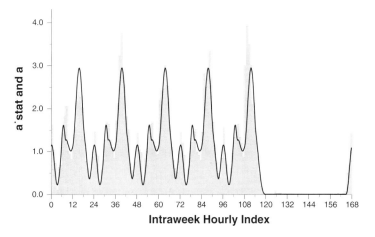

FIGURE 6.3 The histograms of the average hourly activity for a statistical week (over 4 years) for the USD-JPY (above) and USD-CHF (below) rates and the modeled activity.

shown for a particular rate on this page at maximum one price every 6 sec. Some relevant price revisions were therefore lost because of limitations of the data supplier. Whereas the price revisions depend directly on the data supplier's coverage or policy, the prices are issued by market makers who closely follow the real market value and have many data sources available. Thus published prices are conditioned more by other simultaneously available prices, which do not necessarily appear on this data source.

In order to provide some empirical evidence of this dependence, we compare the hourly shares of the weekly number of price revisions in the 168 hr of the statistical week (see Section 6.2.1) of two different data suppli-

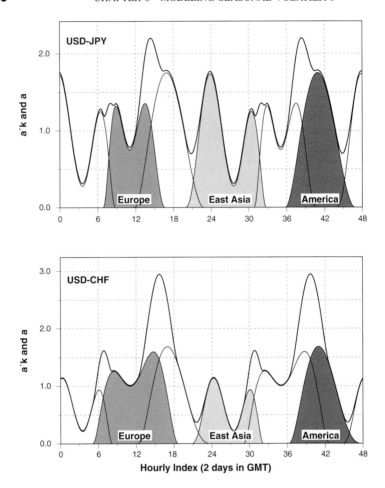

FIGURE 6.4   The model activity decomposed into the three different continental markets over a period of 48 hr during normal business days for the same rates as in Figure 6.3. The top curve is the sum of a_0 and the three market activities.

ers, Reuters and Knight Ridder,[4] for the same period. The two resulting statistical functions differ substantially. Knight Ridder data are about half as frequent as Reuters data and cover the East Asian markets quite poorly. We measure the difference of the two curves in terms of the root mean squared error (RMSE) of all hourly differences.

We then apply the same approach for a comparison of absolute returns between the two suppliers. We analogously measure the difference between the two resulting curves in terms of the RMSE of the hourly differences.

---

[4] Since this study was done, Knight Ridder has been integrated with Telerate to Bridge.

The RMSE ratio R_{RMSE} is defined as follows:

$$R_{RMSE} \equiv \sqrt{\frac{\sum_{i=1}^{24}[(\bar{v}_i^{re} - \bar{v}_i^{kr})/\bar{v}_i^{re}]^2}{\sum_{i=1}^{24}[(\bar{f}_i^{re} - \bar{f}_i^{kr})/\bar{f}_i^{re}]^2}} \qquad (6.16)$$

where $\bar{f}_i$ are the mean hourly number of ticks and $\bar{v}_i$ are the mean hourly absolute returns. The RMSE value here is consistently lower than that for the tick frequency; the ratio is 0.32 for DEM-USD, 0.17 for JPY-USD, 0.20 for USD-GBP, 0.42 for CHF-USD, and 0.52 for XAU-USD. This shows that the volatility is less dependent than the number of price revisions on the data supplier.

Another illustration of this is given in Figure 6.5. We show in these graphs the result of an intraday study of both the tick frequency and the average hourly returns for USD-JPY computed during the same time period on a sample coming from the traditional FXFX page of Reuters (left graphs) and another sample coming from the new method Reuters chose to publish its data, the Reuters Instrument Codes (RICs). This new method, being much more suited for computer manipulations, allows the data vendor to transmit much more information and this is very apparent when examining the two upper graphs on the hourly number of ticks. On the other hand, the two lower graphs show little differences because they are computed directly from the prices, which are not governed by the data vendor policy but rather by the market. We use a similar RMSE ratio as in Equation 6.16 and find values around 0.12. This example indicates clearly the problem one is faced with the activity definition. During the same period and for the same market, the activity should be independent of the data source. This is only the case for the hourly absolute returns.

2. Returns are less sensitive than the tick frequency to data holes. The frequency goes to zero if the communication line is broken (there is no good interpolation method for this variable) whereas, with the proper price interpolation, only the variation around the interpolated line for the returns is lost.

The transaction volume, a potential candidate to describe market activity, is not available in hourly frequency. Transaction volume data are available for particular dates through two surveys published by the Federal Reserve Bank of New York (1986 and 1989). Although these surveys are useful to quantify the amount of capital involved, they do not give any indication about intradaily, daily, and weekly changes. We do not propose our activity model as a direct model for the seasonal patterns of transaction volume, but suggest its usefulness in future research.

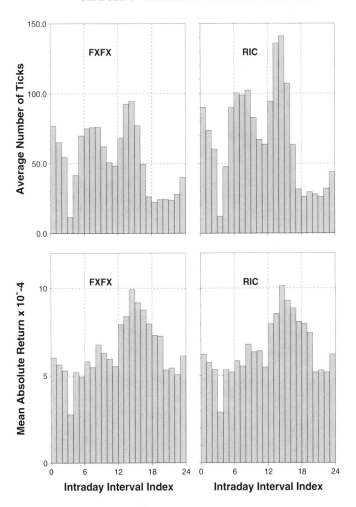

FIGURE 6.5 The comparison of the tick activity (upper graphs) and the hourly absolute return (lower graphs) for two data sources. The old Reuters FXFX page and the new Reuters Instrument Code (RIC) data. The comparison is conducted for the USD-JPY from October 25, 1993 to March 18, 1995.

6.3 A NEW BUSINESS TIME SCALE (ϑ-SCALE)

6.3.1 Definition of the ϑ-Scale

In Section 6.2.2, the time scale ϑ was introduced to model the seasonal, intradaily and intraweekly aspect of heteroskedasticity. In Equation 6.1, the activity variable has been defined as the "speed" of ϑ against the physical time t. The continuous activity function $a(t)$ of Equation 6.7, developed in the previous sections, allows us to define ϑ as its time integral,

$$\vartheta \equiv \vartheta(t) \equiv \int_{t_0}^{t} a(t')\, dt' \equiv a_0\,(t - t_0) + \sum_{k=1}^{3} \vartheta_k(t) \qquad (6.17)$$

The starting date t_0 chosen for the ϑ-scale is arbitrary. The activity is always positive, so its integral $\vartheta(t)$ is a monotonically increasing function. The ϑ_k represents in fact the business time scale of the kth market and is defined as

$$\vartheta_k(t) \equiv \int_{t_0}^{t} a_{1,k}(t')\, dt' \qquad (6.18)$$

This quantity is informative in itself and can be used to model intramarket behavior. Because of the regular weekly pattern of a, ϑ is *predictable* according to Equation 6.17; it may be computed also for the future. Due to normalization (see Equation 6.5), ϑ-time can be measured in the *same units* as physical time (e.g., hours, days, weeks); one full week in ϑ-time corresponds to one week in physical time.

The *relative weight*, W_k, of each market component can be defined with the help of the integral ϑ_k over a full week:

$$W_k = \frac{\vartheta_k(t + 1\ \text{week}) - \vartheta_k(t)}{\vartheta(t + 1\ \text{week}) - \vartheta(t)} = \frac{\vartheta_k(t + 1\ \text{week}) - \vartheta_k(t)}{1\ \text{week}} \qquad (6.19)$$

This is the share of the kth market in the ϑ interval of one week. In Table 6.2, the relative weights of each component, as given by Equation 6.19, are presented together with the fitted parameters. These weights are in fact interesting pieces of information about the market shares of the components defined in Section 6.2.4 and Table 6.1. They are in line with the results of the market surveys regularly made by the (Bank for International Settlements, 1990, 1993, 1995).

The ϑ-scale contracts periods of low activity and expands period of high activity. This is clearly seen on Figure 6.6 where the mapping function between ϑ-time and physical time is shown for USD-DEM over a week. Because the ϑ-time is normalized to physical time over 4 years (see the next section), the two scales almost coincide after a week but not exactly (ϑ-scale is slightly above 168 hr), because we have chosen the week of September 9 to October 1, 1995, where there was no market holiday. This figure shows that during the weekend, ϑ-time flows very slowly, compensating for the low activity during this period in physical time.

6.3.2 Adjustments of the ϑ-Scale Definition

The ϑ-scale defined in Section 6.3.1 reflects a rigid intraweekly pattern of expected market activity. However, there is more relevant information about the activity due to information on business holidays, daylight saving times, and scheduled events in general. In practice, for volatility forecasts, it is desirable to account for this information in the construction of the ϑ-scale. Such adjustments are carried out in Equation 6.17 by recalibrating the factor c^* over the whole sample.

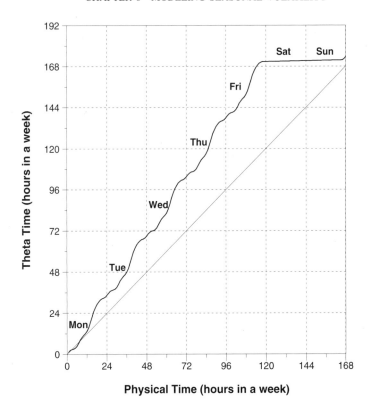

Physical Time (hours in a week)

FIGURE 6.6   The time mapping function between physical time and ϑ time. The week chosen to draw this mapping function is a week with no market holidays (September 25 to October 1, 1995). The thin line represents the flow of physical time.

It is difficult to take into account the different *holidays* of *each* market accurately.[5] In the framework of the three markets of Table 6.1, our approach is an approximate solution. A holiday is considered if it is common to a large part of one of the three markets of the model. On such holidays, the activity $a_{1,k}$ is set to zero for this market. The holiday is treated like a weekend day in Equation 6.10.

In some countries, there are *half-day holidays* . Their treatment would require the splitting of the daily activity functions into morning and afternoon parts. This splitting could also be used to model the few Saturday mornings in Japan (until 1989) when the banks were open. These modifications have not been made as they are beyond our objective of modeling the *main* features of the FX activity patterns.

The *daylight saving time* observed in two of the markets, Europe and America, has an influence on the activity pattern and thus on ϑ . The presence of local markets depends on local time rather than on GMT. One way to deal with this is to convert the time constants of Table 6.2 from GMT to a typical local time scale of the

---

[5] Future holidays are not always known in advance as, for instance, the Islamic holidays. Thus, ϑ might no longer be predictable in those special cases.

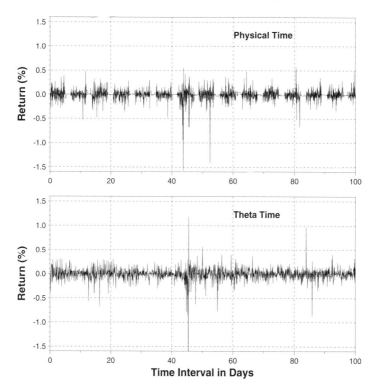

FIGURE 6.7   The hourly returns for USD-DEM from June 3, 1996, 00:00:00 to September 11, 1996, 00:00:00 are plotted using the physical time scale and the ϑ-time scale. Note also the extreme events that are clearly visible on both graphs.

market. This conversion yields different results for the local times in summer and in winter. The time constants are fixed to the *mean* of the summer and winter conversion results, reflecting the fact that the sample used in the activity fitting is composed of approximately half summer and half winter. The computation of the activity and ϑ is then based on Equation 6.10 with these *local* time constants. A better algorithm, which takes into account the difference between summer and winter local market time and which allows a dynamic adaptation to changes in the activity pattern indicates substantial improvement (Breymann, 2000).

So far, volatility patterns with periods of more than one week have been neglected. Yet there may be patterns with longer periods caused by month-end effects, by the monthly or quarterly releases of certain important figures such as the American trade or unemployment figures, and by yearly effects. Moreover, there are long-term changes such as the overall volatility increase over the past 15 years as shown in Chapter 5. None of these effects has been found to be significant in a 4-year sample we studied.

Figure 6.7 illustrates the effect of the time transformation with the hourly returns of USD-DEM over 3 months both in physical and in ϑ-time. It is easy to

TABLE 6.3   Quality test of the ϑ-scale.

Test for the quality of the ϑ-scale as calculated in Equation 6.21. This ratio illustrates the reduction of intraweekly volatility fluctuations when using the ϑ-scale.

	USD-DEM	USD-JPY	GBP-USD	USD-CHF	XAU-USD
Volatility ratio	0.28	0.29	0.25	0.29	0.25

see that the quiet periods during the weekends are in the upper graph in physical time. They give the sense of periodicity. In the lower graph, where hourly returns are computed in ϑ-hours, the seasonality is removed and the picture resembles much more those made with weekly or daily data (omitting weekends). Another remarkable feature of these graphs is the number of large movements. During this period, the USD-DEM experienced price changes as high as 1.5% in an hour.

6.3.3   A Ratio Test for the ϑ-Scale Quality

There are various ways to measure the quality of a ϑ-time scale. Because the goal of such a scale is to remove the daily and weekly seasonality of volatility, it is natural to test the extent to which this has been achieved. Here we define a quantitative test that allows discrimination between various possible business time scales.

The absolute returns on an intraweekly sample as described in Section 6.2.3 are first computed on the physical time scale. We define the size of the weekly fluctuations of mean volatility:

$$F_{v(t)} = \left[\frac{1}{N} \sum_{i=1}^{N} \left(\frac{\sum_{j=1}^{m} |r_j(t_i)|}{m} - \frac{1}{N} \sum_{i=1}^{N} \frac{\sum_{j=1}^{m} |r_j(t_i)|}{m} \right)^2 \right]^{1/2} \tag{6.20}$$

where i is the index of the hourly interval in the statistical week and $N = 168$ the total number of these intervals. Absolute returns are observed and averaged over m weeks with index j, for each hour of the statistical week. The fluctuations, which are large when analyzed in physical time t, should be strongly reduced when analyzed in ϑ-time. For analyzing the fluctuations in ϑ-time, the sampling over one full week is again divided into 168 intervals. Instead of being equally spaced in physical time, they are now equally spaced in ϑ-time. This condition can be formally written as $\vartheta(t_{i+1}) - \vartheta(t_i) = 1$ hr, where the hour is now measured on the ϑ-scale. The sequence t_i that fulfills this condition is computed by numerical inversion of the $\vartheta(t)$ function on one week. The volatiliy ratio is defined by

$$F_{v(\vartheta)} / F_{v(t)} \tag{6.21}$$

where $F_{v(\vartheta)}$ and $F_{v(t)}$ measure the deseasonalized and raw volatility fluctuations. This ratio measures the quality of the extent to which the ϑ scale successfully eliminates the seasonal fluctuations of the volatility.

In Table 6.3, the resulting ratio is between 0.25 and 0.29 for all rates indicating the quality of the ϑ-scale. For a perfect ϑ-scale, the measure tends to zero, and for physical time, the measure is one. Any other ϑ-scale derivation can also be measured the same way, the one with the lowest ratio being the best intraday deseasonalization method. In the next chapter, we will utilize the ϑ-scale in analyzing the autocorrelation function of absolute returns.

6.4 FILTERING INTRADAY SEASONALITIES WITH WAVELETS

The previous sections show that the practical estimation and extraction of the intraday periodic component of the return volatility is feasible. The literature also demonstrated that such extraction of the seasonal volatility component is indispensable for meaningful intraday studies. Earlier studies have shown that strong intraday seasonalities may induce distortions in the estimation of volatility models and are also the dominant source for the underlying misspecifications as studied in (Guillaume et al., 1994; Andersen and Bollerslev, 1997b). Besides, Section 7.3 reveals how such a periodic component pulls the calculated autocorrelations down, giving the impression that there is no persistence other than particular periodicities.

To illustrate the impact of seasonalities, Gençay et al. (2001a) consider the following AR(1) process with a periodic component:

$$y_t = \alpha + \beta y_{t-1} + \sum_{i=1}^{4} 3.0 S_{it} + \epsilon_t \quad t = 1 \dots T \quad (6.22)$$

where $S_{it} = \sin(\frac{2*\pi}{P_i} t) + \eta v_{it}$, $\alpha = 0.0$, $y_0 = 1.0$, $\beta = 0.99$, and $T = 1000$. Periodic components are $P_1 = 3$, $P_2 = 4$, $P_3 = 5$, and $P_4 = 6$ so that the process has 3, 4, 5, and 6 period stochastic seasonality. The random variables ϵ_t and v_{it} are identically and independently distributed disturbance terms with zero mean. The signal-to-noise ratio, η, in each seasonal component is set to 0.30.

Figure 6.8 presents the autocorrelation of the simulated AR(1) process with and without the periodic components. The autocorrelation of the AR(1) process without seasonality (excluding $\sum 3.0 S_{it}$ from the simulated process) starts from a value of 0.95 and decays hyperbolically as expected. However, the autocorrelation of the AR(1) process with the seasonality indicates the existence of a periodic component. The underlying persistence of the AR(1) process in the absence of the seasonality component is entirely obscured by these periodic components. An obvious route is to filter out the underlying seasonalities from the data. A simple method for extracting intraday seasonality that is free of model selection parameters is proposed by Gençay et al. (2001a). The proposed method is based on a wavelet[6] multiscaling approach which decomposes the data into its low and high-frequency components through the application of a nondecimated discrete wavelet transform. In Figure 6.8, the solid line is the autocorrelation of the nonseasonal AR(1) dynamics and the dotted line is the autocorrelation of the deseasonalized series with the method proposed in Gençay et al. (2001a). As

---

[6] An introduction to wavelets can be found in a book by Gençay et al. (2001b).

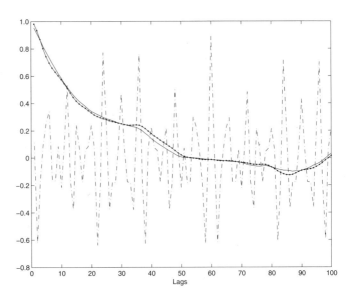

FIGURE 6.8   Sample autocorrelations for the simulated AR(1) process (straight line), AR(1) plus seasonality process (dot-dashed line), and wavelet transformation of the AR(1) plus seasonality process (dotted straight line).

Figure 6.8 demonstrates, wavelet methodology successfully uncovers the nonseasonal dynamics without imposing any spurious persistence into the filtered series.

With this method, Gençay *et al.* (2001a) study two currencies, namely the 5-min Deutschemark – U.S. Dollar (USD-DEM) and Japanese Yen – U.S. Dollar (USD-JPY) price series for the period from October 1, 1992, to September 29, 1993. This data set is also known as the HFDF-I data set. Figure 6.9 presents autocorrelations of the 5-min absolute return series. This shows that the intradaily absolute returns exhibit strong intraday seasonalities. This phenomenon is well-known and reported extensively in the literature; (see for example, Dacorogna *et al.*, 1993; Andersen and Bollerslev, 1997a).

For a long memory process (see Hosking, 1996), the autocovariance function at lag k satisfies $\gamma(k) \sim \lambda k^{-\alpha}$ where λ is the scaling parameter and $\alpha \in [0, 1]$. A leading example is the fractionally integrated process for which $\alpha = 1 - 2d$ and d is the order of fractional integration. In Andersen and Bollerslev (1997a), the fractional order of integration is estimated as $d = 0.36$ for the same USD-DEM series utilized in this example. Andersen *et al.* (2001) calculate six d estimates from various volatility measures for the USD-DEM and USD-JPY series. These six d estimates vary from 0.346 to 0.448. In this example, the fractional integration parameter is set $d = 0.4$ to represent the average of these six estimates. Figure 6.10 presents the autocorrelograms of the filtered 5-min absolute returns along with the estimated autocorrelogram of a long memory process with $d = 0.4$. These

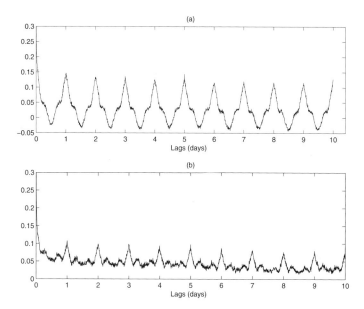

FIGURE 6.9   Sample autocorrelations for the USD-DEM and USD-JPY for the 5-min absolute returns of (a) USD-DEM absolute returns and (b) USD-JPY absolute returns from October 1. 1992. through September 29. 1993.

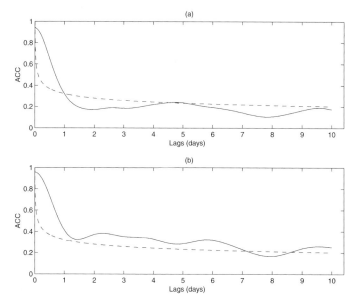

FIGURE 6.10   Sample autocorrelations for the wavelet filtered 5-min absolute returns of (a) USD-DEM and (b) USD-JPY from October 1, 1992 through September 29, 1993. The dotted line is the autocorrelogram for the estimated hyperbolic decay rate for $d = 0.40$— that is, $k^{-.20}$ where k is the number of lags.

findings indicate that the wavelet method is more successful in filtering out intraday seasonalities relative to the method presented in Andersen and Bollerslev (1997a). The persistence of volatility in further lags is also much smaller in Gençay *et al.* (2001a) relative to the Andersen and Bollerslev (1997a). However, the seasonality filters of both Gençay *et al.* (2001a) and Andersen and Bollerslev (1997a) suffer from the fact that the decay of the volatility persistence is slow in the immediate lags relative to the method of Dacorogna *et al.* (1993).

7

REALIZED VOLATILITY DYNAMICS

7.1 INTRODUCTION

High-frequency returns no longer exhibit the seasonal behavior of volatility when investigated in deseasonalized form. Therefore, well-known stylized facts start to be visible in the deseasonalized returns and the corresponding absolute returns. Deseasonalization can be achieved by taking returns regularly spaced in ϑ-time. Absolute returns are just one form of realized volatility whose general definition is given by Equation 3.8.

Realized volatility has a considerable statistical error, which can be reduced by taking returns over short time intervals. This leads to a high number of observations within a given sample.[1] Unfortunately, the choice of a small return interval also leads to a bias caused by microstructure effects. This bias is explained in Section 5.5.3 as a consequence of biased quoting, which leads to a bouncing effect of quotes within a range related to the bid-ask spread. In Section 5.5.3, the bias is treated as a component of the measurement error. In Section 7.2, we study the bias empirically and propose a simple bias correction method that applies to the bias caused by any microstructural effect, not only bid-ask bouncing. Bias-corrected realized volatility has a smaller error than the error attainable without correction.

---

[1] Using overlapping returns is also helpful, as explained in Section 3.2.8.

After appropriately defining realized volatility, we can analyze its dynamical behavior through different statistical methods. The fundamental properties of the volatility dynamics are the conditional heteroskedasticity (also called the volatility clustering) and the long memory of the autocorrelation of volatility.[2] In this chapter, we also examine the asymmetry of information flow between volatilities computed from returns measured at different frequencies which is a typical property to study with high-frequency data. Financial markets are made of traders with different trading horizons. In the heart of the trading mechanisms are the market makers. At the next level up are the intraday traders who carry out trades only within a given trading day but do not carry overnight positions. Then there are day traders who may carry positions overnight, short-term traders and long-term traders. Each of these classes of traders may have their own trading tool sets consistent with their trading horizon and may possess a homogeneous appearance within their own classes. Overall, it is the sum of the activities of all traders for all horizons that generates the market prices. Therefore, market activity would not exhibit homogeneous behavior, but the underlying dynamics would be heterogeneous with each trading horizon (trader class) dynamically providing feedback across all trader classes. Figure 7.1 illustrates such a heterogeneous market where a low-frequency shock to the system penetrates through all layers reaching the market maker in the middle. The impact of these low-frequency shocks penetrates the entire market. The high-frequency shocks, however, would be short lived and may have no impact outside their boundaries. We will study this heterogeneity-driven asymmetry in this chapter.

This book utilizes the deseasonalization method explained in Chapter 6, and Dacorogna et al. (1993), but a flurry of alternative ways of treating the seasonality have also been proposed: the time-of-day dummy variables, Baillie and Bollerslev (1990); a renormalization of the returns by the seasonal volatility, Taylor and Xu (1997); the flexible Fourier framework to model the seasonal pattern, Andersen and Bollerslev (1997b); time deformation with tick frequency, Pecen et al. (1995); Baestaens and Van den Bergh (1995); the use of cubic splines, Engle and Russell (1997); models that include both systematic components and stochastic seasonal components, Beltratti and Morana (1998); and the wavelet multiresolution method of Gençay et al. (2001a) in Section 6.4.

7.2 THE BIAS OF REALIZED VOLATILITY AND ITS CORRECTION

Realized volatility plays a key role both for the exploration of stylized facts and for practical applications such as market risk assessment. When computing it,

---

[2] This clustering property was first noted in Mandelbrot (1963) in his study of cotton prices and the long memory in Mandelbrot (1971). These findings remained dormant until the early 1980s for the volatility clustering until Engle (1982) and Bollerslev (1986) proposed the ARCH and GARCH processes. In the early 1990s, a comprehensive study of the long memory properties of the financial markets had started.

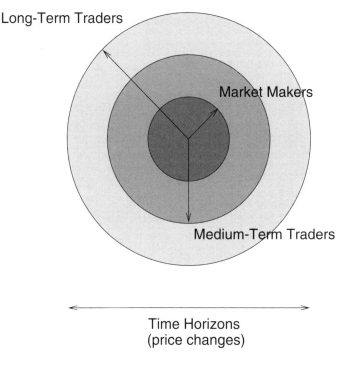

Long-Term Traders

Market Makers

Medium-Term Traders

Time Horizons
(price changes)

FIGURE 7.1   Financial markets are made of traders with different trading horizons. In the heart of the trading mechanisms are the market makers. A next level up are the intraday traders who carry out trades only within a given trading day. Then there are day traders who may carry positions overnight, short-term traders and long-term traders. Each of these classes of traders may have their own trading tool sets and may possess a homogeneous appearance within their own classes. Overall, it is the sum of the activities of all traders for all horizons that generates the market prices. Therefore, market activity is heterogeneous with each trading horizon dynamically providing feedback across the distributions of trading classes.

using Equation 3.8, we can take advantage of high-frequency data by choosing a short time interval Δt of the analyzed returns. This leads to a large number of observations within a given sample and thus a low stochastic error. At the same time, it leads to a considerable bias in most cases.

In the following bias study, Equation 3.8 is considered in the following form:

$$v(t_i) \;=\; v(\Delta t, n, 2; t_i) \;=\; \left\{ \frac{1}{n} \sum_{j=1}^{n} [r(\Delta t; t_{i-n+j})]^2 \right\}^{1/2} \qquad (7.1)$$

The choice of the exponent $p = 2$ has some advantages here. In Section 5.5, we found that the empirical drift exponent of v is close to the Gaussian value 0.5 if v is defined with an exponent $p = 2$. Assuming such a scaling behavior and a fixed sample of size $T = n\Delta t$, v^2 has an expectation independent of Δt:

$$E[v^2(n\Delta t, 1, 2; t_i)] = n E[v^2(\Delta t, n, 2; t_i)] = \sum_{j=1}^{n}[r(\Delta t; t_{i-n+j})]^2 \quad (7.2)$$

Thus v^2 can be empirically estimated as the sum of all squared returns within T, irrespective of the size of Δt. Moreover, the time scale can be changed, such as from ϑ-time to physical time, and the return intervals can be of irregular size. This implies that the estimator is also immune to data gaps within the full sample. If prices are interpolated, previous-tick interpolation (see Equation 3.1) should be used here, because linear interpolation leads to an underestimation of volatility. With all the mentioned modifications, the sum of squared returns remains an estimator for v^2, as long as all the return intervals exactly cover the full sample T. These nice properties may have led Andersen *et al.* (2000) to choose the name "realized volatility" for the sum of squared returns, as on the right-hand side of Equation 7.2.

The empirically found bias violates Equation 7.2, especially if Δt is very small. The deviation of the empirical behavior from Equation 7.2 provides a measure of the bias. We choose a large enough time interval $\Delta t_{\text{ref}} = q\Delta t$ as the bias-free reference case to judge the bias of smaller intervals Δt. In practice, a good choice of Δt_{ref} is between few hours and 1 working day. We define the bias factor $B(t_i)$:

$$B(t_i) = \frac{\sqrt{q}\, v(\Delta t, m\,q, 2; t_i)}{v(\Delta t_{\text{ref}}, m, 2; t_i)} = \sqrt{\frac{\sum_{j=1}^{mq}[r(\Delta t; t_{i-mq+j})]^2}{\sum_{j=1}^{m}[r(\Delta t_{\text{ref}}; t_{i-mq+jq})]^2}} \quad (7.3)$$

where m is the number of analyzed reference intervals of size Δt_{ref}, and $q = \Delta t_{\text{ref}}/\Delta t$ is an integer number. If the scaling assumption of Equation 7.2 is true, $B(t_i)$ converges to 1 for large samples (i.e., large m and q). The bias can be measured in terms of the deviation of $B(t_i)$ from 1.

In Figure 7.2, the bias factor $B(t_i)$ is plotted versus time, for two different markets: the FX rate USD-CHF and the equity index Nikkei-225. The time scale in both cases is a business time: the 49 weekend hr from Friday 8 p.m. GMT to Sunday 9 p.m. GMT are compressed to the equivalent of only 1 hr outside the weekend. The results do not strongly depend on this choice. Similar bias behaviors are obtained when the analysis is done in ϑ-time or physical time. The reference time interval is $\Delta t_{\text{ref}} = 1$ working day. The investigated return intervals Δt are much shorter and vary between 2 min ($q = 720$) and 1 hr ($q = 24$). The number $m = 260$ of reference intervals is chosen high enough to limit the stochastic error of $v(\Delta t_{\text{ref}}, m, 2; t_i)$. This means a bias measurement on a moving sample of about 1 year ≈ 260 working days.

The bias factor distinctly deviates from 1 in Figure 7.2, especially for small values of Δt such as 2 min and 5 min. For $\Delta t = 1$ hr, the bias is still visible but

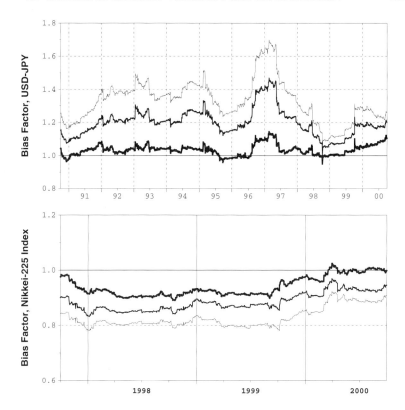

FIGURE 7.2 Bias factors plotted versus time, for the FX rate USD-JPY (upper panel) and the Japanese equity index Nikkei-225 (lower panel). Deviations from 1 indicate a bias in realized volatility. The bias factor is the ratio of two mean realized volatilities over the same sample (see Equation 7.3). The investigated return measurement intervals Δt are as follows. Bold curves: $\Delta t = 1$ hr; middle curves: $\Delta t = 5$ min; thin curves: $\Delta t = 2$ min.

can be neglected more easily. Surprisingly, the biases have different signs. The bias of the foreign exchange (FX) rate is positive, whereas that of the equity index is negative ($B(t_i) < 1$). The bias can be explained by microstructure effects, but these are obviously different for different markets. The microstructure effects of FX rates were discussed in Chapter 5, in particular the negative autocorrelation due to a bouncing effect within the bid-ask spread (Section 5.2.1). The bias due to this effect can be modeled as in Section 5.5.3 and in Corsi *et al.* (2001), where the influence of data gaps on the bias is also analyzed. There is ongoing research aiming at refined versions of this bias model. The negative bias of the equity index has to be explained differently. An equity index is a weighted average of some equity prices. Some of the individual equities play a leading role in price adjustments and establish small trends that the other equities follow. This mechanism causes a short-term (few minutes) positive autocorrelation of the index returns and eventually a negative bias of realized volatility when a very short interval Δt is chosen. The bias factors moderately fluctuate over time, but there are no dramatic shifts. The overall levels are maintained even over the 10-year sample of Figure 7.2 (upper panel).

The bias can be avoided either by taking large return intervals Δt (with the disadvantage of large stochastic errors) or by introducing a *bias correction* for small intervals Δt. Eliminating the bias seems to be a demanding task requiring a model of the microstructure effects. Section 5.5.3 has such a model for FX rates, but other markets such as equity indices need other models.

Instead of developing bias models for each market, we suggest a simple bias correction method that needs no explicit model and only relies on the assumption that the bias-generating mechanism is much more stable over time than the volatility itself. The limited size of bias fluctuations in Figure 7.2 justifies this assumption. The bias correction is simple. Each realized volatility observation is divided by the bias factor as measured in the past:

$$
v_{\text{corr}}(\Delta t, n, 2; t_i) \;=\; \frac{v(\Delta t, n, 2; t_i)}{B(t_i)} \tag{7.4}
$$

where $B(t_i)$ is defined by Equation 7.3. This bias correction can be computed in real time, because it is based on information fully available at time t_i. Some variations of Equation 7.4 are possible, as suggested by Corsi *et al.* (2001). The bias correction factor can be computed by moving average operators as explained in Section 3.3 instead of the sums of Equation 7.3.

Figure 7.3 probes the success of the simple bias correction. The bias factor B_{corr} of the already bias-corrected realized volatility can be measured in the same way as the bias of the uncorrected volatility (Equation 7.3):

$$
B_{\text{corr}}(t_i) \;=\; \frac{\sqrt{q}\; v_{\text{corr}}(\Delta t, m\,q, 2; t_i)}{v(\Delta t_{\text{ref}}, m, 2; t_i)} \tag{7.5}
$$

A perfect bias correction implies $B_{\text{corr}}(t_i) \equiv 1$. However, the bias correction is not perfect. Both the bias correction and its measurement in Equation 7.5 rely on a quantity $v(\Delta t_{\text{ref}}, m, 2; t_i)$, which has a stochastic error. These imperfections are visible in the form of fluctuations of B_{corr} about 1 in Figure 7.3. Figure 7.2 and Figure 7.3 are based on the same samples and parameters and can directly be compared. B_{corr} in Figure 7.3 is much closer to 1 than B in Figure 7.2, in all cases. This fact demonstrates a successful bias correction for both markets, FX and the equity index.

In spite of the success of Equation 7.4 as shown in Figure 7.3, the simple bias correction has some shortcomings, one of them being the multiplicative nature of the formula. Realized volatility values are corrected by a slowly varying correction factor, irrespective of the current volatility level. One can argue that an additive or nonlinear correction of realized volatility would reflect reality better than the multiplicative correction. (An additive correction may lead to impossible negative volatility values, though.) A fair judgment may be as follows. Equation 7.4

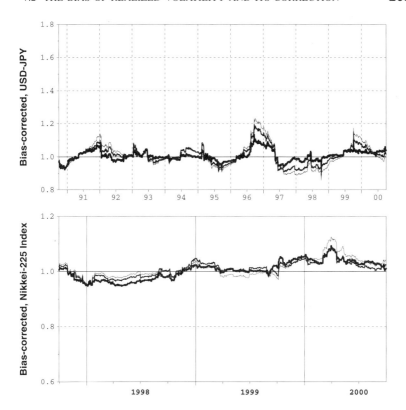

FIGURE 7.3 Bias factors plotted versus time, for the FX rate USD-JPY (upper panel) and the Japanese equity index Nikkei-225 (lower panel), computed by Equation 7.5. The investigated realized volatility values have already been bias-corrected by Equation 7.4, so the small deviations from 1 indicate imperfections of the bias correction. The investigated return measurement intervals Δt are as follows. Bold curves: $\Delta t = 1$ hr; middle curves: $\Delta t = 5$ min; thin curves: $\Delta t = 2$ min. The same scaling as in Figure 7.2 is used.

succeeds in largely reducing the bias and is thus better than no bias correction. As soon as an appropriate model of the bias-generating process for a particular market exists, the corresponding bias-correction method will be clearly superior to Equation 7.4.

Bias correction is a means to compute realized volatility with smaller intervals Δt and, for a given sample of size $T = n\Delta t$, a smaller stochastic error. Unfortunately, the bias correction introduces an additional stochastic error due to the factor $v(\Delta t_{\text{ref}}, m, 2; t_i)$ in Equation 7.3. Corsi *et al.* (2001) show that a bias-corrected volatility with reasonable parameters has a total error that is still distinctly smaller than the error of uncorrected volatility. The following rough calculation also shows this. Uncorrected volatility requires a rather large Δt of about 1 hr (with $q = 24$) to keep the bias at bay. The stochastic error is proportional to $\sqrt{1/24}$, and a bias of roughly of the same size adds to the error. Bias-corrected volatility can have a small $\Delta t = 5$ min ($q = 288$). The stochastic error is proportional to $\sqrt{1/288}$, but the factor $v(\Delta t_{\text{ref}}, m, 2; t_i)$ with $m = 260$ leads to another stochastic error component proportional to $\sqrt{1/260}$. Both error components together are proportional to $\sqrt{1/288 + 1/260} \approx \sqrt{1/137}$. This is distinctly smaller than the value without bias correction, $\sqrt{1/24}$ (where the bias makes the error even larger).

So far, the bias discussion has been restricted to realized volatility with an exponent $p = 2$ in Equation 3.8. When choosing another exponent (such as $p = 1$, a good choice for many following studies), the bias discussion becomes more complicated. The scaling behavior deviates from Gaussian scaling, as seen in Section 5.5, and data gaps have a stronger influence on the bias than in the case $p = 2$. For exponents other than 2, a bias correction with a formula such as Equation 7.4 is less successful, and more research is needed. The technique of bias correction is rather new and will be improved by ongoing research. The realized volatility studies of the following sections are older and do not contain any bias correction. However, the choice of very short return intervals (such as 5 min) has been avoided, so the size of the bias is limited.

7.3   CONDITIONAL HETEROSKEDASTICITY

7.3.1   Autocorrelation of Volatility in ϑ-Time

This section analyzes the autocorrelations of returns and realized volatility in physical and ϑ-time.[3] The study utilizes a 20-min frequency instead of an hourly one. We did not take smaller intervals than 20 min in order to avoid a strong bias, as explained in Section 7.2. The autocorrelation function of the USD-DEM is shown in Figure 7.4 for up to 720 lags. The confidence intervals in Figure 7.4 refer to 95% confidence for a Gaussian random process around the sample mean. Because the distributions of returns and volatility are not Gaussian, the confidence intervals are provided as a reference rather than for exact statistical significance.

In Figure 7.4, the autocorrelation function of volatility has a distinct structure, which is far beyond the confidence intervals. For lags of any integer number of days, clear peaks are found. These peaks indicate the *daily* seasonality. The *weekly* seasonality is highly visible in the form of high autocorrelation for lags around 1 week and low autocorrelation for lags of about *half* a week (which frequently means the correlation of working days and weekends). Finally, there is a finer structure with small but visible peaks at integer multiples of 8 hr, corresponding to a frequency *three* times the daily frequency. Our world market model with *three* continental markets is confirmed by this observation. Apart from these seasonal peaks there must be a positive component of the autocorrelation that declines with increasing lag. In Figure 7.4, this component cannot be observed as it is overshadowed by seasonality.

The autocorrelations of returns, unlike those of volatility (absolute returns), are close to zero and within the confidence intervals for most of the lags. The

---

[3] Absolute returns are studied here.

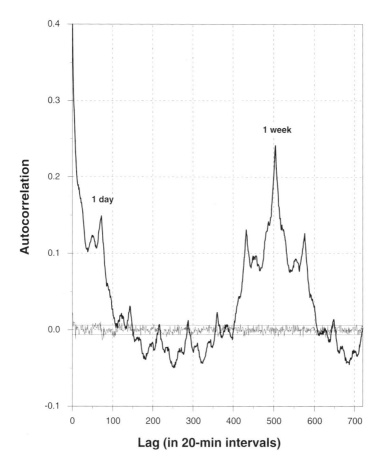

Lag (in 20-min intervals)

FIGURE 7.4 The autocorrelation function of USD-DEM returns and volatility (absolute returns). The data sampling is in 20-min frequency in *physical time* for lags up to 10 days. The 95% confidence interval is for a Gaussian random process. The sampling period is from March 3, 1986, to March 3, 1990.

squared returns, instead of absolute returns, may also be used as a proxy for the underlying volatility. Autocorrelations of square returns also exhibit similar seasonality peaks as those of absolute returns, but are less pronounced. It is well known that the theoretical autocorrelation of squared returns is meaningful only if the *kurtosis* of the return process is finite, which is not guaranteed for currency returns.

A similar autocorrelation analysis is also carried out with the ϑ-time scale instead of the physical time t, and it is presented in Figure 7.5. There are no large seasonal peaks in the volatility autocorrelations of the ϑ-time. This is due to the fact that the ϑ-scale is constructed to eliminate the intraday seasonality. The autocorrelation of volatility is significantly positive and declines at an hyperbolic

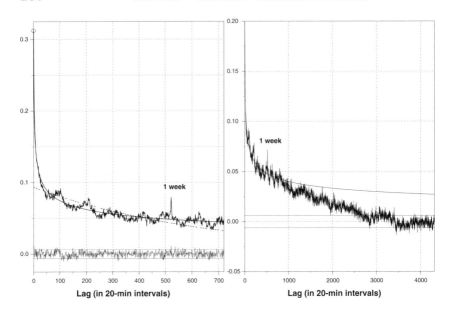

FIGURE 7.5 The autocorrelation function of the USD-DEM returns and the absolute returns at 20-min data frequency in ϑ-*time*. The number of lags is up to 10 ϑ days. The first lag is marked by an empty circle. The exponential decay is shown with a dashed line. The hyperbolically decay fits best to the autocorrelation function of the absolute returns. The figure on the right is the same autocorrelation function for the absolute returns extended to a much larger number of lags with the superimposition of the hyperbolic decay.

rate. This behavior can be explained by the presence of a long memory process in the underlying data-generating process of returns. The rate of decline in the autocorrelation is, however, slower than an exponential decline, which would be expected for a low-order GARCH process, Bollerslev (1986).

The autocorrelation function of volatility (Figure 7.5) is not completely free of seasonalities. A narrow peak can be identified at a lag of 1 week. This peak might be due to the day of the week effects. In our framework, the activity is assumed to be the same for all working days, which may exhibit slight variations across the working days. A small local maximum at a lag of around 1 average business day (one-fifth of a week in ϑ); a small local maximum at a lag of 2 business days and maxima at 3 and 4 business days also exist. A plausible reason for these remaining autocorrelation peaks is a market-dependent persistence of absolute returns. Autocorrelations with a lag of 1 business day compare with the behaviors of the same market participants, whereas autocorrelations with lags of one half or $1\frac{1}{2}$ business days compare with the behaviors of different market participants (on opposite sides of the globe). The market-dependent persistence decreases after 2 business days. The predominance of the "meteor shower hypothesis" found by Engle *et al.* (1990) is confirmed by the fact that the autocorrelation curve in

Figure 7.5 does not exhibit strong maxima for each full business day. Yet the remaining small maxima indicate a certain "heat wave" component.

7.3.2 Short and Long Memory

The autocorrelation function of volatility decays at a *hyperbolic* rate rather than an exponential rate. In studies based on daily FX prices (e.g., Taylor, 1986) or weekly FX prices (e.g., Diebold, 1988), the number of observations is usually too small for outright rejection of either a hyperbolic or an exponential decay of the autocorrelation functions. In studies with longer daily series such as Ding *et al.* (1993), evidence of long memory is found with the S&P 500 from January 1928 to August 1991 (17,055 observations). To illustrate the presence of the long memory, two curves, one hyperbolic and one exponential, are drawn in Figure 7.5 together with the empirical autocorrelation functions. The hyperbolic curve approximates the autocorrelation function much more closely than the exponential curve. This behavior of volatility is similar to the *fractional noise* process of Mandelbrot and Van Ness (1968) and Mandelbrot (1972), which exhibits hyperbolic decay in the autocorrelation function and thus the long memory serial dependence.

The hyperbolic (f_h) and exponential (f_e) functions used in the analysis above have the following form:

$$f_h(\tau) = k\, \tau^{-h}, \text{ and } f_e(\tau) = k\, e^{-\tau/h} \tag{7.6}$$

where the parameters are k, h, and τ. τ determines the lag order of the autocorrelation function. The exponential function cannot simultaneously capture the short and long-term persistence, whereas the hyperbolic function is able to capture both successfully. For the hyperbolic function, k values vary from 0.2 to 0.3 depending on the FX rate, whereas h is remarkably stable around 0.28 for all the rates.

In Figure 7.4 and the first panel of Figure 7.5, the number of lags are limited to 720 intervals (i.e., 10 days) at the 20-min data frequency. In the second panel of Figure 7.5, the number of lags are extended to 4320 (i.e., 60 days) in ϑ-scale. The decay in the volatility autocorrelations is more rapid after 10 days. This type of pattern is not specific to USD-DEM, but is also found in longer time intervals and other FX rates. To explore this behavior further, we compute the autocorrelation function of daily returns (business days) for up to 200 lags and a sample of 20 years. The result is presented in Figure 7.6 and indicates the persistence of the hyperbolic behavior even at the daily frequency.

A process that exhibits a hyperbolic decay in its autocorrelation function is the "fractional noise" of Mandelbrot and Van Ness (1968), which is a purely self-similar fractal. We test the empirical significance for this theoretical process. In Mandelbrot (1972), the autocorrelation function of fractional noise processes is given by

$$a = \frac{|l+1|^{2H} - 2\, l^{2H} + |l-1|^{2H}}{2} \tag{7.7}$$

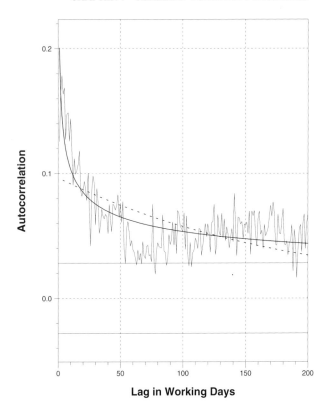

Lag in Working Days

FIGURE 7.6 Autocorrelation function of the absolute business day volatilities in the ϑ-time scale. The data are for the USD-DEM rate from June 1, 1973, to June, 1, 1993. The hyperbolic (solid curve) and the exponential functions (dotted curve) are superimposed on the empirical autocorrelation function. The 95% confidence intervals are for an identically and independently distributed Gaussian process.

where l is the lag parameter and H the Hurst exponent, which lies between 0.5 and 1 for "persistent" fractional noise. For a large number of lags (l), the autocorrelation function converges to

$$a \;\approx\; H\,(2\,H - 1)\, l^{2(H-1)} \tag{7.8}$$

which has a hyperbolic decay. The autocorrelations of absolute returns in Figures 7.5 and 7.6 also follow a hyperbolic decline. The exponent $2(H - 1)$ of Equation 7.8 from the USD-DEM volatilities is $H = 0.87$ in Figure 7.5 and $H = 0.86$ in Figure 7.6. From the H values, the factor $H(2H - 1)$ leads to 0.64 and 0.62, respectively. These values are empirically found to be much lower, which are 0.25 and 0.20, respectively. This indicates that volatility does not follow a *pure* fractional noise process. Volatility is positive definite and has a skewed and fat-tailed distribution, whereas the distribution function of pure fractional noise is Gaussian.

In Peters (1989, 1991), the existence of fractional noise in the returns rather than volatility has been investigated similar to Equation 5.10. These findings claim that a drift exponent different from 0.5 necessarily indicates fractional noise. This conclusion holds only if the distribution forms are stable, but Figure 5.6 does not support this claim. We, therefore, conclude that the return process does not support the fractional noise hypothesis. Unlike volatility, the returns themselves exhibit no significant autocorrelation (see the thin curves in Figures 7.4 and 7.5).

7.4 THE HETEROGENEOUS MARKET HYPOTHESIS

In the earlier sections, we analyzed the presence of two stylized facts. Namely, a hyperbolic decay of the volatility autocorrelations and the "heat wave" effect. Volatility characterizes the market behavior more deeply than just indicating the size of current or recent price movements. It is the visible "footprint" of less observable variables such as market presence and also market volume (for which information is hardly available in FX markets).

The fact is that, contrary to traditional beliefs, volatility is found to be positively correlated to market presence, activity, and volume. Karpoff (1987), Baillie and Bollerslev (1989), and Müller et al. (1990), emphasize the key role of volatility for understanding market structures. The serial correlation studies of LeBaron (1992b,c) show that subsequent returns are correlated in low-volatility periods and slightly anti-correlated in high-volatility periods. In continuous samples mixed from both low-volatility and high-volatility periods, this effect indicates that the forecastability of return is conditional to volatility. Thus, volatility is also an indicator for the persistence of trends.

These properties of volatility lead us to the hypothesis of a heterogeneous market, as opposed to the assumption of a homogeneous market where all participants interpret news and react to news in the same way. The heterogeneous market hypothesis is characterized by the following:

1. Different agents of the heterogeneous market have different time horizons and dealing frequencies. On the side of high dealing frequencies, there are the FX dealers and market makers (who usually have to close all their open positions before the evening); on the side of low dealing frequencies, there are the central banks, commercial organizations, and, for example, the pension fund investors with their currency hedging. The different dealing frequencies clearly mean different reactions to the same news in the same market. The market is heterogeneous with a "fractal" structure of the participants' time horizons as it consists of short-term, medium-term, and long-term components. Each such component has its own reaction time to news, related to its time horizon and characteristic dealing frequency. If we assume the memory of volatility of one component to be exponentially declining with a certain time constant, as in a GARCH(1,1) process, the memory of the whole market is composed of many such exponential declines with different time constants. The superposition of many

exponential declines with widely differing time constants comes close to a hyperbolic decline.

2. In a homogeneous market, the more agents are present, the faster the price should converge to the "real market value" on which all agents have "rational expectations." Thus, the volatility should by negatively correlated with market presence and activity. In a heterogeneous market, different market actors are likely to settle for different prices and decide to execute their transactions in different market situations. In other words, they create volatility. This is reflected in the empirically found, positive correlation of volatility and market presence.

3. The market is also heterogeneous in the geographic location of the participants. This immediately explains the "heat wave" effect. In Section 7.3.1, we indicated that the memory in the volatility process is relatively weak at time lags of about $\frac{1}{2}$ or $1\frac{1}{2}$ business days when market actors on opposite sides of the globe are related to each other and relatively strong at time lags of about 1 or 2 business days when identical groups of participants are considered.

The market participants of the heterogeneous market hypothesis differ also in other aspects beyond the time horizons and the geographical locations. They may have different degrees of risk aversion, face different institutional constraints, and transaction costs.

7.4.1   Volatilities of Different Time Resolutions

The heterogeneous market hypothesis presented in the previous section is associated with fractal phenomena in the empirical behavior of FX markets. A scaling law relating time horizon and size of price movements (volatility) was identified in Chapter 5. This relation is used here to explain why the perception of volatility differs for market agents with different time horizons.

Short-term traders are constantly watching the market to reevaluate their current positions and execute transactions at a high frequency. Long-term traders may look at the market only once a day or less frequently. A quick price increase of 0.5% followed by a quick decrease of the same size, for example, is a major event for an FX intraday trader but a nonevent for central banks and long-term investors.[4] Long-term traders are interested only in large price movements and these normally happen only over long time intervals (see the scaling law of Müller *et al.*, 1990). Therefore, long-term traders with open positions have no need to watch the market every minute.[5] In other words, they judge the market, its prices, and also its volatility with a coarse time grid. A coarse time grid reflects the view of a long-term trader and a fine time grid that of a short-term trader. Bjorn (1994) follows similar methodologies for building an automatic trading model.

---

[4] Small, short-term price moves may sometimes have a certain influence on the *timing* of long-term traders' transactions but not on their investment decisions.

[5] They have other means to limit the risk of rare large price movements by stop-loss limits or options.

The time grid in which real traders watch the market is not strictly regular. In the following lagged correlation study, however, we measure volatilities over different but regularly spaced grids. These volatilities are defined in terms of absolute returns. We prefer mean absolute values to roots of mean squares here because they are statistically less dominated by extreme observations, which are rather important in FX markets with their fat-tailed unconditional distribution functions. The convergence of the fourth moment—a requirement for many types of analysis such as the autocorrelation of squared returns—is not guaranteed for empirical returns. In Chapter 5, we demonstrated that the autocorrelations of the returns indicate a stronger signal for powers around one. This argument is reinforced in Dacorogna *et al.* (2001a), where the autocorrelation of absolute returns is also shown to be much more stable under sample size changes than that of the squared returns. Other studies, such as Ding *et al.* (1993), also find absolute returns to be optimal in the autocorrelation studies.

The volatility based on absolute returns has two essential timing parameters (Guillaume *et al.*, 1997):

- The interval size of the time grid in which returns are observed
- The total size of the sample over which it is computed (the number of grid intervals considered)

For exploring the behavior of volatilities of different time resolution, we define two types of volatility. The "coarse" volatility, v_c, and the "fine" volatility, v_f, are defined by

$$v_c(t_i) = |\sum_{j=1}^{n} r(\Delta t', t_{i-1} + j \Delta t')| \text{ and } v_f(t_i) = \sum_{j=1}^{n} |r(\Delta t', t_{i-1} + j \Delta t')|$$

(7.9)

where $\Delta t' \equiv \Delta t / n$. Figure 7.7 illustrates this definition where at every time point, $t_i = t_{i-1} + 6\Delta t'$, both quantities are simultaneously defined. In this way, the two synchronous time series are obtained whose relation can be explored.

7.4.2 Asymmetric Lead-Lag Correlation of Volatilities

Analyzing the correlation between two time series, such as fine and coarse volatilities, is a standard technique used in empirical finance where the correlation coefficient measures the linear dependence of the two time series. *Lagged* correlation is a more powerful tool to investigate the relation between two time series. The lagged correlation function considers the two series not only simultaneously (at lag 0) but also with a time shift. The correlation coefficient ϱ_τ of one time series and another one shifted by a positive or negative time lag τ is measured and plotted against the value of the lag. The lagged correlation study of this section follows Müller *et al.* (1997a).

Lagged correlation reveals causal relations and information flow structures in the sense of Granger causality. If two time series were generated on the basis of

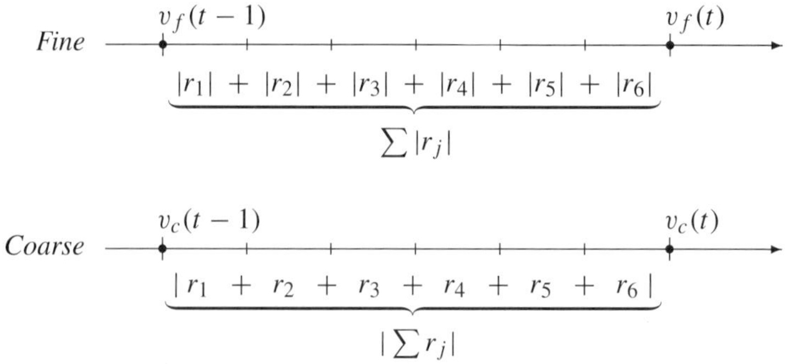

Fine
$$v_f(t-1) \qquad\qquad\qquad v_f(t)$$

$$\underbrace{|r_1| + |r_2| + |r_3| + |r_4| + |r_5| + |r_6|}$$

$$\sum |r_j|$$

Coarse
$$v_c(t-1) \qquad\qquad\qquad v_c(t)$$

$$\underbrace{|\, r_1 + r_2 + r_3 + r_4 + r_5 + r_6\, |}$$

$$\left| \sum r_j \right|$$

FIGURE 7.7 The coarse volatility, $v_c(t)$, captures the view and actions of long-term traders while the fine volatility, $v_f(t)$, captures the view and actions of short-term traders. The two volatilities are calculated at the same time points and are synchronized.

a synchronous information flow, they would have a symmetric lagged correlation function, $\varrho_\tau = \varrho_{-\tau}$. The symmetry would be violated only by insignificantly small, purely stochastic deviations. As soon as the deviations between ϱ_τ and $\varrho_{-\tau}$ become significant, there is asymmetry in the information flow and a causal relation that requires an explanation.

In a first analysis, we consider a working-daily time series where weekends are omitted. The variables under study are the "fine volatility" and the "coarse volatility." Fine volatility is the mean absolute working-daily returns averaged over five observations, so covering a full (working) week. Coarse volatility is the absolute return over a full weekly interval.

The correlation between fine volatility and coarse volatility is a function of the number of lags. When the number of lags is zero, the fine and coarse volatilities are completely identical. In the case of first positive or negative lag, the two intervals do not overlap but follow each other immediately.

The panel on the left hand side of Figure 7.8 shows the lagged correlation function for the USD-DEM in a sample longer than 21 years. The correlation maximum is found at lag zero, which is expected. For the nonzero lags, there is an asymmetry where the coarse volatility predicts fine volatility better than the other way around. The asymmetry is significant for the first two lags where the difference $\varrho_\tau - \varrho_{-\tau}$, represented by the thin curve in Figure 7.8, is distinctly outside the confidence interval for identically and independently distributed observations.

This result can be explained in terms of the heterogeneous market hypothesis presented earlier in this section. For short-term traders, the level of coarse volatility matters because it determines the expected size of trends and thus the scope of trading opportunities. On one hand, short-term traders react to clusters of coarse volatility by changing their trading behavior and so causing clusters of fine volatility. On the other hand, the level of fine volatility does not affect the trading strategies of long-term traders (who often act according to the "fundamentals" of the market).

TABLE 7.1 Difference between lagged correlation for FX rates and gold. The sample period is from June 6, 1973, (August 8, 1980 for gold) to February 1, 1995. The lags are measured in weeks and 3 hr (in ϑ-time), respectively. The negative values indicate the predictability of finely defined volatility from coarse volatility.

Differences	USD-DEM	USD-JPY	GBP-USD	CHF-USD	DEM-JPY	XAU-USD
Weekly						
$\varrho_1 - \varrho_{-1}$	-0.138	-0.127	-0.130	-0.131	-0.129	-0.122
$\varrho_2 - \varrho_{-2}$	-0.105	-0.047	-0.055	-0.076	-0.074	-0.072
3 hourly						
$\varrho_1 - \varrho_{-1}$	-0.117	-0.136	-0.113	-0.093	-0.100	-0.108
$\varrho_2 - \varrho_{-2}$	-0.058	-0.057	-0.059	-0.056	-0.055	-0.068

Similar behavior of the lagged correlation is observed for other FX rates such as USD-JPY and GBP-USD, cross rates such as DEM-JPY, and gold (XAU-USD). Table 7.1 reports the difference $\varrho_1 - \varrho_{-1}$ and $\varrho_2 - \varrho_{-2}$ for a set of these time series. The numbers are similar across the different rates (and also all of the investigated minor FX rates not shown here). The first lag difference is around -0.13 and the second lag difference is around -0.07.

The results with daily data also prevail in high-frequency and in intraday data. Every intra-day study requires an appropriate treatment of the strong intradaily seasonality of volatility. Here we use the predefined business time scale ϑ presented in Chapter 6. A time series with regular intervals in ϑ-time is constructed by selecting the last quote before each point of a regular ϑ-grid. As a basic time interval in ϑ-time, we choose 30 min. This means there is only some 7 min of physical time during the daily volatility peak in the European afternoon and American morning.[6] Fine volatility is now the mean absolute half-hourly returns averaged over six observations, covering a 3-hr time interval. Coarse volatility is the absolute returns over a full 3-hr interval. All these time intervals are calculated in ϑ-time. An interval of 3 ϑ-hr is clearly smaller than the working day of an FX dealer. It often covers a time span with quite homogeneous market conditions.

Figure 7.8 (right panel) provides the lagged correlation function for USD-DEM in 8 years of half-hour returns. Although the half-hour data cover a shorter time span than the daily series, the number of observations is larger. The findings from the half-hourly data confirm the results from the daily series such that coarse volatility predicts fine volatility. We therefore conclude that these findings are independent of the data frequency.

The intradaily behavior of the lagged correlation is similar for other FX rates and gold (see Table 7.1). The empirical findings are similar across the different rates. The first lag difference is around -0.11 and the second lag difference is around -0.06, which are close to the corresponding values of Table 7.1. In the

---

[6] In fact, a much higher frequency of the series should be avoided due to the fact that price changes observed over 5 min or less can be overly biased by microstructure effects (see Section 7.2).

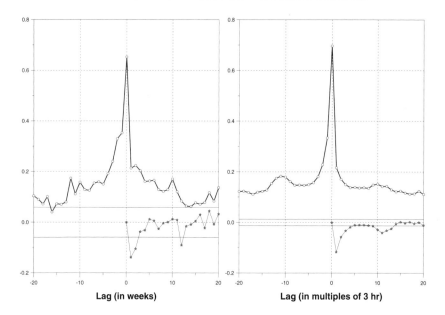

Lag (in weeks)   **Lag (in multiples of 3 hr)**

FIGURE 7.8 Asymmetric lagged correlation of fine and coarse volatilities for USD-DEM. The *left* figure is for working-daily return in a week. The *right* graph is for high resolution study with half-hourly returns within 3 hr (in ϑ-time). The negative lags indicate that the coarse volatility was lagged compared to the fine volatility. The thin curve indicates the asymmetry. The 95% confidence intervals are for identically and independently distributed observations. The sampling period for the left figure is 21 years and 8 months, from June 6, 1973, to February 1, 1995. The sampling period for the right figure is 8 years, from January 1, 1987, to January 1, 1995.

right panel of Figure 7.8, there is also a weak, rather wide local maximum around lag -11, corresponding to -33 hr in ϑ-time. This corresponds to a lag of about 1 working day (because a working day is 1/5 rather than 1/7 of a business week). The difference $\varrho_\tau - \varrho_{-\tau}$ also has a significant (negative) peak around lag 11. This effect has been identified in the right panel of Figure 7.8 and discussed in Section 7.3. Following Engle *et al.* (1990), we call it a "heat wave" effect where traders have a better memory of the events approximately 1 working day ago (when they were active) than a broken number working days ago (when other traders on different continents, with different time zones, were active).

The peak around lag -11 can be explained by a residual seasonality that the ϑ-scale is unable to capture. However, the ϑ-scale is well able to treat *ordinary* seasonality as indicated by the lack of an analogous peak around the positive lag 11. The heat wave effect is more than just seasonality and it cannot be eliminated by a simple time scale transformation. This can be interpreted such that volatility modeling should consider not only volatilities of different time resolutions but also volatilities with the selective memory of individual geographical markets and their time zones.

Assymetric lead-lag correlation is not only present in the FX market but also in the Eurofutures market as shown in Ballocchi *et al.* (1999a). Figure 7.9 presents the results of a lead/lag correlation analysis for forward rates implied from Euromark contracts on the London International Financial Futures Exchange (LIFFE). The asymmetry is highly significant for the first lag and for all maturities. At lag 1, again coarse volatility predicts fine volatility significantly better than the other way around. The study was conducted with a 3-hr grid in ϑ-time where the fine volatility is the mean absolute return measured every 3 hr over 3 days and the coarse volatility is the mean absolute return over the whole 3-day interval. The sample runs from April 1, 1992, to December 30, 1997, which constitutes 700 observations. The effect is rather robust with respect to changes in the definition of the fine and coarse volatilities. Moreover, it is interesting to note that the size of the effect seems to increase when increasing the time-to-start of the forward rate.

To explore this effect on a wider set of parameters, Gilles Zumbach suggested to the following quantities:

$$C(T, n, n') \;=\; \mathrm{Corr}(\,\sigma[T, \frac{T}{2^n}](t)\,,\; \sigma[T, \frac{T}{2^{n'}}](t + T)\,) \qquad (7.10)$$

where $T = 4$ weeks and n and n' are the granularities of our volatility estimator. Then it is possible to compute a quantity I that depends on both n and n':

$$I(n, n') \;=\; C(T, n, n') - C(T, n', n) \qquad (7.11)$$

which means that we look at the first lag difference where the lag is 4 weeks. This quantity should in principle be symmetric but we know from Figure 7.8 that it changes sign and is antisymmetric. Figure 7.10 presents the results of a study conducted by Zumbach (private communication), for the quantity I computed for values of n going from 2 to 12 over a period T of 4 weeks on the ϑ-time scale. This means that the returns are measured at frequencies as low as 2 weeks to frequencies as high as every 10 min in ϑ-time. The FX rate is USD-CHF and the sampling period runs from June 1, 1987, to August 1, 1997. The asymmetry is striking and exists for all these different parameters. The maximum of the effect is obtained for $n = 11$ for the fine volatility and $n' = 7$ with differences as high as 0.29 between the two correlations, about two times more than in Table 7.1. Similar figures were also obtained for other FX rates like USD-DEM or USD-JPY.

7.4.3 Conditional Predictability

The conditional correlation studies of LeBaron (1992b,c) indicate that subsequent returns are correlated in low-volatility periods and slightly anticorrelated in high-volatility periods. In continuous samples mixed from both low-volatility and high-volatility periods, this important effect indicating the forecastability of return does not exist unconditionally. It exists conditional to volatility. Thus, volatility is also an indicator for the persistence of trends. The idea is to compute the following triplet:

$$(\,v(t),\; r(t),\; r(t + \Delta t)\,)$$

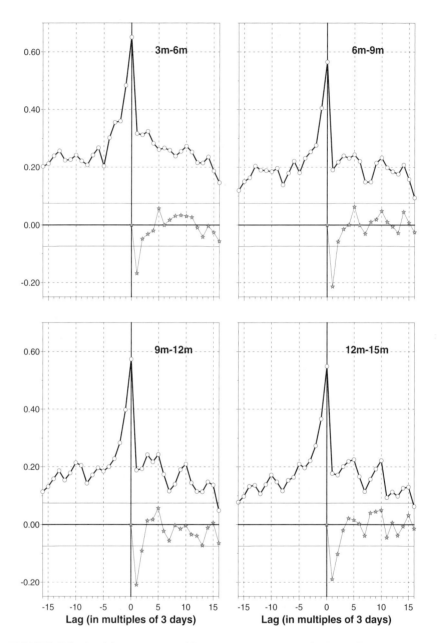

FIGURE 7.9 Lead-lag correlation of fine and coarse volatilities for four different implied forward rates derived from the Three-Month LIFFE Euromark, with a 3-hr grid in ϑ-time. The sampling period is from April 1, 1992, to December 30, 1997. In the panels, a month is represented by m.

Information Flow for the Volatility

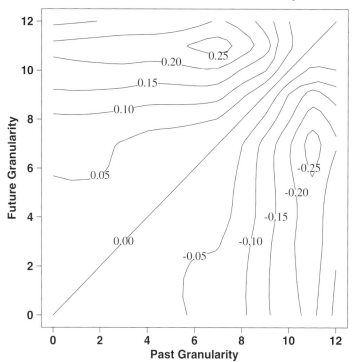

FIGURE 7.10 The correlation difference (Equation 7.11) between coarse and fine volatilities is explored for the USD-CHF FX rate. The asymmetry of the lead-lag correlation (at one lag of 4 weeks) is apparent around the diagonal, which naturally presents a correlation of 1 (and a difference of 0) because we are correlating a quantity with itself. The top half of the graph presents a positive difference in the lagged correlation whereas the bottom half presents the symmetric negative difference. The sampling period is from June 1, 1987, to August 1, 1997. (With permission of Gilles Zumbach.)

where $v(t)$ is a measure of volatility calculated with the weekly variance of daily returns.[7] Then triplets of similar volatility, $v(t)$, are put into the same bin, and the autocorrelation of returns at lag Δt, conditional to $v(t)$, is studied:

$$\rho(v) = \rho(r(t), r(t + \Delta t) \mid v(t)) \tag{7.12}$$

Such an analysis has four parameters, Δt for the returns and the three parameters for the volatility as identified in Section 3.2.4 and in the Equation 3.8: Δt, n, and p.

---

[7] In principle, any definition of volatility along the lines of Equation 3.8 can be chosen and its parameters varied until the conditional correlation reaches a maximum.

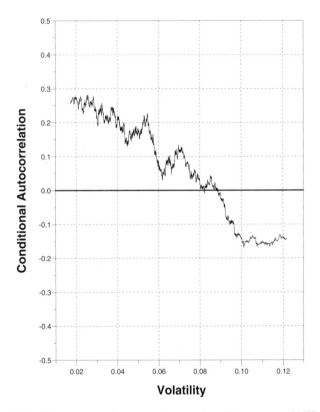

Volatility

FIGURE 7.11 The conditional autocorrelation of weekly returns of USD-DEM as a function of the average absolute weekly return over 5 days. The sampling period is June 1, 1973, to June 1, 1994.

This function $\rho(v)$ is presented for the FX rate USD-DEM on Figure 7.11. It is computed with a Δt of 1 week and a volatility definition that uses the mean weekly absolute returns over 5 weeks. In summary, the parameters for the graph are $\Delta t = 1$ week, $n\,\Delta t = 5$ weeks, and $p = 2$. The conditional correlation appears only for data at low frequency. The effect is quite strong for low volatility with a conditional correlation close to 0.3 at its maximum, decreasing down to negative values of -0.15 for high volatility. The computation is done with overlapping bins containing always the same number of observations to avoid changing the significance of the different results. From this figure, it appears that the "current state" of the market changes the price process behavior and the volatility plays an important role beyond its own dynamics. The results shown here for the most traded FX rates are also present in the other FX rates. It was also reported by LeBaron (1992b) for stock indices. Varying the parameters cause this effect to disappear for Δt smaller than 1 day. In the intraday region, influence of the heat wave effect becomes important and overshadows the findings.

8

VOLATILITY PROCESSES

8.1 INTRODUCTION

One of the many challenges posed by the study of high-frequency data in finance is to build models that can explain the empirical behavior of the data at any frequency at which they are measured from minutes to months. We are now going to examine how conventional models perform when confronted with this problem. In the previous chapter, we discussed the rich structure of the volatility dynamics. We need to introduce new types of volatility models to account for this structure, leading to a higher predictive power.

Many statistical processes proposed in the literature can be described by the following general formula for equally spaced returns r_t:

$$r_t = \sigma_t \, \varepsilon_t \tag{8.1}$$

where ε_t is an identically and independently distributed (i.i.d.) random variable[1] with zero mean and variance 1. In this chapter, t denotes the index of a homogeneous time series rather than time itself. "Homogeneous" means equally spaced on any chosen time scale. We usually choose ϑ-time as introduced in Chapter 6, so

---

[1] In this chapter, normal and Student-t distributions of ε_t are studied.

the model appropriately accounts for seasonalities. The volatility σ_t is the square root of the variance of the return r_t.

Many models are based on Equation 8.1, but they largely differ in the modeling of the volatility variable σ_t. We distinguish three main types of volatility modeling:

1. ARCH-type models. These autoregressive conditional heteroskedastic models define the variance σ_t^2 of the return r_t as a function of *past returns*. This function can be simple or rather complicated. In the GARCH process, for example, σ_t also depends on its own past values, but there is always an equivalent formulation that defines σ_t as a function of past returns only. The volatility σ_t is a model variable that cannot be directly observed, but it can be computed if a sufficiently long series of past return values up to r_{t-1} is known. All the statistical processes discussed in the following sections of this chapter belong to the ARCH type.

2. Stochastic volatility models. In stochastic volatility models, the volatility variable σ_t does not depend on past returns. Instead, it depends on its own past values. The volatility variable σ_t is neither observable nor directly computable from past returns. As a consequence, it is more difficult to estimate the parameters of stochastic volatility models than those of ARCH-type models. The statistical process of σ_t has a memory, so an autoregressive conditional heteroskedastic behavior can be obtained also with stochastic volatility models. There are different types of stochastic volatility models as noted in Taylor (1994); Ghysels and Jasiak (1995), and Ghysels *et al.* (1996). It is possible to model heterogeneous market behavior in the framework of stochastic volatility; a modern example is the cascade model of Ghashghaie *et al.* (1996) and Breymann *et al.* (2000) where volatility modeling is inspired by turbulence models.

3. Models based on realized volatility. Rather than modeling σ_t, (Andersen *et al.*, 2000) propose to define σ_t as the realized volatility computed at index $t - 1$. This realized volatility is computed with high-frequency data, with return intervals of, for example, 30-min, in order to keep stochastic errors low. The time interval of the main model (i.e., the interval between the indices $t - 1$ and t) is usually much larger (e.g., 1 working day). This means using realized volatility at $t - 1$ as a predictor of the volatility between $t - 1$ and t by relying on the volatility clustering. This model has the advantage of using empirical data instead of model assumptions that might be wrong. However, it has some disadvantages:

   ▪ Realized volatility is biased if computed at high frequency (see Section 7.2). A bias correction method such as Equation 7.4 would improve the model.

   ▪ Realized volatility computed at high frequency (fine volatility) lags behind coarse volatility in the lead-lag analysis (see Section 7.4.2). This lag leads to suboptimal forecast quality when predicting the volatility of the next step of the model.

- In general, realized volatility at $t - 1$ may not be the best predictor of volatility between $t - 1$ and t. It should be replaced by a more sophisticated *forecast* of realized volatility at t.

In most of these statistical processes of σ_t^2, it is possible to add some terms modeling external (exogeneous) influences. If volume figures at $t - 1$ are available, for example, they may be a piece of information to predict the volatility σ_t. The processes discussed here are not of this type, they are univariate.

In the remainder of this chapter, we stay within the framework of ARCH-type modeling and compare different models. The ultimate quality criterion of a model is its predictive power. Therefore there are some volatility forecast tests in Section 8.4. Forecasting is further discussed in Chapter 9 where it is the main subject.

8.2 INTRADAY VOLATILITY AND GARCH MODELS

The Autoregressive Conditional Heteroskedastic (ARCH) model of Engle (1982) and its generalized version (GARCH) by Bollerslev (1986) are widely used, not only in the foreign exchange (FX) literature (see, for a review, Bollerslev *et al.*, 1992) but also as the basic framework for empirical studies of the market microstructure such as the impact of news (Goodhart and Figliuoli, 1991; Goodhart *et al.*, 1993) and central bank interventions (Goodhart and Hesse, 1993; Peiers, 1997), or inter and intramarket relationships in Engle *et al.* (1990) and Baillie and Bollerslev (1990). The main assumption behind this class of models is the relative homogeneity of the price discovery process among market participants at the origin of the volatility process. In other words, the conditional density of one GARCH process is assumed to adequately capture all the information and the news. In particular, GARCH parameters for the weekly frequency theoretically derived from daily empirical estimates are usually within the confidence interval of weekly empirical estimates (Drost and Nijman, 1993).

However, we have already seen in this book that several empirical facts are at odds with this homogeneous view of the market. First, the long memory of the volatility (Section 7.3.2) indicates the presence of several market components corresponding to several time horizons. Note that this property of the volatility has already been successfully incorporated in the GARCH setting as the fractionally integrated GARCH (Baillie *et al.*, 1996). Second, at the intradaily frequency, round-the-clock time series reveal seasonal patterns that reflect, among others, the geographical dispersion of the traders, concentrated in three main geographical areas: Asia, Europe, and America. Although the first investigations of the effect of these different geographical locations seemed to indicate that news would uniformly spread out around the world (the so-called meteor shower hypothesis in Engle *et al.*, 1990), we saw traces of heat wave effects in the previous chapter. Third, exchange rates movements are not necessarily related to the arrival of news when inspected at the intraday frequency, Goodhart (1989), reflecting the fact that intraday traders may have other constraints and objectives than, for example, longer-term traders. Fourth, at extremely high frequencies, FX rates exhibit distinct microstructure effects due to the price formation process as studied in Chapter 5.

In this section, we investigate the importance of this heterogeneity for the modeling of the foreign exchange (FX) markets using the GARCH setting. More specifically, we show that estimates of a GARCH process with data in physical time are likely to be spurious, even though estimates for one particular frequency seem to be reasonable. Estimates are only consistent when the seasonal patterns are taken into account. However, even when these seasonal patterns are accounted for, the aggregation properties of the GARCH model break down at the intradaily frequencies, revealing the presence of traders with different risk profiles. In addition to the presence of different trader categories, we observe microstructure effects when analyzing returns over time intervals shorter than about 90 min. At the other extreme, the instability of coefficient estimates over different subperiods of 6 months suggests the presence of seemingly random long-term fluctuations. Finally, these misspecifications of the GARCH process result in its quite poor out-of-sample predictive power for the volatility as compared to realized volatility.

8.2.1 Parameter Estimation of GARCH Models

The GARCH(1,1) process is defined as follows:

$$\sigma_t^2 = \alpha_0 + \alpha_1 \varepsilon_{t-1}^2 + \beta_1 \sigma_{t-1}^2 \tag{8.2}$$

where σ_t^2 is the conditional variance and ε_t^2 is the squared innovation.

To test the effects of the temporal heterogeneity of the markets, this GARCH(1,1) process is estimated for several frequencies. The lowest analyzed frequency is daily and the highest frequency is defined by a homogeneous time series with 10-min intervals. At the higher frequencies (intervals less than 2 hr), we include a fourth-order autoregressive (AR(4)) term $\mu_t = \sum_{i=1}^{4} \phi_i r_{t-i}$ in Equation 8.1 to account for the statistically significant (negative) autocorrelation of the returns at these frequencies (see Section 5.2.1). The regression equation for the return process is

$$r_t = \mu_t + \epsilon_t \tag{8.3}$$

At lower frequencies such a term is not needed, and we use the process of Equation 8.1.

The parameters of the process are estimated as follows. Let θ denote the set of parameters characterizing the process. Assuming that the innovations ε_t are normally distributed, the log-likelihood function is

$$\mathcal{L}(\theta) = -\frac{n}{2} \ln(2\pi) - \frac{1}{2} \sum_{i=1}^{n} \left(\ln(\sigma_i^2) + \frac{\varepsilon_i^2}{\sigma_i^2} \right) \tag{8.4}$$

where the index t has been substituted by i. The number of observations used for the estimation is n. An initial fraction of data must be reserved and used for the build-up of σ_i^2, because of the memory of the volatility process. An estimate $\tilde{\theta}$ for the parameters is given by the solution of the maximization problem

$$\max_{\theta} \; \mathcal{L}(\theta)$$

The log-likelihood procedure has many desirable properties.[2] The solution is independent of the coordinate system in which the parameters are defined, such that the estimation can be done in any parametrization and the results will be identical, up to the chosen parameter transformation. This property is true for finite samples and any data set, assuming a non-degenerate maximum. Even if the process is misspecified (i.e., the data were not generated by the estimated process), the maximum is identical in any coordinate system. Estimating GARCH processes by maximum likelihood is difficult because of the presence of a one-dimensional manifold in the parameter space where the likelihood function is large and almost constant (for a discussion of this point and a good practical solution using the property mentioned above, see Zumbach, 2000).

The assumption of conditional normality can be relaxed by assuming a Student-t distribution for ε_t (Baillie and Bollerslev, 1989) or the generalized exponential distribution (Nelson, 1991). Both of these distributions have fat tails. In the case of the Student-t distribution, the log-likelihood function takes the following form:

$$\mathcal{L}(\theta) = -\frac{n}{2}\left[\ln(\nu - 2) + 2\,\ln\left[\pi^{1/2}\Gamma\left(\tfrac{\nu}{2}\right)\right] - \ln\Gamma\left(\tfrac{\nu+1}{2}\right)\right]$$

$$-\frac{1}{2}\sum_{i=1}^{n}\left[\ln(\sigma_i^2) + (\nu + 1)\ln\left(1 + \frac{\varepsilon_i^2}{\sigma_i^2(\nu-2)}\right)\right] \tag{8.5}$$

where ν is the number of degrees of freedom of the Student-t distribution and Γ is the usual gamma function. Both forms of the log-likelihood function are valid for any process following Equation 8.1, not only GARCH but also the process we shall study in Section 8.3.1.

The maximum of the likelihood function is found by an iterative procedure that combines two methods: a genetic algorithm (GA) (Goldberg, 1989; Pictet *et al.*, 1995) and the Berndt, Hall, Hall, and Hausman (BHHH) algorithm (Berndt *et al.*, 1974) which is a variant of the gradient descent method. The initial solutions are chosen randomly to avoid any a priori bias in the estimation and stored in "genes," which form an initial population. Starting from this population, the genetic algorithm constructs a new population using its selection and reproduction method (Pictet *et al.*, 1995). The solutions with the highest log-likelihood found by the genetic algorithm are used as starting points of the BHHH algorithm, which leads to a further improvement. Once convergence of the BHHH is achieved, the next generation of the GA is computed on the basis of the previous solutions

---

[2] See Davidson and MacKinnon (1993) for a general reference.

obtained with the BHHH algorithm and a set of solutions from the previous generation. This iterative procedure continues until no improvement of the solution is found. The BHHH algorithm alone can be trapped in local maxima of the log-likelihood instead of finding the global maximum. The chosen combination with a genetic algorithm has the advantage of avoiding local maxima. The method is rather fast, notwithstanding the very large number of observations (368,000 data points for the 10-min frequency). Robust standard errors are computed using the variance-covariance matrix estimation of White (1980).

8.2.2 Temporal Aggregation of GARCH Models

If the empirical data can be described as generated by one GARCH(1,1) process at one particular data frequency, the behavior of the data sampled at any other frequency is theoretically determined by temporal aggregation (or disaggregation) of the original process. These theoretically derived processes at different frequencies can be compared to the empirically estimated processes at the same frequencies. Significant deviations between empirical and theoretical results lead to the rejection of the hypothesis of only one GARCH process. We can show then that there is more than one relevant frequency in the volatility generation, and the market can be called temporally heterogeneous, as already found in Section 7.4.

There are two approaches for the theoretical aggregation of GARCH models. The GARCH model can be viewed as either a jump process (Drost and Nijman, 1993) or a diffusion process (Nelson and Foster, 1994). Both approaches lead to very similar results, so we only report results based on Drost and Nijman (1993). In both approaches, the sum of α_1 and β_1 (of Equation 8.2) tends to 1 as the frequency increases. The autoregressive parameter β_1 tends to 1, whereas the moving average parameter α_1 tends to 0. In other words, the higher the frequency, the longer the clusters of volatility as measured in numbers of time series intervals.

Because previous results confirmed the adequacy of these theoretical results at the daily and weekly frequencies (Drost and Nijman, 1993), we use the daily estimations as a starting point to compute the results for the higher frequencies. High frequencies also have the advantage of high statistical significance.

Drost and Nijman (1993) show that symmetric weak GARCH(1,1) processes are closed under temporal aggregation. A process is symmetric if the marginal distribution of returns is symmetric. The term "weak GARCH(1,1)" is exactly defined by Drost and Nijman (1993). It encompasses all processes that essentially follow Equation 8.2 with some weak, nonlinear deviations that are not visible in the autocorrelation of volatility. More precisely, if ε_t is a symmetric weak GARCH(1,1), following the equation $\sigma_t^2 = \alpha_0 + \alpha\varepsilon_{t-1}^2 + \beta\sigma_{t-1}^2$, then the high-frequency parameters α_0, α, and β and the kurtosis $\kappa_\varepsilon = E[\varepsilon_t^4]/(E[\varepsilon_t^2])^2$ determine the corresponding low-frequency parameters. We obtain the symmetric weak GARCH(1,1) process $\overline{\varepsilon}_{(m)tm}$, with

$$\overline{\sigma^2}_{(m)tm} = \overline{\alpha_0}_{(m)} + \overline{\alpha}_{(m)}\overline{\varepsilon}^2_{(m)tm-m} + \overline{\beta}_{(m)}\overline{\sigma^2}_{(m)tm-m} \qquad (8.6)$$

and kurtosis $\bar{\kappa}_{(m)\varepsilon}$ where

$$\bar{\alpha}_{0(m)} = m \,\alpha_0 \frac{1 - (\beta + \alpha)^m}{1 - (\beta + \alpha)} \tag{8.7}$$

$$\bar{\alpha}_{(m)} = (\beta + \alpha)^m - \bar{\beta}_{(m)} \tag{8.8}$$

$$\bar{\kappa}_{(m)\varepsilon} = \quad 3 + (\kappa_\varepsilon - 3)/m + 6(\kappa_\varepsilon - 1)$$

$$\times \frac{\{m - 1 - m(\beta + \alpha) + (\beta + \alpha)^m\}\{\alpha - \beta\alpha(\beta + \alpha)\}}{m^2(1 - \beta - \alpha)^2(1 - \beta^2 - 2\beta\alpha)} \tag{8.9}$$

$\left|\bar{\beta}_{(m)}\right| < 1$ is the solution of the quadratic equation

$$\frac{\bar{\beta}_{(m)}}{1 + \bar{\beta}_{(m)}^2} = \frac{a(\beta, \alpha, \kappa_\varepsilon, m)(\beta + \alpha)^m - b(\beta, \alpha, m)}{a(\beta, \alpha, \kappa_\varepsilon, m)\{1 + (\beta + \alpha)^{2m}\} - 2b(\beta, \alpha, m)} \tag{8.10}$$

with

$$a(\beta, \alpha, \kappa_\varepsilon, m) = \tag{8.11}$$

$$m(1 - \beta)^2 + 2m(m - 1)\frac{(1 - \beta - \alpha)^2(1 - \beta^2 - 2\beta\alpha)}{(\kappa_\varepsilon - 1)\{1 - (\beta + \alpha)^2\}}$$

$$+4\frac{\{m - 1 - m(\beta + \alpha) + (\beta + \alpha)^m\}\{\alpha - \beta\alpha(\beta + \alpha)\}}{1 - (\beta + \alpha)^2}$$

$$b(\beta, \alpha, m) = \quad \{\alpha - \beta\alpha(\beta + \alpha)\}\frac{1 - (\beta + \alpha)^{2m}}{1 - (\beta + \alpha)^2} \tag{8.12}$$

These formulas are used to determine the parameters of the aggregated GARCH processes and can also be used for going from low to high-frequency (i.e., for disaggregation).

When exploring temporal aggregation, we have to choose a time scale. Seasonality is not the subject of an aggregation study, but might disturb it. Eliminating seasonalities by using the ϑ-scale presented in Chapter 6 is a natural choice. However, we have additionally tested an alternative time scale which we call a business time scale in the remainder of this section. This business time simply omits the weekend periods from Friday 22:30 GMT to Sunday 22:30 GMT, when markets are virtually closed.

As a third time scale, we have tried physical time. In physical time, weekends cover two-sevenths of the total sample. This causes a complete breakdown of the estimation procedure, yielding very large α_1 estimates. Physical time including weekends is simply unusable here. The aforementioned business time is a usable substitute of physical time from which it only differs in its omission of weekends.

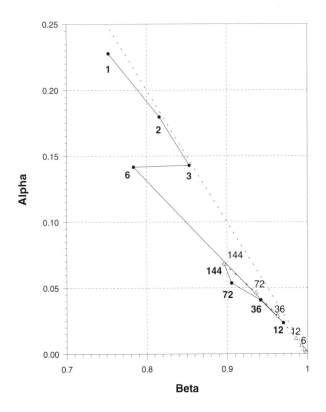

FIGURE 8.1 Aggregation of the GARCH(1,1) for estimated coefficients in business time (●) and theoretically derived coefficients (△) using the (Drost and Nijman, 1993) results for USD-DEM, for different aggregation factors (1 = 10 min; 2 = 20 min; 3 = 30 min; 6 = 1 hr; 12 = 2 hr; 36 = 6 hr; 72 = 12 hr; 144= 24 hr). The labels of the estimated coefficients (●) are printed in bold. The diagonal dotted line represents the stationarity limit for which $\alpha_1 + \beta_1 = 1$. Sampling period: 7 years from January 1, 1987, to December 31, 1993.

8.2.3   Estimates of GARCH(1,1) for Various Frequencies

Time series of USD-DEM have been sampled with frequencies between 10 min and 1 day. For each series, the GARCH(1,1) coefficients have been estimated using the procedure of Section 8.2.1. The resulting coefficients α_1 and β_1 (see Equation 8.2) are plotted in Figure 8.1 in the form of black circles, which are labeled by the number of 10-min intervals contained in the time series interval. The label "144" thus means daily sampling.

For comparison, the theoretical values of α_1 and β_1 are also plotted as triangles. The reference values at daily frequency (label 144) are estimated from real data, but the values at all other frequencies are computed from these reference values according to Drost and Nijman (1993), as explained in Section 8.2.2.A computation according to Nelson and Foster (1994) yields similar results that are not plotted here.

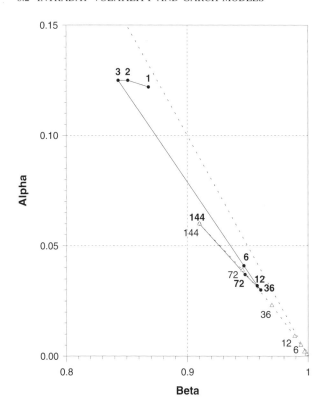

FIGURE 8.2 Aggregation of the GARCH(1,1) for estimated coefficients in ϑ-time ($\bullet$) and theoretically derived coefficients ($\triangle$) using the (Drost and Nijman, 1993) results for the USD-DEM for different aggregation factors (1 = 10 min; 2 = 20 min; 3 = 30 min; 6 = 1 hr; 12 = 2 hr; 36 = 6 hr; 72 = 12 hr; 144= 24 hr). The labels of the estimated coefficients ($\bullet$) are printed in bold. The diagonal dashed line represents the limit for which $\alpha_1 + \beta_1 = 1$. Sampling period: 7 years from January 1, 1987, to December 31, 1993.

Although the coefficient estimates may look quite reasonable for some lower frequencies, the global picture for all frequencies appears quite odd. In particular, the β_1 estimates for frequencies higher than 2 hr decrease down to values close to 0.75, whereas the theory, represented by the triangles in Figure 8.1, suggests that β_1 should tend to one. The triangles are very far from the corresponding black circles. The hypothesis of volatility being generated by only one GARCH(1,1) process is clearly rejected with the high significance of high-frequency data analyzed over 7 years.

The results of Figure 8.1 are computed on the basis of the business time introduced at the end of Section 8.2.2. Figure 8.2 shows the corresponding results based on ϑ-time. The time scale ϑ is in fact a better choice because of its better deseasonalization. However, the results of Figure 8.2 are similar to those of Figure 8.1. The strong deviation between theoretical and empirically estimated

TABLE 8.1 Results of the GARCH(1,1) estimation in business time. GARCH(1,1) parameter estimates for USD-DEM, using the business time scale, for different frequencies. Robust standard errors are given in parentheses. The coefficients with a prime are computed from the (dis)aggregation formulas for the jump hypothesis of Drost and Nijman (1993). The daily interval serves as a reference basis.

Interval	α_0	α_1	β_1	$\alpha_1 + \beta_1$	α_1'	β_1'	$\alpha_1' + \beta_1'$
10 min	$2.15 \cdot 10^{-8}$	0.227	0.752	0.979	0.001	0.999	1.000
	$(0.17 \cdot 10^{-8})$	(0.0013)	(0.0012)				
20 min	$2.66 \cdot 10^{-8}$	0.179	0.816	0.995	0.002	0.997	0.999
	$(0.15 \cdot 10^{-8})$	(0.0037)	(0.0051)				
30 min	$2.65 \cdot 10^{-8}$	0.143	0.853	0.996	0.003	0.996	0.999
	$(0.18 \cdot 10^{-8})$	(0.0062)	(0.0101)				
1 hr	$1.79 \cdot 10^{-7}$	0.142	0.784	0.926	0.006	0.992	0.999
	$(0.42 \cdot 10^{-7})$	(0.0066)	(0.0114)				
2 hr	$3.11 \cdot 10^{-8}$	0.023	0.970	0.993	0.011	0.986	0.997
	$(0.13 \cdot 10^{-8})$	(0.0020)	(0.0015)				
6 hr	$2.43 \cdot 10^{-7}$	0.041	0.941	0.982	0.029	0.962	0.991
	$(0.22 \cdot 10^{-7})$	(0.0039)	(0.0061)				
12 hr	$1.07 \cdot 10^{-6}$	0.054	0.905	0.959	0.046	0.936	0.982
	$(0.17 \cdot 10^{-6})$	(0.0061)	(0.0102)				
24 hr	$1.91 \cdot 10^{-6}$	0.068	0.897	0.965			
	$(0.67 \cdot 10^{-6})$	(0.0095)	(0.0153)				

coefficients already starts with the 6-hr frequency. The conclusions on temporal aggregation of GARCH are the same. The choice of the time scale has no strong impact on a temporal aggregation study, as long as physical time with its high weight of weekends is avoided.

Detailed results for the two time scales are also listed in Tables 8.1 and 8.2. Table 8.1 presents the results obtained for USD-DEM in the business time scale and Table 8.2 for the same rate but in the ϑ-time scale. The error estimates of the results provide more evidence against the hypothesis of only one GARCH(1,1) process generating the data. Even the theoretically computed coefficients at low frequency, which seem quite close to the estimated coefficients, are often outside the confidence intervals. Only the coefficients for the GARCH process are provided in Tables 8.1 and 8.2, even when an AR(4) term was included in Equation 8.1 for frequencies higher than 2 hr (as discussed at the beginning of Section 8.2.1). We have observed that the inclusion of this autoregressive term in the return equation does not significantly change the values of the GARCH coefficients.

The coefficient estimates are quite similar across different FX rates.[3] The hypothesis of only one GARCH(1,1) process is rejected for all the FX rates we tested, not only USD-DEM. The volatility clusters have about the same size—if measured in numbers of time series intervals—for all levels of aggregation. In

---

[3] See Andersen and Bollerslev (1997b) for similar results.

TABLE 8.2 Results of the GARCH(1,1) estimation in ϑ-time.

GARCH(1,1) parameter estimates for USD-DEM, using ϑ-time, for different frequencies. Robust standard errors are given in parentheses. The coefficients with a prime are computed from the (dis)aggregation formulas for the jump hypothesis of Drost and Nijman (1993). The daily interval serves as a reference basis.

Interval	α_0	α_1	β_1	$\alpha_1 + \beta_1$	α_1'	β_1'	$\alpha_1' + \beta_1'$
10 min	$4.09 \cdot 10^{-9}$	0.153	0.839	0.992	0.001	0.999	1.000
	$(0.27 \cdot 10^{-9})$	(0.0047)	(0.0049)				
20 min	$1.24 \cdot 10^{-8}$	0.149	0.830	0.979	0.001	0.998	0.999
	$(0.84 \cdot 10^{-8})$	(0.0057)	(0.0063)				
30 min	$2.56 \cdot 10^{-8}$	0.153	0.815	0.968	0.002	0.997	0.999
	$(0.21 \cdot 10^{-8})$	(0.0077)	(0.0091)				
1 hr	$1.36 \cdot 10^{-8}$	0.047	0.942	0.988	0.004	0.995	0.999
	$(0.46 \cdot 10^{-8})$	(0.0094)	(0.0129)				
2 hr	$1.65 \cdot 10^{-8}$	0.031	0.962	0.993	0.008	0.989	0.997
	$(0.28 \cdot 10^{-8})$	(0.0014)	(0.0022)				
6 hr	$5.93 \cdot 10^{-8}$	0.029	0.963	0.992	0.023	0.971	0.994
	$(0.40 \cdot 10^{-8})$	(0.0011)	(0.0013)				
12 hr	$1.91 \cdot 10^{-7}$	0.039	0.948	0.987	0.038	0.949	0.988
	$(0.45 \cdot 10^{-7})$	(0.0013)	(0.0047)				
24 hr	$8.08 \cdot 10^{-7}$	0.061	0.915	0.975			
	$(2.74 \cdot 10^{-7})$	(0.0119)	(0.0155)				

other words, the volatility memory seems quite short-lived when measured with high-frequency data and long-lived when measured with data of daily or lower frequency. The information content of the volatility variable σ_t is not the same for different frequencies. Different volatilities are relevant at different frequencies. We attribute this, along with other authors (Andersen and Bollerslev, 1997a), to the presence of many independent volatility components in the data. This is again the signature of market heterogeneity. The GARCH model does not capture the heterogeneity of traders acting at different time horizons.

This is a plausible explanation of the abnormal results we obtain at high frequencies from the estimation of the GARCH model using a Student-t distribution instead of the normal distribution such as in Baillie and Bollerslev (1989).[4] GARCH is misspecified, no matter which form of the conditional distribution of returns is chosen.

To further assess the behavior of the volatility as estimated by GARCH(1,1) processes, we have investigated the temporal stability of the coefficient estimates for several subsamples. Figure 8.3 provides the estimations of the GARCH parameters for USD-DEM at the 2-hr time interval, using ϑ-time, for subsamples of 6 months, with about 2,190 observations per subsample. As can be seen, the

---

[4] Although the algorithm converges, the sum of the α_1 and β_1 increasingly exceeds 1 as the frequency becomes higher. One also finds excess residual skewness and kurtosis. Since these results are robust to the size of the sample, they cannot be attributed to a larger number of tail observations.

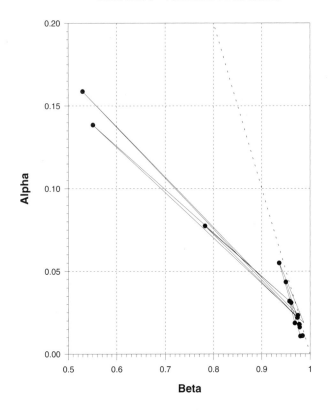

FIGURE 8.3 Temporal stability of the GARCH(1,1) coefficients for subperiods of 6 months for the USD-DEM at the 2-hr frequency. The time scale is ϑ-time. In the parameter space, the coefficients are represented by black circles (•) and connected by lines indicating the temporal sequence. Sampling period: 7 years from January 1, 1987, to December 31, 1993.

coefficients are not stable over time. Some of them are in the left half of Figure 8.3, quite far from the others. Moreover, these aberrant coefficients are not directly connected in the temporal sequence. The shifts in coefficient values have an irregular sequence in time, as shown by the lines connecting the points in Figure 8.3. The hypothesis of all parameters being equal across the subsamples can be rejected by using a likelihood-ratio test (see e.g., Hamilton, 1994) with very high significance. This is again a sign of misspecification of the model, but it may also indicate changes in market behavior.

The forecasting quality of GARCH models will be tested in Section 8.4.2. There we shall see that an increasing sample size does not improve the volatility forecasts from GARCH models. The forecasting quality saturates when increasing the sample size after a certain threshold value. The subsamples used for Figure 8.3 are large enough, so the erratic behavior of GARCH coefficients in that figure cannot be attributed to small sample sizes.

8.3 MODELING HETEROGENEOUS VOLATILITIES

In Chapter 7 we showed that there is asymmetry in the interaction between volatilities measured at different frequencies. A coarsely defined volatility predicts a fine volatility better than the other way around. This effect is not present in a simple GARCH model. More complex types of ARCH models have to be developed to account for the heterogeneity found in high-frequency data, such as the HARCH (Heterogeneous Autoregressive Conditional Heteroskedasticity) model.

The HARCH process proposed in this section has a variance equation based on returns over intervals of *different sizes*. The empirical behavior of lagged correlation can be reproduced well with this new process. At the same time, HARCH is able to reproduce the long memory of volatility,[5] as found in Section 7.3.2, Dacorogna *et al.* (1993), and Ding *et al.* (1993). Moreover, the terms of the conditional variance of HARCH reflect the component structure of the market in a natural way.

As with most processes from the ARCH family, HARCH is based on squared returns,[6] with their good analytical tractability. Whereas the convergence problem of the fourth moment of the return distribution forced us to define volatility in terms of absolute returns in the correlation analysis of Section 7.4.1, there is no such constraint for the volatility equation of the HARCH process.

8.3.1 The HARCH Model

In this section, we present the HARCH model as it was first presented by Müller *et al.* (1997a). This should facilitate the understanding of the approach but this initial formulation as the initial ARCH formulation is cumbersome to compute. In the next sections, we shall see a formulation with a much faster and simpler computation and estimation. As in Equation 8.2, the returns r_t of a HARCH(n) process are defined with the random variable ε_t, which is identically and independently distributed (i.i.d.) and follows a distribution function with zero expectation and unit variance:[7]

$$r_t = \sigma_t \, \varepsilon_t$$

$$\sigma_t^2 = c_0 + \sum_{j=1}^{n} c_j \left(\sum_{i=1}^{j} r_{t-i} \right)^2 \tag{8.13}$$

where

$$c_0 > 0 \, , \ \ c_n > 0 \, , \ \ c_j \geq 0 \ \text{for} \ j = 1 \ldots n - 1 \tag{8.14}$$

---

[5] The FIGARCH process, Baillie *et al.* (1996), has been designed to model the long memory but cannot reproduce the lead-lag correlation of Section 7.4.2 as it is still based on returns observed over intervals of constant size.

[6] Except for a process class proposed by Ding *et al.* (1993), which models volatility in terms of different powers of absolute returns

[7] Here, we utilize a normal distribution and alternatively explore Student-t distributions.

The equation for the variance σ_t^2 is a linear combination of the squares of *aggregated* returns. Aggregated returns may extend over some long intervals from a time point in the distant past up to time $t - 1$. The heterogeneous set of relevant interval sizes leads to the process named HARCH for "Heterogeneous Autoregressive Conditional Heteroskedasticity." The first "H" may also stand for the heterogeneous market if we follow that hypothesis as proposed in Section 7.4.

The HARCH process belongs to the wide ARCH family but differs from all other ARCH-type processes in the unique property of considering the volatilities of returns measured over different interval sizes. The Quadratic ARCH (QARCH) process (see Sentana, 1991) is an exception. Although QARCH was not developed for treating different interval sizes, it can be regarded as a generalized form of HARCH as explained in Section 8.3.3.

The coefficients $c_1 \ldots c_n$ should not be regarded as free parameters of the model. The heterogeneous market approach leads to a low number of free model parameters, which determine a much higher number n of coefficients modeling the long memory of volatility.

The explicit formulation of HARCH(2) may help to illustrate the special properties of the HARCH process.[8] The variance equation of HARCH(2) can be written in two forms:

$$\sigma_t^2 = c_0 + c_1\, r_{t-1}^2 + c_2\, (r_{t-1} + r_{t-2})^2 =$$

$$c_0 + (c_1 + c_2)\, r_{t-1}^2 + c_2\, r_{t-2}^2 + 2\, c_2\, r_{t-1}\, r_{t-2} \quad (8.15)$$

The second form of this HARCH(2) process can be identified as an ordinary ARCH(2) process, except for its last term which contains the mixed product $r_{t-1} r_{t-2}$. In other ARCH-type processes, the absolute values of returns matter where in HARCH, also their *signs* matter. Two subsequent returns of the same size and in the same direction will cause a higher contribution to the variance process than two subsequent returns that cancel out each other.

The variance, the unconditional expectation of squared returns, can be derived from Equation 8.13:

$$E(r_t^2) = E(\sigma_t^2) = c_0 + \sum_{j=1}^{n} c_j \left[\sum_{i=1}^{j} E(r_{t-i}^2) \right] \quad (8.16)$$

The cross products, such as $r_{t-1} r_{t-2}$ in Equation 8.15, have no influence here as their expectation is zero. A necessary condition of stationarity is constant unconditional variance:

$$E(r_t^2) = E(r_{t-i}^2) , \quad i \geq 1 \quad (8.17)$$

---

[8] Whereas HARCH(1) is identical to ARCH(1).

Inserting this in Equation 8.16, we obtain the variance

$$E(r_t^2) = \frac{c_0}{1 - \sum_{j=1}^{n} j\, c_j} \tag{8.18}$$

which must be finite and positive

$$\sum_{j=1}^{n} j\, c_j < 1 \tag{8.19}$$

This necessary stationarity condition is also a sufficient condition for both the stationarity of the process and the existence of the variance, the second moment. Proving this is not trivial and we do not follow here the path chosen by Engle (1982) and Bollerslev (1986) because the mixed products, such as $r_{t-1} r_{t-2}$, make the matrix formulation of the problem difficult. The HARCH process can be seen as a Markov chain. Meyn and Tweedie (1993) have obtained some results for the ergodicity and recurrence of Markov chains that can be used for proving the stationarity and the moment condition. The complete proof is given by Dacorogna *et al.* (1996).

The conditions for the existence and constant unconditional expectation of higher moments can be obtained through steps analogous to Equations 8.16 through 8.19, but the computation becomes increasingly tedious for higher moments and larger n values. The expectation of the $2m^{th}$ moment is

$$E(r_t^{2m}) = E(\sigma_t^{2m})\, E(\varepsilon_t^{2m}) \tag{8.20}$$

Equation 8.13 of the variance is inserted in $E(\sigma_t^{2m})$ and all the terms are explicitly computed. Some products of powers of returns have nonzero expectations, leading to an equation system for these expectations and $E(\sigma_t^{2m})$. The equation system has the dimension m for $n = 2$ and higher for larger n values. In the relatively simple case of the fourth moment ($m = 2$) of HARCH(2) ($n = 2$), the expectation $E(r_t^2 r_{t-1}^2)$ has to be computed and solved together with the equation for $E(r_t^4)$. In the standard case of ε_t following a normal distribution, $N(0, 1)$, $E(\varepsilon_t^4) = 3$ and the following necessary condition is obtained to keep the fourth moment finite

$$3\,[c_2^2 + (c_1 + c_2)^2] + c_2\,[1 + 3\,(c_1^2 + 6c_1 c_2 + 4c_2^2)] < 1 \tag{8.21}$$

The sufficiency of this necessary fourth moment condition is also proven in Dacorogna *et al.* (1996). In Figure 8.4, the second and fourth moment conditions according to Equations 8.19 and 8.21, plus the sixth moment condition following an analogously derived equation, are plotted for a HARCH(2) process. Processes with a finite second and a diverging fourth moment exist in a large part of the c_1-c_2-plane. This is remarkable because half-hourly FX returns have an empirical distribution with a tail index between 2 and 4, as found in Section 5.4.2 and Dacorogna *et al.* (2001a).

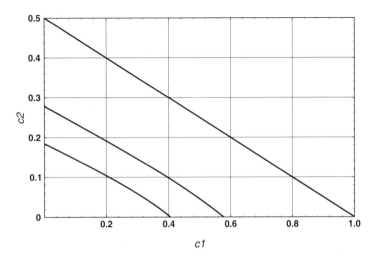

FIGURE 8.4 Moment conditions for the coefficients c_1 and c_2 of a HARCH(2) process with a normally distributed ε_t. The straight line on the right represents the boundary for the stationarity and the existence of the second moment. The curves in the middle and on the left represent the boundaries for the existence of the 4th and 6th moments.

8.3.2 HARCH and Market Components

The memory in the volatility is known to be long, as discussed in Section 7.3.2. Therefore, we need a high order of HARCH, a large n, to model the behavior of empirical time series. This implies a high number of coefficients c_j, which should not be free parameters of HARCH. We need a parsimonious parametrization. In the case of ARCH, some high-order processes can be formulated as low-order GARCH processes (Bollerslev, 1986), but no analogous method is at hand to reduce the number of HARCH parameters.

Our approach of parsimonious parametrization allows for the exploration of the component structure of the market. The coefficients c_j reflect the relative impact of different market components with different relevant time intervals. Therefore, we select m market components corresponding to m free parameters, each associated to some coefficients c_j in a limited range of j. The j ranges are separated by powers of a natural number p, so the typical time interval size of a component differs from that of the neighbor component by a factor of p. All c_j values within one component are assumed to be the same:

$$c_j = C_i = C_{i(j)}$$

$$i(j) = \max\left(k \ \middle| \ k \in \mathbf{N} \ \wedge \ k < \frac{\log j}{\log p} + 2 \right) , \quad j = 1 \dots p^{m-1}$$

$$(8.22)$$

Only m different coefficients C_i have to be estimated to determine the whole set of $n = p^{m-1}$ coefficients c_j.

Table 8.3 presents such a component scheme for a time series in ϑ-time with a basic grid of 30 min, $p = 4$, and 7 components ($m = 7$). An interval of 30-min in ϑ-time means only some 7 min during the daily volatility peaks around 14:00 GMT, some 80 min during the Far Eastern lunch break, and even more during weekends and holidays with their very low volatility. Table 8.3 shows the minimum relevant time intervals of a component rather than the total size of the volatility memory. In fact, the memory of the volatility can greatly exceed the indicated interval. The medium-term traders of component 5, for example, are not interested in the volatility of hourly returns, are most interested in volatilities observed over 1 to $3\frac{1}{2}$ days, and are also interested in volatilities observed over longer intervals.

The choice of the number of components, $m = 7$, and the factor between the typical time resolutions of the components, $p = 4$, is reasonable but somewhat arbitrary. The essential results of this chapter do not strongly depend on this choice and can be found also with other m and p values. The model should cover the variety of relevant time resolutions of the market.[9] A too small choice of m misses the chance of revealing the component structure; a too large m (with a small p) leads to too many parameters to be estimated and an unrealistically narrow definition of market components.

A quantity more suitable for the intuitive understanding than a coefficient C_i is the *impact* I_i of a market component. The expected variance formula, Equation 8.18, strongly suggests a definition of the impact of the jth coefficient as $j c_j$. The impact I_i of the ith component is defined as the sum of the impacts of all its coefficients c_j. By inserting the coefficient definitions of Equation 8.22, we obtain

$$I_1 = c_1 = C_1$$

$$I_i = \sum_{j=p^{i-2}+1}^{p^{i-1}} j c_j = (p-1) p^{i-2} \frac{p^{i-1} + p^{i-2} + 1}{2} C_i \quad \text{for } i > 1$$

$$(8.23)$$

The impact of the long-term components may be considerable even when the coefficients appear to be small. The impact of the fifth component, for example, is $I_5 = 30816 C_5$, where p is assumed to be 4 as in Table 8.3.

The stationarity condition (Equation 8.19) can now be formulated in terms of the impacts. Their sum is smaller than 1:

$$\sum_{i=1}^{m} I_i < 1 \qquad (8.24)$$

---

[9] The choice of Table 8.3 is $m = 7$. An even higher value, $m = 8$, has also been tested, leading to a low, insignificant impact of the eighth component and a rejection in a likelihood ratio test. We conclude that the seventh component is the last relevant one on the long-term side.

TABLE 8.3 Definition of the HARCH components.

A HARCH model with seven market components, each with a range of indices j. All coefficients c_j of a component are identical and only seven parameters need to be estimated. The time intervals are the relevant intervals for the volatility perception of the time components (not the total duration of their memory). These basic intervals are given in ϑ-time and also in physical time. Two columns show the minimum and maximum size of the interval that can occur for a time component, depending also on the daytime. These time component descriptions may contribute to a better understanding of the model.

i	Range of j	Approximate range of time intervals in ϑ-time	Shortest interval (at daily or weekly volatility peaks) in physical time	Longest interval (but avoiding weekends and holidays) in physical time	Description of the time component
1	1	30 min	7 min	80 min	Short-term, intraday dealers (arbitrage opportunities), market makers
2	$2 - 4$	$1 - 2$ hr	16 min	$3\frac{1}{2}$ hr	Intraday dealers with few transactions per day
3	$5 - 16$	$2\frac{1}{2} - 8$ hr	50 min	9 hr	Dealers with overnight positions and occasional intraday transactions
4	$17 - 64$	$8\frac{1}{2} - 32$ hr	4 hr	1 day	Few traders concerned (time intervals often beyond local business hours but less than a business day)
5	$65 - 256$	$1\frac{1}{2} - 5$ days	1 day	$3\frac{1}{2}$ days	Medium-term traders, no intraday trading
6	$257 - 1024$	$5\frac{1}{2} - 21$ days	$3\frac{1}{2}$ days	21 days (weekends always contained)	Long-term traders
7	$1025 - 4096$	$3 - 12$ weeks	3 weeks	12 weeks (weekends always contained)	Long-term investors, central banks

8.3.3 Generalization of the Process Equation

In Equation 8.13, all the returns considered by the variance equation are observed over "recent" intervals ending at time $t - 1$. This strong limitation will be justified by its empirical success, but we can also formulate a more general process equation with observation intervals ending in the past, before $t - 1$,

$$
r_t = \sigma_t \varepsilon_t
$$

$$
\sigma_t^2 = c_0 + \sum_{j=1}^{n} \sum_{k=1}^{j} c_{jk} \left(\sum_{i=k}^{j} r_{t-i} \right)^2 + \sum_{i=1}^{q} b_i \sigma_{t-i}^2
$$

(8.25)

where

$$
\begin{aligned}
c_0 > 0 , \quad c_{jk} \geq 0 \quad &\text{for} \quad j = 1 \ldots n, \quad k = 1 \ldots j; \\
b_i \geq 0 \quad &\text{for} \quad i = 1 \ldots q
\end{aligned}
$$

(8.26)

This generalized process equation considers all returns between any pair of two time points in the period between $t - n$ and $t - 1$. It covers the case of HARCH (all $c_{jk} = 0$ except some c_{j1}) as well as that of ARCH and GARCH (all $c_{jk} = 0$ except some c_{jj}). The last term of the variance equation is a "GARCH term," which may contribute to a parsimonious model formulation. Such a GARCH term may partially model the fading volatility memory of several market components together, but therefore miss the chance of clearly indicating the actual component structure. The main idea of HARCH, taking intervals of different sizes, may also be combined with other ideas from the recent literature about GARCH variations. HARCH can also be regarded as a special case of the Quadratic ARCH model suggested by Sentana (1991). The results obtained for QARCH also apply to HARCH. However, QARCH has been developed in a very different context. Sentana (1991) gives neither a concept of volatilities observed over long intervals nor the stationarity and moment conditions as in Section 8.3.1.

For HARCH, the simple form of Equation 8.13 is preferred. This HARCH is successful in empirical studies, but its computation and estimation is tedious because of the large number of coefficients c_j. This can be strongly improved by introducing the EMA-HARCH process with its partial volatility concept in the next section.

8.3.4 EMA-HARCH Model

In HARCH, the coefficients $c_1 \ldots c_n$ are not regarded as free parameters of the model. The heterogeneous market approach leads to a low number of free model parameters, which determine a much higher number n of dependent coefficients modeling the long memory of volatility.

The approach is to keep in the equation only a handful of representative interval sizes instead of keeping all of them, and replace the influence of the neighboring interval sizes by an exponential moving average (EMA) of the returns measured on each interval. This also has the advantage of including a memory of the past intervals. Let us now introduce the concept of *partial* volatility σ_j^2, which can be regarded as the contribution of the jth component to the total market volatility σ^2. Here the volatility σ_j^2 is defined as the volatility observed over an interval of size k_j. We can reformulate the HARCH equation in terms of σ_j as follows:

$$r_t = \sigma_t \, \varepsilon_t$$

$$\sigma_t^2 = c_0 + \sum_{j=1}^{n} C_j \, \sigma_{j,t}^2 \tag{8.27}$$

where n is now the number of time components in the model. The notation is slightly changed to C_j instead of c_j used in the old formulation to reflect the different meaning of the coefficients. Unlike the standard HARCH, the partial volatility σ_j^2 has a memory of the volatility of *past* intervals of size k_j. The formal definition of σ_j^2 is

$$\sigma_{j,t}^2 = \mu_j \, \sigma_{j,t-1}^2 + (1 - \mu_j) \left(\sum_{i=1}^{k_j} r_{t-i} \right)^2 \tag{8.28}$$

where k_j is the aggregation factor of the returns and takes n possible values, following the relation

$$k_j = p^{j-2} + 1 \quad \text{for} \quad j > 1 \quad \text{with} \quad k_1 \equiv 1 \tag{8.29}$$

When $p = 4$, k_j can only take the values $1, 2, 5, 17, 65, 257, 1025, \cdots, 4^{n-2}+1$. For a 5-min data series, this would mean that the horizons would correspond to 5 min, 10 min, 25 min and so on. The construction of Equation 8.29 ensures that the time components (k_j's) are economically meaningful. Equation 8.28 is the iterative formula for an exponentially weighted moving average, a special application of Equation 3.51. The volatility memory is defined as a moving average of recent volatility. The depth of the volatility memory is determined by the constant μ_j:

$$\mu_j = e^{-\frac{1}{M(k_j)}} \tag{8.30}$$

where the memory decay time constant of the component is given as the function M of the component's volatility interval k_j. Without introducing new parameters, $M(k_j)$ can be defined as

$$M(k_j) = \frac{(k_{j+1} - k_j)}{2} \tag{8.31}$$

This definition is based on the start and the end point of the component interval k_j and makes sure that that the EMA kernel is centered at the characteristic time horizon of the component.

It is easy to prove that a necessary stationarity condition for the new formulation is

$$\sum_{j=1}^{n} k_j C_j \; < \; 1 \tag{8.32}$$

The proof relies on the fact that the expectation of the exponential moving average is the same as the expectation of the underlying time series and that the expectation of cross terms is zero. A similar proof as in Dacorogna et al. (1998a) can be given for the sufficiency of this condition.

We can now define the impact I_j of each component,

$$I_j \; = \; k_j C_j \tag{8.33}$$

Every component with a coefficient C_j has an impact I_j on the conditional volatility process. The stationarity condition, Equation 8.32, can be re-formulated using the sum of impacts:

$$\sum_{j=1}^{n} I_j \; < \; 1 \tag{8.34}$$

An iterative formula needs an initial value for σ_j^2 at the beginning of the time series. A reasonable assumption of that initial value is the unconditional expectation of $\sigma_{j,t}^2$. Here the first value is computed from a data sample prior to the model estimation sample. We term this sample the "build-up" sample.

8.3.5 Estimating HARCH and EMA-HARCH Models

HARCH and EMA-HARCH models are applied to and estimated for empirical FX data here. The time series are homogeneous in ϑ-time, which removes the seasonal pattern of intraday volatility. The time interval is 30 min and the sample includes 10 years of data from January 1, 1987, to December 31, 1996.

For the computation and estimation of both HARCH and EMA-HARCH, we use seven components. For HARCH, the components of Table 8.3 are used. For EMA-HARCH, one component is built from only one time interval but includes, according to Equation 8.28, a moving average that extends over a certain range, which should account for the neighboring time intervals. In fact, there are now two parameters controlling the component definition. The time interval size over which returns are computed, k_j, and the range of the moving average, $M(k_j)$. Both of them are fixed and the optimization is carried out to solve the C_j parameters. The optimization is implemented by searching for the maximum of the log-likelihood function. The procedure we follow to find the maximum is described at the end of Section 8.2.1. It combines two methods: a genetic algorithm (GA) search (Pictet et al., 1995) and the Berndt, Hall, Hall, and Hausman (BHHH) algorithm (Berndt et al., 1974).

TABLE 8.4 HARCH coefficients for USD-DEM.
Comparison between the coefficients and impacts of the two HARCH processes from a half-hourly USD-DEM series, which is equally spaced in ϑ-time over 10 years. Instead of the coefficients C_i, the impacts I_i are given. These provide a direct measure of the impacts of the market components on the HARCH variance. The market components are those of Table 8.3 for HARCH and as in Equations 8.28 and 8.30 for EMA-HARCH. The distribution of the random variable $\varepsilon(t)$ is normal with zero mean and a unit variance.

USD-DEM		HARCH			EMA-HARCH	
Coefficient	Estimate	Standard error	t-statistics	Estimate	Standard error	t-statistics
c_0	1.276×10^{-7}	0.03994×10^{-7}	31.94	0.529×10^{-7}	0.04399×10^{-7}	21.01
I_1	0.1309	0.007151	18.30	0.1476	0.008295	17.80
I_2	0.1930	0.010010	19.28	0.1875	0.012297	15.25
I_3	0.1618	0.009179	17.62	0.1829	0.012545	14.58
I_4	0.0703	0.007363	9.55	0.0507	0.010324	4.91
I_5	0.1003	0.006774	14.81	0.1434	0.010952	13.10
I_6	0.1014	0.006892	14.71	0.1120	0.011835	9.47
I_7	0.0990	0.006118	16.18	0.1145	0.010540	10.86
Log-likelihood	5.7947			5.8014		

The result of the optimization procedure is a set of C_j coefficients from which the component impacts are calculated using Equation 8.23 (for HARCH) or Equation 8.33 (for EMA-HARCH). The sum of impacts I_j must be below one for stationarity of the process (Equations 8.24 and 8.34). In Table 8.4, the coefficients for both the HARCH and EMA-HARCH are shown with their t-statistics for USD-DEM. They are obtained on exactly the same data set. The log-likelihoods can be compared because both models have the same number of independent coefficients. Clearly, the log-likelihood is improved by going to EMA-HARCH. In both cases, all coefficients are highly significant according to the t-statistics and contribute to the variance equation. The stationarity property is fulfilled in both cases. The HARCH and EMA-HARCH have total impacts of 0.8567 and 0.9386, respectively. The impacts of the different components are remarkably similar. Two small differences are worth noticing. The relative importance of the long-term components is slightly higher for EMA-HARCH (37% instead of 35%) and the minimum for the fourth component is more pronounced in EMA-HARCH. The t-statistics are also consistently smaller for EMA-HARCH than for HARCH but still highly significant in all cases. The residuals in both formulations still present an excess kurtosis, as was noticed in Müller *et al.* (1997a) for HARCH.

These results show that we have achieved the goal of redesigning the HARCH process in terms of moving averages. We are able to keep and even improve on the properties of the original HARCH and to considerably reduce the computational

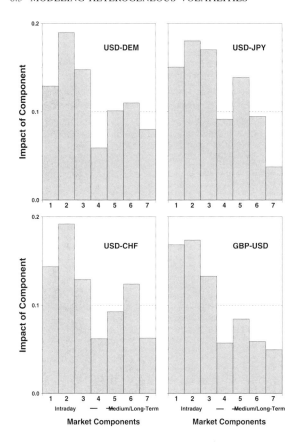

FIGURE 8.5   Impacts of market components of HARCH processes with components as defined in Table 8.3. Each HARCH model has been made for a particular FX rate by fitting a half-hourly time series equally spaced in ϑ-time over 7 years. The differences between the impacts, in particular the low values of the fourth component, are highly significant (see the error values of Table 8.4). The values for USD-DEM are those presented in Table 8.4 and they are not fundamentally different from those of other FX rates.

time to optimize the model. The EMA formulation of the process equation reduces this time by a factor of 1000, making the computation of HARCH volatility much more tractable even with limited computational power. In the next section, we will explore the forecasting ability of these models and compare it to a more traditional approach to volatility.

The impacts I_i are also plotted in a histogram (Figure 8.5) where it is possible to compare the results for different FX rates. The impact of the fourth component is the weakest among all impacts. This is not only for USD-DEM but also many other rates and also for other sampling periods.[10] The fourth component has a

---

[10] When a 7-year sample is split into two parts of 3 1/2 years, the estimated coefficients on both of these subsamples are quite stable.

TABLE 8.5   Results of the EMA-HARCH for the LIFFE Three-Month Euromark.

Results of the EMA-HARCH process estimate for 3-hr ϑ-time intervals for the different forward rates for the LIFFE Three-Month Euromark. The underlying data are from the LIFFE Three-Month Euromark. Standard errors are given. Instead of the coefficients C_i (for $i > 0$), the corresponding impacts I_i are given. Data sample: from April 6, 1992, to December 30, 1997, representing 16,774 observations. The forward rates are labeled according to the market conventions for forward rate agreements, as explained in the text. The 3x6 forward interest rate, for example, applies to the interval starting in 3 months and ending in 6 months.

	3x6	6x9	9x12	12x15	15x18
K_0	2.90 ± 0.15	4.54 ± 0.24	4.29 ± 0.24	6.45 ± 0.39	4.22 ± 0.37
I_1	0.20 ± 0.01	0.17 ± 0.01	0.19 ± 0.01	0.18 ± 0.01	0.12 ± 0.01
I_2	0.01 ± 0.01	0.00 ± 0.02	0.00 ± 0.02	0.01 ± 0.01	0.00 ± 0.02
I_3	0.17 ± 0.02	0.16 ± 0.02	0.16 ± 0.02	0.15 ± 0.02	0.15 ± 0.02
I_4	0.08 ± 0.02	0.11 ± 0.02	0.13 ± 0.02	0.14 ± 0.02	0.12 ± 0.02
I_5	0.11 ± 0.02	0.15 ± 0.02	0.16 ± 0.02	0.15 ± 0.02	0.19 ± 0.02
I_6	0.23 ± 0.02	0.22 ± 0.02	0.19 ± 0.02	0.08 ± 0.02	0.11 ± 0.02
I_7	0.00 ± 0.01	0.03 ± 0.01	0.04 ± 0.01	0.02 ± 0.01	0.03 ± 0.01
L	7.753	7.478	7.345	7.320	7.307

typical time horizon of around 12 hr—too long for intraday dealers and too short for other traders. This naturally explains the weakness of that component.

When comparing the impacts of Figure 8.5 with the component definition of Table 8.3, we see further interesting features captured by HARCH models. First, the short-term components have, in all cases, the largest impacts. These short-term components model essentially the intraday dealers and the market makers who are known to dominate the market. Second, the similarity in the impacts of the USD-CHF and USD-DEM are plausible as it is well known that the Swiss National Bank policy was tightly tied to the USD-CHF to the USD-DEM rates. The relative weakness of the longer-term components for the GBP-USD is another relevant piece of information that can be gathered from this parametrization and has been confirmed to us by market participants. Since the 1992 crisis, the long-term investors have been reluctant to invest in this market and have been more concentrated on the cross rate GBP-DEM. The relative impact of the fifth and the sixth components are in the same order for USD-CHF and USD-DEM but inverted in the case of both USD-JPY and GBP-USD.

8.3.6   HARCH in Interest Rate Modeling

As described in Chapter 7, we haved performed a lead-lag correlation analysis and established the HARCH effect for forward interest rates implied by interest rate futures, constructed according to Section 2.4.2 (see Figure 7.9). In this section, we use the HARCH parametrization in terms of market components to investigate whether we obtain similar features as in the case of foreign exchange rates. To avoid a systematic, deterministic decrease of volatility as explained by Section 5.6.4, we use forward rates for fixed time intervals. The forward rates are labeled according to the market conventions for forward rate agreements. The $I \times J$ forward rate (e.g., the 3x6 forward rate) is the forward rate quoted at time t and applicable for the interval starting at time $(t + I)$ and ending at time $(t + J)$ (I and J are expressed in months). The corresponding time-to-start is I months and the maturity is $(J - I)$ months.

The results of the EMA-HARCH process estimation for 3-hr ϑ-time intervals for the different forward rates for the LIFFE Three-Month Euromark are given in Table 8.5. The EMA-HARCH process is estimated for each forward rate by maximizing the log-likelihood and use data from April 6, 1992, to December 30, 1997, with about 16,800 observations. The distribution of the random variable ε_t is normal with zero mean and a unit variance. The market components (with $p = 4$) are similar to the ones described in the previous section. Like in the case of FX rates, the impact coefficient for the interval range from 6 hr to 1 days (second component) is very small. These results also indicate a decreasing impact of the longer-term components (corresponding to the market actors with the longest time-horizon) going from the first forward rate (i.e., whose time-to-start is closest in the future) to the last one (i.e., whose time-to-start is farthest in the future), reflecting the decrease in the volatility autocorrelation. The sum of the impacts is smaller than one in all cases, meaning that the estimated processes are stationary according to Equation 8.34.

8.4 FORECASTING SHORT-TERM VOLATILITY

The true test of the veracity of a volatility model is its ability to forecast the future behavior of volatility. This means that the data used to test the model are distinct from the data used to find the model parameters. All of the analyses described in this section are performed in an out-of-sample setting.

There is some added complexity in the case of volatility models where there is no unique definition of volatility. Andersen and Bollerslev (1998a) showed that, if the wrong estimators of volatility are taken, it is not possible to really test the forecasting quality of a model. That is why it is important to set a framework in which a forecasting performance analysis can be performed.

8.4.1   A Framework to Measure the Forecasting Performance

We choose here a path similar to that proposed in Taylor and Xu (1997). We construct a time series of realized hourly volatility, $v_h(t)$, from our time series of returns as follows:

$$v_{h,t} = \sum_{i=1}^{a_h} r_{t-i}^2 \qquad (8.35)$$

where a_h is the aggregation factor. In this case, we use data points every 10 min in ϑ-time, so the aggregation factor is $a_h = 6$.

Forecasts of different models are compared to the realized volatility of Equation 8.35. The one-step ahead forecasts are based on hourly returns in ϑ-time. The advantage of using hourly returns instead of 30-min returns as in the previous section is that hourly forecasts are compatible with the historical hourly volatility defined in Equation 8.35. Four models are studied here.

- The first model is used as a benchmark and is a naive historical model inspired by the effect described in Section 7.4.2 and Müller *et al.* (1997a) where low-frequency volatility predicts high-frequency volatility. The historical volatility is computed over a given day measured from the hourly returns. This quantity, properly normalized, is used as a predictor for the next hour volatility, $v(t + 1)$, as defined in Equation 8.35. Formally the forecasting model v_b is

$$v_{b,t} = \frac{1}{24} \sum_{j=1}^{24} \left(\sum_{i=6(j-1)+1}^{6j} r_{t-i} \right)^2 \tag{8.36}$$

where the factor in front of the summation is here to normalize v_b to hourly volatility.

- GARCH(1,1) is

$$v_{garch,t} = h_t = \alpha_0 + \alpha_1 \varepsilon_{t-1}^2 + \beta_1 h_{t-1} \tag{8.37}$$

where ε_t is i.i.d. and follows a normal distribution function with zero mean and unit variance.

- The HARCH model in Equation 8.13 and the seven components of Table 8.3, introduced by Müller *et al.* (1997a).

- The EMA-HARCH model in Equation 8.27 and 8.28 with seven components.

The three parameter models are optimized over a sample of 5 years of hourly data using the estimation procedure described in Section 9.3.5. The forecasts are then analyzed over the 5 remaining years. We term this procedure the static optimization. To account for possible changes in the model parameters, we also recompute them every year using a moving sample of 5 years. We term this procedure dynamic optimization. In this case, the performance is always tested outside of the gliding sample to ensure that the test is fully out-of-sample. In both cases, we use an out-of-sample period of 5 years of hourly data, which represents more than 43,000 observations.

We compare the accuracy of the four forecasting models to the realized hourly volatility of Equation 8.35. The quantities of interest are the forecasting signal,

$$s_f = \tilde{v}_{f,t} - v_{h,t} \tag{8.38}$$

where $\tilde{v}_f$ is any of the forecasting models, and the realized signal,

$$s_r = v_{h,t+1} - v_{h,t} \tag{8.39}$$

The quantity $\tilde{v}_{f,t}$ is taken in the estimation sample either directly or rescaled by the ratio of the averages $\bar{v}_h$ and $\bar{\tilde{v}}_f$. This makes the forecast values on average closer to the historical volatility. In the rest of this chapter, we call the quantity, $(\bar{v}_h \cdot \tilde{v}_{f,t})/\bar{\tilde{v}}_f$, the rescaled forecast.

In this formulation, performance measures proposed in Dacorogna *et al.* (1996) can be applied because the quantities defined in Equations 8.38 and 8.39 can take positive and negative values contrary to the volatilities, which are positive definite quantities. One of these measures is the direction quality,

$$Q_d = \frac{\mathcal{N}(\{\tilde{v}_f \mid s_f \cdot s_r > 0\})}{\mathcal{N}(\{\tilde{v}_f \mid s_f \cdot s_r \neq 0\})} \tag{8.40}$$

where $\mathcal{N}$ is a function that gives the number of elements of a particular set of variables. It should be noted that this definition does not test the cases where either the forecast is the same as the current volatility or the volatility at time $t+1$ is the same as the current one. This is, of course, unlikely to occur in our particular case. A detailed statistical discussion of this measure can be found in Pesaran and Timmerman (1992).

In addition to this measure, we use a measure that combines the size of the movements and the direction quality. It is often called the *realized potential*,

$$Q_r = \frac{\sum \text{sign}(s_f \cdot s_r) \, |s_r|}{\sum |s_r|} \tag{8.41}$$

In fact, the measures Q_r and Q_d are not independent and Q_r is a weighted average of $\text{sign}(s_f \cdot s_r)$ whereas $2Q_d - 1$ is the corresponding unweighted average. It is easy to show that if

$$Q_r > 2\,Q_d - 1 \tag{8.42}$$

the forecast of the sign of s_r for large $|s_r|$ values is better than average.

A more traditional measure such as the comparison of the absolute error of a model to a benchmark model can also be used. This benchmark model is chosen to be the historical volatility as defined in Equation 8.36, v_b. The quantity

$$Q_f = 1 - \frac{\sum |s_r - s_f^{model}|}{\sum |s_r - s_f^{benchmark}|} \tag{8.43}$$

is a quality measure, which increases with an increasing performance of the model. If $Q_f > 0$, the model outperforms the benchmark. If $Q_f < 0$, the benchmark outperforms the model. The second part of Equation 8.43 is similar to the known Theil's U-statistic, Makridakis *et al.* (1983), except that we use the absolute value instead of the squared errors.

TABLE 8.6   Forecasting performance for USD-DEM.

Forecasting accuracy of various models in predicting short-term market volatility. The performance is measured every hour over 5 years, from January 1, 1992, to December 31, 1996, with 43,230 observations. In parentheses, the accuracy of rescaled forecasts is shown.

USD-DEM	Q_d	Q_r	Q_f
	Static Optimization		
Benchmark	67.7% (67.6%)	54.2% (54.3%)	0.000
GARCH(1,1)	67.8% (67.3%)	58.5% (59.7%)	0.085 (0.072)
HARCH(7c)	69.2% (68.7%)	58.3% (59.2%)	0.134 (0.129)
EMA-HARCH(7)	69.4% (68.8%)	60.7% (62.5%)	0.140 (0.128)
	Dynamic Optimization		
Benchmark	67.7% (67.4%)	54.2% (54.6%)	0.000
GARCH(1,1)	67.0% (66.0%)	59.5% (59.8%)	0.074 (0.057)
HARCH(7c)	67.7% (66.8%)	60.1% (60.8%)	0.113 (0.102)
EMA-HARCH(7)	68.8% (67.7%)	62.4% (62.9%)	0.133 (0.117)

The summations (including $\mathcal{N}$) in Equations 8.40, 8.41, and 8.43 are over all hours in the out-of-sample period. The number of independent observations is large so that the degrees of freedom of the calculated tests are sufficiently large. Performance measures based on squares such as the signal correlation or squared errors are not used because our interest is in squared returns and the fourth moment of the distribution of returns may not be finite, as discussed in Section 5.4.2.

8.4.2   Performance of ARCH-Type Models

In Table 8.6, the results for the different performance measures are presented for the most traded FX rate, USD-DEM, for the static and dynamic optimizations. In parentheses, the results for the scaled forecasts are presented. For all measures, three parameter models perform better than the benchmark and the EMA-HARCH performs the best. The forecast accuracy is remarkable for all ARCH-type models. In more than two-thirds of the cases, the forecast direction is correctly predicted and the mean absolute errors are smaller than the benchmark errors for all models. The realized potential measure shows that the forecast of volatility change is accurate not only for small $|s_r|$ but also for large ones. The condition expressed in Equation 8.42 is always satisfied for all models. Neither the scaled forecast nor the dynamic optimization seems to significantly improve the forecasting accuracy. The realized potential Q_r is the only measure that consistently improves with dynamic optimization. Examining the model coefficients computed in moving samples shows that they oscillate around mean values. No structural changes in the coefficients were detected. The accuracy improvement in Q_r together with the loss in Q_f in the case of dynamic optimization indicates that the prediction of large movements is improved at the cost of the prediction of direction of small real movements. From the point of view of forecasting short-term volatility, the EMA-HARCH is the best of the models considered here and compares favorably to HARCH. Similar conclusions can be drawn from the results for four other FX rates.[11] The cross rate JPY-DEM presents results slightly less accurate than the other currencies, but it should be noted that the early half of the sample has been synthetically computed from USD-DEM and USD-JPY. This may lead to noise in the computation of hourly volatility and affect the forecast quality.

---

[11] The interested reader will find them in Dacorogna *et al.* (1998b), where similar tables are listed for USD-JPY, GBP-USD, USD-CHF, and DEM-JPY.

9

FORECASTING RISK AND RETURN

9.1 INTRODUCTION TO FORECASTING

This section examines forecasting models for different variables. The predicted variable should be observable, so the forecasts and the true variable values can be compared in the future to allow for statistical forecast quality tests. The following variables can be predicted:

- The absolute size of future returns. This can be done in different mathematical forms, one of them using *realized volatility* as defined in Section 3.2.4. We ignore the direction of the future price returns here and assume their probability distribution function to be symmetric by default. Under this assumption, the chosen forecast variable also measures the *risk* of holding a position in the financial asset.

- The future return over the forecast period, including its sign. This also implies a price forecast because the future price is the price now plus the future return.

- A full probability distribution function of future returns. This is the most comprehensive goal. Given the natural uncertainty of forecasting, we are rarely able or willing to forecast details of the distribution function, and we are more than happy to have good forecasts of its center and its width.

248

There are basically two approaches for constructing forecasting models. The foreign exchange market again serves as our main example. The first approach builds upon structural economic models testing various forms of market efficiency[1] or the study of the issues such as the purchasing power parity model and the modeling of risk premia (see Baillie and McMahon, 1989; MacDonald and Taylor, 1992). Meese and Rogoff (1983) carried out the first comprehensive out-of-sample tests of these models, which they call structural models.

Models following the second approach are often called time series models and are based on information extracted from the past of the time series through various forms of linear and nonlinear statistical operators and prefiltering techniques. These types of models can be univariate or multivariate.[2] In this chapter, we adopt the second approach and study univariate time series models by utilizing only past prices to forecast a given series. There are two main motivations for this approach. First, the absence of any theory for the short-term movements of the foreign exchange (FX) rates makes the structural models irrelevant for these horizons. Second, the availability of high-frequency data can capture many of the market effects that are relevant to the short-term movements, (e.g., the behavior of different market participants).

The forecasting models presented in this chapter are *univariate* where only one time series is predicted. They are univariate not only in the predicted target variable but also in the information set used. Multivariate forecasting as an important but complex subject is not discussed here, but Chapter 10 has some relevant discussions.

The models work with high-frequency data as described by Chapter 2 and take into account every tick in the market. The predicted quantity (e.g., the price or future realized volatility) is related to a *time horizon*, (e.g., the return of the next hour or the volatility of one full business day from now.) The use of high-frequency data allows us to make short-term forecasts for time intervals less than a day. This leads to a large number of observed forecast intervals and thus high statistical significance.

In principle, the knowledge of the "true" data-generating process in the sense of Chapter 8 should also lead to the "true" forecasting model. We have indeed used statistical processes to generate forecasts and measured the success of these statistical processes in terms of their forecasting quality in Chapter 8. In practice, the way from a statistical process to a good forecasting model is not as straightforward. Many otherwise popular statistical processes have serious shortcomings when looking at the intradaily and temporally aggregated behavior, as shown in Section 8.2. Moreover, the statitical processes of that section are volatility models. The price aspect of these models is trivial by having the current price as expectation value for future prices. When moving to forecasting models, we can be more ambitious by also constructing nontrivial price forecasts. We also introduce new

---

[1] The reader may refer to Fama (1970, 1991).

[2] Granger and Newbold (1977) and Priestley (1989) are introductions to these types of models.

testing methods for forecasts. Thus the two topics, data-generating processes and forecasting, are only loosely related.

Forecasting models can be tested by comparing the forecasts to the actual values of the predicted variable. A possible test criterion is the standard deviation of the forecasts from the actual values. Different test criteria can be computed by statistical means, using a test data sample as discussed in Section 9.4. The test result consists of not only a quantitative quality measure but also a statistical significance measure of this quality. The test sample can also be used to optimize the forecasting model and its parameters. In that case, the resulting optimized model should be tested in *another* sample (i.e., out-of-sample). The test results of the original sample (in-sample) cannot be used as an unbiased measure; they only give an upper limit of the otherwise unknown forecasting model quality.

Two examples of univariate time series models are given: volatility forecasting models used for risk assessment in Section 9.2 and a large real-time price forecasting system with live data feeds in Sections 9.3 and 9.4.3.[3]

9.2   FORECASTING VOLATILITY FOR VALUE-AT-RISK

Risk can be measured by different means, for example, through an extreme value analysis as in Sections 5.4.2 and 5.4.3. Here we follow a simpler approach by regarding volatility as the variable that determines the risk. This is also the view of popular risk assessment methods. In these methods, the volatility value is inserted in a standard model to compute the Value-at-Risk (VaR): the expected loss of a portfolio after one business day corresponding to the 1% quantile,[4] (i.e., in a scenario that is worse than 99% of the expected cases and better than the remaining 1%). Inserting a volatility figure (computed from variances and covariances of returns of the portfolio assets) may not be enough to compute a reliable VaR. This is discussed by Davé and Stahl (1998), but is not the focus of interest here.

The required volatility value is in fact a volatility *forecast* for the period from "now" to "now plus one business day." In this section, we discuss univariate volatility forecasting models. Multivariate volatility models need separate treatment because they depend on the intradaily covariance or correlation between assets. This poses some problems as discussed in Chapter 10.

9.2.1   Three Simple Volatility Forecasting Models

Müller (2000) has a discussion of volatility forecasts based on time series operators as presented in Section 3.3. Following that paper, we consider three operator-based volatility forecasting methods of increasing sophistication and quality: (1) the volatility forecasts of RiskMetrics[TM] developed by J. P. Morgan (1996) as a

---

[3] This forecasting model is running in real time as a part of the Olsen & Associates Information System (OIS).

[4] Our scientific interest also extends to forecast intervals other than one business day and quantiles other than 1%, of course.

well-known example, (2) an improved version based on tick-by-tick data, and (3) a further improved multi-horizon version.

All of these volatility models can be seen as observations of volatility in the past (i.e., realized volatility measurements as Equations 3.8 or 3.68, for example). However, the models are intended to be applied to the future. The computed volatility values, although measured in the past, are estimates of the *future* volatility and thus measures of risk. Autoregressive heteroskedasticity as discussed in Section 5.6.1 is the stylized fact that justifies using a certain past volatility as an estimate of future volatility. Section 9.3 has another approach where the volatility forecast is no longer a realized volatility of the past, and Section 8.4.2 considers volatility forecasts directly derived from statistical processes.

The RiskMetrics methodology uses a well-known example of a simple volatility forecast based on an IGARCH process with the following conditional expectation of the squared return:

$$\sigma^2(t) = \mu \, \sigma^2(t - \Delta t) + (1 - \mu) \, [x(t) - x(t - \Delta t)]^2 \qquad (9.1)$$

with $\mu = 0.94$. This formula is evaluated only once per business day, at a given daytime; the resulting volatility value is valid until it is replaced by a new one, one business day later. The time scale t is thus a business time scale omitting weekends, with $\Delta t = 1$ business day. Equation 9.1 is an exponential moving average (EMA) iteration as explained in Section 3.3.5 and can be written as such, using the notation of Equation 3.51,

$$\sigma^2(t) = \text{EMA}\left[\tau; \, [x(t) - x(t - \Delta t)]^2\right] \qquad (9.2)$$

evaluated at discrete time points separated by $\Delta t = 1$ business day, with an EMA range of $\tau = \mu/(1 - \mu) = 15.67$ business days. The EMA operator is explained in Section 3.3.5, but Equation 3.52 has to be replaced here by a version for discrete, homogeneous time series,

$$\mu = \nu = \frac{1}{1 + \alpha} = \frac{\tau}{\tau + 1} \qquad (9.3)$$

as explained by Müller (1991). The only parameter, $\mu = 0.94$, has been chosen to optimize the volatility forecasting quality of Equation 9.1 over a wide range of financial assets and test periods according to J. P. Morgan (1996).

In Figure 9.1, two volatilities are presented. The difference between the two curves solely originates from the choice of daytime when the price x is sampled and the volatility is computed by Equation 9.1 or 9.2. One curve is sampled at 7 a.m. (Greenwich Mean Time) GMT which is a time in the late afternoon of East Asian time zones or a suitable daytime for the daily risk calculations of an East Asian risk manager. The other curve is sampled at 5 p.m. GMT, a suitable daytime for a risk manager in London.

The differences between the two curves are surprisingly large: up to 25%, an alarming uncertainty for risk managers. In our case, two risk managers measure

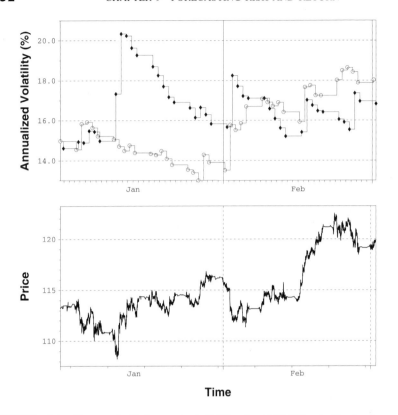

FIGURE 9.1 Top panel: Daily standard RiskMetrics USD-JPY volatility for January, 1999 to February 1999. Circles: Data sampled at 7 a.m. GMT. Diamonds: Data sampled at 5 p.m. GMT. Bottom panel: The USD-JPY price plotted against time.

very different volatility and thus risk levels for the *same* financial instrument, just because they live in different time zones. A difference can persist over weeks, as shown in Figure 9.1. This figure is just an example. The same surprisingly strong effect can also be found for other financial instruments, sampling periods, choices of daytime, and process equations.

Both deviating volatility values cannot be right at the same time; there must be an error in these values. This error is of stochastic nature; there is no systematic bias dependent on the daytime. In Figure 9.1, the difference between the two curves is neither always positive nor negative; it changes its sign.

Figure 9.1 demonstrates the large stochastic error of the RiskMetrics method. The large size of this error has two main reasons:

1. The rather small range of the kernel of about 16 business days. The number of independent observations is limited. We cannot essentially change this fact, because the choice of a short range is also motivated by the goal of fast adaptivity to new market events.

2. The results depend on only one observation per day, taken at a certain daytime. All the other information on prices of the day is thrown away. The value at that daytime may have little representation for the full day: it may be located on top of a short-lived local peak of the price curve.

The second investigated volatility forecasting model was introduced by Müller (2000). It follows RiskMetrics as closely as possible. There are only two innovative modifications:

- The squared volatility $\sigma^2(t)$ is computed at every available tick, not only once per business day.
- Simple returns are replaced by operator-based, smoothed returns.

Nothing is changed otherwise; the sampling range of 15.67 business days and the business-daily nature of (smoothed) returns are preserved. The formula is again written with the help of time series operators:

$$\sigma^2 = c\,\text{EMA}\left[\tau;\ (x - \text{EMA}[\Delta t, 4;\ x])^2\right] \tag{9.4}$$

again with $\Delta t = 1$ business day and $\tau = 15.67$ business days. Equation 9.4 is iteratively evaluated tick by tick. The iterated operator $\text{EMA}[\tau, 4; x]$ is defined by Equation 3.53. As the simple EMA operator, it can be efficiently computed by using the iterative Equation 3.51.

The constant c compensates for the fact that we use smoothed returns, $x - \text{EMA}[\Delta t, 4; x]$, instead of the simple returns, $x(t) - x(t - \Delta t)$. In the case of x following a Gaussian random walk, the theoretically correct value is $c = 128/93$. Using this factor eliminates a systematic bias of the tick-by-tick volatility as compared to the RiskMetrics volatility.

Equation 9.4 is computed on a special business time scale defined as follows. The 49 weekend hours from Friday 8 p.m. GMT to Sunday 9 p.m. GMT are compressed to the equivalent of only 1 hr outside the weekend. This fully corresponds to the time scale of RiskMetrics, which omits the weekend days. A more sophisticated and appropriate choice of the business time scale would be the ϑ-time of Chapter 6, but this is avoided here in order to keep the approach as close to RiskMetrics as possible.

The advantages of the tick-by-tick volatility forecast are demonstrated in Figure 1.3. The volatility as a function of time appears as one continuous, consistent curve. We obtain volatility values at any daytime now, not just once or twice a day. A risk manager in London measures the risk of the instrument on the same basis as a risk manager in East Asia, as should be expected. The variations of the volatility level over time are more moderate in Figure 1.3 than the corresponding variations of the RiskMetrics volatility, although the kernel range of 15.67 business days is the same.

The tick-by-tick volatility forecast is based on (almost) continuously overlapping returns. Overlapping returns lead to reduced stochastic noise of volatility measurements, as shown in Section 3.2.8. In addition to this, the tick-by-tick volatility is based on smoothed rather than simple returns, which also leads to a reduction of stochastic noise.

The third volatility model is a multiple-horizon version of the second model:

$$\sigma^2 = \frac{\sum_{k=0}^{n-1} f_w^k \, \sigma_k^2}{\sum_{k=0}^{n-1} f_w^k} \tag{9.5}$$

with

$$\sigma_k^2 = c \, \text{EMA} \left[\tau_0 \, f_\tau^k; \left(x - \text{EMA}[\Delta t_0 \, f_{\Delta t}^k, 4; x] \right)^2 \right] \tag{9.6}$$

where the partial volatility forecasts of Equation 9.6 are like the volatility forecasts of Equation 9.4. The weights f_w^k of the partial volatility forecasts, their return intervals $\Delta t_0 \, f_{\Delta t}^k$, and their sampling ranges $\tau_0 \, f_\tau^k$ are in geometric sequences and can be flexibly chosen and optimized by setting the parameters n (the number of partial forecasts), f_w, Δt_0, $f_{\Delta t}$, τ_0, and f_τ.

The third volatility model (Equation 9.5) shares the advantages of the second one (Equation 9.4) and has the additional multiple-horizon property, which leads to superior volatility forecast quality. This is in analogy to the multiple-horizon EMA-HARCH process shown in Section 8.3.4, which is also superior to single-horizon processes such as GARCH.

9.2.2 Choosing the Best Volatility Forecasting Model

The quality of volatility forecasting models has to be measured in statistical tests, comparing the forecasts to the actual values of the target variable, which is a form of realized volatility here.

In out-of-sample tests of the three volatility forecasting models presented in Section 9.2.1, the tick-by-tick model of Equation 9.4 has distinctly better volatility forecasts than the RiskMetrics model of Equation 9.1 or 9.2. Equation 9.5 leads to even better volatility forecasts.

Testing the quality of volatility forecasts implies some technical difficulties. First, there are several quality measures to choose from. This is discussed in Sections 9.4.1 and 8.4.1, where volatility forecasts are derived from process equations and tested by several criteria.

A second difficulty lies in the bias of both realized volatility (the target variable) and volatility forecasts which appears if the return intervals chosen are too small. This bias is discussed in Section 3.2.4 and in Andersen *et al.* (2000). Volatility forecast tests are affected by this bias. A treatment of the bias is almost inevitable when designing volatility forecasting models and tests based on high-frequency returns over intervals of less than an hour. Corsi *et al.* (2001) propose a suitable bias correction method.

Due to these technical difficulties, there is no comprehensive study of high-frequency volatility forecasts and their qualities yet. The final goal is the development of a consistent methodology of risk analysis based on high-frequency data with superior forecasting quality: *real-time risk assessment*.

9.3 FORECASTING RETURNS OVER MULTIPLE TIME HORIZONS

This section examines the forecasting model of Dacorogna *et al.* (1996). This model supports several forecast intervals. Hourly returns are predicted as well as daily, weekly, monthly, and quarterly returns. The forecasting model of returns relies on an underlying volatility forecast. Both the volatility and return forecasts use the same methodology. Volatility is treated with the help of an alternative time scale, the *intrinsic time* of the time series.

9.3.1 Intrinsic Time

The foreign exchange returns exhibit conditional heteroskedasticity which can be treated through a change of time scale. This is the second layer of our forecasting model on top of the business time ϑ-scale. Some literature followed a similar approach to treat the conditional heteroskedasticity, such as Stock (1988), who uses two types of time deformation, one based on the time series itself and one on business cycle variables.[5] In our approach, we also use the underlying time series to construct a time deformation. It is based on the scaling law defined in Equation 6.2 and on the price volatility:

$$\tau(t_c) \equiv \tau(t_{c-1}) + k \frac{\vartheta(t_c) - \vartheta(t_{c-1})}{\Delta\vartheta} \frac{|\Delta x|^E}{c} \qquad (9.7)$$

where t_c is the current time, the price difference is taken on the same interval as $\Delta\vartheta$, and E and c are the scaling law inverse exponent and factor, respectively. The constant k is a calibration factor dependent on the particular time series. Its role is to keep τ in line with physical time in the long run. This relationship is in fact the reverse of the scaling law for a particular return taken on a constant ϑ-time interval size.

This second new time scale, the τ-scale, does not directly use the physical time t, and does not need to have fundamental information about the behavior of the series. The only information needed to define the scale are the values of the time series themselves. Thus we have chosen to call this time scale *intrinsic time*. The consequence of using such a scale is to expand periods of high volatility and contract those of low volatility, thus better capturing the relative importance of events to the market. Any moving average based on the intrinsic time τ dynamically adapts its range to market events. Therefore a forecasting model based on the τ-scale has a *dynamic memory* of the price history.

There is, however, a problem when using such a time scale. The intrinsic time τ is only known for the past, contrary to the business time scale ϑ, which is known also for the future, because it is based on average behavior. Thus a forecasting model for the price actually needs to be composed of *two* forecasting models, one for the intrinsic time and one for the price. The first requires forecasting of the size (not the direction) as time cannot flow backward.

---

[5] In the same paper Stock (1988) indicates how this approach can be compared to the ARCH models.

9.3.2 Model Structure

The price generating process is far from stationary in physical time. In Section 9.3.1, the geographic seasonality and conditional heteroskedasticity are modeled through successive changes of the underlying time scales. After these transformations, the remaining structure and the dynamics of the transformed series can be analyzed. The model presented in this section captures the dynamics through the computation of nonlinear indicators. Because the model is on the business-time scale ϑ, all equations are written in terms of this new scale. The relation to the physical time scale is given by Equation 6.17.

9.3.3 A Linear Combination of Nonlinear Indicators

The model equations are based on nonlinear *indicators*, which are modeled with moving averages. Indicators for market prices come conceptually from simple trading systems used in practice by market participants.[6] Those trading systems yield *buy* and *sell* signals by evaluating an indicator function. The crossing of a certain threshold by the indicator on the positive side is regarded as a *buy* signal, on the negative side as a *sell* signal. An indicator is thus used as a *predictor* of a variable or its change, for instance, a price change (i.e., a return).

Finding an ideal indicator, if it exists at all, would be enough to make a good price forecast. We, however, have no ideal indicators. Therefore there is need to combine different indicators appropriately to optimize their respective influence. Partly, the forecasting models presented here are based on a *linear combination* of price indicators z_x where the relative weights are estimated by multiple linear regression. For a fixed forecasting horizon $\Delta\vartheta_f$ (corresponding to a Δt_f in physical time), the price forecast $\tilde{x}_f$ is computed with

$$\tilde{x}_f = x_c + \sum_{j=1}^{m} c_{x,j}(\Delta\vartheta_f)\, z_{x,j}(\Delta\tilde{\tau}_f, \tau_c) \qquad (9.8)$$

where x_c is the current price, and m is the number of indicators used in the model (from two to five per horizon). All the indicators are estimated in intrinsic time scale (τ-scale). The coefficients $c_{x,j}(\Delta\vartheta_f)$ are estimated with a multiple linear regression model.

$\Delta\tilde{\tau}_f$ in Equation 9.8, the forecasting horizon expressed in intrinsic time, is not yet defined. This quantity must be computed from its own forecasting model, which is similar to that in Equation 9.8. The forecasting horizon, $\Delta\tilde{\tau}_f$, can be written as an intrinsic time forecast,

$$\Delta\tilde{\tau}_f \equiv \tilde{\tau}_f - \tau_c = \sum_{j=1}^{m} c_{\tau,j}(\Delta\vartheta_f)\, z_{\tau,j}(\Delta\vartheta_f, \vartheta_c) \qquad (9.9)$$

---

[6] See for instance Dunis and Feeny (1989); Murphy (1986).

where the forecasting model is computed in ϑ-scale. The coefficients $c_{\tau,j}(\Delta\vartheta_f)$ are estimated through a multiple linear regression and $z_{\tau,j}(\Delta\vartheta_f, \vartheta_c)$ are the intrinsic time indicators.

Contrary to most traditional forecasting models, this model does not rely on a fixed basic time interval but is designed with a concept of continuous time. In fact, the time when a price is recorded in the database is unequally spaced in time. Moreover, the use of the τ-scale implies that our forecasting models must be computed simultaneously over several fixed time horizons $\Delta\vartheta_f$.

Given a forecasting horizon in physical time Δt_f and the price history until x_c, one can compute $\Delta\vartheta_f$ with Equation 6.17 and τ_c with Equation 9.7. With a sufficiently large set of indicators, $z_{\tau,j}(\Delta\vartheta_f, \vartheta_c)$, $z_{x,j}(\Delta\tilde{\tau}_f, \tau_c)$, and coefficients, $c_{\tau,j}(\Delta\vartheta_f)$ and $c_{x,j}(\Delta\vartheta_f)$, the price forecast can be computed by choosing the appropriate $\Delta\tilde{\tau}_f$ with Equation 9.9 and substituting it into Equation 9.8. In the next two sections, we define the indicators and study how to compute the coefficients $c_{x,j}$.

9.3.4 Moving Averages, Momenta, and Indicators

In Equations 9.8 and 9.9, the indicators are based on momenta, which are based on moving averages. In particular, we work with *exponential* moving averages (EMA) because they may be conveniently expressed in terms of recursion formulae (see Chapter 3).

The momentum indicator is

$$m_x(\Delta\tau_r, \tau_c) \equiv x_c - EMA[\Delta\tau_r; x](\tau_c) \tag{9.10}$$

which compares the most recent price to its own exponential moving average (EMA), using the notation in Section 3.3.5 and computed by the recursion formula of Equation 3.51. This is done by using intrinsic time as the time scale. It is also possible to define the *first* and the *second* momenta. The first momentum, $m_x^{(1)}$, is the difference of two exponential moving averages (or momenta) with *different ranges*. This can be considered as the first derivative of $x(\tau)$. The second momentum, $m_x^{(2)}$, is the linear combination of three exponential moving averages (or momenta) with different ranges, which provide information on the *curvature* of the series over a certain past history.

In section 9.3.3 we introduce the concept of indicators. Here we want to define those that are used in our forecasting models.

There are a large number of technical indicators (Murphy, 1986; Dunis and Feeny, 1989) and momenta indicators are widely used in technical trading systems. We limit our focus on momenta type indicators. Following Equation 9.8, let an indicator for returns with a range $\Delta\tau_r$, $z_x(\Delta\tau_r, \tau_c)$ be defined as follows:

$$z_x(\Delta\tau_r, \tau_c) = \left[\frac{m_x^{(o)}(\Delta\tau_r, \tau_c)}{\sqrt{1 + (m_x^{(o)}(\Delta\tau_r, \tau_c)/m_{max})^2}} \right]^p \tag{9.11}$$

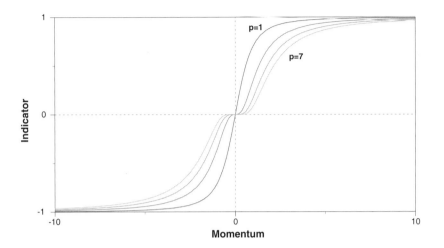

FIGURE 9.2 The nonlinear function for computing the momentum indicator. This function is presented for different values of the parameter p.

where $m_x^{(o)}(\Delta\tau_r, \tau_c)$ are normalized momenta of order o of returns, m_{max}^p is the maximum value the indicator can take, and the power p is the accentuator of the indicator movements. In the case of price indicators, p must be an odd number to keep the sign of the moving average. The shape of the nonlinear function is illustrated in Figure 9.2 for different powers p and for a m_{max} of one. This functional shape illustrates how the indicator plays the role of a primitive trading system. If the momentum has a high positive or negative value, the indicator z_x saturates, which is when the indicator is fully exposed in a *long* or *short* position. The power p both plays the role of a threshold (no threshold if $p = 1$) and influences how the model approaches its full long or short position. The m_{max}^p value plays the role of the *quantity* of capital invested and also influences the shape of the indicator function.

The definition given in Equation 9.11 can easily be extended to other types of problems. For instance, the same definition can be used for constructing indicators for the intrinsic time in the ϑ-scale, $z_\tau(\Delta\vartheta_r, \vartheta_c)$ where the parameters are now defined as functions of τ_c computed using Equation 9.7 on the ϑ-scale. The function $\tau(\vartheta)$ is a monotonic positive definite function so that all of its momenta are positive.[7] When the function is raised to an even power, only the upper right quadrant of Figure 9.2 becomes relevant. The primitive trading system analogy does not work in this case but the emphasis on large movements can be avoided by leveling off the indicator.

In the implementation of this algorithm, the indicators are *continuously up-dated*. Every new price received from the market makers causes the model to

---

[7] Time never flows backward.

recompute all its indicators for all the horizons. It then updates the forecasts for each time horizon.

9.3.5 Continuous Coefficient Update

The forecasting model environment is such that the indicators and the corresponding coefficients are continuously updated. Each coefficient $(c_{x,j}, c_{\tau,j})$ is updated by estimating the model in the most recent past history. The length of the past history is a function of the forecasting horizon.[8] The motivation for horizon-dependent finite samples for optimization is motivated from the fact that there are different regimes in the market and short-term horizons are particularly sensitive to them. Furthermore, short-term traders are not influenced by a past much older than 3 months. The use of samples extending into the far past to optimize short forecasting horizons will make the model less adaptive to regime changes.

Adaptation to long-term regime or structural changes is enabled by re-evaluation of the optimization as soon as enough new information becomes available. The optimization sample size is kept fixed (in ϑ-time), rolled forward, and then linear regression is reapplied to the new sample. This technique is similar to that used in Schinasi and Swamy (1989) and Swamy and Schinasi (1989) except that we use a fixed sample size while they add on the new data to their sample. The model is optimized through the usual generalized least-square method, except for two modifications.

Our forecasting models run in real time and the continuous reoptimization can generate instabilities (rapid jump from positive to negative forecast) when standard linear regression techniques are used. The instabilities originate from both the indicators and their coefficients in the linear combination (Equations 9.8 and 9.9). The indicators are moderately volatile and we avoid indicators that are too volatile by limiting the power of the exponents in the indicator construction to 3 for simple momenta and 7 for higher momenta. Moderately volatile indicators can cause instabilities only if their coefficients are large. The coefficients are less volatile than the indicators (due to the large optimization samples), but they may have high values if the regression by which they are optimized is near-singular because of high correlation between the indicators. Within a particular sample, the high positive and negative coefficients typical in the solution of a near-singular regression matrix would balance each other out. However, as soon as these coefficients are used with changing indicator values outside this sample, the equilibrium is lost and the high coefficients may boost the forecast signal. We have already eliminated one source of near-singularity by avoiding indicators that are too similar in the same forecast.

The standard regression technique is applied under the assumption of precise regressors and a dependent variable with a Gaussian error. Our regressors (indicators), however, originate from the same database as the dependent variable (the return); thus, they are prone to database errors (missing data, badly filtered data, and so on) and to errors in the construction of the ϑ and τ time scales. Taking into

---

[8] A few months for hourly forecasts, up to a few years for 3-month forecasts.

account the regressor errors allows a solution to the problem of near-singularities in a natural way. Instead of considering the jth regressor $z_{j,i}$ at the ith observation (where we have dropped the variable index and the horizon for ease of notation), we consider the *imprecise* regressors $\hat{z}_{j,i} = z_{j,i} + \varepsilon_{j,i}$ where $\varepsilon_{j,i}$ is the random error with variance of ϱ^2 times that of z_j. We call the small parameter ϱ the typical relative error of the indicators and we assume it is roughly the same for all indicators of the type we defined in Section 9.3.4. Without going into the details of the calculation, such a change modifies the final version of the system of k equations. The kth equation can be written as follows:

$$\sum_{j=1}^{m} c_j \left(1 + \varrho^2 \, \delta_{jk} \right) \sum_{i=1}^{N} w_i \, \hat{z}_{j,i} \, \hat{z}_{k,i} = \sum_{i=1}^{N} w_i \, Y_i \, z_{k,i} \qquad (9.12)$$

where N is the number of observations used in the regression, m is the number of indicators (same as in Equation 9.8), w_i is a weighting function depending on the type of moving averages used (here it is an exponential), and δ_{jk} is the usual Kronecker symbol: 1 for $j = k$ and 0 for $j \neq k$. The quantity Y_i is the usual response term of the regression: $x(\vartheta_i + \Delta\vartheta_f) - x(\vartheta_i)$. There is only one addition to the original regression: the diagonal elements of the system matrix are multiplied by a constant factor $1 + \varrho^2$, slightly greater than 1.

The effect of increasing diagonal values of the original matrix by the factor ϱ^2 is to guarantee a minimum regularity of the modified matrix even if the original one is near-singular or even singular. The variable ϱ^2 can be interpreted as the parameter of this minimum regularity. This desired effect is also accompanied by a slight decrease of the absolute values of the coefficients c_j, because the right-hand side of the equation system remains unaffected by the modification. The decreases are insignificant, the only exceptions being for coefficients inflated by near-singularity in the original regression: there, the absolute values decrease substantially, which is what we want anyway.

The other departure from the usual regression technique is a modification of the regression response Y_i necessitated by the leptokurtic behavior of returns. The forecast signals are much less leptokurtic than the returns, hence the optimization is dominated by exceptionally large real price movements rather than the "normal" price movements. This is also accentuated by the fact that it is squared returns that enter into the computation of the least square fit. Furthermore, the users of our forecasting models are more interested in the correct direction of the forecast than in the absolute size of a return forecast. A pure linear regression is thus inappropriate.

The minimization of the sum of squared deviations, however, has an important advantage: it can be reached by solving a system of linear equations. Theoretically though, the least sum of squares could be replaced by any utility function. Our problem is thus to find, within the framework of the regression technique, a more appropriate optimization (or utility) function. The best way to achieve this goal is through a *mapping function* of the returns: the forecast should fit the mapped returns $\tilde{Y}_i$ rather than the *real* returns Y_i.

A suitable mapping function makes the mapped returns less leptokurtic than the original ones. The rest of the regression problem remains unchanged. The desired effects can be obtained with an underproportional mapping function presenting the following properties:

- Small returns should be amplified when considered in the regression, in order to establish a sufficient penalty against forecasts of the wrong direction.

- Large returns should be reduced when considered in the regression, so the distribution function of mapped returns is no longer leptokurtic.

- The mapping effects should decrease with the increasing time horizon size.

The choice of such a mapping function M is arbitrary provided it has the above properties. The one function used in our model is

$$\hat{Y}_i = M(Y_i) = \frac{AY_i}{[Y_i^2 + B]^\alpha} \tag{9.13}$$

with the parameters A, B, and α depending on the time horizon $\Delta\vartheta_f$. The same parameters are used for all different FX rates. They have been calibrated by trial and error in order to keep the full sample variance of the mapped returns on the same level as that of the original returns. The parameter α must follow the condition $0 \le \alpha < 0.5$ because the mapping function must be an underproportional bijection.

9.4 MEASURING FORECAST QUALITY

Two questions are relevant for testing any forecasting model of foreign exchange (FX) rates:

- What data should be used for testing?

- What is a good measure of forecasting accuracy?

Since the classical paper by Meese and Rogoff (1983), researchers in this field have been aware of the need for out-of-sample tests to truly check the forecast validity. Because of the statistical nature of FX rates, there would be little significance in the forecast accuracy measured on the same data that were used for optimizing the models. The real test comes when the model is run on data that were not used in constructing the model. In our case, our model being run in real-time, we have a continuous out-of-sample test. Besides the question of in and out-of-sample, there is a question as to what constitutes the relevant quantity for measuring the accuracy of forecasting methods. In Makridakis *et al.* (1983) the main measures are reviewed. We limit ourselves here to presenting the reasons as to why we chose certain types of measures and how we compute the uncertainty of these measures.

9.4.1 Appropriate Measures of Forecast Accuracy

Most standard measures rely on the mean square error (MSE) and the mean absolute error (MAE) for each time horizon. These errors are then compared to the similar ones produced by a naive forecasting model serving as a benchmark. One naive model may be the random walk forecast where expected returns are zero and the best forecast for the future is the current price. These accuracy measures are, however, all parametric in the sense that they rely on the desirable properties of means and variances, which occur when the underlying distributions are normal. The selection of the random walk model to derive the benchmark MSE or MAE is inherently inappropriate. It is in effect comparing the price volatility (MSE or MAE) with the forecasting error. There is no reason to expect that the heteroskedasticity and the leptokurticity of returns would not affect their MSE or MAE for a particular horizon. Thus the significance of their comparison with the forecast MSE or MAE is unclear. It might only reflect the properties of price volatility.

Such considerations have led us to formulate here nonparametric methods of analyzing forecast accuracy. These are generally "distribution free" measures in that they do not assume a normally distributed population and so can be used when this assumption is not valid. One measure that has this desirable property is the percentage of forecasts in the right direction. To a trader, for instance, it is more important to correctly forecast the direction (up or down) of any trend than its magnitude. We term this measure the *direction quality*, also known as the sign test:

$$D(\Delta t_f) \equiv \frac{N(\{\tilde{x}_f \mid (\tilde{x}_f - x_c)(x_f - x_c) > 0\})}{N(\{\tilde{x}_f \mid (\tilde{x}_f - x_c)(x_f - x_c) \neq 0\})} \tag{9.14}$$

where N is a function that gives the number of elements of a particular set of variables $\{x\}$, and x_c and $\tilde{x}_f$ have the same definition as in Equation 9.8. We give the forecasting horizon in physical time Δt_f because the quality must be measured in the time scale in which people look at the forecasts. It should be clarified here that this definition does not test the cases where either the forecast is the same as the current price or when the price at time $\vartheta_c + \Delta\vartheta_f$ is the same as the current one. To illustrate this problem, let us note that the random walk forecast cannot be measured by this definition. Other definitions could be used, like counting the case when the direction is zero as half right and half wrong. Excluding the cases where one of the two variables is zero would be a problem if this would occur very often. Our results show that it only occurs quite seldom and for the real signal $(x_f - x_c)$ (few percent of the observations on the very short horizons) and almost never for the forecast signal $(\tilde{x}_f - x_c)$.

Unlike more conventional forecasts, for instance, a weather forecast, an FX rate forecast is valuable even when its direction quality is slightly above 50% and statistically significant. No trader expects to be right all the time. In practice we assume that a D significantly higher than 50% means that the forecasting model is better than the random walk. The problem lies in defining the word "significant."

As much as one would like to be independent of the random walk assumption, we are still forced to go back to it in one way or the other, as here, when we want to define the significance level of the direction quality. As a first approximation, we define the significance level as the 95% confidence level of the random walk:

$$\sigma_D \approx \frac{1.96}{2\sqrt{n}} \tag{9.15}$$

where n is the number of tests. The factor 2 comes from the assumption of an equal probability of having positive or negative signals. It is a similar problem to the one of tossing a coin.

Another measure we use in conjunction with the previous one is the *signal correlation* between the forecasting signal and the real price signal:

$$C(\Delta t_f) \equiv \frac{\sum_{i=1}^{n'}(x_{f,i} - x_{c,i})\,(\tilde{x}_{f,i} - x_{c,i})}{\sqrt{\sum_{i=1}^{n'}(x_{f,i} - x_{c,i})^2\,\sum_{i=i'}^{n}(\tilde{x}_{f,i} - x_{c,i})^2}} \tag{9.16}$$

where n' is the number of possible measures in the full sample, n the number of full forecasting horizons in the full sample, and i' is $n - n'$. Here again the forecasting horizon is given in physical time, Δt_f. We estimate the significance of this quantity using $1.96/\sqrt{n'}$.

Both the direction quality and the signal correlation unfortunately have a slight drawback. They do not provide a measure of the forecast effectiveness. Nevertheless, we believe that they are superior to standard measures due to the nonnormality of the return distributions. The direction quality, which for all practical purposes is the most relevant indication of the forecast, and the signal correlation must be highly significant before we accept a model as being "satisfactory."

9.4.2 Empirical Results for the Multi-Horizon Model

Optimization consists of two distinct, but interrelated operations, corresponding to the two main types of parameters in the models. The linear model coefficients $c_{\tau,j}$ and $c_{x,j}$ are optimized through least squares (see Section 9.3.5), and under the control of this process, always fulfill the strict out-of-sample condition when applied to a forecast. On the other hand, the nonlinear parameters of the indicators described in Section 9.3.4 must be optimized by trial and error to meet the above criteria: the direction quality and the signal correlation. The data set used in selecting the best combination of indicators is termed the *in-sample* period where the model parameters are fully optimized.

In Table 9.1 we indicate how our sample is divided to satisfy the different requirements of model initialization, in-sample optimization, and out-of-sample tests. The initialization period is needed for both initializing the different EMAs (see the discussion in Section 3.3.3) and computing the first set of linear coefficients $c_{\tau,j}$ and $c_{x,j}$. The results presented in the next section are computed over two specific periods using our database of intraday market makers' quotes. The first

TABLE 9.1 The sampling periods of the forecast study. The data samples used for initialization, model training (in-sample), and testing (out-of-sample).

Data range	Data types	Data size	Usage
June 1, 1973, to Feb. 2, 1986	Daily data	152 months	Model initialization
Feb. 3, 1986, to Dec. 1, 1986	Intraday	10 months	Model initialization
Dec. 1, 1986, to Sep. 1, 1990	Intraday	46 months	In-sample period
Sep. 3, 1990, to Nov. 3, 1992	Intraday	25 months	Out-of-sample tests

runs from December 1, 1986, to September 1, 1990 (46 months), and is our in-sample period. The second runs from September 3, 1990, to October 3, 1992 (25 months). This second period is pure *post ex-ante* testing—that is, data from this period were not used at all for building the model. These 25 months constitute our out-of-sample test.

9.4.3 Forecast Effectiveness in Intraday Horizons

The forecast horizons here are for 2, 4, and 8 hr. This choice was made for two reasons. First, there is almost no literature to study models for such short horizons. Second, the statistical significance of the findings can be enhanced due to a large number of observations within a few years at the intraday frequency.

The quality measures are computed for each time horizon at an interval of 1/12 of the horizon. As mentioned earlier, the forecast accuracy is always measured in the physical time scale because it is in this scale that the different forecasts are useful. The number of relevant points in the statistical computation varies depending on the horizon and on the number of missing data for the different currencies. For the 2 hr horizon it varies from around 70,000 tests to 140,000, for 4 hr from 35,000 to 70,000, and for 8 hr 24,000 to 37,000. These very large numbers ensure that our statistical results are highly significant. We currently have 41 currencies running on the Olsen Information System (OIS), but in order not to overwhelm this study with numbers, we only show results for the 10 most important FX rates against the USD and 10 of the most traded cross rates. For the other currencies the results are very similar. The direction quality and the signal correlation are given in percentage for the in and out-of-sample testing periods in Table 9.2 for the USD rates and in Table 9.3 for the cross rates. Juxtaposing both results show clearly that, except for the 2 hr in the USD rates and for GBP-USD, the quality achieved in-sample is in most cases maintained out-of-sample and sometimes even slightly improved.

In Table 9.4 we summarize the significance of these results. For each horizon and for each currency we write a "+" sign if *both* the direction quality and the signal correlation are above the significance levels computed using Equation 9.15 for the direction quality and $1.96/\sqrt{n'}$ for the signal correlation. If one of the two

TABLE 9.2 Direction quality and signal correlation for 10 USD rates.

Direction quality and signal correlation, in-sample and out-of-sample, for 9 FX rates and gold price against the USD. The numbers are expressed in percentage.

FX	Hor.	Direction	Correlation	FX	Hor.	Direction	Correlation
USD-DEM	2hr	52.1 / 51.6	+2.8 / +0.7	USD-NLG	2hr	51.5 / 50.8	+2.0 / -0.0
	4hr	52.6 / 52.1	+4.9 / +3.0		4hr	51.5 / 51.8	+1.9 / +1.2
	8hr	52.0 / 52.5	+2.8 / +2.0		8hr	50.5 / 51.8	+0.1 / +3.2
USD-JPY	2hr	51.5 / 52.2	+1.8 / +3.2	USD-ITL	2hr	51.5 / 50.8	+1.6 / -1.3
	4hr	51.7 / 52.9	+2.1 / +6.0		4hr	51.8 / 51.8	+2.4 / +1.4
	8hr	51.8 / 52.1	+4.0 / +5.4		8hr	51.7 / 52.4	+1.9 / +4.3
GBP-USD	2hr	51.8 / 50.5	+1.1 / -1.9	USD-CAD	2hr	51.8 / 52.6	+3.0 / +3.5
	4hr	51.5 / 51.7	+1.6 / +0.9		4hr	51.9 / 52.9	+4.8 / +5.2
	8hr	50.6 / 51.3	+1.9 / +2.1		8hr	52.4 / 53.6	+2.9 / +6.0
USD-CHF	2hr	51.5 / 51.2	+1.7 / -0.7	AUD-USD	2hr	51.8 / 53.4	+0.8 / +3.5
	4hr	52.2 / 52.1	+2.7 / +1.9		4hr	51.7 / 54.2	+2.7 / +6.5
	8hr	52.5 / 51.5	+2.4 / -0.4		8hr	51.4 / 53.7	+4.0 / +6.1
USD-FRF	2hr	51.0 / 50.8	+1.1 / -0.4	XAU-USD	2hr	52.5 / 53.0	+3.5 / +2.3
	4hr	52.2 / 51.6	+3.1 / +2.2		4hr	53.5 / 53.1	+4.3 / +3.8
	8hr	50.7 / 51.5	+0.1 / +0.4		8hr	53.5 / 52.9	+3.9 / +2.9

measures or both are below the significance level we write a "−" sign. Except for two USD rates (GBP-USD and USD-FRF), two cross rates (CAD-CHF and XAU-CHF), and the 2 hr horizon for the USD rates, which do not sustain conclusively the out-of-sample test, the other cases confirm the success of the model. The 2 hr cross-rates pass the out-of-sample test for 80% of the cases (only 40% of the cases for the USD rates) and the 4 hr for 80% and 8 hr for 90% of the cases. The USD rates for the 4 hr pass the test in 90% of the cases and for 8 hr in 80% of the cases.

In this chapter, we have shown that with the help of high-frequency data the statistical properties of FX rates can be better understood and that specifying forecasting models for very short-term horizons is possible. These models contain ingredients all designed to better capture the dynamics at work in the FX market. The most important characteristics of the models are as follows:

- Univariate time analysis type of model but based on intraday nonhomogeneous data,

- Variable time scales to capture both the seasonal heteroskedasticity (ϑ-scale) and the autoregressive conditional heteroskedasticity (τ-scale)

- Linear combination of nonlinear indicators

- Multiple linear regression with two modifications to avoid instabilities and to correct for the leptokurtic behavior of the returns

TABLE 9.3 Direction quality and signal correlation for 10 cross rates.

Direction quality and signal correlation, in-sample and out-of-sample, for 9 FX cross rates and gold price. The numbers are expressed in percentage.

FX	Hor.	Direction	Correlation	FX	Hor.	Direction	Correlation
JPY-DEM	2hr	52.5 / 51.7	+2.3 / +1.0	GBP-CHF	2hr	54.4 / 55.1	+7.4 / +6.5
	4hr	51.8 / 51.0	+3.0 / +2.5		4hr	53.5 / 54.1	+6.2 / +5.0
	8hr	52.0 / 51.0	+4.0 / +1.3		8hr	53.8 / 54.2	+6.4 / +8.0
GBP-DEM	2hr	54.0 / 55.2	+6.1 / +5.6	JPY-CHF	2hr	52.6 / 51.7	+3.1 / +0.9
	4hr	53.3 / 54.5	+5.3 / +4.4		4hr	52.2 / 50.8	+3.5 / +2.1
	8hr	53.3 / 54.2	+4.7 / +8.7		8hr	54.1 / 51.4	+9.1 / +1.5
CHF-DEM	2hr	57.1 / 55.5	+12.5 / +8.1	GBP-JPY	2hr	52.8 / 53.3	+4.5 / +4.0
	4hr	54.9 / 54.6	+9.7 / +6.2		4hr	52.3 / 53.0	+4.6 / +4.8
	8hr	55.2 / 54.4	+10.0 / +6.7		8hr	52.8 / 52.8	+6.5 / +6.2
FRF-DEM	2hr	62.0 / 62.7	+20.4 / +22.0	CAD-CHF	2hr	51.1 / 51.2	+1.9 / -0.4
	4hr	59.7 / 59.5	+15.0 / +16.1		4hr	52.0 / 51.7	+2.6 / +0.4
	8hr	57.6 / 56.3	+14.3 / +13.2		8hr	52.3 / 51.8	+4.3 / +1.6
DEM-AUD	2hr	51.4 / 51.1	+2.5 / +1.2	XAU-CHF	2hr	51.0 / 50.6	+1.0 / -0.8
	4hr	51.2 / 51.1	+3.1 / +2.1		4hr	52.1 / 51.0	+3.2 / -0.2
	8hr	50.5 / 51.2	+4.0 / +3.2		8hr	52.0 / 52.4	+3.0 / +5.1

- Continuous optimization of the model coefficients in a finite size, forecasting horizon-dependent sample.

The forecast quality of these models is evaluated on a very large sample with two different measures that avoid statistical problems arising from the nature of the FX rate time series. The rigorous separation of in and out-of-sample measures, the large number of observations, and the stringent significance levels mean that the statistical results of the forecast evaluation are convincing evidence for our models having beat the random walk for most of the 20 studied currencies and for the very short-term forecasting horizons. These results are also corroborated by those we obtain on the other 21 rates that run on the Olsen Information System (OIS).

What are the consequences of such results on the economic theory of market efficiency? We believe that they point to the extension and improvement of methods and tools for defining and analyzing market efficiency. The accepted theory was probably never conceived for such short horizons, and even more important, it takes an unrealistic view of market response to new information. Being developed only in a statistical framework, the theory assumes that economic actors integrate new price information *instantaneously*, and very little attention is paid to the time needed for a piece of information to be available to all market participants and to the diverse interpretation of that information. In the context of very short time horizons these factors play critical roles in market adjustments. It is reasonable

TABLE 9.4 Significance of the forecast quality for 20 exchange rates.

The in-sample and out-of-sample forecast significance for 10 USD rates and 10 cross rates. The "+" sign indicates a forecast quality above the significance limits of all test criteria, otherwise the "-" sign is used. Example: "+/-" means a significant in-sample quality and an insignificant out-of-sample quality.

2 hr	USD-DEM	+/-	USD-NLG	+/-	JPY-DEM	+/+	GBP-CHF	+/+
	USD-JPY	+/+	USD-ITL	+/-	GBP-DEM	+/+	JPY-CHF	+/+
	GBP-USD	+/-	USD-CAD	+/+	CHF-DEM	+/+	GBP-JPY	+/+
	USD-CHF	+/-	AUD-USD	+/+	FRF-DEM	+/+	CAD-CHF	+/-
	USD-FRF	+/-	XAU-USD	+/+	DEM-AUD	+/+	XAU-CHF	+/-
4 hr	USD-DEM	+/+	USD-NLG	+/+	JPY-DEM	+/+	GBP-CHF	+/+
	USD-JPY	+/+	USD-ITL	+/+	GBP-DEM	+/+	JPY-CHF	+/+
	GBP-USD	+/-	USD-CAD	+/+	CHF-DEM	+/+	GBP-JPY	+/+
	USD-CHF	+/+	AUD-USD	+/+	FRF-DEM	+/+	CAD-CHF	+/-
	USD-FRF	+/+	XAU-USD	+/+	DEM-AUD	+/+	XAU-CHF	+/-
8 hr	USD-DEM	+/+	USD-NLG	-/+	JPY-DEM	+/-	GBP-CHF	+/+
	USD-JPY	+/+	USD-ITL	+/+	GBP-DEM	+/+	JPY-CHF	+/+
	GBP-USD	+/+	USD-CAD	+/+	CHF-DEM	+/+	GBP-JPY	+/+
	USD-CHF	-/-	AUD-USD	+/+	FRF-DEM	+/+	CAD-CHF	+/+
	USD-FRF	-/-	XAU-USD	+/+	DEM-AUD	-/+	XAU-CHF	+/+

to assume that the markets need a *finite time* to adjust to any information and that this time depends on the nature of the information.

We think that these adjustments can be modeled and hence that a certain predictability of price movements exists. Our forecasting models, while a positive step in this direction, are nevertheless only a first one and there is still room for improvement through a better understanding and definition of intrinsic time and through the search for better indicators.

10

CORRELATION AND MULTIVARIATE RISK

10.1 INTRODUCTION

Correlations and covariances between returns of different financial assets play an important role in fields such as risk management and portfolio allocation. This chapter addresses three problematic issues concerning linear correlation coefficients of returns, computed from high-frequency data:

1. The correlation of intraday, equally spaced time series derived from unevenly spaced tick-by-tick data deserves careful treatment if a bias resulting from the classical missing value problem is to be avoided. We propose a simple and easy-to-use method, which corrects for different data frequencies and gaps by updating the linear correlation coefficient calculation with the aid of covolatility weights. This is a bivariate alternative to time scale transformations which treat heteroskedasticity by expanding periods of higher volatility while contracting periods of lower volatility.

2. It is generally recognized that correlations between financial time series vary over time. We probe the stability of correlation as a function of time for 7 years of high-frequency foreign exchange rate, implied forward interest rate, and stock index data. Correlations as functions of time in

turn allow for estimations of the memory that correlations have for their past values.

3. It has been demonstrated that there is a dramatic decrease in correlation, as data frequency enters the intrahour level (the "Epps effect"[1]). We characterize the Epps effect for correlations between a number of financial time series and suggest its possible relation to tick frequency.

10.2 ESTIMATING THE DEPENDENCE OF FINANCIAL TIME SERIES

Measuring the dependence or independence of financial time series is of increasing interest to those concerned with multivariate decision formation (e.g., in risk assessment or portfolio allocation). Often this is estimated quantitatively using the linear correlation coefficient,[2] which is a basic measurement of the dependence between variables. Zumbach (1997) reviews many interesting measures of associations besides the linear correlation. The popularity of this measure stems from its simple definition, practical ease of use, and its straightforward results, which are easily interpreted, scale free, and directly comparable. Although the calculation of the correlation coefficient is well defined and rather simple, a number of unresolved issues exist with respect to application of the rule and interpretation of results in the high-frequency data domain.

- The data input for the correlation coefficient calculation are two time series with equal (i.e., homogeneous) spacing between ticks. This necessity is easily satisfied for low frequency ($\leq$ one tick per week) data. However, the intraday case deserves more careful treatment if a resulting data bias is to be avoided. A problem arises when the two time series of unevenly spaced tick-by-tick data have different frequencies or active hours within a day, which may or may not overlap. We propose a simple and easy-to-use normalization method, which corrects for frequency differentials and data gaps. This alternative formulation updates the correlation calculation only where data exists, ensuring that there is no measurement bias resulting from the classical missing value problem (see Krzanowski and Marriott, 1994, 1995) or from differences in the active hours of the financial time series. In addition, this formulation remains scale free and straightforward to understand and implement.

- The linear correlation coefficient calculation largely discards the time variable. The variances of two time series and their covariance are constructed

---

[1] Epps (1979).

[2] The use of the linear correlation coefficient is appropriate not only for multivariate normal joint distributions but also for multivariate elliptical joint distributions. Many financial joint return distributions have been observed to fall into or close to this latter category. Also for fat-tailed return distributions, the linear correlation coefficient remains a useful and relevant measure of association; only the interpretation of results and, more specifically, the determination of accurate confidence limits is problematic. Correlations of *squared* returns from fat-tailed distributions are even more problematic.

either with the assumption of being constant or as a type of average value if value changes are recognized. It is generally accepted that correlations in financial time series vary over time (Longin and Solnik, 1995) and are even subject to correlation "breakdown" or large changes in correlation in critical periods. In the discussion that follows, we probe the stability of correlation as a function of time, for a number of financial instruments, in order to determine the relevance of using high-frequency data. We go on to investigate the manner in which present correlation values are in turn correlated to their past values (autocorrelation of correlations). A model of the self-memory of correlation is proposed as the basis for the formulation of a long-term correlation forecast.

- The impact of time series data frequency on correlations should also be clearly established. This is especially relevant as higher frequency data becomes more widely available and more often used in order to improve statistics. Previous authors have demonstrated a dramatic decrease in correlation as data frequency enters the intra-hour level, for both stock (Epps, 1979) and foreign exchange returns (see Guillaume *et al.*, 1997; Low *et al.*, 1996). This discussion attempts to characterize and investigate more deeply the Epps effect in a number of financial time series through the examination of 7 years of high-frequency data.

10.3 COVOLATILITY WEIGHTING

The calculation of correlation coefficients is straightforward but some inconvenience is introduced via its simple definition. The correlation calculation requires two equally spaced (i.e., homogeneous) time series as input. This necessity is easily satisfied where low-frequency ($\leq$ one tick per week) data are concerned. However, the problem requires more careful treatment at higher data frequencies where one cannot dictate the time or number of observations. One often faces two main problems when estimating correlation between two high-frequency time series. The first involves correlating two time series of inherently different frequencies. If the two time series are both regular with respect to data arrival intervals but of different frequencies, one might create from them two equally spaced, homogeneous time series, which both have frequencies equal to the lesser frequent of the two. This easy situation does not occur very often, though. It is more common to be faced with time series such as foreign exchange (FX) rates, where data frequency can vary from very few quotes to hundreds of quotes per hour. What is the best way to measure the dependence between an FX rate and another one that is perhaps less active or has activity peaks and valleys at completely different daytimes? Ideally, one would prefer the correlation calculation to be updated more often when more information exists and less often when it does not exist. A way to do this is to introduce a time scale that compresses physical time if there is no information and to expand it when it exists. This is similar to the idea presented in Chapter 6, where ϑ-time was introduced to model volatility patterns. This method has been found useful for a number of applications, but is time-consuming to implement in practice. Moreover, we have the multivariate problem of two time series for which we would need a common time scale.

A second problem arising when estimating correlation between two high-frequency financial time series is that of missing values or data gaps. Large data gaps are actually an extreme case of the first problem (varying and nonmatching data arrival frequencies), but there is no harm in discussing the two problems separately. Despite one's best efforts, data gaps sometimes occur due to failures in the data acquisition chain. One can only make an educated guess about the correlation between two time series when such a gap occurs; it cannot be measured. More commonly, there are financial instruments whose time series have regular and large data gaps as part of their inherent character. Consider, for example, attempting to correlate a stock index (e.g., the Dow Jones Industrial Average,) which exists for 8 hr per day, 5 days per week (except holidays), with another stock index that exists for a similar amount of time each day but with a relatively large time shift (e.g., the Financial Times 100 index). There are a number of different schools of thought regarding the correlation between two financial instruments when one or both are not actually active. These sometimes consider derivatives of the instruments rather than the underlying instruments themselves. Other arguments confuse time-lagged correlation with direct correlation, but these are entirely different issues. When faced with varying activity rates and data gaps, it would be convenient to use some form of data interpolation to solve these problems. Unfortunately, the experience of many practitioners has not been reassuring (see Press *et al.*, 1992).

Some methods for approximating a homogeneous time series from unevenly spaced, tick-by-tick data involve some form of data imputation. Methods of imputing data vary in complexity and effectiveness and most have been found to be beneficial under at least some set of conditions and assumptions. However, all forms of imputation rely on a model, and a standard supposition is that critical characteristics of the data do not change between in-sample and out-of-sample periods. There is always the possibility that imputation will introduce a false bias into variance and covariance calculations, but nevertheless it is difficult to avoid some form of it in cases where data is not of an infinitely high frequency. Some useful attempts have been made to circumvent imputation all together. One interesting and recent example is described in de Jong and Nijman (1997). This work builds on efforts described in Cohen *et al.* (1983) and Lo and MacKinlay (1990a,b). The authors develop a covariance estimator, which uses irregularly spaced data whenever and wherever it exists in either of two time series. However, methods such as this one rest on the assumption that the processes generating transaction times and the prices themselves are independent. This assumption may be quite reasonable, depending on the instruments involved, but proving so is rarely trivial and we prefer to avoid it altogether.

In this discussion, we propose and illustrate a simple measure of correlation that avoids imputation based on data models or assumptions on distributional characteristics. Although the inputs for this alternative measure are homogeneous time series derived through simple linear interpolation, the method filters out any underestimation of variances and covariances caused by lack of sampling variation. In addition, rather than making the strong assumption that price and transaction time are independent, this method makes use of the arrival time variable in order to compensate for the sometimes large differences that can exist in financial time series frequencies. Data gaps of varying size are common and we ignore any discussion of whether correlation actually exists during this period, because in any case we cannot measure it directly. Our goal is rather to develop a measure of correlation where information exists and to avoid updating our measure where data do not exist, a fact that should be recalled when results are interpreted. This implies that a lower data frequency or data gaps in one time series may limit the use of another one, and the unavoidable price to pay is a certain loss of statistical significance. However, the method is specifically meant to measure correlations at high data frequencies where statistical significance is high by nature.

10.3.1   Formulation of an Adjusted Correlation Measure

The standard linear correlation coefficient is a measure of correlation between two time series Δx_i and Δy_i and is defined as follows:

$$\varrho(x_i, y_i) \equiv \frac{\sum_{i=1}^{n} (\Delta x_i - \langle \Delta x \rangle)(\Delta y_i - \langle \Delta y \rangle)}{\sqrt{\sum_{i=1}^{n} (\Delta x_i - \langle \Delta x \rangle)^2 \sum_{i=1}^{n} (\Delta y_i - \langle \Delta y \rangle)^2}} \tag{10.1}$$

with the sample means,

$$\langle \Delta x \rangle \equiv \sum_{i=1}^{n} \frac{\Delta x_i}{n} \quad \text{and} \quad \langle \Delta y \rangle \equiv \sum_{i=1}^{n} \frac{\Delta y_i}{n} \tag{10.2}$$

The sample is of size T with $n = T/\Delta t$ homogeneously spaced observations. Correlation values are unitless and may range from -1 (completely anticorrelated) to 1 (completely correlated). A value of zero indicates two uncorrelated series.

The two variables Δx_i and Δy_i are usually returns of two financial assets. In risk assessment (but not in portfolio allocation), the deviation of returns from the zero level is often considered instead of the deviation from the sample means $\langle \Delta x \rangle$ and $\langle \Delta y \rangle$. In this special case, we can insert $\langle \Delta x \rangle = \langle \Delta y \rangle = 0$ in Equation 10.1.

An estimate of the *local* covolatility for each of these observations is defined by further dividing each time span (Δt) over which Δx_i and Δy_i are calculated into m equal subintervals from which subreturn values, $\Delta \tilde{x}_j$ and $\Delta \tilde{y}_j$, can be obtained. This redefined time series now consists of $\tilde{n} = T/\Delta \tilde{t}$ equally spaced return observations where $\Delta t \equiv m \Delta \tilde{t}$. The return definitions conform to Equation 3.7, based on logarithmic middle prices as in Equation 3.6. To obtain a homogeneous series, we need linear interpolation as introduced in Equation 3.2. The choice of linear interpolation method is essential.

For each of the previous coarse returns, Δx_i (as for Δy_i), there exists a corresponding estimation of covolatility between the two homogeneous time series of returns

$$\omega_i(\Delta\tilde{x}_j; \Delta\tilde{y}_j; \Delta\tilde{t}) \equiv \sum_{j=1}^{m} \left(\left| \Delta\tilde{x}_{i\cdot m-j} - \langle \Delta\tilde{x}_{i\cdot m} \rangle \right| \cdot \left| \Delta\tilde{y}_{i\cdot m-j} - \langle \Delta\tilde{y}_{i\cdot m} \rangle \right| \right)^{\alpha}$$

(10.3)

where

$$\langle \Delta\tilde{x}_{i\cdot m} \rangle = \sum_{j=1}^{m} \frac{\Delta\tilde{x}_{i\cdot m-j}}{m} \quad \text{and} \quad \langle \Delta\tilde{y}_{i\cdot m} \rangle = \sum_{j=1}^{m} \frac{\Delta\tilde{y}_{i\cdot m-j}}{m}$$

(10.4)

The most obvious choice for α is 0.5, though this can be investigated as a way to magnify or demagnify the weight given to farther outlying return values. A value of 0.5 is used in all cases described in this discussion.

Equation 10.3 formulates covolatility around the mean rather than around zero and it therefore follows that $\omega_i = 0$ for the case of returns derived from two linearly interpolated prices existing outside of our region of interest, Δt. These covolatility estimates can be inserted as weights in all the sums computed to obtain the variances and covariance of the correlation calculation:

$$\tilde{\varrho}(\Delta x_i, \Delta y_i, \omega_i) \equiv$$

$$\frac{\sum_{i=1}^{T/\Delta t} \left[(\Delta x_i - \langle \Delta x \rangle)(\Delta y_i - \langle \Delta y \rangle)\omega_i \right]}{\sqrt{\sum_{i=1}^{T/\Delta t} \left[(\Delta x_i - \langle \Delta x \rangle)^2 \omega_i \right]} \sqrt{\sum_{i=1}^{T/\Delta t} \left[(\Delta y_i - \langle \Delta y \rangle)^2 \omega_i \right]}}$$

(10.5)

Note that Δx_i and Δy_i from Equation 10.5 are the same values as used in Equation 10.1, as they are logarithmic returns taken over the same time period, Δt. These coarse return values can then be defined as the sum of the fine return values

$$\Delta x_i \equiv \sum_{j=1}^{m} \Delta\tilde{x}_{i\cdot m-j}$$

(10.6)

The sample means $\langle \Delta x \rangle$ and $\langle \Delta y \rangle$ have to be reconsidered in Equation 10.5. In the special case of risk assessment, we can still replace them by zero. Otherwise, we prefer that they are calculated again in a weighted fashion so that returns are considered only when observations over intervals of size Δt exist. Rather than keeping Equation 10.2, we define covolatility weighted mean values for both time series:

$$\langle \Delta x \rangle \equiv \frac{\sum_{i=1}^{T/\Delta t} (\Delta x_i \cdot \omega_i)}{\sum_{i=1}^{T/\Delta t} \omega_i} \quad \text{and} \quad \langle \Delta y \rangle \equiv \frac{\sum_{i=1}^{T/\Delta t} (\Delta y_i \cdot \omega_i)}{\sum_{i=1}^{T/\Delta t} \omega_i}$$

(10.7)

In this way, the means are calculated over the identically weighted data sample also used for the rest of the correlation calculation. The weights adjust for periods of lower or higher activity.

Equation 10.3 is formulated in such a way that $\omega_i = 0$ for the case of returns interpolated over a data gap—that is, a tick interval that fully contains the analyzed interval of size Δt. Data gaps have no influence on the means, and the sums of Equations 10.5 and 10.7 are not updated there. The covolatility adjusted measure of correlation described by Equation 10.5 also retains the desirable characteristics of the original, standard linear correlation coefficient; it is scale free, and completely different measurements are directly comparable. In addition, this alternative method is only slightly more complicated to implement than the standard linear correlation coefficient and can easily be implemented on a computer.

As will be applied later, this correlation measure easily fits into the framework of autocorrelation analysis. Given a time series of correlations $\tilde{\varrho}_t$, it can be correlated with a copy of itself but with different time lags (τ) between the two, as shown in Equation 10.8:

$$R(\tilde{\varrho}(\Delta x_i, \Delta y_i, \omega_i), \tau) =$$

$$\frac{\sum_{t=\tau+1}^{n}(\tilde{\varrho}_t - \langle\tilde{\varrho}_1\rangle)(\tilde{\varrho}_{t-\tau} - \langle\tilde{\varrho}_2\rangle)}{\left[\sum_{t=\tau+1}^{n}(\tilde{\varrho}_t - \langle\tilde{\varrho}_1\rangle)^2 \sum_{t=\tau+1}^{n}(\tilde{\varrho}_{t-\tau} - \langle\tilde{\varrho}_2\rangle)^2\right]^{1/2}} \tag{10.8}$$

for $\tau > 0$, where

$$\langle\tilde{\varrho}_1\rangle = \frac{1}{n-\tau}\sum_{t=\tau+1}^{n}\tilde{\varrho}_t \quad \text{and} \quad \langle\tilde{\varrho}_2\rangle = \frac{1}{n-\tau}\sum_{t=\tau+1}^{n}\tilde{\varrho}_{t-\tau} \tag{10.9}$$

For the discussions that follow, we measure correlation using the covolatility adjusted method described by Equation 10.5, unless otherwise stated, and always with $m = 6$ and $\alpha = 0.5$ (see Equation 10.3). Any subsequent use of the commonly recognized linear correlation coefficient (Equation 10.1) will be referred to as the "standard" method.

10.3.2 Monte Carlo and Empirical Tests

Various tests were performed on the covolatility adjusted correlation measure in order to test its behavior when applied to time series with differing frequencies and data gaps.

A first test used synthetic Monte Carlo data to illustrate the effectiveness of the method. Two separate, uncorrelated, normally distributed, i.i.d. random time series, A_i and B_i, were produced, each with zero mean, standard deviation $\sigma = 0.01$ and size $m = 10,000$. A third series, C_i, can then be formed as a linear combination of the previous two:

$$C_{i=1}^{m} \equiv kA_{i=1}^{m} + (1 - k)B_{i=1}^{m} \tag{10.10}$$

TABLE 10.1 Results of a Monte Carlo simulation of correlations. Comparing the covolatility adjusted linear correlation $\tilde{\varrho}$ to the standard linear correlation ϱ, both applied to synthetic time series. The series D_i is like C_i, but regularly spaced sections of the data are replaced by linearly interpolated data. Details are described in the text. Note the similarity of the $\varrho(A_i, C_i)$ and $\tilde{\varrho}(A_i, D_i)$ columns.

Multiplier k Equation 10.10	$\varrho(A_i, C_i)$ Equation 10.1	$\varrho(A_i, D_i)$ Equation 10.1	$\tilde{\varrho}(A_i, D_i)$ Equation 10.5
0.0	0.00	0.00	0.00
0.1	0.12	0.10	0.12
0.2	0.23	0.15	0.22
0.3	0.38	0.28	0.38
0.4	0.52	0.40	0.51
0.5	0.69	0.51	0.69
0.6	0.83	0.62	0.82
0.7	0.92	0.67	0.91
0.8	0.97	0.72	0.95
0.9	0.99	0.74	0.97
1.0	1.00	0.74	0.99

where the constant k is selected such that $0 \leq k \leq 1$. In this way, the new series C_i has a controllable correlation to the original data series A_i.

The synthetic returns C_i were then cumulated to synthetic prices P_i, with starting value $P_1 = 10$ and sample size $m + 1 = 10,001$:

$$P_{i=2}^{m+1} \equiv e^{\ln(P_{i-1}) + C_{i-1}} \tag{10.11}$$

The pure cumulation of C_i leads to synthetic logarithmic prices that are transformed to synthetic nonlogarithmic prices by the exponential function.

Repeated data sections, each consisting of 50 price observations, were then deleted in the time series P_i and replaced by prices linearly interpolated from the prices bracketing the deleted sections. The distance between these artificial data gaps also consisted of 50 observations, creating an alternating series of original data patches followed by data gaps filled with linearly interpolated prices. Finally, the first differences of this altered price series were taken to build a new series of returns, D_i.

Equation 10.5 was then used to measure the correlation between one of the original return distributions, A_i, and the manipulated return distribution, D_i, given various values of the constant multiplier k. Results are shown in comparison to the standard linear correlation calculation in Table 10.1.

A comparison of columns two ($\varrho(A, C)$) and four ($\tilde{\varrho}(A, D)$) shows that the covolatility adjusted correlation measure described by Equation 10.5 successfully approximates the original standard linear correlation between distributions A and C before some data patches were replaced by linearly interpolated values. Any small deviations that exist are due to the statistical error ($\sim 2\%$) of these tests. The third column of Table 10.1, by contrast, shows standard correlation values severely affected by the interpolation-filled data gaps. This simple example illustrates one of the original design goals of the covolatility adjusted linear correlation measure: correlation is measured where data exist, and the calculation is not updated where data do not exist.

Tests with foreign exchange data were performed to exemplify the effect of the covolatility adjusted correlation measure on time series with fluctuating data frequency and volatility. Homogeneous time series of USD-DEM prices were generated according to Section 3.2.2, equally spaced by 3-min intervals, once in physical time, once in ϑ-time as explained in Chapter 6. USD-DEM has a high data frequency (see Table 2.2), but is also characterized by large intraday and intraweek fluctuations of both data frequency and volatility as shown in Section 5.6.2 and Figure 5.12. Absolute value of USD-DEM returns were used because they are known to have autocorrelations of greater magnitude than actual returns. Three autocorrelation functions are investigated: (1) standard autocorrelation (Equation 10.8) of 18-min returns in physical time, (2) standard autocorrelation of 18-min returns in ϑ-time (see Chapter 6), and (3) autocorrelation measured by the covolatility adjusted correlation coefficients (Equation 10.5), analyzing 18-min in physical time. The covolatility computation was done in 3-min intervals and with $m = 6$ (Equation 10.3), resulting in a covolatility value every 18 min. Results of these measurements are shown in Figure 10.1. A total data period of 6 months was used, ranging from January 1, 1996, to July 1, 1996.

The covolatility adjusted autocorrelation values (bullets in Figure 10.1) are significantly lower than the corresponding standard autocorrelation values, but close to the standard autocorrelation of the series equally spaced in ϑ-time. We ascribe the high level of standard autocorrelation in physical time to the weekly seasonality of the data. The high absolute returns during working days and the low values on weekends are responsible for part of the high standard autocorrelation at lags up to about 1 day. As described in Chapter 6, ϑ-time eliminates seasonality and thus the part of the autocorrelation caused by seasonality. The covolatility behaves similarly in the following respect. Weekends with their data gaps have extremely low covolatility values, so they are practically eliminated from the statistics. Weekly seasonality no longer affects the statistics. At lags around 24 hr, the picture is different. The covolatility adjusted autocorrelation approaches the value of the standard autocorrelation in a clear peak which indicates daily seasonality. Unlike ϑ-time, which deforms time to eliminate seasonality, the covolatility adjusted correlation measure was designed to give a high weight to the most active periods, with no intention to hide all the seasonalities. Removing seasonality is not always desirable, so we find the covolatility adjusted correlation estimation to be a suitable method for many applications. In addition, the simplicity of this methodology lends itself to wider use.

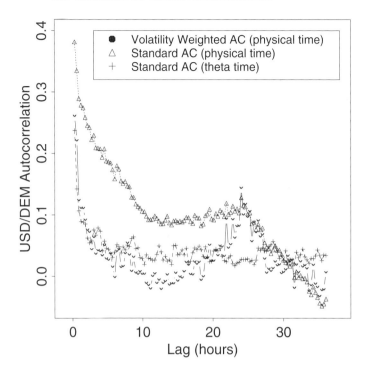

FIGURE 10.1 Autocorrelation of the absolute values of USD-DEM returns as a function of the time lag. The triangles ($\triangle$) refer to standard autocorrelation of absolute returns, equally spaced in physical time. Bullets ($\bullet$) refer to the covolatility adjusted autocorrelation of the same absolute returns. Crosses ($+$) refer to standard autocorrelation of absolute returns, equally spaced in ϑ-time. Sampling period: January 1, 1996, to July 1, 1996.

10.4 STABILITY OF RETURN CORRELATIONS

When correlation is calculated between two time series, the assumption is that this quantity does not vary over time. For the case of financial time series this is seldom occurs, although time variance of the correlation coefficient over time can sometimes be small. This issue is critical for portfolio pricing and risk management where hedging techniques can become worthless when they are most needed, during periods known as correlation "breakdown," or relatively rapid change. Boyer *et al.* (1997) have also demonstrated that a detection of correlation breakdown or other structural breaks by splitting a return distribution into a number of quantiles can yield misleading results. We use high-frequency data to estimate correlations literally as a function of time for a number of different financial time series in an effort to better understand the level of change that can occur. High-frequency correlation estimations are contrasted with lower-frequency estimates for the same sample periods. The "memory" that correlation coefficients have for their past values is also estimated for a number of examples using a simple

TABLE 10.2   Data sampling for correlation as function of time.
Four different sampling schemes are selected to divide the total sampling period of size T
from January 7, 1990, to January 5, 1997.

Correlation calculation period T/N	Data frequency (number of returns per day) $f = nN/T$	Number of returns per correlation calculation n	95% confidence band $1.96/\sqrt{n}$
365 days	1	365	0.10
128 days	3	384	0.10
32 days	12	384	0.10
7 days	72	504	0.09

and appropriate parameterization. Such estimations can be applied to long-term correlation forecasting, which is required, for example, to price or hedge financial options involving multiple assets, Gibson and Boyer (1997).

10.4.1   Correlation Variations over Time

The general stability of correlation coefficients was examined using various correlation calculation intervals and data frequencies. This involved examination of a fixed historical time series over a time period T, from January 7, 1990, to January 5, 1997. The time series of returns ($r(t_i)$) was then divided into N subsets of equal duration (T/N) from which correlation coefficients were computed according to Equation 10.1. Four values of N were selected, while the total period T always remained constant. A homogeneous series of n returns was then chosen inside each period of size T/N via linear interpolation, so each correlation coefficient is based on n observations. Similar numbers n were selected for all the four values of N in order to maintain nearly uniform statistics, as shown in Table 10.2. In this table, the number of return observations per day, $f = nN/T$, is also given.

Results from these calculations are shown in Figures 10.2 to 10.7, where correlations versus time are displayed, and dashed lines above and below zero correlation are 95% confidence ranges assuming normally distributed random distributions. The confidence limits are slightly nonuniform due to small variations in statistics. Some correlations were computed with fewer observations than n because of missing observations. Whenever a weight ω_i from Equation 10.3 was equal to zero, the corresponding observation was ignored. The weights ω_i were not used for any other purpose, and the correlations remain standard linear correlations defined by Equation 10.1.

Correlation coefficient mean values and variances are given for each pair of financial instruments and for each of the four calculation frequencies in Table 10.3. Having virtually the same statistical significance for all correlation calculations shown in Figures 10.2 through 10.7, we can make a number of observations about

TABLE 10.3   Means, variances, maxima and minima of correlation.
Means, variances, maxima and minima of the linear correlation coefficients as shown in Figures 10.2 through 10.7. For each pair of financial instruments, four correlation intervals T/N of decreasing size are investigated. The total sampling period T is from January 7, 1990, to January 5, 1997.

Instrument pair	Correlation period	Mean value	Variance (σ^2)	Max	Min.
USD-DEM – USD-NLG	1 year	0.99	0.000026	0.99	0.98
USD-DEM – USD-NLG	128 day	0.99	0.00012	1.00	0.95
USD-DEM – USD-NLG	32 day	0.96	0.0029	1.00	0.54
USD-DEM – USD-NLG	7 day	0.88	0.0067	0.98	0.41
USD-DEM – USD-GBP	1 year	0.76	0.029	0.96	0.42
USD-DEM – USD-GBP	128 day	0.79	0.015	0.98	0.57
USD-DEM – USD-GBP	32 day	0.76	0.031	0.98	0.09
USD-DEM – USD-GBP	7 day	0.69	0.030	0.97	0.20
USD-DEM – USD-ITL	1 year	0.76	0.040	0.99	0.41
USD-DEM – USD-ITL	128 day	0.75	0.057	0.99	0.18
USD-DEM – USD-ITL	32 day	0.76	0.044	0.99	0.07
USD-DEM – USD-ITL	7 day	0.68	0.044	0.97	0.07
DJIA – AMEX	1 year	0.73	0.0083	0.84	0.60
DJIA – AMEX	128 day	0.70	0.0087	0.85	0.57
DJIA – AMEX	32 day	0.41	0.041	0.78	-0.29
DJIA – AMEX	7 day	-0.01	0.030	0.62	-0.50
DEM 3-6m – DEM 9-12m	1 year	0.84	0.00074	0.88	0.81
DEM 3-6m – DEM 9-12m	128 day	0.78	0.0084	0.90	0.57
DEM 3-6m – DEM 9-12m	32 day	0.71	0.025	0.96	0.13
DEM 3-6m – DEM 9-12m	7 day	0.54	0.074	1.00	-1.00
USD 3-6m – DEM 3-6m	1 year	0.33	0.024	0.51	0.13
USD 3-6m – DEM 3-6m	128 day	0.30	0.028	0.59	-0.10
USD 3-6m – DEM 3-6m	32 day	0.30	0.051	0.85	-0.34
USD 3-6m – DEM 3-6m	7 day	0.28	0.066	1.00	-0.52

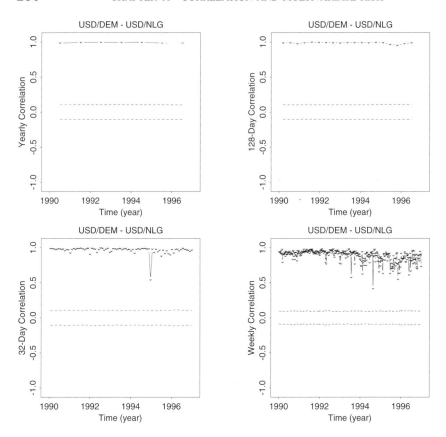

FIGURE 10.2 Linear correlation coefficients calculated using increasingly small sub-intervals, T/N = (365 days, 128 days, 32 days, and 7 days), for the FX return pair USD-DEM – USD-NLG. The dashed lines above and below zero correlation are 95% confidence ranges assuming normally distributed returns.

correlation stability. The highly correlated USD-DEM – USD-NLG returns shown in Figure 10.2 appear largely constant over the total sample period of 7 years. As the subperiod width for correlation calculation decreases (and the number of correlation calculations inside the total period increases), more structure becomes apparent. This additional structure is reflected by an increasing variance in Table 10.3. Correlations calculated with lower data frequency are not simply an average of those calculated with higher quotation frequencies; Table 10.3 shows the mean value for USD-DEM – USD-NLG correlations moving steadily downward with increasing correlation resolution (an -11% change between yearly data resolution and weekly resolution). This can be partially explained by considering that error distributions for empirically computed correlations are not symmetric when coefficients differ from zero. However, such drops in correlation with higher data frequency as can be observed with the DJIA-Amex pair point to a stronger effect which will be addressed in more detail in Section 10.5.

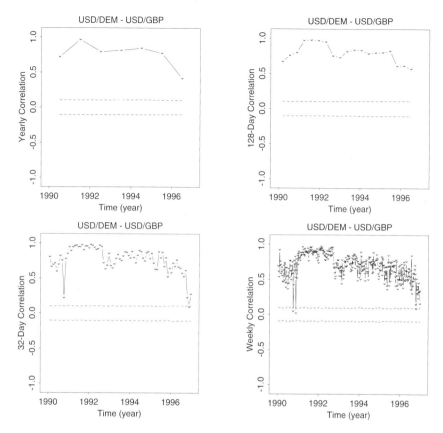

FIGURE 10.3 Linear correlation coefficients calculated using increasingly small subintervals, $T/N =$ (365 days, 128 days, 32 days, and 7 days), for the FX return pair USD-DEM – USD-GBP. The dashed lines above and below zero correlation are 95% confidence ranges assuming normally distributed returns.

Figures 10.3 and 10.4 show correlations for the FX rate pairs USD-DEM – USD-GBP and USD-DEM – USD-ITL. Note that the inverse rate USD-GBP was used instead of the more usual GBP-USD, in order to be in line with other currencies and to obtain positive correlation. Both figures exhibit fast and large drops in correlations during the second and third weeks of September 1992. Presumably, this directly reflects the turmoil of the European Monetary System (EMS) at that time, when GBP and ITL left the system. This appears to be a clear example of correlation breakdown.

Recapitulating the major points of Section 10.4, correlation was examined as a function of time for a number of different financial instruments. The time frame of 7 years was divided in four different ways, using subperiods of 365, 128, 32, and 7 days. The number of subperiods over the total 7 year period was then 7, 19, 79, and 365, respectively. The subperiods of different size were divided into n intervals for return observations. This number n had roughly the same size in all cases,

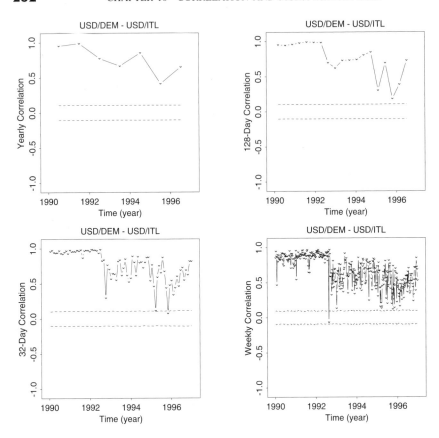

FIGURE 10.4 Linear correlation coefficients calculated using increasingly small sub-intervals, $T/N = $ (365 days, 128 days, 32 days, and 7 days), for the FX return pair USD-DEM – USD-ITL. The dashed lines above and below zero correlation are 95% confidence ranges assuming normally distributed returns.

between 365 and 504, so the statistical significance of correlation values was always comparable. The correlation between some financial instruments can be described as reasonably stable. However, brief but large breaks can be observed in almost all cases, and the additional statistics provided by time series of higher frequency are essential to detect such occurrences. In addition, we observed decreasing absolute values all the correlations we examined when going to higher data frequencies. This will be further discussed further in Section 10.5.

10.4.2 The Exponential Memory of Return Correlations

The linear correlation values shown in Figures 10.2 through 10.7 can be seen as time series in their own right. A certain stability of correlation levels seems to indicate that markets have a memory for these levels. This memory can be investigated by considering the autocorrelation of the correlation time series. We

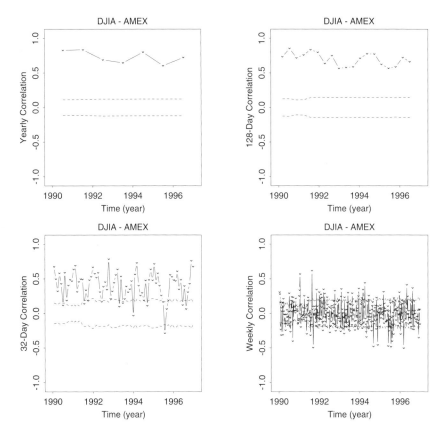

FIGURE 10.5 Linear correlation coefficients calculated using increasingly small sub-intervals, $T/N = $ (365 days, 128 days, 32 days, and 7 days), for the stock index pair DJIA − AMEX (both expressed in USD). The dashed lines above and below zero correlation are 95% confidence ranges assuming normally distributed returns.

focus on the weekly correlation measurements displayed in the lower right plots of Figures 10.2 through 10.7. These weekly correlations are computed from 20-min returns. The autocorrelation analysis was performed for different lags (τ), using Equation 10.8.

Results of these calculations are shown in Figure 10.8. Shown along with each autocorrelation curve are the 95% confidence limits for a normally distributed random process. The differences in the behaviors of the six correlation pairs are striking. For foreign exchange rate correlations, we observe a significantly positive autocorrelation extending to long lags up to 50 to 100 weeks. Correlation structures have a long memory. For correlations between implied forward interest rates, we find a positive autocorrelation above the significance limit for lags up to 3 or 4 months, which means a reduced but still long memory. The correlation of the stock index pair (Down Jones and AMEX Stock Index) behaves differently as it dives below significance already at the first lag of 1 week. The market has no consistent

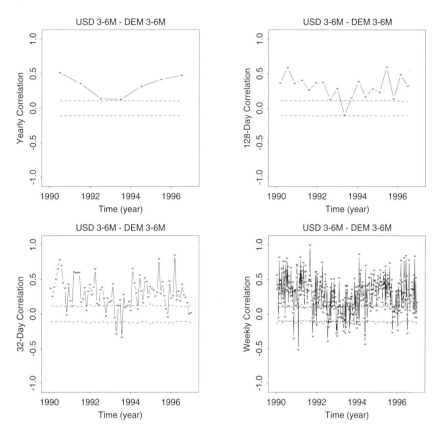

FIGURE 10.6 Linear correlation coefficients calculated using increasingly small sub-intervals, $T/N = $ (365 days, 128 days, 32 days, and 7 days), for the implied forward interest rate pair USD 3-6 months – DEM 3-6 months. The dashed lines above and below zero correlation are 95% confidence intervals assuming Linear correlation coefficients calculated using increasingly small subintervals, $T/N = $ (365 days, 128 days, 32 days, and 7 days), for the implied forward interest rate pair USD 3-6 months – DEM 3-6 months. The dashed lines above and below zero correlation are 95% confidence ranges assuming normally distributed returns.

memory of the level, but this may be due to the strong Epps effect of the 20-min returns, explained in Section 10.5. Figure 10.8 also shows that autocorrelation values for each of the six instrument pairs decline roughly exponentially but with markedly different attenuation rates.

To better gauge the difference in autocorrelation attenuation for these correlation pairs, the autocorrelations shown in Figure 10.8 were modeled by a simple exponential function:

$$Y \equiv Ae^{-x/\lambda} \qquad (10.12)$$

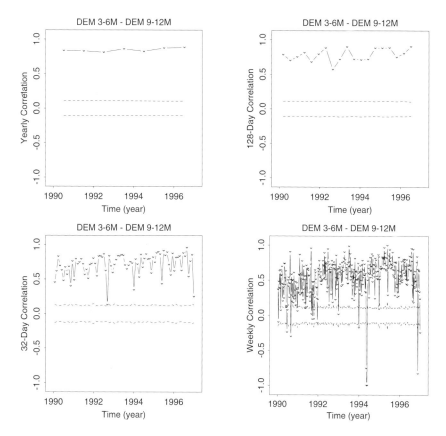

FIGURE 10.7 Linear correlation coefficients calculated using increasingly small sub-intervals, T/N = (365 days, 128 days, 32 days, and 7 days), for the implied forward interest rate pair DEM 3-6 months – DEM 9-12 months. The dashed lines above and below zero correlation are 95% confidence ranges assuming normally distributed returns.

where λ is an exponential attenuation length and A is a simple weight. These parameters were fitted to the data in Figure 10.8, starting with the first lag (neglecting the zeroth lag, which is equal to one by definition) and only to the point where autocorrelation data fell below the 68% of the upper confidence limit, thus focusing on the initial decay of autocorrelation. The autocorrelations of USD-DEM – USD-GBP correlations are shown in Figure 10.9. The results for the autocorrelations of correlation data shown in Figure 10.8 are also reported in Table 10.4. The DJIA-AMEX pair is excluded here due to the lack of correlation in the 20-min returns, as mentioned above.

The goodness of fit can be judged by the χ^2 value, divided by the degree of freedom m in fitting. This is also shown in Table 10.4. Each autocorrelation value was assumed to have a stochastic error of $1/\sqrt{N}$, where N is the total number of correlation observations considered when calculating an individual autocorrelation value. All χ^2/m values are below 1 or just slightly above 1, indicating

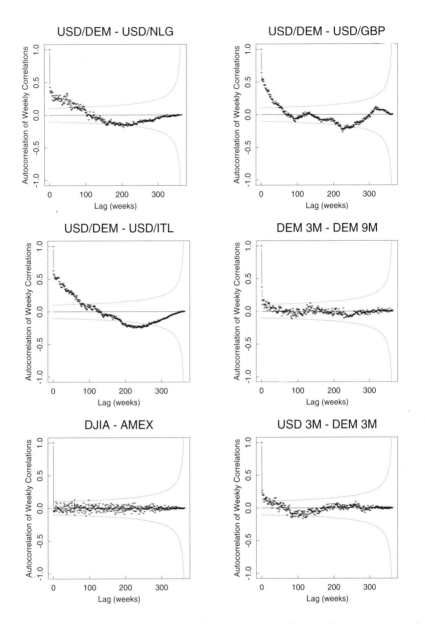

FIGURE 10.8   Autocorrelations of weekly correlation coefficients of returns, as plotted in Figures 10.2 through 10.7. The 95% confidence ranges corresponding to normally distributed random distributions are shown as dotted curves, where the curvature is caused by the decreasing size of the sample with growing lags. The total sampling period T is from January 7, 1990, to January 5, 1997.

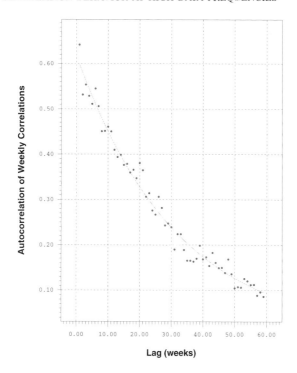

FIGURE 10.9 Fit of an exponential function to the autocorrelation of USD-DEM – USD-GBP weekly correlation coefficients.

that Equation 10.12 describes the data rather well. Adding a second exponential function to Equation 10.12 did not significantly improve the goodness of fit in all cases unless the data point at zero lag (defined as being equal to one) was added to the data set.

Table 10.4 shows considerable values of the amplitude A (which cannot exceed 1) and a long memory of the correlation level. The pair USD-DEM – USD-NLG has the longest memory with an exponential attenuation length of more than 80 weeks, which is just over one and a half years. The autocorrelation model of Equation 10.12 with the parameters of Table 10.4 can be the basis of a correlation forecast. This forecast could be remarkably long-term due to the long memory in correlation, depending on the instrument pair.

10.5 CORRELATION BEHAVIOR AT HIGH DATA FREQUENCIES

Previous authors have observed a dramatic decrease in correlation as the time intervals of the returns enter the intrahour level, for both stock (Epps, 1979) and FX returns (Guillaume *et al.*, 1997; Low *et al.*, 1996). We follow the suggestion of Low *et al.* (1996) by referring to this phenomenon as the Epps (1979) effect after the first identifiable author to thoroughly document it. In this discussion, the Epps

TABLE 10.4 Autocorrelation study.

The autocorrelations of weekly correlation data shown in Figure 10.8 are fitted to the parametrization given in Equation 10.12, for five financial instrument pairs. A large value of λ indicates a long, exponentially decaying memory of the correlation level. The variable χ^2/m indicates the goodness of fit (good fits have a value around 1 or preferably below); m is the degree of freedom of fitting.

Instrument	A	λ (weeks)	χ^2/m
USD-DEM – USD-NLG	0.35 ± 0.01	80.9 ± 7.1	0.65
USD-DEM – USD-GBP	0.62 ± 0.02	31.5 ± 1.8	0.15
USD-DEM – USD-ITL	0.61 ± 0.02	59.8 ± 3.0	0.34
DEM 3-6m – DEM 9-12m	0.27 ± 0.04	10.0 ± 2.6	1.30
USD 3-6m – DEM 3-6m	0.23 ± 0.03	21.8 ± 5.4	0.41

effect is characterized and investigated for a number of foreign exchange rates, stock indices, and implied forward interest rate pairs through the examination of the same 7 years of high-frequency return values as used in the previous sections.

The basis of our exploration was a set of homogeneous time series of returns, equally spaced by 5-min intervals, for several financial instruments. Linear interpolation was used in the sense of Equtions 3.2 and 3.6. For each time series of 5-min returns, we obtained 499 additional time series through aggregation: 10-min returns, 15-min returns, ... , 2500-min returns. To cover longer time intervals, 877 more time series were obtained by further aggregation in coarser steps: 2530-min returns, 2560-min returns, ... , 28810-min returns, where a 28810-min interval roughly corresponds to 20 days. Various calculations were performed with these many times series. The most interesting results are the correlation coefficients for returns of different financial instruments, using the same time interval size. This can be done for all interval sizes of the aggregated time series.

The resulting correlation coefficients are plotted as a function of the time interval size in Figure 10.10. When returns are computed with high frequency, over intervals distinctly shorter than 1 day, the correlation levels diminish in Figure 10.10. The same effect is better viewed in Figure 10.11, where the same data are shown with a logarithmic scale of interval sizes and where the data point farthest to the left (highest data frequency) corresponds to the correlation calculated using linearly interpolated, homogeneous time series of 5-min returns.

Table 10.5 gives the minimum and maximum values for the linear correlation coefficient data shown in Figure 10.10. Also given are the time intervals at which maxima occurred. We noted several problems when taking the maximum of correlation as a function of the time interval. The correlation graphs reach a more or less stable maximum level at time intervals exceeding one day, but this stability is not perfect for any correlation graph. Moreover, the maximum of correlation is affected by increasing stochastic noise for large time intervals. In an attempt

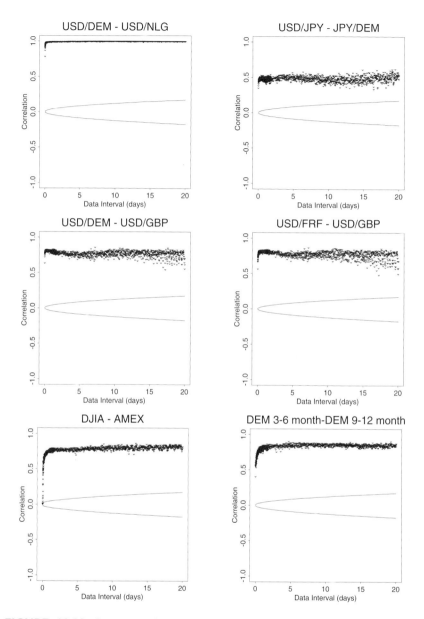

FIGURE 10.10 Linear correlation coefficients calculated for six pairs of financial instruments as a function of the size of the time interval of returns. For all calculations the total sampling period remained constant (from January 9, 1990, to January 7, 1997,) causing the 95% confidence ranges to be narrow at high data frequencies and wider as the time interval increases. Rapid declines in correlation at very high data frequencies are noted in all cases.

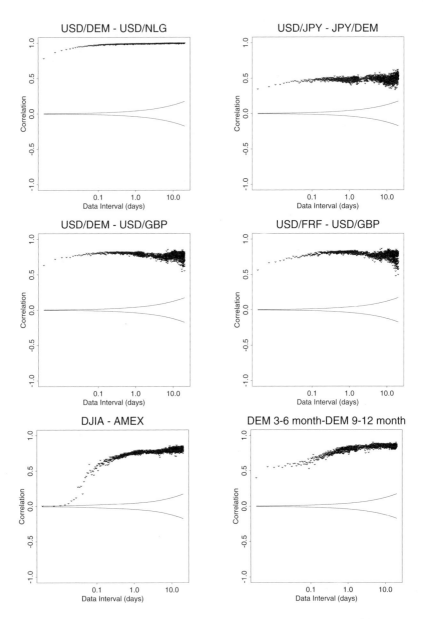

FIGURE 10.11 Linear correlation coefficients calculated for six pairs of financial instruments as a function of the size of the time interval of returns. The same data as in Figure 10.10 are shown with a logarithmic horizontal axis. Rapid declines in correlation at very high, intraday data frequencies are noted in all cases.

TABLE 10.5   Correlation results characterizing the Epps effect.

Minima, maxima, and mean values (averaged over time intervals between 1 and 2 days) of correlation coefficients. These correlations are functions of the time interval of return measurement, as plotted in Figures 10.10 and 10.11. Also given are the time intervals at which the maxima occurred and the time intervals where the coefficient reaches 90% of the mean value. This latter time interval in the last column is called the stabilization interval—the threshold after which the Epps effect no longer affects correlation results. The sampling period was from January 9, 1990, to January 7, 1997.

Instrument pair	Min. corr.	Max. corr.	Interval of max. (days)	Mean corr. (1–2 days)	90% of mean	Stabiliz. interval (min)
USD-DEM – USD-GBP	0.55	0.86	7.2	0.79	0.71	10
USD-DEM – USD-NLG	0.78	1.00	14.0	0.99	0.89	15
USD-FRF – USD-ITL	0.49	0.86	12.0	0.79	0.71	25
USD-NLG – USD-FRF	0.69	0.99	16.9	0.97	0.87	25
USD-FRF – USD-GBP	0.48	0.86	7.2	0.80	0.72	30
USD-JPY – DEM-JPY	0.34	0.62	19.4	0.48	0.43	30
DEM-GBP – USD-GBP	0.23	0.75	17.0	0.45	0.41	170
DJIA – AMEX	0.00	0.86	13.3	0.77	0.69	320
DEM 3-6M – DEM 9-12M	0.40	0.90	19.2	0.82	0.74	340

to give a more accurate reference level of the correlation drop due to the Epps effect, Table 10.5 also reports the arithmetic mean of all correlation values based on time intervals between 1 and 2 days. A total of 224 correlation values (i.e., 224 aggregated time series) belong to this range of time intervals. Although there is no best choice of time interval for the general case, this mean value is considered as a reasonable reference level of correlation in its stable region. When moving to shorter time intervals, the Epps effect makes the correlation values decline. As a threshold value of the Epps effect, Table 10.5 also shows the time interval at which correlations drop to 90% of the reference level. This estimation of the Epps threshold or, seen from the other side, the correlation stabilization interval has the advantage that it can be uniformly applied to all cases, and it does not deliver obviously misleading results based on the maximum value of correlation.

We find that even currency pairs that are highly correlated in the long term become much less correlated in the intrahour data frequency range. Müller *et al.* (1997a) propose a hypothesis of heterogeneous markets where the market agents differ in their perception of the market, have differing risk profiles, and operate under different institutional constraints (see also Section 7.4). If the financial markets are indeed composed of heterogeneous agents with different time horizons of interest, then the Epps effect in correlation estimations can be interpreted as a cut-off between groups of agents. Short-term traders focus on the rapid movements of individual rates rather than multivariate sets of assets. For these short-term agents, correlations between instruments play a secondary role. Other, less rapid agents reestablish "correct" correlations after market shocks, but this takes some time.

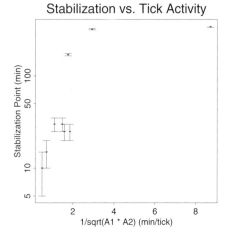

FIGURE 10.12 Correlation stabilization intervals (= stabilization points, in min) as a function of the inverse square root of the product of the tick frequencies. The same instrument pairs and stabilization intervals as in Table 10.5 are plotted.

When considering the stabilization interval in the last column of Table 10.5, we find that the Epps effect already vanishes at return measurement intervals of 10 min for the correlation of the most frequently quoted financial instruments. For pairs of less frequently quoted instruments, the Epps effect may last for hours, up to 6 hr in Table 10.5. This indicates a relationship between tick frequencies (and perhaps liquidity) of instruments and the duration of the Epps effect. Two correlation studies were made to probe this relationship: (1) standard correlation between the stabilization interval and the tick frequency of the more frequently quoted instrument of the pair and (2) standard correlation between the stabilization interval and the tick frequency of the less frequently quoted instrument. Mean tick frequencies per business day were taken, as listed in Table 2.2.

The greater of the two tick frequencies is estimated to have a standard correlation of -0.59 to the stabilization interval. The corresponding standard correlation of the lower tick frequency is -0.65. These values are significant to 92% and 95% confidence levels, respectively, assuming a normal random distribution. Therefore we conclude that, to a reasonable level of confidence, both of the tick frequencies substantially affect the stabilization interval after which the Epps effect of correlations vanishes. Tick frequency and stabilization interval are inversely related. This can be seen graphically in Figure 10.12 where the stabilization interval is plotted versus the inverse geometric mean of the two tick frequencies. When two tick frequencies are very high, as on the left-hand side of Figure 10.12, the stabilization interval becomes small. On the other side, at very low data frequencies, a plateau in the correlation stabilization interval appears to exist at a data interval of 300 to 400 min. This would indicate that the Epps effect does not play a substantial role in attenuating correlation values beyond 6-hr return measurement intervals, even if the instruments involved are very inactive ($<$ 100 data updates per business day). It should be stated that these are indicative and preliminary results and an enhanced study with more instruments and statistics is called for.

10.6 CONCLUSIONS

The problems associated with estimation of correlation at higher data frequencies have been discussed and illustrated using examples. An easy-to-use covolatility adjusted correlation estimator, which correctly accounts for missing or nonexistent data, has been proposed. The effect of this new formulation is to estimate correlation when data exist, and to make no update to the correlation calculation when data do not exist. The input of the method is homogeneous time series linearly interpolated between the ticks. At times when tick intervals are longer than the return measurement intervals, the weight of the return observations tends to zero. Because the estimator is adjusted by covolatility, some of the information from the more frequent of the two time series involved will not be fully utilized, and statistical significance can be degraded. With growing data frequency, this degradation is inevitable but tolerable because the statistical significance based on high-frequency sampling is high by nature. Covolatility adjusted correlation is an estimator complementary to other estimators. Its fluctuating weighting of observations is an alternative to time scale transformations such as the ϑ-time discussed in Chapter 6.

Empirically estimated linear correlation coefficients of returns vary over time. The return correlations of some financial instrument pairs widely fluctuate from week to week, whereas other correlations are very stable over periods of many years. It was observed that long-term historical stability is not a guarantee of future correlation stability. This was evidenced through the examination of USD-ITL and USD-GBP return correlations with the USD-DEM rate. The crisis of 1992, when the involvement of ITL and GBP in the European Monetary System (EMS) was suspended, was reflected by a dramatic and rapid change in their correlations with other currencies thereafter. Correlation calculated over a long data sample (years) has an averaging effect, and increased structure in correlations is observed when correlations are calculated over smaller periods (weeks). Depending on the time horizon of interest, there is pertinent information to be gained when calculations are performed over smaller periods using high-frequency data. The self-memories of return correlations have been modeled as exponential attenuations through estimation of the autocorrelation of linear correlation coefficients. Correlation values have memories for their past values that differ between instument pairs and often extend over years rather than only weeks. The understanding of this correlation memory is a first step toward correlation forecasting.

The behavior of the correlation coefficient as a function of the time interval of return measurement has been investigated. Nonzero correlations of returns are dramatically attenuated when this interval decreases and enters the intrahour region. This behavior is called the Epps effect and depends on the pair of investigated financial instruments. When the measurement interval exceeds a threshold value called the stabilization interval, the Epps effect gives way to a rather stable behavior of the correlation. There is some preliminary evidence of an inverse relationship between the stabilization interval and the mean tick frequency of the instruments involved. If financial markets are composed of heterogeneous agents as suggested in Section 7.4, the stabilization interval can be interpreted as a threshold between groups of agents. For extremely short-term traders focusing on time horizons below the stabilization interval, correlations between instruments may be less of an issue than for other agents.

In applications such as asset allocation or risk assessment, the return measurement intervals should preferably be chosen longer than the stabilization interval. However, there is no general "best" time interval for measuring correlation. It is important to choose the most relevant interval size for a specific application.

I I

TRADING MODELS

I I.I INTRODUCTION

Recently, the skepticism among academics to the possibility of developing profitable trading models has decreased with the publication of many papers that document profitable trading strategies in financial markets, even when including transaction costs.

In the earlier literature, simple technical indicators for the securities market have been tested by Brock *et al.* (1992). Their study indicates that patterns uncovered by technical rules cannot be explained by simple linear processes or by changes in the behavior of volatility.[1] LeBaron (1992a), LeBaron (1997) and Levich and Thomas (1993b) follow the methodology of Brock *et al.* (1992) and use bootstrap simulations to demonstrate the statistical significance of the technical

---

[1] In Gençay (1998b), the DJIA data set of Brock *et al.* (1992) is studied with simple moving average indicators within the nonparametric conditional mean models. The results indicate that nonparametric models with buy-sell signals of the moving average models provide more accurate sign and mean squared prediction errors (MSPE) relative to random walk and GARCH models. Gençay (1999) shows that past buy-sell signals of simple moving average rules provide statistically significant sign predictions for modeling the conditional mean of the returns for the foreign exchange rates. The results in Gençay (1999) also indicate that past buy-sell signals of the simple moving average rules are more powerful for modeling the conditional mean dynamics in the nonparametric models.

trading rules against well-known parametric null models of exchange rates. Sullivan *et al.* (1999) examine the trading rule performance by extending the Brock *et al.* (1992) data for the period of 1987–1996. They show that the trading rule performance remains superior for the time period that Brock *et al.* (1992) studied; however, these gains disappear in the last 10 years of the Dow Jones Industrial Average (DJIA) series. Lo *et al.* (2000) have proposed an approach to evaluate the efficacy of technical analysis based on technical pattern recognition using nonparametric kernel regression. They apply their method to a large number of U.S. stocks and they report that several technical indicators provide incremental information of practical value. Overall, the scope of the most recent literature supports the technical analysis, but it is generally limited to simple univariate technical rules. One particular exception is the study by Dacorogna *et al.* (1995), which examines real-time trading models of foreign exchanges under heterogeneous trading strategies. They conclude that it is the identification of the heterogeneous market microstructure in a trading model which leads to an excess return after adjusting for market risk.

Trading models are investment tools that provide explicit buy and sell trading recommendations. A clear distinction should be made between a price change forecast (presented in Chapter 9) and an actual trading recommendation. A trading recommendation naturally includes a type of price change forecast, but must also account for the specific risk profile of the dealer or user of the respective trading model. Another distinction is that a trading model must take into account its past trading history. This decision might be biased by the position it is currently holding and the price paid for entering in this position, whereas a price forecast is not submitted to such asymmetries. A trading model thus goes beyond predicting a return. It must decide if a certain action is to be taken. This decision is subject to the specific risk profile, the trading history, and institutional constraints such as opening hours or business holidays.

The purpose of this chapter is not to provide *ready-to-use* trading strategies, but to give a description of the main ingredients needed in order for any real-time trading model to be usable for actual trading on financial markets. Any reasonable trading strategy is composed of a set of tools that provides trading recommendations within a capital management system. In this book we shall not discuss the capital management part, but we wish to show that with a reasoned approach and high-quality data, it is possible to design practical and profitable trading models. Indeed, we have developed our own trading models and this presentation builds on this experience. Our models anticipate price movements in the foreign exchange (FX) market sufficiently well to be profitable for many years yet with acceptable risk behavior, and, they have been used by many banks.

Market investors mainly use trading models as decision tools, but in this chapter we will also illustrate that profitable trading models with robust performance measures can be employed as a statistical tool to study the market structure and to test the adequacy of price-generation processes.

A robust performance measure of trading strategies is one of the most important ingredients in the development of new models and also in their use. In Section 11.3, we discuss different possible performance measures and we derive two risk-adjusted ones for investors with risk-averse preferences. Maximizing these measures is equivalent to maximizing the expected utility of an investor.

To construct successful trading strategies is not an easy task and many possible mistakes must be avoided during the different development phases of new models. We shall describe here some of the main traps in which new system designers generally fall and provide some ideas as to how to construct more robust trading strategies. In the following sections we will also give a short description of the various components needed in trading models and a specific approach using genetic algorithms to obtain more robust optimization results.

11.2 REAL-TIME TRADING STRATEGIES

In the assumption of a heterogeneous market, there is no trading strategy that is absolutely better than other ones. Which strategy to choose will depend on the trading and risk profile of the investor. This is confirmed by the existence of many different types of portfolio and investment strategies in the financial markets. It is also why we use in this study different trading model algorithms. We believe that these new investment strategies will simply contribute to, and not fundamentally change, the heterogeneous composition of financial markets.

To be useful, real-time trading models must provide realistic trading recommendations that the user can follow. This means that the models should do the following:

- Give a warning a few minutes in advance of a deal.

- Not change recommendations too rapidly.

- Not give recommendations outside business hours.

- Take into account market holidays.

- Support stop-loss (around the clock).

In this section, we present the basic system architecture that we use in our real-time trading models and discuss the main components needed to transform available price quotes into actual trading recommendations. The model is divided in three main parts, that is,

- Generation of the *trading model* recommendations.

- Receipt of the simulated positions by the *simulated trader*.

- Generation of the model statistics by the *performance calculator*.

Figure 11.1 depicts the overall structure and data flow of a simple real-time trading model. The next subsections describe these different components.

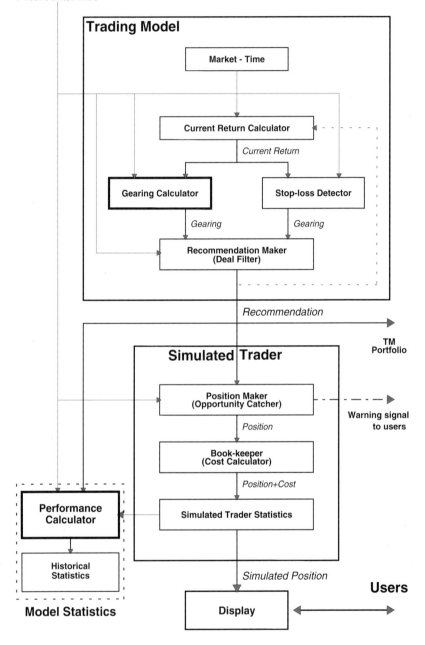

FIGURE 11.1   Data flow of prices and deal recommendations within a real-time trading model.

TABLE 11.1 Market constraints.

FX market business time constraints for the trading models running for different geographical markets. The markets are listed roughly in the order of their opening times in GMT.

Market	Time zone	Opening time (local time)	Closing time (local time)	Holidays (per year)
Tokyo	JPT	09:00:00	18:00:00	15 Days
Singapore	PRC	09:00:00	18:00:00	11 Days
Frankfurt	MET	08:30:00	17:00:00	12 Days
Vienna	MET	08:00:00	17:30:00	15 Days
Zurich	MET	08:00:00	17:30:00	10 Days
London	UKT	07:30:00	17:00:00	10 Days
New York	EST	08:00:00	14:00:00	12 Days

11.2.1 The Trading Model and Its Data-Processing Environment

As in forecasting or other applications, trading models depend heavily on the quality of the financial data that are fed to the program. Problems related to bad or invalid data can play an important role at different stages of the decision process. For instance, bad data can disturb the computation of the model indicators and then imply a partial or complete loss of the prediction power related to these indicators. One other sensitive part is the computation of the current return of the open positions. The current return is often used to trigger stop-profit algorithms, or exit specific positions. Any invalid price that passes through the filter incorrectly can produce a long-term perturbation effect on the trading abilities of the system, especially if it is used as a transaction price. To avoid data-related problems, a good trading system must include a special filter to cancel or postpone recommendations until a realistic transaction price is selected.

Trading Hours and Market Holidays Although some markets like the FX market operate continuously, individual traders or institutions generally partake of this market only for a portion of each day. Our models accommodate such users by incorporating the notion of business hours and holidays. Every trading model is associated with a local market that is identified with a corresponding geographical region. In turn, this is associated with generally accepted office hours and public holidays. The local market is defined to be open at any time during office hours provided that the trading model does not operate on a weekend or a public holiday. Typical opening hours for a model are between 9:00 and 17:00 local time, the exact times depending on the particular local market and traded instruments. In the case of FX, Table 11.1 presents typical opening hours of different geographical markets. Except for closing an open position if the price hits a stop loss limit (described in section 11.2.1), a model may not deal outside of the market's opening hours.

Current Return Calculations   In the trading room, people seldom take a full exposure at once. The traders like to build their positions in steps (gearing steps). In such cases, it is useful to introduce an auxiliary variable, the average price $\overline{p}$ paid for achieving the current exposure (gearing). This variable simplifies the computation of the return of a position built in steps. After a new deal with index i, the average price depends on the type of transaction as follows:

$$
\overline{p}_i \equiv
\begin{cases}
\overline{p}_{i-1} & if \quad |g_i| < |g_{i-1}| \ \text{and} \ g_i g_{i-1} > 0 \\[2ex]
g_i \left[\frac{g_i - g_{i-1}}{p_i} + \frac{g_{i-1}}{\overline{p}_{i-1}} \right]^{-1} & if \quad |g_i| > |g_{i-1}| \ \text{and} \ g_i g_{i-1} > 0 \\[2ex]
p_i & if \quad g_i g_{i-1} < 0 \ \text{or} \ g_{i-1} = 0 \\[2ex]
undefined & if \quad g_i = 0
\end{cases}
\tag{11.1}
$$

where g_{i-1} and g_i are the previous and current gearings, respectively, p_i is the current transaction price, and $\overline{p}_{i-1}$ is the average price before the deal. In the initial case, when the current gearing is neutral, the average price $\overline{p}$ is not yet defined. If we start from a neutral position $g_{i-1} = 0$ or reverse a position $g_i g_{i-1} < 0$, the price to build the position is simply the current price p_i. If the new position is built on top of a previous position, then we need to compute the average price paid from the price paid for each fraction of the full position. If the new position is just unfolding part of the previous position, then the average price paid for the position does not change. It is simply either profit taking or stop loss.

The average price $\overline{p}$ is needed to compute a quantity central to a trading model, the *return* of a deal,

$$
r_i \equiv (g_{i-1} - g_i') \left(\frac{p_i}{\overline{p}_{i-1}} - 1 \right)
\tag{11.2}
$$

where the gearing g_i' is equal to 0 if the model takes an opposite position ($g_i g_{i-1} < 0$) and g_i otherwise. There are deals with no return: those starting from a neutral gearing, $g_{i-1} = 0$, and those increasing the absolute value of the gearing while keeping its sign.[2] In these cases, Equation 11.2 does not apply (whereas Equation 11.1 applies to all deals).

The *current return*, r_c, is the unrealized return of a transaction when the current position is off the equilibrium ($g_i \neq 0$). If p_c is the current market price required

---

[2] The example below demonstrates the accounting of a trading model of USD-CHF, where CHF is the *home (numeraire)* currency and USD is the foreign *exchanged* currency. The trading model is played with a limit of 100 CHF. The usual practice for the capital flow in foreign exchange trading is that it is started from a capital of zero with credit limit. This is what is assumed here. All of our return calculations are expressed in terms of the home currency. In other words, the returns are calculated in terms of DEM for USD-DEM, CHF for USD-CHF, FRF for USD-FRF, and JPY for DEM-JPY.

for going back to neutral, generalizing Equation 11.2 yields the current return,

$$r_c \equiv g_i \left(\frac{p_c}{p_i} - 1 \right) \tag{11.3}$$

Gearing Calculation A gearing calculator lies at the heart of a trading model. The gearing calculator provides the trading model with its intelligence and the ability to capitalize on movements in the markets. The gearing calculator also provides the trading model with particular properties. These include the frequency of dealing and the circumstances under which positions may be entered.

In other words, the gearing calculator is the *real* model. In contrast, the other trading model components form a shell around the gearing calculator, providing it with price data, detecting if the stop-loss is hit, and examining the trading recommendations made by the gearing calculator. The gearing calculator reevaluates its position every time a new price quote is received from the data-vendors. (As previously noted, a filter validates each price beforehand in order to eliminate outliers and other implausible data.)

The gearing calculator employs two kinds of ingredients: a set of indicators, which are produced from the input price data, and trading rules, which are functions of the past dealing history, the current position, and other quantities such as the current unrealized return of an open position.

The models described here give a recommendation not only for the direction but also for the amount of the exposure. In our models, the possible exposures (gearings) are $\pm\frac{1}{2}$, ± 1 (full exposure) or 0 (no exposure).

Recommendation Maker The fact that the gearing calculator's indicators and rules suggest entering a new position does not necessarily mean that the model will make such a recommendation. Whether it does or not depends on various secondary rules that then take effect.

These rules constitute the deal acceptor. This determines whether the deal proposed by the indicators is allowed to be made. The prime constraint is the timing of the proposed deal. First, no deal other than a stop-loss deal (see Section 11.2.1) may take place within a few minutes of a deal already having occurred. This is to prevent overloading a human dealer who may be following the models. Second,

Time	Gearing	Current position in CHF	Current position in USD	FX
0	0	0	0	Don't care
1	0.5	-50	35.71	1.4
2	1	-100	69.04 (33.33 more)	1.5
3	0	10.46 (69.04*1.6 more)	0	1.6

In the example above, the trading lots in CHF are always 50 (half gearing step) or 100 (full gearing step) when increasing the (long or short) position, whereas decreasing the position means selling the full current USD amount (when going to neutral) or half the current USD amount (when going from gearing 1 to 1/2). There can be other accounting conventions, but they hardly differ numerically.

the gearing calculator may make a recommendation to enter a new trading position but this recommendation can be followed only if the local market is open.

The quality of the most recent price imposes another constraint. A stringent filter determines if a given price is suitable for dealing. This is to ensure that recommended deals are made only with genuine prices rather than extraneous data. The deal acceptor permits a new deal only with a price passing the deal-filter.

If the gearing calculator suggests entering a new position but the deal acceptor decrees otherwise, the suggestion is simply ignored. Eventually, when timing and other factors are right, the gearing calculator will suggest entering a new position and the deal acceptor will approve.

Stop-Loss Detection Besides being passed on to the gearing calculator, the filtered price quotes are also sent to the stop-loss detector. The stop-loss detector is triggered if the market moves in an unexpected direction. That is, if the model enters a trading position because it anticipates the market to move in a certain direction but in fact the market then moves the other way, the stop-loss may be hit. The trading model defines a stop-loss price when a position is entered. If the current price – that is, the most recent price – moves below the stop-loss price (for a long position) or above the stop-loss price (for a short position), the stop-loss is said to be hit. Hitting the stop-loss causes a deal to close the current open position (i.e., return to the neutral position). In effect, the stop-loss prevents excessive loss of capital when the market moves in an unexpected direction. The stop-loss price may change when a new position is entered or as the current price changes (see Section 11.2.1). The current stop-loss price is displayed on the user-agent.

For 24-hr markets like FX, a stop-loss deal may occur at any time, even outside local market hours. In this case, the assumption is that a position that is kept open outside market hours is handled by a colleague present in another market-place who will deal appropriately if the stop-loss is hit. Should this happen, no further change in position occurs until the local market opens once again.

Stop-Profit Control The concept of stop-profit is associated with that of stop-loss. The stop-loss price starts to move in parallel with the current price once a trading model has achieved a potential profit (3% or slightly less in FX market) since entering the latest position. In other words, being in a situation whereby the model could realize such a gain by immediately entering a neutral position causes the stop-loss price to start moving. The difference between the stop-loss and current prices is kept constant as long as the current price continues moving in a direction that increases the potential profit of the open position. That is, the stop-loss price moves as a ratchet in parallel with the current price. The stop price is allowed to move only during opening hours. It is never adjusted when the market is closed.

The model then enters a neutral position if it detects prices slipping backward. This allows a model to save any profit it has generated rather than lose it when the market abruptly turns. This one-directional movement of the stop-loss price allows the model to capitalize on a price trend.

11.2.2 Simulated Trader

The simulated trader allows the system to control continuously its performance by simulating a trade every time the trading model gives a recommandation. In the following, we shall describe the different part that composes the simulated trader.

Opportunity Catcher   The trading model may make a deal recommendation in two distinct ways. One, the gearing calculator may make a recommendation that is then authorized by the deal acceptor. Two, hitting the stop-loss price activates the stop-loss detector.

Whichever way a deal comes about, the *opportunity catcher* is activated. The opportunity catcher manifests itself on the user-agent as an eye-catching signal for the FX dealer to buy or sell according to the recommendation.

While he or she is actively dealing, the opportunity catcher in the trading model collects the transaction price with which to deal, either the median bid price if going from a longer position to a shorter one or the median ask price if going from a shorter position to a longer one. This search for the transaction price lasts for 2 or 3 min depending on the currency, the assumption being that a quoted price has a life-time of about 2 or 3 min even if it is superseded by later quotes.

After the 2 or 3 min search period, a second signal appears on the user-agent signifying that the trading model has made a simulated deal using the transaction price found by the opportunity catcher. The FX dealer then concludes his or her deal-making activities and waits until the trading model produces another recommendation.[3]

Bookkeeper   The *bookkeeper* executes simulated deals on behalf of the trading model. It keeps track of all deals that have been made and evaluates statistics demonstrating the performance of the trading model. The bookkeeper computes a set of quantities that are important for the different trading rules like the following:

- The *maximum return when open*, which is the maximum value of r_c from a transaction i to a transaction $i + 1$ reached during opening hours,

- The *minimum return when open*, which is the minimum value of r_c from a transaction i to a transaction $i + 1$ reached during opening hours.

In this section we describe some of the important variables that need to be watched for deciding on the quality of a specific model. These are the following:

- The *total return*, R_T, is a measure of the overall success of a trading strategy over a period T, and is defined by

$$R_T \equiv \sum_{j=1}^{n} r_j \qquad (11.4)$$

---

[3] As a point of detail, the opportunity catcher is not activated for a stop-loss deal occurring outside market hours. In this case the trading model deals directly. A human trader following the model should then make a corresponding deal for himself as quickly as possible.

where n is the total number of transactions during the period T, j is the jth transaction and r_j is the return from the jth transaction. The total return expresses the amount of profit (or loss) made by a trader always investing up to his/her initial capital or credit limit in his/her home currency.

- The *cumulated return*, C_T, is another measure of the overall success of a trading model wherein the trader always reinvests up to his/her current capital, including gains or losses

$$C_T \equiv \prod_{j=1}^{n} (1 + r_j) - 1 . \qquad (11.5)$$

This quantity is slightly more erratic than the total return.

- The *maximum drawdown*, D_T, over a certain period $T = t_E - t_0$, is defined by

$$D_T \equiv \max(R_{t_a} - R_{t_b} \mid t_0 \le t_a \le t_b \le t_E) \qquad (11.6)$$

where R_{t_a} and R_{t_b} are the total returns of the periods from t_0 to t_a and t_b, respectively.

- The *profit over loss ratio* provides information on the type of strategy used by the model. Its definition is

$$\frac{P_T}{L_T} \equiv \frac{N_T(r_j \mid r_j > 0)}{N_T(r_j \mid r_j < 0)} \qquad (11.7)$$

where N_T is a function that gives the number of elements of a particular set of variables under certain conditions during a period T. Here the numerator corresponds to the number of profitable deals over the period T and the denominator is the number of losing deals over the same period.

11.3   RISK SENSITIVE PERFORMANCE MEASURES

Evaluating the performance of an investment strategy generally gives rise to many debates. This is due to the fact that the performance of any financial asset cannot be measured only by the increase of capital but also by the risk incurred during the time required to reach this increase. Returns and risk must be evaluated together to assess the quality of an investment. In this section we describe the various performance measures used to evaluate trading models.

The annualized return, $\bar{R}_{T,A}$, is calculated by multiplying the total return (Equation 11.4) with the ratio of the number of days in a year to the total number of days in the entire period.[4] In order to achieve a high performance and good

---

[4] If it is the annualization of one particular return (for one trade going from neutral to neutral), one simply needs to multiply the return by the ratio of 1 year in days to the time interval from neutral to neutral. Usually, the annualization of the total return is calculated for all the trades during a whole year. This is simply the sum of all trade returns not annualized during the whole year. If at the end of the year there is an open position, the current return of your open position is added to the total return.

acceptance among investors, investment strategies or trading model performance should provide high annualized total return, a smooth increase of the equity curve over time, and a small clustering of losses. The fulfilment of these conditions would account for a high return and low risk. In addition to favoring this type of behavior, a performance measure should present no bias toward low-frequency models by including always the unrealized return of the open position and not only the net result after closing the position.

Already in 1966, Sharpe (1966) introduced a measure of mutual funds performance, which he called at that time a *reward-to-variability ratio*. This performance measure was to later become the industry standard in the portfolio management community under the name of the Sharpe ratio, Sharpe (1994). Practitioners frequently use the Sharpe Ratio to evaluate portfolio models. The definition of the Sharpe ratio is

$$S_T \equiv A_{\Delta t} \frac{\bar{r}}{\sqrt{\sigma_r^2}} \tag{11.8}$$

where $\bar{r}$ is the average return and σ_r^2 is the variance of the return around its mean and $A_{\Delta t}$ is an annualization factor,[5] depending on the frequency at which the returns are measured Sharpe (1994).[6] Unfortunately, the Sharpe ratio is numerically unstable for small variances of returns and cannot consider the clustering of profit and loss trades.

There are many aspects to the trading model performance; therefore, different quantities have to be computed to assess the quality of a model. In the section on the bookkeeper, we already described some of the important variables that need to be watched for deciding on the quality of a specific model. Here we introduce the two risk-sensitive measures that are the basic quantities used in further sections to analyze the behavior of trading models.

11.3.1 X_{eff}: A Symmetric Effective Returns Measure

As the basis of a risk-sensitive performance measure, we define a cumulative variable $\tilde{R}_t$, at time t, as the sum of the total return R_T of Equation 11.4 and the unrealized current return r_c (Equation 11.3) of the open position. This quantity reflects the current value of the investment and includes not only the results of previously closed transactions but also the value of the open position (mark-to-market). This means that $\tilde{R}_t$ is measuring the risk independently of the actual trading frequency of the model. Similar to the difference between price and returns, the variable of relevance for the utility function is the change of $\tilde{R}$ over a time

---

[5] $A_{\Delta t} = \sqrt{12}$ for monthly frequency.

[6] Here the Sharpe ratio refers to the calculation of the returns in the expressed currency and the variance is computed with monthly returns. The monthly returns are the total return achieved to the end of the month (sum of all returns up to now, including the current return of the open position) minus the total return achieved at the end of the previous month.

interval Δt,

$$X_{\Delta t} = \tilde{R}_t - \tilde{R}_{t-\Delta t} \tag{11.9}$$

where t expresses the time of the measurement. Generally Δt is allowed to vary from 7 days to 301 days. A risk-sensitive measure of trading model performance can be derived from the utility function framework (Keeney and Raiffa, 1976). Let us assume that the variable $X_{\Delta t}$ follows a Gaussian random walk with mean $\overline{X}_{\Delta t}$ and the risk aversion parameter α is constant with respect to $X_{\Delta t}$. The resulting utility $u(X_{\Delta t})$ of an observation is $-\exp(-\alpha X_{\Delta t})$, with an expectation value of $\overline{u} = u(\overline{X}_{\Delta t}) \exp(\alpha^2 \sigma_{\Delta t}^2/2)$, where $\sigma_{\Delta t}^2$ is the variance of $X_{\Delta t}$. The expected utility can be transformed back to the *effective return*, $X_{eff} = -\log(-\overline{u})/\alpha$ where

$$X_{eff} = \overline{X}_{\Delta t} - \frac{\alpha \sigma_{\Delta t}^2}{2} \tag{11.10}$$

The risk term $\alpha \sigma_{\Delta t}^2/2$ can be regarded as a risk premium deducted from the original return where $\sigma_{\Delta t}^2$ is computed by

$$\sigma_{\Delta t}^2 = \frac{n}{n-1} \left(\overline{X_{\Delta t}^2} - \overline{X}_{\Delta t}^2 \right) \tag{11.11}$$

Unlike the Sharpe ratio, this measure is numerically stable and can differentiate between two trading models with a straight-line behavior ($\sigma_{\Delta t}^2 = 0$) by choosing the one with the better average return.[7] The measure X_{eff} still depends on the size of the time interval Δt. It is hard to compare X_{eff} values for different intervals. The usual way to enable such a comparison is through the annualization factor, $A_{\Delta t}$, where $A_{\Delta t}$ is the ratio of the number of Δt in a year divided by the number of Δt's in the full sample

$$X_{eff,ann,\Delta t} = A_{\Delta t} X_{eff} = \overline{X} - \frac{\alpha}{2} A_{\Delta t} \sigma_{\Delta t}^2 \tag{11.12}$$

where $\overline{X}$ is the annualized return and it is no longer dependent on Δt. The factor $A_{\Delta t} \sigma_{\Delta t}^2$ has a constant expectation, independent of Δt. This annualized measure still has a risk term associated with Δt and is insensitive to changes occurring with much longer or much shorter horizons. To achieve a measure that simultaneously considers a wide range of horizons, a weighted average of several $X_{eff,ann}$ is computed with n different time horizons Δt_i, and thus takes advantage of the fact that annualized $X_{eff,ann}$ can be directly compared,

$$X_{eff} = \frac{\sum_{i=1}^n w_i X_{eff,ann,\Delta t_i}}{\sum_{i=1}^n w_i} \tag{11.13}$$

---

[7] An example for the limitation of the Sharpe ratio is its inability to distinguish between two straight line equity curves with different slopes.

where the weights w are chosen according to the relative importance of the time horizons Δt_i and may differ for trading models with different trading frequencies. Generally, α is set to $\alpha = 0.1$ when the returns are expressed as a percentage. If they are expressed in numbers, α would be equal 10. The risk term of X_{eff} is based on the volatility of the total return curve against time, where a steady, linear growth of the total return represents the zero volatility case. This volatility measure of the total return curve treats positive and negative deviations symmetrically, whereas foreign exchange dealers become more risk averse in the loss zone and hardly care about the clustering of positive profits.

11.3.2 R_{eff}: An Asymmetric Effective Returns Measure

A measure that treats the negative and positive zones asymmetrically is defined to be R_{eff}, (Müller *et al.*, 1993b; Dacorogna *et al.*, 2001b) where R_{eff} has a high risk aversion in the zone of negative returns and a low one in the zone of profits, whereas X_{eff} assumes constant risk aversion. A high risk aversion in the zone of negative returns means that the performance measure is dominated by the large drawdowns. The R_{eff} has two risk aversion levels: a low one, α_+, for positive $\Delta \tilde{R}_t$ (profit intervals) and a high one, α_-, for negative $\Delta \tilde{R}_t$ (drawdowns),

$$
\alpha = \begin{cases} \alpha_+ & for \quad \Delta \tilde{R}_t \geq 0 \\ \alpha_- & for \quad \Delta \tilde{R}_t < 0 \end{cases} \tag{11.14}
$$

where $\alpha_+ < \alpha_-$. The high value of α_- reflects the high risk aversion of typical market participants in the loss zone. Trading models may have some losses but, if the loss observations strongly *vary* in size, the risk of very large losses becomes unacceptably high. On the side of the positive profit observations, a certain regularity of profits is also better than a strong variation in size. However, this distribution of positive returns is never as *vital* for the future of market participants as the distribution of losses (drawdowns). Therefore, α_+ is smaller than α_- and we assume that $\alpha+ = \alpha_-/4$ and $\alpha_- = 0.20$. These values are under the assumption of the return measured as *percentage*. They have to be multiplied by 100 if the returns are not expressed as percentage figures.

The *risk aversion* α associated with the utility function $u(\Delta \tilde{R})$ is defined in Keeney and Raiffa (1976) as follows:

$$
\alpha = -\frac{\dfrac{d^2 u}{[d(\Delta \tilde{R})]^2}}{\dfrac{du}{d(\Delta \tilde{R})}} \tag{11.15}
$$

The utility function is obtained by inserting Equation 11.14 in Equation 11.15 and integrating twice over $\Delta \tilde{R}$:

$$
u = u(\Delta \tilde{R}) = \begin{cases} -\dfrac{e^{-\alpha_+ \Delta \tilde{R}}}{\alpha_+} & \text{for } \Delta \tilde{R} \geq 0 \\ \dfrac{1}{\alpha_-} - \dfrac{1}{\alpha_+} - \dfrac{e^{-\alpha_- \Delta \tilde{R}}}{\alpha_-} & \text{for } \Delta \tilde{R} < 0 \end{cases} \tag{11.16}
$$

The utility function $u(\Delta\tilde{R})$ is monotonically increasing and reaches its maximum 0 in the case $\Delta\tilde{R} \to \infty$ (infinite profit). All other utility values are negative. (The absolute level of u is not relevant; we could add and/or multiply all u values with the same constant factor(s) without affecting the essence of the method.)

The inverse formula computes a return value from its utility:

$$
\Delta\tilde{R} = \Delta\tilde{R}(u) = \begin{cases} -\dfrac{\log(-\alpha_+ u)}{\alpha_+} & \text{for } u \geq -\dfrac{1}{\alpha_+} \\[3mm] -\dfrac{\log(1-\frac{\alpha_-}{\alpha_+}-\alpha_- u)}{\alpha_-} & \text{for } u < -\dfrac{1}{\alpha_+} \end{cases} \tag{11.17}
$$

The more complicated nature of the new utility definition, Equation 11.16, makes deriving a formula for the *mean* utility quite difficult and offers no analytical solution. Moreover, the R_{eff} is dominated by the drawdowns that are in the *tail* of the distribution, not in the center. The assumption of a Gaussian distribution, which may be acceptable for the distribution as a whole, is insufficient in the tails of the distribution, where the stop-loss, the leptokurtic nature of price changes, and the clustering of market conditions such as volatility cause very particular forms of the distribution.

Therefore, the use of *explicit* utilities is suggested in the R_{eff} algorithm. The end results, R_{eff} and the effective returns for the individual horizons, will however, be transformed back with the help of Equation 11.17 to a return figure directly comparable with the annualized return and X_{eff}. The utility of the jth observation for a given time interval Δt is

$$
u_{\Delta t, j} = u(\tilde{R}_{t_j} - \tilde{R}_{t_j - \Delta t}) \tag{11.18}
$$

The total utility is the sum of the utility for each observation

$$
u_{\Delta t} = \frac{\sum_{j=1}^{N_j} v_j \, u_{\Delta t, j}}{\sum_{j=1}^{N_j} v_j} \tag{11.19}
$$

In this formula, N_j is the number of observed intervals of size Δt that overlaps with the total sampling period of size T and the weight v_j is the ratio of the amount of time during which the jth interval coincides with the sampling period over its interval size Δt. This weight is generally equal to one except for the first observation(s), which can start before the sample starts, and the last one(s), which can end after the sample ends. To obtain a lower error in the evaluation of the mean utility, different regular series of overlapping intervals of size Δt can be used. The use of overlapping intervals is especially important when the interval size Δt is large compared to the full sample size T. Another argument for overlapping is the high, overproportional impact of *drawdowns* on R_{eff}. The higher the overlap factor, the higher the precision in the coverage of the worst drawdowns.

The mean utility $u_{\Delta t}$ can be transformed back to an *effective* return value by applying Equation 11.17:

$$\Delta \tilde{R}_{eff,\Delta t} \;=\; \Delta \tilde{R}(u_{\Delta t}) \tag{11.20}$$

This $\Delta \tilde{R}_{eff,\Delta t}$ is the typical, effective return for the horizon Δt, but it is not yet annualized. As in the case of the X_{eff}, an annualization is necessary for a comparison between R_{eff} values for different intervals. The annualization factor, $A_{\Delta t}$, is the ratio of the number of Δt in a year divided by the number of nonoverlapping Δt's in the full sample of size T. We have

$$\tilde{R}_{eff,ann,\Delta t} \;=\; A_{\Delta t}\, \Delta \tilde{R}_{eff,\Delta t} \tag{11.21}$$

To achieve a measure that simultaneously considers a wide range of horizons, we define R_{eff} as a weighted mean over all the n horizons,

$$R_{eff} \;=\; \frac{\sum_{i=1}^{n} w_i\, R_{eff,ann,\Delta t_i}}{\sum_{i=1}^{n} w_i} \tag{11.22}$$

where the weights w_i are chosen according to the relative importance of the time horizons Δt_i and may differ for trading models with different trading frequencies. In the case of the trading models described in this book, we have choosen a weighting function

$$w_i \;=\; w(\Delta t_i) \;=\; \frac{1}{2 + \left(\log \frac{\Delta t_i}{90 \text{ days}}\right)^2} \tag{11.23}$$

with the maximum for a Δt of 90 days.

Both X_{eff} and R_{eff} are quite natural measures. They treat risk as a discount factor to the value of the investment. In other words, the performance of the model is discounted by the amount of risk that was taken to achieve it. In the X_{eff} case the risk is treated similarly both for positive or negative outcome, whereas in the case of R_{eff} negative performance is more penalized.

11.4 TRADING MODEL ALGORITHMS

We turn now to the description of the techniques used to build the real-time trading models. Trading models have been developed for many decades by a large number of people and applied in all types of financial markets. These models have been designed from a broad class of indicators ranging from classical technical analysis up to chaotic theory. It is just not possible to provide a comprehensive list of the various approaches used in trading system design and the literature in this field is so large that we will leave this exercise to other authors. As in the case of technical analysis, hundreds of articles and books have been written.

Generally, trading systems are built from a few classes of indicators providing specific types of information on the underlying financial time series. For instance, we have these:

- The *trend following* indicators, which allow to detect and follow major market trends.

- The *overbought and oversold* indicators, which allow to detect important market turning points.

- The *cycle* indicators, which try to emphasize periodic market fluctuations.

- The *timing* indicators, which provide optimum exit conditions.

As an example we will describe one model that we have developed for the FX market and that many large banks have actively used for a decade. As we have pointed out earlier, a trading strategy is built from some indicators and a set of decision rules. Indicators are variables of the trading system algorithm whose values, together with the system rules, determine the trading decision process. In Chapter 3.3 we gave different descriptions of indicators that have been used in conjunction with trading models.

11.4.1   An Example of a Trading Model

The real-time trading model (RTT) studied in this section is classified as a one-horizon, high-risk/high-return model. The RTT is a trend-following model and takes positions when an indicator crosses a threshold. The indicator is momentum based, calculated through specially weighted moving averages with repeated application of the exponential moving average operator (see Section 3.3.6). In the case of extreme foreign exchange movements, however, the model adopts an over-bought/oversold (contrarian) behavior and recommends taking a position against the current trend. The contrarian strategy is governed by rules that take the recent trading history of the model into account. The RTT model goes neutral only to save profits or when a stop-loss is reached. Its profit objective is typically at 3%. When this objective is reached, a gliding stop-loss prevents the model from losing a large part of the profit already made by triggering it to go neutral when the market reverses.

At any point in time t, the gearing function for the RTT is

$$g_t(I_x) = sign(I_x(t)) \; f(|I_x(t)|) \; c(I(t))$$

where

$$I_x(t) = x_t - MA(\tau = 20 \text{ days}, 4; x)$$

where x_t is the logarithmic price at time t and the moving average (MA) of x follows the definition and notation of Equation 3.56 (where the last argument x of

MA indicates the time series to which the MA operator is applied),

$$
f(|I_x(t)|) = \begin{cases} if & |I_x(t)| > b & 1 \\ if & a < |I_x(t)| < b & 0.5 \\ if & |I_x(t)| < a & 0 \end{cases}
$$

and

$$
c_t(I) = \begin{cases} +1 & if & |I_x(t)| < d \\ -1 & if & |I_x(t)| > d \ and \ g_{t-1} \cdot sign(I_x(t)) > 0 \ and \ r_l > P \end{cases}
$$

where $a < b < d$ and r_l is the return of the last deal and P the profit objective. The function, $f(|I_x(t)|)$, measures the size of the signal at time t and the function, $c(|I_x|)$, acts as a contrarian strategy. The model will enter a contrarian position only if it has reached its profit objective with a trend following position. In a typical year, the model will play against the trend two to three times while it deals roughly 60 to 70 times. The hit rate of the contrarian strategy is of about 75%.

The parameters a and b depend on the position of the model,

$$
a(t) = \begin{cases} a & if & g_{t-1} \neq 0 \\ 2a & if & g_{t-1} = 0 \end{cases}
$$

and $b = 2a$. The thresholds are also changed if the model is in a position $g_t \neq 0$ and the volatility of the price has been low, in the following way:

$$
a(t) = \begin{cases} a & if & |x_e - x_t| > v \\ 10a & if & |x_e - x_t| < v \end{cases}
$$

where x_e is the logarithmic entry price of the last transaction and v is a threshold, generally quite low $< 0.5\%$. This means that the model is only allowed to change position if the price has significantly moved from the entry point of the deal.

Because X_{eff} and R_{eff} are implicit functions of the gearing, the optimization of the RTT model is based on the X_{eff} and R_{eff} performance. The parameters subject to optimization are; τ, a, d, and v. There are two other auxiliary parameters, which are the stop loss, S, at which an open position is automatically closed and the profit objective, P. These parameters are only optimized at the end once the others have been found and they are also not allowed to vary all the way because maximum stop-loss and maximum gain limits are set by the environment.[8] The model is subject to the open-close and holiday closing hours of the Zurich market.

11.4.2 Model Design with Genetic Programming

The major problem with trading models is the large amount of time needed to develop and optimize new trading strategies. As we said before, a trading strategy is a small computer program composed of some indicators to forecast price trends combined with a set of rules to determine the trading decision process.

---

[8] For more details on the optimization procedure, see Pictet *et al.* (1992).

One very promising approach in the search of new trading strategies is provided by genetic programming (GP) method (Koza, 1992; Banzhaf *et al.*, 1998). This is an evolutionary algorithm that allows to automatically discover computer programs that solve a given problem. Evolutionary algorithms tend to find globally satisfactory solutions to the problem and, much in the same way as in nature, populations of organisms tend to adapt to their surrounding environment. Such an approach has been applied to stock indices, as noted in Allen and Karjalainen (1999), and to exchange rates, as noted in Oussaidène *et al.* (1997); Neely *et al.* (1997); Bhattacharyya *et al.* (1998).

Individual programs in GP are represented as parse trees with ordered branches in which the internal nodes are functions (with subtree branches as function arguments) and the leaves or terminal nodes are variables. The functions are chosen from a user-defined *function set*, those that are a priori believed to be useful for the problem at hand, and the leaves are selected from a *terminal set* containing the principal variables or constants of the problem.

Once an initial population has been created, the genetic algorithm enters a loop. At the end of each iteration (or generation), a new population has been created by applying a certain number of stochastic operators to the members of the previous population. A *selection* operator is first applied in order to extract some above-average individuals for reproduction. When a population of parents has been extracted, two reproduction operators are used: *crossover* and *mutation*. As shown on Figure 11.2, the crossover operator starts by selecting a random crossover point in each parent tree (*a* and *b*) and then exchanging the subtrees, giving rise to two offspring trees (*c* and *d*). The crossover sites, $c1$ and $c2$, are usually chosen with nonuniform probability, in order to favor internal nodes with respect to leaves. In the same figure we can observe that from two parents trees, which are not interesting, the crossover is able to generate the offspring (*c*), which correspond to a well-known simple trading strategy using the difference between two moving averages. After crossover, a certain proportion of the offspring are subject to mutation. The mutation operator is implemented by randomly removing a subtree at a selected point and replacing it with a randomly generated subtree.

In the basic genetic programming approach, it is generally required that all elements of a tree return the same data type, so as to allow arbitrary subtrees to be recombined by the crossover and mutation operators. This *closure property* (Koza, 1992) can be a potential limitation in some applications like the trading strategies search process. In earlier studies, on the use of GP for searching new trading strategies (Oussaidène *et al.*, 1997), a large proportion of the population members were noted to be irrelevant and resulted in a wasteful search. For instance, if you carefully study the different GP trees in Figure 11.2, you can easily conclude that only the offspring (*c*) corresponds to a reasonable indicator.

As mentioned, trading models are a function of the price history. In the case of the FX market, it is common to consider the logarithmic middle price x, which possesses an exact symmetry $x \rightarrow -x$, corresponding to the interchange of the expressed and exchanged currencies. Consider the U.S. Dollar to German Mark

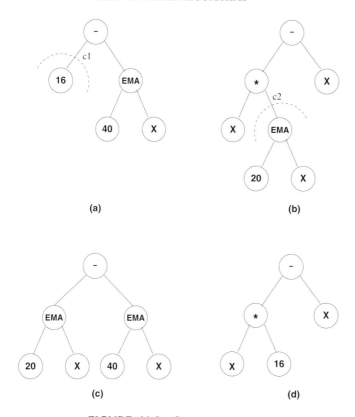

FIGURE 11.2 Crossover operator.

(USD-DEM) exchange rate. A trading model that is optimum for the USD-DEM rate is also expected to be optimum for the inverted DEM-USD rate. For this to hold, the model for the inverted DEM-USD rate should provide a signal, at any time t, that has exactly the reverse sign than the one for the USD-DEM rate. It means the output signal $g_t(x)$ of a consistent trading model must be an antisymmetric function of the return. Enforcing the symmetry condition on the trading model thus requires that $g_t(x) \rightarrow g_t(-x) = -g_t(x)$. Maintaining this property in a GP tree requires tracking the symmetry property at individual nodes in the tree, and forms the basis for defining syntactic restrictions. To enforce the symmetry, three possible types are defined:

- Antisymmetric type A (e.g., a moving average of x):
  $A(-x) = -A(-x)$
- Symmetric type S (e.g., a volatility): $S(-x) = S(x)$
- Constant type C (numerical constants)

Constants are in essence of symmetric type; however, there are many advantages to considering the constant type separately. In specifying a GP trading model,

+ −	A	S	C
A	A	−	−
S	−	S	S
C	−	S	−

* /	A	S	C
A	S	A	A
S	A	S	S
C	A	S	−

FIGURE 11.3 Syntactic restrictions for basic arithmetic operators.

every node evaluation is considered to return both a value and a type (A, S, or C as defined above). The typing mechanism is used to categorize the symmetry properties. A variety of functions may be considered for formulating trading models. Each function must be specified in terms of syntactic restrictions relating to symmetry, and guiding their combination with terminals and other functions. As an example, the syntactic restrictions for the basic arithmetic operators are provided in Figure 11.3. In these tables, the first row and column correspond to the type of the two arguments, with the intersection cells showing the type of the result. The symbol "−" represents a combination of arguments that is disabled. Operation on two constants is generally disabled to avoid wasteful computation of constants through the regular crossover and mutation operators (Evett and Fernandez, 1998). The constants are generally mutated using specific non-uniform mutation operators (Michalewicz, 1994).

Other classes of functions are useful in the construction of the trading strategies. The important one is the class of the time series convolution operators described in Section 3.3. For instance, in Figure 11.2, we see exponential moving averages of the middle logarithmic price x for the two ranges of 20 and 40 days. Such operators can be used as function nodes if their syntactic restrictions are provided. They can also be used directly as input variables of the antisymmetric or symmetric type, depending on their symmetry properties when x is replaced by $-x$. In the case of a moving average operator, syntactic restrictions are forced to have the same symmetry type for the input and output signals.

Other operators often used in trading strategies are the classes of:

- Logic operators: AND, OR,
- Comparison operators: greater than, smaller than,
- Conditional operators: IF-then, IF-then-else.

As we expect an asymmetric output trading signal, it is suitable to use for these operators a ternary Boolean logic, Oussaidène *et al.* (1997).

In using such trading strategies, like in Bhattacharyya *et al.* (1998), we clearly depart from the closure property. In fact, we consider here a strongly typed GP approach (see Montana, 1995), where the evolution procedure needs to define a random tree initialization routine, and crossover and mutation operators respecting the defined restrictions.

As an example, we describe a study by Chopard *et al.* (2000) who analyze five exchange rates (USD-DEM, USD-JPY, USD-CHF, GBP-USD, and USD-FRF), where each time series contains 9 years of hourly data from January, 1, 1987, to December, 31, 1995. The data are divided into alternate training (in-sample) and test (out-of-sample) periods of $1\frac{1}{2}$ year each. We have used the four arithmetic functions $(+,-,*,/)$, the basic comparison $(<,>)$, and the logical operators (AND,OR,IF), which were defined in Bhattacharyya et al. (1998). Both comparison and logical operators are defined for a ternary logic $\{-1,0,+1\}$, which corresponds to the signal returned by a trading model. As in the case of the arithmetic functions, these operators are used with syntactic restrictions to preserve the overall symmetry properties of the generated GP trees. Indicators reported in earlier studies (Oussaidène et al., 1997; Bhattacharyya et al., 1998) are also used for this application. The terminals used are as follows:

- Antisymmetric indicators: M_n that represent the momentum of price x over n days. Here we consider three different ranges: M_8 and M_{16}, M_{32}.

- Symmetric indicators: V_n that are volatility indicators over n days: V_8 and V_{16}.

- Constant values in the range [-2, +2].

As a last step, the output value of the GP tree is mapped to a gearing value in the range [-1, +1] to obtain a gearing signal. For the purpose of reducing overfitting, each trading model is tested on many exchange rate time series. The fitness measure, X_{eff}, of a GP-tree is then defined as the average fitness over each exchange rate, decreased by a penalty proportional to the standard deviation of these values.

Five independent optimization runs are performed. In each run, we evolve four subpopulations of 100 individuals each. All subpopulations are created randomly using the *ramped half-half* approach (Koza, 1992) with a maximum depth of 4. In the reproduction phase, we use the *tournament* selection. The mutation and crossover operators are used with corresponding probabilities of 20% and 80% and the maximum depth allowed for generated trees is fixed to 6. Each subpopulation sends periodically 5% of its best individuals to another, randomly selected, subpopulation. A given subpopulation includes its local buffer of received migrants when the difference between the best and the average scores of the current population is smaller than half the standard deviation of the scores. The new individuals replace an equal number of low-fitness ones in the receiving population. The evolution is stopped when a maximum number of 10,000 individuals have been evaluated. The selected solution is the best solution found by the four subpopulations.

Table 11.2 presents the performance results of the different runs. The first entry gives the average quality of the basic antisymmetric momentum indicators M8, M16, and M32. The results of the optimization runs are given in decreasing order of their out-of-sample performance. The results of this table indicate that on average the performance of the solutions provided by the genetic algorithm are significantly higher than the performance of the basic momentum indicators.

TABLE 11.2   Trading model results versus tree complexity.

Tree complexity, yearly return R, and fitness value X_{eff} (in percent) corresponding to the in-sample and out-of-sample periods. The results are given for preoptimized indicators and for the best solution of each optimization run.

Run	Tree complexity	In-sample $\bar{R}$	In-sample X_{eff}	Out-of-sample $\bar{R}$	Out-of-sample X_{eff}
Indicators	1	4.23%	-1.84%	3.61%	-3.77%
Run 1	21	8.12%	3.86%	6.29%	1.09%
Run 2	17	9.49%	4.16%	5.80%	0.47%
Run 3	19	7.45%	2.82%	5.06%	-2.34%
Run 4	24	7.71%	3.55%	4.87%	-3.28%
Run 5	28	6.84%	2.63%	3.10%	-5.85%

For instance, the solution selected in the second run that provides the best in-sample result is given by the GP-tree:

```
(IF (> V8 0.027)
        (IF (> V16 0.108)
                (+ M16 M32)
                (* M32 1.957) )
        (* M8 1.542)
)
```

The use of syntatic restrictions allows the discovery trees of lower complexity on average, compared with the previous study of Oussaidène *et al.* (1997), and all the generated GP trees are valid. However, there may exist some solutions that do not generate any trades, because some conditions always evaluate the same value. These solutions are quickly eliminated in the selection process. On average the solutions seem to be more robust and to provide higher out-of-sample performance.

One limiting problem in these optimizations was implied by the use of "hard" logical and basic comparison operators that give rise to undesirable discontinuities due to the jumps of the Boolean variables that can occur for tiny changes of the basic indicators. One better way of implementing these operators would be through the use of fuzzy-logic. A smoother transition between different logical states can probably provide better performances.

All these optimization runs are done using hourly data, for obvious efficiency reasons. Then, when such optimization is completed, the final selected solution(s) must be tested in the complete real-time trading model environment with tick-by-tick data to check its behavior and to do some fine-tuning needed for the understanding of the final users.

11.5 OPTIMIZATION AND TESTING PROCEDURES

When the main trading strategy has been selected, one of the most difficult tasks is to optimize the parameters present in the model and to test the different solutions in order to select the most robust trading model to be used in the real time data. The goal is to select robust solutions that have desirable generalization properties to provide satisfactory performance in the future.

In the optimization process we expect the selection of a trading model that realizes large profits from the price moves present in the time series. We assume that these profits will be maximized when the trading model catches the dynamics of the price-generation process. Unfortunately, during the optimization phase the trading model repeatedly sees the same data set and discovers how to profit from some specific price moves that could be due to some random fluctuation of the prices. This will lead a trading model to provide poor results on real-time data. Such a model is called an "overfitted" model. To minimize overfitting during optimization, a few important elements are to be present:

- A good measure of the trading model performance
- Indicator evaluation for different time series
- Large data samples
- A robust optimization technique
- Strict testing procedures

An optimization algorithm will always try to find the best solution in the parameter space. In the case of trading models, optimization of such properties is not suitable, because a solution corresponding to the best possible parameters generally corresponds to an overfitted solution. As we argued earlier, such solutions will often generate poor generalizations in a real-time trading setting. In the next section, we shall concentrate on one robust optimization technique based on the genetic algorithm approach. This method allows the selection of a group of solutions that correspond to broad regions of the parameter space where the trading performance is higher *on average*, rather than the highest.

11.5.1 Robust Optimization with Genetic Algorithms

The new element we want to present in this section is a way to automatize the search for improved trading models. Genetic algorithms offer a promising approach for addressing such problems (Allen and Karjalainen, 1999). Genetic algorithms consider a population of possible solutions to a given problem and evolve it according to mechanisms borrowed from natural genetic evolution: reproduction and selection. The criterion for selecting an individual is based on its fitness to the environment, or more precisely to the quality of the solution it bears. A possible solution is coded as a chromosome (gene), which is formally the data structure containing the values of the quantities characterizing the solutions.

In the framework of the present optimization, a gene will contain the indicator parameters, a time horizon, a weighting function of the past, and the type of operations used to combine them. Contrary to GP, the gene does not offer the flexibility to the algorithm but only to the parameters. The fitness function will be based on the return obtained from the recommendations of a given trading model.

Sharing Scheme For Multi-Modal Functions   A major problem in trading model optimization is to obtain models that are robust against market changes and random noise in data collection. In such optimization problems, sharp peaks of high fitness are usually not representative of a general solution, but rather they indicate accidental fluctuations. Such fluctuations may arise out of inherent noise in the time series or due to threshold effects in the trading model performance. Peaks in such a discontinuous, noisy and multimodal fitness space generally correspond to trading models that will not perform well in out-of-sample tests.

In the context of genetic algorithms, optimizing multimodal functions has been investigated using methods inspired from the natural notions of niche and species, as noted by Goldberg and Richardson (1987); Deb and Goldberg (1989), and Yin and Germay (1993). The general goal is to be able to create and maintain several subpopulations, ideally one per major peak of the fitness function, instead of having the whole population converging to one global optimum.

One of the best methods was proposed by Goldberg and Richardson (1987). The idea is that the GA perception of the fitness function is changed in such a way that when individuals tend to concentrate around a high peak, the fitness is reduced by a factor proportional to the number of individuals in the region. This has the effect of diminishing the attractiveness of the peak and allowing parts of the population to concentrate on other regions. This effective fitness of an individual i, called shared fitness s_f, is given by

$$s_f(i) = \frac{f(i)}{m(i)} \tag{11.24}$$

where $f(i)$ is the original fitness and $m(i)$ is called the niche count. For an individual i, the quantity $m(i)$ is calculated by summing up the sharing function values contributed by all N individuals of the population,

$$m(i) = \sum_{j=1}^{N} \text{sh}(d_{ij}) \tag{11.25}$$

where d_{ij} is the distance between two individuals i and j and

$$\text{sh}(d_{ij}) = \begin{cases} 1 - \left(\frac{d_{ij}}{\sigma_s}\right)^{\alpha} & \text{if } d_{ij} < \sigma_s \\ 0 & \text{otherwise} \end{cases} \tag{11.26}$$

The quantities α and σ_s are constants. A difficulty of this method is in choosing the value of σ_s. This requires prior knowledge about the number of peaks in the solution space. In our economical application as well as in many realistic problems, this information is not readily available.

A method is proposed in Yin and Germay (1993) based on a different sharing scheme and using an adaptive cluster methodology. The authors show that this method is effective in revealing unknown multimodal function structures and is able to maintain sub-population diversity. This method establishes analogies between clusters and niches in the following way. The GA population is divided by the adaptive MacQueen's KMEAN clustering algorithm, in K clusters of individuals that correspond to K niches. The shared fitness calculation is the same as in the classical sharing method, but the niche count $m(i)$ is no longer associated with σ_s. In this case, the number of individuals within the cluster to which the individual i belongs plays a central role in the niche count calculation. As the number of clusters is associated with the number of niches (peaks), the individuals are put into a single partition of K clusters, where K is not fixed a priori but is determined by the algorithm itself. Therefore no a priori knowledge about the numbers of peaks of the fitness function is required as in the classical sharing method. The niche count $m(i)$ is computed as

$$m(i) \ = \ N_c \ - \ N_c * \left(\frac{d_{ic}}{2 \, D_{max}} \right)^{\alpha} \qquad \qquad x_i \ \in \ C_c \qquad (11.27)$$

where N_c is the number of individuals in the cluster c, α is a constant, and d_{ic} is the distance between the individual i and the centroid of its niche. The algorithm requires a distance metric in order to compute the distance between two clusters and the distance between one individual and one cluster. Two clusters are merged if the distance between their centroids is smaller than a threshold parameter D_{min}. Moreover, when an individual is further away than a maximum distance D_{max} from all existing cluster centroids, a new cluster is formed with this individual as a member. The efficiency of the algorithm is improved by sorting the population in descending order according to the individual's fitness before the application of the clustering.

Such genetic algorithm with sharing and clustering has been applied to standard multimodal and continuous fitness functions by Yin and Germay (1993) and Chopard et al. (1995) with promising results. One example of a more complex application was the determination of the optimum parameters of the *business* time scale,[9] which is used for analyzing price history and computing indicators. In this example, the optimization is quite difficult because we have to optimize simultaneously 17 parameters and the function is nonlinear in some of its parameters. To solve such a problem, it was necessary to add a normalization of the parameter space in the genetic algorithm—that is, each parameter is only allowed to vary in the range [0,1]. In simple problems, the two clustering parameters are generally set to $D_{min} = 0.05$ and $D_{max} = 0.15$. But here, because of the large dimensionality of the parameter space, the value of the clustering parameters D_{min} and D_{max} must be much larger. In this case, the two parameters are multiplied by $\sqrt{n}$ where n is the number of parameters to be optimized. The results obtained with this genetic algorithm are very promising and the sharing and clustering approach clearly increases

---

[9] This is a time scale that contracts and expands time based on seasonal activity or volatility of the time series (see Chapter 6).

the speed of convergence compared to the simple genetic algorithm described in the previous section.

When applied to the indicator optimization problem, the genetic algorithm with sharing and clustering runs into difficulties. If the fitness landscape contains too many sharp peaks of high fitness, all the selected clusters concentrate around these peaks and the genetic algorithm is unable to find robust solutions. In the next section, we propose some modifications to the genetic algorithm to detect clusters in the parameter space that correspond to more general and robust solutions.

Modified Sharing Function for Robust Optimizations   We need to find a new genetic algorithm that avoids the concentration of many individuals around sharp peaks of high fitness but detects broad regions of the parameter space containing a group of individuals with a high average fitness level and a small variance of the individual fitness values.

To solve this problem, we propose a new sharing function that penalizes clusters with large variance of the individual fitness values and also penalizes clusters with too many solutions concentrated inside too small a region. The distance metric considered here is the Euclidean distance computed in the real parameter space (phenotypic sharing). In the proposed sharing scheme, all the individuals that belong to a given cluster c will share the same fitness value,

$$s_f(i) = \overline{f_c} - \left(\frac{N_c}{N_{av}} + \frac{1 - r_d}{r_d} \right) \sigma(f_c) \qquad \forall x_i \in C_c \qquad (11.28)$$

where N_c is the number of genes in the cluster c, $\overline{f_c}$ is the average fitness value, and the standard deviation of the individual fitness values $\sigma(f_c)$ is defined by

$$\overline{f_c} = \frac{1}{N_c} \sum_{i=1}^{N_c} f(i) \qquad \text{and} \qquad \sigma(f_c) = \sqrt{\frac{1}{N_c - 1} \sum_{i=1}^{N_c} (f(i) - \overline{f_c})^2}$$

$$(11.29)$$

As the method is based on the distribution of gene fitness inside each cluster, we keep only the clusters that contain at least a minimum number of members. We use a minimum cluster size of two individuals. As we also need to keep enough clusters of reasonable size, we have to limit the size of the largest clusters. The term N_c/N_{av} in Equation 11.28 is used to control the number of genes inside each cluster. If N_c is smaller than the expected average number of genes inside each cluster N_{av}, the correction is reduced, otherwise it is increased. Here, the constant N_{av} is chosen such that the population size is divided by the (preconfigured) expected number of clusters.

The second term $(1 - r_d)/r_d$ in Equation 11.28 is used to penalize clusters with too high a concentration of genes around their centroid. The value r_d is defined as

$$r_d = \sqrt{\frac{1}{N_c} \sum_{i=1}^{N_c} \left(\frac{d_{ic}}{D_{max}} \right)} \qquad (11.30)$$

where d_{ic} is the distance of the gene i to the centroid of the corresponding cluster c. Here the square root is used to avoid too large a correction for an average concentration of genes, as is often the case.

To keep the cluster's space as large as possible, we also have to minimize the overlap between different clusters. To reduce this overlap, the clustering parameter $D_{\min}$ must be quite large and here we use $D_{\min} = D_{\max}$. In order to have a reasonable clustering parameter for large dimensionality of the parameter space, the values of the two clustering parameters $D_{\min}$ and $D_{\max}$ are multiplied by $\sqrt{n}$ where n is the number of parameters to be optimized.

With this new sharing scheme, the selection pressure is no more specific to each individual, as in a standard GA, but is the same for all genes present in a given cluster. This allows us to get a selection mechanism that looks for subpopulations of solutions with an average high quality instead of the best individual solution. Of course, the overall convergence speed is slightly reduced.

The selection pressure toward robust solutions is still present through the adaptive cluster methodology that tends to create clusters around a group of good individuals and through the reproduction technique, which uses elitism and mating restriction inside each cluster. Moreover, to keep a larger variety in the population, all the individuals who do not really belong to any clusters (i.e., who are further than the maximum distance $D_{\max}$ from all existing cluster centroids) will have an unmodified fitness value. During the reproduction phase these individuals will have no mating restriction and generally a slightly higher selection probability.

To speed up the full process, the result of each different gene is stored and not recomputed when this gene appears again in the next generations. Moreover, the information of all the previously computed solutions can be used at the end to assess the reasonableness of the optimum solution.

Eventually, the algorithm selects, for each cluster, the best solution that is not farther than the distance $D_{\max}/2$ from the cluster centroid. The final solution is the solution selected for the cluster that has the maximum average fitness corrected by the variance—that is, for the maximum value of $\overline{f_c} - \sigma(f_c)$.

The success of this type of genetic algorithm is still quite sensitive to the quality of the fitness measure but also to the normalization of the parameter space (i.e., to the quality of the metric used in the cluster construction). If the parameters do not have all the same sensitivity, this should also be reflected in the clustering algorithm. That is why we introduce the possibility of modifying the normalization of the parameter space, but in many applications this is not enough and some parameter mapping functions are needed. These functions depend on the specific problem to solve.

11.5.2 Testing Procedures

Strict optimization and testing procedures are a necessary condition to obtain robust trading strategies. The three main phases in the development of new trading models are as follows:

- The development and optimization of new trading strategies

- The historical performance tests to select the strategies from data that were not used to optimize the models

- Real-time tests to confirm the performance of the selected models

The amount of historical data available for both the development (optimization) and the testing of a new trading model is always of finite size. On one side, to obtain meaningful and robust optimization results, a data sample as large as possible is requested. On the other side, the same is true for the statistical tests of the performance of a new model. Of course, the same data cannot be used for both the optimization and for the test of a trading strategy. The available historical data must be split into a minimum of two different sample periods. One period, named the *in-sample*, is used for the optimization and the other one, named the *out-of-sample*, for the performance tests. Such splitting must never be modified during the optimization or the testing phase, otherwise the risk of overfitting the historical data becomes very large and the statistical tests on the model performance are unreliable.

Another problem to take into account with financial data is the long-term heteroskedasticity (i.e., the presence of clusters which correspond to periods where the average price volatility is higher and other ones where the average price volatility is lower). As many trading models can react quite differently according to the average volatility of the market prices, it is not very convenient if the two selected data sets for optimization and testing present significant differences in their statistical properties.

A rule that provides reasonable results is to use two-thirds of the historical data for the optimization and one-third for the tests. The first part of the optimization data must be kept for the indicator initialization. The size of this initialization period, also named the *build-up* period, depends on the type of the indicators. In the case of exponential moving averages, the size of the initialization must be approximately 12 times larger than the range of the slower moving average.

At the end of the optimization process, the performance tests are executed once. If these performance tests do not provide good results, then the new trading model must be rejected.

It is strongly recommended to avoid tiny modifications of the initial model until good performance tests are obtained, because such procedure implies that the out-of-sample data period is, in fact, used indirectly for the optimization process itself, and again opens the door to overfitting problems.

When a new model is selected and passes the historical performance tests, the final phase is to check it in real-time for a few months. These last tests, named *ex-ante* tests, are useful to confirm the historical performance of the model and to check its reaction to real-time data flow. At Olsen & Associates (O&A), only the models that pass with success, both the historical test and the real-time ex-ante period, are used for real trading.

11.6 STATISTICAL STUDY OF A TRADING MODEL

11.6.1 Heterogeneous Real-Time Trading Strategies

The idea of this section is to use some trading models developed at Olsen & Associates as a tool to study the market structure (work presented in Dacorogna *et al.*, 1995). These models act like filters that concentrate on typical price movements and give us information about the market itself. The hypothesis of a heterogeneous market leads to three conjectures:

1. In a heterogeneous market, no particular trading strategy is systematically better than all the others. Excess return can be gained for different trading profiles, so various ways of assessing the risk and return of trading models are needed.

2. The different geographical components of the FX market have different business hours according to different time zones and, on the assumption of the heterogeneous market hypothesis, different strategies. Therefore, there are disruptions in the market behaviors from one geographical component to the next. Trading models that do not explicitly analyze the geographical components can avoid these disruptions only by restricting their active hours to the normal business hours of one geographical market. For such models, trading 24 hr a day does not pay.

3. The most profitable models actively trade when many agents are active in the market (liquid periods) and do not trade at other times of the day and on weekends. The heterogeneous market hypothesis attributes the profitability of trading models to the simultaneous presence of heterogeneous agents, whereas the classical efficient market hypothesis relates this profitability to inefficiencies. (This would imply that the illiquid periods of the market are the most favorable for excess returns.) If our conjecture is right, the optimal daily trading time interval should depend on the traded FX rate rather than the model type. Trading will be most profitable when the main markets for a particular rate are active.

Two trading models based on different algorithms are used in this study. The performance of these models is analyzed against changing market conditions, trading intervals, opening and closing times, and market holidays. The first trading model (RTT) is the one described in Section 11.4.1. Whereas the RTT model relies on one indicator with one time horizon, the second type of trading model (named here RTM) uses three different time horizons simultaneously to incorporate the views of three different market components. Like the RTT model, the RTM models have a profit objective of 3%, but the stop-loss value and profit objective are much smaller. The dealing frequencies of the RTM models are often higher than those of the RTT models, and they are also neutral more often.

The study presented here does not try to optimize the models in any way, so the distinction between in and out-of-sample is of little relevance. All the tests were conducted in a 7-year period from March 1986 to March 1993 for

TABLE 11.3 Performance comparison between models.

Performance comparison between the O&A class RTT, RTM trading models, and a (benchmark) 20-day moving average model. The displayed performance measures are the annualized total return R, the risk-sensitive performance measure X_{eff}, the maximum drawdown D, the profit-loss ratio P/L and the dealing frequency F. These performance measures are explained in Sections 11.2.2 and 11.3.1.

FX rate	Model	R	X_{eff}	D	P/L	F
USD-DEM	MA(20)	5.5%	-0.9%	21.1%	0.57	1.0
	RTT	16.9%	11.2%	9.6%	0.41	1.7
	RTM	11.3%	8.6%	8.4%	0.68	2.0
USD-JPY	MA(20)	6.6%	0.6%	21.3%	0.53	0.9
	RTT	9.6%	4.2%	10.9%	0.59	1.5
	RTM	6.0%	3.5%	9.6%	0.45	1.9
GBP-USD	MA(20)	10.7%	5.5%	14.0%	0.58	1.0
	RTT	11.9%	7.1%	14.6%	0.40	1.6
	RTM	10.6%	8.2%	7.9%	0.66	2.1
USD-CHF	MA(20)	8.0%	0.9%	19.2%	0.59	1.1
	RTT	11.6%	6.1%	14.5%	0.55	1.3
	RTM	14.0%	10.1%	16.9%	0.65	1.9
USD-FRF	MA(20)	7.1%	4.0%	15.8%	0.56	1.0
	RTT	15.5%	11.2%	7.5%	0.75	1.1
	RTM	10.7%	8.6%	5.3%	0.60	2.1
USD-NLG	MA(20)	7.5%	3.3%	16.6%	0.55	1.0
	RTT	16.4%	10.9%	8.7%	0.50	1.7
	RTM	14.0%	11.2%	7.4%	0.69	2.1
USD-ITL	MA(20)	8.5%	1.7%	21.7%	0.57	1.0
	RTT	14.6%	7.2%	10.5%	0.42	1.6
	RTM	9.4%	6.1%	9.3%	0.65	1.9
DEM-JPY	MA(20)	1.4%	0.8%	4.9%	2.00	0.1
	RTT	10.9%	8.7%	6.5%	0.66	1.9
	RTM	10.1%	8.6%	5.9%	0.73	1.6
Average	MA(20)	7.7%	2.2%	18.5%	0.56	1.0
	RTT	13.4%	8.3%	10.4%	0.54	1.6
	RTM	10.8%	8.1%	8.8%	0.64	2.0

TABLE 11.4 Performance comparison between markets.

The average risk-adjusted return X_{eff} for the different markets is shown as a percentage the average dealing frequency F is given in number of deals per week. The markets are listed in the order of their opening times in GMT.

Market	X_{eff}		Dealing frequency (F)	
	RTT	RTM	RTT	RTM
Tokyo	-0.8	1.6	1.3	1.4
Singapore	-0.4	2.3	1.4	1.4
Frankfurt	7.5	6.7	1.5	1.8
Vienna	8.3	7.8	1.5	2.0
Zurich	8.3	8.1	1.6	2.0
London	8.6	8.2	1.6	2.0
New York	6.3	6.7	1.5	1.9

USD-DEM, USD-JPY, GBP-USD, USD-CHF and DEM-JPY, and a $6\frac{1}{2}$ year period from December 1986 to March 1993 for USD-FRF, USD-NLG, and USD-ITL.

Table 11.3 shows the comparative performance of the two types of models (RTT and RTM) together with the performance of a simple 20-day moving average model tested with the same high frequency data and the same environment. All models produce a significant profit even when transaction costs are fully accounted for. However, they differ both in the size of the average profit and in the risk of temporary losses. This was formulated as the first conjecture in the introduction. These results are a good illustration of the possibility of having diversified strategies that are all profitable but correspond to different risk profiles.

Realistic trading models should be configured for traders located in particular geographical locations. Our high-frequency data give us the flexibility of configuring different opening hours for different markets. In Table 11.3, the models were computed within the market constraints of Zurich. Now we want to show how the effective return varies if the market constraints are changed. Six other markets are tested: Frankfurt, London, New York, Singapore, Tokyo, and Vienna. Table 11.4 shows the different parameters related to the active times of these markets.

The same eight FX rates used for the performance comparison in Table 11.3 were tested here. In Table 11.4, we present the average of X_{eff} over the eight FX rates for the seven markets and the corresponding mean dealing frequency. The bad results for Tokyo and Singapore are not surprising because these markets are the least liquid. Good results in these markets are only obtained for USD-JPY and DEM-JPY. For the other five markets, X_{eff} generally does not vary much (within 1 to 2%), but it clearly peaks on the most active market (London) although the models were optimized for the Zurich market. This presents the first empirical evidence for our third conjecture that within the active times, the performance is not very sensitive to certain changing conditions.

TABLE 11.5 The best X_{eff} as a function of opening hours.

The best X_{eff}, in percent, as a function of the number of daily business hours and the opening and closing times in MET. The sixth column shows the X_{eff} reached when the models are allowed to trade 24 hr. The last column shows the hour that produces the best X_{eff} when only 1 hour per day is allowed for trading.

FX rate	Model	Best X_{eff}	Interval size	Daytime	$X_{eff}(24hr)$ 24hr trading	Best 1-hr trading
USD-DEM	RTT	9.7	12hr	7:00 – 19:00	6.7	16:30 – 17:30
	RTM	9.0	11hr	8:30 – 19:30	2.8	12:00 – 13:00
USD-JPY	RTT	4.3	9hr	8:30 – 17:30	-4.2	10:00 – 11:00
	RTM	7.6	9hr	3:00 – 12:00	0.5	17:00 – 18:00
GBP-USD	RTT	13.4	10hr	9:00 – 19:00	6.9	16:30 – 17:30
	RTM	9.0	8hr	6:00 – 14:00	5.8	13:00 – 14:00
USD-CHF	RTT	7.4	1hr	16:30 – 17:30	-5.8	16:30 – 17:30
	RTM	5.1	8hr	9:30 – 17:30	-0.6	18:30 – 19:30
USD-FRF	RTT	11.2	8hr	11:00 – 19:00	0.5	17:00 – 18:00
	RTM	9.4	9hr	8:00 – 17:00	1.6	16:00 – 17:00
USD-NLG	RTT	12.3	8hr	12:00 – 20:00	6.9	16:00 – 17:00
	RTM	8.8	10hr	8:30 – 18:30	4.6	15:30 – 16:30
USD-ITL	RTT	9.2	9hr	12:00 – 21:00	0.3	16:30 – 17:30
	RTM	6.6	8hr	11:00 – 19:00	1.3	13:00 – 14:00

At the beginning of this Section 11.6.1, we introduced two conjectures as subjects of research: it is not favorable to extend the dealing period to more than the normal business hours or even to 24-hr trading for our model types (conjecture 2); and the most profitable dealing periods should be the most active and liquid ones (conjecture 3). To test these conjectures, two main questions were asked: Is there an optimal daily business interval and do these optimal opening and closing hours differ for different rates? We present here the results of a study where we vary both the length and the starting point of the daily opening period. The two real-time model classes were tested with daily working intervals of 1, 8, 9, 10, 11, 12, 13, and 24 hr, shifting the opening time in 30-min steps from 0:00 to 24:00.

Table 11.5 shows the best X_{eff} values together with their corresponding working hours in Middle European Time (MET) for all rates and trading models used in this study. The models were optimized in-sample on $9\frac{1}{2}$ hours from 8:00 to 17:30. Some first remarks can be made by looking at the results: shorter time intervals (8–10 hr) are generally preferred to longer ones (11–13 hr), thus confirming conjecture 2. There is not much profit in long working time intervals; these only tend to increase the number of bad deals because the indicators are more sensitive to noise. Yet, because longer time intervals cover a larger period, the X_{eff} values of longer time intervals are more stable against changing opening and closing hours, that is, their variance is clearly smaller than that of shorter intervals. One exception is model RTT for USD-CHF where the 1-hr time interval is best, but the models still have significant peaks at the 9-hr interval (from 8:30 to 17:30, 4.9%).

Further evidence in support of conjecture 2 is given by the sixth column in Table 11.5, listing the X_{eff} values for 24-hr trading for comparison with the best X_{eff} values attained for shorter trading intervals. The X_{eff}(24-hr) values are much lower than the best X_{eff} values for almost all rates and models. This failure of 24-hr trading can be interpreted as an insufficiency of the models to deal with short-term price movements, in particular the disruptive market behaviors arising when the main dealing activity shifts from one geographical location to another (with a different time zone). A 24-hr trading interval leads to a dealing frequency higher than that of a 12-hr interval. Contrary to the 24-hr trading interval, the best 1-hr intervals that coincide with the most active times of the day are seldom significantly worse than the rest of the intervals tested.

In Table 11.5, there are also indications that conjecture 3 is valid. The USD-JPY models show a strong tendency toward favoring opening hours early in the European morning (or closing times early in the afternoon), whereas GBP-USD and USD-ITL prefer opening times in the late morning. These results are in line with the time zones of the home markets of the currencies and must be related to market liquidity. For JPY, better results are obtained when its main market (Far East) is active, for GBP and ITL, when London (1-hr behind the Zurich market) is active (ITL is traded more in London than in Milan). The results of the RTT model for USD-NLG seem to contradict this conjecture, but it should be qualified. There is, in fact, another peak with an X_{eff} of 11.3% at a 12-hr trading interval from 7:30 to 19:30.

In conclusion, the systematic analysis of the influence of the trading hours on these models reveals some important facts. First of all, if we regard our model classes as representing medium-term components in the market, we see that it is not useful to stay active 24-hr a day. Without a much more sophisticated treatment of the intraday movements, it does not pay for a medium-term trader to be active all the time. Second, it shows that, contrary to assumptions based on the classical efficient market hypothesis, a trading model is profitable when its active hours correspond to the most active hours of one of the main geographical components of the market. It is essential that the models execute their deals when the market is most liquid. This fact is illustrated by three empirical findings:

- The maxima of performance are clustered around opening hours when the main markets are active.

- The best active times are shifted for certain currencies to accommodate their main markets (Japan for JPY, London for GBP).

- If the models are only allowed to trade for 1 hour, the best choice of this hour is usually around the peaks in the daily activity of the market.

The systematic variation of the business hours of the trading models again reveals the geographical structure of the FX market and its daily seasonality by the most profitable trading times being concentrated where the market is most liquid.

11.6.2 Price-Generation Processes and Trading Models

Instead of feeding the trading models with real data, we can use simulated data from different price-generation processes. The results indicate that the performance of the trading models with real FX data is much higher relative to the simulated price processes. This demonstrates that the trading models successfully exploit a certain predictability of returns that exists beyond the scope of the studied price-generation processes. The results also provide opportunity to compare different statistical price processes with each other. In the case of the RTT model described in Section 11.4.1, the out-of-sample test period is 7 years of high-frequency data on three major foreign exchange rates against the U.S. Dollar and one cross rate. From its launch in 1989 until the end of 1996, the model had not been reoptimized and was running on the original set of parameters estimated with data prior to 1989. This allows us a unique advantage that there is no socially determined coevolutionary relationship between our data set and the technical strategies used in implementing our specification tests.

The trading model yields positive annualized returns (net of transaction costs) in all cases. Performance is measured by the annualized return, X_{eff}, R_{eff}, deal frequency and maximum drawdown. Their simulated probability distributions are calculated with the three traditional processes, the random walk, GARCH, and AR-GARCH, but also with an AR-HARCH. The null hypothesis of whether the real-time performances of the foreign exchange series are consistent with these traditional processes is tested under the probability distributions of the performance measures. As expected from the discussions of the previous chapters, the results from the real-time trading model are not consistent with the random walk, GARCH(1,1) and AR-GARCH(1,1) as the data-generating processes. It is also the case with the AR-HARCH processes.

Simulation Methodology   The distributions of the performance measures under various null processes are calculated by using a simulation methodology. In our trading model simulations, we use a 5-min interval sampling of the prices in order to keep the computation within manageable bounds. It is a good compromise between efficient computation and realistic behavior when compared to the real-time trading model results generated from all ticks. The main information used by a trading model to update its indicators is the *returns*. The return between two consecutive selected ticks at time t_{j-1} and t_j is defined as

$$r_j = x_j - x_{j-1}$$

and the corresponding elapsed ϑ-time (described in Section 6.2) between these two ticks is

$$\Delta\theta_j = \theta_j - \theta_{j-1}$$

By construction, in the sampled time series, the average elapsed ϑ-time between two ticks, $\overline{\Delta\theta}$, is nearly 5 min.

Multiple time series from a given theoretical price generation process need to be generated. To keep the impact of special events like the data holes in the model behavior, we decided to replace the different bid-ask price values but always keep the recorded time values. As the different ticks are not exactly regularly spaced, even in ϑ-time, the average return corresponding to a 5-min interval needs to be calculated. This is calculated by rescaling the observed return values

$$r_j^* = r_j \left(\frac{\overline{\Delta\theta}}{\Delta\theta_j} \right)^{1/E}$$

where the exponent $1/E$ is called the drift exponent and it is set to 0.5 under the random walk process.

To obtain meaningful results, a simulated time series should have the same average drift α and average variance σ^2 as the observed returns. This is done by generating returns, $\hat{r}_j$, corresponding to a 5-min interval in ϑ-time. In the case of a random walk process, the returns $\hat{r}_j$ are computed with

$$\hat{r}_j = \alpha + \epsilon_j$$

where $\epsilon_j \sim N(0, \sigma^2)$.[10] When the effective elapsed time between two ticks, $\Delta\theta_j$, is not exactly 5-min, we scale again the generated return using the same scaling formula

$$r_j' = \hat{r}_j \left(\frac{\Delta\theta_j}{\overline{\Delta\theta}} \right)^{1/2}$$

where $\overline{\Delta\theta}$ is 5 min. If there is a data hole, the sum of the generated return $\hat{r}_i$ is computed until the sum of the added 5-min intervals is larger than the size of the data hole measured in ϑ-time. The sum of the returns is scaled with the same technique as individual returns.

The simulated logarithmic prices, x_j', are computed by adding the generated returns r_j' to the first real logarithmic price value x_0. The bid-ask prices are computed by subtracting or adding half the average spread, that is,

$$p_{ask,j}' = \exp\left(x_j' + \frac{\overline{s}}{2} \right)$$

and

$$p_{bid,j}' = \exp\left(x_j' - \frac{\overline{s}}{2} \right)$$

---

[10] In the simulations, ϵ is specified to be normally distributed. We also explored bootstrapping the residuals of the studied models. The main findings of the study remain unchanged between these two approaches.

The parameters and the normalized residuals of the GARCH(1,1) process are estimated using the maximum likelihood procedure presented in Chapter 8. The simulated returns are generated from the simulated normalized residuals and the estimated parameters. The estimated parameters of the AR(p)-GARCH(1,1) processes together with the simulated residuals are used to generate the simulated returns for this process. As before, half of the average spread is subtracted (added) from the simulated price process to obtain the simulated bid (ask) prices.

For each replication we start by generating the simulated data a year before the model is tested. This year is 1989 and it is used to create the history dependency in returns and to initialize the different trading model indicators.

Empirical Results The simulated data are the 5-min ϑ-time series,[11] from January 1, 1990, to December 31, 1996, for three major foreign exchange rates, USD-DEM, USD-CHF (Swiss Franc), USD-FRF (French Franc), and the most liquid cross-rate DEM-JPY (Deutsche Mark – Japanese Yen). From Chapter 6, we know that high-frequency data inherits intraday seasonalities and require deseasonalization. We use for this study the deseasonalization methodology presented in Chapter 6. Our data set contains 671,040 observations per currency. The simulations for each currency and process are done for 1000 replications.

Before discussing the details of different studies, we present in Table 11.6 results that substantiate the claims made at the beginning of this section. We give a summary of the p-values of the main performance measures for the USD-DEM, USD-CHF, USD-FRF, and DEM-JPY. The p-value[12] represents the fraction of simulations generating a performance measure larger than the original.

The methodology of this study places a historical realization in the simulated distribution of the performance measure under the assumed process and calculates its one-sided p-value.[13] This indicates whether the historical realization is likely to be generated from this particular distribution or not. More important, it indicates

---

[11] The real-time system uses tick-by-tick data for its trading recommendations. The simulations in this study are carried out with 5-min data as it is computationally expensive to use the tick-by-tick data for the simulations. The historical performance of the currency pairs from the 5-min series are within a few tenths of a percent for all performance measures with the performance of the real-time trading models utilizing the tick-by-tick data. Therefore, there is no loss of generality from the use of the 5-min frequency for the simulations instead of the tick-by-tick feed.

[12] The p-value represents a decreasing index of the reliability of a result. The higher the p-value, the less we can believe that the observed relation between variables in the samples is a reliable indicator of the relation between the respective variables in the population. Specifically, the p-value represents the probability of error that is involved in accepting our observed result as valid, that is, as *representative of the population*. For example, a p-value of 0.05 indicates that there is a 5% probability that the relation between the variables found in our sample is *purely coincidental*. In other words, assuming that in the population there was no relation between those variables whatsoever, and by repeating the experiment, we could expect that in approximately every 20 replications of the experiment there would be one in which the relation between the variables in question would be equal or stronger than ours. In many areas of research, the p-value of 5% is treated as a *borderline acceptable* level.

[13] p-value calculations reported in this study are the *simulated* p-values obtained from the distribution of 1000 replications of a given performance measure. For brevity, we simply refer to it as p-value in the text.

TABLE 11.6 *p*-value Comparisons.

p-value comparisons with random walk (RW), GARCH(1,1), and AR(4)-GARCH(1,1). The *p*-values are expressed in percentage. The definitions of the three performance measures are presented in Section 11.3.

Currency	RW	GARCH(1,1)	AR(4)-GARCH(1,1)
Annual return			
USD-DEM	0.3	0.4	0.1
USD-CHF	8.9	8.4	3.7
USD-FRF	1.2	0.9	0.3
DEM-JPY	2.1	1.2	0.5
Xeffective			
USD-DEM	0.0	0.1	0.1
USD-CHF	0.7	1.4	1.9
USD-FRF	0.2	0.1	0.2
DEM-JPY	0.2	0.4	0.1
Reffective			
USD-DEM	0.0	0.0	0.0
USD-CHF	0.6	0.9	2.3
USD-FRF	0.1	0.1	0.1
DEM-JPY	0.1	0.4	0.1

whether the historical performance is likely to occur in the future. A small *p*-value (less than 5%) indicates that the historical performance lies in the tail of the distribution and the studied performance distribution is not representative of the data-generating process, given that the trading model is a good one. If the process that generates the performance distribution is close to the data-generating process of the foreign exchange returns, the historical performance would lie within two standard deviations of the performance distribution, indicating that the studied process may be retained as representative of the data-generating process.

Random Walk Process   The results for the random walk process for USD-DEM time series are reported in Table 11.7. The first and the second columns are the historical realization and the *p*-value of the corresponding performance measures. The remaining columns report the $5th$ and the $95th$ percentiles, mean, standard deviation, skewness, and the kurtosis of the simulations.

After the transaction costs, actual data with the USD-DEM, USD-CHF, USD-FRF and DEM-JPY yield an annualized total return of 9.63, 3.66, 8.20, and 6.43%, respectively. The USD-CHF has the weakest performance relative to the other three currencies. The X_{eff} and R_{eff} performance of the USD-DEM, USD-FRF, and DEM-JPY are all positive and range between 3 and 4%. For the USD-CHF, the X_{eff} and R_{eff} are -1.68 and -4.23%, reflecting the weakness of its performance.

TABLE 11.7 Random Walk Simulations for USD-DEM.

The second column presents the performance of the trading model with the actual data. The results under columns p-value, percentile, mean, standard deviation, skewness, and kurtosis present the values of these statistics from 1000 replications with the random walk process computed every 5-min for a period from 1990 to 1996. The p-values are reported in percentage terms (e.g., 0.3 refers to 0.3%). The definitions of the performance measures are presented in Sections 11.2.2 and 11.3.

Description	Historical realization	p-value (in %)	Percentile (5%, 95%)	Mean	St.Dev	Skew.	Kurt.
Annual return	9.63	0.3	-11.38, 4.03	-3.44	4.74	0.09	-0.13
Xeffective	3.78	0.0	-20.25, -4.14	-12.11	5.09	0.13	-0.23
Reffective	4.43	0.0	-26.42, -7.70	-16.80	5.90	0.03	-0.20
Max drawdown	11.02	100.0	25.26, 94.86	53.79	21.36	-0.71	0.21
Deal frequency	1.68	100.0	2.20, 2.71	2.46	0.16	-0.10	-0.19
Horizon:	7 days						
Xeffective	3.47	0.0	-19.65, -4.24	-11.83	4.76	0.08	-0.15
Reffective	1.80	0.0	-24.14, -7.21	-15.51	5.20	0.05	-0.15
Horizon:	29 days						
Xeffective	3.27	0.0	-20.21, -4.36	-12.10	4.95	0.07	-0.23
Reffective	2.16	0.0	-27.05, -8.07	-17.45	5.91	0.02	-0.28
Horizon:	117 days						
Xeffective	4.07	0.0	-20.85, -3.42	-12.21	5.44	0.10	-0.32
Reffective	5.10	0.0	-31.01, -6.53	-18.10	7.49	0.26	0.25
Horizon:	301 days						
Xeffective	4.62	0.0	-23.37, -2.42	-11.89	6.32	0.39	0.02
Reffective	6.83	0.0	-27.85, -3.25	-14.56	7.49	0.35	0.16

The p-values of the annualized return for the USD-DEM, USD-CHF, USD-FRF, and DEM-JPY are 0.3, 8.9, 1.2, and 2.1%, respectively. For the USD-DEM and USD-FRF, as reported in Table 11.6, the p-values are less than the 2% level and it is about 2% for the USD-CHF. In the case of the USD-CHF, the p-value for the annualized return is 8.9, which is well above the 5% level. As indicated in Section 11.3, the annualized return only utilizes two points of the equity curve leaving a large degrees of freedom to infinitely many paths that would be compatible with a given total return. X_{eff} and R_{eff} are more stringent performance measures, which utilize the entire equity curve in their calculations. The p-values of X_{eff} and R_{eff} are 0.0, 0.0% for USD-DEM, 0.7 and 0.6% for USD-CHF, 0.2 and 0.1% for USD-FRF, and 0.2 and 0.1% for DEM-JPY. The p-values for the X_{eff} and R_{eff} are all less than 1%, rejecting the null hypothesis that the random walk process is consistent with the data-generating process of exchange rate returns.

The maximum drawdowns for the USD-DEM, USD-CHF, USD-FRF and DEM-JPY are 11.02, 16.08, 11.36, and 12.03%. The mean maximum drawdowns from the simulated random walk processes are 53.79, 63.68, 47.68, and 53.49 for the USD-DEM, USD-CHF, USD-FRF, and DEM-JPY, respectively. The mean of the simulated maximum drawdowns are three or four times larger than the actual maximum drawdowns. The deal frequencies are 1.68, 1.29, 1.05, and 2.14 per week for the four currency pairs from the actual data. The deal frequencies indicate that the RTT model trades on average no more than two trades per week although the data feed is at the 5-min frequency. The mean simulated deal frequencies are 2.46, 1.98, 1.65, and 3.08, which are significantly larger than the actual ones.

The values for the maximum drawdown and the deal frequency indicate that the random walk simulation will yield larger maximum drawdown and deal frequency values relative to the values of these statistics from the actual data. In other words, the random walk simulations deal more frequently and result in more volatile equity curves on average relative to the equity curve from the actual data. Correspondingly, the p-values indicate that the random walk process cannot be representative of the actual foreign exchange series under these two performance measures. The summary statistics of the simulated performance measures have negligible skewness and statistically insignificant excess kurtosis. This indicates that the distributions of the performance measures are symmetric and do not exhibit fat tails.

The simulation results with the random walk process demonstrate that the real-time trading model is a consistent model. In other words, a process with no mean and a homoskedastic variance should only perform to generate an average return that would match the mean transaction costs. This consistency property is an essential ingredient of a trading model and the real-time trading model passes this consistency test. The means of the simulations indicate that the distributions are correctly centered at the average transaction costs, which is expected under the random walk process. For instance, the mean simulated deal frequency of the USD-DEM is 2.46 deals per week or 127.92 (2.46×52) deals per year. The relative spread for the USD-DEM is 0.00025, which in turn indicates an average transaction cost of -3.20% per year. Given that the mean of the simulated annualized return is -3.44, we can conclude that the mean of the simulated annualized return distribution is centered around the mean transaction cost.

The behavior of the performance measures across 7-day, 29-day, 117-day and 301-day horizons is also investigated with X_{eff} and R_{eff}. The importance of the performance analysis at various horizons is that it permits a more detailed analysis of the equity curve at the predetermined points in time. These horizons correspond approximately to a week, a month, 4 months and a year's performance. The X_{eff} and R_{eff} values indicate that the RTT model performance improves over longer time horizons. This is in accordance with the low dealing frequency of the RTT model. In all horizons, the p-values for the X_{eff} and R_{eff} are less than a half a percent for USD-DEM, USD-FRF, and DEM-JPY. For USD-CHF, the p-values are less than 2.4% for all horizons. Overall, the multihorizon analysis indicates that the random walk process is not consistent with the data-generating process of the foreign exchange returns.

TABLE 11.8   GARCH(1,1) parameter estimates.

The sample is 5-min returns from 1990–1996.

	USD-DEM	USD-CHF	USD-FRF	DEM-JPY
α_0	4.95 (4.23)	0.11 (0.12)	9.38 (7.09)	2.97 (4.03)
α_1	0.1111 (0.0005)	0.1032 (0.0007)	0.1572 (0.0007)	0.0910 (0.0005)
β_1	0.8622 (0.0007)	0.8578 (0.0009)	0.8137 (0.0009)	0.8988 (0.0006)
LL	6.45	6.17	6.29	6.34
$Q(12)$	4810	4201	4256	3089
$\hat{\epsilon}_{\sigma^2}$	1.04	1.03	1.07	1.05
$\hat{\epsilon}_{sk}$	-0.07	-0.03	-0.05	0.16
$\hat{\epsilon}_{ku}$	11.73	7.28	22.93	27.73

GARCH(1,1) Process   A more realistic process for the foreign exchange returns is the GARCH(1,1) process, which allows for conditional heteroskedasticity. The GARCH(1,1) estimation results are presented in Table 11.8. The numbers in parentheses are the robust standard errors and the GARCH(1,1) parameters are statistically significant at the 5% level for all currency pairs. The Ljung-Box statistic is calculated up to 12 lags for the standardized residuals and it is distributed with χ^2 with 12 degrees of freedom. The Ljung-Box statistics indicate serial correlation for the USD-DEM. The variances of the normalized residuals are near one. There is no evidence of skewness but the excess kurtosis remains large for the residuals.

In Table 11.9, the simulation results with the GARCH(1,1) process are presented for the USD-DEM rate. Because GARCH(1,1) allows for conditional heteroskedasticity, it is expected that the simulated performance of the RTT model would yield higher p-values and retain the null hypothesis that GARCH(1,1) is consistent with the data-generating process of the foreign exchange returns. The results, however, indicate smaller p-values, which is in favor of a stronger rejection of this process relative to the random walk process.

One important reason for the rejection of the GARCH(1,1) process as well as the random walk model is that these are pure volatility processes without predictability of the direction of returns, which matters for trading models. Another reason is the aggregation property of the GARCH(1,1) process. The GARCH(1,1) process behaves more like a homoskedastic process as the frequency is reduced from high to low frequency. Because the RTT model trading frequency is less than two deals per week, the trading model does not pick up the 5-min level heteroskedastic structure at the weekly frequency. Rather, the heteroskedastic structure behaves as if it is measurement noise where the model takes positions, and this leads to the stronger rejection of the GARCH(1,1) as a candidate for the foreign exchange data-generating process.

TABLE 11.9 GARCH(1,1) simulations for USD-DEM.

Description	Historical realization	p-value (in %)	Percentile (%, 95%)	Mean	St.Dev	Skew.	Kurt.
Annual return	9.63	0.4	-11.14, 5.12	-3.27	4.90	-0.08	-0.01
Xeffective	3.78	0.1	-20.40, -3.16	-11.88	5.18	-0.07	-0.11
Reffective	4.43	0.0	-26.60, -6.37	-16.50	6.10	-0.14	-0.05
Max drawdown	11.02	100.0	24.17, 93.96	53.33	21.50	-0.73	0.30
Deal frequency	1.68	100.0	2.14, 2.64	2.39	0.15	-0.02	-0.15
Horizon:	7 days						
Xeffective	3.47	0.2	-19.56, -3.49	-11.64	4.90	-0.06	-0.03
Reffective	1.80	0.0	-24.19, -6.58	-15.37	5.38	-0.08	-0.05
Horizon:	29 days						
Xeffective	3.27	0.2	-19.95, -3.29	-11.86	5.00	-0.12	-0.04
Reffective	2.16	0.1	-26.92, -6.75	-17.20	6.04	-0.20	-0.03
Horizon:	117 days						
Xeffective	4.07	0.1	-21.24, -2.77	-11.91	5.56	0.03	-0.28
Reffective	5.10	0.1	-30.17, -5.44	-17.57	7.60	0.29	0.31
Horizon:	301 days						
Xeffective	4.62	0.2	-22.73, -1.48	-11.73	6.42	0.28	0.16
Reffective	6.83	0.3	-27.64, -2.01	-14.28	7.72	0.26	0.38

In a GARCH process, the conditional heteroskedasticity is captured at the frequency that the data have been generated. As it is moved away from this frequency to lower frequencies, the heteroskedastic structure slowly dies away leaving itself to a more homogeneous structure in time. More elaborate processes, such as the multiple horizon ARCH models (as in the HARCH process of Müller *et al.*, 1997a), possess conditionally heteroskedastic structure at all frequencies in general. The existence of a multiple frequency heteroskedastic structure seems to be more in line with the heterogeneous structure of the foreign exchange markets.

Table 11.6 we presented a summary of the p-values of the annualized return for the USD-DEM, USD-CHF, USD-FRF and DEM-JPY. In the case of the GARCH(1,1) simulation, they are 0.4, 8.4, 0.9, and 1.2%, respectively. All four currency pairs except USD-CHF yield p-values, which are smaller than 1.3%. The X_{eff} and R_{eff} are 0.1 and 0.0% for USD-DEM, 1.4 and 0.9 percent for USD-CHF, 0.1 and 0.1% for USD-FRF, and 0.4 and 0.4 percent for DEM-JPY.

The historical maximum drawdown and deal frequency of the RTT model is smaller than those generated from the simulated data. The maximum drawdowns for the USD-DEM, USD-CHF, USD-FRF, and DEM-JPY are 11.02, 16.08, 11.36, and 12.03 for the four currencies. The mean simulated drawdowns are 53.33, 60.58, 46.00, and 48.77 for the four currencies. The mean simulated maximum drawdowns are three to four times larger than the historical ones. The historical deal frequencies are 1.68, 1.29, 1.05, and 2.14. The mean simulated deal frequencies are 2.39, 1.87, 1.59, and 2.66 for the four currencies. The differences between the historical deal frequencies and the mean simulated deal frequencies remain large. Therefore, the examination of the GARCH(1,1) process with the maximum drawdown and the deal frequency indicates that the historical realizations of these two measures stay outside of the 5% level of simulated distributions of these two performance measures.

The mean simulated deal frequency for the USD-DEM is 2.39 trades per week. In annual terms, this is approximately 124.28 deals per year. The half spread for the USD-DEM series is about 0.00025 and this yields 3.11% when multiplied with the number of deals per year. The -3.11% return would be the annual transaction cost of the model. For the model to be profitable, it should yield more than 3.11% per year. Table 11.9 indicates that the RTT model generates an excess annual return of 9.63%, whereas the mean of the annualized return from the GARCH(1,1) process stays at the -3.27% level.

The multi-horizon examination of the equity curve with the X_{eff} and R_{eff} performance measures indicates that the GARCH(1,1) process as a candidate for the data generation mechanism is strongly rejected at all horizons from a 7-day horizon to a horizon as long as 301 days. The overall picture coming out of the test is not very different for the GARCH(1,1) than that of the random walk process.

AR(4)-GARCH(1,1) Process   A further direction is to investigate whether a conditional mean dynamics with GARCH(1,1) innovations would be a more successful characterization of the dynamics of the high-frequency foreign exchange returns. The conditional means of the foreign exchange returns are estimated with four lags of these returns. The additional lags did not lead to substantial increases in the likelihood value.

The results of the AR(4)-GARCH(1,1) optimization are presented in Table 11.10. The numbers in parentheses are the robust standard errors and all four lags are statistically significant at the 5% level. The negative autocorrelation is large and highly significant for the first lag of the returns. This is consistent with the high-frequency behavior of the foreign exchange returns and is also observed in Dacorogna *et al.* (1993). The Ljung-Box statistics still indicate serial correlation in the normalized residuals. The variances of the normalized residuals are near one. There is no evidence of skewness but the excess kurtosis remains large for the residuals.

The p-values of the annualized returns are presented in Table 11.6. They are 0.1, 3.7, 0.3, and 0.5% for the USD-DEM, USD-CHF, USD-FRF, and DEM-JPY. The results indicate that the AR(4)-GARCH(1,1) process is also rejected under the RTT model as a representative data generating process of foreign exchange returns. Here again, a possible explanation of this failure is the relationship between the dealing frequency of the model and the frequency of the simulated data. The AR(4)-GARCH(1,1) process is generated at the 5-min frequency but the model dealing frequency is between one or two deals per week. Therefore, the model picks up the high-frequency serial correlation as noise and this serial correlation works against the process. This cannot be treated as a failure of the RTT model.

TABLE 11.10 AR(4)-GARCH(1,1) parameter estimates.

The sample is 5-min return from 1990–1996. α_0 values are 10^{-9}. The numbers in parentheses are the standard errors. The standard errors of α_0 are 10^{-11}. LL is the average log likelihood value. $Q(12)$ refer to the Ljung-Box portmanteau test for serial correlation and it is distributed χ^2 with 12 degrees of freedom. The $\chi^2_{0.05}(12)$ is 21.03. $\hat{\epsilon}_{\sigma^2}$, $\hat{\epsilon}_{sk}$ and $\hat{\epsilon}_{ku}$ are the variance, skewness, and the excess kurtosis of the residuals.

	USD-DEM	USD-CHF	USD-FRF	DEM-JPY
α_0	3.90 (3.40)	8.19 (9.03)	7.28 (5.80)	2.92 (3.93)
α_1	0.099 (0.0005)	0.0874 (0.0006)	0.1349 (0.0007)	0.088 (0.0005)
β_1	0.8796 (0.0006)	0.8833 (0.0007)	0.8411 (0.0008)	0.9008 (0.0006)
γ_1	-0.176 (0.001)	-0.208 (0.001)	-0.200 (0.002)	-0.130 (0.002)
γ_2	-0.011 (0.001)	-0.031 (0.002)	-0.025 (0.002)	-0.090 (0.002)
γ_3	0.003 (0.001)	-0.001 (0.002)	-0.005 (0.002)	-0.005 (0.002)
γ_4	-0.004(0.001)	-0.002 (0.001)	-0.008 (0.002)	-0.010 (0.002)
$\bar{LL}$	6.46	6.19	6.30	6.35
$Q(12)$	623	531	492	374
$\hat{\epsilon}_{\sigma^2}$	1.04	1.03	1.07	1.05
$\hat{\epsilon}_{sk}$	-0.07	-0.04	-0.05	0.15
$\hat{\epsilon}_{ku}$	12.29	7.86	21.84	27.98

Rather, this strong rejection is evidence of the failure of the temporal aggregation properties of the AR(4)-GARCH(1,1) process at lower frequencies.

The rejection of the AR(4)-GARCH(1,1) process with the X_{eff} and R_{eff} is even stronger and very much in line with the results for the random walk and the GARCH(1,1). The p-values of the X_{eff} and R_{eff} are 0.1, 0.0 percent for USD-DEM, 1.9, 2.3% for USD-CHF, 0.2, 0.1% for USD-FRF, and 0.1, 0.1% for DEM-JPY. The p-values remain low at all horizons for the X_{eff} and R_{eff}. The p-values of the maximum drawdown and the deal frequency also indicate that in almost all replications the AR(4)-GARCH(1,1) generates higher maximum drawdowns and deal frequencies.

Conclusions This extensive analysis of real-time trading models with high-frequency data suggests two main conclusions. First, technical trading models can generate excess returns, which are explained neither by traditional theoretical processes nor by luck. Second, the foreign exchange rates contain conditional mean dynamics that are neither present in the random walk nor GARCH(1,1), and AR-GARCH(1,1) processes.

The dealing frequency of the model is approximately between one and two per week although the data feed is at the 5-min frequency. Because the model's trading frequency is less than two deals per week, it does not pick up the 5-min level heteroskedastic structure at the weekly frequency. Overall, the results presented in this section have a general message to the standard paradigm in econometrics. It is

TABLE 11.11   AR(4)-GARCH(1,1) simulations for USD-DEM.

Description	Historical realization	p-value (in %)	Percentile (5%, 95%)	Mean	St.Dev	Skew.	Kurt.
Annual return	9.63	0.1	-10.46, 3.13	-3.68	4.13	-0.01	-0.16
Xeffective	3.78	0.1	-16.72, -3.16	-9.95	4.27	-0.02	-0.18
Reffective	4.43	0.0	-21.37, -5.28	-13.37	4.93	-0.07	-0.15
Max drawdown	11.02	100.0	21.73, 84.55	49.07	19.16	-0.59	0.03
Deal frequency	1.68	100.0	1.89, 2.35	2.12	0.14	-0.04	-0.26
Horizon:	7 days						
Xeffective	3.47	0.1	-16.53, -2.86	-9.72	4.13	0.01	-0.18
Reffective	1.80	0.2	-19.63, -4.95	-12.33	4.45	-0.01	-0.17
Horizon:	29 days						
Xeffective	3.27	0.1	-16.90, -3.24	-9.94	4.21	0.00	-0.11
Reffective	2.16	0.1	-21.54, -5.87	-13.67	4.87	-0.02	-0.02
Horizon:	117 days						
Xeffective	4.07	0.1	-17.37, -2.83	-9.97	4.50	0.00	-0.26
Reffective	5.10	0.0	-24.10, -4.75	-14.17	5.98	0.23	0.21
Horizon:	301 days						
Xeffective	4.62	0.1	-18.19, -2.01	-9.83	4.95	0.19	0.16
Reffective	6.83	0.1	-22.90, -2.91	-12.15	6.15	0.34	0.53

not sufficient to develop sophisticated statistical processes and choose an arbitrary data frequency (e.g., 1 week, 1 month, annual) claiming afterward that this particular process does a "good job" of capturing the dynamics of the data-generating process. In financial markets, the data generating process is a complex network of layers where each layer corresponds to a particular frequency. A successful characterization of such data generating processes should be estimated with models whose parameters are functions of *intra* and *inter*-frequency dynamics. In other fields, such as in signal processing, paradigms of this sort are already in place. Our understanding of financial markets would be increased with the incorporation of such paradigms into financial econometrics. Our trading model, within this perspective, helps us to observe this subtle structure as a diagnostic tool.

11.7   TRADING MODEL PORTFOLIOS

In the previous sections we have described what trading models are and how we can optimize and test them. In this section we will briefly study the combination of different trading model strategies into portfolios and discuss the particular case of currency risk hedging.

Any trading strategy is based on some specific indicators and decision rules and then will perform better in some market conditions. To reduce the risk implied by the use of such trading models, it is common to combine various trading strategies, which provide different trading signals for the same asset, in a

portfolio of models. As these models generally do not have the same clustering of good and bad periods, the overall risk is then reduced. But this is true
only if the composition of the trading model portfolio is not changed too often.
Dynamic modifications of the trading model portfolio, which keep a reasonable
risk profile, are very hard to obtain and at O&A we advocate choosing static
portfolio strategies where the dynamic behavior is left to the trading models themselves.

The optimal trading model portfolio strategy depends on certain decisions of
the investor such as the choice of the investment assets, frequency of changes,
and limits of risk and exposure. One of the main problems is the selection of
the trading models to be used in such a portfolio. It is easy to test many different combinations and to select the best one, but such a procedure can produce
undesirable results. In fact, during this selection procedure, the risk of overfitting particular historical data may again occur from the back door. To overcome these types of problems, it is often desirable to use an equally weighted
portfolio—that is, a portfolio where the same proportion of capital or credit limit
is invested in each trading model. Another possibility is to select the optimal
trading model portfolio using a robust optimization procedure, like in trading
model optimization (Section 11.5.1), but we will not discuss such an approach
here.

Table 11.12 compares the performance obtained for a trading model portfolio,
which corresponds to an equally weighted portfolio strategy, to the performance
of the individual trading models on the same period. The analysis period is from
January 1993 to December 1997. During this period, all these trading models
were running in the real-time O&A information system with no reoptimizations.
On this table we observe very well that for the same annualized total return the
risk of the portfolio is considerably lower than the average risk on the individual
models. The maximum drawdown of the portfolio is about half of the average
maximum drawdown of the models and the annualized X_{eff} is one of the largest.
The variation of the total return of the portfolio over the years is plotted on Figure 11.4.

Portfolios of trading models can be used as dynamic investment strategies in
many financial markets, but the complexity of the optimization of such portfolios
based on a very large number of trading models (needed for a good diversification)
would be extremely hard to control. As we observed in the previous sections, the
optimization of the different trading strategies is in itself a complicated process
that needs to be done at regular intervals to take into account the nonstationarity
of the underlying time series.

In the case of foreign exchange, an interesting application of portfolio trading
models is the dynamic hedging of currency risk. In this case, the number of models
to optimize is reduced and it is reasonable to consider a dynamic hedging strategy
based on the trading recommendations. In the next section we will provide a brief
description of this approach.

TABLE 11.12   Portfolio performance of O&A trading models.

Performance comparison between 10 O&A class RTT, RTM trading models, and an equally weighted portfolio of the same models. The different performance measures displayed are the annualized total return R, the risk-sensitive performance measure X_{eff}, the maximum drawdown D, and the annualized Sharpe ratio S.

FX rate	Model	R	X_{eff}	D	S
USD-DEM	RTT	6.8%	2.3%	10.2%	0.73
	RTM	3.4%	1.3%	9.8%	0.51
DEM-JPY	RTT	1.7%	-2.6%	16.1%	0.19
	RTM	9.3%	6.4%	8.9%	1.32
USD-CHF	RTT	3.7%	-1.2%	10.9%	0.38
	RTM	2.5%	-0.3%	13.7%	0.36
USD-FRF	RTT	9.2%	4.7%	9.9%	1.03
	RTM	5.6%	2.5%	10.0%	0.71
GBP-DEM	RTT	5.6%	2.2%	14.3%	0.69
	RTM	5.0%	2.8%	8.1%	0.79
Average values		5.2%	1.8%	11.2%	0.71
Portfolio		5.2%	4.1%	5.5%	1.09

11.8 CURRENCY RISK HEDGING

Hedging problems arise whenever an investor, for example, a fund manager or a commercial organization, is holding foreign assets such as foreign securities over a period of time. The foreign assets are denominated in a foreign currency. The investor measures the performance of his/her investment in terms of the investor's home currency. The foreign assets have a degree of volatility in terms of their own currency. Due to the foreign exchange rate movements the volatility is, however, higher when expressed in terms of the investor's home currency. This implies additional risk. By additionally taking a short position in the foreign currency, this implicit foreign currency exposure can be compensated and the risk can be reduced; this is the basic idea of hedging. Whereas a constant short position is referred to as *static* hedging, this section deals with *dynamic* hedging where the foreign currency positions vary over time.

In this section, a strategy of hedging the foreign exchange (FX) risk associated with foreign investment is specified. As an innovative element of this strategy, real-time trading models are used. The whole strategy can then be called a dynamic overlay. To be successful, we need profitable trading models that are only weakly

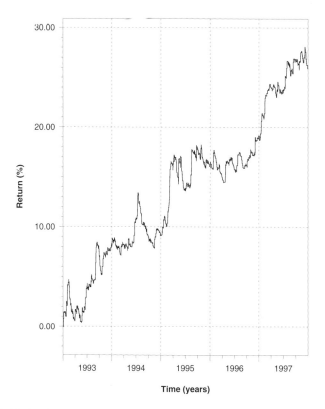

FIGURE 11.4 Total return of a portfolio of 10 O&A trading models over 5 years.

correlated or anticorrelated to the usual primary investments, because positive correlation would imply an increased risk.

An investor's risk/return decisions must be matched to the set of all possible investments (including dynamic allocation of capital to the foreign currencies), the *feasible set*. Figure 11.5 shows this feasible set as a shadowed region. The upper-left border of this set is termed the *efficient frontier*; those investment portfolios lying along this frontier deliver the maximum possible return for the minimum possible risk or the minimum risk for the set of best possible returns. The point at which an investor's indifference curve has a common tangent with the efficient frontier represents the best possible match between the investor's preferences and the possible investment portfolios. The right, dashed vertical line in Figure 11.5 indicates the expectation for the risk of a primary investment, which is left completely unhedged. A circle is drawn where this vertical line intersects with the horizontal line indicating the expected return of the primary investment.

The dashed vertical line to the left in Figure 11.5 indicates the reduction of risk achieved through an optimal static hedge of the primary investment, which usually implies short positions in all foreign currencies in which the foreign assets

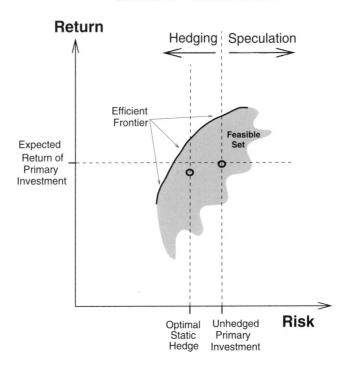

FIGURE 11.5 Set of feasible portfolios available to an investor when he/she implements a currency hedging strategy. The efficient frontier lies on the upper-left edge of the set (gray area), or along the darkened edge in the figure.

of the primary investment are denominated. In practice, this reduction in risk may be purchased at the price of slightly reduced returns due to transactions costs, thus the circle that intersects this risk line is lowered to slightly below the expected return of the primary investment in this example.[14] This optimal static hedge has succeeded in reducing risk. However, note that there may still be some distance between the static point and the efficient frontier of the feasible set, which is defined by the use of dynamic allocation to foreign currencies through trading models. The distance between the statically hedged portfolios and the efficient frontier marks the improvement that can be attained through a dynamic currency overlay using trading models.

The subject of currency hedging has been discussed in the literature for some time. In Froot (1993), full hedging is recommended for minimizing the risk due to *short-term* FX volatility. On the other hand, it is also shown that a lower amount of hedging or even no hedging is better for minimizing the risk of *long-term* value

---

[14] Whereas the transactions costs of a one-time, static FX transaction are minimal, the short positions in the foreign currencies may imply considerable costs of carry due to interest rate differential between the two currencies. These costs, which are sometimes also in favor of the investor, may lead to a distinct return difference between statically hedged and unhedged portfolios.

fluctuations of the investment. Depending on the time horizon, there is thus a certain range, a scope within which the hedging ratio can be chosen.

Levich and Thomas (1993a) go one step further. They hedge a position *dynamically* by varying the hedge ratios over time. They show that this is *profitable* as compared to no hedging or static hedging. In their most successful strategy, a "currency overlay" with many currencies involved, they change the hedge ratios by following simple "technical trading signals."

In the overlay strategy described here, the allowed ranges of static hedging and the exposure due to dynamic hedging are limited.[15] Thus the main purpose of hedging, which is reducing the risk due to FX rate volatility, is maintained. On the other hand, we have a well-founded additional profit expectation, based on the profitability of the trading models and trading model portfolios.

11.8.1 The Hedging Ratio and the "Neutral Point"

Currency hedging means, for an investor who has bought a foreign asset such as equity of value s, holding a short position of size $-s_h$ in the foreign currency in order to minimize the volatility of the value of his/her total position due to FX rate fluctuations. The hedging ratio h is defined as

$$h = \frac{s_h}{s} \tag{11.31}$$

The study by Froot (1993) shows that choosing the best h, the one that minimizes the total volatility, is not trivial and depends on the time horizon of the investor. For short-term investors, the best h is 1 or slightly less; for long-term investors, who hold their position over many years, the best choice of h is about 0.35. In Froot (1993), the hedging ratio h is assumed to be constant over time.

In our *dynamic* hedging approach (we follow here the method suggested in Müller *et al.*, 1997b), we want to vary h over time, following some real-time trading models to reach an additional profit or to reduce the risk of the primary investment expressed in the home currency. This requirement will, when used during optimization, automatically set limits to the type of hedging strategy to use. In the lack of a clear criterion like reducing the risk, some rules could be introduced to achieve desirable features like, for instance, h would not depart too much from the best value—that is, in most cases, between 0.35 and 1 according to Froot (1993). Each of the individual foreign currencies has its own hedging ratio h_i, but there is also the option of taking only one *global* hedging ratio h for all currencies. The following discussion applies to both the individual h_i and h.

In lack of an objective risk criterion, most investors set some limits $h_{\min}$ and $h_{\max}$ on the choice of the hedging ratio, often to satisfy some institutional constraints or to limit the risk if they have no other quantitative criterion to do this. A typical choice might be $h_{\min} = 0$ (no hedging) and $h_{\max} = 1$ (full hedging).

---

[15] Interested readers are referred to our internal paper where the methodology is described in detail, Müller *et al.* (1997b).

In the middle between the extreme h values, we define the *neutral point*, h, of the hedging strategy to be

$$h_{\text{mid}} = \frac{h_{\min} + h_{\max}}{2} \qquad (11.32)$$

and the total possible range Δh of dynamic hedging is

$$\Delta h = h_{\max} - h_{\min} \qquad (11.33)$$

We have seen that the O&A real-time trading models vary their gearings between two limits called "gearing -1" and "gearing 1" as explained in Section 11.2.1. If the neutral point h_{mid} is chosen for static hedging and if there is only one foreign currency and one trading model (for the FX rate between that foreign currency and the home currency), these trading limits directly correspond to the limits $h_{\min}$ and $h_{\max}$. However, the investor may decide to allow wider exposure limits for the dynamic positions than those of the static positions. The situation becomes more complicated in the presence of many currencies and many trading models.

11.8.2   Risk/Return of an Overlay with Static and Dynamic Positions

To solve the allocation problem, a basis of portfolio theory has to be applied to our particular overlay problem.

A portfolio Π can be written in terms of the sum of the primary investment (PI), a static foreign exchange position placed in order to hedge foreign exchange risk (SH) and a series of variable positions placed to dynamically hedge foreign exchange risk (DH)

$$\Pi = PI + SH + DH \qquad (11.34)$$

In what follows, we refer to a portfolio diversified in $i = 1$ to n currencies and dynamically hedged by $j = 1$ to m trading models:

$$\Pi = \sum_{i=1}^{n} \alpha_i I_i + \sum_{i=1}^{n} h_i \alpha_i R_i^{FX} + \sum_{j=1}^{m} \omega_j R_j^{TM} \qquad (11.35)$$

Expectation of portfolio returns, or changes in value, can then be written as $E[\Delta\Pi]$, or as a sum of the expectation values of its comprising parts:

$$E[\Delta\Pi] = E[\Delta I] + E[\Delta R^{FX}] + E[\Delta R^{TM}] \qquad (11.36)$$

that is,

$$E[\Delta\Pi] = \sum_{i=1}^{n} \alpha_i E[\Delta I_i] + \sum_{i=1}^{n} h_i \alpha_i E[\Delta R_i^{FX}] + \sum_{j=1}^{m} \omega_j E[\Delta R_i^{TM}] \qquad (11.37)$$

where

ΔI_i = the fractional return of the ith underlying foreign investment component at a given time, t, and over a time horizon, Δt; $\Delta I_i \equiv \Delta I_i(\Delta t, t) \equiv (I_t - I_{t-\Delta t})/I_{t-\Delta t}$, where I_i are in units of the home currency,

α_i = the amount of the portfolio allocated to the ith currency in units of the home currency,

h_i = the unitless static hedging ratio for the ith foreign currency,

ΔR_i^{FX} = the portfolio returns due to fluctuations in the static hedge positions,

ω_i = the weights given to each trading model (in units of the home currency), and

ΔR_j^{TM} = the trading model return values.

The risk of the portfolio is characterized by the variance of the portfolio returns $\sigma_{\Delta\Pi}^2$:

$$\sigma_{\Delta\Pi}^2 = E\left[(\Delta\Pi - E[\Delta\Pi])^2\right] \qquad (11.38)$$

11.8.3 Dynamic Hedging with Exposure Constraints

To compute the efficient frontier of the dynamic hedging strategy, we need to optimize the return given the risk or conversely optimize the risk given the return. Such an optimization is suitably done using the Lagrange multiplier technique. We can maximize the quantity[16] $E[\Delta\Pi] - \lambda' \sigma_{\Delta\Pi}^2$ or, more conveniently, minimize $\sigma_{\Delta\Pi}^2 - \lambda E[\Delta\Pi]$. The parameter λ is the Lagrange multiplier and can be varied from 0 (considering risk only) to high positive values (considering mainly return while keeping risk under some control) to get the whole efficient frontier. Each value of λ corresponds to a point on the efficient frontier. Let us call U the target function to be minimized,

$$U = \sigma_{\Delta\Pi}^2 - \lambda E[\Delta\Pi] \qquad (11.39)$$

where $E[\Delta\Pi]$ and $\sigma_{\Delta\Pi}^2$ have been defined and expressed in Equations 11.37 and 11.38.

Some components of the total portfolio have free coefficients, which can be determined with the goal of minimizing the target function U: the hedging ratios h_i and the amounts of money (maximum exposures) ω_j allocated to the trading models. These coefficients are generally subject to constraints:

1. The trading model sizes ω_j must not be negative: $\omega_j \geq 0$. In fact, such negative ω_j would mean doing the opposite of the trading recommendations. In these cases, this will lead to new transaction costs, which make the actual returns much worse than the formal results suggest. Therefore, we exclude negative trading model coefficients.

---

[16] This first quantity is very similar to X_{eff}, the risk-corrected return derived in Section 11.3.1. The optimization problem comes back to optimizing X_{eff} for different risk aversion constants.

2. The static hedging ratios h_i are limited to an allowed range between $h_{\min,i}$ and $h_{\max,i}$. Generally there are regulations or risk management rules that do not allow the investors to take too extreme positions, therefore hedging ratios that are above $h_{\max,i}$ or below $h_{\min,i}$ are generally excluded.

The constraints make a direct solution of the allocation problem impossible. The minimization of U (a quadratic function of the coefficients) under linear constraints on the coefficients is a special case of *quadratic programming*. A technique developed by Markowitz (1959), based on the simplex method, can solve this problem; we follow Markowitz (1987). There is no local minimum of U in the space of the coefficients; this can be proven. The solution, once found, always represents the global minimum.

Currency-wise exposure limits may be less rigid than those on the hedging ratios. But exposure limits on foreign currencies are not simple, as they involve several assets together. The exposure constraints are linear in ω_j and h_i. As the simpler constraints, they can be fully accounted for in the framework of the solution method presented by Markowitz (1987).

The whole efficient frontier can be obtained by minimizing U for different choices of the Lagrange multiplier λ. The left-hand side of the efficient frontier obviously starts at $\lambda = 0$ where the return of the portfolio has no influence and only risk counts. The right-hand side limitation of the efficient frontier is less evident. For unconstrained dynamic strategies, the efficient frontier normally extends to infinity (when more and more money is allocated to trading models). A hedging strategy should obviously not deal with infinite risks. There should be a risk limit beyond which the strategies are considered unacceptable even if the formal exposure limits are not yet reached. But in the case of constraints, the efficient frontier generally has a genuine end on the right-hand side. Therefore, we use a "shooting" strategy for determining the λ value that approximately leads to the desired maximum risk at the right end of the efficient frontier. The method by Markowitz (1987) helps us to find this value.

11.8.4 Concluding Remarks

This problem turns out to be rather difficult and requires many different inputs and programs to solve it in a practical way. The algorithm needs the following main ingredients:

- The user-defined investment goals such as primary investment and exposure limits.
- Time series of returns of all assets in the portfolio: FX rates, interest rates (or their differentials), and typical primary investments such as stock indices and bond indices of many currencies.
- Time series of returns of the trading models used for dynamic hedging (including transaction costs).
- The computation of mean returns and the covariance matrix of all relevant assets.

- A target function to be optimized, measuring risk and return, with a Lagrange multiplier that sets the balance between risk and return. This function depends on two types of parameters, which are static hedging ratios and trading model allocation sizes.

- A method to solve the quadratic programming problem with linear constraints (exposure limits).

In conclusion, we are able to solve the dynamic overlay problem under exposure constraints with a quite complex but well-understood algorithm. The result is the efficient frontier of feasible solutions, each with a particular risk/return profile. It is the choice of the investor to decide which portfolio on the efficient frontier he/she wants to follow.

12

TOWARD A THEORY OF
HETEROGENEOUS MARKETS

At the end of this in-depth review of some of the techniques and models used with high-frequency data, there is clear evidence that price movements of foreign exchange rates and other financial assets for short to medium-term horizons are predictable to some extent. This is substantiated by a positive forecast quality and high real-time trading model returns (e.g. Dacorogna *et al.*, 1992; Pictet *et al.*, 1992; Gençay *et al.*, 2001c, 2002). More generally, financial returns of whatever asset substantially depart from the random walk model and are being predicted with some success by market participants.

Where does this sustained predictability originate? Are the real-time trading models, for instance, successful in capturing the inefficiencies of the foreign exchange (FX) market? Because this market is widely held to be the most efficient of the financial markets, does this success conflict with the theory of efficient markets, which precludes the ability to forecast and denies the existence of profitable trading models? Should we conclude from this evidence that markets are inefficient? We believe that we should rather adapt our theory of the financial market to the reality of the stylized facts and of markets that are very efficient in a newly defined way.

The motivation of this chapter is to explain why and how markets can be at the same time highly efficient and to some extent predictable. There are a number of reasons for this that are all associated with market dynamics. We want to put in perspective the current theory of efficiency and suggest to move beyond it. This is one of the big challenges ahead in the theory of finance. Many researchers are working in this special field, such as the whole movement of "behavioral finance" around Robert Shiller,[1] or parts of the econophysics group and many others who see the need to find ways of moving from a rather static definition to a more dynamic one.

12.1 DEFINITION OF EFFICIENT MARKETS

In conventional economics, markets are assumed to be efficient if all available information is reflected in current market prices (Fama, 1970, 1991). Economists have embarked on weak, semi-strong, and strong-form efficiency tests. The weak-form tests investigate whether market prices actually reflect all available information. The semi-strong tests are based on so-called event studies, where the degree of market reaction to "news announcements" is analyzed. The strong-form tests, finally, analyze whether specific investors or groups have private information from which to take advantage. By and large, most studies conclude that the major financial markets are efficient and that all information is reflected in current prices. However, the conclusions of such studies have been bogged down by methodological questions: in particular, whether any observed departures from market efficiency are due to any genuine market inefficiency or whether a deficiency of the market pricing model is being used as a yardstick to compare actual with theoretical prices.

The inference that in an efficient market no excess return can be generated with trading models is based on the assumption that all investors act according to the rational expectation model (Shiller, 1989; Fama, 1970). If this assumption is wrong, the conclusion that forecasting is impossible is also questionable. The assumption of rational expectations has been called into question on various platforms and the idea of heterogeneous expectations has become of increasing interest to specialists. Shiller (1989), for example, argues that most participants in the stock market are not "smart investors" (following the rational expectation model) but rather follow trends and fashions. The modeling of "noise trader" has become a central subject of research in market microstructure models. On the FX market, there is much investigation of "speculative bubbles" and the influence of technical analysis on the dealer's strategy (see, for example, Frankel and Froot, 1990). Some attention has also been caught by the possibility of time-varying expectations, which better reflect to our view of the market (Bekaert and Hodrick, 1992). Variation over time in expected returns poses a challenge for asset pricing theory because it requires an explicit dynamic theory in contrast to the traditional static capital asset pricing model (CAPM).

---

[1] See, for instance, Shiller (2000) where the author claims that the market agents are essentially acting irrationally.

In summary, the conclusion that financial asset prices are not predictable is based on three assumptions: market prices reflect all the information available, news and events that hit the market are normally distributed, and the market is composed of homogeneous agents. The two first assumptions are reasonable starting points for the definition. The third assumption poses a real problem. It is clear that all market agents have in fact bounded rationality. They cannot be omniscient and do not all enjoy the same freedom of action and access to the markets. Recent works by Kurz (1994) and Gouree and Hommes (2000) present new theoretical models to tackle this problem. Introducing the heterogeneity of agents can give rise to very interesting nonlinear effects in the models. They show that many of the price fluctuations can be explained by endogenous effects. Similar conclusions are reached by Farmer and Lo (1999) in their discussion of market efficiency. They base their analysis on a comparison with the evolution of ecological systems. Farmer (1998) develops a market model inspired by ecological systems that contains agents with various trading strategies.

12.2   DYNAMIC MARKETS AND RELATIVISTIC EFFECTS

We just saw that conventional economics makes its inferences on efficient markets on the basis of a model in which economic agents are entities that act according to the rational expectation strategy. Any differences in planning horizons, frequency of trading, or institutional constraints are neglected. However, there is substantial empirical evidence that investors have heterogeneous expectations, as noted in Müller *et al.* (1993a) and Müller *et al.* (1997a). Surveys on the forecasts of participants in the FX market reflect the wide dispersion of expectation at any point in time. The huge volume of FX trading is another indication reinforcing this idea because it takes differences in expectation among market participants to explain why they trade.[2] In Chapter 7, we presented the heterogeneous market hypothesis; at the end of this book the need for such a view becomes clear. It is the most elegant way to reconcile market efficiency with the stylized facts. Lux and Marchesi (1999) have developed simulation models of financial markets that include agents with different strategies (fundamentalists and chartists). They were able to show (Lux and Marchesi, 2000) that this model can reproduce most of the empirical regularities (fat tails, long memory, and scaling law) even though they use normally distributed news in their simulations.

The theoretical work on financial markets with heterogeneous agents has also gained momentum in the literature. Among this literature, Brock (1993), Brock and Kleidon (1992), Brock and LeBaron (1996), Brock and Hommes (1997), and Hommes (2000) investigate the underlying source for the structural heterogeneity of financial markets. Brock (1993) studies the interacting particles system theory to build structural asset pricing models. Brock and Hommes (1997) build a general theory of expectation formation, which nests rational expectations in an

---

[2] Over $1500 billion US is traded every day in the different centers like Tokyo, London, and New York according to a survey taken every 3 years by the Bank for International Settlements (1999).

econometrically tractable system. Brock and Kleidon (1992) show how bid-ask spreads fluctuate over the day by firm size categories as a measure of "thickness" of the market. Brock and LeBaron (1996) stress not only the standard asymmetric information theory in matching key stylized facts, but also the importance of the role of multiple time scales. Hommes (2000) provides a review of recent work on heterogeneous agent financial theory.

There are many ways to describe heterogeneous expectations. We believe that the most promising approach is to differentiate the expectations according to their time dimension because we consider the *different time scales* of the market participants the key characteristic of the market. Some are short-term traders, others have long-term horizons with market makers at the short-term end of the scale and central banks at the long-term end. Contrary to the usual assumption, there is no privileged time scale in the market. The interaction of components with different time scales gives rise to characteristically relativistic effects[3] such as certain properties of volatility clusters, trend persistence, lag between interest rate adjustment, and FX rate adjustment. The latter is a good example of what conventional theory considers an inefficiency whereas we see it as an effect arising from the different time scales involved in the market. To take advantage of the lag in adjustment between interest rate and exchange rate moves, an investor needs to tie up his/her money for months or even years. This is a very long time for an FX trader. Some investors will thus tend to ignore these profit opportunities whereas others invest in them, as is testified by the development of managed currency funds based on this property. The combination of all of these effects ultimately enables the construction of successful forecasting and trading models.

In long time intervals, market price changes are "flatter" and have fewer relevant movements (trend changes) than in short-term intervals. The higher the resolution and the smaller the intervals, the larger the number of relevant price movements. The long and the short-term traders thus have different trading opportunities: the shorter the trading horizon, the greater the opportunity set. A market participant's response to outside events should always be viewed as relative to one's intrinsic opportunity set. A short-term trader does not react in the same way as a long-term trader. Economic decision makers, such as traders, treasurers, and central bankers, interpret the same information differently. The variation in perspective has the effect that specific price movements cannot lead to a uniform reaction; rather, they result in individual reactions of different components. In turn, these reactions give rise to secondary reactions, with the different components reacting to their respective initial response. Watching the intraday price movements, one clearly sees the sequences of secondary reactions triggered by the initial events. See, for example, Goodhart and Curcio (1991); Almeida *et al.* (1998) on news effect on the FX market or Franke and Hess (1997) on the

---

[3] We use here the term "relativistic" to express the dynamic interaction between different market components relative to each other rather than relative to the news that has impacted the market. These effects are sometimes called endogenous effects in the literature, Kurz (1994).

Deutsche Termin-Börse. The existence of different trading strategies in the market was also put forward in Chapter 7 to explain the HARCH effect of asymmetry in the information flow at different frequencies. LeBaron (2000) shows that introducing agents with different time horizons in his market model gives rise to heteroskedasticity effects in the resulting price volatility.

The delay with which the secondary reactions unfold is called the *relaxation time*. If diverse components with different time scales interact in the market, there is typically a mixture of long and short relaxation times following the impact of outside events. If different relaxation times are combined, the resulting autocorrelation decays hyperbolically or almost hyperbolically. This is a natural explanation of the long memory effects detected in financial markets. Dacorogna *et al.* (1993) studied the autocorrelation function for short-term absolute returns, confirmed the hyperbolic decay, and revealed that volatility clusters tend to have a longer memory than assumed by other studies of the subject. We saw in Chapter 7 that many studies confirm this effect.

There is yet another phenomenon, which originates from the fact that financial markets are spread worldwide. Economic and political news and trading activity are not stationary. They have a clear-cut pattern of moving around the world in a 24-hr cycle. The price data of foreign exchange rates reflect this in terms of a 24-hr seasonality in market volatility, Müller *et al.* (1990). This seasonality can be accounted for by introducing a *business time scale* such as in Dacorogna *et al.* (1993). The 24-hr cycle implies that market reactions to an event cannot be simultaneous and that there are distinct relaxation times following the event. Geographical components related to the business hours of the different trading centers must be added to the time components. The interaction of geographical components leads to behaviors such as the "heat wave" effect proposed by Engle *et al.* (1990).

12.3 IMPACT OF THE NEW TECHNOLOGY

The realization that there is value in the data to define an investment strategy has brought to life many new firms that specialize in modeling financial markets and in providing trading advices on the basis of technical models. The question is, of course, will the impact of the new technology be a passing phenomenon or will it have a long-term effect? As the relativistic phenomenon arises from the interaction of components with different time scales, it will remain appropriate as long as heterogeneous expectations continue to exist in the market. The interaction process may become more complex, but it cannot disappear.

News technologies enable users to identify additional trading opportunities to increase their profits. This quickens their pace of trading and contributes to higher market volume and liquidity. The improved liquidity lowers the spreads between bid and ask prices. Lower spreads imply lower transaction costs, which in turn increase the opportunity horizon for profitable trading. The new technology introduces a shift in perspective, with components starting to focus on more numerous short-term time intervals.

As components become increasingly short-term in their focus, the spectrum of short-term components increases. This has the effect that relative differences among components become more significant and the relativistic effects more pronounced. Contrary to accepted notions, which assume that sufficient buying power can "trade away" any phenomenon, the increased buying power will have the overall effect of enhancing the relativistic effects. Thus the very basis of our ability to forecast and build profitable trading models will be enhanced. This statement must be qualified in the sense that the reaction patterns will become increasingly diversified, and therefore more complex, and the speed of adjustment will increase requiring more and more sophisticated models.

12.4 ZERO-SUM GAME OR PERPETUUM MOBILE?

Conventional thought has it that financial markets must be a zero-sum game. This is true if we take a static view. In reality, the financial markets are dynamic and they are highly complex.

Markets are a platform for components to take advantage of the diversity of interests. They are able to match their opposing objectives when one component buys and another component sells. The lower the friction, the easier a counterpart for a particular transaction is found and the larger, therefore, is the particular component's opportunity set. By being able to go ahead with a particular transaction, the flexibility of the respective components is increased and their profit potential improved.

The new technology fosters the ability of the market to provide an environment for the generation of wealth. As explained, interaction within the market gives rise to relativistic effects and relaxation times. To the extent that these relativistic effects are understood and incorporated into forecasting and trading model technology, market participants have the opportunity to generate additional profit or limit their losses. In our terminology, the profit that is generated is energy extracted from the market. Improved efficacy of component interaction generates additional energy and reduces the friction associated with buying and selling within the market. The process may be compared to the search for more efficient engines in the automobile industry where everybody gains from it in the long term.

Have we achieved a *perpetuum mobile*? The answer is clearly no. Like any other technological innovation, the new technology does not generate energy from nothing, but it does take advantage of the energy potential existing in the financial markets. By offering a service to the economic agents, financial markets are not closed systems but do get a permanent input of money. This makes them highly open systems in terms of energy. Besides, a lot of resources have been put into the new technology in the form of extensive research, development work, and hardware to treat the information. Numerous studies have shown that simple trading rules do not work in efficient markets. Only elaborated treatment of the data allows the identification of profitable trading rules. This treatment is not free, it has a price. Moreover, as the relativistic reaction patterns become increasingly diversified, research and development efforts will have to increase in the future to keep up with the ever-changing nonlinear patterns.

12.5 DISCUSSION OF THE CONVENTIONAL DEFINITION

As the markets consist of a diversity of components, different relaxation times occur because of the underlying relativistic effects between different components. It follows that the weak form of efficiency coupled with the rational expectation model cannot be attained. Because of the presence of different time components with heterogeneous expectations, current market prices cannot reflect all available information. The price discovery mechanism follows rather a dynamic "error correction model" where the successive reactions to an event unfold in the price. Why, then, did this not show up more clearly in previous scientific investigations? Some of the several reasons include the following:

- High-frequency data are a prerequisite for the empirical investigation of relativistic phenomena.

- Extensive computing power is needed to show the predictability in financial markets. Access to reasonably priced computing power has become available only recently.

- It is in the past few decades that an increasing awareness for dynamic and nonlinear processes has been gained. Such an awareness is crucial for the study of relativistic effects.

The presumption of conventional economics that forecasting is impossible per definition has had a powerful impact on the research on market efficiency. Economists have focused on structural studies that were hamstrung by a lack of high-frequency data and theoretical shortcomings. Little academic research has been invested in actually trying to predict shorter-term price movements and build successful trading models.

12.6 AN IMPROVED DEFINITION OF "EFFICIENT MARKETS"

Although the current definition of efficient markets has shortcomings, we do not think that this concept should be abandoned; rather, it should be adapted to the new findings. It is important to find a good measure of how well a market operates.

From a dynamic perspective, the notion of reduced friction should be central to the notion of efficiency. We consider an efficient market to be a market where all market information must be available to the decision makers and there must be participants with different time scales and heterogeneous expectations trading with each other to ensure a minimum of friction in the transaction costs.

A quantitative measure of efficiency might be derived from the bid-ask spreads (those between real bid and ask prices being more appropriate for such a measure than the nominal spreads quoted in information systems). Spreads are not only a measure of "friction," they also contain a risk component. The volatility or, more precisely, the probability of extreme returns within short time intervals should be considered together with the spread in the quantitative measure of market efficiency to be proposed. We are sure that in the years to come this definition will prevail and we shall find precise measures of efficiency as it is the case in thermodynamics and engineering.

BIBLIOGRAPHY

Admati, A. R., and Pfleiderer, P. (1988). A theory of intraday patterns: Volume and price variability, *Review of Financial Studies*, 1, 3–40.

Ahn, D.-H., Boudoukh, J., Richardson, M., and Whitelaw, R. F. (2000). Partial adjustment or stale prices? Implications from stock index and futures return autocorrelations, *Stern Business School Working Paper*.

Allais, M. (1974). The psychological rate of interest, *Journal of Money, Credit and Banking*, 3, 285–331.

Allen, F., and Karjalainen, R. (1999). Using genetic algorithms to find technical trading rules, *Journal of Financial Economics*, 51, 245–271.

Almeida, A., Goodhart, C. A. E., and Payne, R. G. (1998). The effects of macroeconomic news on high frequency exchange rate behavior, *Journal of Financial and Quantitative Analysis*, 33, 383–408.

Andersen, T. G. (1996). Return volatility and trading volume: An information flow interpretation of stochastic volatility, *Journal of Finance*, 51, 169–204.

Andersen, T. G., and Bollerslev, T. (1997a). Heterogeneous information arrivals and return volatility dynamics: Uncovering the long-run in high frequency returns, *Journal of Finance*, 52, 975–1005.

Andersen, T. G., and Bollerslev, T. (1997b). Intraday periodicity and volatility persistence in financial markets, *Journal of Empirical Finance*, 4, 115–158.

Andersen, T. G., and Bollerslev, T. (1998a). Answering the skeptics: Yes, standard volatility models do provide accurate forecasts, *International Economic Review*, 39, 885–905.

Andersen, T. G., and Bollerslev, T. (1998b). Deutsche Mark-Dollar volatility: Intraday activity patterns, macroeconomic announcements, and longer run dependencies, *Journal of Finance*, 53, 219–265.

Andersen, T. G., Bollerslev, T., Diebold, F. X., and Labys, P. (2000). Exchange rate returns standardized by realised volatility are (nearly) Gaussian, *NBER Working Paper No: 7488*.

Andersen, T. G., Bollerslev, T., Diebold, F. X., and Labys, P. (2001). The distribution of realized exchange rate volatility, *Journal of the American Statistical Association*, forthcoming.

Baestaens, D. J. E., and Van den Bergh, W. M. (1995). The marginal contribution of news to the DEM/USD swap rate, *Neural Network World*, 5, 371–381.

Baillie, R. T., and Bollerslev, T. (1989). The message in daily exchange rates: A conditional-variance tale, *Journal of Business and Economic Statistics*, 7, 297–305.

Baillie, R. T., and Bollerslev, T. (1990). Intraday and intermarket volatility in foreign exchange rates, *Review of Economic Studies*, 58, 565–585.

Baillie, R. T., and McMahon, P. C. (1989) *The Foreign Exchange Market*, Cambridge University Press, Cambridge.

Baillie, R. T., Bollerslev, T., and Mikkelsen, H.-O. (1996). Fractionally integrated generalized autoregressive conditional heteroskedasticity, *Journal of Econometrics*, 74, 3–30.

Ballocchi, G. (1996). Interbank money market rate statistics: Results for the forecaster optimization, Internal document GBA.1996-03-01, Olsen & Associates, Seefeldstrasse 233, 8008 Zürich, Switzerland.

Ballocchi, G., and Hopman, C. (1997), Bond futures: From statistical properties to forecasting, Internal document GBA.1997-10-28, Olsen & Associates, Seefeldstrasse 233, 8008 Zürich, Switzerland.

Ballocchi, G., Dacorogna, M. M., Hopman, C. M., Müller, U. A., and Olsen, R. B. (1999a). The intraday multivariate structure of the Eurofutures markets, *Journal of Empirical Finance*, 6, 479–513.

Ballocchi, G., Dacorogna, M. M., Gençay, R., and Piccinato, B. (1999b). Intraday statistical properties of Eurofutures, *Derivatives Quarterly*, 6, 28–44.

Ballocchi, G., Gençay, R., Piccinato, B., and Dacorogna, M. M. (2001). Time-to-expiry seasonalities in Eurofutures, *Studies in Nonlinear Dynamics and Econometrics*, forthcoming.

Bank for International Settlements (1990). Survey of foreign exchange market activity, *Document from the Monetary and Economic Department*, Basle, February 1990.

Bank for International Settlements (1993). Central bank survey of foreign exchange market activity, *Document from the Monetary and Economic Department*, Basle, February 1993.

Bank for International Settlements (1995). Central bank survey of foreign exchange market activity, *Document from the Monetary and Economic Department*, Basle, February 1995.

Bank for International Settlements (1999). Central bank survey of foreign exchange and derivatives market market activity, *Document from the Monetary and Economic Department*, Basle, May 1999.

Banzhaf, W., Nordin, P., Keller, R. E., and Francone, F. D. (1998). *Genetic Programming: An Introduction*, Morgan Kaufmann, San Francisco, CA.

Barndorff-Nielsen, O. E. (1998). Processes of normal inverse Gaussian type, *Finance and Stochastics*, 2, 41–68.

Barndorff-Nielsen, O. E., and Prause, K. (1999). Apparent scaling, *Finance and Stochastics*, forthcoming.

Bekaert, G., and Hodrick, R. J. (1992). Characterizing predictable components in excess returns on equity and foreign exchange markets, *Journal of Finance*, 47, 467–509.

Beltratti, A., and Morana, C. (1998). Estimating variance in the foreign exchange market with high frequency data, *Bocconi University*, manuscript.

Beltratti, A., and Morana, C. (1999). Computing value at risk with high frequency data, In *Journal of Empirical Finance*, 6, 431–455.

Berndt, E., Hall, B., Hall, R., and Hausman, J. (1974). Estimation and inference in nonlinear structural models, *Annals of Economic and Social Measurement*, 3, 653–665.

Bhattacharyya, S., Pictet, O. V., and Zumbach, G. (1998). Representational semantics for genetic programming based learning in high-frequency financial data, In *Genetic Programming 1998: Proceedings of the Third Annual Conference*, Madison, Wisconsin, M. Kaufmann, Ed., 11–16.

Bjorn, V. (1994). Optimal multiresolution decomposition of financial time-series, In *Proceedings of the Conference on Neural Networks in the Capital Markets*, Pasadena, November 1994.

Black, F., and Scholes, M. (1973). The pricing of option and corporate liabilities, *Journal of Political Economy*, 81, 637–659.

Bollerslev, T. (1986). Generalized autoregressive conditional heteroskedasticity, *Journal of Econometrics*, 31, 307–327.

Bollerslev, T., and Domowitz, I. (1993). Trading patterns and prices in the interbank foreign exchange market, *Journal of Finance*, 48, 1421–1443.

Bollerslev, T., and Melvin, M. (1994). Bid-ask spreads and volatility in the foreign exchange market: An empirical analysis, *Journal of International Economics*, 36, 355–372.

Bollerslev, T., Chou, R. Y., and Kroner, K. F. (1992). ARCH modeling in finance, *Journal of Econometrics*, 52, 5–59.

Boothe, P., and Glassman, D. (1987). The statistical distribution of exchange rates, empirical evidence and economic implications, *Journal of International Economics*, 22, 297–319.

Bouchaud, J.-P., Potters, M. (2000). Theory of financial risks, *From Statistical Physics to Risk Management*, Cambridge University Press, Cambridge.

Bouchaud, J.-P., Potters, M., and Meyer, M. (2000). Apparent multifractality in financial time series, *European Physical Journal B*, 13, 595–599.

Boyer, B. H., Gibson, M. S., and Loretan, M. (1997). Pitfalls in tests for changes in correlations, *Federal Reserve Board International Finance Discussion Paper No: 597*.

Breymann, W. (2000). Dynamic theta time: Algorithm, configuration, tests, Internal document WAB.2000-07-31, Olsen & Associates, Seefeldstrasse 233, 8008 Zürich, Switzerland.

Breymann, W., Ghashghaie, S., and Talkner, P. (2000). A stochastic cascade model for FX dynamics, *International Journal of Theoretical and Applied Finance*, 3, 357-360.

Brock, W., Lakonishok, J., and LeBaron, B. (1992). Simple technical trading rules and the stochastic properties of stock returns, *Journal of Finance*, 47, 1731–1764.

Brock, W. A. (1993). Pathways to randomness in the economy: Emergent nonlinearity and chaos in economics and finance, *Estudios Economicos*, 8, 3–55.

Brock, W. A. (1999). Scaing in economics: A reader's guide, *Industrial and Corporate Change*, 8, 409–446.

Brock, W. A., and Hommes, C. (1997). A rational route to randomness, *Econometrica*, 65, 1059–1095.

Brock, W. A., and Kleidon, A. (1992). Periodic market closure and trading volume: A model of intraday bids and asks, *Journal of Economic Dynamics and Control*, 16, 451–489.

Brock, W. A., and LeBaron, B. (1996). A dynamical structual model for stock return volatility and trading volume, *Review of Economics and Statistics*, 78, 94–110.

Burghardt, G., and Hoskins, B. (1995). The convexity bias in Eurodollar futures: Part I, in *The Handbook on Derivative Instruments*, Atsuo Konishi and Ravi E. Dattareya, Eds., Ch. 4, 81–120.

Calderon-Rossel, J. R., and Ben-Horim, M. (1982). The behavior of the foreign exchange rates, empirical evidence and economic implications, *Journal of International Business Studies*, 13, 99–111.

Calvet, L. E., Fisher, A. J., and Mandelbrot, B. B. (1997). Large deviations and the distribution of price changes, *Cowles Foundation Working Paper No: 1165*.

Campbell, J. Y., Lo, A. W., and MacKinlay, A. C. (1997). *The Econometrics of Financial Markets*, Princeton University Press, Princeton, New Jersey.

Chopard, B., Oussaidène, M., Pictet, O., Schirru, R., and Tomassini, M. (1995). Evolutionary algorithms for multimodal optimization in financial applications, In *Proceedings of the SPP-IF Seminar*, Zürich, 139–142.

Chopard, B., Pictet, O., and Tomassini, M. (2000). Parallel and distributed evolutionary computation for financial applications, *Parallel Algorithms and Applications Journal*, 15, 15–36.

Clark, P. K. (1973). A subordinated stochastic process model with finite variance for speculative prices, *Econometrica*, 41, 135–155.

Cohen, K., Hawawimi, G., Maier, S., Schwartz, R., and Whitcomb, D. (1983). Friction in the trading process and the estimation of systematic risk, *Journal of Financial Economics*, 12, 263–278.

Corsi, F., Zumbach, G. O, Müller, U. A., and Dacorogna, M. M. (2001). Consistent high-precision volatility from high-frequency data, *Economic Notes*, forthcoming.

Cox, J. C., and Rubinstein, M. (1985). *Options Markets*, Prentice-Hall, Englewood Cliffs, NJ.

Dacorogna, M. M., Gauvreau, C. L., Müller, U. A., Olsen, R. B., and Pictet, O. V. (1992). Short-term forecasting models of foreign exchange rates, Presentation at the IBM Summer Research Institute in Oberlech Austria on "Advanced Applications in Finance, Investment and Banking", July 27-July 31, 1992; MMD.1992-05-12, Olsen & Associates, Seefeldstrasse 233, 8008 Zürich, Switzerland.

Dacorogna, M. M., Gauvreau, C. L., Müller, U. A., Olsen, R. B., and Pictet, O. V. (1996). Changing time scale for short-term forecasting in financial markets, *Journal of Forecasting*, 15, 203–227.

Dacorogna, M. M., Müller, U. A., Nagler, R. J., Olsen, R. B., and Pictet, O. V. (1993). A geographical model for the daily and weekly seasonal volatility in the FX market, *Journal of International Money and Finance*, 12, 413–438.

Dacorogna, M. M., Müller, U. A., Jost, C., Pictet, O. V., Olsen, R. B., and Ward, J. R. (1995). Heterogeneous real-time trading strategies in the foreign exchange market, *European Journal of Finance*, 1, 243–253.

Dacorogna, M. M., Müller, U. A., Embrechts, P., and Samorodnitsky, G. (1996). How heavy are the tails of a stationary HARCH(k) process?, published in "Stochastic Processes and Related Topics" book in memory of Stamatis Cambanis edited by Yannis Karatzas Balram S. Rajput and Murad Taqqu published by Birkhäuser, Boston.

Dacorogna, M. M., Embrechts, P., Müller, U. A., and Samorodnitsky, G. (1998a). How heavy are the tails of a stationary HARCH(k) process? In *Stochastic Processes and Related Topics*, Y. Rajput and M. Taqqu, Eds., pp. 1–31, Birkhäuser, Boston.

Dacorogna, M. M., Müller, U. A., Olsen, R. B., and Pictet, O. V. (1998b). Modelling short-term volatility with GARCH and HARCH models, In *Nonlinear Modelling of High Frequency Financial Time Series*, C. Dunis and B. Zhou, Eds., pp. 161–176, John Wiley & Sons, Chichester.

Dacorogna, M. M., Pictet, O. V., Müller, U. A., and de Vries, C. G. (2001a). Extremal forex returns in extremely large data sets, *Extremes*, forthcoming.

Dacorogna, M. M., Gençay, R., Müller, U. A., and Pictet, O. V. (2001b). Effective return, risk aversion and drawdowns, *Physica A*, 289, 66-88.

Danielsson, J., de Haan, L., Peng, L., and de Vries, C. G. (1997). Using a bootstrap method to choose the sample fraction in tail index estimation, *Journal of Multivariate Analysis*, forthcoming.

Davé, R. D. (1993). Statistical correlation of data frequency price change and spread results, Internal document RDD.1993-04-26, Olsen & Associates, Seefeldstrasse 233, 8008 Zürich, Switzerland.

Davé, R. D., and Stahl, G. (1998). On the accuracy of var estimates based on the variance-covariance approach, In *Proceedings of the 6th Karlsruher Ökonometrie-Workshop*, March 1997, Springer Verlag.

Davidson, R., and MacKinnon, J. G. (1993). *Estimation and Inference in Econometrics*, Oxford University Press, Oxford, England.

Davis, R., Mikosch, T., and Basrak, B. (1999). Sample ACF of multivariate stochastic recurrence equations with applications to GARCH, *Department of Mathematics and Computing Science of the University of Groningen Working Paper*.

de Haan, L. (1990). Fighting the ARCH-enemy with mathematics, *Statistica Neerlandica*, 44, 45–68.

de Haan, L., Jansen, D. W., Koedijk, K. G., and de Vries, C. G. (1994). Safety first portfolio selection, extreme value theory and long run asset risks, In *Extreme value Theory and Applications*, J. Galambos, J. Lechner, and E. Simiu, Eds., pp. 471–488, Kluwer, Dordrecht.

de Jong, F., and Nijman, T. (1997). High frequency analysis of lead-lag relationships between financial markets, *Journal of Empirical Finance*, 4, 259–277.

de Vries, C. G. (1992). Stylized facts of nominal exchange rate returns, in *Handbook of International Macroeconomics*, F. van der Ploeg, Ed., pp. 1–57.

Deb, K., and Goldberg, D. E. (1989). An investigation of niche and species formation in genetic function optimization, In *Proceeding of the Third International Conference on Genetic Algorithms*, pp. 42–50.

Demos, A. A., and Goodhart, C. A. E. (1992). The interaction between the frequency of market quotations, spread, and volatility in the foreign exchange market, *Applied Economics*, 28, 28, 377–386.

Diebold, F. X. (1988). Empirical modeling of exchange rate dynamics, *Lecture Notes in Economics and Mathematical Systems*, Vol. 3030, Springer Verlag, Berlin.

Ding, Z., Granger, C. W. J., and Engle, R. F. (1993). A long memory property of stock market returns and a new model, *Journal of Empirical Finance*, 1, 83–106.

Drost, F., and Nijman, T. (1993). Temporal aggregation of GARCH processes, *Econometrica*, 61, 909–927.

Dunis, C., and Feeny, M. (1989). *Exchange Rate Forecasting*, Woodhead-Faulkner, Cambridge.

Dunis, C., and Keller, A. (1993). Implied versus historical volatility: An empirical test of the efficiency of the currency options market using non-overlapping data, *Conference on Financial Markets Dynamics and Forecasting*, Paris, 2–4 Sep 1993.

Eben, K. (1994). Arbitrage alerts and changing interrelations between FX rates, *Institute of Computer Science, Academy of Sciences of the Czech Republic*, manuscript.

Eberlein, E., Keller, U., and Prause, K. (1998). New insights into smile – mispricing and value at risk: The hyperbolic model, *Journal of Business*, 71, 371–405.

Ederington, L. L., and Lee, J. H. (1993). How markets process information: News releases and volatility, *Journal of Finance*, 48, 1161–1191.

Ederington, L. L., and Lee, J. H. (1995). The short-run dynamics of the price adjustment to new information, *Journal of Financial and Quantitative Analysis*, 30, 117–134.

Edison, H. (1993). The effectiveness of central bank intervention: A survey of the post-1982 literature, *Essays in International Finance*, Princeton University.

Embrechts, P., Klüppelberg, C., and Mikosch, T. (1997). *Modelling Extremal Events, Applications of Mathematics Stochastic Modelling and Applied Probability*, Vol. 33, Springer, Berlin.

Engle, R. F. (1982). Autoregressive conditional heteroskedasticity with estimates of the variance of U.K. inflation, *Econometrica*, 50, 987–1008.

Engle, R. F., and Russell, J. R. (1997). Forecasting the frequency of changes in quoted foreign exchange prices with the autoregressive conditional duration model, *Journal of Empirical Finance*, 4, 187–212.

Engle, R. F., and Russell, J. R. (1998). Autoregressive conditional duration: A new model for irregularly spaced transaction data, *Econometrica*, 66, 1127–1162.

Engle, R. F., Ito, T., and Lin, W.-L. (1990). Meteor showers or heat waves? Heteroskedastic intra-daily volatility in the foreign exchange market, *Econometrica*, 58, 525–542.

Epps, T. (1979). Co-movements in stock prices in the very short-run, *Journal of the American Statistical Association*, 74, 291–298.

Evett, M., and Fernandez, T. (1998). Numeric mutation improves the discovery of numeric constants in genetic programming, In *Genetic Programming 1998: Proceedings of the Third Annual Conference*, M. Kaufmann, Ed., pp. 66-71, Madison, Wisconsin.

Fama, E. F. (1970). Efficient capital markets: A review of theory and empirical work, *Journal of Finance*, 25, 383–417.

Fama, E. F. (1991). Efficient capital markets: II, *Journal of Finance*, 46, 1575–1617.

Farmer, J. D. (1998). Market force, ecology, and evolution, *Santa Fe Institute Working Paper*.

Farmer, J. D., and Lo, A. W. (1999). Frontiers of finance: Evolution and efficient markets, *Proceeding of the National Academy of Science, U.S.A.*, 96, 9991–9992.

Feinstone, L. J. (1987). Minute by minute: Efficiency, normality, and randomness in intradaily asset prices, *Journal of Applied Econometrics*, 2, 193–214.

Feller, W. (1971). *An Introduction to Probability Theory and Its Applications*, Wiley Series in Probability and Mathematical Statistics, Vol. 2, 2nd ed., John Wiley & Sons, New York.

Fisher, A. J., Calvet, L. E., and Mandelbrot, B. B. (1997). Multifractality of Deutschemark U.S. Dollar exchange rates, *Cowles Foundation Working Paper No: 1166*.

Flood, M. D. (1991). Microstructure theory and the foreign exchange market, *Federal Reserve Bank of St. Louis Review*, 73, 52–70.

Flood, M. D. (1994). Market structure and inefficiency in the foreign exchange market, *Journal of International Money and Finance*, 13, 131–158.

Frances, P. H., and van Griensven, K. (1998). Forecasting exchange rates using neural networks for technical trading rules, *Studies in Nonlinear Dynamics and Econometrics*, 4, 109–114.

Franke, G., and Hess, D. (1997). Information diffusion in electronic and floor trading, *University of Konstanz Working Paper*.

Franke, G., and Hess, D. (1998). The impact of scheduled news announcements on T-bond and Bund futures trading, *University of Konstanz Working Paper*.

Frankel, J. A. and Froot, K. A. (1990). Chartists, fundamentalists, and trading in the foreign exchange market, *American Economic Review*, 80, 181–185.

Friedmann, D. and Vandersteel, S. (1982). Short-run fluctuations in foreign exchange rates, evidence from the data 1973–79, *Journal of International Economics*, 13, 171–186.

Frisch, U. (1995). *Turbulence*, Cambridge University Press, Cambridge, U.K.

Froot, K. A. (1993). Currency hedging over long horizons, *National Bureau of Economic Research Working Paper No: 4355*.

Froot, K. A., Kim, M., and Rogoff, K. (1995). The law of one price over 700 years, *National Bureau of Economic Research Working Paper No: 5132*.

Fung, H.-G., and Leung, W. K. (1993). The pricing relationship of Eurodollar futures and Eurodollar deposit rates, *Journal of Futures Markets*, 13, 115–126.

Gallant, A., Rossi, P., and Tauchen, G. (1993). Nonlinear dynamic structures, *Econometrica*, 61, 871–907.

Garbade, K. D., and Silber, W. L. (1985). Price movements and price discovery in futures and cash markets, *Review of Economics and Statistics*, 65, 289–297.

Gençay, R. (1998a). Optimization of technical trading strategies with neural network models and evidence of profitability in security markets, *Economics Letters*, 59, 249–254.

Gençay, R. (1998b). The predictability of security returns with simple technical trading rules, *Journal of Empirical Finance*, 5, 317–345.

Gençay, R. (1999). Linear, nonlinear and essential foreign exchange prediction with simple technical rules, *Journal of International Economics*, 47, 91–107.

Gençay, R., and Stengos, T. (1998). Moving average rules, volume and the predictability of security returns with feedforward networks, *Journal of Forecasting*, 17, 401–414.

Gençay, R., Selcuk, F., and Whitcher, B. (2001a). Differentiating intraday seasonalities through wavelet multiscaling, *Physica A*, 289, 543–556.

Gençay, R., Selçuk, F., and Whitcher, B. (2001b). *An Introduction to Wavelets and Other Filtering Methods in Economics and Finance*, Academic Press, forthcoming, San Diego, CA.

Gençay, R., Dacorogna, M. M., Olsen, R., and Pictet, O. V. (2001c). Real-time foreign exchange trading models and market behavior, *Journal of Economic Dynamics and Control*, forthcoming.

Gençay, R., Selcuk, F., and Whitcher, B. (2001d). Scaling properties of foreign exchange volatility, *Physica A*, 289, 89–106.

Gençay, R., Ballocchi, G., Dacorogna, M. M., Olsen, R., and Pictet, O. V. (2002). Real-time trading models and the statistical properties of foreign exchange rates, *International Economic Review*, forthcoming.

Ghashghaie, S., Breymann, W., Peinke, J., Talkner, P., and Dodge, Y. (1996). Turbulent cascades in foreign exchange markets, *Nature*, 381, 767–770.

Ghose, D., and Kroner, K. F. (1995). The relationship between GARCH and symmetric stable processes: Finding the source of fat tails in financial data, *Journal of Empirical Finance*, 2, 225–251.

Ghysels, E. and Jasiak, J. (1995). Stochastic volatility and time deformation: An application of trading volume and leverage effects, In *Proceedings of the HFDF-I Conference*, Zurich, Switzerland, March 29-31, 1995, 1, 1–14.

Ghysels, E., Harvey, A., and Renault, E. (1996). Stochastic volatility, *in Handbook of Statistics 14, Statistical Methods in Finance*, G. S:. Mandala and C. S. Rao eds., North holland, Amsterdam.

Gibson, M. S., and Boyer, B. H. (1997). Evaluating forecasts of correlation using option pricing, *Federal Reserve Board International Finance Discussion Paper Series No: 1997-600*.

Gielens, G., Straetmans, S., and de Vries, C. G. (1996). Fat tail distributions and local thin tail alternatives, *Communications in Statistics, Theory and Methods*, 25, 705–710.

Glassman, D. (1987). Exchange rate risk and transactions costs: Evidence from bid-ask spreads, *Journal of International Money and Finance*, 6, 479–490.

Glosten, L. R. (1987). Components of the bid-ask spread and the statistical properties of transaction prices, *Journal of Finance*, 42, 1293–1307.

Goldberg, D. E. (1989). *Genetic Algorithms in Search, Optimization & Machine Learning*, Addison-Wesley, Reading, MA.

Goldberg, D. E., and Richardson, J. (1987). Genetic algorithms with sharing for multimodal function optimization, In *Proceeding of the Second International Conference on Genetic Algorithms*, pp. 41–49.

Goldie, C. M., and Smith, R. L. (1987). Slow variation with remainder: Theory and applications, *Quarterly Journal of Mathematics, Oxford 2nd series*, 38, 45–71.

Goodhart, C. A. E. (1989). News and the foreign exchange market, In *Proceedings of the Manchester Statistical Society*, pp. 1–79.

Goodhart, C. A. E., and Curcio, R. (1991). The clustering of bid/ask prices and the spread in the foreign exchange market, *LSE Financial Market Group Discussion Paper No: 110*.

Goodhart, C. A. E., and Demos, A. (1990). Reuters screen images of the foreign exchange market: The Deutschemark/Dollar spot rate, *Journal of International Securities Markets*, 4, 333–348.

Goodhart, C. A. E. and Figliuoli, L. (1991). Every minute counts in financial markets, *Journal of International Money and Finance*, **10**, 23–52.

Goodhart, C. A. E., and Figliuoli, L. (1992). The geographical location of the foreign exchange market: A test of an "islands" hypothesis, *Journal of International and Comparative Economics*, 1, 13–27.

Goodhart, C. A. E. and Hesse, T. (1993). Central bank FX intervention assessed in continuous time, *Journal of International Money and Finance*, 12, 368–389.

Goodhart, C. A. E., and Payne, R. G. (1996). Microstructural dynamics in a foreign exchange electronic broking system., *Journal of International Money and Finance*, 15, 829–852.

Goodhart, C. A. E., Hall, S. G., Henry, S. G. B., and Pesaran, B. (1993). News effects in a high frequency model of the Sterling-Dollar exchange rate, *Journal of Applied Econometrics*, 8, 1–13.

Goodhart, C. A. E., Ito, T., and Payne, R. G. (1995). One day in June, 1993: A study of the working of Reuters 2000-2 electronic foreign exchange trading system, *NBER Technical Working Paper No: 179*.

Gouree, J. K., and Hommes, C. H. (2000). Heterogeneous beliefs and the nonlinear cobweb model, *Journal of Economic Dynamics and Control*, 24, 761–798.

Granger, C., and Ding, Z. (1995). Some properties of absolute return: An alternative measure of risk, *Annales d'Economie et de Statistique*, 40, 67–91.

Granger, C. W. J., and Newbold, P. (1977). *Forecasting Economic Time Series*, Academic Press, London.

Groenendijk, P. A., Lucas, A., and de Vries, C. G. (1996). Stochastic processes, nonnormal innovations, and the use of scaling ratios, In *Proceedings of the third*

International Conference on Forecasting Financial Markets, London March 27-29, 1996, 1, 1–38.

Guillaume, D. M. (1994). On the trend-following behavior of intradaily foreign exchange market and its relationship with the volatility, *Center for Economic Studies, Catholic University of Leuven*, manuscript.

Guillaume, D. M., Dacorogna, M. M., and Pictet, O. V. (1994). On the intradaily performance of GARCH processes, In *Proceedings of the First International Conference on High Frequency Data in Finance, HFDF-I*, Zürich, Switzerland.

Guillaume, D. M., Dacorogna, M. M., Davé, R. D., Müller, U. A., Olsen, R. B., and Pictet, O. V. (1997). From the bird's eye to the microscope: A survey of new stylized facts of the intradaily foreign exchange markets, *Finance and Stochastics*, 1, 95–129.

Gwilym, O. and Sutcliffe, C. (1999). *High-Frequency Financial Market Data*, Risk Books, London.

Hall, P. (1982). On some simple estimates of an exponent of regular variation, *Journal of the Royal Statistical Society, Series B*, 44, 37–42.

Hall, P. (1990). Using the bootstrap to estimate mean square error and select smoothing parameter in nonparametric problem, *Journal of Multivariate Analysis*, 32, 177–203.

Hamilton, J. D. (1994). *Time Series Analysis*, Princeton University Press, Princeton, NJ.

Hansen, L. P., and Hodrick, R. J. (1980). Forward exchange rates as optimal predictors of future spot rates: An econometric analysis, *Journal of Political Economy*, 88, 829–853.

Harris, L. (1987). Transaction data tests of the mixture of distributions hypothesis, *Journal of Financial and Quantitative Analysis*, 22, 127–141.

Hartmann, P. (1998). Do reuters spreads reflect currencies' differences in global trading activity, *Journal of International Money and Finance*, 17, 757–784.

Hasbrouck, J. (1998). Security bid/ask dynamics with discreteness and clustering: Simple strategies for modeling and estimation, In *Proceedings of the HFDF-II Conference*, Zurich, 2, pp. 1–24.

Hasbrouck, J. (1999). Trading fast and slow: Security market events in realtime, *Stern School of Business Working Paper*.

Hill, B. M. (1975). A simple general approach to inference about the tail of a distribution, *Annals of Statistics*, 3, 1163–1173.

Hols, M. C., and De Vries, C. G. (1991). The limiting distribution of extremal exchange rate returns, *Journal of Applied Econometrics*, 6, 287–302.

Hommes, C. (2000) Financial markets as nonlinear adaptive evolutionary systems, *Quantitative Finance*, 1, 149–167.

Hosking, J. (1996). Asymptotic distribution of the sample mean, autocovariances and autocorrelations of long memory time series, *Journal of Econometrics*, 73, 261–284.

Hsieh, D. A. (1988). The statistical properties of daily foreign exchange rates: 1974–1983, *Journal of International Economics*, 24, 129–145.

Hull, J. C. (1993). *Options, Futures and other Derivative Securities*, Prentice-Hall International, Englewood Cliffs, NJ.

Ibragimov, I., and Linnik, Y. V. (1971). *Independent and Stationary Sequences of Random Variables*, Wolters-Noordhoff, Groningen.

International Monetary Fund, (1993). International capital markets. Part I: Exchange rate management and international capital flows, *World Economic and Financial Surveys*, Washington DC, April 1993.

Ito, T., and Roley, V. V. (1987). News from the U.S. and Japan: Which moves the yen/dollar exchange rate? *Journal of Monetary Economics*, 19, 255–277.

J. P. Morgan (1996). RiskMetrics — Technical document. J. P. Morgan and International Marketing – Reuters Ltd.

Jones, C. M., Kaul, G., and Lipson, M. L. (1994). Transactions, volumes and volatility, *Review of Financial Studies*, 7, 631-651.

Karpoff, J. M. (1987). The relation between price changes and trading volume: A survey, *Journal of Financial and Quantitative Analysis*, 22, 109–126.

Keeney, R. L., and Raiffa, H. (1976). *Decisions with Multiple Objectives: Preferences and Value Tradeoffs*, John Wiley & Sons, New York.

Kendall, M., Stuart, A., and Ord, J. K. (1987). *Advanced Theory of Statistics*, Vol. 1, 5th ed., Charles Griffin & Company Limited, London.

Koedijk, K. G., Schafgans, M. M. A., and De Vries, C. G. (1990). The tail index of exchange rate returns, *Journal of International Economics*, 29, 93–108.

Koza, J. R. (1992). *Genetic Programming*, The MIT Press, Cambridge, MA.

Krzanowski, W. J., and Marriott, F. H. C. (1994). *Multivariate Analysis, Distributions, Ordination and Inference*, Vol. 1, 1st ed., Kendall's Library Statistics, Edward Arnold, London.

Krzanowski, W. J., and Marriott, F. H. C. (1995). *Multivariate Analysis, Classification, Covariance Structures and Repeated Measurements*, Vol. 2, 1st ed., Kendall's Library Statistics. Edward Arnold, London.

Kurz, M. (1994). *Endogenous Economic Fluctuations, Studies in the Theory of Rational Beliefs*, Vol. 6, Studies in Economic Theory. Springer, Berlin.

Leadbetter, M., Lindgren, G., and Rootzén, H. (1983). *Extremes and Related Properties of Random Sequences and Processes*, Springer Series in Statistics. Springer-Verlag, New York-Berlin.

LeBaron, B. (1992a). Do moving average trading rule results imply nonlinearities in foreign exchange markets?, *University of Wisconsin-Madison, SSRI Working Paper*.

LeBaron, B. (1992b). Forecast improvements using a volatility index, *Journal of Applied Econometrics*, 7, 137–149.

LeBaron, B. (1992c). Some relations between volatility and serial correlations in stock market returns, *Journal of Business*, 65, 199–219.

LeBaron, B. (1997). Technical trading rules and regime shifts in foreign exchange, *Advanced Trading Rules, E. Acar and S. Satchell, Eds., Butterworth-Heinemann.*

LeBaron, B. (1999a). Technical trading rule profitability and foreign exchange intervention, *Journal of International Economics*, 49, 125–143.

LeBaron, B. (1999b). Volatility persistence and apparent scaling laws in finance, *Brandeis University*, manuscript.

LeBaron, B. (2000). Evolution and time horizons in an agent based stock market, *Brandeis University*, manuscript.

Levich, R. M., and Thomas, L. R. (1993a). Internationally diversified bond portfolios: The merit of active currency risk management, *National Bureau of Economic Research Working Paper No:4340.*

Levich, R. M. and Thomas, L. R. III. (1993b). The significance of technical trading-rule profits in the foreign exchange market: A bootstrap approach, *Journal of International Money and Finance*, 12, 451–474.

LIFFE (1995a). *Government Bond Futures.* The London International Financial Futures and Options Exchange, London, United Kingdom.

LIFFE (1995b). *International Bond Market.* The London International Financial Futures and Options Exchange, London, United Kingdom.

Lo, A., Mamaysky, H., and Wang, J. (2000). Foundations of technical analysis: Computational algorithms, statistical inference, and empirical implementation, *Journal of Finance*, LV, 1705–1765.

Lo, A. W., and MacKinlay, A. C. (1988). Stock market prices do not follow random walks: Evidence from a simple specification test, *Review of Financial Studies*, 1, 41–66.

Lo, A. W., and MacKinlay, A. C. (1990a). An econometric analysis of nonsynchronous trading, *Journal of Econometrics*, 45, 181–211.

Lo, A. W., and MacKinlay, A. C. (1990b). When are contrarian profits due to stock market overreaction? *Review of Financial Studies*, 3, 175–205.

Longin, F. and Solnik, B. (1995). Is the correlation in international equity returns constant: 1960–1990? *Journal of International Money and Finance*, 14, 3–26.

Loretan, M., and Phillips, P. C. B. (1994). Testing the covariance stationarity of heavy-tailed time series, *Journal of Empirical Finance*, 1, 211–248.

Low, A., Muthuswamy, J., and Sarkar, S. (1996). Time variation in the correlation structure of exchange rates: High frequency analyses, In *Proceedings of the Third International Conference on Forecasting Financial Markets*, London, England, March 27–29, 1996, 1, 1–24.

Lux, T., and Marchesi, M. (1999). Scaling and criticality in a stochastic multi-agent model of a financial market? *Nature*, 397, 498–500.

Lux, T. and Marchesi, M. (2000). Volatility clustering in financial markets: A micro-simulation of interacting agents? *International Journal of Theoretical and Applied Finance*, 4, 1–20.

Lyons, R. K. (1995). Test of microstructural hypotheses in the foreign exchange market, *Journal of Financial Economics*, 39, 321–351.

Lyons, R. K. (1996a). Foreign exchange volume: Sound and fury signifying nothing? In *The Microstructure of Foreign Exchange Markets*, J. Frankel et al., Eds., University of Chicago Press, pp. 183–201.

Lyons, R. K. (1996b). Optimal transparency in a dealership market with an application to foreign exchange, *Journal of Financial Intermediation*, 5, 225–254.

Lyons, R. K. (1998). Profits and position control: A week of FX dealing, *Journal of International Money and Finance*, 17, 97–115.

MacDonald, R., and Taylor, M. P. (1992). Exchange rate economics, *IMF Staff Papers*, 39, 1–57.

Makridakis, S., Wheelwright, S. C., and McGee, V. E. (1983). *Forecasting Methods and Applications*, 2nd ed., John Wiley & Sons, New York.

Mandelbrot, B. B. (1963). The variation of certain speculative prices, *Journal of Business*, 36, 394–419.

Mandelbrot, B. B. (1971). When can price be arbitraged efficiently? A limit to the validity of the random walk and martingale model, *Review of Economics and Statistics*, 53, 225–236.

Mandelbrot, B. B. (1972). Statistical methodology for nonperiodic cycles: From the covariance to R/S analysis, *Annals of Economic and Social Measurement*, 1, 259–290.

Mandelbrot, B. B. (1983). *The Fractal Geometry of Nature*, W. H. Freeman and Company, New York.

Mandelbrot, B. B. (1997). *Fractals and Scaling in Finance*, Springer Verlag.

Mandelbrot, B. B., and Taylor, H. M. (1967). On the distribution of stock prices differences, *Operations Research*, 15, 1057–1062.

Mandelbrot, B. B., and Van Ness, J. W. (1968). Fractional brownian motions, fractional noises and applications, *SIAM Review*, 10, 422–437.

Mandelbrot, B. B., Fisher, A. J., and Calvet, L. E. (1997). A multifractal model of asset returns, *Cowles Foundation Discussion Paper No: 1164*.

Mansfield, P., Rachev, S. T., and Samorodnitsky, G. (1999). Long strange segments of a stochastic process and long range dependence, *Cornell University, School of Operations Research and Industrial Engineering, Technical Report No: 1252*.

Mantegna, R. N., and Stanley, H. E. (1995). Scaling behavior in the dynamics of an economic index, *Nature*, 376, 46–49.

Mantegna, R. N., and Stanley, H. E. (2000). *An Introduction to Econophysics — Correlations and Complexity in Finance*, Cambridge University Press, Cambridge.

Markowitz, H. M. (1959). *Portfolio Selection: Efficient Diversification of Investments*, Wiley, Yale University Press (1970), New York.

Markowitz, H. M. (1987). *Mean-Variance Analysis in Portfolio Choice and Capital Markets*, Basil Blackwell, Oxford, Cambridge, MA.

Mason, D. M. (1982). Laws of large numbers for sums of extreme values, *Annals of Probability*, 10, 754–764.

McCulloch, J. H. (1997). Measuring tail thickness in order to estimate the stable index α: A critique, *Journal of Business and Economic Statistics*, 15(1), 74–81.

McFarland, J. W., Petit, R. R., and Sung, S. K. (1982). The distribution of foreign exchange price changes: Trading day effects and risk measurement, *Journal of Finance*, 37, 693–715.

McNeil, A. J. and Frey, R. (2000). Estimation of tail-related risk measures for heteroscedastic financial time series: An extreme value approach, *Journal of Empirical Finance*, 7, 271–300.

Meese, R. A., and Rogoff, J. (1983). Empirical exchange rate models of the seventies, do they fit out of sample? *Journal of International Economics*, 14, 3–24.

Melvin, M. T., and Yin, X. (2000). Public information arrival, exchange rate volatility and quote frequency, *Economic Journal*, 110, 465–490.

Meyn, S. P. and Tweedie, R. L. (1993). *Markov Chains and Stochastic Stability*, Springer Verlag, Heidelberg.

Michalewicz, Z. (1994). *Genetic Algorithms + Data Structures = Evolution Programs*, Springer-Verlag, 2nd ed., Berlin.

Mikosch, T. and Starica, C. (1999). Change of structure in financial time series, long range dependence and the GARCH model, *University of Groningen*, manuscript.

Montana, D. J. (1995). Strongly typed genetic programming, *Evolutionary Computation*, 3, 199–230.

Moody, J. and Wu, L. (1995). Statistical analysis and forecasting of high frequency foreign exchange rates, In *Proceedings of the HFDF-I Conference*, Zurich, Switzerland, March 29-31, 1995, 3, 29–31.

Morgan Guaranty (1996). *RiskMetrics^{TM} – Technical Document*, 4th ed., Morgan Guaranty Trust Company of New York, New York.

Mosteller, F., and Tukey, J. W. (1977). *Data Analysis and Regression*, Addison-Wesley, Reading MA.

Müller, U. A. (1991). Specially weighted moving averages with repeated application of the EMA operator, Internal document UAM.1991-10-14, Olsen & Associates, Seefeldstrasse 233, 8008 Zürich, Switzerland.

Müller, U. A. (1993). Statistics of variables observed over overlapping intervals, Internal document UAM.1993-06-18, Olsen & Associates, Seefeldstrasse 233, 8008 Zürich, Switzerland.

Müller, U. A. (1996). Generating a time series of fixed-period spot interest rates from interest rate futures, Internal document UAM.1996-04-19, Olsen & Associates, Seefeldstrasse 233, 8008 Zürich, Switzerland.

Müller, U. A. (1999). The O&A filter for data in finance, Internal document UAM.1999-04-27, Olsen & Associates, Seefeldstrasse 233, 8008 Zürich, Switzerland.

Müller, U. A. (2000). Volatility Computed by Time Series Operators at High Frequency, In *Statistics and Finance: An Interface*, W. S. Chan, W. K. Li and Howell Tong, Eds., Imperial College Press, London.

Müller, U. A., and Sgier, R. G. (1992). Statistical analysis of intraday bid-ask spreads in the foreign exchange market, Internal document UAM.1992-04-10, Olsen & Associates, Seefeldstrasse 233, 8008 Zürich, Switzerland.

Müller, U. A., Dacorogna, M. M., Olsen, R. B., Pictet, O. V., Schwarz, M., and Morgenegg, C. (1990). Statistical study of foreign exchange rates, empirical evidence of a price change scaling law, and intraday analysis, *Journal of Banking and Finance*, 14, 1189–1208.

Müller, U. A., Dacorogna, M. M., Davé, R. D., Pictet, O. V., Olsen, R. B., and Ward, J. R. (1993a). Fractals and intrinsic time — A challenge to econometricians, in "Erfolgreiche Zinsprognose' ', Ed. by B. Lüthje, Verband öffentlicher Banken, Bonn 1994.

Müller, U. A., Dacorogna, M. M., and Pictet, O. V. (1993b). A trading model performance measure with strong risk aversion against drawdowns, Internal document UAM.1993-06-03, Olsen & Associates, Seefeldstrasse 233, 8008 Zürich, Switzerland.

Müller, U. A., Dacorogna, M. M., and Pictet, O. V. (1995). The error of statistical volatility of intradaily quoted price changes observed over a time interval, Internal document UAM.1995-07-31, Olsen & Associates, Seefeldstrasse 233, 8008 Zürich, Switzerland.

Müller, U. A., Dacorogna, M. M., Davé, R. D., Olsen, R. B., Pictet, O. V., and von Weizsäcker, J. E. (1997a). Volatilities of different time resolutions – analyzing the dynamics of market components, *Journal of Empirical Finance*, 4, 213–239.

Müller, U. A., Dacorogna, M. M., and Lundin, M. C. (1997b). Currency overlay using trading models under exposure constraints, Internal document UAM.1997-07-06, Olsen & Associates, Seefeldstrasse 233, 8008 Zürich, Switzerland.

Müller, U. A., Dacorogna, M. M., and Pictet, O. V. (1998). Heavy tails in high-frequency financial data, In *A Practical Guide to Heavy Tails: Statistical Techniques for Analysing Heavy Tailed Distributions*, R. J. Adler, R. E. Feldman and M. S. Taqqu, Eds., pp. 55–77, Birkhäuser, Boston, MA.

Murphy, J. J. (1986). *Technical Analysis of the Futures Markets*, New York Institute of Finance, Prentice-Hall, New York.

Mussa, M. (1979). Empirical regularities in the behavior of exchange rates and theories of the foreign exchange market, *Carnegie-Rochester Series on Public Policy*, 11, 9–58.

Neely, C., Weller, P., and Dittmar, R. (1997). Is technical analysis in the foreign exchange market profitable? A genetic programming approach, *Journal of Financial and Quantitative Analysis*, 32, 405–426.

Neftci, S. N. (1991). Naive trading rules in financial markets and Wiener-Kolmogorov prediction theory: A study of technical analysis, *Journal of Business*, 64, 549–571.

Nelson, D. B. (1991). Conditional heteroskedasticity in asset returns: A new approach, *Econometrica*, 59, 347–370.

Nelson, D. B., and Foster, D. P. (1994). Asymptotic filtering theory for univariate ARCH models, *Econometrica*, 62, 1–41.

Oussaidène, M., Chopard, B., Pictet, O. V., and Tomassini, M. (1997). Parallel genetic programming ans its application to trading model induction, *Parallel Computing*, 23, 1183–1198.

Pecen, L., Ramešová, N., Pelikán, E., and Beran, H. (1995). Application of the GUHA method on financial data, *Neural Network World*, 5, 565–571.

Peiers, B. (1997). Informed traders, intervention, and price leadership: A deeper view of the microstructure of the foreign exchange market, *Journal of Finance*, 52, 1589–1614.

Pesaran, M. H., and Timmerman, A. (1992). A simple nonparametric test of predictive performance, *Journal of Business and Economic Statistics*, 10, 461–465.

Peters, E. E. (1989). Fractal structure in the capital markets, *Financial Analysts Journal*, 1989, 32–37.

Peters, E. E. (1991). *Chaos and Order in Capital Markets*, A Wiley Finance Edition, John Wiley & Sons, New York.

Petersen, M. A. and Fialkowski, D. (1994). Posted versus effective spreads, good prices or bad quotes? *Journal of Financial Economics*, 35, 269–292.

Piccinato, B., Ballocchi, G., and Dacorogna, M. M. (1997). A closer look at the Eurofutures market: Intraday statistical analysis, Internal document BPB.1997-08-25, Olsen & Associates, Seefeldstrasse 233, 8008 Zürich, Switzerland.

Pictet, O. V., Dacorogna, M. M., Müller, U. A., Olsen, R. B., and Ward, J. R. (1992). Realtime trading models for foreign exchange rates, *Neural Network World*, 2, 713–744.

Pictet, O. V., Dacorogna, M. M., Chopard, B., Oussaidène, M., Schirru, R., and Tomassini, M. (1995). Using genetic algorithms for robust optimization in financial applications, *Neural Network World*, 5, 573–587.

Pictet, O. V., Dacorogna, M. M., and Müller, U. A. (1998). Hill, bootstrap and jackknife estimators for heavy tails, In *A practical guide to heavy tails: Statistical Techniques for Analysing Heavy Tailed Distributions*, R. J. Adler, R. E. Feldman and M. S. Taqqu, Eds., pp. 283-310, Birkhäuser, Boston, MA.

Poterba, J. M., and Summers, L. H. (1988). Mean reversion in stock prices: Evidence and implications, *Journal of Financial Economics*, 22, 27–59.

Press, W. H., Flannery, B. P., Teukolsky, S. A., and Vetterling, W. T. (1986). *Numerical Recipes. The Art of Scientific Computing*, Cambridge University Press, Cambridge.

Press, W. H., Teukolsky, S. A., Vetterling, W. T., and Flannery, B. P. (1992). *Numerical Recipes in C. The Art of Scientific Computing*, Cambridge University Press, Cambridge.

Priestley, M. B. (1989). *Nonlinear and Nonstationary Time Series Analysis*, Academic Press, London.

Rogalski, R. J., and Vinso, J. D. (1978). Empirical properties of foreign exchange rates, *Journal of International Business Studies*, 9, 69–79.

Roll, R. (1984). A simple implicit measure of the effective bid-ask spread in an efficient market, *Journal of Finance*, 39, 1127–1139.

Roy, A. D. (1952). Safety first the holding of assets, *Econometrica*, 20, 431–449.

Rydberg, T. H., and Shephard, N. (1998). Dynamics of trade-by-trade price movements: Decomposition and models, *Aarhus Center for Analytical Finance Working Paper Series No: 21*.

Schinasi, G. J., and Swamy, P. A. V. B. (1989). The out-of-sample forecasting performance of exchange rate models when coefficients are allowed to change, *Journal of International Money and Finance*, 8, 375–390.

Schnidrig, R. and Würtz, D. (1995). Investigation of the volatility and autocorrelation function of the USD/DEM exchange rate on operational time scales, In *Proceedings of the HFDF-I Conference*, Zurich, Switzerland, March 29-31, 1995, 3, 1–19.

Sentana, E. (1991). Quadratic ARCH models: A potential reinterpretation of ARCH models, *LSE Financial Markets Group Discussion Paper No: 122*.

Sharpe, W. F. (1966). Mutual fund performance, *Journal of Business*, 39, 119–138.

Sharpe, W. F. (1994). The Sharpe Ratio, *Journal of Portfolio Management*, 21, 49–59.

Shiller, R. J. (1989). *Market Volatility*, The MIT Press, Cambridge, MA.

Shiller, R. J. (2000). *Irrational Exuberance*, Princeton University Press, Princeton.

Stock, J. H. (1988). Estimating continuous-time processes subject to time deformation, *Journal of the American Statistical Association*, 83, 77–85.

Subrahmanyam, A. (1991). Risk aversion, market liquidity, and price efficiency, *Review of Financial Studies*, 4, 417–441.

Sullivan, R., Timmermann, A., and White, H. (1999). Data-snooping, technical trading rule performance and the bootstrap, *Journal of Finance*, 54, 1647–1692.

Surajaras, P., and Sweeney, R. J. (1992). *Profit-Making Speculation in Foreign Exchange Markets, The Political Economy of Global Interdependence*, Westview Press, Boulder, CO.

Suvanto, A. (1993). Foreign exchange dealing, Essays on the Microstructure of theForeign Exchange Market, *ETLA, The Research Institute of the Finnish Economy Working Paper A19*.

Svensson, L. E. (1992). An interpretation of recent research on exchange rate target zones, *Journal of Economic Perspectives*, 6, 119–144.

Swamy, P. A. V. B., and Schinasi, G. J. (1989). Should fixed coefficients be re-estimated evry period for extrapolation? *Journal of Forecasting*, 8, 1–17.

Tauchen, G. E., and Pitts, M. (1983). The price variability-volume relationship on speculative markets, *Econometrica*, 51, 485–505.

Taylor, M. P., and Allen, H. (1992). The use of technical analysis in the foreign exchange market, *Journal of International Money and Finance*, 11, 304–314.

Taylor, S. J. (1986). *Modelling Financial Time Series*, John Wiley & Sons, Chichester.

Taylor, S. J. (1994). Modeling stochastic volatility: A review and comparative study, *Mathematical Finance*, 4, 183–204.

Taylor, S. J. and Xu, X. (1997). The incremental volatility information in one million foreign exchange quotations, *Journal of Empirical Finance*, 4, 317–340.

Tucker, A. L. and Scott, E. (1987). A study of diffusion processes for foreign exchange rates, *Journal of International Money and Finance*, 6, 465–478.

Walmsley, J. (1992). *The Foreign Exchange and Money Market Guide*, Wiley Finance Edition, John Wiley & Sons, New York.

Wasserfallen, W. (1989). Flexible exchange rates: A closer look, *Journal of Monetary Economics*, 23, 511–521.

Wasserfallen, W., and Zimmermann, H. (1985). The behavior of intradaily exchange rates, *Journal of Banking and Finance*, 9, 55–72.

Westerfield, R. (1997). The distribution of common stock price changes: An application of transactions time and subordinated stochastic models, *Journal of Financial and Quantitative Analysis*, 12, 743–765.

White, H. (1980). A heteroscedasticity-consistent covariance matrix and a direct test for heteroscedasticity, *Econometrica*, 48, 421–448.

Yin, X., and Germay, N. (1993). A fast genetic algorithm with sharing scheme using cluster analysis methods in multimodal function optimization, In *Proceedings of International Conference on Artificial Neural Nets and Genetic Algorithms*, Innsbruck, Austria, pp. 450–457.

Zhou, B. (1993). Forecasting foreign exchange rates subject to de-volatilization, *MIT Sloan School Working Paper No: 3510*.

Zimmermann, H. J. (1985). *Fuzzy Set Theory and Its Applications*, Kluwer-Nijhoff Publishing, Boston, Dordrecht, Lancaster.

Zumbach, G. (1996). Time series and operators, Internal document GOZ.1996-05-23, Olsen & Associates, Seefeldstrasse 233, 8008 Zürich, Switzerland.

Zumbach, G. (1997). Measure of association, Internal document GOZ.1997-11-21, Olsen & Associates, Seefeldstrasse 233, 8008 Zürich, Switzerland.

Zumbach, G. (2000). The pitfalls in fitting GARCH processes, In *Advances in Quantitative Asset Management*, C. Dunis, Ed., Kluwer, Amsterdam.

Zumbach, G. O. and Müller, U. A. (2001). Operators on inhomogeneous time series, *International Journal of Theoretical and Applied Finance*, 4(1), 147–178.

Zumbach, G. O., Dacorogna, M. M., Olsen, J. L., and Olsen, R. B. (2000). Measuring Shock in Financial Markets, *International Journal of Theoretical and Applied Finance*, 3(3), 347-355.

Zumbach, G. O., Dacorogna, M. M., Olsen, J. L., and Olsen, R. B. (2000). Market crises, shock of the news, *Risk Magazine*, 13, 110–114.

INDEX

A

activity
    activity variable, *see* variable
    market activity, 175, 177, 183
approach
    macroeconomic, 5
    microstructure, 2
    time series, 2
arbitrage
    formula, 29
    opportunities, 28
    riskfree, 22
    triangular arbitrage, 118, 127
ARCH, *see* model

B

Bank for International Settlements, 137
basis point, 23, 125, 171
BHHH algorithm, 223
bias, 44
    bias of realized volatility, *see* volatility
    market maker bias, 154
bid-ask bounce, 124
Black and Scholes, 43
Brownian motion, 49
build-up, 52, 87, 223, 263
    error, 56
    time interval, 56

business-time scale, *see* time scale

C

call for margin, 12
capital management system, 296
cash interest rates, 21
cheapest-to-deliver, 29, 31
conditional heteroskedasticity, 204
conditional predictability, 215
convergence, 163, 320
    model estimation, 223
correlation, 268
    adjusted correlation measure, 272
    breakdown, 270, 277
    covolatility weighting, 268, 270
    Epps effect, 269, 288
    linear correlation coefficient, 272
    memory, 293
    variations, 278
counterparty default risk, 11
covariance, 268
    cross-covariance, 124
    matrix, 116, 346
    realized, 50
credit ratings, 28
credit risk, 128
credit spread, 21
cross rate, 16, 19
cross-covariance, 124

376

cumulative distribution function, 173

D

daily time series, 174
data
  ask, 12, 15
  bid, 12, 15
  bid-ask price, *see* price
  bid-ask spread, *see* spread
  daily, 14
  data cleaning, *see* filter
  data filter, *see* filter
  dependent quote, 95
  effective price, *see* price
  effective spread, *see* spread
  empirical, 132
  high-frequency, 1, 10, 32, 33
  historical, 16
  homogeneous, 35
  inhomogeneous, 35
  interest rate, 21
  intraday, 14
  irregularly spaced, 1
  low-frequency, 14
  quote, 1
  quoted spread, *see* spread
  quotes, 15
  regularly spaced, 1
  sparse, 3
  synthetic regular, 54
  tick, *see* tick, 38
  tick-by-tick, 1, 4, 6, 51
  time stamp, 15
  traded spread, *see* spread
  transaction price, 1, 15
  weekly, 14
data cleaning, 82
data error, 85
  decimal error, 85
  human error, 85
    intentional error, 85
    unintentional error, 85
  repeated ticks, 86
  scaling problem, 86
  system error, 85
  test, 85
    early morning test, 86
    monotonic series, 86
  tick copying, 86
data providers, 11
  Bloomberg, 11, 15
  Bridge, 11, 46, 186
  Knight Ridder, 15, 186
  Reuters, 11, 15, 46, 186

  Telerate, 15, 128, 186
data-generating process, 122, 328, 338, *see* model
day-of-the-week effect, 169
daylight saving time, 164, 190
delivery risk, 170
deseasonalized returns, 197
directing process, 176
direction change indicator, 47
direction quality, 262
distribution, *see* probability distribution
  nonstable, 142
Dow Jones Industrials, 8
dynamic memory, 255
dynamic optimization, 246
dynamic overlay, *see* hedging

E

economic forecast, 129
economic news announcement, 130
econophysicist, 9
effective news, 130
effective number of observations, 50
efficient frontier, 341
efficient markets, 349, 354
electronic order-matching system, 15
  Electronic Broking Services (EBS), 15
  Reuters Dealing 2000, 15
EMA-HARCH, *see* model
Epps effect, *see* correlation, 293
equity indices, 32
EUREX, 24
EURIBOR, 25
Euro, 24
Eurodeposits, 21
Eurofutures contracts, 121
Eurolira, *see* market, Eurofutures
European Monetary System (EMS), 127
Euroyen, *see* market, Eurofutures
expiry, 12, 29, 31
  quarterly expiry, 24
  time-to-expiry, 31
exponential attenuation, 293
exponential decline, 209
exponential memory, 282
exposure, 339
extreme events, 6
extreme risks, 144
extreme value theory, 138

F

fat-tailedness, 132
FIGARCH, *see* model

filter
    adaptive method, 98
    after-jump algorithm, 105
    artificial quote method, 118
    ask quote, 110
    bid quote, 110
    bid-ask quote, 110
    bid-ask spread, 110
    build-up period, 87
    credibility, 93, 114
    data cleaning, 82
    data filter, 82
    decimal error, 113
    domain error, 111
    filter configuration, 113
    filter parameters, 116
    filtering algorithm, 89
        credibility, 89
        full-tick filtering window, 89
        scalar filtering window, 89
        univariate filter, 89
    filtering hypothesis, 113
        error hypothesis, 113
        winning hypothesis, 113
    forward premiums/discounts, 111
    full-quote filtering window, 109
        quote splitting, 110
    high-quality data, 100
    historical mode, 115
    historical operation, 87
    interest rate, 111
    level filter, 88, 91
    level quote, 110
    multivariate filtering, 100, 116
        filtering sparse data, 116
    next point interpolation, 96
    pair filtering, 88, 93, 98
    price, 111
    real-time mode, 115
    real-time operation, 87
    repeated quotes, 100
    scalar filtering window, 103
        filter test, 104
        the normal update, 104
    scalar quote, 110
    scalar window
        dismissing scalar quotes, 107
    scaling factor, 113
    second scalar window, 108
    sensitivity analysis, 120
    short-term interest-rate futures, 111
    spread filter, 98
    spread quoting, 98
    strong filter, 116
    time scale, 100

    timing, 87
    trust capital, 90, 104
    univariate filtering, 113, 116
    validity test, 110
    weak (tolerant) filter, 116
finite variance, 132
first position, 30
forecasting, 248
    forecast accuracy, 246, 262
    forecast effectiveness, 264
    forecast horizon, 264
    forecast quality, 261
    forecasting model, 249
    multivariate forecasting, 249
    real-time price forecasting system, 250
    signal correlation, 263
        forecasting signal, 263
        real signal, 263
    volatility forecast, 250
forecasting performance, 243
    benchmark comparison, 245
    direction quality, 245
    realized potential, 245
foreign exchange (FX) market, *see* market
forward discount, 23
forward interest rate, 25
forward points, 23
forward premium, 23
forward rate, 22, 25
fractal behavior, 8, 209
fractional noise process, 207
FXFX page, 16

G

GARCH, *see* model
Gaussian distribution, 135, 155
genetic algorithm, 223, 317
    adaptive clustering, 319
    multi-modal function, 318
    sharing scheme, 319
genetic programming, 311
    closure property, 312
    function nodes, 312
    syntactic restrictions, 313
    terminal nodes, 312
    tournament selection, 315
geographical components, 179
geometric mean, 170
goodness-of-fit, 285
granularity, 171

H

HARCH, *see* model

heat-wave component, 207
heat-wave effect, 209, 214, 352
hedge funds, 17
hedging, 31
  currency overlay, 343
  currency risk, 209, 340
  dynamic hedging, 340, 345
  instruments, 24
  neutral point, 343
  ratio, 343
heterogeneity, 44
heterogeneous market hypothesis, *see* hypothesis
heteroskedasticity, 35, 162
  autoregressive conditional, 265
Hill estimator, 145
holiday
  half-day, 190
holidays, *see* market
hyperbolic decline, 210
hypothesis
  heat wave hypothesis, 179
  heterogeneous market hypothesis, 209, 210, 224
  island hypothesis, 179
  meteor shower hypothesis, 179, 206

I

IGARCH, *see* model
implied interest rate, 25
implied volatility, *see* volatility
index
  AMEX Stock Index, 283
  Down Jones Index, 283
indicator, 257
  antisymmetric, 315
  cycle, 310
  overbought and oversold, 310
  symmetric, 315
  timing, 310
  trend following, 310
  volatile indicator, 259
information set, 82, 249
instability, 259
institutional constraints, 14, 128
institutional framework, 127
institutional investors, 17
interbank interest rates, 21
interbank money market rates, 121
interpolation, *see* method
intervention, 129
  official, 129
intraday
  analysis, 127

  movements, 174
  prices, 174
  statistics, 163
  volatility, 174
intraweek
  analysis, 177
  statistics, 163
  volatility, 174
intrinsic time, *see* time scale, τ-scale
investment assets, 339

J

J. P. Morgan, 6

K

kernels, 52
Kronecker symbol, 260
kurtosis, 134, 205
  operator, 71

L

lagged correlation, 211
lead-lag, 20
lead-lag correlation, 211
leptokurticity, 173
LIBOR, 25
LIFFE, 24, 31
likelihood
  likelihood-ratio test, 230
  log-likelihood, 222
  maximum likelihood, 223, 330
Ljung-Box, 334
long memory, 8, 198, 207
long-term regime, 259

M

mapping function, 261
mark-to-market, 305
market
  Asian stock, 52
  bond, 28
  centralized, 11
  decentralized (OTC), 11
  derivative, 11
  equity, 32
  Eurofutures, 169
    Eurodollar, 169
    Eurolira, 24, 169
    Euromark, 169
    Euroyen, 24

Short Sterling, 169
foreign exchange (FX), 11, 13
  FX forward, 15
  FX forwards, 14
  FX futures, 14
  FX spot, 13, 15
futures, 11, 12
  bond futures, 28
  commodity futures, 31
  Eurofutures, 24
  individual equity futures, 33
geographical market, 214
German bond market, 131
heterogeneous market, 210
holidays, 190
homogeneous market, 210
interest rate futures, 23, 25
liquid, 1
market microstructure, 5
opening hours, 176
option, 11, 13, 33
over-the-counter (OTC), 2, 12, 19, 21, 24
over-the-counter interest rate, 23
participants, 10
  anonymity, 10
spot, 11, 12
spot interest rate, 24
U.S. treasury bond market, 131
market activity, 175, 177, 183
market efficiency, 14, 45, 156, 249, *see* efficient markets
market expectation, 130
market makers, 19
market microstructure effect, 197, 201
market risk, 158
market-dependent persistence, 206
Markov chain, 233
maturity, 22
maximum likelihood, *see* likelihood
mean absolute error (MAE), 262
mean square error (MSE), 262
mean squared prediction errors (MSPE), 295
measure
  asymmetric effective returns, 307
  reward-to-variability ratio, 305
  risk-sensitive performance, 304
  symmetric effective returns, 305
method
  distribution free measure, 262
  interpolation, 37
    linear, 54
    previous-tick, 37
  nonparametric method, 262
  overlapping, 44
  panel regression, 47

polynomial, 25
polynomial interpolation, 26
microstructure, 2, 5, 14
Middle European Time (MET), 326
middle price, 122
misspecification, 222
mixture of distributions, 131
model
  ARCH, 221
  capital asset pricing model (CAPM), 349
  EMA-HARCH, 237, 254
  FIGARCH, 221, 231
  GARCH, 44, 146, 221, 222, 224, 328
    AR-GARCH, 328
    diffusion process, 224
    estimation problems, 226
    jump process, 224
    temporal aggregation, 224
  HARCH, 146, 231, 335
    AR-HARCH, 328
    HARCH components, 236
  IGARCH, 251
  in-sample optimization, 263
  intraweek market activity, 179
  lagged adjustment model, 124
  macroeconomic, 5
  market activity, 175, 183
  market maker bias, 154
  market microstructure, 14
  model initialization, 263
  model structure, 256
  moving average model, 295
  multi-horizon, 263
  multicascade model, 148
  multifractal model, 148
  multivariate volatility model, 250
  nonparametric conditional mean models, 295
  Normal Inverse Gaussian (NIG) Lévy process, 151
  out-of-sample test, 263
  purchasing power parity model, 249
  QARCH, 232
  random walk, 54, 147, 150, 152, 253, 331
  risk premia, 249
  structural model, 249
  time series model, 249
  trading, *see* trading model
  trading model, 295
  volatility, 6
moment, 55, 132, 135, 137
  finite second moment, 142
  nonconverging fourth moment, 142
momenta, 257
Monte Carlo simulations, 145

multifractal model, 8
multifractality, 148
multiple assets, 278

N

near-singularity, 259
neutral point, *see* hedging
noise trader, 349
nonstable distribution, 142
notional deposit, 26

O

official intervention, 129
Olsen & Associates (O&A), 4, 11, 18
open position (mark-to-market), 305
opening hours, *see* trading hours
operator, 35
    average, 55
    backward shift, 77
    causal, 54
    comparison, 314
    complex moving average, 75
    conditional, 314
    convolution, 51
    crossover, 312
    derivative, 55, 66
    difference, 78
    differential, 64
    exponential moving average (EMA), 59
        iterated, 59
    homogeneous, 58
    linear operator and kernels, 54
    logic, 314
    microscopic, 36, 76
    moving average (MA), 61
    moving correlation, 71
    moving kurtosis, 71
    moving norm, 63
    moving skewness, 71
    moving standard deviation, 63
    moving variance, 63
    mutation, 312
    nonlinear, 58
    regular time series, 77
    tick frequency, 79
    time translation, 77
    time-translation invariant, 54
    volatility, 68, 79
    windowed Fourier transform, 74
optimization
    robust optimization, 317
option pricing, 3
out-of-sample, 222

outright forward rate, 22
outright forward transactions, 23
overlap
    method, 44
    overlap-free, 50
    overlapping returns, *see* return
overshooting, 27

P

performance index, 32
periodicity, 160, *see* seasonality
permanence hypothesis, 5
perpetuum mobile, 353
physical delivery, 31
portfolio
    pricing, 277
    trading model portfolio, 338
post ex-ante testing, 264
prefiltering technique, 249
price, 37, 38
    bid-ask, 17
    effective price, 40, 125
    middle, 122
    price formation, 3, 123
    synthetic, 275
    transaction, 1, 15
probability density function (pdf), 54
probability distribution, 54, 132
process, *see* model
psychological time, 176

Q

quadratic programming, 346
quote, *see* data

R

random walk, *see* model
rational expectations, 210
real market value, 210
realized volatility, *see* volatility
regime shifts, 8
relaxation time, 352
return, 37, 40
    deseasonalized, 197
    mean, 48
    nonoverlapping, 50
    overlapping, 47
    synthetic, 275
Reuters, 1, 21
Reuters Instrument Code (RIC), 15
risk management, 3, 14, 52, 277

risk profiles, 14
risk-sensitive measures, 305
RiskMetrics, 251
    methodology, 251
    volatility, 253
robustness, 58
rolling over, 13
rollover scheme, 29
root mean squared error (RMSE), 186

S

safety margins, 171
scaling laws, *see* stylized facts
    empirical, 177
scaling properties, 8
    significance, 9
seasonality, 35, 44, 175
    daily seasonality, 204
    geographical seasonality, 181
    ordinary seasonality, 214
    seasonal heteroskedasticity, 175, 265
    seasonal volatility, 174
    weekly seasonality, 204
second position, 30
segmentation, 128
serial expiry contracts, 24
settlement rules, 12
Sharpe ratio, 305
short memory, 207
signal processing, 338
Singapore International Monetary Exchange,
    24
skewness, 173
    operator, 71
    realized, 46
slippage, 32
speculative bubbles, 349
spot
    interest rates, 21
    market, *see* market
    trading, 11
    transaction, 23
spread
    average, 46, 172
    bid-ask, 17, 19, 23, 40, 45, 91, 124, 125,
        154, 170, 354
    credit spread, 21
    effective, 126
    log, 45
    quoted, 171
    relative, 45
    traded, 171
spurious persistence, 194
stability, 143

standard limit theory, 153
stochastic process, *see* model
stock indices, 32
stock splits, 32
stop-loss deal, 301
stop-profit algorithm, 299
stringent filter, 302
structural change, 259
stylized facts, 2, 14, 121, 127
    autocorrelation of return, 121
    autocorrelation study, 161
    bid-ask bounce, 124
    bid-ask spread, 170
    daily and weekly patterns, 122
    deterministic volatility, 169
    discreteness, 125
    distribution of returns, 122
        fat-tailed, 122
    distributional issues, 121
    distributional properties, 132
        bounded distributions, 135
        fat-tailed distributions, 135
        thin-tailed distributions, 135
    negative first-order autocorrelation of re-
        turns, 123
    scaling laws, 122, 147
        apparent scaling, 152
        fat tails, 142
        interquartile range, 150
        limitations, 158
    scaling properties, 121
    seasonal heteroskedasticity, 122, 163
    seasonal volatility, 163, 167
        U-shaped, 167
    seasonality, 121
subordinated process, 176
swap, 23
    FX swap rates, 23
symmetry, 132
synthetic price, *see* price
synthetic return, *see* return

T

tail
    index, 6, 132, 135
    statistics, 6
Taylor expansion, 62
technical analysis, 3, 14, 129
technological change, 8
temporal aggregation, 224
test
    ex-ante test, 322
    likelihood ratio, 7
    Monte Carlo, 274

out-of-sample test, 249
  ratio test, 192
tick, 1, 10
  tick frequency, 37, 46
    log, 46
  tick time, 124
tick-by-tick, *see* data
time horizon, 209, 210, 249, 307, 309
time scale, 8, 176
  τ-scale, 255
  ϑ-scale, *see* time scale, ϑ-time
  ϑ-time, 174, 176, 188
  business, 174, 188, 225
  tick time, 124
  variety of time scales, 8
time stamp, 10, 15
trading horizon (trader class), 198
  day trader, 199
  intraday trader, 199
  long-term trader, 199
  market maker, 199
  short-term trader, 199
trading hours, 174, 299, 327
trading model, 295
  current price, 302
  current return, 300
  gearing calculator, 301
  market constraints, 299
  performance calculator, 297
  performance measures, 304
    R_{eff}, 307
    X_{eff}, 305
    Sharpe ratio, 305
  portfolios, 338
  real-time trading models, 296, 310, 323
  real-time trading strategies, 297
  recommendation maker, 301
  simulated trader, 297, 303
    bookkeeper, 303
    opportunity catcher, 303
  stop-loss deal, 301
  stop-loss detector, 302
  stop-loss price, 302
  stop-profit algorithm, 299
  stop-profit control, 302
  symmetry properties, 315
  testing procedures, 317
  trading hours, *see* trading hours
  transaction costs, *see* transaction
transaction
  clock, 176
  costs, 170, 295, 325, 331, 333
  price, 1, 15
  volume, 46, 176
trust capital, *see* filter

U

uncertainty, 154
undershooting, 28

V

Value-at-Risk (VaR), 6, 250
variable
  activity, 176
  direction change indicator, 47
  price, *see* price
  realized covariance, *see* covariance
  realized skewness, *see* skewness
  return, *see* return
  spread, *see* spread
  tick frequency, *see* tick
  volatility, *see* volatility
vehicle currency, 19, 172
volatility
  annualized, 41
  coarse volatility, 211
  conditional heteroskedasticity, 198
  daily volatility, 158
  deterministic volatility, 170
  expected volatility, 96
  fine volatility, 211
  historical, 41
  implied, 43
  model, 43
  patterns, 176
  realized volatility, 37, 41, 197, 248
    bias, 154, 159, 198
    bias correction, 202
  volatility clustering, 122, 161, 198, 228
  volatility ratio, 47, 192

W

wavelet, 193
  multiscaling approach, 193
  signal-to-noise ratio, 193
  wavelet transform, 159
  wavelet variance, 160
weekend effect, 172
White's variance-covariance matrix
    estimation, 224

Y

yield curve, 25

Z

zero-sum game, 353